W9-DHW-442

# Contents at a Glance

# SUSE™ Linux 10

## UNLEASHED

Michael McCallister

**SAMS**   800 East 96th Street, Indianapolis, Indiana 46240

# SUSE™ Linux 10 Unleashed

International Standard Book Number: 0-672-32726-0

Library of Congress Catalog Card Number: 2004095632

Printed in the United States of America

First Printing: October 2005

08   07   06   05        4   3   2   1

## Trademarks

## Warning and Disclaimer

## Bulk Sales

Sams Publishing offers excellent discounts on this book when ordered in quantity for bulk purchases or special sales. For more information, please contact

**U.S. Corporate and Government Sales**
**1-800-382-3419**
corpsales@pearsontechgroup.com

For sales outside of the U.S., please contact

**International Sales**
international@pearsoned.com

**Acquisitions Editor**
Jenny Watson

**Development Editor**
Scott Meyers

**Managing Editor**
Charlotte Clapp

**Project Editor**
Mandie Frank

**Copy Editor**
Barbara Hacha

**Indexer**
John Sleeva
Aaron Black

**Proofreader**
Kathy Bidwell

**Technical Editors**
Robert Shimonski
Emmett Dulaney

**Publishing Coordinator**
Vanessa Evans

**Multimedia Developer**
Dan Scherf

**Designer**
Gary Adair

**Page Layout**
Susan Geiselman

# Table of Contents

# About the Author

**Michael McCallister** has spent the last decade making computing easier for the full spectrum of user levels and experience. He is currently a technical writing consultant with Compuware.

Michael has run a SuSE Linux desktop at home since version 5.3 and knows firsthand how far the distribution has come over the years. He is the author of *Computer Certification Handbook*, published by Arco Press (2000), and his technology stories have been published in places such as *Linux Journal*, *Java Developer's Journal*, *Internet Voyager*, and *Isthmus*. He is a member of the Society for Technical Communication, the Milwaukee Linux Users Group, and the National Writers Union.

# About the Contributors

**Timothy Boronczyk** is a native resident of Syracuse, New York. He has been involved in web design since 1998 and has written several articles on PHP programming and other design topics. In his spare time he enjoys photography, listening to and composing music, spending time with friends, solving sudoku puzzles, and sleeping with his feet off the end of the bed.

**Emmett Dulaney** has worked with UNIX since 1990 and Linux since its debut. He is the author of several books from Novell Press including *Novell Linux Desktop 9 Administrator's Handbook* and the upcoming *Novell Linux Practicum Lab Manual*.

**Robert J. Shimonski** is a well-known industry specialist, speaker, trainer, and author. He works within today's most challenging technological and business environments. Rob brings proven frontline industry knowledge to the reader. He can be found online at www.RSNetworks.net.

**Robb H. Tracy** has a Master of Science degree in instructional technology from Utah State University. He has designed and implemented technical training curricula for major industry hardware and software vendors since 1994. Robb is currently the president of Nebo Technical Institute, Inc., a provider of content development services for the information technology training industry.

# Dedication

*To Jeanette, who smoothes the edges and keeps everything together.*

# Acknowledgments

Writing can be a lonely endeavor, but in the course of writing a book like this, there are all sorts of people whose paths you cross and who make the result better. Many thanks to Jenny Watson, my acquisitions editor, who gave me the chance to do this. Also thanks to my agent, Carole McClendon at Waterside Productions. Endless props to Rob Shimonski, who tech edited the bulk of the text and pitched in at the end to get this project completed. Scott Meyers offered excellent advice, Mandie Frank shepherded the review process, and Barbara Hacha did a marvelous copy edit. Special thanks to Scott Villinski at Novell, who helped with the installation chapter, and offered a few tips (with Tim Kresler) to the Milwaukee Linux Users Group; and Don Bangs, who got me my first computer and always responds to hardware emergencies.

To all the developers, testers, documenters, and users of SUSE Linux and all the wonderful applications that go with it: Thank you isn't enough, but I hope it'll do for now. To the participants on all the mailing lists: Your helpfulness to me and all the other users should never go unnoticed. To my friends in the Boulder and Milwaukee Linux Users Groups: Couldn't have done any of this without you.

Finally, to my wife Jeanette, who always believed I was a writer and my two favorite distractions, Hannah and Ben (and their parents, Bev and Bob): May you grow up happy and in a Linux world.

# We Want to Hear from You!

As the reader of this book, *you* are our most important critic and commentator. We value your opinion and want to know what we're doing right, what we could do better, what areas you'd like to see us publish in, and any other words of wisdom you're willing to pass our way.

You can email or write me directly to let me know what you did or didn't like about this book—as well as what we can do to make our books stronger.

*Please note that I cannot help you with technical problems related to the topic of this book, and that due to the high volume of mail I receive, I might not be able to reply to every message.*

When you write, please be sure to include this book's title and author as well as your name and phone or email address. I will carefully review your comments and share them with the author and editors who worked on the book.

E-mail:    opensource@samspublishing.com

Mail:      Mark Taber
           Associate Publisher
           Sams Publishing
           800 East 96th Street
           Indianapolis, IN 46240 USA

## Reader Services

For more information about this book or another Sams Publishing title, visit our website at www.samspublishing.com. Type the ISBN (excluding hyphens) or the title of a book in the Search field to find the page you're looking for.

# Introduction

Welcome to *SUSE Linux 10 Unleashed*! This book is going to help you get the most out of your SUSE Linux system, and it includes a fully functional copy of the operating system distribution.

Since SUSE Linux A.G. was acquired by networking pioneer Novell in 2003, more North Americans are becoming familiar with the SUSE Linux distribution that has long been popular in Europe. SUSE Linux offers an incredibly easy installation and a large number of applications that have been tested for stability.

SUSE Linux 10 marks a new way of doing things for both Novell and SUSE, and this book can help you join the excitement. SUSE Linux 10 is the first SUSE release built and tested through the OpenSUSE project. Thousands of people around the world downloaded and ran four beta releases, contributed bug reports, feature wish lists, and postings on the OpenSUSE mailing list. Novell has committed to opening up the process even further in 2006. You'll read more about the OpenSUSE project in the next chapter.

Whether you're completely new to Linux or coming to SUSE Linux from another distribution, you're going to find solid information in a slightly more relaxed style than you're used to in a computer book.

SUSE Linux has always been known as a distribution packed with applications, and version 10 is no exception. This book, as always, includes a complete copy of the distribution on CDs and DVD. The Linux kernel forms the core of a truly modern operating system that can power anything from wrist watches to supercomputers. SUSE Linux can run on computers running processors ranging from the Intel 486 through 64-bit processors from AMD and Intel.

This book will be especially helpful to the millions using Linux as their everyday desktop system. After first sweeping over the server landscape in the late 1990s, Linux is gaining ground in the desktop arena. More Linux developers have become interested in writing software for the masses of ordinary users. You'll learn how to use several open-source office productivity applications, access the Internet, work with digital music and video, and even play a few games.

*SUSE Linux 10 Unleashed* contains everything you need to get started and be productive.

> **NOTE**
>
> This book includes a copy of SUSE Linux 10, but readers owning earlier versions of SUSE Linux should find nearly all the advice contained here useful.

You'll get a little bit of Linux history before jumping into the preparation needed for a successful installation and long-term operation of SUSE Linux. Then you'll get step-by-step instructions in using the SUSE Linux standby, Yet another Setup Tool (YaST), to install SUSE Linux and configure your hardware. Next, you'll learn about the everyday applications you need to run Linux on the desktop, and then you'll learn about using the Internet, creating websites, and running web and FTP servers.

System administration is the next major topic, where you'll learn how to manage your files, users, and data, and how to keep your system current by updating it with the same tool you use to install the system.

Finally, because Linux has always been a playground for programmers, we'll cover both the classic tools for creating new programs and the newer scripting languages.

## Why Use Linux?

More than a decade has passed since Linus Torvalds put his operating system code on the Internet, and millions have been putting Linux to good use. It's been a while since Linux was viewed as a "toy operating system" used only by geek computer hobbyists.

Big corporations, colleges, governments, school districts, nonprofit organizations, and everyday users are all turning to Linux to boost productivity at a low cost.

There are a lot of reasons why running Linux is a good idea. If you're still thinking about it, here are a few of them:

- Linux puts you in control of your computing environment. Although much of the buzz around "free software" revolves around cost (and we'll get to that argument in a moment), what's really important is that the user is really in charge. Choices abound in the Linux space. If you're not happy with the way one application works, there's usually something else out there that can make you happy. Most applications are also endlessly customizable, so just because there's an annoying feature included as a default, you can always turn things off or modify its functioning.

- Linux is inexpensive to install, run, and update. Unlike proprietary operating systems, you can take the CDs and DVD from this book and install SUSE Linux 10 on as many computers as you need to. Configure Linux individually for your file servers, routers, web servers, and desktops. All these systems will run crash-free with little maintenance required and (if you like) automated updates that don't even need user intervention to install.

- Linux is ready for the desktop. Nearly everything you can do on a Windows machine can be done on SUSE Linux 10, from creating professional office documents and presentations to getting files on the Internet. It's also not that hard to get used to after you've made the switch. When Grandma is running Linux, she's less likely to see error messages and crashing programs, too.

- Linux is a rock-solid server performer. The operating system (OS) made its first impression as a fast, secure, stable, scalable, and robust server OS. The current kernel easily handles multiprocessor machines, gigabytes of system memory, and terabytes of data. Most Enterprise-level applications have Linux versions. Although this book does not cover the Novell Open Enterprise Server, SUSE Linux 10 serves as a proving ground for new enterprise applications to be included in OES.

- Linux thrives in a variety of environments. Linux drives many personal digital assistants, laptops, desktops, and specialized computers. You can put your ancient 486 processor to work as a router or file server with SUSE Linux 10. It also runs on AMD 64-bit Opteron processors, and did so for a year before 64-bit Windows XP was released.

- Linux offers a royalty-free development platform for several operating systems. Because of the open-source development model and the high-quality, free tools available to developers, anyone from 13-year-old budding programmers to massive development shops can produce quality software relatively inexpensively.

- Linux now offers big player support. Although the Linux community is still the best place to go for support when things go wrong, the presence of IBM, Novell, and other big companies in the support space can make even the most uneasy bean counter relax a little.

## Who This Book Is For

This book will get you going on SUSE Linux 10. Novell now targets this version for the "computer enthusiast" and personal user, and this is especially true with the new OpenSUSE development project. The contents are aimed at the intermediate to advanced user, but even the newest Linux users should find much useful information, especially in Part 1. The end of each chapter offers pointers to excellent resources on the World Wide Web (WWW) to keep you current and help you delve deeper into the subject areas covered here.

The YaST installer is better than most at identifying and configuring hardware, but you should have at least some familiarity with your system and the types of hardware it contains before installing any Linux system. Knowing your way around the command line never hurts either. This book will help you gain and refine those skills and show you how to learn more about your computer, Linux, and the applications included in the distribution.

System administrators of all experience levels will be able to use this book to install, set up, and run common network services, including the Apache web server, FTP servers, and Samba for cross-platform networking. You'll also get comfortable with using YaST to update your systems.

Programmers will learn about the tools available to help you be productive, with summaries of many professional-grade text editors, integrated development environments, and web programming languages and tools.

## What This Book Contains

*SUSE Linux 10 Unleashed* is organized into six parts, covering installation and configuration, everyday usage, Internet access and usage, basic and advanced system administration, and programming. The idea is to work from the very basics of using the OS into more difficult and advanced tasks. With the accompanying CD-ROMs and DVD-ROMs, you have everything you need to get started.

New Linux users will find the first three parts most helpful. You'll get valuable information on the following topics:

- An overview of SUSE Linux.

- Getting help through the printed and online documentation provided with SUSE Linux 10, through the Internet, and through Linux User Groups (LUGs).

- Planning for your installation by looking at the reasons and tasks you have for your computer, and then examining your hardware.

- A detailed walk-through of the installation process.

- Preserving an existing Windows installation for dual-boot launching.

- Configuring and using the X Window System, the Linux graphical interface, and the two primary desktop environments for Linux—KDE and GNOME.

- Making friends with your command line.

- Printing in Linux.

- Running OpenOffice and other productivity tools.

- Accessing the Internet.

- Managing email, Usenet, and file transfer with both FTP and peer-to-peer protocols.

- Playing music, video, and games.

- Burning CDs and DVDs.

- Turning your PC into a personal video recorder a la TiVo.

- Creating your own websites and weblogs.

Parts 4 and 5 are about system administration. New users should at least review Part 4 to learn how to manage data and users and use YaST and other tools to keep the system updated. Professional system administrators can go deeper, with material on the following:

- Managing the boot process.

- Securing your system and network.

- Managing the kernel and its modules.

- Setting up networks.

- Working with Samba to network Linux and Windows systems together.

- Running the Apache web server.

- Managing Internet domains.

Part 6 covers programming in SUSE Linux. You'll learn about these topics:

- Tools for the C, C++, and Java programmer.

- Managing databases and using them in programming.

- The LAMP web programming "suite": Linux, Apache, MySQL, and the scripting languages Perl, Python, and PHP.

The appendixes describe the various permutations of SUSE Linux offered by Novell and deliver an expanded list of Internet resources for learning about the topics introduced here.

## Conventions Used in This Book

*SUSE Linux 10 Unleashed* is intended to be as complete as possible, but with all the applications included in the distribution, it's impossible to cover every option. You'll find a lot of lists and tables to help you through, however.

Where there are graphical tools to use, you'll find screenshots giving you visual cues to the steps you're working through.

To help you better understand code listing samples and the command-line interface, several formatting techniques are used to show input and responses. For example, where you have to type something in, the typeface looks like this:

```
ls
```

If typed input is in response to a prompt, what you type will also be in bold:

```
Delete files? [y/n]  y
```

Words in commands that are between brackets are placeholders. If you see

```
<username>
```

Enter the username at that spot.

The following elements give you useful tidbits of information that relate to the surrounding text.

> **NOTE**
>
> Notes give you additional information that may help you perform a task, give you some ancillary detail, or point to another spot in the book, or online, for more information about the current topic.
>
> Longer notes, or sidebars, will help you with specific tasks, related technologies, and things on the horizon.

> **TIP**
>
> A tip will have a timesaving technique, a special insight, or something else to make you a smarter user.

> **CAUTION**
>
> Cautions will warn you about potential mishaps or steps to take before doing something potentially dangerous, such as running a command, editing configurations, or choosing a setting.

You should know that everything in this book was developed using SUSE Linux and open-source tools.

As you work through this book and learn more about the OS and its tools, always keep in mind the admonition SUSE Linux developers try to remind us of at the end of every installation: "Have a lot of fun!"

# PART I

# Installation and Configuration

## IN THIS PART

# Welcome to SUSE Linux

Ａnd a fine place it is to begin! Whether you are brand new to Linux or moving from another distribution, you will find SUSE Linux easy to use and powerful to work with. *SUSE Linux Unleashed* is here to help you get the most out of it. This chapter will give you a brief overview of SUSE Linux, with hints on how to use the rest of this book.

## What Is SUSE Linux?

The first thing anyone wants to know is "where does this SuSE thing come from, why is it spelled funny, and how do I pronounce it?" Fair questions.

- The Gesellschaft für Software- und System-Entwicklung (Corporation for Software and System Development) was founded in 1992 in Nuremberg, Germany, and released its first distribution of the Linux kernel and associated software a year later. SuSE began publishing its distribution in English in 1997; it opened an office in Oakland, California, at that time.

- The spelling, as you can see, is not derived from some marketer's branding idea. It really is the corporate acronym. However, since being acquired by Novell in 2004, the distribution is now called SUSE (no lowercase letters) Linux, and the acronym no longer stands for anything.

- In German, there are no silent letters, and the letter E is almost always short (as in "the"), so the company's name is pronounced "Sue-suh." Often as not, though, you'll hear it referred to as "Susie" or some variation.

But what is Linux? More properly known as GNU/Linux, it is an operating system born in 1991, when Linus Torvalds, then a computer science student at the University of Helsinki, wanted to run a variation of Unix on his home computer. At that time, Unix ran only on big workstations with lots of power and memory, not Intel-based personal computers. Using tools from the GNU (GNU's Not Unix) project, Torvalds was able to port a usable operating system to PCs. He then made the source code available on the Internet, licensed under the GNU General Public License (GPL).

As a result of that generosity, Linux now runs on nearly every platform and architecture, from cell phones and personal digital assistants to Intel- and Macintosh-based PCs to mainframes and workstations running global enterprises.

SUSE Linux is one of dozens of distributions of Linux. What does this mean? The Linux kernel is really just the central piece of any distribution. Each distribution bundles different pieces of compatible software (most, if not all, licensed under the GPL or other free software license), an installation program, perhaps some documentation and some level of support.

---

**TIP**

Want to learn more about other distributions? See http://distrowatch.com/ for listings of more than 300 distinct offerings.

---

SUSE offers a variety of versions of its core distribution to meet differing needs. This book focuses on SUSE Linux 10, which Novell calls the "community supported" product targeted to home and home-business users. This is the version now created by the OpenSUSE project, which launched in August 2005. The next sections include descriptions of the other versions available.

All these versions use the SUSE install program, YaST (Yet another Setup Tool), to install, configure, and update your Linux installation. Besides being one of the tools that makes SUSE Linux unique, YaST is such a useful and pervasive tool, you'll find mention of it in nearly every chapter in this book. YaST simplifies nearly all your administrative tasks: managing users and groups, updating applications, installing new hardware and maintaining security. YaST also manages your printers through the Common Unix Printing System (CUPS), which contains drivers for more than 1,000 printers.

## SUSE Linux

SUSE has always been well known for having the biggest distribution among the "majors." Hundreds of open-source applications are bundled with SUSE Linux—so many that it takes five CD-ROMs (or one DVD) to hold them all. Half of that includes the source code for the applications, but there are still more applications than you will probably ever use. But consider this: If you have instant access to all these programs, you are less of a prisoner of your installed applications. If you find an application installed with SUSE Linux that isn't doing the job right, chances are that there's another application you can install that will be more to your liking.

If your business needs change and you need some other software tool to get things done, odds are you don't have to pull out your checkbook to get the functionality you need. You just need to fire up YaST and search for the appropriate tool, and in minutes, you're ready to go.

Both Unix and Linux began as systems oriented toward the command line (or *shell*), and the command line is often the fastest and easiest way to get computing tasks done. But just as DOS begat Windows, Unix begat the X Window System. Proprietary X servers later begat the XFree86 project, which became the default GUI for Linux systems. In 2004, the X Consortium, which originally oversaw the development of X, revived and put out its own free server. SUSE Linux opted to use this (referred to as X.org) as the basis for its X Server beginning with v9.1.

Sitting on top of most copies of X these days is a desktop environment: The K Desktop Environment (KDE) or the GNU Network Object Model Environment (GNOME—pronounce the G). Both provide the same sort of look and feel and functionality of proprietary desktops, but each has its own personality. Historically, the SUSE team has been involved in developing KDE practically from the beginning, and so KDE has been the default SUSE desktop, although GNOME was always an option. With SUSE Linux v9.4, you can choose your preferred desktop. You'll learn more about X, KDE, and GNOME in Chapter 6, "Launching Your Desktop."

SUSE Linux also comes with two complete office suites (OpenOffice.org and KOffice), two minisuites (GNOMEOffice, with word processor, database, and spreadsheet, and SoftMaker Office, with word processor and spreadsheet), two industrial strength open-source relational database management systems (PostgreSQL and MySQL), two financial programs (GnuCash and KMyMoney), two personal information managers (Ximian Evolution and Kontact), and just about everything you need to be productive.

When you consider that the Internet largely runs on Unix, there should be no surprise that you can find on your SUSE Linux discs just about anything you need to connect with or do work on the Internet. And many functions have a selection of tools: multiple web browsers (all the browsers you've heard of, except for Internet Explorer, and many you haven't), email clients, chat and instant messaging tools, and newsreaders (for both Usenet and RSS feeds). Web developers and designers also have two web-page creators in Bluefish and Quanta Plus.

Programmers at all skill and experience levels will find practically all the necessary tools for their craft. Text editors galore, starting with the venerable GNU Emacs and vim and including many others of more recent vintage, the GNU Compiler Collection (gcc), support for Perl, Python, Ruby, PHP, Java, and just about any other language you can think of, and at least two integrated development environments (IDEs) in KDevelop and Eclipse. Manage your large projects with the Concurrent Versioning System (CVS) or Subversion, too.

Generally, SUSE Linux is updated with point releases twice a year, but because applications get revised with bug fixes, security fixes, and feature enhancements all the time, you can stay on the cutting edge. Many developers package their applications using the Red Hat Package Management System (RPM). SUSE has always used this method to build its distribution, and many SUSE-specific RPMs have been written. Use the YaST Online Update (YOU) or the Advanced Package Tool (APT) created for Debian systems and adapted for RPM.

With SUSE Linux, you can create many types of systems: a networked file server, a Web server, a DNS server, a mail server, a router, or a plain old desktop workstation.

You can string together several machines to make your own super computer, known as a Beowulf cluster. The choice is yours.

## OpenSUSE.org

On August 9, 2005, Novell announced the OpenSUSE project at the LinuxWorld conference in San Francisco. For the first time, the SUSE community at-large would get to participate in the testing and development process for SUSE Linux. Novell's stated goal in this venture is to make it easy for anyone to get access to "the world's most usable Linux distribution," and to welcome new open-source developers into the SUSE fold.

The OpenSUSE process offers a freely-downloadable distribution that contains only open-source software, with the ability to add non–open-source packages (like the Java Runtime Engine) separately. In addition, OpenSUSE serves as the basis for the boxed, retail version of SUSE Linux, which is the traditional distribution.

To participate in the project, and get the latest installable version of SUSE Linux, visit www.opensuse.org and click the download link (see Figure 1.1).

**FIGURE 1.1**    The OpenSUSE.org website lets you participate in the SUSE Linux development process.

There is much useful content at this site, besides getting both the latest release and the latest test version. How often have you run into a problem that might be a bug, and asked yourself whether the software company is aware of the problem, and on the road to fixing it? With SUSE Linux, now you can check. Novell has opened up its SUSE bug database, Bugzilla; if you run into trouble, you can search the database, and if necessary, submit the problem directly to Bugzilla.

On the OpenSUSE.org site, you can learn more about the distribution. View official documentation, and read posted articles from the Novell website and elsewhere on the Web. View the roadmap for the next release, subscribe to the OpenSUSE discussion/support mailing list, and peruse the FAQs. One of the more interesting aspects of OpenSUSE.org is that it is a Wiki. This means that you—and every other user of the page—can submit content to any page on the site. You are especially encouraged to add content to the Documentation page, so as you learn more about SUSE Linux, you can share that knowledge with other users. You'll learn more about wikis in Chapter 16, "Collaborating with Others."

Users will also be the driving force in future development. Like Red Hat's Fedora Core project, OpenSUSE will be the place where new features and applications first appear. What works will then appear in the regularly updated boxed version of SUSE Linux, and, where appropriate, into the corporate Novell Linux Desktop and SUSE Linux Enterprise Server (SLES).

## The SUSE Linux Install Program

There are several ways to install SUSE Linux, but the easiest is to boot from the CD-ROM that accompanies this book. Your initial install is not the only thing you can do with this CD. You can use it to

- Test your computer's memory—This test confirms that your installed RAM chips are working properly.

- Rescue a troubled system—If you cannot boot your computer at all, booting from the CD gives you access to an emergency command line that can help you access your files and troubleshoot the problem.

## File Systems in SUSE Linux

By default, SUSE Linux uses the ReiserFS v3 file system written by Hans Reiser and maintained by the Namesys team. This is faster and more efficient than the traditional Linux ext2 file system. ReiserFS and other journaling file systems make crash recovery much simpler. When changes (such as creating, deleting, saving, or executing a file) are about to be made to the file system, ReiserFS writes this information in a journal file that exists on the disk. Should the system crash before the change is finished, the repair utility needs to search only the journal to locate the problem, rather than searching the entire disk surface. This makes it easier to repair and preserve your data.

What if you don't like ReiserFS? No problem! The install program will create volumes in ext2, ext3, the IBM Journaling File System (JFS), and XFS, originally developed for the SGI Irix. You will learn more about file systems in Chapter 18, "Managing Files, Volumes, and Drives."

## 64-Bit SUSE Linux

Personal computers have been getting ever more powerful as time goes on. A decade ago, the 32-bit microprocessor, and the new operating systems that could support it, were the focus of attention. The transition from 16-bit processors like the Intel 80286 and its predecessors, to 32-bit processors and the graphical operating systems that supported them, was rapid and changed people's lives. These processors could support four gigabytes of memory, just a phenomenal amount in the days when RAM was measured in mega-bytes. We got genuine multitasking, prettier interfaces—and yes, the ability to think about running UNIX-like systems on PCs.

We are now standing at the dawn of the next revolution in personal computing, as 64-bit processors have come down in price to the point where it's quite possible that your next computer will have one. Servers have been running 64-bit processors for some time now. Since September 2003, AMD has been selling 64-bit Opteron and Athlon chips for ordinary PCs, and the Apple G5 is a 64-bit processor.

What does this mean? A couple of things for the average user. First, your system will (theoretically) support up to 16 million gigabytes of RAM. In practice, however, your system will probably be limited to a mere 256 terabytes or less. This means that applications can run much faster. Chances are they will also be larger, because they can now have more code running at the same speed.

The Linux kernel has supported 64-bit processors from the beginning, and SUSE Linux has run on the x86_64 architecture since version 9.0. If you install the 64-bit version of SUSE Linux (not included with this book's media), nearly all the applications you install will be the 64-bit versions. SUSE Linux will still run 32-bit applications as well, but you are a little more likely to run into problems. Some of the known problems will be mentioned in Notes in this book.

# Getting Help: Documentation and Other Sources

With more than 1,000 programs included in the distribution, even a book this size cannot cover everything in your copy of SUSE Linux.

There are plenty of places to go to learn more about Linux and help you troubleshoot problems with applications. Many of these are included in the references at the end of this and the other chapters of this book.

## Printed Documentation and the SUSE Help Center

SUSE is one of the few software companies anywhere that still provides printed manuals that try to help users beyond installing the product. Buying the boxed version of SUSE Linux gives you two thick books, the Administration Guide and User Guide. Although you can sometimes tell that they have been translated from German, these books have a fairly easy-to-read style that will get you using the product in short order.

Both manuals were also converted into HTML pages and integrated into the electronic SUSE Help Center. This is a boon for the user in two ways: You don't have to rummage around the office to find the books, and you can run a full-text search of both books for the information you're looking for.

The online versions of the manuals are updated regularly, even after your version of the distribution is current, so check for updates at least a couple times a year to be sure you have the latest version.

## Searching the Help Center

Open the Help Center by typing **susehelp** from the shell, or click the life preserver icon in KDE or GNOME. Putter around the Table of Contents to see what is included, or click the Search tab to find something specific. Help-Center search uses the ht://dig engine used on many websites (see Figure 1.2).

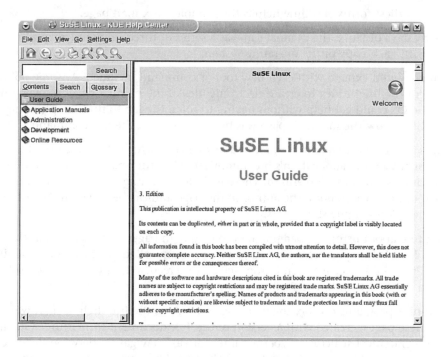

**FIGURE 1.2**    The SUSE Linux Help Center offers the full text of the SUSE Administration Guide and User Guide. It's searchable, too.

The first time you want to run a search, click Create Search Index first so the engine has something to look at. You'll see a set of online books to index; check them all so you can access everything. If you happen to be on a slower machine, results may come faster if you just index the two guides. Click the HTML Search tab to learn a little more about ht://dig and where it is installed on your system (along with learning that the SUSE developers use a Perl script to create the index). When you're ready, click OK to create the index. When you're finished, check the Status column in the main window. Each indexed book should say OK, and what you did not index will say Missing.

The search screen is much like an advanced web search screen where you can select what to search, how many results to return, and how to treat multiple word searches. By default, if you ask Help Center to find the terms "spam" and "filter," the engine will search for documents with both words in it (a Boolean AND). If you want to find either term, choose OR in the Method box. The default search scope is the two manuals. To search all the components, choose All. If you think your answer may be in an info or man page (more on these later), check these boxes, too; the Scope Selection box will switch to Custom automatically. Click Search to find your answer. Results will appear in the right window. Click a hyperlink to see the pertinent article.

## Man and Info Pages

One of the earliest forms of online help is the humble Unix man page.

In the early days of Unix, the manual came as a series of three-ring binders sent out from Bell Labs with each copy of the operating system.

The manual would expand with each new tool or command included. At some point, someone got the bright idea to create electronic files of the manual pages so everyone running the OS could get help without having to roam the lab to find the page they needed. This is how the man(ual) page was born, along with the man command.

Man pages are compressed text files, located in /usr/share/doc. They are usually tersely written (usually by the application's programmers), with information listed under particular categories specified by convention. These include a command reference, a summary of what each option/switch does, the author of the page and/or the program. Occasionally, there are even known bug statements.

To learn more about using the man program to read man pages, type **man man** at the command line. When you press Enter, a paging program called groff will load and display the page. Press the spacebar to scroll from screen to screen. When you're done reading, press the q key to return to the shell prompt.

More complex programs can tax the man page format, so the info help format was created. These pages, created with a version of the TeX document formatting system, include a hierarchical structure, hypertext links for easy navigation between documents, and keyboard and mouse navigational tools. The first time you use info (often when looking for help in the Emacs text editor), it can be a little overwhelming, but it is not too hard to deal with after you have a feel for it. Read the info tutorial (type **info info**) to learn more.

Many man pages are on the web, and you can search both man and info pages in the SUSE Help Center. Start looking for man pages at the Linux Documentation Project (see the following tip). Then try going to http://www.google.com/linux and search.

> **TIP**
>
> Use apropos and whatis to find what you need. If you know what you want to do but are not sure about the tool to use, type `apropos <keyword>` at the shell prompt. Apropos will search the NAME section of each man page (which includes a brief description of the tool's purpose) and display a list of programs and commands that may help. It's not foolproof, but even if you don't find exactly the right tool, you may get on the road to finding what you really need.
>
> The whatis program does the inverse of apropos. Suppose you couldn't remember what the acronym "bash" stood for. Type `whatis bash` and you'll know!

## SUSE Online Support

The SUSE support website at http://www.suse.com/us/private/support/index.html is a great resource for getting help. There is a mix of paid and free online support.

When you're trying to find a solution for a problem, click Support Database from the main Support menu, or just go directly to the Support Database at http://portal.suse.com/sdb/en/index.html. This database is searchable, either via keyword or full text. Besides German and English, the database exists in French, Spanish, Czech, and Hungarian (Magyar).

> **NOTE**
>
> At the time of writing, Novell was still in the process of converting the suse.com web pages to novell.com servers. If you can't find a page listed here, check the http://www.novell.com/linux home page to see where it may have moved to.

The Online Support menu on the main support page links to some interesting HOWTO documents, showing you step-by-step how to accomplish many tasks, from partitioning your hard drive to comparing HTML editors to encrypting email.

Novell also offers what they call "Cool Communities," on their website. This is an area where assorted experts offer tips on a regular basis. There's even a Wiki page, where you can post your own articles and questions, at http://wiki.novell.com/index.php/SUSE_LINUX_Professional.

> **TIP**
>
> Learn more about wikis in Chapter 16.

## The Linux Documentation Project

The place to start for more user-friendly guides to Linux tools and applications is the Linux Documentation Project. Frequently Asked Questions (FAQ) lists, HOWTO pages, and more detailed guides to applications are written, reviewed, and edited by a team of volunteers and compiled at the LDP site, www.tldp.org.

Because all the documents here are formatted in DocBook XML, everything here is presented in a variety of formats; at least one should meet your needs. Site search is powered by Google and is right on the home page, so finding items related to your question is quick and easy. You can also easily see the most recently updated documents or just browse through categories to educate yourself.

The howtoenh packages included on the SUSE Linux disk are not updated often, but can be helpful. They are not installed by default, so if you want them, use YaST.

## The SUSE Mailing Lists

SUSE sponsors 51 electronic mailing lists in multiple languages to allow users to help each other with problems and questions. The general list in English, suse-linux-e, generates some 150 messages per day on all topics, but most lists are more specialized. Read descriptions of all the lists, with links to the list archives, at http://www.suse.com/us/private/support/online_help/mailinglists/. You can also subscribe to multiple lists on this page; just check the box next to the list you want to subscribe to and type your email address at the bottom of the page. You must subscribe to a list to post a question.

The chief problem with the archives is that they are not directly searchable. You can browse the monthly archives, which are sorted by thread for solutions, but this can be time consuming. Fortunately, Google and most other search engines can do site-specific searches.

To search all the lists for Perl-related issues, the Google syntax is

```
perl site:lists.suse.com.
```

To search just suse-linux-e, change the site to lists.suse.com/archive/suse-linux-e/.

Your favorite search engine may use different syntax; check the engine's support page for specific information.

Because these lists are high traffic, make sure to check the archives before posting a question yourself. Chances are whatever you are experiencing, someone else is, too. To get the best help from the list, keep these things in mind:

- When you ask a question, describe any problem as specifically as possible. Include pertinent sections of log files, with the error messages you received.

- Describe your efforts to solve the problem. "I've searched the Help Center and the archives. I saw the discussion about a similar problem and tried the solution, but it didn't work (or here's why my problem is different from that one)."

- Be patient! Although sometimes questions can be answered and problems solved in minutes, that's not the norm. If people don't respond, wait a few days (if you can) before asking again. The person who has your answer just may be busy at that moment. If you can't wait for a solution, try another list, or contact your local Linux User Group (see the next section).

- After you have asked a question, hang around for a while. Perhaps you can answer someone else's question—what goes around comes around.

There is also a SUSE Users Yahoo Group. Sign up or view the archives at http://groups.yahoo.com/group/suselinuxusers/.

## Linux User Groups

When you really want a live, knowledgeable human being to help you with a problem or teach you something, most users have just two choices: hire a consultant for big bucks or find your closest friend who knows something about computers. Problem is, that tech-savvy friend is probably pretty well versed in working with one or another of the propri-etary operating systems produced on the West Coast, but might not know a lot about Unix or Linux. What do you do now?

Fortunately, if you live reasonably close to a decent-sized population center or town with a college campus, there is likely to be a gaggle of Linux-savvy people just a few mouse clicks away—your local Linux User Group (LUG). These people usually meet once a month for speakers, demonstrations, occasional door prizes, and general camaraderie. Most active LUGs have websites, and many have email lists where problems get solved, equipment gets traded, and opinions about various technical and Linux-related issues are shared. If you are slightly intimidated by the thought of installing Linux on your computer, LUGs frequently hold "install fests" where experienced folks will install SUSE or another distribution (your choice) on your system and give you pointers along the way. As with most everything Linux, this all comes free of charge.

Now you can't just pick up a phone book and call the LUG office to get started, but it is not especially hard to find one either. You can check your daily newspaper for meeting notices (these are often found on the business pages) or call your public library for infor-mation. Some communities still have specialty computer magazines left over from the tech boom days that list user groups of all kinds.

The fastest way to find a LUG is probably online. Linux Gazette magazine hosts the Groups of Linux Users Everywhere (GLUE) site at http://glue.linuxgazette.com. They are organized geographically, so you can browse through the listings or search from the main page. Every group has an email contact, and many have a URL listed. If a website is not listed here, do not assume the group doesn't have one. Searching is an option. Both Google and Yahoo have Linux User Group directories, but rather than sort through a complicated directory structure, just type "**<yourtown> Linux User Group**" into the regular search box.

# References

Each chapter in this book includes a reference section with links to more or related infor-mation about the subject of the chapter. Use it to build a set of bookmarks to help you learn more about Linux in general, and SUSE Linux in particular.

- http://www-1.ibm.com/linux/—The Linux portal at IBM, which has news, reports, and white papers related to this important Linux player. Check the SUSE Linux link under "Linux Distributors" for material related to IBM support for SUSE Linux products.

- http://www.novell.com/linux/suse/—The English-language home of SUSE Linux. News, downloads, support.

- http://support.novell.com/linux/—Search the support database, read HOWTOs, and subscribe to a mailing list.

- http://portal.suse.com/sdb/en—Direct link to the SUSE support database.

- http://www.opensuse.org—The home of the OpenSUSE project. Download the latest version for testing and use. Sign up for a mailing list and contribute to the OpenSUSE wiki.

- http://www.namesys.com—Learn about the ReiserFS file system here.

- http://www.tldp.org/—The Linux Documentation Project. Where to go for general Linux questions and to learn about many of the applications included in your SUSE Linux distribution.

- http://glue.linuxgazette.com/—Groups of Linux Users Everywhere. Find your nearest Linux Users Group.

- http://linuxgazette.net/—The Linux Gazette, "making Linux just a little more fun." This electronic magazine is oriented toward new Linux users. Ask The Answer Gang your question.

- http://www.google.com/linux—The Google Linux-specific search page.

# CHAPTER 2

# Preparing to Install SUSE Linux

It is easier to buy a Linux PC today than it was a few years ago, but manufacturers still don't see the need, even if they are strong Linux proponents (such as IBM and Novell).

So the odds are very good that you will have to install SUSE Linux yourself, especially if you want to use it as your everyday desktop system.

Even if you are not planning to install SUSE Linux on 10 different servers and 47 desktops, changing operating systems is not a matter to be taken lightly. You should give as much consideration to the questions of meeting hardware requirements, dual-boot arrangements, what applications to install, and how your one new SUSE Linux system relates to the other machines on your network as any Chief Information Officer (CIO) would.

If you are approaching this installation with some trepidation, relax!

Although some of the horror stories of the bygone past may have been true, your experience installing SUSE Linux is much more likely to be a pleasant memory down the road. If you have a typical system with reasonably modern hardware, installing should be a snap. To make that even more likely, it is important to plan ahead. This chapter and the next two will help you make an easy transition.

In this chapter, we will think carefully about all the things that you need to consider before installing SUSE Linux.

We will go over the minimum and recommended system requirements for using SUSE Linux and try to help you avoid some of the potential driver-related problems with some peripherals.

Finally, there are the questions of partitioning your hard drive(s), which you should definitely think about before starting to install.

SUSE Linux is very flexible, and can meet most any computing need you have. This chapter is about figuring out what those needs are.

# Planning Your SUSE Linux Installation

Even if you are installing SUSE Linux on a single computer (which is a basic assumptions in this book), there may be some business-related considerations to make before getting started with SUSE Linux.

If you know ahead of time what you need and want from your new system, you will save time. You can always make changes down the road.

The most important consideration is: What do you want to do with your SUSE Linux system? Will it run just the Apache web server or be your network file server? Will the computer be connected to the Internet? If so, how? Do you want to launch a web-hosting business? Will it be just a toy to practice on or a full-time tool?

Will you have to access Windows files on other computers or on the same machine?

If you have some other operating system (OS) now performing the task(s) you want Linux to do, you should think about why you want to make a change.

There is a cost to migrating in time and training, although in most cases, Linux makes that cost very worthwhile.

---

**TIP**

As you plan for your install, keep a notebook handy to write things down as you think of them, and always keep it around to make notes as things happen while you're running Linux. Text files typed into the machine are handy, as are sticky notes. But when something breaks and you can't get to those electronic notes, you'll be happy you have something to refer to.

I got this tip from Matt Welsh's *Running Linux* when I was starting out, and it is still one of the best tips I ever got.

---

Another thing to consider is what to do with your existing OS. Later on in this chapter, you'll learn about setting up your machine to dual boot Windows and SUSE Linux.

This is an easy thing to do, assuming you have the space. Before you decide, make a list of all the things you use your computer for and the applications you use. Look at the list of applications in your Windows Start menu to be thorough; it's easy to forget some of the things that are second nature to use. Try to find a Linux counterpart. Start with the list at http://linuxshop.ru/linuxbegin/win-lin-soft-en/table.shtml and match the Linux applications to your Windows list.

To get you started, look at Table 2.1. This is a sampling of the list I made for myself. The list of applications features some of the best-known applications for their category, but the list is not comprehensive by any means.

**TABLE 2.1**   Selected Computing Tasks and Linux Applications

| Task | Windows Application | Linux Application |
| --- | --- | --- |
| Browsing the Web | Internet Explorer | Netscape/Mozilla/Firefox, Opera, Konqueror, Galeon, Epiphany |
| Budget stretching | Quicken, Money, QuickBooks | Gnucash, KMyMoney |
| Developing websites | Dreamweaver, FrontPage, HomeSite | Quanta, Bluefish, emacs |
| Editing photos and graphics | Photoshop, Paint Shop Pro | The GIMP |
| Editing plain text | Notepad/WordPad, JEdit, NoteTab | KWrite, Emacs, XEmacs, vim, JEdit |
| Number crunching | Excel, Paradox OpenOffice.org Calc | OpenOffice.org Calc, KSpread, Gnumeric |
| Opening and creating Zip archives | WinZip, ZipMagic, PKZip | Ark, GNOME File Roller, command-line |
| Playing MP3 and other multimedia content | WinAmp, MusicMatch, RealPlayer, Windows Media Player | XMMS, Xine, Kaffeine, FreeAmp, RealPlayer (Helix Community version) |
| Playing RealAudio streaming audio files | RealPlayer | RealPlayer (Helix Community version), XMMS |
| Reading and writing email | Outlook/Outlook Express, Mozilla Thunderbird, Eudora, Pegasus Mail | KMail, Mozilla Thunderbird, Evolution, Sylpheed |
| Word processing | Word, WordPerfect, OpenOffice.org, Writer, Abiword | OpenOffice.org Writer, Abiword, Kword |
| Managing personal information (contacts, calendar) | Outlook, Lotus Notes, Groupwise | Evolution, Kontact, Groupwise |

# System Requirements

The first thing to know and understand is that the days of worrying whether your current hardware setup will run Linux are largely over. SUSE Linux will run on most any Intel-based hardware. Novell/SUSE promises full support on anything Pentium-classed, including Celerons and AMD K5 processors.

SUSE will also handle DEC Alpha and various multiprocessor systems quite well. Two ends of the aging process present difficulties: Aging 486 machines and brand-new machines with 64-bit processors and the high-performance gaming video card just released last week may have problems (though perhaps fewer than you might think).

> **NOTE***
>
> Do you have a 64-bit processor on your PC? See the section on 64-bit SUSE Linux in Chapter 1, "Welcome to SUSE Linux."

Hardware problems generally stem from vendors not writing Linux drivers for their equipment. This is distinctly true for laptop manufacturers. Because of Linux's recent gain in popularity, the biggest hardware vendors are beginning to support Linux with their hardware, either providing drivers directly or providing open-source developers with software development kits (SDKs) for writing open-source drivers. The drivers often wind up directly in the Linux kernel for all distributions.

SUSE recommends three basic system requirements for running SUSE Linux 10:

- Processor—Pentium 1–4; AMD Duron, Athlon, Athlon XP, Athlon MP, or Athlon 64; Intel Celeron or EMT 64

- Main memory—At least 128MB; 256MB recommended

- Hard disk—At least 500MB; 2.5GB recommended for standard system

Before installing SUSE Linux, you should spend some time and compare your existing hardware with the SUSE Linux Hardware Database at http://cdb.suse.de/.

The site offers two types of hardware search. The Express Search lets you type in a vendor or device type, or you can browse from the preselected hardware categories.

> **TIP**
>
> If you are migrating from Microsoft Windows and are unsure of the details (manufacturer, type, and so on) of your hardware, go to the Device Manager to find out. Right-click My Computer and choose Properties from the context menu. Go to the Hardware tab and click Device Manager. Select the system at the top of the list. Click Print to get a list of all your devices.
>
> This can be quite lengthy. For something a little more configurable, try downloading the shareware product mvPCinfo or using another third-party system utility.

The results of the Express Search is just a Yes or No, with some listings of "partial." Click the Details button for more information on a specific item, including whether older versions of SUSE Linux support an item. Results are printable; click the link at the top of the page.

The Extended Search offers many more categories and many more ways of sifting the data. Use this search if you want to check whether your Zip drive, ham radio card, or your ISDN high-speed connection will work under DEC Alpha (see Figure 2.1).

The main results page is similar to the Express page, but the honesty level of the Status column is refreshing. Some printers, for example, are listed as Problematic. You are encouraged to click the Details button for more information. Here, too, results are printable.

> **NOTE**
>
> Do not panic if you search for a specific item and it is not in the database. With the number of vendors and different pieces of hardware out there, it's hard to test everything, especially when you are also trying to write and test software! For example, there are very few ADSL high-speed modems in the SUSE database, but judging from personal experience and what comes up on the SUSE support lists, the record is quite good on recognizing and supporting these devices.

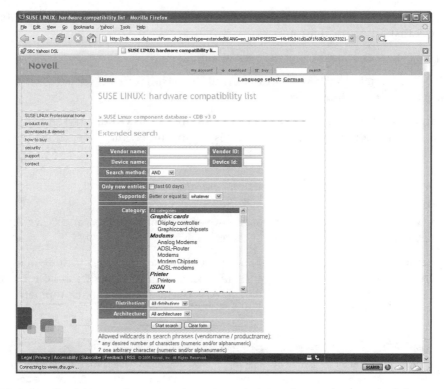

**FIGURE 2.1** The SUSE Hardware Database Extended Search page lets you look for just about anything.

When searching the database, here are some of the categories you'll want to confirm:

- Controller cards—Particularly if you have SCSI or FireWire.

- CPUs—As listed before, virtually every modern CPU is supported, but there's no harm in checking.

- Input devices—If you have an ancient keyboard, there might be an issue.

- Modems—See the section on WinModems later in this chapter.

- Network cards—Generally not an issue, but if you're planning on Linux managing your network resources, it would be bad to have a nonsupported card.

- Pointing devices—Mice and tablets, especially for laptops.

- Printers—Consult http://www.linuxprinting.org in addition to the SUSE hardware database for current information about printers on Linux.

- RAM—Some chipsets have problems.

- Sound cards—Most popular cards are fine, but might not have every feature.

- Motherboards—If you've built your PC from scratch with a relatively obscure board, check first for compatibility.

- Storage devices—Some Zip drives have issues.

- Universal Serial Bus (USB) devices—Consult the USB-Linux device page http://www.qbik.ch/usb/devices/ for current information.

- Video cards—Occasional problems occur running the X Window System. You may not get the highest resolutions the card is capable of. Nvidia drivers must be downloaded separately via YaST.

## Linux on Laptops

SUSE Linux 10 has improved support for the Advanced Configuration and Power Interface (ACPI) standard, so your laptop battery will last longer.

If you plan to run Linux on your laptop, be aware that manufacturers include many proprietary drivers for their hardware, and Linux support may be spotty at best. But don't be completely discouraged. The Linux on Laptops page at http://linux-laptop.net/ has the latest news and HOWTOs on its subject.

> **TIP**
>
> If you are in the market for a new Linux laptop, a few companies have sprung up to preinstall SUSE Linux, or any other distribution you want, on a name-brand portable. Browse the ads in your favorite Linux magazine or head over to http://www.linuxcertified.com/ or http://emperorlinux.com/.

## SUSE Linux and Legacy Hardware

The problem with older hardware and Linux is, as stated earlier, a general lack of device drivers. This is somewhat reasonable, in that the operating system was being built from the ground up, both in terms of people hacking on the Linux kernel and using it. As Linux grew in usage, at least on the server, more hardware manufacturers took notice, and more active support existed for server-side cards and peripherals. Only recently have advanced video cards, dial-up modems, and printers started shipping with Linux drivers.

Do not fret if you have an ancient Pentium box with the 33MHz processor, built-in sound and video cards, and the 1 gigabyte hard drive. Although you may not be able to install a GUI on it, there are several valuable modern-day uses you can put that box to. These include the following:

- Save tons of space on your other machines by installing all your fonts on this one and attaching it to the network.

- Store and play your MP3 (or Ogg Vorbis) music collection.

- Store data backups from CD or tape.

- Build a hardware firewall for your network.

- Make it a web server for your intranet.

- Make it your email box with fetchmail, postfix, and a text-based email client (mutt, pine, emacs).

- Put a fax modem in it and make it your fax machine.

- Host a remote printer.

- Build an FTP server.

With pre-Pentium processors (386/486), you will probably not be able to run any current version of SUSE Linux. You should be able to install a basic Debian GNU/Linux, though. Check out the Debian Project at http://www.debian.org.

## Avoiding Potential Hardware Problems

It should come as no surprise that no operating system is perfect. With every Windows service pack, some software breaks, and that often includes hardware drivers. The same is true with Linux. Many devices will work out of the box or at the point of install. More and more, manufacturers are providing Linux drivers for their equipment. But some pieces of hardware always seem to have at least some trouble working under Linux. This section is designed to help you through the special minefields.

## Software-Based Modems

Most computer peripherals handle whatever task they are built for by themselves; all that's needed is a device driver that integrates with the operating system. Tell an application you want to print the file on your screen, the application tells the OS, which tells the driver, which tells the printer. Done!

An exception to this rule exists that most users may never realize until they install Linux on their computer. Suddenly the modem doesn't work anymore, and you can't access the Internet. Welcome to the world of WinModems! Many popular modem models, both the internal and external varieties, work as you would expect. Driver support for modems is excellent under Linux. Some modems, though, move much of the functioning to software—software designed for Microsoft Windows.

The argument for this setup is that it is easier and cheaper to update software than hardware, but making hardware functioning dependent on having a specific operating system seems difficult, at best. This is somewhat like Michelin deciding to make tires only for General Motors, telling Ford owners they'd have to make their own if they wanted to use the features Michelin had, only they won't tell you how they did it.

Nonetheless, many open-source software developers have taken on the challenge of making Winmodems work under Linux. Not that many years ago, the only choice available to users was to buy another modem, but that is no longer true. Some Winmodem makers have helped provide details and development kits to create open-source drivers. IBM has integrated support for software-based modems on the ThinkPad 600/E and 770 in the Linux kernel.

It's always best to check for Linux compatibility before buying a modem, but you don't always get that choice. The place to turn for information on Winmodems on Linux is http://www.linmodems.org.

## Universal Serial Bus Devices

The Universal Serial Bus (USB) specification was designed to allow PCs to support more peripheral devices without adding serial or parallel connections to an already overburdened pile of cables. It also allows devices that don't need a permanent connection to the PC (such as digital cameras and audio players) to plug in and out only as needed, without having to reboot, much less open the box every time you needed it.

Nearly all PCs produced since the late 1990s have included at least two ports based on v1.1 of the USB specification. Devices built to this specification move data to and from the device to the PC at speeds between 1.5 and 12 megabytes per second (MBps). USB V2.0 permits much faster transfer speeds (up to 480 MBps), and so now you see even portable hard drives plugging into USB 2.0 ports and moving data swiftly.

Among the types of devices you'll see that plug into a USB port are keyboards, mice, modems, scanners, printers, digital cameras, webcams, and network cards (both wired and wireless).

The Linux kernel has supported the USB standard since v2.2.18, so all recent versions of SUSE Linux support at least USB 1.1 through the uhci kernel module. Developers working on the 2.6 kernel created the ehci module to support USB 2.0 and have since included compatible modules for earlier kernel versions, going back to v2.4. Still, some USB devices still have problems, mainly wireless (802.11b) network adapters, scanners, and some webcams.

Visit http://www.qbik.ch/usb/devices/ to search an excellent database of USB devices, and visit http://www.linux-usb.org/ for general information on this topic.

## "Peripherals" on the Motherboard

Most laptops and some less-expensive desktop PCs include built-in video, audio, and network support right on the motherboard. This practice lowers power requirements and simplifies the design, although these units often don't have all the power and features of more expensive PCI cards.

If these are new devices, Linux support can be flaky.

When buying these machines, be careful to check for Linux support. Ask the vendor questions, and get answers. That's good advice for anything, but especially if you have a new, cutting-edge notebook, because you can't replace just one piece of a notebook yourself. It almost always has to go back to the factory.

## Thinking About Dual Booting, Partitioning, and Other Worries

The last thing you need to think about before beginning your SUSE Linux installation is the question of what to do with your current installed OS. Chances are you have perfectly good data on your computer that you want to keep. This should already be backed up on some other media (CD-ROM, Zip drive, tape) in any case. But what about that copy of Windows XP under which you have created all that data? Do you want to start over from scratch, or should you keep it around? This goes back to the original question asked at the beginning of the chapter—what do you want to do with your PC?

Unless you have a small hard drive packed with applications and data, installing SUSE Linux alongside your existing Windows and using a boot manager to switch back and forth is a simple matter. Installing a standard Office package with X, KDE, and OpenOffice would not take up more than 1 gigabyte of space. Table 2.2 shows you what SUSE recommends in the way of partition sizes for various uses:

**TABLE 2.2**    Recommended Partition Sizes

| Type of Install | Partition Size |
| --- | --- |
| Minimum install (no X Window System) | 180MB |
| Minimum with X Window System | 500MB |
| Standard graphical install | 1–2GB |
| (one desktop environment, | |
| OpenOffice, web browser) | |
| Storing multimedia | 2GB |
| (music and video clips) | |
| CD burning | 1GB |
| All of the above | 4GB |

As you can see, SUSE Linux won't eat up your 80GB drive all at once—or even after a lot of usage. And even if you're a glutton for choices, it's not really a problem. A system with both KDE and GNOME desktop environments, three office suites, five browsers, six text editors (both graphical and plain), a couple of personal information managers, and a fair amount of data still barely takes up 10GB.

So if for any reason you want to keep Windows around, this is easily done.

## Dual Booting with Windows

When installing SUSE to dual boot with Windows, YaST installs SUSE Linux into an "extended" partition, leaving Windows with the primary partition.

> **NOTE**
>
> On any dual-boot machine, Windows must *always* be installed first.

SUSE Linux comes with a free software-partitioning tool, GNU Parted, that works much like the commercial products Partition Magic and Partition Commander. This makes it easier to create and organize data on your drive. Unlike the `fdisk` tool (both the DOS/Windows and UNIX/Linux versions) that destroys data when modifying partitions, Parted protects the data on partitions that are being resized. YaST uses a version of Parted called Expert Partitioner during the initial install, and the root user can run it directly from YaST at any time to resize, delete, or add partitions. Learn more about Parted/Expert Partitioner in Chapter 18, "Managing Files, Volumes, and Drives."

---

**CAUTION**

Anytime you want to play with the partition table, be aware that you are putting your data at some risk, even if it is a small one. Power surges, fuse burnouts, and temporary blackouts happen, and never at a convenient time. Always back up critical data. Have an emergency boot disk on hand. Create one when the SUSE Linux install asks you to. See Chapter 20, "Managing Data: Backup, Restoring, and Recovery," for more information.

---

The downside to dual booting is that you must reboot every time you want to use a different OS. Shutdown and startup time can add up when you are trying to get things done. The good news is that you don't have to do this to access and use a data file on the Windows side of your box. SUSE Linux will read and open (with an appropriate application) any file on your system. Linux supports both FAT and NTFS file systems. When detecting the presence of a Windows file system, SUSE Linux creates a `/windows` directory where it stores and displays your directories and files. How much you can move and copy files to and from these directories depends on the underlying Windows file system. Linux permissions won't transfer from a Linux file system to the Windows File Allocation Table (FAT), and copying from a Linux file system to the NT File System (NTFS) used by default in Windows NT/2000/XP is nearly impossible. Unfortunately, no Windows OS supports any Linux file system. Third-party Windows utilities allow you to view and copy files from a Linux ext2 file system, but none will let you open a file directly from your `/home` directory.

---

**NOTE**

Want to work with files on a Windows box on your network? For that you need Samba. See Chapter 25, "Setting Up Networks and Samba."

---

## How to Partition Your Drive(s)

Whether you dual boot or not, you will need at least two partitions to run SUSE Linux properly. You can do this before the install with a commercial product if you're comfortable doing that, or YaST will help you with the process during the install. If you are not planning to dual boot, you are probably better off waiting for the install, as YaST will reformat the drive for you.

The two minimum partitions are the root partition, signified with a forward slash (/), and a swap partition, which Linux uses as virtual memory. Traditionally, the size of the swap partition is equivalent to (or a multiple of) the amount of hardware RAM you have installed. So if you have 256MB of RAM, your swap should be 256MB (or even 512MB) as well. YaST will configure this automatically during the install.

If you have only these two partitions, YaST will put all the other standard directories on the same partition as /. These are

- /bin—Binary files.
- /boot—Files to boot Linux.
- /dev—Device drivers.
- /etc—Configuration files.
- /home—Each user gets a data directory under this one.
- /lib—Libraries, the underlying code for many applications.
- /media—Removable disks and drives (floppy discs, CD-ROMs, Zips).
- /mnt—The mount directory, where all partitions (mount points) are listed.
- /opt—Some applications install to this directory instead of /usr.
- /proc—A dynamic directory where all running processes are logged. Constantly changing.
- /root—Not to be confused with plain / (also called "root"), this is the home directory for the root user.
- /sbin—System binaries, usually files that need to run during startup.
- /srv—Services.
- /tmp—Temporary files.
- /usr—Most applications install themselves here.
- /var—Variable files and programs, including print spoolers, mail clients, and security logs, are stored here.

You may want to consider putting one or several of these directories on a separate partition (mount point), because doing so can make a drive more efficient and ready for expansion. Candidates for separate mount points include /home (especially with multiple users on the same system), /opt (if you find several applications installing here, setting aside a gigabyte as a mount point could improve performance), and /usr (this would enable you to further separate programs from data and may improve performance; make this partition up to 6GB if you plan to install everything on the SUSE install disks).

## References

This set of links points to useful resources on partitioning, installing Linux on a variety of hardware, and other installation tools.

- http://linux.dell.com—Home of the Dell Linux Community. Dell is focused on Enterprise Linux and will sell you servers with either SUSE Linux Enterprise Server or Red Hat Enterprise Server, but the community site offers mailing lists to support Linux users on desktops and laptops as well.

- http://linuxshop.ru/linuxbegin/win-lin-soft-en/table.shtml—Look here for Linux equivalents of Windows applications.

- http://cdb.suse.de—The SUSE hardware compatibility database.

- http://www.linuxprinting.org—Want to see if your printer works in Linux? Here's the place.

- http://www.linux-usb.org—The Linux-USB project, with information on supported devices and drivers.

- http://www.qbik.ch/usb/devices—The Linux USB devices database to search for compatible devices.

- http://www.linmodems.org—Linux drivers for software-based modems.

- http://www.linuxcertified.com and http://emperorlinux.com—Two companies that deliver laptops with Linux preinstalled.

- http://linux-laptop.net—More information on Linux-friendly laptops.

- http://www.linux1394.org—The Linux FireWire project with information on drivers for these devices.

- http://elks.sourceforge.net—The Embeddable Linux Kernel Subset, an attempt to build some Linux functionality that will run on an Intel 286 and earlier processor.

- http://www.lnx-bbc.org—Home of the Linux Bootable Business Card project, producing a "live CD" in the shape of a standard business card.

- http://www.knoppix.org—Another Live CD project; stick the CD in the drive and run Linux, no matter what OS is installed on the hard drive.

- http://www.gnu.org/software/parted/parted.html—Home of GNU Parted, the free software disk-partitioning tool.

# CHAPTER 3

# Installing SUSE Linux

Installing SUSE Linux is a simple process. The SUSE Linux YaST application (Yet another Setup Tool) walks you through the process, detects and configures your hardware, and generally takes charge. In this chapter, you learn how to complete a basic installation of SUSE Linux using the CDs included with this book.

At this stage of the game, you're probably anxious to get started, but a brief introduction helps you make sure everything is ready. Then you can begin the installation and follow this chapter's advice all the way through.

By the end of the chapter, you will have logged in for the first time, ready to use SUSE Linux.

## Methods of Installing SUSE Linux

SUSE Linux can be installed on a workstation through a plethora of possibilities. The installation can be done from a central server, across the network, or using any of the media types available (CD ROM/DVD).

Because this book includes the operating system on accompanying media, we will focus on installing it using those. While the method is different with the other types of installation, most follow the same steps and you can easily find information specific to those installations on the website.

# Preparing to Install from a CD-ROM or DVD

The media included with this book is bootable and will install SUSE Linux directly when you start your computer. The main thing you need to know before starting the process is whether your BIOS is set to boot from your CD-ROM or DVD-ROM drive.

---
**CAUTION**

Changing BIOS settings can be dangerous, and it's not hard to make a computer unbootable with the wrong setting. Follow these instructions carefully and don't change any other setting unless you know what you're doing.

---

To check this, reboot your computer. Among the first things you see on your screen as the computer starts up is the method of accessing your BIOS settings. Often this is the Delete or Escape key; other times, it is one of the function keys at the top of the keyboard. Each BIOS manufacturer does things differently. Press this key as soon as you see it. Shortly, the settings will appear.

Look for a setting title called Boot Sequence, Boot Order, or something similar. This setting determines where the BIOS looks for a bootloader code that tells it the volume is bootable. The setting itself should look something like this if the CD-ROM is to be checked first:

```
CD-ROM, C:, floppy
```

---
**TIP**

Change the order accordingly if you are installing from DVD.

---

Every drive that may be bootable should be listed here. This order points first to the CD drive, then the hard drive (which may be identified as either IDE or SCSI instead of the Windows drive letter), and then the floppy. It's possible that either the hard drive or the floppy may come first in the sequence. In this instance, you should adjust the setting so that the CD is checked before the hard drive. To change the setting, use the Tab key to highlight the Boot Sequence, then press Enter to change the setting. This process, again, varies from BIOS to BIOS. You should get a list of possible sequences from which you can choose, or you may have to select each drive in the order you want.

---
**NOTE**

Checking other drives before the hard drive will slow your boot time a few seconds, so you may want to reset the Boot Sequence after your SUSE Linux installation is completed.

Learn more about your BIOS and the boot process in Chapter 22, "Managing the Boot Process and Other Services."

---

Select a sequence similar to the one listed in this section, and save your new choice. If the first SUSE Linux CD or the SUSE DVD is in the drive, it should now boot. If not, and another operating system is installed, the computer may boot to that OS. If the computers boots to another OS, make sure the SUSE CD is in the drive and then restart your computer.

# Installing SUSE Linux with YaST

The installation begins when you insert the first SUSE Linux CD into your drive and boot up. A menu appears with several startup choices (see Figure 3.1). Select Installation. YaST will identify and initialize the hardware it needs to begin, and then display the Novell Software License Agreement. Click I Agree to continue to the first installation screen. Select your preferred language from the extensive list.

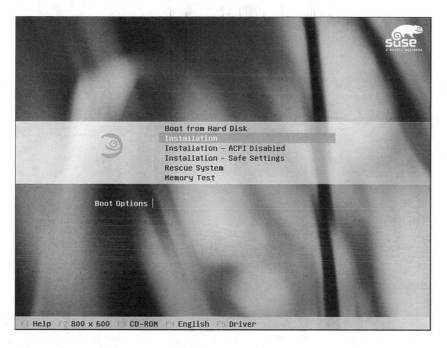

**FIGURE 3.1**    Select an Installation option from this initial screen.

## Initial Installation Settings

YaST loads the kernel modules for your hard drive and then displays a list of Installation Settings (see Figure 3.2). Review carefully all the settings for accuracy and click either the heading of each section or the Change button on the bottom to correct any errors.

> **TIP**
>
> If you have a two-button mouse, notice that YaST will automatically emulate a three-button mouse. This lets you access many middle-button features by clicking both buttons at the same time.

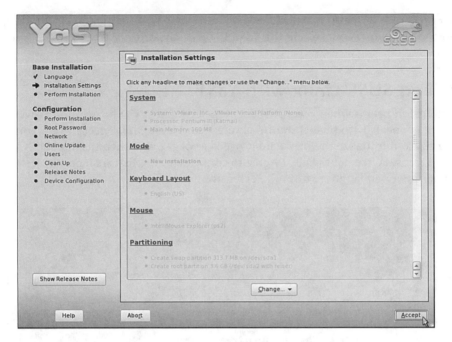

**FIGURE 3.2**   YaST autodetects your hardware and makes some default choices about your installation. Edit any default selection by clicking the heading or using the Change button.

## Partitioning

You learned most of what you need to know about how disks are partitioned under Linux in Chapter 2, "Preparing to Install SUSE Linux." YaST creates a Root and swap partition by default. If you want to add partitions or use a different file system than ReiserFS, select the Partitioning heading and make your changes.

> **TIP**
>
> If YaST detects the presence of another operating system, it will ask whether you want to replace that OS with SUSE Linux or dual boot both. YaST will use the GNU Parted partitioning tool to shrink the existing partition and allow SUSE Linux to install. If you have two physical hard drives and want to install Linux on the second drive, it will format that drive accordingly.
>
> See "Thinking About Dual Booting, Partitioning, and Other Worries," in Chapter 2, and Chapter 11, "Going Cross-Platform," for more information.

## Setting Your Time Zone

Use the Time Zone section to identify your location so that the system time will be correct for your time zone. By default, time is marked using a 24-hour clock, rather than the AM/PM divide. You can change this in YaST later. See "Setting Date and Time" in Chapter 4, "Further Configuration with YaST2 and SaX2."

## Installing Software Packages

By default, YaST installs the Standard System with KDE, a selection of basic applications and the K Desktop Environment. If you prefer the other leading Linux desktop environment, you can install the Standard System with GNOME. Click the Software section of the Installation Settings, and click the appropriate button.

Click Accept when you are ready to install the base system. Depending on the software packages you selected, you may have to view and accept other license agreements for certain applications (for example, the Macromedia Flash player).

---

**CAUTION**

YaST will also warn you that it is formatting a partition and that any data on that partition will be destroyed. This gives you one more chance to turn back in case you have data on your computer that you want to preserve. Click Install to begin the process.

---

YaST formats the designated partition for the data drive and the swap partition and then begins installing the operating system and the designated software packages. Depending on the amount of software to be installed and the speed of your processor and CD drive, the time it takes to do this will vary. The right side of your screen contains a progress bar that gives you a total estimate of the time remaining.

If you are installing from the CD set (rather than from the DVD), you'll see a few horizontal bars crossing the progress bar; they represent the approximate time until you'll have to swap CDs again. Feel free to walk away from the keyboard while the installation proceeds. The DVD contains all the files on the single disk and frees you from the worry of needing to be ready to swap media as needed.

---

**NOTE**

To pass the time while YaST is installing, you can watch the slide show, which (as is traditional in lengthy software installations) presents a rundown of some of the new features in this version, or click the Details tab (see Figure 3.3) to see the list of packages being installed (and an overview of the number of packages installed from each CD).

---

After the base system is installed, YaST reboots your computer to make sure things are in good shape to begin (you will have a 10-second warning when you can stop the reboot, if necessary). Leave the first CD in the drive for the reboot. When the reboot is complete, the Package Installation screen appears, and you'll be asked to insert the second CD.

Packages will continue to install, and the blue progress bar will continue to shrink. You'll be asked again to swap out CDs occasionally until the installation is complete.

## Creating the root User

When all the packages have been installed, you will become the system administrator for the first time. Your task is to create the first user on the system: root. This is done simply enough: In UNIX and Linux, a user equals a password.

**FIGURE 3.3**    View the details of the software package installation in this screen.

The first password you create, for the root user, is by far the most important. The root user has complete control over the system, for good or evil. Therefore, the root password must be secure and easy to remember. If you forget the root password, it becomes extremely difficult (although not impossible) to access any system files. At minimum, the root password must be at least five characters and should have a mixture of letters, cases, and numbers.

> **TIP**
>
> See "Selecting Passwords" in Chapter 19, "Managing Users, Managing Security," for tips on creating secure passwords.

Click Expert Options to choose the encryption method for your passwords (see Figure 3.4). By default, SUSE Linux uses the DES standard, but it is much safer to use the Blowfish encryption standard because it allows for up to 72 characters in the password string. This is much harder to crack randomly. When you have typed and confirmed the root password, click Next.

## Configuring Network and Internet Connections

Next, YaST checks for networking hardware: Ethernet cards, dial-up modems, or high-speed connections. You have the option to configure these yourself later (click Skip Configuration), but it is a good idea to set this up during the installation. YaST will use this connection to go online to update your installation in the next step.

**FIGURE 3.4**     Strengthen the encryption of your Root password by clicking Expert Options.

Figure 3.5 shows the default network settings screen. As before, if YaST failed to detect all your networking hardware, or misidentified something, click the appropriate heading or use the Change button to make adjustments.

> **NOTE**
>
> If more than one network interface card (NIC) is found, you may be asked to configure the second card. This might be the case if this computer is going to function as a router or Internet gateway. One card, labeled eth0, will be the first active interface when you boot.

Note that the SUSE Firewall is turned on by default. This is a good thing, unless you are already protected by a hardware router, which is included with many Digital Subscriber Line (DSL) accounts, and in business network settings. Click Next to confirm the network settings.

YaST tests your connection as you set it up. It connects to a nearby SUSE Linux update server to retrieve the latest Release Notes and any updates to your installed software. If you have any problem connecting, review the network settings and make sure everything is correct.

> **TIP**
>
> Learn more about your Internet connection in Chapter 12, "Connecting to the Internet."

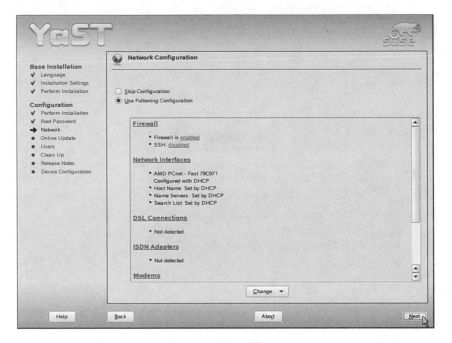

**FIGURE 3.5**    Confirm or edit your network hardware and configuration on this screen.

## Creating a User

Now it's time to set up your first user—you! As with the root user, the central task in creating a user on a Linux system is to make a password. YaST first asks whether this user will log in locally or from another computer, using either the Lightweight Directory Access Protocol (LDAP), the Network Information Service (NIS), or from a Windows PC through Samba. In all likelihood, the first user on the system will log in locally on this PC; select this option and click Next.

Type the relevant information into the Add a New Local User screen (see Figure 3.6), including the user password. This should always be different from the root password, but use the same general rules. For further information and advice on New User settings, see "Setting Up User Accounts in YaST" in Chapter 19. Click Next to create this and all other system users.

YaST now runs the SUSEConfig file to add the user and confirm the other changes made to this point. This can take a minute or longer, depending on your system. It then displays the Release Notes, with current information on new features and known problems. Click Next when you have reviewed this information.

**FIGURE 3.6**    Add your first user (usually you) in this screen.

## Configuring Hardware for the X Window System

The last step in the installation is identifying and configuring the hardware you'll need for the graphical X Window System and your chosen desktop environment. YaST autodetects your graphics card, connected printers, sound card, and a few miscellaneous peripherals. Again, if the autodetection failed or misidentified a card, select the appropriate heading or click the Change button and make any necessary changes. Click Next when you're ready. YaST confirms the changes and writes the default configuration files.

You will now see the Congratulations! screen (see Figure 3.7), signifying the end of the installation process. You are ready to log in for the first time. If you want to check other settings or add more software packages next, check the Start YaST Control Center box before clicking Finish. You may remove your CD at this time.

The system will then begin the boot process, finishing by displaying the green screen with the login prompt.

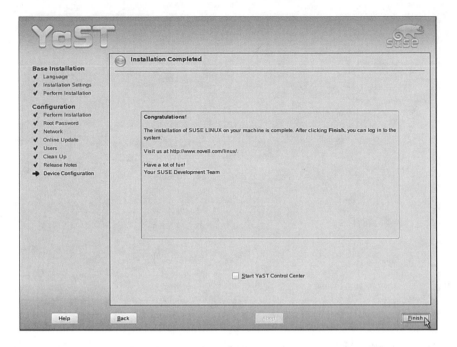

**FIGURE 3.7**   You've finished!

# Logging In and Shutting Down the First Time

When you boot your SUSE Linux system after running the startup scripts, your Linux kernel will display the login screen (see Figure 3.8). You'll be asked to type the username and the password. Only rarely should you log in as root, and then only for specific purposes.

Looking in the lower-left corner of the login screen, you'll see that you have some options in logging in. You can change the language of the display manager by selecting your language from the menu. By clicking the appropriate choice, you can choose to shut down or reboot your computer instead of logging in.

The Session menu allows you to change your desktop environment for this session if you have other window managers or desktop environments installed. Although this is probably not the case in your first login, if you like variety in your computing experience, you may want to play with this function later.

> **TIP**
>
> For the first login, it is always recommended to keep it as simple as possible. Your primary purpose is to make sure that the installation was successful and there are no problems. After you have assured yourself that this is the case, you can get more creative with login choices.

**FIGURE 3.8**    Log in here.

When you have entered your username and password, your selected desktop environment loads. This is KDE by default or GNOME by selection. Take a look around; click and right-click to your heart's content. Visit the Novell SUSE website and get comfortable. You should then log out and reboot your system to make sure everything is in proper order.

Find the Logout command from the desktop menu and click Restart Computer. That's all there is to it. The computer will shut down and then restart.

Welcome to Linux! You have now begun the journey.

## References

- http://www.novell.com/linux/suse—Always the place to start if you want to know something about SUSE Linux.

- http://tldp.org/HOWTO/Installation-HOWTO/index.html—From 2002, this Linux Installation HOWTO was written by programming guru Eric S. Raymond.

- http://www.pcguide.com/ref/mbsys/bios/set—A detailed description of most BIOS settings. Go to the Advanced Settings page to review the boot sequence/order options.

- http://www.pcworld.com/howto/article/0,aid,107870,00.asp—This article from *PC World* magazine runs through various BIOS settings in a more popular style.

- http://www.gnu.org/software/grub—The GRUB bootloader home page.

# Further Configuration with YaST and SaX2

In the previous chapter, you saw how easy it is to get SUSE Linux up and running. In this chapter, you'll learn more about configuring hardware after the installation. You'll start with the no-longer-inevitable but still troublesome post-installation glitches, and you'll finish with peripherals and portables.

## Troubleshooting Installation Problems

Linux applications, and the kernel itself, are much more fault tolerant than they used to be. It's hard to render a system completely unbootable. At the same time, it's much easier to overlook certain problems that may be affecting performance on a system that seems to be running well. Services may not start, modules don't load, or the hard drive does not respond as quickly as it should. It's a good idea to run the dmesg program occasionally to review the information the kernel is getting during bootup. Also review /var/log/messages regularly to see everything that goes into the log. Anyone can view this file in a text editor, but you can also view it in YaST. Go to the Misc page and click View System Log.

> **TIP**
>
> Besides /var/log/messages, you can view other logs, such as /var/log/warn and several process tables from the /proc directory in this YaST module. Use the drop-down menu to change the file you're viewing.

Messages in /var/log/messages are generated by the kernel and other applications run by sysinit. Many "errors" noted here are not really errors. If the system has configured a device you don't have, it will generate an error, but that's harmless. But look for errors that appear to affect devices and processes that you use. Investigate the causes of these errors.

When you're troubleshooting problems, search the SUSE help pages and check the man page for the problem application (along with modules.conf for kernel modules that are not loading). Paste the error message (up to 10 words) into an Internet search engine and see what comes up. Then head over to the "Getting Help" section of Chapter 1, "Welcome to SUSE Linux," to look deeper into the problem.

# Configuring Hardware with YaST

YaST autodetects and configures many types of peripheral hardware. But it's not really Linux if you can't tweak the default settings. In this section, you look at the YaST Hardware page and learn what you can configure, and how.

---

**TIP**

In both the KDE and GNOME desktop environments, the green "card" icon in the taskbar represents the YaST Hardware Tool, also called the SUSEplugger. It loads selected hardware-related applications at startup and handles autodetection of new hardware after the initial installation. Right-click to configure its functioning.

---

## Gathering Information About Your Hardware

Before tweaking away, you may want a snapshot of what hardware is already recognized and functioning. The YaST Hardware Information module is a graphical version of the hwinfo command-line utility. It probes your system and displays a comprehensive report on what hardware (cards, controllers, devices, and the like) is on your system, along with fairly in-depth information about most of the items. To start this program, open YaST and go to the Hardware page. Click Hardware Information and you're on your way. Figure 4.1 gives you an idea of what it looks like.

Click the plus (+) sign next to an item to see detailed information on that item. To save the results to a file readable in a text editor, click Save to File. Name the file (hwinfo<date-run>, for example) and put it somewhere in your home directory. Click Close to return to YaST.

## Modifying Disk Controller Settings

Your hard disk controller (HDC) is located on the motherboard. The Linux kernel loads the disk controller early in the boot process. You can set optional parameters here to improve system performance, if you know what you're doing. These parameters and modules will vary depending on your system. Your motherboard's manual may have some suggestions, and Googling "<module_name> parameters" may offer valuable advice.

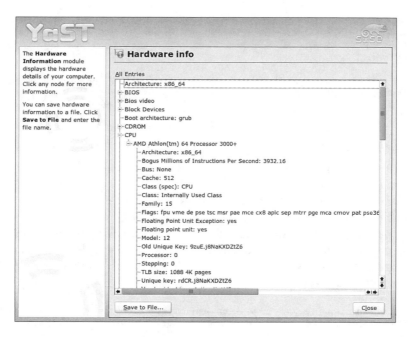

**FIGURE 4.1** The YaST Hardware Information module provides detailed information on your system.

> **CAUTION**
>
> *Always* test the loading of modules when changing disk controller parameters! If your hard disk does not load when you boot, you will be able to launch Linux only from the CD-ROM and will not have access to any files on your hard drive!

If you have more than one HDC on your system, you can use the Move Up or Move Down buttons to choose what loads first. If you don't want an HDC to load on boot, uncheck the Load Module in initrd box. Initrd is a file the kernel accesses to determine what modules it should load at boot.

Click Finish to confirm your settings and return to YaST.

▶ Learn more about the Linux boot process in Chapter 22, "Managing the Boot Process and Other Services."

## Configuring a Joystick

If YaST did not detect your joystick, use the Joystick module to select one yourself. It has a Test button so you can confirm that the joystick works properly with the selected driver.

## Adjusting Your Keyboard Layout

Do you occasionally type in a different language from your primary tongue? Do you use a Dvorak keyboard? The YaST Keyboard Layout module can change how the OS and all applications respond to your individual keystrokes. Open the module and you will see a long list of layout styles. Select a different language and tab to the Keyboard Test. Chances are that most of the letter keys will be the same as what you are used to, but the punctuation and symbol keys will be different. In some languages, even the number keys will be changed. The changes generally involve accented letters and common symbols used in a particular language.

Click Expert Settings to change certain system defaults. If you don't use the keypad on the right of your keyboard to enter numbers and don't like the NumLock light on all the time, you can turn off NumLock on startup here. The same is true for Caps Lock. You can even disable Caps Lock completely. These settings are written to /etc/sysconfig/keyboard, so you can review and adjust them manually if you prefer.

## Configuring Your Mouse

In all likelihood, YaST autodetected your mouse and loaded appropriate drivers during the installation. If you had the capability to use your mouse during the installation, your mouse should be installed properly. Feel free to check what driver SUSE Linux is using in the YaST Mouse Model module.

Although many drivers are included in the list, options are minimal. Consult the documentation for your mouse to check for appropriate drivers. If you don't have a working mouse, use the Tab key to maneuver to the module and then to the list. If you see your model, arrow down to select it. Tab again to highlight the Test button. You should be able to click it. If you can't, you will have to work your way through the list, testing one by one to find a working driver.

> **TIP**
>
> You can configure (even without SuperUser access) many more mouse options in the settings for your desktop environment. These include selecting left-handed mouse behavior, cursor themes, and acceleration settings.
>
> In the KDE Control Center, go to Peripherals, Mouse. In the GNOME Control Center, go to Hardware, Mouse.

## Configuring Your Scanner

If YaST did not autodetect your scanner when you first installed (or when you hooked it up to your PC), you've got problems. Manual configuration of USB-connected scanners is complex and dangerous (it is possible to damage your scanner with the wrong settings). Manually configuring a SCSI scanner is a little easier, but you can't do it without shutting down your system first.

Common reasons for a scanner not being detected include the following:

- The scanner is not supported. Check http://cdb.suse.de/index.php?LANG=en for a list of Linux-compatible devices.

- The SCSI controller was not installed correctly.

- There are termination problems with your SCSI port.

- The SCSI cable is too long.

- The scanner has a SCSI light controller that is not supported by Linux.

- The scanner is defective.

## Configuring Your TV or Radio Card

With a TV card, you can turn an ordinary PC into a home entertainment system. You'll learn more about this, including how to make your own personal video recorder, in the "TV and Video" section of Chapter 10, "Sights, Sounds, and Other Fun Things."

As with the other cards and peripherals in this chapter, YaST should have recognized your TV or radio card on installation. If not, you can install it manually with the TV Card module. Open the module in YaST and click Configure. A list of manufacturers and models (see Figure 4.2) appears. Select yours.

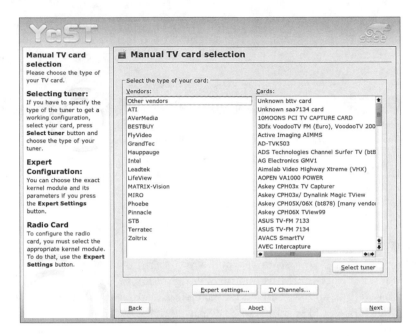

**FIGURE 4.2**    Select your TV card from the list.

Depending on your card, you may also have to select a tuner model. Click Select Tuner and choose from the list. To get a list of TV stations and channels available to you, click TV Channels and use the drop-downs to set your location and type (TV Norm) of signal. North Americans should set the TV Norm for NTSC and choose one of the US Frequency Tables. Click Scan the Channels to get the list. You can then use the Add, Edit, or Delete buttons to customize the list.

Click Next to specify how to manage audio output. By default, SUSE Linux sends it to your sound card. If you have multiple sound cards, you can select one here to work with your TV card. If no sound cards are set up, click Configure Sound Cards to open that YaST module (this configuration is discussed in Chapter 10). Click Next to continue.

This screen configures the infrared control mechanism for your card. You can choose from two different kernel modules to load and then click Test to see which one works. Click Next to complete the process.

## Setting Date and Time

During the installation, YaST will ask for your time zone and set your clock accordingly. If you move, or if you have a laptop that travels with you, it's easy to change time zones with the YaST Date and Time module (see Figure 4.3), located on the System page. When you open it, select your region in the left pane and your time zone in the right.

**FIGURE 4.3**    Select the desired time zone in the Date and Time module.

If you prefer to have your clock set in relation to the Universal Time (also known as Greenwich Mean Time), click the Etc region. The Global region includes several non-standard zones, such as South Pole time and Navajo time.

In this module, you can also specify how the kernel sets your hardware clock at boot. If you are dual booting with Windows, this should be set for Local Time. Otherwise, it is good to use the Unix Universal Time standard.

When your settings are correct, click Accept to confirm.

You can also configure your time and date settings in your desktop environment. Change time and clock settings in KDE by right-clicking on your taskbar clock, usually located on the right end of the taskbar. This context menu gives you the option to change your time-zone, manually adjust the time, and change the display settings. Because the clock displays 24-hour time by default, you may want to switch this to AM/PM right away. You have to reboot for changes to stick, though.

In GNOME, right-clicking the clock opens the Clock Preferences dialog box. You can choose from four display types: the traditional 12-hour (AM/PM) and 24-hour standards, or the less traditional UNIX or Internet times. UNIX Time counts seconds since January 1, 1970, while Internet Time was invented by the Swatch watch company. Here's how they describe the format on their website:

"Internet Time is a new universal time created by Swatch. With this new way of timekeep-ing, there are no more time zones, as the entire world is happening at the same time, at the same moment. Internet Time divides the 24 hours of a day into 1,000 units called beats. 1 beat represents 1 minute, 26.4 seconds. Internet Time is displayed by @ and three digits, ranging from @000 to @999. The internet day starts at midnight (@000) in Biel, the home of Swatch."

Use the checkboxes to decide whether to display the passing seconds and/or the current date on your clock, and whether to use Universal Time (called UTC here).

## Using the Network Time Protocol (NTP) to Keep Accurate Time

If you have an always-on connection to the Internet, either through a LAN or broadband modem, consider running a Network Time Protocol (NTP) client. You can use NTP to connect to public servers attached to an atomic clock. These clocks, which measure the resonance of a cesium atom, will lose a second every million years. The NTP client included with SUSE Linux checks with a specified public time server and resets your system's clock accordingly.

Go to the YaST Network Services page to open the NTP Client module (see Figure 4.4). Turn the client on by clicking When Booting System where it asks when to start the client. This will load the NTP client daemon. To make it work, the daemon needs a time server to connect to.

**FIGURE 4.4**    Set up your NTP client to use the pool NTP servers to reduce the load on high-traffic servers.

There are two ways to set up your NTP connection, simple and complex. The Simple way is to identify another machine on your LAN (which, presumably, is then connected to a time server), or choose from a selection of public time servers that SUSE has found. Click Select to choose a server to connect to. Another screen will come up. Now choose Public NTP Server, and you will see a list of predefined servers for your country. Select one geographically close to you. It's a little better if the server is in your time zone, but it does not matter greatly. Click Test to confirm the server is active and then click OK to confirm the selection.

Click Complex Configuration to set up a backup server. Click Add from the first screen (Figure 4.5). After choosing Server from the Peer Type choices (Figure 4.6), click Next.

**FIGURE 4.5**    Configure the Network Time Protocol daemon in YaST.

To ease the burden on public time servers—and keep them going—the Server Pool Project was created. This is a system where the client points to a nearby pool server (such as north-america.pool.ntp.org) and this site points to a different public server every hour. It is most courteous to do this, so enter this server in the appropriate box. Click Test again to confirm that this connection is working. Check the Use for Initial Synchronization box so the kernel defaults to this server at boot, and then click OK to add this server to the list.

---
**NOTE**

If you are not in North America, visit http://ntp.isc.org/bin/view/Servers/NTPPoolServers for the current list of "subzone" pool servers. You can also use pool.ntp.org as a last resort.

---

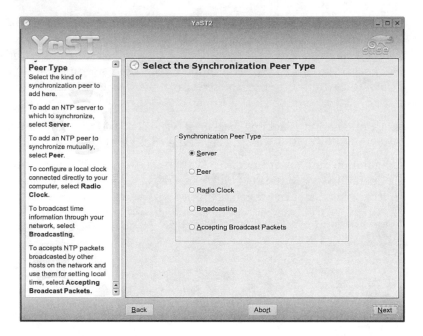

**FIGURE 4.6**   You can select from many types of timekeepers, but most likely you will choose a public time server to manage your clock.

There are other settings in the Complex Configuration dialog box. Accepting the defaults, as always, is OK.

- Run NTP Daemon in chroot jail: Never underestimate the creativity of bad guys who want to interfere with your system. When you are contacting remote public servers, there is a risk (however slight) that malware could exist on that server that could compromise security on your system. Checking this box (which is the default setting) puts the NTP daemon in a special /home/jail directory, where it cannot access any part of your system.

- Configure NTP Daemon with DHCP: If there is a DHCP server on your network, it may help you connect to NTP servers. This provides another security layer, because the information passes through another secure machine before getting to you. Check with your network administrator to see if the DHCP server is set up to look for NTP servers before turning this option on.

- Open Port in Firewall: Say you're traveling with your laptop, and want to connect to this machine through a Wide Area Network to set your laptop time. You must first open the firewall to get access. Do that by checking this box. Click Firewall Details to choose a network interface that you'll use. It's best to only open one port in the firewall.

Click Finish to confirm your choices. The NTP daemon will connect to your designated server(s) the next time you boot to Linux. If you change settings while the daemon is running, YaST will restart it when you click Finish.

# Power Management

There's no getting around this fact: Computers and peripherals consume a lot of electricity. With dwindling supplies of fossil fuels leading to ever-higher energy bills, it's good to minimize the power drain.

We are in a transition phase for power management on PCs and laptops, with one standard replacing another. Advanced Power Management (APM) is supported by most hardware manufacturers and BIOS routines.

Advanced Configuration and Power Interface (ACPI) is a power-management specification that allows the operating system (OS) to control the amount of power distributed to the computer's devices. Devices not in use can be turned off, reducing unnecessary power expenditure. ACPI is the latest generation of DOS-based power management software for PCs. ACPI replaces the older Intel APM software utility. ACPI does more than just manage timeouts during periods of inactivity; it dynamically monitors power usage within the computer's systems and assigns power accordingly. ACPI controls are found in your PC's BIOS, and ACPI will work only if supported by the systems BIOS and your systems OS, such as SUSE Linux as of Kernel release 2.6.

> **NOTE**
>
> One place where ACPI alone is supported is in SUSE Linux for the AMD 64-bit processor.

APM allows workstations and servers to automatically shut down when told to. ACPI provides more control over the process. Depending on your system, you may want to configure for both standards. In this section, you'll learn how to use YaST to configure your desktop PC. In the next, you'll see how to configure your laptop.

## YaST Power Management

The Power Management module is located under the System page. It is shown in Figure 4.7.

By default, a PC is set for best performance, but you can adjust this scheme in favor of Powersave (for the least energy consumption) or Acoustic (for quiet operation). The fourth scheme, Presentation, is the same as Performance, but turns the screensaver off. You can add your own scheme or edit existing ones by clicking Edit Schemes.

# Portable PC Issues

Laptop computers are finicky beasts with many proprietary bits of hardware and software. These issues can make it difficult to install SUSE Linux. After you have the OS installed and running, though, you don't have to settle for a lesser system when you're on the move. This section will offer some tips to help.

**FIGURE 4.7**    YaST offers several power management schemes, or you can adjust it your own way or even make your own.

## Power Management for Laptops

SUSE Linux configures laptops for saving power and prolonging battery life, whether you have an APM or ACPI system (see the earlier "YaST Power Management" section if you missed those definitions). The YaST Power Management module lets you tweak those settings.

Choose Edit Schemes to make changes to the default settings or add your own. Use the three buttons on the main screen (refer to Figure 4.7) for quicker adjustments.

Battery Warning lets you set three levels of warnings that your battery is going dead. You decide both when the threshold is met (through a numerical scheme), and what warning SLP issues. By default, SLP sends a popup to the screen for the first two levels, and then shuts down automatically when the power situation becomes Critical. Use the drop-down menu to change these actions; perhaps you want the screensaver to come on at the second (Low Capacity) warning level, or for the machine to suspend itself.

ACPI Settings: Defines what actions occur when you press the Power and Sleep buttons, or when you close the laptop cover. Use the drop-down menu to choose from the same actions used in Battery Warning (Notify, Shutdown, Logout, Standby, Suspend to RAM, Suspend to Disk, Start Screensaver, Ignore).

Enable Suspend: Three ways to do this. Suspend to Disk is checked by default. This protects your data most effectively, but takes longer to revive than suspending to RAM. Suspending to RAM recovers quickly, but if you happen to run out of power while you are suspended to RAM, you could lose unsaved data on the screen.

Switch to Standby Mode: This shuts down power to your screen, turns off the fan, and other power drains until you power back up. Designed for brief respites, data is not saved before going to Standby.

YaST checks to see if your machine supports all these options. Unsupported options may not be available.

## Working with PCMCIA Cards

Laptops often use PCMCIA (Personal Computer Memory Card International Association) cards to add functionality, memory, or peripherals.

To activate support for PCMCIA cards, use the YaST Runlevel Editor. This module is on the System page.

## Configuring Bluetooth Wireless Support

When the Swedish telecommunications company Ericsson developed a new wireless tool that allowed different electronic components to communicate without being attached by heavy cables, it wanted a snappy name for it. Reaching back into the Scandinavian past, someone discovered a Danish king, Harald Blaatand, who united Denmark and Norway in the tenth century. Blaatand translated into English is *Bluetooth*. And that is how this trademark was born.

SUSE Linux should autodetect your Bluetooth device and load the appropriate drivers. YaST should also install the `bluez-libs` and `bluez-utils` software packages to manage your connection.

> **TIP**
>
> Install `bluez-cups` if you need to print via Bluetooth.

You can enable Bluetooth support manually through the YaST Bluetooth module, located on the Hardware page. This tells the kernel to "hot-plug" the Bluetooth kernel module and its daemon at boot. Click Advanced Daemon Configuration to further set up Bluetooth support (see Figure 4.8).

If you want Bluetooth communication channels to be encrypted, click Security Options. First, enable Authentication to force users to enter a password before making a Bluetooth connection; then enable Encryption to further protect data passing through the connection.

> **NOTE**
>
> Not all Bluetooth devices support authentication or encryption. You may have to turn these options off when connecting to that type of device.

Click Finish to confirm your changes.

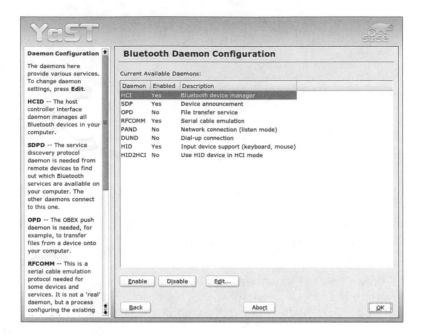

**FIGURE 4.8**   Configure the Bluetooth daemon here.

## Configuring Infrared Interface (IrDA) Mode

Chances are good that your laptop uses either Bluetooth or Infrared Data Association (IrDA) to communicate with other devices. IrDA's differences with Bluetooth are minimal, but significant:

- In Bluetooth, the individual devices do not need to "see" each other directly.

- In Bluetooth, several devices can be connected in a network. However, the maximum data rate is 720 Kilobits per second (in the current version 1.2). The next version of Bluetooth is expected to improve that rate to more than 2 Megabits per second.

- Theoretically, Bluetooth can even communicate through walls. In practice, however, this depends on the properties of the wall and the device class. There are three device classes with transmission ranges between 10 and 100 meters.

There are two IrDA operation modes. The standard mode, SIR, accesses the infrared port through a serial interface. This mode works on almost all systems and is sufficient for most requirements. The faster mode, FIR, requires a special driver for the IrDA chip. Not all chip types are supported in FIR mode because of a lack of appropriate drivers. Set the desired IrDA mode in the BIOS of your computer. The BIOS also shows which serial interface is used in SIR mode.

IrDA is a major drain on your battery, so SUSE Linux does not automatically turn IrDA on at boot. You must go to the YaST IrDA module located on the Hardware page.

Click Start IrDA and then set the proper serial port for the connection (consult your laptop manual). Test the connection and then click Finish to get to work.

# Configuring CD, DVD, and Rewritable Drives

So much of our entertainment now comes on compact disks of various types, it is essential for our computers and operating systems to keep up. Although it has had some obstacles to surmount, Linux developers have made it relatively easy to run CDs, DVDs, and the gamut of recordable CD formats. This section focuses on the technical end of providing device drivers for these types of drives and disks. To learn more about the Linux multimedia experience, including how to burn CDs and DVDs, see Chapter 10.

## Integrating CD and DVD Drives into Your System

YaST simplifies the process of mounting your CD and DVD drives (see Figure 4.9). The CD-ROM module identifies your drive(s) and adds a reference and mount point to your `/etc/fstab` file.

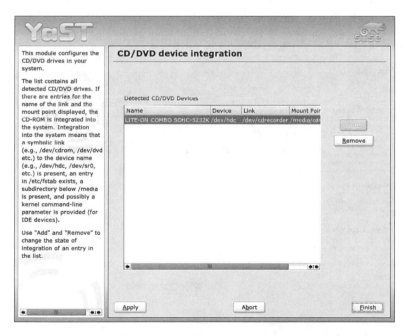

**FIGURE 4.9**    Make sure your CD and DVD drives are mounted in this module.

The CD-ROM module is very limited in what it can do. If YaST autodetects a drive (which it will nearly always do, especially when you install via CD/DVD), you cannot manually set up and integrate the drive. It also does not permit changing any of your settings (you can still edit /etc/fstab yourself).

Essentially, the only option in this module is to "remove" (or unintegrate) a drive. This removes the symlink to the drive in the /dev directory and the mount point in the /media directory. To restore the drive, click Add. Click Finish to return to YaST.

▸ Learn more about mounting drives and /etc/fstab in Chapter 18, "Managing Files, Volumes, and Drives."

## Speeding Up Your CD Drive Through Direct Memory Access (DMA)

By default, your IDE hard drive can bypass the processor and call on memory directly. This is referred to as Direct Memory Access or DMA. Bypassing the processor using DMA frees up the processor to continue with other tasks and can greatly enhance system performance.

At one time, SUSE Linux set the defaults so all IDE drives could use DMA, but problems with systems locking up or losing data occurred when some CD-ROM drives had DMA turned on. Thus, DMA is turned on for hard drives by default, but not CD drives. You can change this setting yourself in the IDE DMA Setup module (see Figure 4.10).

---

**CAUTION**

Back up your data before changing this setting, just in case.

---

**FIGURE 4.10**   The IDE DMA Setup screen.

Select the CD drive in the list and then click the DMA Mode drop-down menu. Choose the DMA On default setting for starters. If that works trouble-free, consider changing to a higher speed. You will get another warning about the potential for problems, so you can back off before making the change. Click Finish to confirm the new setting or click Abort to return to YaST.

## References

- http://www.bluetooth.com—The Bluetooth website.

- http://www.holtmann.org/linux/bluetooth—Marcel Holtmann's Linux and Bluetooth page. Articles in English and German, plus downloads.

- http://www.cs.ucl.ac.uk/staff/s.zachariadis/btpalmlinux.html—A guide to connecting your Palm PDA to your PC with Bluetooth.

- http://tuxmobil.org—The place to get information on Linux on all sorts of mobile hardware: laptops, PDAs, and cell phones. A monthly newsletter is available as well.

- http://tuxmobil.org/Infrared-HOWTO/Infrared-HOWTO.html—The Linux Infrared HOWTO. Configuring and using IrDA.

- http://linux-laptop.net—Another portable Linux site.

- http://www.sane-project.org—Home of the Linux scanner driver project "Scanner Access Now Easy." Search to see if your scanner is supported by Linux.

- http://www.ntp.org—Network Time Protocol home.

- http://ntp.isc.org/bin/view/Servers/WebHome—The Public NTP Server list. Find a Network Time Protocol server to connect to. Contains much more helpful information, too.

- http://www.cpqlinux.com/acpi-howto.html—The Linux ACPI HOWTO.

# PART II

# Using SUSE Linux

## IN THIS PART

# Getting Started with SUSE Linux

In the days before the X Window System made things a little more soft and cuddly, Unix was labeled the most user-unfriendly operating system known to humanity.

There was the cold, forbidding command-line interface (CLI) with seemingly millions of obscure commands to learn. Today both Unix and Linux have an assortment of terrific graphical interfaces to give you point-and-click ease for your computing tasks, but even if you use them all the time, it is good to have access to and an understanding of that command line (usually called the shell or console). When you want something done quickly, or want to understand what's going on under the hood when you ask Linux to do something, the shell is the place to go.

In this chapter, you will learn the basics of interacting with SUSE Linux, from logging in to understanding the file system to dealing with file permissions.

You'll pick out the best shell for your working style and play with some text editors, too. By the end of the chapter, you'll be able to handle the power of being the Root user and know when and how to wield that power.

Read this chapter in particular if you are transitioning from a proprietary OS (even more so if that OS was Windows 98 or earlier, which had no conception of logging in multiple users and dealing with security via file permissions). Read this chapter whether you are the administrator (Root user) of your system, have some administrative privileges (via sudo), or are just an ordinary user in an office with an IT staff. If you are more experienced using Unix or another Linux distribution, you may still find some new tricks, or just get a refresher on the basics.

# Logging In to SUSE Linux

After you have installed SUSE Linux and created at least one user (yourself) on the system, you must log in. The standard login is pretty straightforward. By default, SUSE Linux boots to a KDE-based graphical login screen, known as the display manager. You enter your username (or click the icon representing you) and password and identify whether you want to start KDE, GNOME, some other X Window manager or a shell/command line (what appears in this drop-down menu is set by the Root user, so your options may differ). Press Enter to finish booting.

## Logging In from the Shell

What about those times when you don't need to load graphics just to log in, get a piece of information, and shut down? Or what if X has a problem loading? The text login is a simple process. SUSE Linux boots to a login shell. Type your username and press Enter to get the password prompt. Enter your password and you have full access to your system (or at least as much access as you have with the graphical interface).

> **NOTE**
>
> In this book, you will see some terms for the Linux command-line interface used somewhat interchangeably.
>
> Most often, you'll see *shell* or *command line* to refer to this interface. When you read about a command to run at the shell prompt, you can run that command whether or not you have a graphical interface loaded.
>
> Occasionally, you will see a reference to a *console*, or *X Terminal* (*xterm*, for short). These refer to graphical shells within an X environment. Some consoles have additional tricks they can do that a standard shell can't. When you see these terms, understand that the instructions apply only to the graphical shell.

> **NOTE**
>
> If you get the text login prompt as a result of something bad happening and X won't boot, it is always better to log in as Root because you will have more tools to fix what went wrong. If you are not Root (the system administrator), go get the person who is.

## Logging Out of the Shell

Typing **exit** or **logout** logs you out of the shell. At this point, another user can log in, or you can shut down your computer. Depending on your settings, users may be able to use the shutdown or reboot commands to perform these tasks.

# Working with the Linux File System

As the Internet has just a few specific but well-known top-level domains (.com, .net, .org, .edu, and the like), so are Linux files organized in a particular hierarchy, with specific directories that hold specific types of files.

Virtually all Linux distributions have the same structure, and this is likely to become more entrenched with the Linux Standard Base specifications becoming more universal. The Linux Standard Base (www.linuxbase.org) is an effort to make all Linux distributions more compatible with each other, and with most applications. SUSE is a longtime supporter of this effort, and has been compliant with LSB standards since LSB v1.0. In addition, the Filesystem Hierarchy Standard seeks specifically to standardize the contents of the top-level Unix/Linux directories. This structure is beautiful for software developers because they can know what directories will be present on each user's machine and can install programs into the appropriate directory. It also enables programmers to build more modular programs, which depend on other standard libraries. It helps packaging systems—such as the Red Hat Package Manager (RPM) that SUSE uses—check and confirm that a file on which a package depends is present on a user's system. Testing goes easier, too, because fewer things can go wrong.

We went over that structure briefly in Chapter 2, "Preparing to Install SUSE Linux." To have another look and get your first lesson in using a shell, open the KDE Konsole and type `ls` /. You should see the following:

```
bin     dev     home    media   opt     root    srv     usr     windows
boot    etc     lib     mnt     proc    sbin    tmp     var
```

For a more detailed view of the file system from the shell, use the `tree` command. This program might not be installed by default, but it is on the CD-ROM. The results displayed by this program include all the top-level directories listed in "How to Partition Your Drive(s)" in Chapter 2, along with a few levels of subdirectories.

> **NOTE**
>
> When you're typing into the KDE Konsole, you're using the bash shell in an X Terminal (or Xterm). You'll learn more about shells and terminals, including how to change the defaults, later in the chapter.

In Windows, you have the capability to create, delete, and rename as many top-level directories and subdirectories as you want, and very few bad things can happen to you as a result. Renaming the Program files or Windows directories would cause problems, but the system won't come to a halt if you installed a program to a directory outside of Program files. Although you have the same technical ability to manipulate the directory structure in SUSE Linux, at least if you have Root privileges, *don't*!

The sole exception to this otherwise ironclad rule is in your home directory. As a user, you can and should organize your documents and other data any way you see fit. You will see several recommendations in this book to put particular files and programs in your home directory because it can be the best place for them. If you find it useful, put every file you create in its own directory (although that might be a little extreme).

This recommendation extends to putting files of your own creation into one of the system directories. Say you create a text file that has a collection of tips and tricks you've learned about the bash shell over the years, called BashTips. Because you know that man pages and other documentation for bash goes in the /usr/share/doc/bash directory, you might be tempted to store the file there. No problem—unless somewhere down the road one of the developers or documentation writers adds a BashTips file to the bash package. When that file gets installed, your file is replaced with no questions asked, never to be recovered. No program will ever try to copy a file in your home directory, so put things that are yours there.

---

**TIP**

If you ever find the need to have files in two places at once, use symbolic links, usually called *symlinks*. In the preceding example, keep the file in /home/documents/bash. Then open a shell and type **ln -s /documents/bash/BashTips /usr/share/doc/bash/MyBashTips**. Now if you look for MyBashTips in this directory, it will open your file. More about this later.

---

## Essential File System Commands from the /bin and /sbin Directories

The /bin (short for binary) directory holds your shell applications and many essential shell commands you need when running and booting Linux. The /sbin (or system binary) directory contains the various installed file systems, YaST, the SUSE Firewall, and other commands needed at boot or for the Root user to solve systemwide problems. On the average system, each directory will have 5–8MB worth of files in them, with /sbin a little bit bigger than /bin. Many, if not all, of these commands are statically linked, not dependent on other software libraries located in other directories (mostly /lib and /usr/lib). Nearly every other application on your system relies on one or more of these external (or shared) libraries to run. These dynamically linked applications create a software ecosystem that ties an application to its operating system. Statically linked applications and commands, along with the kernel, represent the operating system itself.

## Using the /boot and /dev Directories

The /boot directory contains a compressed version of the Linux kernel that loads at boot (earlier versions of the startup script delivered a message that the kernel was "exploding," which undoubtedly unnerved more than a few novices in those days). When you rebuild or install a new kernel, the new kernel and related files go first into this directory (see Chapter 24, "Kernel and Module Management," for more information on updating your kernel).

Linux device files are located in the /dev directory. As noted earlier, nearly everything in Linux is represented as a file. No further proof is needed than a peek into this directory. There you will find about 7,500 files representing devices that are or may some day be attached (or not) to your system. The more commonly used devices include the following:

- IDE and SCSI hard drives, represented as hda and sda, respectively.

- CD-ROM, CD-R, and CD-RW drives (and their DVD counterparts), some of which are IDE; others are viewed by the system as SCSI.

- Serial ports, marked `tty`.

- Pointing devices, such as `/dev/input/mouse`.

- Universal Serial Bus (USB) devices, in the `dev/usb` directory.

- Printers, marked `lp`.

If you're running short of disk space, you might think cleaning out some of these files would help you. Closer inspection reveals that they are all 0byte files. Leave them alone.

## Editing Configuration Files in the /etc Directory

One of the beauties of Linux applications is the way you can make software your own. Whether it's changing the behavior of a command, adding a keyboard shortcut, or changing the color of the application title bar, there are lots of ways to make the applications you use work the way you want them to. Often, you don't even have to open the application you want to modify to make the changes you want. Most applications store their configurations in a simple text file located in the /etc directory. Scroll through the directory to see exactly what is there. Check to see which user owns a file before trying to edit it—if Root owns the configuration file, you'll have to log in as the SuperUser to make changes.

Some of the more important system-related configuration files in this directory are

- `fstab`—This file system table lists each mountable storage device on your computer. These include hard drives, floppy drives, CD and DVD drives, and removable drives. The file displays each device's mount point, its location on the partition table, instructions on whether it should mount automatically on boot, and a few other options. See the section "Mounting a File System" in Chapter 18, "Managing Files, Volumes, and Drives," for more information on /etc/fstab.

- `inittab`—The system initialization table defines the different runlevels that the system uses at boot to start your computer. Changes to this file (which can be made manually, but also in YaST's `suseconfig` editor) can determine whether you boot to a graphical or text login screen, as well as whether someone can log in to the machine remotely with a dial-up modem. You will learn more about the boot process and runlevels in Chapter 22, "Managing the Boot Process and Other Services."

- `modprobe.conf` and `modprobe.conf.local`—The main `modprobe.conf` file contains directions and options used when loading kernel modules to operate various pieces of hardware, such as sound cards, USB devices, network cards, and the like. The contents of this file are used during boot. SUSE engineers update this file from time to time and recommend that if you want to do your own editing, you use `modprobe.conf.local` to keep those changes from being overwritten. You will learn more about `modprobe.conf` in Chapter 24, "Kernel and Module Management."

- passwd and shadow—The passwd file and its more secure counterpart, shadow, contain the list of all users on the system, along with their account information. It's often said in Unix circles that a user doesn't exist until she has a password. This is one of the reasons why. You will learn more about users and passwords in Chapter 19, "Managing Users, Managing Security."

## Where All the Good Stuff Goes: Your /home Directory

Ultimately, the most important data on any computer belongs in this directory—the files you create for yourself. Every "real" (in contrast to a system) user on a Linux system gets a /home directory labeled with their username. That user has complete control over folders and files created in this directory and control over all access to those files except for the Root user.

In an effort to be helpful, SUSE Linux adds a few subdirectories to the /home directory by default:

- /bin can hold binary (program) files, but is usually empty to begin with.

- /Desktop holds your KDE desktop icons. GNOME users tend to have a cleaner look, but the subdirectory is there if you want it.

- Documents is a lovely place to store word processing files and other, well... documents.

- /public_html is a place to store your website. If you have a web server, such as Apache, installed, this directory links directly to your localhost URL. Read more about building websites in Chapter 14, "Creating Basic Websites," and Chapter 31, "Programming Dynamic Websites." Learn more about the Apache web server in Chapter 26, "Managing Your Apache Web Server."

You can work with these subdirectories, create more, delete some—your /home is your playground. But remember, back up your /home directory regularly. It's designed for that.

## Finding Desktop Programs in /opt

The Filesystem Hierarchy Standard (FHS) says, "The /opt/ directory provides storage for large, static application software packages." In practice, this seems to mean applications oriented to the desktop. Confined within /opt are all the built-in KDE and GNOME applications, Mozilla and its Firefox progeny, Softmaker Office files, and the Zope web application server. Depending on what you have installed, your mileage may vary.

## Where Most of the Programs Go: The /usr Directory

The /usr directory is somewhat surprising when you look at it, because it has a parallel structure to the main (/) directory. This is why some folks give /usr its own mount point (that is, in DOS/Windows it would have its own drive letter). This directory is usually quite large (in the multigigabyte range, depending on how many applications you install) and contains many shared files and applications. It also houses the X Window System for graphical and remote computing. This directory is the place to start when looking for a particular application on your system, to handle troubleshooting, desktop icon placing, and everything in between.

## Variable Data: The /var Directory

The /var directory holds subdirectories used by various system services for spooling and logging. Some of the files in this directory are temporary, like a printer queue spooler file. System and kernel logs keep much longer and so are renamed and rotated through periodically. Incoming local email is usually directed to /var/spool/mail as well.

Linux also uses /var for other system services. YaST keeps backup boot sectors and YaST Online Update files, among other things, in /var/lib/YaST2. The RPM package database is also stored in /var/lib/rpm.

## Changing User Information and the Finger Program

Unix was born in a multiuser environment at Bell Labs and was widely used in university computer science labs with a bunch of students floating in and out using whatever terminal was available. Defining users in a system was a necessity in the early days of Unix. As more users came on to systems with the advent of the PC, requiring users to log in was the touchstone of security measures. Today, because of viruses, worms, and assorted evildoers trying to break into networks almost constantly, named users and passwords are essential elements in any secure computing environment.

The Root user, who is responsible for all administrative tasks on the system, creates an account for each user. This involves assigning a username and creating an initial password for that user. You created the first user account for your system during the installation in Chapter 3, "Installing SUSE Linux."

The Root user can delegate responsibilities to a single user or a group of users by sharing the Root password. Those users can then run the SuperUser program (su) to act as the Root user. You will learn more about SuperUsers in Chapter 19.

Individual users cannot change their usernames. System administrators of large user communities like to have some consistency in usernames, especially considering that a username is a central element of that user's email address. Users can, however, change the information associated with their name and contained with your other login information in /etc/passwd and in your public "finger" file. This is generally phone-directory information that may need to be public, but that otherwise may be an artifact of a bygone era.

Finger was a program developed to help Unix users find each other, both electronically and physically. Typing **finger *&lt;username&gt;*** delivered whatever was in that user's finger file. To see what's in yours, type **chfn** (change finger information) at the shell prompt. By default, SUSE Linux does not create additional user information with new users, but it is easily configured by Root. You'll see something like this:

```
Name:
Office:
Office Phone:
Home Phone:
```

You're led through a series of prompts to enter new or updated information. Feel free to leave items blank (or change them appropriately).

# Choosing and Using a Shell

The shell is perhaps the most underappreciated feature of a modern Linux system. New users try to avoid it, preferring the GUI tools that they are used to. Old-timers are wedded to the shell they learned at school. There's no real reason to give the shell a second thought, is there? Of course there is!

By default, SUSE Linux (and pretty much all the other Linux distributions) installs the bash (Bourne Again SHell) shell as the standard command-line interface. There's certainly no reason not to take this fine choice and run with it. But this is Linux, and there's absolutely no reason not to explore some or all of the alternatives to bash included in SUSE Linux. This section will introduce you to these options, tell you how to change shells temporarily and permanently, and then offer pointers on how to use a shell productively.

> **NOTE**
>
> Learn even more about using shells, including writing shell scripts to automate tasks, in Chapter 8, "Shaking Hands with Your Shell."

## Cool Stuff That All Shells Have in Common

The shell is not just a keyboard-based program launcher. It is a powerful tool you can use to get lots of things done quickly—if you know how to use it. Some shells are designed for running scripts to automate tasks, and others work best interacting with its favorite user—you! Following are some of the things that all shells have in common:

- Command history—The shell stores every command you enter (up to a limit, which is configurable). This feature lets you easily access and repeat commands from the history. Press the up-arrow key to see the last command and keep pressing to view each previous command. Pressing the down-arrow key moves forward in time, as it were, returning you back to an empty prompt. To reuse a command, locate it and press Enter to run the command.

  This works over sessions, too. Even if you run the shell only once a month (or once a decade), the command history stays current.

- Filename completion—Another terrific tool for lazy typists. Start typing a filename and press the Tab key.

The shell checks the path for files that start with the keys you typed, and a suggestion appears.

This is especially helpful when performing actions on files with long names, or deep in a directory. Some shells will also complete commands. See the sections on running tcsh and zsh later in the chapter.

- Command-line editing—Did you mistype a letter in a command and get an error? Don't retype the whole thing; use the command history and left- and right-arrow keys to get to the error, or change the options.

- Many utilities to work with—Tools such as sed and awk can help with commands and scripts.

- Aliasing—Another typing shortcut, similar to a symlink. One command (or set of letters) stands in for another. This is set up in the shell configuration file. Among other things, aliasing allows bash to run when you type sh and the tcsh shell to run when you call csh.

- Background processing—If one command is taking a long time to complete, you can move it to the background and run another command.

- Multiple sessions—You can have more than one shell (and multiple instances of the same shell) open at the same time, even without a graphical interface, and switch back and forth.

- Programmable everything—The shell is a programming environment with languages on par with any other programming language.

These are just some of the advantages of most all shells. But how does one shell differ from another? We will look at the three most popular shells—bash, tcsh, and zsh—in some detail, and then look at Midnight Commander (mc), a specialized shell for managing files and directories. Finally, there is a very brief introduction to the Korn (ksh) and the Almquist (ash) shells.

## Running bash

Just about every Linux user has used bash at least once. As one of the original GNU projects, it has been in development since 1987. Version 3.0 was released in July 2004 and is included in SUSE Linux Professional 9.2. As you might guess from the name, bash (Bourne Again Shell) is the logical successor to the venerable Unix shell (sh) written by Steve Bourne. This is a shell best adapted for running scripts to automate tasks.

You can tweak bash's performance by editing the .bashrc configuration file. Root can edit the systemwide .bashrc, and each user on the system may have his or her own configuration file, although a user cannot override the system configuration.

Looking at a configuration file provides both a sample of the kinds of things you can do with a shell and offers a glimpse at the syntax each shell uses to perform its tasks.

The default system configuration in SUSE Linux, `bash.bashrc`, is located, like other configuration files, in the `/etc` directory. Let's look at some of the settings defined here.

This section lets you display directory listings in different colors.

The colors are set in another file, `DIR_COLORS`. In this setting, bash looks for `DIR_COLORS` first in the home directory, then in `/etc`.

```
#
# Colored file listings
#
if test -x /usr/bin/dircolors ; then
    #
    # set up the color-ls environment variables:
    #
    if test -f $HOME/.dir_colors ; then
    eval `dircolors -b $HOME/.dir_colors`
    elif test -f /etc/DIR_COLORS ; then
    eval `dircolors -b /etc/DIR_COLORS`
    fi
fi
```

Note the hash mark (#) in front of some of the lines. This indicates a comment line. The line is not processed by the shell, but usually describes what the next batch of code is supposed to do.

This next section defines some aliases. As mentioned before, aliases are command-line shortcuts that allow you to substitute one command for another.

```
#
# Set some generic aliases
#

alias rd=rmdir
alias md='mkdir -p'
alias which='type -p'
alias rehash='hash -r'
alias you='yast2 online_update'
```

This alias is a nice one. If you often mistype a command, you can specify a little reminder. You may think that the opposite of the `mount` command to display a drive or partition is unmount, but really it's umount (no N). This alias tells bash to remind you of the right command every time you add the extra N. Sure, you could just have unmount replace umount on your system, but what if you are working on someone else's system that does not have this alias? You may just forget the real command.

With this method, you might train your fingers to type the right thing after a few gentle nudges.

```
alias unmount='echo "Error: Try the command: umount" 1>&2; false'
test -s $HOME/.alias && . $HOME/.alias
fi
```

This section modifies how the command history is handled, by making sure the History file doesn't get too big with many duplicate listings of the same file.

```
# Do not save dupes and lines starting by space in the bash history file
HISTCONTROL=ignoreboth
if test "$is" = "ksh" ; then
# Use a ksh specific history file and enable
    # emacs line editor
    HISTFILE=$HOME/.kshrc_history
    VISUAL=emacs
fi
;;
esac
```

SUSE recommends not editing this default system file, because it can be overwritten in a system update. With this bit of code, bash checks for a local configuration file edited by the system administrator, saved as /etc/bash.bashrc.local.

```
if test "$is" != "ash" ; then
    #
    # And now let's see if there is a local bash.bashrc
    # (for options defined by your sysadmin, not SuSE Linux)
    #
    test -s /etc/bash.bashrc.local && . /etc/bash.bashrc.local
fi
```

As noted at the beginning of this section, bash is a shell environment for scripting. Other shells are designed to be more interactive. Let's look at the leading example: the C shell.

## Running tcsh

Bill Joy (later to become a founder of Sun Microsystems) wrote the original C shell in college. He aimed to provide a more interactive work environment, with a syntax more like the C programming language.

Interactive shells are focused on directly processing commands you type in, rather than running scripts or files. Script-oriented shells such as bash can be used interactively, but it is rarely a good idea to make a C shell run scripts.

The version of the C shell included in SUSE Linux is called tcsh, a tribute to the TENEX mainframe operating system. It has programmable command completion and a referable command history.

The best thing about tcsh, though, is its command spell checker.

If you type **frotune** at a tcsh prompt, it will ask if you mean **fortune**. A yes answer gives you a fortune cookie.

## Running zsh

The Z shell strives to be the best of both worlds, enabling you to safely write scripts or use it interactively. It is based on the Korn shell (ksh) written by David Korn, with tons of extra features. Many folks love zsh to bits for its power and flexibility, but with great power comes great complexity. This shell's Info file has 21,530 lines of documentation in 11 subnodes. We won't cover all of that here.

zsh has virtually all the neat features previously listed and works quite well with the default configuration file (etc/zshrc).

Some features, such as command spell check, are not set by default, but it is a fairly easy task to edit them.

This shell also checks your default text editor, and if it is emacs or vim, it will adopt that editor's key bindings (aka keyboard shortcuts) in addition to its own.

## Managing Files with Midnight Commander

Whatever shell you choose for your everyday use, you may find the Midnight Commander a handy in-between tool for moving files around. In between? Suppose you don't need to load a full GUI desktop to move a batch of files, but even all the wildcards and completion shortcuts offered by your shell won't let you easily copy a set of files from different directories into one other directory. You need something else—something that will display two directories side by side and let you drag or move things from one place to another. You need Midnight Commander!

To open Midnight Commander, type **mc** at the shell prompt. Figure 5.1 shows the initial default display of your home directory on both sides of the screen. Use the arrow keys to navigate in the left pane. Use the Tab key to move from one side to the other, and then move around. Select a file or folder and press Enter to open that item. Mouse support is excellent; click any menu at the top to see your choices. Along the bottom are the F-key bindings: pressing F1 brings up the Help file, F2 displays a context-sensitive menu of choices for the selected file or directory, and so on.

To copy a set of documents with the .sxw extension from ~/documents to a directory on a remote server called /backup/mikemc, follow these steps:

1. In the left pane, use the arrow keys to navigate to the /Documents directory. Press Enter to open this directory.

2. Tab to the right pane. At the bottom of the Midnight Commander, you will see a flashing cursor. This is a shell prompt. Type **cd /backup/mikemc** to navigate to this directory. You could use the parent folders, marked .., to find the directory, but this is faster.

3. Tab back to the left pane. Press Alt-+ to open the Select Group dialog. Type **\*.sxw** and press Enter to select all files with the .sxw extension.

4. Press F5 to open the Copy dialog box. Confirm that the correct files are going to the correct directory. Select any options you want by navigating with the Tab key and selecting with the spacebar. Press Enter to complete the operation.

**FIGURE 5.1**   The Midnight Commander shell.

Midnight Commander is a program ripe for exploration. The first few times you work with it, play around a little. Go to a menu, or press an F key to see what a command does.

The help files are indeed helpful! This is a full-featured file manager: View hidden files if you like, access FTP sites, and upload or download files (at the same time, if you want to), run executables, and change permissions (if you can) and owners with the ChMod and ChOwn commands. In short, just about everything you can do with a file in a shell, you can do with Midnight Commander. It even has a command history.

> **TIP**
>
> The KDE Konsole lets you open a new Midnight Commander session from the Session menu. Choose regular or Root (with your password).

### ksh **and** ash

The other shell choices may be less popular, but are still valid. Here's a quick overview:

- Korn shell (ksh)—This shell, written by David Korn, was the first popular shell to try to combine the scripting features of the Bourne shell and the interactive features of the C shell. AT&T tried to turn ksh into a commercial product, with limited success. There are two versions of the "pure" Korn shell: ksh88 and ksh93. The version included with SUSE Linux is the public domain pd-ksh. It has reproduced most of the features of ksh88, with a few new ones of its own.

The Z shell is also one of the Korn shell descendants, and if you know ksh well, you should be able to function well with zsh.

- Almquist shell (ash)—This lightweight Bourne-like shell has but 17 built-in commands, so as a shell it's perfect for embedded and other tight spaces and login shells. In fact, it is the SUSE login shell.

## Choosing a Shell

You now know a little bit about each shell. How do you decide which to use? The easiest thing is, of course, to stick with what you know. If you have used a shell before, there should be some compelling reason to switch. Similarly, if you don't ever intend to do anything fancy with your shell, you might as well stick with bash. You can certainly do very fancy things with bash, but why change from the default?

Bash is also a great tool to learn scripting from. Resources abound on the Net to help you do that, and you'll learn more about that in Chapter 8 as well. If you don't want to write scripts, use an interactive shell such as tcsh, pd-ksh, or zsh.

If you are a lousy typist, you should certainly consider one of the shells with a spell checker. tcsh spell checks by default; zsh spell checks with a very quick configuration file edit. The fancier you want to get with file and command completion, the more you'll probably want zsh.

As recommended at the beginning of this section, try out all the shells, at least once. All you have to do is type the name of the shell at any other shell prompt. When you're done and want to return to bash, type **exit**. Look over the documentation. All the shells have extensive man or info pages. After you've settled on a shell, run the Change Shell (chsh) program to identify your choice. Then take some time to read those docs thoroughly.

Now that you've settled one of the interminable Linux wars to your satisfaction, you can choose a text editor.

---

**Running YaST from the Shell**

YaST is a tool older than most GUI desktop environments, and it runs beautifully from any shell. Log in as the SuperUser with the su command, and then type **yast** at the prompt. Figure 5.2 shows the opening screen in a KDE Konsole.

This is especially useful in an emergency, when the system won't boot to the GUI login screen. To restore your system from a previous backup (see Chapter 20, "Managing Data: Backup, Restoring, and Recovery," for more information on backing up and restoring your system), follow these steps:

1. Run YaST by typing **yast** at the rescue prompt.
2. Use the arrow key to select System from the listing on the left.
3. Tab to the module section on the right, and then arrow down to Restore System.

4. Follow the instructions on the page or view details in the "Using System Restore" section of Chapter 20.

To maneuver around the menus and choices, use the accelerator keys highlighted on each screen. Press the Alt key with the highlighted letter to move to the item you want. For example, in any screen, press Alt+H to get Help on that screen. When finished, press Alt+Q to Quit and return to the shell prompt.

All YaST modules that are in the GUI version work in the command-line version as well, although Online Update (YOU) is dependent on the state of your Internet connection.

**FIGURE 5.2**    YaST works just as well from the shell as from a GUI environment.

# Editing Text

Because Unix and Linux are rooted in the hacker/geek/programmer culture, where coding was (and is) the most important function of any computer, having robust shells and editors were essential parts of the experience. It is no accident that Bill Joy wrote both the C shell and the `vi` editor, nor that Richard Stallman created the GNU Project and the `emacs` editor (and that each has completely different views about how to create and license software).

Of course, that was in the bygone early days of Unix. Why does it matter what text editor you should use now? And why do you need one, anyway? Consider this: Word processors are wonderful things, but often they are the very essence of overkill. One of the beauties of Linux is that nearly all the configuration and customization options for applications are contained in simple text files. This is true whether the program has a GUI or not. So making changes in the way a program works doesn't necessarily have to require opening the program; just open the config file in a text editor!

There's one other reason to be at least somewhat comfortable with at least one nongraphical editor. One of the truly cool things about Linux is the capability to access many different computers regardless of where you happen to physically be located at a given moment.

Remote access to other servers and workstations is another beauty of Linux, but most times, those remote machines (especially the servers) don't even have X installed. To get any work done, you need a text editor.

SUSE Linux offers no fewer than 22 text editors through YaST, as shown in Table 5.1. Don't be overwhelmed by the number of choices, though. Basically, text editors fall into one of two major camps: editors that behave like vi and editors that behave like emacs. This list also has a few line editors that work directly in the shell.

**TABLE 5.1**   Types of Editors in SUSE Linux

| Vi-type | Emacs-type | Other |
|---------|------------|-------|
| Vim | Emacs | Ed |
| Gvim | Xemacs | Joe |
| Nvi | TeXmacs | Pico |
| Kvim | Uemacs | E3 |
| | Zile | FTE |
| | Qemacs | Mined |
| | | THE (the Hessling Editor) |
| | | JEdit |

The next few sections will help you work with these various editors.

## Working with vim and Its Clones

They say that vi is hard to learn, but once you get there, you can do amazing things with it. That hard-to-learn part is evident from the first time you use it (unless you have a *vi* user nearby). When you first open the vi editor (and these days, typing vi actually opens its "improved" version, vim), you cannot type anything. By default, vi opens in its command/viewing mode. You can maneuver around a file, provided you know that commands in vi begin with a colon (:). To edit a file, you must press the Insert key (or Esc-i) first.

After you know this secret handshake, vim can be very useful and, with practice, very powerful. It also comes with extensive documentation. The documentation page at the Vim.org site says it best: "The most useful software is sometimes rendered useless by poor or altogether missing documentation. Vim refuses to succumb to death by underdocumentation."

To quickly get up to speed in vim, you don't have to run the editor. Run vimtutor from the shell prompt to get a brief tutorial, estimated to take about 30 minutes to complete.

Following are a few commands that will help you get started with vim:

Simple navigation: Your arrow keys work fine, but these characters also move the cursor:

| | |
|---|---|
| h | left |
| l | right |
| k | up |
| j | down |

| | |
|---|---|
| Delete character | x |
| Delete line | dd |
| Save | :w (write) |
| Find text in file | /<string> |
| Changing mode from Insert to Command | Esc |
| Quit | :q |
| Quit without saving | :q! |

Gvim and Kvim both offer GUIs for the basic editor. They were written for GNOME and KDE, respectively, but you can use either one in either environment. The primary development team for Kvim has moved on to produce another GUI-based vi clone called Yzis.

Nvi is a slightly different version of vi from the University of California at Berkeley.

## Working with Emacs and Its Clones

GNU emacs is the infinitely customizable, everything-but-the-kitchen-sink editor/work environment. It was the first product of the GNU Project, and so is beloved by many free-software purists.

It is the text editor that keeps your hands busy over the keyboard with seemingly odd multiple keybindings (Ctrl+X to begin a command and another combination to complete it). Learning emacs is a supremely geeky thing to do.

If vim has everything an editor should have in one pretty, if sometimes impenetrable, package, emacs is a modular monster. Emacs reads email and Usenet newsgroups, browses the web and composes web pages in HTML, XHTML, XML, and sundry other formats as well. It offers a development environment for practically every extant programming language. You can even see a sublimely odd conversation between Zippy the Pinhead and a psychoanalyst. But to do all this, you must have the proper mode installed. Emacs is a big program (taking up to 30MB), but it does not include every mode that has been written. Sometimes you have to go hunting for the thing you need.

Emacs is easy to start up (type emacs <filename> from the shell prompt), and navigation can be pretty easy.

Unlike vim, Emacs has its own interface (vim just shows up in the shell) with menus and mouse support, although not quite as pretty as under X. Unless you include a mode command when you launch it, emacs assumes you want to write text and loads in text fill mode. If you don't want words to wrap at the end of a line, go to the Options menu or type Alt+X+auto-f[TAB] to change the mode.

Emacs also has a tutorial that will walk you through the basic commands and navigation tools. In emacs, use Ctrl+H, and then press "T" to get to it.

Most of the other clones of emacs (aficionados use the plural emacsen) are subsets of the original designed for specific uses. XE began as a GUI version, but has a separate group of developers that have done some things differently from its parent. Generally speaking, XEmacs is faster to add new features and does not require packagers to assign copyright to the Free Software Foundation (that administers the GNU Project).

## Some of the Others

You don't need to follow the crowd when choosing an editor. Choices are not limited to the big two. Take these for a spin:

- ed—The first Unix line editor. It opens by default in viewing/command mode and is the reason vi does the same.

  You could put it in the vi-clones category, if it didn't predate vi. If you need a shell script to edit or perform commands on some text, ed is the editor to invoke. It's fast and functional for basic line editing.

- Joe—You say you can't decide whether emacs or vi is cooler? Do you still remember all those WordStar commands and macros? You just might love Joe's Own Editor. Joe is a flexible beast that wants to work the way you want it to. It can emulate any of the previously mentioned editors with a simple command switch. You can open and edit multiple files at once and provide different environments for each one. Like emacs, it can read email and news, too. Help is extensive and can put a command template right on your screen so you don't have to think about how to save a file (Ctrl+K, and then D, if you must know).

- JEdit—This is a Java-based graphical editor that many folks swear by. Although powerful by itself, it also has a plug-in architecture that can bulk it up even more. The nice thing is that it is incredibly easy to add and update any plug-in you have with the built-in plug-in manager. The commands are relatively easy to learn, and the user's guide is helpful.

- The Hessling Editor (the)—This is a specialized editor for people used to working in VMS/CMS and another example of how niches get served in an open-source environment. There may not be millions of VMS veterans with wallet in hand transitioning to Linux, but it takes only one person with some programming skills to write that editor and make it available to the rest of us.

# Why Can't I Edit This File? How Permissions Work

If there's one thing that is important to know about Linux, it is that everything on your computer exists as a file. Your printer, sound card, hard-drive partitions, monitor, directories—a file on your system represents that item. And each file has rules about who can access it and in what manner.

In this section, you will get an introduction to permissions. This is covered in more depth in Chapter 19. No matter what your skill level is, you should read the "User Accounts and Permissions" section of that chapter.

Linux is a multiuser operating system, with a minimum of two users on any machine: the Root user and a "generic user.

> **NOTE**
>
> The Root user is also the SuperUser when logged in as such, and other users can become the SuperUser with the Root password.

Each file (again, that means everything on your system) has an owner and is assigned to a group when it is created. Read, write, and execute permissions are set for three types of user: Owner, group, and the rest of the world.

The `ls -l` (long format) directory listing command displays the permissions for each file. To see the system default permissions for a file, use the touch command to create an empty file and then run `ls -l`, like this:

```
touch file
mikemc@linux:~> ls -l file
-rw-r--r--   1 mikemc   users          0 2004-12-08 09:43 file
```

> **TIP**
>
> Touch will also change the access time of any existing file.

Looking at this listing, you see a 10-character block of dashes and letters (-rw-r--r--). These characters identify the permissions for this file.

The first character in the block indicates whether it is a special file in some way (d identifies it as a directory, c is for a character device, and b is for a block device, such as a hard drive). We know this is a plain data file because there is a dash, noting it is not any of these special types.

The default permissions for this file show us that the Owner of the file can Read and Write it (rw-); it is Read-Only (r--)for both the Group and Others (the rest of the world). If this was supposed to be an executable program file, a problem would exist, because no one has permission to execute it.

The next columns tell us other important things about this file:

- The number next to the permissions block shows the number of hard links to a file.

You may better understand this as the number of copies of this file that exist on the system. Files almost always have just one link/copy. Directories nearly always have at least two because it is linked in its parent directory.

- After the link counter, you see the Owner of the file. Because we created the file logged in as user mikemc, mikemc is the owner. In this case, this user is the only person who can edit this file (that is, make changes to and write back to the hard drive). The owner can be changed by either the current owner or by Root using the chown command.

- After the Owner is identified, you see the group (users) assigned to this file. This means that all users on the system can read the file, but cannot write (save changes) to it. As with any read-only file, other users can save changes in a different location or with a different filename. The group assignment can be changed by the owner or by Root using the chgrp command.

- The file size and creation date are defined in the last columns. This file is empty, but the size is defined in bytes.

## Changing Permissions

When you are the owner of a file (or the SuperUser), you have the right to make that file more (or less) accessible by adjusting its permissions. You do that with judicious use of the chown (Change Owner), chgrp (Change Group) and chmod (Change Mode) commands.

> **NOTE**
>
> You can make these changes in any of the GUI file managers (Konqueror, Nautilus, and so on) by opening the Properties dialog box of a file (or group of files). See Chapter 18.

To make user2 the owner of the file we created in the last section, type the following:

```
chown user2 file
```

> **CAUTION**
>
> If your system administrator has imposed disk quotas for users, only Root can change owners. This prevents you from exceeding your quota by fobbing off your excess files on another user. Disk quotas are covered in Chapter 18.

This works for multiple files, too. Name each file or use wildcards to specify similar files. For example, if you have a bunch of files in this directory that begin with "file" and you want to change ownership of them, modify the previous command to

```
chown user2 file*
```

As with many Linux commands, when you run this command the shell prompt will reappear unless there is a problem or error.

Our file allows only the owner to make changes (write) to the file. If you want anyone in the writers group to be able to edit it directly, you should change the group assigned to this file from users (which are all system users) to writers (a previously defined select group of users):

```
chgrp writers file
```

> **CAUTION**
>
> chgrp works only if you are both the Owner of a file and a member of the group you're changing to. If you want to change permissions to a different group, you may be able to use the newgrp command to temporarily join that group, if you know the group password. Otherwise, Root must make the change.

But we're not done; the group permission is still set for Read-Only. We complete the task here:

```
chmod g+w file
```

As noted in the previous section, permissions are defined as Read, Write, and eXecute--rwx. With the g+w switch, we've told chmod to add (+) Write (w) privileges to the group (g).

The choices for chmod include the following:

> u—user
>
> g—group
>
> o—others
>
> a—all users
>
> Plus sign (+)—add a Read, Write, or eXecute permission
>
> Minus sign (-)—remove a Read, Write, or eXecute permission

Some people prefer using octal (base 8) numbers when using chmod. This way, instead of adding or subtracting individual permissions, you can specify exactly what you want them to be when you complete the command. Using octals to make the same change we made previously, the command looks like this:

```
chmod 664 file
```

Why these numbers? Each digit represents one set of permissions: Owner Group Others. Each number represents the rights each entity has

> 4 = Read permission
>
> 2 = Write permission
>
> 1 = Execute permission

Add each permission number to signify the permission level the file should have. So, as shown, the Owner and Group has Read and Write (4+2=6); Others just has Read.

To confirm the changes you've made, just run `ls -l` again.

### Directory Permissions

Directories also have permissions assigned to them. Use `ls -dl` (d for Directory, l for Long version) to see the permissions of your current directory (most likely, the home directory). You should see something like this:

```
drwxr-xr-x   64 mikemc   users      4056 2004-12-09 15:02
```

The distinguishing mark here is the leading `d` in the permissions block. This tells you that you are looking at a directory. Looking carefully, you can see that the Owner (`mikemc`) can do everything (`rwx`), whereas the Users group and Others can read a list of the directory's contents. You have to have execute rights (`r-x`) to view directory contents. Looking at this octally, permissions are set at 755.

You can perform the same permission changes on directories as with files, using the same tools, provided you have the rights to do so.

## Working as Root

Permissions, more importantly the lack of them, mean a lot on a Linux (or Unix) system, especially if you're "just a user." Permissions are all about security—keeping the system safe from harm. In this case, harm can come from many directions. When you think about computer security, the vision that comes to your head is mostly likely that of the evil hacker who attempts to steal your passwords, credit card numbers, critical data, or even your identity. Security on the Internet is certainly an important consideration, and protecting your networks and systems against that type of criminal activity is essential.

> **TIP**
>
> If you spend any time hanging around the Linux community, you will probably get a lecture about the hacker previously described. Don't be put off; Unix and Linux were both forged out of the more noble "hacker culture" devoted to making better technology, not to busting into other people's machines.

In Linux and Unix, however, security and permissions also keep you from the more mundane harm and the bad things that can happen to any user at any time, such as the time you accidentally deleted an entire folder of documents relating to your company's latest merger from your machine, and it took the IT staff a week to reconstruct it from backups.

As Root, you have inestimable power at your fingertips. You can keep the system humming, or you can bring it down with a few keystrokes. All you have to do to destroy a system is type this command (*Don't* try this at home!):

```
rm -fr /
```

This command removes (rm) all files and directories recursively from the root of the tree. If you're dual-booting with a mounted Windows partition, that partition will be gone, too. If you happen to be logged in to some remote machine somewhere that is now part of your system, it's best to get on the phone now. The remote files are disappearing, too.

> **TIP**
>
> This scenario is another reason to not mount your Windows partition(s) automatically at boot time.

So don't take chances. Even if you are the all-powerful Root on your machine, always log in as the humble user unless you have system work to do. Even though you can add the Root user to your SUSE Linux graphical Login screen, don't. Save it for emergencies.

Now that you're properly terrified, let me tell you that there are essential tasks that must be performed by the Root user. You can do these things safely, too. We will go into detail about many of these things in Parts 3 and 4, but for now here is a small list:

- Install and update most software
- Run YaST
- Set the clock
- Turn the firewall on and off
- Add and delete users
- Kill some services

The best way to perform all these tasks is to use the su (SuperUser) command and type the Root password. You can do whatever tasks you need to, then return to the shell prompt, and type **Exit** to return to your user prompt.

> **NOTE**
>
> When you run YaST and some other graphical programs that need Root access, they will offer to remember the Root password for you. If there is any chance that some day you will forget the Root password when you need it the most, don't take them up on this offer. Just keep typing it in.
>
> For more tips on passwords, see Chapter 19.

As Root, you can allow specific users to perform specific tasks using the sudo command. This is described in detail in Chapter 19.

## Creating and Deleting Users

A user is not a user until he or she has a password. All user passwords (and occasionally some other information) are stored in the /etc/passwd file. You can create new users in SUSE Linux in two ways—through YaST or through the shell.

When you first installed SUSE Linux, you created your first user—you. If different people use the computer, giving them their own accounts is essential. If you happen to be the only one planning to use Linux, why would you need to create another? Think about the different roles you play when you're at your computer. You might want to create different users to play those roles, without distraction.

In YaST, managing users and groups comes under the Security tab. To add a user, go to Manage Users and click Add. You'll be asked to supply a username and an initial password. You'll also be asked if you want to set an expiration date for that password. Changing passwords regularly is a good idea, especially on networked computers, including ones that access the Internet.

From the shell, adding users is a two-step process. After logging in with su, use the useradd command to quickly create a user:

```
useradd drone77
```

You must now create an initial password (remember: no password, no user) by running passwd:

```
passwd drone77
Changing password for user drone77
New password:
Retype new password:
passed: all authentication tokens updated successfully.
```

Enter the new password twice. If you don't do this, drone77 will not be able to log in. The first time drone77 logs in, she will be given the opportunity to create her own password.

Type **useradd -D** to confirm the new user's default settings. You will see the Group ID, home directory, account and password policy, default shell, and the directory holding the configuration file for that shell.

As you might expect, if useradd adds users, userdel will delete users from your system. It is best to delete the user's home directory when you remove the user from the passwd file as well. Do this using the -r (recursive) switch:

```
userdel -r drone77
```

This also removes the user from the mail queue.

## Shutting Down and Rebooting the System

By default, only Root can shut down the system. This is especially important when the system is a server, but it is also good for any networked device where people may depend on a file being available.

Root can allow users to perform this function, which is a good idea when you are using your computer as a desktop or a dual-boot system. This is done in YaST.

To shut down the system from the shell, log in as su and run the shutdown command. The fastest way to do this is with the -h (halt) switch:

```
shutdown -h now
```

or

```
shutdown -h 0
```

If you are on a network, you may want to specify a time for shutdown, and send the other users a message:

```
shutdown -h 18:30 "System is going down for maintenance this evening"
```

The message will go out 15 minutes before shutdown (in this case, at 6:15 p.m.).

To reboot a system, you use the same shutdown command, this time with the -r (reboot) switch. Set the time as you did previously.

If this system is a server, make sure you don't shut it down while something else is happening (such as a backup). Again, with awesome power comes awesome responsibility.

# References

This chapter covered a lot of ground. The references will help you go into more depth on the Linux file system, shells, editors, and permissions. When choosing a shell or an editor, I highly recommend reviewing their man (or info) pages, as well as their websites.

## File System

- http://www.pathname.com/fhs—Probably more than you want to know about the new Linux Filesystem Hierarchy Standard.

- http://www.linuxbase.org—The Linux Standard Base page.

- http://standards.ieee.org/regauth/posix—The IEEE POSIX information page.

## Shells

- http://cnswww.cns.cwru.edu/~chet/bash/bashtop.html—Chet Ramey's bash page. He is the current maintainer of the bash project.

- http://www.tldp.org/LDP/Bash-Beginners-Guide/html/—The Bash Beginners Guide as a web page. If you visit you can get this in other formats, along with other excellent Linux resources.

- http://web.cs.mun.ca/~michael/pdksh/—The Public Domain Korn Shell home page.

- http://www.tcsh.org/Welcome—The tcsh Wiki. Learn more and contribute your own knowledge about this C Shell.

- http://www.zsh.org/—Home of the Z Shell. Select a nearby mirror.

- http://www-106.ibm.com/developerworks/linux/library/l-z.html—Good introduction to the Z shell from IBM.

- http://www.ibiblio.org/mc/—Home of the Midnight Commander. Screen shots, FAQs, and a TODO list for the developers.

- http://www.dotfiles.com/—Explore contributed configuration files for various shells, editors, and other tools.

- http://www.shelldorado.com/—Heiner's Shelldorado. Much scripting information for all shells, but a good introduction, too.

## Editors

- http://www.gnu.org/software/emacs/emacs.html—The GNU/Emacs home page.

- http://www.dotemacs.de/—The "very unofficial dotemacs home." Explore the many ways to configure your emacs.

- http://www.emacswiki.org—Find new modules and helpful people here.

- http://www.vim.org/—The Vim home page.

- http://vimdoc.sourceforge.net/—Where to find documentation of all sorts for Vim.

- http://www.yzis.org/—The new project from the developers of Kvim for the K Desktop Environment.

- http://sourceforge.net/projects/joe-editor/—The home for Joe's Own Editor.

- http://jedit.org/—The Java-based editor.

## Working as Root

- http://linux.about.com/od/embedded/l/blnewbie_toc.htm—The Linux Newbie Administrator Guide. A basic overview.

- http://www.gratisoft.us/sudo/—The sudo main page. Downloads, documentation, and resources for this command.

# CHAPTER 6

# Launching Your Desktop

When you normally log in to SUSE Linux, you use a graphical login screen. That screen, a display manager, is your first taste of the X Window System, more often called X11R6, X11, or just plain X. X has a much longer history than Microsoft Windows, but it is similar in many ways. It has also gone through more than a few changes along the way. The most recent change is a revival of development from the X.org Foundation, the official owners of X. Earlier versions of SUSE Linux included an open-source version of X for the Intel platform called XFree86; SUSE Linux 9.3 uses X.org version X11R6.8.2.

X uses a client/server model in its architecture, but it's a little different from what you may think. Normally, you are working with a client on your PC that makes requests on your server, which is remote. With X, the server is installed on your machine. It accepts requests from any number of clients, which can also be on your machine, or connected from a remote location (like a Telnet session). X Servers supply the graphics drawing protocols and much of the network communication to support clients' libraries.

Most SUSE Linux users boot to an X-based graphical desktop environment. By default, that has always been the K Desktop Environment (KDE). SUSE developers have long worked on KDE, and continue to do so. But in recent years, many users have gravitated toward the GNU Network Object Model Environment (GNOME, pronounced with a hard G sound). Among those were Miguel De Icaza, Nat Friedman, and their Ximian development team. Novell purchased Ximian shortly before acquiring SuSE, Inc., and has been working to promote compatibility between the two desktops and their applications. The Novell Linux

Desktop (NLD) seeks the best of both worlds, and SUSE Linux offers you the choice to install either or both desktop environments.

This chapter covers the basics of the X Window System and how it works in SUSE Linux. You'll learn about the primary desktop environments—KDE and GNOME—and get a brief introduction to some other X Window managers, if you don't need all that overhead.

# Understanding the X Window System

The X Window System represents two primary concepts. The X Window System was created to keep the UNIX kernel and GUI code separate. It was also designed for distributed processing based on the client/server model. That is, with X you don't need to have a computer with massive amounts of hard drive space and RAM to run graphical applications. A thin client with a connection to an X server is all you need. Nonetheless, if you have the aforementioned massive hard drive and hundreds of megabytes of RAM, you can host both the X server and many clients on your own machine.

The X server's primary job is to create and manage windows, dialog boxes, buttons, and other graphical elements on a screen. That screen can be located practically anywhere in the world, and perhaps even on a laptop on the International Space Station. X is extremely portable, too. After you have configured X the way you (or your system administrators) want it, you can take that configuration file with you and copy it into any other X-capable machine and it will run the same way.

Dozens of applications have been developed to manage windows for X, and hundreds of X client programs exist to help users work in the graphical environment X provides. It all begins, however, with the fundamental question: What do you want your window decorations to look like?

## Configuring X in SUSE Linux

SaX (also referred to as SaX) is the X configuration tool for SUSE Linux. It runs for the first time during the initial SUSE Linux installation, where it identifies your graphics card, installs the graphics drivers, and sets up X to its default configuration. The settings are stored in the /etc/X11/XF86Config file. You can edit this file manually, but that would be unnecessary risky behavior.

To open SaX after the initial installation, go to YaST, Hardware, Graphics Card and Monitor. A second window will open with your initial monitor and card listed, along with the resolution and whether the card supports 3D acceleration. Click Change to open SaX and configure X.

---

**CAUTION**

SaX usually does a terrific job of identifying your video card and setting up the X environment. It can make mistakes, but before you hand edit XF86Config, try choosing the Reprobe button in SaX. With the wrong Monitor Frequency settings, it is possible (if quite rare) to blow out your monitor.

---

When you open SaX, you can see that it manages much more than your desktop settings (see Figure 6.1). The Multihead section will configure a multiple monitor setup; Input Devices include keyboard, mouse, touchscreen, and graphics tablet; and Access Control covers Virtual Network Client (VNC) access and XAccess, a tool for controlling your mouse with the keypad (especially useful for people who can't see the screen).

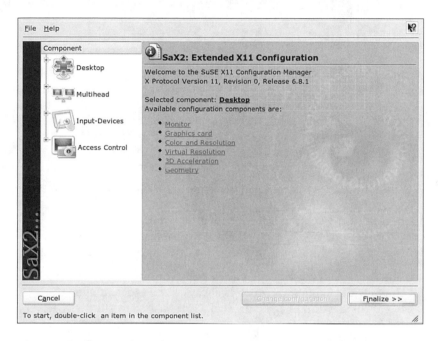

**FIGURE 6.1**    SaX2 offers a safe and graphical way to configure the X Window System.

If SaX has incorrectly identified either your monitor or graphics card, click the appropriate link and then click Properties. You will get a list of manufacturers and models to select from. Select the correct one; if you have a Linux driver disk for the item, click the Manufacturer's Disk button to install the new drivers. You can read and make changes to the frequency range and other settings in the Frequencies and Expert tabs, but don't do this unless you are absolutely sure you know what you're doing. Click OK and Finish to confirm your choices.

> **NOTE**
>
> As you make changes in each SaX component, be aware that nothing is written into the configuration file until you click Finalize and test the new setup.

There's not much to do in the Color and Resolution section. SaX detects the maximum color depth and all the resolutions your card will support and sets both defaults to the highest possible. Unless you have a fairly ancient machine, the color depth will be set at 16-bit True Color. This is the only thing you can change.

If you see some black edges on your screen and want to adjust this, go to the Geometry section. SaX puts up a window (see Figure 6.2) that will help.

**FIGURE 6.2**    Adjust the size of your screen display with the SaX Geometry screen.

Change the position if the desktop is large enough in width and height, but you are seeing empty space on one side. Change the size if you're seeing empty space on both sides. Keep pushing the appropriate arrow buttons until it looks right; then click Save.

When you're finished changing settings, click Finalize on the main SaX screen. You'll be asked to test the new configuration, which is always a good idea. If everything looks good, click Save; if the desktop image fails, click Ctrl+Alt+Esc to kill the X server and review your selections.

---

**TIP**

In most cases, you'll be using a display manager to log in and start X, but there may come a time when something breaks and you can't get into the display manager. Don't panic! You may still be able to get into X.

If this happens at boot, you will get a text-based login prompt. Log in as user, and you should be sitting in your home directory (type **pwd** to make sure). Look for the .xinitrc file: ls -a .xinitrc.

SUSE Linux puts a default file in Home called .xinitrc.template. Make a copy of this file to activate it:cp .xinitrc.template .xinitrc

Now, type the magic word: **startx**

This should get you in and may help you solve the original problem.

---

# Choosing a Desktop Environment: KDE and GNOME

With Windows and the Macintosh, the desktop is just that—the desktop. Linux is all about choices, and so is X. We'll talk about your choices in more lightweight window managers later, but chances are you are going to spend a good chunk of your computing time in one or another of these two desktop environments: KDE or GNOME.

One of the cool things is that you can remain indecisive your whole life: You can choose what desktop to load every time you log in. Of course, you don't have to choose that often either; SUSE Linux will load whatever desktop you loaded last time by default (and the initial default, assuming you installed it, is KDE).

When you first install SUSE Linux, YaST will recommend installing just the KDE desktop. You can choose to install GNOME instead, or install both if you have enough disk space.

With very few exceptions, all software designed for one desktop will happily run on the other, and will even show up in the other's Start menu. A trivial example is that SUSE installs identical default wallpaper for both desktops. You might find that one application designed for GNOME runs a little slower on KDE (or vice versa), but these types of issues are rarely catastrophic. All the Linux products not designed with either desktop (like OpenOffice.org and the Mozilla family) will also run beautifully in both.

Another key similarity is the capability to display multiple virtual desktops. If you regularly run one of those other operating systems and if you're a busy person, the desktop can get awfully crowded with a web browser, email client, word processor, and project manager all up at the same time. You can wind up Alt+Tabbing between apps, resizing and minimizing windows, or heavily working the taskbar to keep up. Wouldn't it be nice to have each application in its own desktop, away from the others? By default, GNOME and KDE offer you two virtual desktops (GNOME calls them workspaces). You can have up to 16 in KDE and 36 in GNOME. You can switch between them by pressing the Ctrl key along with the F key corresponding to the desktop number (that is, to switch to Desktop 2, press Ctrl+F2; for Desktop 3, press Ctrl+F3, and so on). For the incurable customizers, you can use descriptive names for each desktop, and even have different wallpaper on each one! You can have some applications (such as your schedule or time tracker) appear on all desktops, and choose whether you want to see the applications on other desktops in the taskbar. The taskbar will always show you your desktop lineup, with representations of the windows, as shown in Figure 6.3.

**FIGURE 6.3**    One busy desktop displayed as four busy desktops. This diagram shows active applications in virtual desktops 1–4, with one small window in all six. Click any of the images to work on that desktop.

In this section and the next, you will learn more about each desktop environment and the tools specifically designed for it. This should guide you in selecting the right desktop for you. Try them both, though. As with most things, choosing a desktop is largely a matter of personal preference.

KDE is older, more stable, and has more applications designed for it. Its technological underpinnings come from the commercial Qt libraries from Trolltech, and for a long time Qt's licensing scheme was not open source.

GNOME is the relative newcomer and has only recently become a stable system. Its technological underpinnings come from the first Linux killer app: The GNU Image Manipulation Program (The GIMP) (see the section "Editing Images with The GIMP" in Chapter 10, "Sights, Sounds, and Other Fun Things"). It began as an open-source rebellion, but has the support of many leading Linux-oriented corporations.

GNOME was the first desktop project to put usability at the top of its concerns, producing a truly admirable Human Interface Guidelines (HIG) document that has been a model for later efforts (including KDE's forthcoming HIG project). It has ambitions beyond the desktop as well. Many of its most partisan developers believe it provides a model framework for all software development.

> **TIP**
>
> One more common function for both desktop environments is a very handy application launcher. Press Alt+F2 to bring up a dialog box. Enter the name of an application to launch it. If you enter a URL, the default browser (Konqueror in KDE, Epiphany in GNOME) opens on that site. This way, you save time browsing through menus or opening new shells.

## KDE: The K Desktop Environment

The KDE project began in 1996 and has been the default desktop environment for SUSE Linux for nearly all that time. SUSE Linux 9.2 includes KDE 3.3. SUSE Linux also uses the KDE Display Manager to provide a graphical login screen after it has booted.

When you first log in to KDE, it will take a few seconds to load, but when it's finished you will see the basic elements of the desktop, looking much like Figure 6.4. Windows users should feel pretty comfortable with this opening experience—a few icons on the desktop, a taskbar (called the Kicker in KDE parlance) along the bottom, with assorted applications ready for quick access and a clock in the right corner (optionally configured to show the seconds passing by).

By default, KDE loads any applications that were running when your last session ended, so you can pick up where you left off. The SUSE icon in the left corner of the Kicker opens the application menus. To its right, the icons on the left side give you access to your home directory (via the Konqueror file manager), the Konsole Xterminal shell, the SUSE Help Center, the Konqueror web browser, and the Kontact personal information manager (the Outlook-style combined email, address book, and calendar program).

You will notice that KDE developers have a fetish for naming their programs with a K in front. This can be kreative, or just a little too kute, but it is a handy way of identifying what applications are K-specific. The Kicker panel is highly customizable; right-click anywhere to add or remove icons from the panel. The Configure Panel screen also lets you put the panel on a different side of the screen and set several other options.

**FIGURE 6.4**    The SUSE default KDE desktop. Along the bottom are the standard application icons, virtual desktops, and applications that run at startup.

In the right corner of the Kicker, next to the clock, are more application icons that always run. Mouse over each to see what they are. The smaller SUSE icon is the SUSEWatcher application, which checks the YaST Online Update (YOU) servers regularly to see if updates are available. These fix security problems and occasionally give you new versions of installed applications. Watch for an exclamation mark on this icon to get new updates. See Chapter 21, "Keeping Your System Current: Package Management," for more information on YOU.

The Klipper clipboard utility offers much more than its Windows counterpart. Among other things, Klipper stores your last seven cut/copy actions by default, so you can paste several items in sequence if you choose. Klipper will remember your clipboard actions over sessions, too.

So many applications have been written for KDE that the YaST initial installation menu separates out some from the default KDE installation. It's all there if you want it, though. KDE includes a complete office suite (KOffice, see Chapter 9, "Being Productive: Office Suites and Other Tools"), a programming integrated development environment (KDevelop, see Chapter 28, "Using the GNU Compiler Collection and Other Programming Tools"), a CD/DVD burning utility (K3b, see Chapter 10, "Sights, Sounds, and Other Fun Things"), and an outstanding printer support tool (KPrint, see Chapter 7, "Printing with SUSE Linux"). The Konqueror file manager is also a web browser with its own interface. All these tools are covered in greater depth in their relevant chapters.

## GNOME: The GNU Network Object Model Environment

When you open GNOME for the first time, you may notice two differences between it and KDE: The look is a lot less cluttered, and the taskbar is at the top of the screen. You might even miss it the first time you look.

The GNOME panels are highly configurable with a curious collection of applications that you have much more control over than in KDE. Displaying many of the same characteristics and applications by default as KDE, the whole look is a bit cleaner with the much smaller icons. See Figure 6.5 for a look.

**FIGURE 6.5**  The default GNOME desktop is much cleaner than KDE, with a smaller and more configurable set of panels.

The Programs menu was built for SUSE (indicated by the Novell icon attached to it) and is identical to the default Kicker menu in KDE, but there is a separate menu for quick access to System tools, including YaST, the file finder, and the logout button. The left side default applications include the Epiphany web browser, the Evolution groupware/personal information manager tool, and OpenOffice.org Writer, along with SUSEWatcher and SUSEPlugger. On the right, in addition to the clock, is the volume control and the list of all open applications.

In the bottom panel is your task/workspace switcher (right-click it to change the number of workspaces/desktops) and a window hiding tool to show just the desktop. Active applications and documents also appear in the bottom panel.

To add an icon to either panel, right-click exactly in the spot where you want the item to appear and choose Add to Panel. You can then select your item from the menu. Among the choices is a weather report with the current temperature and conditions for many global cities. Select your own location—or the place you want to be.

---

**TIP**

To get quick access to the standard GNOME menus, add the Main Menu to your top panel. This is much more extensive, and GNOME-specific, complete with the GNOME footprint logo.

---

# Managing Files from Your Desktop

Sooner or later, you will need to move or copy files from one directory (or device) to another. Chances are, at one time or another you have used Windows Explorer (and/or its slightly less useful companion, My Computer) to perform this task. Perhaps you've thought that there has to be a better way to do this than Microsoft's way. Thus, even in the Windows world, there are third-party file managers that reinvent that task in several ways.

Both Linux desktop environments have file managers that seek to ease this task. In this section, we'll look at both of them, plus a third KDE-based file manager included in SUSE Linux, Krusader.

## Using Konqueror in KDE

KDE's Konqueror takes an Explorer-like approach (to the point of being a web browser as well), with mount points (drives) and directories in the left pane and the contents of the selected directory displayed as large icons with the file or subdirectory name on the right, with a toolbar across the top. If you're comfortable working in the Windows file manager, you should find Konqueror easy to work with, but it won't take long for you to see that Konqueror has more to offer than Explorer. You will also see that Konqueror can be configured to work in whatever style you want.

There are several ways to launch Konqueror:

- To see the contents of your /home directory, click the House icon on the left end of the KDE Kicker taskbar.

- Clicking the My Computer icon runs Konqueror in the /media directory. You should see the contents of your hard drive(s) and floppy drive in this view.

- Press Alt+F2 and type in a path to a directory. Konqueror will open in that directory (typing a web address will open Konqueror in browser mode).

- From the Kicker menu, go to System, File Manager. You should see Home and Computer, as listed previously. You should also see File Manager—Super User Mode in this menu. This mode is especially helpful when you're troubleshooting permissions problems, if you are the SuperUser.

The first time you open your home directory, you'll see something similar to Figure 6.6.

**FIGURE 6.6**    The KDE Konqueror file manager offers an Explorer-like interface with lots of extras.

This is Konqueror's default File Management profile, in Icon view. On the left side is the familiar directory tree, focused on the /home directory, with the files and folders in that directory displayed with icons on the right. To see more details on your files, click the Tree View icon in the toolbar, or go to the View menu at the top, select View Mode, Tree (or Detailed List) View. On the far left of the Konqueror screen, you can also change what you see in the left pane of the window. Click each icon to display various system services, the Root (/) folder, your network (including FTP sites configured by Konqueror's own team or added manually), or your current Konqueror web browser history and bookmarks. What's nice about this is that changing the display in the left pane does not automatically change the display in the right File pane—until you click something in the new left pane. This makes dragging and dropping files just a bit easier when you have quick access to nearly every place you'd want to send a file to.

Konqueror takes another cue from modern web browsers by enabling tabbed navigation even on your file system. To open a new, empty tab, press Ctrl+Shift+N (for New), or right-click in the tab area and select New Tab from the context menu. You can then use the Location bar to type in a destination, or use one of the left-pane options to open a folder in the new tab. Should you desire, you can detach the tab and put it in its own window. Unfortunately, you cannot drag files from one tab to another, but there's a way around that. Go to the Window menu, select Split View Top Bottom, and then select another location. You'll see something like Figure 6.7.

**FIGURE 6.7**    Drag and drop items from one pane to another in Konqueror.

Now you can drag from one pane to another. Should you happen to have something in the other tab to send to the bottom folder (in this case, a USB "keychain" drive), you can drag that down as well. By default, Konqueror always asks you what to do (copy, move, or create a link) when you drop something, so you are always in control of what happens.

When you get Konqueror configured the way you like it (or at least one of the ways you like it), go to Settings, Save View Profile. By default, the current profile name comes up in the Profiles screen (see Figure 6.8). Unless you want your new setup to become the default File Management settings, change the name as shown.

> **NOTE**
>
> When saving a profile, you can tell Konqueror to remember the directories you are currently in by checking the Save URLs in Profile box. Same thing for the Save Window Size box.

## Using Krusader in KDE

When you look at a power user's file manager, such as Midnight Commander and others like it, one thing that makes it stand out is this notion of double panes. When you're moving files from one place to another, it is comforting to be able to see both the original location and the target at the same time. This way, you know that things worked out as you intended. This is Krusader's mantra.

**FIGURE 6.8** Set a desired configuration as a Profile in Konqueror, and you can load that configuration with a few mouse clicks.

When you open Krusader (see Figure 6.9), it will certainly remind you of the Midnight Commander interface. Krusader does dual panes by default—in fact, you can't get rid of them. It has the mc-like F-key command menu on the bottom, along with the standard GUI menus and toolbars on top. But that's only the beginning of this very feature-full file manager.

**FIGURE 6.9** Krusader gives you a dual-pane interface and will synchronize the files in each pane if you want it to.

Although it will not browse the Web for you, it will do just about everything else Konqueror does, and more:

- Compare and synchronize two directories.

- Create compressed archives in one of several formats (including standard tarballs, gzip, and bzip).

- Mount a drive.

- Open and edit a file as Root (if you have the rights to do that).

- Split one file into smaller pieces (to fit on a portable drive), or combine several files into one.

Krusader also has a fairly fast search engine that will locate files and directories using a specified pattern. For example, in Konqueror, you can search your entire computer or individual directories, but not selected multiple directories. In Krusader, you can specify multiple directories to look in or directories to not search in (such as /proc or /var). You'll learn more about finding files in Chapter 18, "Managing Files, Volumes, and Drives."

You can be quite productive with Krusader if you are busy with files all the time. You might even find Krusader fun to use, even if it won't burn a new CD for you.

## Using Nautilus in GNOME

Once upon a time at the turn of the millennium, a group of former Apple developers were converted to the open source cause. They founded a company called Eazel and announced their determination to make Linux as easy to use for the ordinary person as the MacOS. Their plan was to begin with a simple file manager and work from there. But the economy turned bad, and venture capital was no longer throwing money at even promising startups. Just 16 months after announcing their big plans, Eazel was dead, but not before their file manager, Nautilus, was born. Through the miracle of open-source licensing, Nautilus lives on as the default file manager for the GNOME desktop.

Nautilus seems to operate from the principle that if two windows make file management easier, more windows are even better. Each time you double-click a directory in Nautilus, the directory opens in what Nautilus calls an object window. This has, by default, a set of icons representing files and folders and a small menu bar. After you have all the windows open that you need, you can then arrange them to your satisfaction and drag and drop to your heart's content. Figure 6.10 shows the Nautilus List view, which you can access by choosing View as List from the View menu. You can choose a third view, called Browser View, by right-clicking a folder and selecting Browse Folder from the context menu. Whatever your view, you'll see that directory hierarchies are downplayed somewhat in Nautilus, with parent directories accessible only in the drop-down menu in the lower-left corner.

Drag-and-drop can be tricky if you are not careful. Dragging a file from one directory to another only moves the file. If you want to copy files, you must first select your files, right-click, and choose Copy Files from the menu. Then open the destination folder and right-click again to Paste.

**FIGURE 6.10**    Nautilus has a clean interface with multiple windows to work with.

The Places menu points to several common starting points (Computer, Home, Trash) and will also open the GNOME CD Creator for easy CD burning.

# Configuring Your Desktop Environment

You can choose to customize your experience with both desktops as much as you like. KDE has a simple and comprehensive Control Center where this happens. GNOME gives you a choice in how and where to customize. Following is a brief guide to some of the highlights.

## KDE Control Center

When you open the KDE Control Center, you get a quick summary of your system information: versions for KDE and the Linux kernel release, the machine name, and your username. Down the left side are the configuration categories.

In Appearance and Themes, you can set the wallpaper (called Background here), the screensaver, window colors, and other look-and-feel items. Each can be set individually, or themes can do this all at once. Go to the Theme Manager and click Get New Themes to visit http://www.kde-look.org for downloadable themes, wallpaper, and screensavers. The Background and Screen Saver pages show you what each option looks like in a test screen, so you don't have to commit before seeing it.

The Desktop area lets you set up the number of virtual desktops you want and sets various options for the Kicker panels and taskbar. Choose the Device Icons tab under Behavior to include links to devices and directories on your desktop.

The Internet and Network area lets you configure Konqueror's web-browsing functions, share your desktop with other KDE users on the network, and set up your Samba client

configuration for accessing Windows shares on your network (SuperUsers can also configure a Samba server). If you're on a laptop with Bluetooth capabilities, you can add and
manage your Bluetooth services here as well.

In KDE Components you can set default applications for mail, Konqueror's embedded text
editor (for viewing text files in the file manager), instant messaging, and Xterminal. You
can also change the default web browser from Konqueror so that Internet links open in
your browser of choice. The Session Manager also sets the behavior for shutdown and
startup.

Peripherals sets mouse, keyboard, and joystick behaviors. The Power Control settings,
which turn off the screensaver and monitor when not in use, are located under Display
(and laptop power controls are in Power Control). Regional and Accessibility settings
define your keyboard layout and how times, dates, and money are displayed depending
on the norm for your country. Set keyboard shortcuts for various KDE functions in the
Keyboard Shortcuts section and define other keyboard shortcuts and mouse gestures in
KHotKeys, a new addition. Figure 6.11 shows the Keyboard Shortcuts screen.

**FIGURE 6.11**    Define keyboard shortcuts for several KDE applications in the Control Center
Regional and Accessibility area.

Security and Privacy lets you take some security measures for yourself. The KDE Wallet
function will remember website passwords and other private information if you choose.
This is kept in a password-protected file that only you have access to.

Don't like the startup music that KDE plays? Head over to Sound & Multimedia, System
Notifications. You can turn off or replace many automatic sounds associated with various

actions—and not only sounds. You can assign a log file to an action, display a message, or specify any combination of notifications for any action.

Most of the System Administration tools and all the YaST tools require SuperUser (su) access to manipulate, but the Administrator Mode button is a handy way to make that happen.

If you are dual booting Windows and SUSE Linux, the Font Installer lets you include all your Windows fonts in Linux. Click Add Fonts and then navigate to /windows/c/ Windows/Fonts. Select all (or only the ones you want) and click Open.

When making changes in the Control Center, you must click Apply before moving away from that window. If you forget, you'll get a message asking if you want to apply the changes you made. With a few exceptions, all changes take place immediately.

## Customizing GNOME

Making the desktop work the best way for you is one of the stated goals of the GNOME project. If something doesn't look or work right, right-click it, and you should see a way to fix it. In the panels, you can add or remove items and panels easily enough, and you can set the size, color, and autohide capability in the Properties screen. Want to use a 24-hour clock instead of the AM/PM variety? Right-click the clock and you can make those changes.

The centralized Settings customization tool is in the System menu in the top panel (see Figure 6.12). Double-click any of the Settings icons to open the relevant screen.

**FIGURE 6.12**    The GNOME Settings Control Panel gives each area its own page.

The first section deals in the Personal, or so the menu says. The Accessibility and Assistive Technology Support pages confirm the GNOME project's commitment to usability. Some of the tools here can even help people with ordinary abilities and without physical disabilities get more done.

The Menus screen can be confusing. It opens a series of Nautilus file manager windows, where you can add or remove menu items. The shortcuts screen is much like the KDE screen shown in Figure 6.11. It's easy to create a new shortcut (highlight the action on the screen and then press the key[s] you want to use as the shortcut), but there's only one option. In KDE, you can choose an alternative.

The Appearance section covers the usual window decorations and such. GNOME is famed for its dashing GTK-based Themes, which are really more about color schemes than wallpaper and screensavers. Some themes come with suggestions for these elements as well. As with KDE, you can select screen fonts, wallpaper (Desktop Background), and screensavers separately. The Window preferences let you select a window just by passing the mouse cursor over it.

In the Hardware section, you are dealing with keyboard, mouse, and screen resolution issues. The keyboard settings here are the same as in the Accessibility area (and there's a link to those preferences, too), but one tab is of note to those of us who don't want to be disabled: GNOME will enforce a three-minute typing break every hour (by default, this is configurable, of course) to keep you away from repetitive stress syndrome. You can postpone the break, but I don't recommend that you do. Screen resolution should generally not be changed.

The System section covers Sound events, applications associated with file types, and whether you're using a proxy server to access the Internet. The Sessions page lets you define what applications should run at startup. It shows you the currently active programs and gives you the option to save that configuration for your next session start. You can also add applications manually to the startup.

## What Is a Window Manager and Why Would I Want to Use It?

Full-blown desktops for X did not come around until the mid-1990s. Before their arrival, there were window managers. From the humble Tabbed Window Manager (twm) that is about as basic as you can get to the very ambitious nearly complete desktops WindowMaker and fvwm, there are X window managers to fit every taste. Most of the widely used window managers are still in active development, and some work on top of the desktop environments as well as with just plain X.

Window managers are essential to any X installation, because without them, while X draws the window, it relies on window managers to move, resize, minimize, or maximize the window.

This section covers some of the window managers included in SUSE Linux and describes how they work. Like the desktop environments, window managers can be quite customizable and offer several goodies on their own.

## Why Run a Window Manager?

Following are a few reasons to know at least one window manager, even if you normally run a full desktop environment.

- Window managers are generally lightweight; they don't take a long time to load and don't suck up memory.

- If you just need X to connect to a remote machine and move some files, you don't need to load all the libraries for all the KDE utilities.

- If you ever have to connect to a remote X server halfway around the world on a phone line that transfers data at 33Kbps on a good day, knowing how to navigate in a window manager can save time and your sanity.

- Window managers tend to focus on performance at the expense of eye candy.

- OpenOffice.org, your favorite text editor, and your graphical browser work just as well under a window manager as they do in a desktop.

## Starting Up with a Window Manager

When you install a window manager with YaST, another entry is put into the display manager's boot menu. When you log in, click the Options button, go to Session Type, and choose your window manager.

## Running fvwm

This window manager, which started life as the Feeble Virtual Window Manager, but is no longer an acronym, is a favorite of more than a few alpha geeks. Gushing quotes from such Linux stars as Eric Raymond, Alan Cox, and Linus Torvalds himself appear on FVWM's website.

The default FVWM desktop (Figure 6.13) is somewhat plain, but clearly you can get some work done on it.

The FVWM menu bar at the top displays the multiple workspaces FVWM supports; it loads an analog clock and the playful "Eyes" toy that follows your mouse around while you're working. FVWM loads an Xterm by default for command-line work, but the SUSE menu gives you access to most of the same applications that run on the meatier desktops, including OpenOffice.org. The Graphics menu will run The GIMP (which took the screenshot), and the Tools menu runs Mozilla.

> **TIP**
>
> Right-clicking anywhere in an FVWM workspace brings up the SUSE Applications menu for easy program launching.

**FIGURE 6.13**    FVWM can run Mozilla, and its menu bar helps you get to work.

When you launch a program in FVWM, a shadow window attaches to your cursor so you can place it exactly where you want it on your screen (or in another workspace). Clicking the mouse draws the application window at the spot you select.

FVWM is a modular program. To view the currently available modules, click Modules from the FVWM menu. The Config module helps you customize your .fvwm2rc configuration file. You can also edit it manually, from /etc/X11/fvwm2 (for a systemwide configuration). If you want your own, copy the systemwide file to your home directory and edit it.

## Running WindowMaker

WindowMaker's roots are deep in the alternative-OS world. It is an attempt to re-create the look of NeXTSTEP, the operating system for the NeXT Cube. NeXT was the second big idea from Apple Computer founder Steve Jobs. It may not have been great from a marketing standpoint, but it certainly has its fans.

WindowMaker (you'll find that the team of developers has not yet fully resolved whether the application is one word or two) takes a little getting used to, but is a fast and powerful system.

When you load WindowMaker for the first time, the main thing you'll notice is that you don't have to wait. Log in and before you blink your eyes, it's up and ready for work. This may depend somewhat on your processor and RAM, but it should be quick. WindowMaker, by default, loads just two things on the desktop: on the left is the Workspaces Clip, on the right, the Applications Dock (see Figure 6.14).

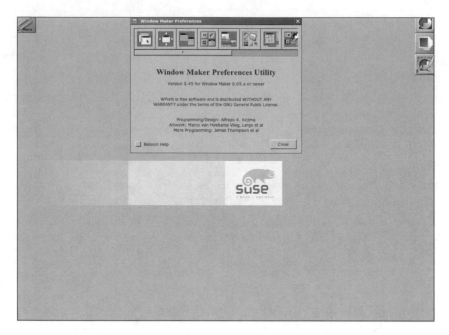

**FIGURE 6.14**    The Applications Dock (right corner) and Workspaces Clip make WindowMaker distinctive. Customize your WindowMaker in the separate WmakerPrefs package.

The Dock is a place to quickly launch applications, although there is not much there to start with. The Clip manages workspaces and applications. To create a new workspace, right-click anywhere on the desktop and choose Workspaces, Create New from the context menu. The context menu is also where you will see the familiar SUSE Applications menu from which to launch apps.

When you launch an application in WindowMaker, an icon square will appear in the lower-left corner of the screen; it may have the application's real icon or just a generic one. Drag that application icon to the Dock to add it to the Dock for this session. To put it on the Dock permanently, right-click and go to Workspaces, Save Session. You also get that opportunity when you exit WindowMaker.

Use the Clip to navigate between workspaces and applications, or use Alt plus number keys; that is, Alt+2 moves you to Workspace 2, Alt+3 to Workspace 3, and so on. The Clip will tell you what workspace you're in.

Customize WindowMaker with the Wprefs utility that installs separately from the main WindowMaker package; download the wmakerprefs package. Wprefs is fairly easy to understand and gives you no fewer than 13 categories of settings. Novices should activate the button help located in the last (Expert) category. This category is also where you can set WindowMaker to always save the session at shutdown. You can also customize the context menu in the Applications Menu Editor.

## Running IceWM

IceWM is another straightforward window manager that SUSE does not dress up too much in its incarnation. The SUSE menu is there, of course, and the multilingual Welcome wallpaper used in the KDM login screen is used instead of something more scenic.

Otherwise, IceWM behaves like the others. It's effective without being flashy. It is highly configurable, but don't use the GUI iceprefs package included in SUSE Linux. For some reason, an ancient package that relies on an ancient version of Python is still included in this distribution.

This is another open source success story. When David Mortenson, the original developer of iceprefs, stopped updating the program without formally relinquishing control of the project, the program lay dormant for three years. As Erica Andrews explains on the project website: "I love IceWM and IcePref...and IcePref needed a SERIOUS upgrade—so I did it, as everybody else seemed too lazy to do it."

IcePref2 is now a component of the IceWM Control Center, a series of utilities for this still-active window manager. Download the RPM from the project website (http:// icesoundmanager.sourceforge.net) and install it using YaST (see Chapter 21 for more information). You may get a complaint about a missing file (pygtk), but if you have the Python-GTK package installed, you have this.

Log in to IceWM and you'll get that nice clean screen. Open an Xterminal and type **icepref** at the prompt. You'll see the endlessly customizable IcePref dialog boxes (see Figure 6.15).

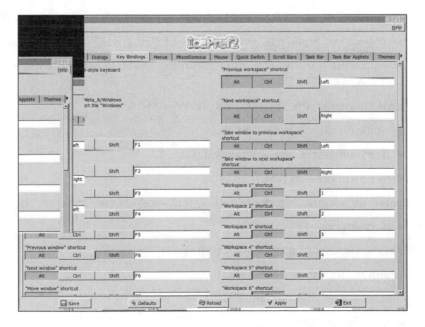

**FIGURE 6.15**   Use IcePref to customize just about anything you want in IceWM, including keyboard shortcuts.

A look along the row of tabs shows you the types of changes you can make. Some options will be confusing to novices, but window managers are for the more sophisticated users.

## References

- http://www.x.org—The X.org Foundation, the hub of X Window System development activity.

- http://freedesktop.org—The effort to produce minimum standards for free desktop software. Not a formal standards body, but a "collaboration zone" where projects are hosted and KDE and GNOME developers can discuss concerns.

- http://www.kde.org—The home of the K Desktop Environment. A well-organized site, with links to nearly everything relevant to KDE.

- http://dot.kde.org—The KDE News site, with links to online articles about KDE and its applications, along with press releases and the like.

- http://www.gnome.org—The GNOME home.

- http://www.gnomedesktop.org—"Footnotes," the GNOME News site.

- http://www.novell.com/linux/ximian.html—The Ximian area of Novell.com. Information about Evolution, Mono, and the Ximian Desktop.

- http://konqueror.kde.org/—The Konqueror site, covering both the file-management and web-browsing functions of this versatile tool.

- http://krusader.sourceforge.net/—The Krusader dual-pane file manager for KDE.

- http://www.gnome.org/projects/nautilus/—Nautilus, the GNOME file manager.

- http://xwinman.org—An Internet hub for learning about and trying Window Managers for X.

- http://www.gnomefiles.org/app.php?soft_id=599—Metacity.

- http://sawmill.sourceforge.net—Sawfish.

- http://www.windowmaker.org—WindowMaker.

- http://www.icewm.org—IceWM.

- http://icesoundmanager.sourceforge.net/IcePref2—IceWM configuration tool.

- http://www.fvwm.org—FVWM.

- http://blackboxwm.sourceforge.net—BlackBox wiki.

- http://icculus.org/openbox/2—OpenBox.

- http://enlightenment.org—Enlightenment.

- http://www.xfce.org—Xfce.

# CHAPTER 7

# Printing with SUSE Linux

Until relatively recently, printing in Linux has been something of a chore. As the hardware got cheaper, the proprietary drivers got more specialized and more valuable to their vendors. Open-source drivers for the most popular inkjet printers were hard to come by, and different distributions did printing differently, even though the protocol they used was the same. This situation has changed dramatically since the advent of the Common Unix Printing System (CUPS), a protocol that simplified things greatly.

Today, SUSE Linux supports hundreds of printers to one degree or another, and YaST makes it easy to set up, test, and configure your printer. In this chapter you will walk through a printer setup, learn to manage multiple printers on your system, and use the command line to print documents directly.

You will also learn a little about PostScript, the primary UNIX/Linux printing language, and its cousin, the Portable Document Format (PDF). Linux has always had applications that read PDF files, and Adobe has occasionally released Linux versions of Acrobat Reader. Several Linux applications (chief among them OpenOffice.org) now support making PDF documents as well.

## Printing: An Overview

The most important thing to understand about printing in Linux is that it is largely a conversion process. Whenever you issue a print command in an application, you are actually creating a PostScript (.ps) file that is sent to the printer.

The problem is that most printers, except for relatively high-end laser printers, do not have the power to process PostScript commands directly.

To solve this problem, Peter Deutsch of Aladdin Enterprises wrote a program called Ghostscript and released it under an open source license, the Aladdin Free Public License (AFPL). Subsequently, another version was released under the GNU General Public License. The primary difference between the two licenses is that the AFPL does not allow for commercial distribution. Both versions (and a commercial version produced by Artifex) are still being produced, with AFPL Ghostscript at v8.11 and GPL Ghostscript at v7.05. CUPS incorporates a specially patched version of GPL Ghostscript, called ESP Ghostscript, that SUSE Linux uses in its distribution.

Ghostscript lets you view raw PostScript and Portable Document Format (PDF) files. With the right drivers, it can also convert them into files that non-PostScript printers can process.

This following steps describe what happens when you press Print:

1. The data you want to print is stored in the print queue.

2. The print spooler retrieves the data and sends it on to the print filter.

3. The filter then determines whether the data is already in PostScript; if not, it converts it to PostScript.

4. The PostScript data is then sent on directly to a PostScript printer (if that's available), or the filter runs Ghostscript.

5. Ghostscript, in turn, uses its driver to convert the PostScript into another standard printer language. That data is then sent to the printer.

6. When all the converted data is in the printer, the spooler deletes it from the print queue.

## Common Unix Printing System (CUPS)

CUPS made printing a lot easier for ordinary users. Before CUPS, printing could involve navigating around the Internet trying to find the right drivers. For system administrators, it was worse because the admin had to set up all printing configurations for each system.

CUPS, developed by Easy Software Products, pulled all the drivers together in one place. It also allows users to set different printing options on a job-by-job basis, at least within the context of general limits set by the administrator.

CUPS is a standards-based print system. It uses the Internet Printing Protocol (IPP) developed by the Internet Engineering Task Force (IETF) Printing Working Group. It runs as a server daemon that receives print data from Ghostscript and then communicates with the printer.

The CUPS daemon on your computer can also communicate with other printers on its dedicated communications port 631. This makes it possible for your computer to "see" other printers without having to configure them.

You can configure a printer with CUPS with a built-in web-based administrative tool, but the potential exists for a security breach because you are typing the Root password into your browser. As always, doing your configuration through YaST is safer, and probably easier.

## Configuring Printers with YaST

YaST attempts to detect active printers on install, and if you have a fully supported printer, it should find it. Do not give up hope if YaST does not detect it, because it is a simple task to configure your printer manually in YaST as well. To set up a local printer, follow these steps:

> **NOTE**
>
> YaST will let you manually configure your printer even if it is not connected to your computer. Obviously, you won't be able to run any of the tests, but go ahead and walk through the steps.

1. Open YaST, go to Hardware, Printers.

2. YaST checks its settings and tries to detect any active printer(s); then it displays the first Printer Configuration page (see Figure 7.1).

**FIGURE 7.1**   If YaST cannot detect your printer, it displays this empty screen. You can then manually configure your printer.

- If YaST finds no active printers, it will display the basically blank screen you see in Figure 7.1. Click Add to start manual installation of a local printer.

- The first step in adding a printer queue is identifying how your printer is connected to your system. Older printers use the parallel port, which is the default in the YaST settings (see Figure 7.2). Newer printers usually plug in to your system via a USB port. If you are trying to attach a network printer, you need to know the protocol the printer uses: If it's on a Windows network, use the Samba (SMB) option; if it's on an older Novell NetWare network or you otherwise need to use this protocol, choose IPX. When you have selected the type, click Next.

**FIGURE 7.2**    You should know how your printer is connected to your system: parallel port or USB for most local connections, or the protocol your network printer uses.

- This screen lets you test your connection before loading a driver. Figure 7.3 shows the parallel printer test screen. Your screen may differ slightly. Make sure your printer is on before testing the connection. When you click Test Printer Connection, YaST sends a message ("Hello World") to the printer. Depending on your printer, it should light up, print the message, or just send a form feed (that is, move the paper down). If it does, click Next.

- In this screen shown in Figure 7.4, you name the printer (actually, the print queue). The first field, Name for Printing, is how the machine identifies the printer. By default, YaST assigns the name "printer," but you should name it something else, especially if it is a network printer. This is usually the model name or location. The queue name cannot have spaces in it (you can do that in the Description line). The Description is what you call the printer and has no rules. The Location is optional, but can help you figure out which printer is yours.

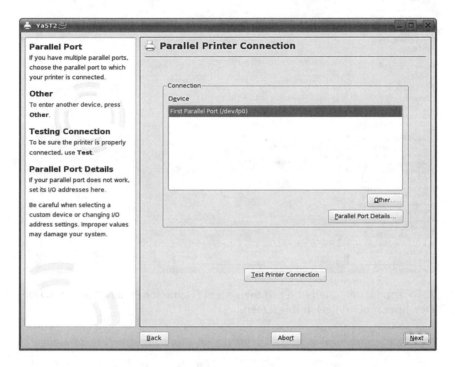

**FIGURE 7.3** Test your parallel printer connection on this screen. YaST sends a test message, and your printer should respond.

> **NOTE**
>
> All local printers "Do Local Filtering," so leave this box checked and do not click Test Printing on this page. You'll do that after you identify your printer model.

- Figure 7.5 shows where you identify your printer model. Select one of the 49 manufacturers on the left side, and then select a model on the right. If you have a PPD file from your manufacturer, click Add PPD File to Database. You'll get the choice to install from a local file or download from the manufacturer's FTP site (you have to enter the site name). Click Next to confirm your settings and test your configuration.

> **NOTE**
>
> Although the model list seems pretty thorough, don't panic if you don't see your model. There are often common drivers for many manufacturers. Check the printer database at Linuxprinting.org for the right driver for your model.

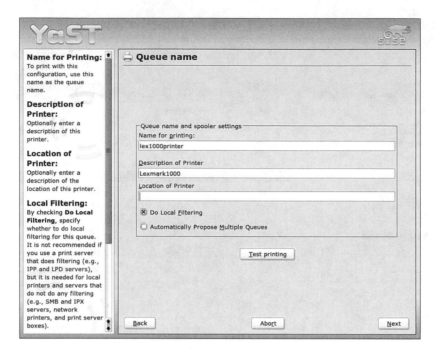

**FIGURE 7.4**    You identify the printer to the system (Name for Printing) and describe it for yourself (Description of Printer) in this screen.

**FIGURE 7.5**    Select your printer from the list.

- Your settings should appear on the final screen, shown in Figure 7.6. Make sure everything is correct in the Current Values list, and then check (double-click) the Printing Filter Settings. These may be set to A4 paper and other items that may not work for your printer in this test. Click Test to send a test page to the printer, and select one of the test versions from the dialog box. Ideally, the page should print. Click OK when it does.

Your printer should now be set up for all applications. If you need to make changes in your configuration, you can always come back here to do that.

**FIGURE 7.6**    Test your printer here.

# Configuring CUPS and Network Printers with KDEPrint

Setting up remote network printers is not substantially different from the local setup process, but because SUSE Linux 10 gives you a choice, let's show you how to set this up in the KDEPrint wizard.

To open KDEPrint, go to Printers in the KDE menu. Figure 7.7 shows you the existing printers it has autodetected.

Click Add to select your remote printer. You have several choices of network printer interfaces. Both Network Printer and Network Printer w/IPP options allow you to scan your network for printers to connect to. The Remote CUPS Server and Remote LPD Queue (which you should only use if the printer you are trying to use does not support CUPS) require you to enter an IP address manually.

**FIGURE 7.7**    KDEPrint displays autodetected and manually added printers.

When you select Network Printer, Figure 7.8 appears.

**FIGURE 7.8**    Scan your network for available printers with this wizard screen.

Click Scan to check your network for printers, which will appear in the main window on the left. If you know the location of the printer already, you can also enter the address and port manually. Click Next to confirm your settings.

To connect to a remote CUPS server, you must know the IP address of the server. You will first be asked if the remote server requires authentication, or is anonymous. If necessary, type your username and password for the CUPS server (which may be the same as your SUSE Linux login). Click next, and enter the IP address of the server, and the wizard will connect to the address. Confirm your settings, and you're in.

You can also connect to Windows printers through Samba. See Chapter 25, "Setting Up Networks and Samba," for more information on this.

As a last resort, SUSE Linux also will try to connect with remote CUPS servers that may be available on the Internet. As noted previously, CUPS uses the Internet Printing Protocol to connect to printers. Network printers can thus communicate with CUPS clients via port 631. If configured properly, the network printer can send out broadcast packets when it is available for printing jobs. In the YaST Printer Configuration dialog box (refer to Figure 7.1), you can set your computer to Listen to Remote CUPS Servers to Get Comfortable Access to Remote Queues.

The problem with this method is that you risk the possibility that an attacker sends IPP broadcasts to your computer announcing available print queues, and you accidentally print to a counterfeit queue. You may believe the job is sent to a local server, whereas in reality it is sent to the attacker's server.

To use this method, port 631/UDP must be open for incoming packets from the network, but not from outside your network or the Internet. The way to solve this problem is to configure the SUSE Firewall appropriately. This means enabling listening only via the Internal Network interface, not the External (Internet) interface.

If your firewall is not turned on when you configure your printer, you are putting your print data at risk. If necessary, open the YaST Firewall module and turn it on before setting up Listen mode (you can have two YaST modules open simultaneously). Pay attention to how the Firewall has identified your Internal and External interfaces, because you will need to know the External interface in the Printer setup.

When you have the firewall turned on, go back to the Printer setup and click Change next to the line telling you Port for Listening to Remote CUPS Servers is Closed by Firewall. Now check the Open Port in Firewall box; the Firewall Details button will become active. Click the button; both interfaces will be checked, but won't be identified as Internal and External. Uncheck the box matching the External interface. Click OK to confirm your choice and return to the main Printer menu; then click Finish to complete the operation.

## Printing with CUPS

After you have set up your printer, printing is an easy chore from the user's standpoint. In most cases, you'll just click Print (Ctrl+P) from your application, bring up the print dialog box, and accept the defaults. You have many choices, however, when that dialog box appears.

Take a look at Figure 7.9. It is the Print dialog box in the Konqueror web browser, but the options are common to many applications. At the top is the Printer ID section, with the default printer showing. By default, this is all that shows when you first click Print.

**FIGURE 7.9**    CUPS enables the user to make lots of choices on-the-fly, as shown in this Konqueror print dialog box.

---

**TIP**

Need to add a printer? Just click the icon that looks like a magic wand to the left of the Properties dialog box. This opens the KDEPrint application.

---

You can change many of the default settings by clicking the Properties button at the top, but Konqueror makes nearly all of them available in this dialog box when you click Expand. The tabbed properties pages let you choose a page range if you don't want to print the whole document, and you can print them last-page-to-first if you have an inkjet that spits out paper print-side up.

In the Advanced Options page, you can schedule a print job for later. If you're in a networked setting and need to enter a job or budget code into the printer, you can enter that information here, too, under Billing Information.

# Working with the Portable Document Format (PDF)

You have no doubt seen and worked with Adobe Acrobat documents in the Portable Document Format. Software manuals, government documents, and electronic books of all kinds have been published and distributed on the Web for years. The idea behind PDF is simple: create and distribute electronic documents in a manner that the layout of the page is controlled (that is, every reader sees it the same way), and with no barriers to reading it (a free Reader exists for every system).

Adobe Systems, the owners of the Acrobat software and inventors of the PDF format, has been inconsistent in its Linux support over the years. The Reader supplied with SUSE Linux and other Linux distributions is version 5.0. There has never been a Linux version of the full Acrobat product, either. Ghostscript has become the default Linux PDF reader over time, but its interface is a bit more clunky than Adobe's own product.

> **NOTE**
> Adobe has delivered a Linux version of Adobe Reader 7.0. This is retrievable in YaST or from the Adobe site directly: http://www.adobe.com/products/acrobat/readstep2.html

Considering that PDF is a slight variation on the UNIX/Linux PostScript print standard, it's a little surprising that free, open source PDF creation tools have not been forthcoming. The exceptions are the TeX publishing tool and a pstopdf shell utility that did not produce a quality transformation from plain PostScript (ps) to PDF. You can indeed make PDF files with TeX, but it is notoriously difficult to learn and operate.

This changed with OpenOffice.org v1.1. Finally, there was an easy-to-use method of creating good-looking PDF documents in Linux. All you need to do to create a PDF is click the PDF Export tool on your default toolbar.

Suppose you have a holiday letter with graphics that you send out to friends and family every year. You can easily create a PDF version right in OpenOffice.org that you can send to your email buddies or put on your personal website:

1. Create your document as you would normally.

2. Insert graphics and watermarks and position them where you want.

3. Save the document as an OpenOffice.org document first so that you have an "original" copy that you can edit.

4. When everything's ready to go, click the Acrobat toolbar button (or go to File, Export as PDF).

5. A dialog box will come up. If you want to give the PDF file a distinct name, that's OK. OOo will automatically add the `.pdf` extension to your file.

6. A PDF Options screen will appear, allowing you to choose how many pages of your document to include in your PDF, how to handle graphics, and a couple of other options. If you have a long document with headings, you may want to check the Tagged PDF box. Your headings will then appear as Bookmarks in the PDF, making for easier navigation. When you've made your choices, click Export to create the PDF.

7. Your OOo file will still be onscreen so that you can edit it. To open your new PDF document, locate it in your favorite file manager. Acrobat Reader (or Ghostview, depending on how your system is configured) will display your exported file.

Figure 7.10 shows a PDF created with OpenOffice.org in Acrobat Reader.

**FIGURE 7.10**    Create your own PDF documents with OpenOffice.org.

> **TIP**
>
> Learn more about the things you can do with OpenOffice.org and other Linux office suites in Chapter 9, "Being Productive: Office Suites and Other Tools."

# Console Print Control

As with nearly everything else in Linux, you don't need X running to print a file. CUPS answers shell commands very well, and if for some reason the CUPS daemon won't run, you still have access to the old UNIX/Linux print standard, LPRng, which responds to the same commands. This section will cover how to print from your command line.

> **TIP**
>
> If you don't know much about the shell or console, there's much more in Chapter 8, "Shaking Hands with Your Shell."

## Using Basic Print Commands

It's good to know these five basic shell commands if you just need to print something quickly without having to launch a program or wait for a GUI to load. These will work from any shell prompt, whether you have X running or not. In some cases, you need to be logged in as the SuperUser to have access to all options.

- `lp <options> <filename> <printer>`—The basic "line printer" spooling command.

- `lpq - the "line printer queue,"`—Tells you what print jobs are currently being processed. It will also give you the name(s) of the printer queue(s) installed on this machine if you do not know what's available.

- `lpstat`—Statistical information from the server and printer.

- `lprm`—Cancels the current print job.

- `lpadmin`—The CUPS line printer administration system. You must be Root (or SuperUser) to use. This command manages spooling, the print daemon, and all printer activity.

All these commands have reasonably good man pages, and you can also examine the CUPS Administration Guide in `/usr/share/doc/packages/cups/sam.html`.

Don't be afraid to use wildcards when using the `lp` command to print from the shell. To print all OpenOffice.org Writer documents in the current directory to a printer called "lp," type the following:

```
lp -dlp *.sxw
```

Now if you run the queue command, `lpq`, you will see the file(s) being printed. This includes other pertinent information, such as the owner, the job number, and size of the job. CUPS uses the job number to handle multiple orders.

Armed with a job number, you can cancel that specific job with `lprm <jobnumber>`.

# Avoiding Printing Problems

Before buying a new printer, always research its Linux compatibility first. SUSE Linux and CUPS can run most current printer models, especially if they are standard printers connected by a parallel cable. Some vendors support Linux better than others, and it is always a good idea to visit www.linuxprinting.org to get the current thinking on each printer vendor.

The following sections contain a few tips on the more problematic devices.

## Multifunction (Print/Fax/Scanner) Devices

The more you try to do, the harder it is to succeed. These printing triathletes need the full support of the manufacturer to make a go of it in Linux, and that support has been spotty. In response to a clamor from Linux users, the leading producer of budget-priced multifunction devices, Brother, has begun writing Linux print and scan drivers. They are still rated "Useless" at linuxprinting.org, but your mileage may vary. See http://solutions.brother.com/linux/en_us for current information on Brother drivers.

Consider yourself lucky, however, if you have an HP OfficeJet multifunction device. SUSE Linux supports these devices out of the box.

### USB and Older Inkjet Printers

More printers run from the USB port these days. You learned something about Linux and vendor support for USB devices in Chapter 2, "Preparing to Install SUSE Linux." Although there's nothing special to note about USB printers, you should still check out http://www.linux-usb.org if you have or are considering one of these printers.

Generally, you should avoid inexpensive older inkjet printers that came out at the end of the last century. Manufacturers didn't know much about Linux when these printers were new, and they certainly aren't going back to add support now.

Like the Winmodems that rely on software to perform many essential communications tasks, quite a few of these printers shaved a few bucks off their cost by using the Microsoft Graphic Device Interface (GDI). Essentially, the printers run only because they have access to this Windows-only interface.

The SUSE Linux Administration Guide offers a partial list of these printers, and linux-printing.org has a broader listing in its database.

## References

- http://linuxprinting.org—A central compendium of information on printing in Linux. Download official and unofficial open source drivers. Read the recommendations in the Suggested Printer List when you're in the market for a new printer. Ask questions in the forums.

- http://h10018.www1.hp.com/wwsolutions/linux/products/printing_imaging—Hewlett Packard's Linux driver efforts.

- http://www.tldp.org/HOWTO/Printing-HOWTO—From the page, "A collection of information on how to generate, preview, print and fax anything under GNU/Linux."

- http://www.cups.org—The place to keep up with the Common Unix Printing System.

- http://www.pwg.org/ipp—The IETF Printer Working Group's page on the Internet Printing Protocol (IPP), used by CUPS. Very technical, but a good FAQ.

- http://www.ghostscript.com—The Ghostscript news and community page. New release announcements and a community component based on "diary entries."

- http://www.cs.wisc.edu/~ghost—The Ghostscript home page.

- http://www.adobe.com/products/acrobat—Learn more about Acrobat and PDF from the official site. You can also download the free Reader here.

- http://solutions.brother.com/linux/en_us—The Brother Linux support and driver status page.

# CHAPTER 8

# Shaking Hands with Your Shell

"In the beginning was the command line," sayeth Neal Stephenson in his wonderful essay on the history of computer operating systems. And so it is true. The easiest and fastest way to get things done in Linux is directly from the command line, called the *shell*. Why a shell? If the heart of the operating system is the kernel of the nut, clearly you have to crack the shell to get at it.

The point-and-click graphical interface is easy, once you've learned it. Yet there is so much power behind a couple of keystrokes in the shell that it's sometimes hard to think of an easier way to do things. The big difference is the learning curve. In the GUI, after you've figured out how a mouse works, you're well on your way to getting work done. As opposed to this, that cold empty shell prompt gives you no advice on what to do with it.

No matter how expert you are with the graphical interface, there may be times when you have to rescue a system, and a shell prompt is all you have to work with. It's important to know at least a few commands to get things going. Throughout this book, you'll find plenty of ideas on using your shell to quickly get computing tasks done.

In this chapter, we will focus on understanding the shell as a programming language. Most of the shells included in SUSE Linux allow you to string commands together in an editor and save them as a script. Knowing the shell's syntax, you can define variables, assign values, create functions, and evaluate different results—most everything a "real" programming language such as C, Java, or C++ can do. Many of the standard shell commands are really just shell scripts. Perhaps your script will one day find itself in common usage, too.

# The Power of the Command Line

Understanding the shell's capabilities is the first step to writing good scripts. The shell is much more than a program launcher, although it does that very well. The shell is also called the "command interpreter," because it takes your typed command and does several things with it:

1. First, it determines whether the command is something built into it. If it is, it runs the command.

2. If not, it checks the search path environment variable to find the command (unless you've located the command yourself by typing in the full path).

3. When it locates the command you've asked for, the shell makes a fork call on the Linux kernel to copy the program (so it will return to the shell prompt after the program completes its task). The program then makes another exec call on the kernel to execute the command.

4. Finally, the shell uses some rules to determine what a command like `cat *.txt *.sxw > doclist` is trying to accomplish (this is where the interpretation comes in) and delivers a result.

A shell can run several commands included in a single string, like the preceding example. This is a relatively simple command, but while executing it, the shell does several things:

- Launches a program—It runs cat, a program that displays files on the screen.

- Does job control and gets out of the way—The shell pretends it isn't there while Cat searches for the text of all files in the current directory with `.txt` and `.sxw` extensions and then displays it.

- Redirects output—Before the text display hits the screen, the shell leaps back into action and intercepts the system call, putting the display (that is, the text of all files with those extensions) into a file called doclist and saving it to the same directory.

---

**RUNNING SHELL COMMANDS IN KONQUEROR**

Do you want to combine the power of the shell with the relative convenience of a GUI file manager? The KDE file manager, Konqueror, lets you run any shell command from its interface.

Go to Tools, Execute Shell Command (or press Ctrl+E). If you have a file or directory selected, you will see its name in the edit box, but running a command on that file isn't necessary. Type any command (or series of commands) and it will run; any messages pop up in a separate window.

If you have opened Konqueror as the SuperUser, you will have all the privileges of rank when you run commands, but you cannot log in as SuperUser (or run any command that requires extra input) from a plain Konqueror window.

---

Among the other things a shell can do (besides the "Cool Stuff That All Shells Have in Common" listed in Chapter 5, "Getting Started with SUSE Linux") are the following:

- Search files and directories for patterns or regular expressions using locate, gawk, or grep.

- Feed the results or output of one program into another program for further processing.

- Run multiple commands separated by a semicolon.

- Create five empty files with a single command:

  ```
  touch file {a,b,c,d,e}
  ```

- Run a program in the background.

You will use all of these little wonders when writing your scripts in this chapter.

> **NOTE**
>
> The examples in this chapter will be for bash shell scripts, as it is by far the most popular (and the default) shell in SUSE Linux. You can write scripts to perform practically all the tasks included here on other shells as well. Consult the man page for your shell to check the proper syntax. You might also want to check out *Sams Teach Yourself Shell Programming in 24 Hours* by Sriranga Veeraraghavan or *Linux Shell Scripting with Bash* by Ken O. Burtch.

## Pattern-Matching in the Shell

The shell command line allows you to use strings of specially constructed patterns for wildcard matches. This is a different simpler capability that supported by GNU utilities such as grep, which can use more complex patterns, known as expressions, to search through files or directories or to filter data input to or out of commands.

The shell's pattern strings can be simple or complex, but even using a small subset of the available characters in simple wildcards can yield constructive results at the command line. Some common characters used for shell pattern matching are:

- `*`   Matches any character. For example, to find all files in the current directory ending in .txt, you could use

  ```
  ls *.txt
  ```

- `?`   Matches a single character. For example, to find all files in the current directory ending in the extension d?c (where ? could be 0-9, a-z, or A-Z):

  ```
  ls *.d?c
  ```

- `[xxx]` or `[x-x]`   Matches a range of characters. For example, to list all files in a directory with names containing numbers:

  ```
  ls [0-9]*
  ```

To find only those with characters 1, 5, or 8, this would be

```
ls [158]*
```

- \x    Matches or escapes a character such as ? or a tab character. For example, to create a file with a name containing a question mark:

```
touch foo\?
```

Table 8.1 shows a few more common special characters. For a more comprehensive list, see the Advanced Bash Scripting Guide, listed in the References section.

**TABLE 8.1**    Special Characters in bash

| Character | Meaning |
| --- | --- |
| # | Beginning of a comment line (except when it's part of a #!). |
| $ | Shell variable name. |
| ; | Command separator. |
| . | Current directory. |
| .. | Parent directory. |
| ~ | (tilde) Home directory (this character is located to the left of the number 1 on your keyboard; hold down the shift key to use it). |
| ` | (backtick) Command substitution; tells the shell to use the results of the upcoming command as part of the next task. |
| > | Redirects the output of a script to a file. If the file exists, it will be overwritten. |
| >> | Appends the output of a script to an existing file. If the file does not exist, it will be created. |
| ¦ | Pipe. Helps to chain commands and scripts together, passes the output of one command as an argument in the next. |
| & | Run this in the background; it allows you to return to the shell prompt. |

Always be careful when using special characters. As you can see, some special characters have different meanings depending on their context, so your script may not behave if you don't use the character properly. Some characters can also be destructive, so make sure you use the right one.

If you want to use a special character in a "normal" way, use the backslash (\) as an *escape character* in the script. To display the result of some calculation involving U.S. or Australian money, for example, include this string:

```
echo \$(5153.27 + 654863.15)
```

Note that mixing wildcards and regular expressions in shell scripts can lead to problems if you're not careful. For example, finding patterns in text is best left to regular expressions used with commands such as grep; simple wildcards should be used for filtering or matching filenames on the command line. Although both Linux command expressions and shell scripts can recognize the backslash as an escape character in patterns, the dollar sign ($) will have two wildly different meanings (single-character pattern matching in expressions and variable assignment in scripts).

## Redirecting Input and Output

You can create, overwrite, and append data to files at the command line, using a process called input and output redirection. The shell recognizes several special characters for this process, such as >, <, or >>.

In this example, the output of the `ls` command is redirected to create a file named `textfiles.listing`:

```
ls *.txt >textfiles.listing
```

Use output redirection with care because it is far too easy to overwrite existing files. All you need to do is redirect a different command to any existing file. The shell will perform the task you ask it to without checking for a file with the same name, or prompting you about your wishes concerning the soon-to-be-departed file.

On the bright side, you can redirect output to add content to an existing file with the append operator, >>. So if you find something interesting to add to your textfiles collection, use two angle brackets instead of one in your command:

```
ls /usr/share/doc/packages/emacs/doc/gnus tut.txt >>textfiles.listing
```

You can also turn your angle bracket around to take data and feed it to a command with input redirection, like this:

```
cat < textfiles.listing
```

## Piping Data

Many Linux commands can be run together in a single, connected command line to transform data from one form to another. Stringing commands together this way is known as using or creating pipes. Pipes take the output of one command and use it as input for the next command. This can be done nearly endlessly.

Use the bar operator (|) to create pipes in the shell (it is used most often in this role, so many folks know the bar operator as the pipe already). Say you were the system administrator and needed to know who was currently logged in at a given moment. A piped command like this would give you a nice, tidy list:

```
who | cut -ci-8 | sort -u | pr -l1 -8 -w78 -t
```

You can see four commands at work here:

1. `who` tells you the users who are logged in. This result is processed by

2. `cut`, which outputs only the usernames to the screen (instead of the whole line), but first

3. `sort` puts the names in alphabetical order, and removes from the list those users who are logged in more than once. Finally,

4. `pr` takes the list, one per line, and delivers it to the screen in eight columns.

8

This is simple, and as your shell wizard skills improve, you will be able to do simply amazing things with a few keystrokes and some pipes.

## Background Processing

Often in this book, you'll see a shell command with an ampersand (&) at the end of it. This is especially true when you use the shell to launch a graphical application. You may wonder what this is there for. The & takes advantage of the shell's ability to process commands in the background, while still running other programs from the same command line.

Let's say you want to run the GKrellM system monitor from the shell. If you just type **gkrellm** at the prompt, the program will run, of course. But if you look at the shell, you'll see a dead cursor that cannot complete any more commands, at least until you exit out of GKrellM.

If you then exit out of the monitor (right-click anywhere in the program and select Quit), your shell prompt returns, and you can type commands again. Using the up arrow to recall your last command from the command history, gkrellm again appears at the prompt. This time, add the background processing operator &, and press Enter. GKrellM runs as before, but bash now tells you the process number for this application, and then returns you to the prompt. You can now enter any other command you like.

# Writing a Shell Script: The Basics

Having a command history available at your shell prompt is a great tool, but what if you run variations on some of the same commands every day? What happens when you run a complicated set of commands every other week, but not necessarily on the same day of the week? These are the times when a script comes in handy.

Shell scripts won't necessarily run any faster than a C program, but because they don't have to be compiled, they can be a lot smaller. That makes them more portable as well; they will always fit on a floppy. You don't have to install extra libraries on your system unless you need to access some other language as part of your script. The process of writing scripts is also simpler and faster than any compiled language.

If you're just starting out in shell scripting, go easy. It's like a new exercise program. Don't try to do too much all at once. Concentrate on automating a process you're already doing, or would be doing if it didn't seem so complicated.

Most important, when doing scripting, do not open a word processor—ever! You are just producing a text file, and an editor will do just fine. Leaving aside all the formatting that a word processor will add to your script, it also has automatic word wrap, which could easily mess things up when you run your script. Review the text editor choices in Chapter 5, and play with a few before deciding which is the best editor for you.

> **NOTE**
>
> SUSE Linux automatically creates a /bin subdirectory in your home directory. This is a good place to store your scripts because this is the first item in your search path.

# Scripting in bash

To get started, you can create some command aliases to simplify a few command-line tasks. Aliases in Linux are environment variables that behave in the same way they sound—as another name for a command. You can define aliases on-the-fly at the command line, but those are good for only one session. It's preferable to have these available to you all the time.

Before beginning to write your script, take a look at the default aliases defined by SUSE. Go to a shell and type **alias** at the prompt. You will see the following listing. If you are migrating from Windows, try not to be too offended.

```
alias +='pushd .'
alias -='popd'
alias ..='cd ..'
alias ...='cd ../..'
alias A:='echo -e '\''Error: There is no such thing as a drive
    A: in Linux.\n
If you want to access your floppy, try "mount /dev/fd0"
    and then look\n
in the directory /media/floppy !'\'''
alias C:='echo -e '\''Error: There is no such thing as a drive
    C: in Linux!\n
Your harddisk should already be mounted (via /etc/fstab or
    autofs).'\'''
alias a:='A:'
alias beep='echo -en "\007"'
alias c:='C:'
alias cd..='echo '\''Error: Try: cd ..'\'''
alias chkdsk='echo -e '\''Error: Your filesystems are
    checked on bootup.\n
If you want to do it manually, use fsck.\n
Use df and mount for an overview of your disks.'\'''
alias copy='echo '\''Error: Try the command: cp -piv'\'''
alias del='echo '\''Error: Try the command: rm -iv'\'''
alias dir='ls -l'
alias format='echo -e '\''Error: The DOS concept of formatting
    disk media is screwed.\n
If you want to create a filesystem use "mkfs". To format
    a floppy, use\n
"fdformat /dev/fd0" and then "mkfs.minix /dev/fd0".'\'' #'
alias l='ls -alF'
alias la='ls -la'
alias ll='ls -l'
alias ls='/bin/ls $LS_OPTIONS'
alias ls-l='ls -l'
alias md='mkdir -p'
```

```
alias mem='echo '\''Error: Try the command: free'\'''
alias move='echo '\''Error: Try the command: mv -iv'\'''
alias o='less'
alias rd='rmdir'
alias rehash='hash -r'
alias sys='echo -e '\''Error: Linux cannot be transferred
    like that.\n
If you want to install Linux or create bootfloppies,
    please use YaST.'\'' #'
alias unmount='echo "Error: Try the command: umount" 1>&2; false'
alias ver='echo '\''Error: Try the command: uname -a'\'''
alias which='type -p'
alias you='yast2 online_update'
```

These aliases are set in the systemwide environment settings files: /etc/profile and /etc/bash.bashrc and they apply to every user by default. Any user can customize his or her own aliases by modifying the ~/.bashrc file and you can write a script containing any aliases you want and then reference that script in .bashrc.

For example, open a text editor and type these lines:

```
#!/bin/sh
alias ls='ls -l'
alias ldir='ls -aF'
alias copy='cp'
alias ft='fortune -a'
```

Here's what you've done with this script:

- In line 1, you declare that this is a (bash) shell script. This line has several colorful nicknames that refer to the two characters at the front: hash-bang, sh-bang, or just plain bang.

- Line 2 tells bash that when you type ls to get a directory listing, you *always* want it to give you the detailed (long) listing, with permissions, size, and date/time information. This results in the same display as the default alias ll.

- Line 3 gives you a list of files and directories in color, with no details, when you type ldir.

- Line 4 changes what the shell does when you type the DOS command copy: instead of getting the slightly rude reminder of proper Linux syntax, the shell will actually do what you meant it to.

- Line 5 defines a shortcut to getting a fortune cookie as ft. The -a switch means that fortune will consult all of its fortune collections and may result in something crude displayed on your screen. Use this switch carefully.

Add other aliases as you choose, and then save the file to ~/bin/myaliases. There's no extension required. When you're done editing your script, you have two tasks remaining. First, this is just a text file as it is. To make it a script, it must be executable. Open your shell, change to the /bin directory and type **chmod +x myaliases**. Because you have ownership of all files in your home directory, this file is now executable.

> **TIP**
>
> Get into the commenting/documentation habit early in your scripting career. At the top of each script, explain what the purpose of the script is. For the preceding example, the comment could be
>
> #This script adds some directory listing #aliases to the default set.
>
> Be sure to add the hash mark (pound sign) to the beginning of each line of your comment, otherwise the shell will try to interpret your comment as a command.

To add these aliases to your basic configuration, open ~/.bashrc in your editor and add this line to the bottom of the file:

~/bin/myaliases

Save and exit. Restart your computer. Open a shell and type **alias**. Your four new aliases should now be on the list.

## Variables in Shell Scripts

As a programming language, shells can process variables in your scripts. Following are the three types of variables shell scripts you can work with:

- Environment variables are part of the system, and you worked with two of them, Aliases and PATH, in the previous example. You can define new environment variables, and some environment variables (like Alias and PATH) can be modified in a script.

- Built-in variables, like command switches, are provided by the operating system and cannot be modified.

- User variables are defined and used by the script writer.

> **NOTE**
>
> If you have experience with other programming languages, you'll notice one difference with shell programming: variables are not typed in shell scripts.
>
> Conversely, if you learn shell scripting first and go on to other programming languages, you will need to learn how to identify variables as numbers, strings, or other data types that exist in that language.

## Assigning Values to Variables

Declaring and initializing variables in bash is straightforward. To use a variable called lcount to count the number of iterations in a loop, type **lcount=0**.

To store a string in a variable, just declare and identify:

```
myname=mikemc
```

If the string has embedded spaces, use quotes:

```
myname="Michael McCallister"
```

## Accessing Variable Values

Access the value of a variable by prefixing the variable name with a dollar sign ($). To display your search path, for example, use $PATH. If the variable you want to access is var, use $var.

To assign the value of var to the lcount variable, type

```
lcount=$var
```

# Positional Parameters

You can pass options from the command line or from another script to your shell program. These options are called *positional parameters* and have special names provided by the system. You must understand how to use positional parameters and pull in variables retrieved from the command line to develop more advanced shell programs.

The names for positional parameters are really numbers; the first parameter is 1, the second 2, the third 3, and so on. Access the parameter using $1, $2, and so on. You cannot invoke 2 before 1, but you can omit 3 to get a result if 1 and 2 are present.

Let's say we have a shell program that expects two parameters—a first name and a last name. If you have only a first name (1), that's OK. If you just have the last name (2), you'll get an error.

This shell program, myname1, takes one parameter (a name) and displays it onscreen:

```
#!/bin/sh
#Name display program
if [ $# -eq 0 ]
then
    echo "Name not provided"
else
    echo "Your name is "$1
fi
```

Notice that in shell scripting, every `if` statement must end with `fi`.

If you run myname1 like this:

```
bash myname1
```

You'll get this result:

```
Name not provided
```

If you run myname1 like this:

```
bash myname1 Mike
```

This is the output:

```
Your name is Mike
```

You may have wondered what that $# code was in myname1. This is a built-in variable provided by the kernel to the shell, returning the number of positional parameters passed to the shell program. There's more about these built-in variables in the next section.

## Using Positional Parameters to Get Command-Line Variables

Positional parameters can be really useful if you have piped commands using complex arguments, especially if the commands aren't used frequently. For example, you can use your system with a voice modem to serve as an answering machine. If you do, you can write a script that retrieves and plays the messages. This script, called pvm, converts a saved sound file (in .rmd or voice-phone format) and pipes the sound to your audio device:

```
#!/bin/sh
# play voice message(s) in /var/spool/voice/incoming
rmdtopvf /var/spool/voice/incoming/$1 | pvfspeed -$ 0000 ; \
pvftobasic >/dev/audio
```

Play the message by typing the following at the shell prompt:

```
pvm name_of_message
```

## Automating Tasks with Scripts

Shell scripts with positional parameters are often used for automating routine and mundane jobs, such as generating system log reports, checking the file system, user resource accounting, printer use accounting, and other system, network, or security administration tasks.

This script, if added to your /etc/crontab scheduling table, can help you monitor your system by running a keyword search on your logs for important information.

```
#!/bin/sh
#   name:     greplog
#    use:      mail grep of designated log using keyword
#
# author: bb
# usage: greplog {keyword} {logpathname}
#
# bugs: does not check for correct number of arguments

# build report name using keyword search and date
log_/report=/tmp/$1.logreport.`date '+%m%d%y'`

# build report header with system type, hostname, date and time
echo "===============================================================" \
    >$log_report
echo "            S Y S T E M   M O N I T O R   L O G" >>$log_report
echo uname -a >>$log_report
echo "Log report for" `hostname -f` "on" `date '+%c'`    >>$log_report
echo "===============================================================" \
    >>$log_report ; echo "" >>$log_report

# record log search start
echo "Search for->" $1 "starting" `date '+%r'` >>$log_report
echo "" >>$log_report

# get and save grep results of keyword ($1) from logfile ($2)
grep -i $1 $2 >>$log_report

# build report footer with time
echo "" >>$log_report
echo "End of" >>$log_report at `date '+%r'` >>$log_report

# mail report to root
mail -s "Log Analysis for $1" root <$log_report

# clean up and remove report
rm $log_report
exit @
```

This script creates the $log_report variable, which stores the report. The $1 keyword and first argument on the command line is used as part of the filename, along with the current date. The report header has some formatted text, the system name (output of the uname command), the hostname, and date. The script records the start of the search, and any keyword matches in the log are added to the report. A footer containing the report name and time is added. The report is mailed to root, with the search term as the subject of the message, and the `$log_report` file is deleted.

Test the script by running it yourself. Make sure that the system is running the syslogd daemon. Feed it a keyword and a pathname to the system log `/var/log/messages`, like this:

```
greplog FAILED /var/log/messages
```

If any login failures have occurred on your system, root should get an email message. If you have correctly configured your email services (see "Setting Up Your SUSE Linux Email Account" in Chapter 13, "Using the Internet: Browsing the Web and Writing Email"), the SuperUser should get that email.

## Built-In Variables

The Linux kernel provides the shell with several built-in variables. You cannot modify the results of these variables. These include

- $#—Number of positional parameters passed to the shell (which we used in the last section)

- $?—Completion code of the last command or shell program executed within the shell (returned value)

- $0—The name of the shell program

- $*—A single string of all arguments passed at the time of invocation of the shell program

These are just a few of the basic tasks and things you can do with your shell. We'll go even deeper in Chapter 33, "Command-Line Master Class."

## References

- http://www.cryptonomicon.com/beginning.html—The Neal Stephenson essay, "In the Beginning Was the Command Line." See also an authorized "update" by Garrett Birkel, "The Command Line in 2004," at http://home.earthlink.net/~android606/commandline.

- http://www.gnu.org/software/bash—The official bash site at the GNU Project. Download the latest, and read the Introduction to Bash.

- http://cnswww.cns.cwru.edu/~chet/bash/bashtop.html—Chet Ramey's bash site. Ramey is the current bash maintainer. Looks very much like the official page, but also has the bash FAQ list.

- http://www.tldp.org/LDP/Bash-Beginners-Guide/html—A bash guide for beginners.

- http://ldp.nllgg.nl/LDP/abs/html—The Advanced bash scripting guide. "This tutorial assumes no previous knowledge of scripting or programming, but progresses rapidly toward an intermediate/advanced level of instruction." Read online, or download the PDF or the SGML source.

- http://www.filibeto.org/sun/lib/development/shell/config_the_bash_shell.html— Configuring the bash shell.

- http://www.justlinux.com/nhf/Shells/Basic_Console_Commands.html—Learn these commands and you can be comfortable saying you know bash "well enough."

- http://www.kornshell.com/doc—Assorted documentation for the commercial Korn shell, ksh.

- http://web.cs.mun.ca/~michael/pdksh—The public domain Korn shell site. This is the version included with SUSE Linux.

- http://www.tcsh.org—The tcsh wiki. Although it does not contain a wealth of information, check out the FAQ and TipsNTricks page. You can also subscribe to the two tcsh mailing lists.

- http://www.faqs.org/faqs/unix-faq/shell/csh-whynot—Perl guru Tom Christiansen's famous 1996 essay, "Csh Programming Considered Harmful." Why it's a bad idea to script in the C shell.

- http://www.zsh.org—Home of the Z shell. Very useful.

# CHAPTER 9

# Being Productive: Office Suites and Other Tools

We are at the dawn of the age where businesses and ordinary people are using Linux as their everyday computing platform. There have been Linux tools for word processing, making presentations, managing finances, personal calendars, and other such tasks for a long time. Productivity tools are now coming into their own, and more people are starting to recognize that.

SUSE has always been in the forefront of desktop Linux, marketing the first Linux Office Suite in 1999. Based on the Applixware suite now produced by VistaSource, this suite didn't exactly set the world on fire, but marked the beginning of the Linux desktop revolution.

There is hardly a task you can complete in Windows that cannot be done in Linux, and often you will find that your Linux application does it better, or faster, or easier. This chapter explores the office productivity applications included in SUSE Linux and shows you how to get started with them. Many of these applications install by default with the Office install option, and others can be added through YaST. All will make you a more productive user.

## Comparing Linux Office Suites

Today, four competitive open-source suites operate under SUSE Linux. They each come with a word processor and spreadsheet program, and some have additional elements. Some have versions for Windows and/or the Apple Macintosh. All will help you get your work done.

OpenOffice.org (and its commercial sibling StarOffice) is probably the best known of the four. Its backing from Sun Microsystems, its variety of applications, and its multiplatform character make it a very big player. But it is not the only game in town. Both KDE and GNOME desktop environments have associated office suites that may not get all the publicity OpenOffice.org gets, but are fine tools nonetheless. A new suite from German company Softmaker made its debut in SUSE Linux 9.2, and there are other commercial choices for your consideration.

This chapter gives you a quick rundown on all the office suite choices available under SUSE Linux to help you decide what you need. As always, play around with each of them.

## Running OpenOffice.org

If your primary concern when choosing an office suite is the capability to read and write Microsoft Office-compatible files, OpenOffice.org (OOo) is probably your best bet. The notoriously finicky proprietary formats remain dominant in modern business, and OOo offers the best filters currently available. Although it is impossible to be 100% compatible without access to the format's structure, OOo does a terrific job. Microsoft Office users will also find OpenOffice.org's interface quite familiar, making the transition a little easier as well.

But OpenOffice.org is not just a Microsoft clone. There are some things it does differently, and more than a few things that it does better. We'll explore these in the next section.

### What Is OpenOffice.org?

This product began its life as a fully integrated productivity suite for the OS/2 operating system. Produced by the German company StarDivision, it had everything wrapped up in one desktop interface. StarOffice 5 was the first major suite produced for Linux (just beating out WordPerfect for that honor). It was important for Linux to have this type of software available, but there were problems with it. Chief among these problems was that it took forever to load. The interface took over the entire desktop and loaded all its components—word processor, spreadsheet, database, presentation, even a web browser, calendar, and email client—into memory at once.

When Sun Microsystems bought StarDivision in 2002, it made two decisions that put the product on the very successful path it is now on. First, it released the StarOffice code under an open source license (the Lesser General Public License, or LGPL), creating the OpenOffice.org project and allowing developers and users to contribute. Second, it scrapped the integrated features that bogged down its predecessors. Although it would always be easy to access different parts of the suite and put data from a spreadsheet into a document, the desktop interface would disappear, and not all components would load simultaneously. Sun also scrapped some of the "feature creep" that had set in and focused on delivering the core elements of a suite.

So what are these elements? OpenOffice.org 2.0, shipping in a beta version with SUSE Linux 9.3, will have the following programs:

- Writer—This word processor should be very familiar to users of just about any other similar application. It creates documents with amazing complexity, handles collaborative tools such as Comments, and exports to a variety of non-native formats. You can even turn any document into a Portable Document Format (PDF) that anyone with the Adobe Acrobat Reader (or the open source Ghostview) can open and read. The Writer/Web tool offers a slightly different toolbar layout, but delivers much cleaner HTML code than its Microsoft counterparts (Word and FrontPage).

- Calc—This spreadsheet program is the number-cruncher's delight. Although it uses a different macro language than Microsoft Excel uses, nearly all standard functions are supported. Calc supports several data exchange formats, as well.

- Impress—The presentations you make with this tool may not be any more informative than its PowerPoint counterpart, but they are just as professional. When you start Impress, a wizard walks you through the steps to create a new presentation. Impress comes with two presentation templates: Introducing a New Product and Recommending a New Strategy.

- Draw—A vector drawing program similar to CorelDraw or Adobe Illustrator. Create polygonal drawings for your documents, presentations, or web pages. Use connectors for Visio-like flowcharts and brainstorms. You can even do Flash animations if you're so inclined.

- Math—This is a formula editor for higher math equations. Create and edit formulas for insertion into a spreadsheet or for display in a document. Math includes a number of fonts and symbols rarely needed in standard word processing documents, but essential for academic science and math writing.

- Base—The first effort at a database product by the OpenOffice.org team will create new databases and import from a selection of database formats, including Microsoft Access, MySQL, and Java Database Connectivity (JDBC)—even the flat-file dBASE database.

## Installing OpenOffice.org

When you install SUSE Linux with the Office components included, YaST will install the English version of OOo by default. If you prefer to install OOo later, this is easily done through YaST. Run YaST and choose Install and Remove Software. Either Search for the OpenOffice package or use the Package Groups to locate Productivity, Office, Suite. You will find several language versions of OOo on the SUSE Linux CD/DVD.

YaST takes care of all the details related to an install, which is good. Installing a downloaded version can be messy. If you download a new version directly from the OOo site, you must run the installer twice. First install OOo as Root (that is, using su).

This will allow all users to run OOo and install some files that are owned by Root. Each user who wants to use OOo should then install the client, using the same process. The second install places many OOo files into your home directory.

As you might expect from a Sun product, OOo uses Java-based files for some tasks and requires that the Java Runtime Environment v1.4 or later be installed for best results. However, the OOo install program doesn't always look in the right place for the JRE. In SUSE Linux, the JRE is stored in the /usr/lib/SunJava2 directory.

## Starting OpenOffice.org

You can start OpenOffice.org in any of several ways. OOo is integrated into both the KDE and GNOME menus, under `Office`. In KDE, each application is listed under the appropriate type (word processor, spreadsheet, and so on). At the bottom is the Office Suite icon with the OOo logo. This opens the Documents and Templates window.

OOo also provides a separate QuickStarter program that places an OOo icon in both the KDE and GNOME taskbars. Install `ooqstart` from YaST and then right-click the icon when you want to load a OOo component. Double-clicking the QuickStarter icon brings up a new Writer document by default. This is configurable. Choose Configure OpenOffice.org QuickStarter from the QuickStarter menu.

With either method, you are presented with the OOo menu. Depending on your OOo version, you may be presented with either the list of programs or the type of document you want to open or create: Text Document, HTML Document, Spreadsheet, Drawing, Presentation. Choosing From Template brings up a list of existing templates, and Open Document lets you choose from existing documents.

## Configuring OpenOffice.org

Regardless of the method, after you have OOo installed, you are ready to go and can begin creating documents and other files. You may, however, want to customize standard OOo behavior before you begin. Go to Tools, Options in any OOo application to open the dialog box.

As you can see in Figure 9.1, there are many choices to make in configuring OOo.

Following are some of the many things you can define in the Options dialog box:

- Define your mail client (should you want to email a document directly from OOo) and other external programs you may want to access. See more about setting up and using email in Chapter 13, "Using the Internet: Browsing the Web and Writing Email," and Chapter 15, "Managing Email Servers."

- Tell OOo to automatically save your work at regular intervals.

- Locate where OOo keeps those backups.

- Turn on (or off) the automatic spell checker.

- Use a Direct Cursor tool to put text wherever you click (and not just at the beginning of the next line).

- Define your default document fonts.

**FIGURE 9.1** The OpenOffice.org Options dialog box lets you set up OpenOffice.org and its various tools the way you want. In this dialog box, the default path for saved documents is changed.

You may also want to set up and customize your toolbars and keyboard shortcuts at some point. Do this by going to the Tools, Customize menu.

These dialog boxes are improved in version 2.0, but can still be confusing to the beginner.

Suppose you needed to keep track of the word count of a document and wanted to check it periodically. This information is displayed in the Document Properties dialog box under the File menu. To change the toolbar, go to Tools, Customize (or right-click in the toolbar). Click the Toolbars tab. The dialog box shown in Figure 9.2 appears.

At the top, you see a listing of the various toolbars in a drop-down menu, with the standard toolbar displayed. In the middle are the available commands for this toolbar.

Notice that some items in the Commands window don't have a check next to them. If you click the check box, it becomes active. Looking over the list, you'll see that there's no Document Properties there. Fortunately, there's an Add button on the right. This brings up the Add Commands dialog box, with Categories on the left and related Commands on the right. There are a lot of categories, and they don't match up completely with the menus, but if you click the Document category, Document Properties appears, and it has an icon.

Select Document Properties on the right, and click Add in the middle (or drag the button over with your mouse).

If an item you want on the toolbar doesn't have a default icon, add it to the toolbar and then click the Icons button to select a new icon. You can also move the existing icons using the Move Up/Move Down buttons. Add separators from the bottom of the Available Buttons list.

9

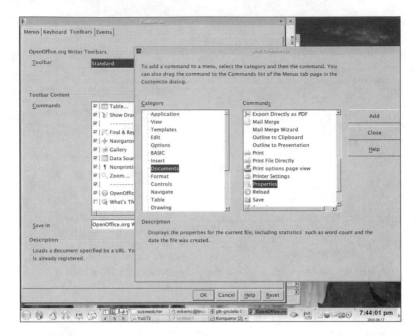

**FIGURE 9.2**    The Customize Toolbars page is a little tricky to deal with, but will put nearly any OpenOffice.org command a click away.

Click to Close the Add Commands window, and then click OK to return to your document. Done! To see your word count, click the new Document Properties icon, and then click Statistics.

### Using OpenOffice.org

A few things are different about OOo that may take some getting used to, especially if you are migrating from Microsoft Office. Some of these are shown in Figure 9.3, as you look at a typical Writer document.

For the most part, this is an interface that should be familiar to anyone who has used a word processor. But what's that extra toolbar on the left of the screen? This is called the main toolbar, which appears in basically the same configuration regardless of what application you're using. The top toolbars change depending on the application, but some tools you will always need.

The other item here that seems extraneous, but that can save you tons of time, is the Stylist. When you first open any document or spreadsheet, this thing is sitting in the middle of your document, making a nuisance of itself. Your first inclination might be to make it go away, but resist that. Move it over so it's not blocking out your document, and then use it.

Have you ever wondered where a signature line is supposed to start in a letter? How to properly do a block quote in a school paper? How much space is supposed to be between the number and the text in a list? Have you ever spent a half-hour trying to get any of these things to line up right in a document? If so, you need to start working with styles and the Stylist.

**FIGURE 9.3**   A typical document window in OpenOffice.org. Note the vertical component toolbar down the left side of the window and the Stylist on the right.

What is the Stylist? It is a handy way to apply standard formats to blocks of text or spreadsheet cells. In Microsoft Word, styles are easy to ignore and most people don't ever change from the Normal style. In OOo, you can continue to go through life using only the Default style, but the Stylist is there to at least make you think about using it.

Use the Stylist to set up paragraphs (the most-often-used styles), characters (such as a book title), pages, and whole documents. If you have a certain way you want your styles to look, you can edit the properties of existing styles or create new styles of your own.

One default setting in OOo that takes more than a little getting used to (if you don't put it to pasture early) is autocompletion mode. As you type, you will suddenly find green-highlighted letters on the screen. Press Enter to accept Writer's suggestion or keep typing or hit the space bar to make it go away. Lazy typists may love this as much as autocompletion in their favorite shell, but Writer is frequently wrong in its guesses, and that can make for complications or embarrassing typos.

You can make it work for you, but if it's just too maddening, turning autocompletion off is fairly simple: Go to Tools, AutoCorrect/AutoFormat. Click the Word Completion tab and uncheck Enable Word Completion. You can make other tweaks in this dialog box, too.

> **TIP**
>
> There are two boons for formal or academic writers in OpenOffice.org that are not obvious to the casual observer.
>
> - You can use the Navigator tool to build outlines of your documents. Your Headings are listed in the Navigator, and you can drag them around, promote, and demote them.
>
> - You can also create a bibliographic database for use in either a single document or across documents. Go to Tools, Bibliography Database to give it a spin.

## Running KOffice

The K Desktop Environment (KDE) team began building an office suite in 2001. Although it does not have all the polish (and certainly not the level of publicity) of OpenOffice.org, it is a very good suite.

KDE users should especially appreciate KOffice and its tools. KOffice is designed to integrate well with this popular desktop and with the other tools in the suite. Although each component launches separately from either the shell or the KDE Kicker menu, there is also a launch interface, called koshell, that includes icons for all the office tools.

KOffice uses a technology, called KParts, that allows for integration of many tools under one umbrella, but does not require every piece to be present for everything to work. Thus, although you have to download and install the entire OpenOffice.org suite, you may need only the word processor. Each KOffice tool is a single KPart, and if you want only KWord, that's all you need to get.

The primary weakness of KOffice is its lack of compatibility with most modern Microsoft formats. The KOffice tools will read the vast majority of Microsoft Office documents, spreadsheets, and so on, but cannot produce complex documents in the current Office formats, although it can do Rich Text Format and WordPad (that is, Microsoft Word 6). Communicating with Office users is not impossible, as KOffice will Save to the OpenOffice.org format (which is an encapsulated XML format), WordPerfect, and standard HTML or XML.

### What's in KOffice?

The KOffice tools rival OOo in number, if not always in quality. As with many things related to KDE, they also tend to run the "K" references into the ground. Following is what you'll find if you install the entire suite:

- Koshell—The integrated launch tool for all KOffice tools. Use this if you need access to all the tools in the kit.

- KWord—A frames-based word processor that also serves as a fine desktop publishing tool. If you have experience with Adobe PageMaker, InDesign, or FrameMaker, you will find much that is familiar in KWord.

- KSpread—This spreadsheet is scriptable and can handle complex formulas as well.

- KPresenter—Another presentation program.

- Kivio—A flowcharting and diagramming program similar to Visio under Windows.

- Karbon14—The basis for all life  on earth, it is also the KOffice vector drawing program.

- Krita—This paint program hopes one day to replace The GIMP in the hearts of Linux designers everywhere.

- Kugar—Something different for an office suite under any OS: a business report developer/generator.

- KChart—A chart generator.

- KFormula—A formula editor.

### Installing and Configuring KOffice

YaST does not install KOffice by default, even if you choose KDE as your primary desktop. To install KOffice, follow these steps:

1. Go to the YaST Software page and click Install and Remove Software. Have your SUSE Linux CD ready.

2. Either Search for KOffice (which is faster) or go to the Package display under Productivity, Office.

3. Select the KOffice modules you want to install. They are listed by function (word processing, spreadsheet, and so on).

4. Check for compatibility (if that was not done automatically) and then click Accept to install the selections. You may get a notification that other files are being installed as well.

5. YaST will install KOffice and, barring any problems, will return to the main screen.

6. Run YaST Online Update (YOU) to check for updates to the software.

Customizing and configuring KOffice tools is very much like configuring any KDE tool. Go to the Settings menu and choose from any of five Settings dialog boxes. Opening the Configure KWord dialog box displays something similar to Figure 9.4.

Using sliders to change settings is a little unusual and is just one option for making changes in this dialog. Click each icon on the left to view and edit settings related to those items. Use different dialog boxes to edit toolbars, keyboard shortcuts, and automatic word completion and corrections.

### Using KOffice

When you launch a KOffice application, you get choices from some basic templates, recent documents, and the contents of your Documents directory (see Figure 9.5). If you like using styles, be sure to select one of the letter (US or A4) templates. The plain text option is literally that—only one Standard style.

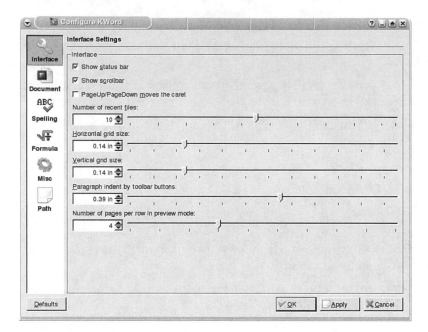

**FIGURE 9.4**    The KWord configuration dialog box lets you use sliders to change settings.

**FIGURE 9.5**    The KWord Open dialog box lets you select from several blank templates or from existing documents.

What makes KWord stand out is its page layout formats. Inspired by the indispensable technical writer's tool, Adobe FrameMaker, KWord helps you create frames to hold text, graphics, white space and other design elements with relative ease.

The KWord interface includes a document structure map that lets you quickly add frames to fill in later. The software isn't yet ready for really long documents, but is certainly up to the task of a company newsletter or holiday message.

KSpread also has templates for many standard tasks—invoices, balance sheets, and family budgets. You can even use KSpread to calculate your body mass index.

## Running GNOME Office

Despite having a pair of fine and well-built applications, GNOME Office (GO) is still a project in formation. As of this writing, GNOME Office is a very loose confederation of tools, with no common interface or direct integration. The applications are built on the GTK widget set that underlies everything in the GNOME desktop.

### What's in GNOME Office?

For now at least, GNOME Office consists of three key applications:

- AbiWord—A cross-platform word processor with a pluggable architecture allowing you to have just the functionality you want, and not so much bloatware.

- Gnumeric—A spreadsheet with all the features you would expect. It will read your Excel files, too.

- GNOME-DB—A GUI front end to all popular open source databases that can also connect to LDAP directories, mail data, and the like. The libraries associated with this project provide data management functions to many GNOME applications.

Other productivity tools running under the GNOME desktop may one day be part of the GO project, but today this is it. We will cover Evolution, the GNOME personal information manager, in Chapter 13 and The GIMP in Chapter 10, "Sights, Sounds, and Other Fun Things."

### Installing and Configuring GNOME Office

GO has no single install, but all the components are installable from YaST. There are three GNOME-DB files to install: libgda, libgnomedb, and mergeant.

> **TIP**
>
> Are you running KDE as your main desktop? You can still run any or all of the GNOME Office tools. YaST will install any of the necessary GNOME libraries if you choose to install AbiWord or Gnumeric.
>
> Both of these tools have Windows versions, should you want to try them out there. GNOME-DB will also run on Macintosh OS X.

6

## Using GNOME Office

AbiWord has a very nice, clean interface based on the Microsoft Works word processor. It has a pretty good Save as Word function, so it should be easy to trade documents with the Microsoft world. As always, some of the more esoteric functions are hard to reproduce.

Abiword 2.2 is a word processor with a difference: its default file format is the Extensible Markup Language (XML). Any document created by Abiword can be viewed in a web browser that supports XML, or any text editor. In the latter, you can see the markup tags. Abiword will export documents to standard HTML or with PHP instructions and display the results in a browser with a default or custom cascading stylesheet.

Abiword handles right-to-left text with ease, giving support to those who craft words in Arabic and Hebrew. You can even manipulate this feature paragraph-by-paragraph if you are writing for multiple audiences.

You can use styles in AbiWord, and you can modify them on-the-fly. AbiWord also comes with a few templates, including a most interesting Resume template, using their mascot, Abi the Ant.

Gnumeric delivers on its promise to be Fast, Free, and Accurate. It will import your Excel files and should also handle most other popular spreadsheet formats (including OpenOffice.org Calc and Quattro Pro). It boasts of more than 100 functions that are unique to Gnumeric (that is, not available in Excel).

There is fine documentation at http://www.gnome.org/projects/gnumeric/doc/. Newcomers to spreadsheets should certainly read Chapter 3 of the online manual, which is a Quick-Start tutorial in using Gnumeric.

# Running Softmaker Office

Softmaker Office 2004 is a new addition to SUSE Linux 9.2. This small commercial suite promises a small memory footprint, fast loading, and seamless conversion to and from Microsoft formats. As with GNOME Office, Softmaker is a very loosely connected collection of two applications: word processor Textmaker 2002 and spreadsheet Planmaker 2004.

Like KOffice, Textmaker offers some desktop publishing features as well as ordinary word processing. Its Object Mode makes it easy to create and place new text or graphics frames (see Figure 9.6).

The built-in templates are interesting, with several business card designs, letters, faxes, memos, and a phone list template.

Textmaker's chief weakness is that the spell checker is disabled in this version.

Planmaker is a perfectly serviceable spreadsheet—nothing fancy—but with all the features you would expect from this application. It does a great job of importing Excel worksheets (see Figure 9.7) and has 320 built-in functions.

**FIGURE 9.6**    Textmaker lets you easily create multicolumn layouts with text and graphics frames.

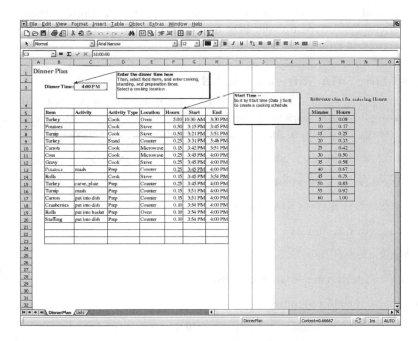

**FIGURE 9.7**    Planmaker smoothly imports Microsoft Excel worksheets.

## Other Commercial Suites

Although not included with SUSE Linux, a few other commercial products in this category might interest you.

Hancom Office is produced by a South Korean firm. Version 2.0 offers a word processor, a spreadsheet, a presentation tool, and a paint program.

ThinkFree Office for Linux was released just days before the OpenSUSE project was announced in August 2005. Its chief claim to fame is even easier document sharing with Microsoft Office tools. ThinkFree saves files to the Microsoft format by default and also makes Acrobat PDF files for use in the Adobe Reader. ThinkFree Office contains a word processor (Write), a spreadsheet (Calc), and a presentation (Show) package. You can try it out free at the ThinkFree website: http://www.thinkfree.com.

Applixware, by VistaSource, has been around for a while. The recently released v4.3.3 has a word processor, a spreadsheet, a presentation product, a graphics generation toolkit, a database management integration client, and an email client.

WordPerfect, one of the first big-name products to enter the Linux market, no longer develops a Linux version, but you can still buy a copy of Corel WordPerfect Suite 2000 for Linux.

# PDA Connectivity

SUSE Linux provides programs and clients you can use with your Palm-style personal digital assistants (PDAs). Sync up your PDA data with your PC, send and retrieve mail, keep your calendar in order, and more.

## Command-Line PDA Software for SUSE Linux

The most popular PDA-related applications are bundled in a single package, called pilot-link. You can organize and work with your Palm OS-compatible PDA directly from your shell prompt—no GUI required. Among pilot-link's amazing capabilities are

- Extracting and uploading addresses from your address book(s)

- Installing datebook information

- Transferring text memos to and from the PDA

- Managing your to-do lists

- Managing user settings

- Sending and retrieving email documents

- Installing new PDA programs

- Backing up, synchronizing, and restoring the contents of a PDA

- Acquiring expense-account database information

The suite has 31 tools for you to use, and after you've connected your Palm cradle to your PC, you should be able to use any of them to manage your information. For example, to back up the contents of your Palm device to your Linux system, type this command at the shell:

```
pilot-xfer -p /dev/ttyS1 -b backupdirectory
```

This command creates a directory called backupdirectory, and then downloads and saves the contents of the PDA to backupdirectory. Explore the range of pilot-link tools in the suite's man page, or visit http://www.pilot-link.org to connect with the pilot-link community.

### Connecting with Your PDA in KDE and GNOME

If you want to know how good a tool pilot-link really is, all you need to know is that all the GUI tools mentioned here are just different ways of putting a pretty face on the underlying command-line tools offered by pilot-link. KPilot and Gnome-Pilot are the "official" Palm interfaces for their respective desktop environments (although KPilot is considerably more powerful than its counterpart), and a third, J-Pilot, also works well.

J-Pilot will manage, retrieve, install, back up, and sync any information for your Palm-compatible PDA. Click the Date Book, To-Do List, Address Book, and Memo Pad buttons to perform related tasks. Use the Sync and Backup buttons to update or preserve a copy of a PDA's data. KPilot integrates with the Kontact personal information manager for KDE, allowing you to quickly transfer mail and contact information between your devices.

> **NOTE**
>
> If you need to sync up information only periodically, the GNOME-based Multi-Sync and KDE-based KitchenSync may be just what you need.

## Managing Your Finances

For even the most rabid Linux fan, financial software was (and maybe still is) the final frontier for the Linux desktop. Many people keep Windows around just to run Quicken (and maybe a couple of games).

Now there are two open source projects that want to make you feel comfortable managing your (or your business's) money in Linux. GnuCash is the veteran, with KMyMoney the upstart challenger. Both are set up to do standard double-entry bookkeeping and can import Intuit Quicken QIF files.

GnuCash 1.8 has a very nice account setup wizard and handles QIF file transfer very well. GnuCash supports creating accounts in nearly every currency imaginable. After you've set up at least one account, the opening screen gives you a list of your accounts, a description, and your current balance. To open an existing account, select it from the list and click Open.

Quicken users will be very comfortable with the register interface, seen in Figure 9.8.

**FIGURE 9.8**    The GnuCash register screen is very similar to Quicken's.

Organizing your income and expenses into categories is a little different in GnuCash than in its Windows counterpart, however. Both Income and Expenses exist as separate accounts alongside your bank account, and you must create subaccounts for each expense. Quicken categories may transfer over, but you might have to create subaccounts manually. GnuCash does not have any defaults, but that means you can identify as many categories as you want to track.

KMyMoney works pretty much the same way as its counterparts do, but it is definitely a work in progress. This should be a fine application by the time it gets to v1.0.

When you open KMyMoney for the first time, you see a template screen with just one (Blank) template. You must select this icon before creating your first account. You must first identify the Institution this account falls under and then set up the account. The wizard to do this is straightforward, and though the terminology may be a little off-putting at first, it is easy to get started.

The Ledgers screen that displays your data is not as attractive as GnuCash (see Figure 9.9), but manually entering transactions is less confusing. KMyMoney will automatically add a new payee when you enter it in the Edit box. Categories are not fully implemented in version 0.6.4.

Both tools support scheduled transactions and will alert you to bill-sending due dates.

Neither tool does direct online banking, but this is in the long-term plans. For financial institutions that allow customers to download account information through QIF files, these can be easily imported into either application. Intuit is now encouraging its partners to switch to a new format, one which the open source tools do not yet support.

**FIGURE 9.9**   KMyMoney's Ledgers screen displays your account information and lets you enter transactions manually.

# More Tools to Make You Productive

To round out this chapter, here are a few more tools that will help you get more done, and often in less time. Some of these tools are alternatives to others already in a suite; others are unique in their categories.

> **TIP**
>
> Managing personal information is essential to a productive life. Because so many of the Linux tools for managing personal information include email clients, these tools are described in Chapter 13.

## Desktop Publishing with Scribus

Several of the word processing applications we've discussed here have had some desktop publishing features, but if you've got experience with dedicated publishing software such as Quark Xpress, Microsoft Publisher, or Adobe PageMaker/InDesign, you may find that Scribus is the tool you want. You may even find yourself abandoning these other apps for good!

You can create newsletters and magazines, and at least one complete book has been published with Scribus. It will do heavy-duty high-resolution print-production work, but can also do simple PDF flyers and posters. You can also produce HTML files for posting on the Web.

Curiously, Scribus adds itself to the KDE menu as a word processor (under the Office menu). This is not to say that its Story Editor won't do the job of writing good text, but Scribus is a page designer. It is best suited for taking already written text and graphics and placing them on a page.

If you're not familiar with desktop publishing, be sure to visit the Scribus documentation site, docs.scribus.net, and work through the Get Started with Scribus tutorial. You will walk through the entire process of producing a print magazine with Scribus, using all the tools, and learning a bit about page design as well.

Figure 9.10 shows you the various windows that you will work with in Scribus. The main window (with the colored squares and swatch of dull text) is where the work gets done. You can place frames in this window, drag them around the page, and tweak them (and any objects within) using the Properties dialog box (in the lower left). Use the Outline tool (lower right) to plan the elements of your document and where you want to place them. You can easily change your mind and move each element around when using this tool. The page map in the upper left lets you easily navigate among multiple pages. Keep frequently used clips of text or graphics in the Scrapbook, and drag them into your new document at any time.

Play with Scribus and get your documents out.

**FIGURE 9.10**   Scribus makes it easy to create and publish professional documents.

## Diagramming and Flowcharting with Dia

Dia seeks to be the Linux version of Microsoft Visio, the business tool that enables IT managers to diagram their networks and enables human resource folks to build their organizational charts. And it does a pretty nice job of it.

Dia is a GNOME application with dozens of default shapes, from general polygons to network diagrams to Uniform Modeling Language programming charts that can be quickly slapped together and connected with each other in no time. Figure 9.11 shows a very simple network configuration created in less than five minutes.

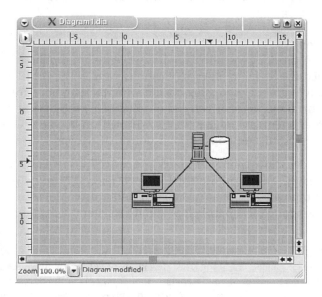

FIGURE 9.11    A simple Dia networking diagram.

Making connections between objects—that is, grouping them so they move together—is two clicks away. Select an object, right-click, and choose Select, Connected from the context menu.

Dia works much better in GNOME than in KDE, but it is easy to work with, whatever your environment. KOffice's counterpart, Kivio, still has some distance to cover before equaling Dia.

## Mindmapping with VYM

View Your Mind is a nifty little tool that is similar to Dia, but with a specific purpose: helping your brain make the connections it needs to resolve all those little ideas running around in it.

VYM lets you develop your ideas on things great and small. It can serve as a visual document outline or help you develop a plan for your next job search or career change. Your maps can be deeply hierarchical or with thought balloons randomly strewn around the screen. Connect headings with more detailed musings, or attach other documents to your map.

## Fax and Scanner Applications

As the countless owners of multifunction printers can attest, scanning and faxing documents are just other ways of printing. Although email and FTP may now be the document-transfer methods of choice for many, digitizing paper documents and sending them across phone lines as a fax are still widely used methods of getting information into the hands of your clients. Linux can easily handle both tasks, and SUSE Linux provides the tools to handle them.

### Scanner Applications

The use of a scanner provides a wealth of options to enhance productivity. You can manipulate scanned images in graphics applications such as The GIMP, and then print, fax, or embed them in a word processing document or presentation. You can scan paper documents for archival purposes, or you can process them with optical character recognition (OCR) software to translate images into words that can be put in an editable form. SUSE Linux offers the SANE and Kooka applications to assist you with scanning.

Scanner support under Linux is provided by Scanner Access Now Easy (SANE). If your scanner is supported, it is listed on the SANE support page at http://www.sane-project.org/sane-supported-devices.html. You can find it using the search engine or browse the list of supported scanners before you make your purchase.

> **NOTE**
>
> If you have a newer scanner, check the latest development versions of SANE. Each new version adds support for more devices. If your scanner is supported only in the development version, you need to download and compile the CVS version. This is a complex operation suitable for advanced Linux users only, and it is beyond the scope of this book. For information on that process, see the CVS HOWTO at the Linux Documentation Project: http://www.tldp.org.

Kooka is a KDE application that provides standard scanning capabilities along with OCR functions and its own image gallery. Because Kooka is a KDE application, it can also provide scanning services to other KDE applications, such as the KOffice suite.

### Fax Client Software

SUSE Linux provides several clients that handle different aspects of composing, viewing, and sending faxes. KDE has two graphical applications: Kfax, which views incoming electronic faxes, and KDEprintFax, which writes them. The actual sending and receiving of faxes is handled by the command-line fax server HylaFax.

You can use any text editor or word processor to create a document to fax. OpenOffice Writer even has a wizard that will create a fax cover sheet template for easy use. Go to File, Wizards, Fax to set that in motion. KDEprintFax also lets you write a cover page in its interface, which you can see in Figure 9.12.

**FIGURE 9.12**   KDEprintFax lets you send faxes directly from your desktop. It serves as a graphical front-end to the command-line HylaFax fax server.

To open KDEprintFax, go to the Utilities menu in KDE and select Printing. Click Add File from the toolbar to locate the file(s) you want to fax. View the file with the View File button. To select a recipient, you can either retrieve the information from your address book or type in a name, company, and fax number using the Add Recipient dialog box. Click Send Fax to complete the operation.

> **NOTE**
>
> Using multiple fax applications might seem unnecessarily complicated if you're used to sending and receiving faxes with the same interface and/or with a modem connected to the fax machine. The Unix/Linux approach is more complicated because it is network focused. A single computer can be set up to send and receive faxes for the entire network of hundreds of computers. Not every machine on the network needs a fax modem to send faxes if one machine can. All any one node on the network needs is a way to view faxes and send them via the fax server. In some ways, that's simplicity itself.

Besides HylaFax, which is capable of handling faxes for a large network, the traditional way of handling faxes is with the command-line combination **mgetty+sendfax**. Although SUSE Linux includes the RPM packages for both of these tools, configuration is a bit complex and too big a subject for our context.

## References

- http://www.OpenOffice.org—The home of the open source productivity suite. Extended documentation, a knowledge base, and links to the various mailing lists that keep this project running.

- http://wwws.sun.com/software/star/staroffice/—OpenOffice.org's commercial big brother, produced and marketed by Sun Microsystems. This version includes a database and a few other closed-source widgets and tools.

- http://www.taming-openoffice-org.com/—Aimed at the person who wants to get more out of OOo. Contains many valuable tips, links, and pointers to other books that cover OOo in depth.

- http://www.KOffice.org—The KDE Office Suite home. Downloads, news, mailing lists and archives.

- http://www.gnome.org/gnome-office—The umbrella home for the GO Suite.

- http://www.abisource.com—The AbiWord page.

- http://www.gnumeric.org—The Gnumeric page.

- http://www.softmaker.de/index_en.htm—Softmaker Office.

- http://www.vistasource.com/page.php?id=86—Applixware.

- http://en.hancom.com/products/hancomoffice20.html—Hancom Office.

- http://kmymoney2.sourceforge.net/index.html—KMymoney.

- http://www.gnucash.org—GnuCash.

- http://www.scribus.net—Home of the Scribus desktop publishing tool. Be sure to check out the detailed and very helpful tutorial at docs.scribus.net.

- http://www.gnome.org/projects/dia/—The Dia diagramming tool. Useful documentation not included in the package.

- http://www.insilmaril.de/vym/—The View Your Mind page. Written in VYM and exported to HTML. Nice way to see how the program works.

# CHAPTER 10

# Sights, Sounds, and Other Fun Things

There is more than work to be done on your SUSE Linux machine. Your desktop can play music and serve as a radio. Movies are indeed made on Linux boxes. You can create and edit images of all types and move pictures from your digital camera to your PC. You can even watch TV on your monitor (with the right video card)!

Linux is not yet the gamers' OS of choice, but there are more ways to have fun on Linux than you may have thought. You'll learn what's available in this chapter, too.

Because most of this is visually oriented, we'll emphasize the tools for GNOME and KDE, but there are some interesting command-line tools for multimedia to learn about, too.

## Starting Out: Configuring Your Sound and Video Cards

An impression exists that Linux is weak in multimedia (especially sound card) support. This is largely because of some mixed results for the very popular Creative Labs (SoundBlaster) products under Linux. Today, multimedia support is great and continually improving.

SUSE Linux supports most current sound cards out of the box. During the SUSE Linux installation, YaST should recognize and give you a default configuration for both your sound and video cards, enough to get you up and running. Although you can further configure both cards during the setup, it's better to get your system going and then tweak later through YaST.

Sound support for SUSE Linux is provided through ALSA, the Advanced Linux Sound Architecture. ALSA began as a simple project to write better drivers for a single sound card, and it blossomed. It has been supported in the kernel since v2.5, and been the default sound system since v2.6. It supports everything from consumer sound cards to multichannel interfaces and will play multiple audio streams simultaneously if you want.

YaST handles all the configuration tasks for ALSA, and you are no longer required to load the kernel modules manually. This is the topic of the next section.

## Configuring Sound Cards in YaST

Most settings for audio and video are set in YaST. To do this, open YaST and click Hardware to start the configuration. When you click Sound, YaST checks your current configuration and displays all detected sound cards.

You can set some advanced options for the card, but unless you are trying to solve some problem and know what to change, you should leave these alone. Click Volume to change the default volume settings for every channel on your card. The Start Sequencer check box loads kernel modules for MIDI sounds at boot, and is checked by default.

If YaST does not automatically recognize your card, you can add it manually in this dialog box.

Choose the card from the menu or use the Search tool to find your card. Click Next to confirm the changes.

Reconfiguring your video card and monitor should also be done automatically if you change your hardware. Clicking Video Card and Monitor in YaST's Hardware section will tell you the current settings. Click Change to run SaX2 (see Chapter 4, "Further Configuration with Yast2 and Sax2," to learn more about configuring the X Window System with SaX2).

---

**TIP**

Need to test your sound quickly? Head for the KDE or GNOME Control Center and set a system notification. In KDE, go to Sound & Multimedia, and then System Notifications. In KDE System Notifications, select KDE Is Starting Up and click the > icon to play the sound. In GNOME, open Multimedia (if necessary) and then Sound. Select the Sound Events tab and pick a random sound (you must have the gnome-audio package installed for the default sounds to work).

---

# Playing Music and Listening to the Radio

After your sound card is working, perhaps the only thing you want to do, audiowise, is to play your CDs and MP3s, and access your favorite Internet radio stations. SUSE Linux provides a wealth of ways to do this and more.

The most mature all-purpose media player for Linux (and all X Window Systems) is the X Multimedia System (XMMS). XMMS modeled its GUI after Winamp, the popular media player for Windows.

Its display is very modular, so you can have as much (or as little) eye candy to visually enhance your audio experience. Figure 10.1 shows what happens if you display everything in a default installation.

XMMS plays most every audio format, with the exception of Windows Media (`.wma`, `.asf`) files. It will play your audio CDs out of the box, as well as MPEG movies.

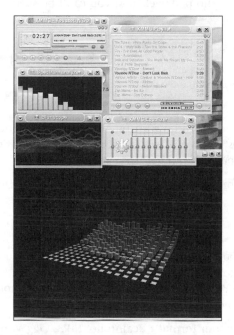

**FIGURE 10.1**   Arrange the XMMS display any way you like to enhance your audio experience. Equalizers, playlists, sound analyzers, and oscilloscope meters are all showing here in addition to the simple player in the upper left.

If you have a live Internet connection, both XMMS and the KDE CD player (KSCD) will contact the CD Database (CDDB) of your choice (XMMS defaults to FreeDB) to deliver track information when you play a CD.

## Sound Formats

Digital sound recordings appear in several formats. You can create and listen to files in the following formats with SUSE Linux:

- Raw—More properly known as the headerless format, audio files using this format contain an amorphous variety of specific settings and encodings. All other sound files have a short section of code (the header) that identifies the format type.

- MP3—Perhaps the most popular audio format ever. MP3 uses a commercial, proprietary compression scheme, which can create licensing issues for both creators and users.

10

- WAV—These days, WAV (Windows Audio Visual format) files are mostly used as brief sound effects to accompany error messages and other computer events. This is because WAV files are not compressed and so take up a lot of room even for a short clip.

- Ogg-Vorbis—This format is the open source competitor to MP3. You'll enjoy better compression, better audio playback, and you can't be sued for using it.

> **TIP**
>
> Want to learn more about these and other audio formats? Head over to the Audio Format FAQ at http://www.cnpbagwell.com/audio.html.

Should you need to convert an audio file from one format to another, various utilities can help you do that. The best known is Sound Exchange (SoX). This command-line utility is not installed by default, but you can get it via YaST.

Timidity is a cross-platform MIDI-to-WAV converter and player. It handles karaoke files, too, displaying the words so you can sing while it plays.

## Internet Radio and Other Streaming Media

One of the best things about your Internet connection, even under dial-up, is the capability to hear hundreds of radio stations broadcasting music, news, and information globally through the World Wide Web. What was once the province of hobbyists with expensive radio equipment is now available to anyone with an Internet connection.

Streaming audio comes in four formats: RealAudio, MP3, Ogg Vorbis, and Windows Media (wma). SUSE Linux media players handle all these formats except for Windows Media.

XMMS does streaming audio quite well, though occasionally it will ask you for a file to play.

The Linux player made for streaming audio is the Helix Community Player. RealNetworks open-sourced the code for its various media formats and the RealPlayer client some time ago.

SUSE Linux 9.2 was the first SUSE version to come equipped by default with RealPlayer Gold, although earlier UNIX versions of the RealAudio player worked with Linux. RealPlayer (owned by RealNetworks) and its completely open-source cousin, the Helix Community Player, play most audio types, streaming or not. SUSE Linux 10 includes RealPlayer 10.0.5 in both the open-source and retail versions.

If you happen to be fond of the built-in browser included in the Windows version of RealPlayer, you may be disappointed with the Linux version, but even though it may lack visual appeal, it performs its actual function—playing audio—quite well.

> **NOTE**
>
> If you're running SUSE Linux 9.2 on a 64-bit processor, you may have trouble running RealPlayer inside Mozilla-based browsers (including Firefox, Epiphany, and Galeon). The 32-bit RealPlayer package included with the distribution does not install the Mozilla plug-in, and attempting to install it manually results in the browser crashing on launch. The Helix community is working on a 64-bit version of both the Helix and RealPlayer applications, including the plug-ins, which may be released by the time you read this.
>
> RealPlayer works fine as a standalone player under an AMD Athlon 3000+.

Both versions of the Helix player have the plug-in architecture that should, in time, yield a player that does what every user wants it to. This depends on whether enough users make their wishes known.

## Making Your Own Music

SUSE Linux has a number of tools to help you record your own sounds.

Icecast is a streaming-audio server application that enables you to play your MP3 collection over a LAN, or even over the Internet.

## Burning CDs and DVDs

Burning your own CDs is a fundamental skill for Linux multimedia enthusiasts. Compact discs and digital versatile discs (DVDs) are the standard media for multimedia data of all types because they are cheap to produce, ultra portable, and can hold the large files that carry audio, and especially video, signals. Even the standard three-minute pop song requires a few megabytes of space to store. For multimedia, you can use CD/DVDs to

- Record, play, and store graphical images, music, video, and playlists

- Rip audio tracks from your own music CDs and create "mix tapes" to your liking

Of course, CDs can store many other types of files, not only audio and visual files. They are an excellent medium for storing backups of all data stored on your hard drives. See Chapter 20, "Managing Data: Backup, Restoring, and Recovery," for more information.

It may be obvious to state, but if you want to record multimedia (and other) data on a CD, you must have a drive that supports writing data to discs. A simple CD-ROM player does just that—plays already-recorded material that is read-only. What you need is a CD-RW (Read/Write) or DVD-RW/DVD+RW drive. The discs themselves must also be writable (CD-R or CD-RW and the corresponding DVD formats). YaST will configure your hardware at installation; see Chapter 4 to see how that is done. To ensure that your hardware is configured properly, use cdrecord -scanbus to get information on using the CD drive under SCSI emulation. When you type the following:

```
cdrecord -scanbus
```

10

You should see something like this:

```
Cdrecord-Clone 2.01 (x86_64-suse-linux) Copyright (C) 1995-2004 Jörg Schilling
Note: This version is an unofficial (modified) version
Note: and therefore may have bugs that are not present in the original.
Note: Please send bug reports or support requests to http://www.suse.de/feedback
Note: The author of cdrecord should not be bothered with problems in this version.
Linux sg driver version: 3.5.27
Using libscg version 'schily-0.8'.
cdrecord: Warning: using inofficial libscg transport code version
(okir@suse.de-scsi-linux-sg.c-1.83-resmgr-patch '@(#)scsi-linux-sg.c 1.83 04/05/20
Copyright 1997 J. Schilling').
scsibus0:
0,0,0 0) 'LITE-ON ' 'COMBO SOHC-5232K' 'NK07' Removable CD-ROM
0,1,0 1) *
0,2,0 2) *
0,3,0 3) *
0,4,0 4) *
0,5,0 5) *
0,6,0 6) *
0,7,0 7) *
scsibus2:
2,0,0 200) 'Memorex ' 'TD 2C ' '1.04' Removable Disk
2,1,0 201) *
2,2,0 202) *
2,3,0 203) *
2,4,0 204) *
2,5,0 205) *
2,6,0 206) *
2,7,0 207) *
```

The CD writer is present and is known by the system as device 0,0,0. The numbers represent the scsibus/target/lun (logical unit number) of the device. You will need to know this device number when you burn a CD from the command line, so write it down or remember it.

When you're first getting started with CD burning, it's good to have the comforting approach of a GUI wizard to walk you through the process. You can tackle the command-line approach eventually, but because SUSE Linux offers a pair of very good GUI tools for burning multimedia discs, you are indeed in good hands. In this section, you'll first learn about the CD creation tools that come with KDE and GNOME. Then you'll see the shell tools that let you burn at your keyboard.

## Creating CDs and DVDs from Your Desktop

KDE's graphical CD/DVD "Kreator" is called K3b, and it makes CD burning pretty much a matter of dragging and dropping files into a project and going about your business.

Perhaps it's not quite that simple, but close enough for rock 'n' roll (or whatever style you prefer).

When you open K3b (see Figure 10.2), you see a familiar three-pane interface. On the upper left is your directory structure, with your last directory selected. In the upper right are the files contained in the selected directory. At the bottom is where the action happens. K3b offers four options in the main window:

- New Audio CD Project
- New Data CD Project
- New Data DVD Project
- Copy CD

**FIGURE 10.2**  K3b knows what the typical CD-burning projects are and puts them in easy reach on the main screen.

These items are not the only things you can do with K3b, but they are the most typical. Go to New Project in the File menu to see your other selections.

> **TIP**
>
> The Copy CD feature in K3b is pretty cool. Want a copy of a favorite CD to play in your car while the original sits in your home stereo? Put that CD in your computer's drive. Run K3b and choose Copy CD (you may have to turn off the default CD player first). K3b will first copy the tracks of the CD to a temporary directory on your hard drive. It will then prompt you to insert a writable CD and burn the tracks to the blank CD.

Let's make an audio CD. Click the appropriate button and the bottom pane effectively becomes a representation of your CD. Find your digital music files using the two upper panels, and drag the files you want to burn into the bottom pane. K3b should identify the track information from the tags included in every digital music file. If you don't see the title, artist, or other information for a track in the pane after you drag them in, select the track and click Query Cddb if you are online to check the CD Database, or type the information in yourself.

As you drag files into the bottom pane, the progress bar tells you how much room you have remaining on the disk. When you have dragged all the files you want (or have reached the end of the disc), you can rearrange them in any order you want. To create an ordered M3u playlist file for your MP3 audio files, click the Convert Audio Tracks icon from the toolbar and check the box. You can also use this dialog box to convert files from one audio format to another if you choose.

When all is well, and you have your tracks in order, click the Burn button on the toolbar. Another dialog box will appear. If you want to give your CD a title, click the Description tab in this dialog box. There are many settings available here, but accepting the defaults is the way to go for the novice. Click OK to start burning. A progress bar will appear to let you know how the burn is going. When the burn is complete, K3b will eject your new CD and play a happy bugle tune to announce its success. Your new CD will now play in any computer, stereo, or other CD player.

### Burning CDs with Nautilus in GNOME

In GNOME, basic CD burning is built right in to the Nautilus file manager. Insert a blank CD in your CD-RW drive. Go to the Places menu in Nautilus and select CD/DVD Creator. Open a second (or more) Nautilus window(s) containing the files you want to burn to the CD. Drag and drop the files into the CD/DVD Creator window (which is really a special directory called burn:///).

When you have your files selected, select Write to Disc from the File menu in the CD/DVD Creator window. This opens a dialog box (see Figure 10.3) where you can name the CD. There are no special features for building multimedia collections (such as playlist orders), but if you just want to get some files (music or otherwise) onto a CD or DVD, Nautilus gives you the tool to do that.

## Creating a CD from the Shell

Under the hood of the CD writing process, you'll find that this takes two steps. First, you create the iso9660-formatted image, and then you burn (or write) that image onto the CD. The iso9600 is the default file system for CD-ROMs.

Use the mkisofs command to create the ISO image. This command has many options (see the man page for a full listing), but use the following for quick burns:

```
mkisofs -r -v -J -l -o /tmp/our_special_cd.iso /source_directory
```

**FIGURE 10.3**    Nautilus gives you a simple tool to create CDs.

The options used in this example are

> -r—Sets the permission of the file to more useful values. UID and GID (individual and group user ID requirements) are set to zero, all files are globally readable and searchable, and all the files are set as executable (for Windows systems).

> -v—Displays verbose messages (rather than terse messages) so that you can see what is occurring during the process; these messages can help you resolve problems if they occur.

> -J—Uses the Joliet extensions to ISO9600 so that Windows can more easily read the CD. The Joliet (for Windows), Rock Ridge (for Unix), and HSF (for Mac) extensions to the ISO9600 standard are used to accommodate long filenames rather than the eight-character DOS filenames that the standard supports natively.

> -l—Allows 31-character filenames; plain DOS will not like it, but everyone else does.

> -o—Defines the directory where the image will be written (that is, the output) and its name. The /tmp directory is convenient for this purpose, but the image could go anywhere that you have room and write permissions.

> /source_directory—Indicates the path to the source directory—that is, the directory containing the files you want to include on your CD. There are ways to append additional paths and exclude directories (and files) under the specified path; it is all explained in the man page if you need that level of granularity. Our simple solution is to construct a new directory tree and populate it with the files we want to copy, and then make the image using that directory as the source.

Many more options are available, including options to make the CD bootable.

After you have created the ISO image, you can write it to the CD with the cdrecord command.

```
cdrecord -eject -v speed=12 dev=0,0,0 /tmp/our_special_cd.iso
```

10

The options used in this example are

-eject—Ejects the CD when the write operation is finished.

-v—Displays verbose messages.

speed=—Sets the speed; the rate depends on your drive's capabilities. If the drive or the disc itself does not support a faster speed (or burns poorly at the higher speed), you can use lower speeds to get a good burn.

dev=—Specifies the device number of the CD writer (I told you that you'd need this).

---

**TIP**

If you have CD-RW (read/write) discs, you can use the cdrecord blank= option to erase all the existing files on the CD.

cdrecord also gives you the option (when the disc supports it) of making multisession CDs. Without this option, when you remove a CD from the drive after writing files to it, your disc can no longer be written to, even if it still has space available. Using cdrecord -multi gives you the choice to put more files on the disc later.

Current standard capacity for a CD is 700MB of data, or 80 minutes of music. Some CDs can be overburned; that is, recorded to a capacity higher than the standard. You can overburn with cdrecord as long as your drive supports it. Find out more at http://www.cdmediaworld.com/hardware/cdrom/cd_oversize.shtml.

---

## Creating DVDs from the Shell

Many new computers now come with DVD-writing drives, and costs have come down to where ordinary users can buy them as well. Unfortunately, the standards-making bodies have not kept up with the increasing availability of these drives, so there are two competing formats for writing DVDs. Commonly known as the + and – formats, DVD+R, DVD+RW, DVD-R, and DVD-RW are the ones we have to live with for now.

Differences between the two have mostly to do with how the data is modulated onto the DVD itself, with the + format having an edge in buffer underrun recovery. How this is achieved impacts the playability of the newly created DVD on any DVD player. The DVD+ format also has some advantages in recording on scratched or dirty media. Most drives support the DVD+ format, and some support both.

This section will focus on the DVD+RW drives because most drives sold support this standard. The software supplied with SUSE Linux supports both formats. It will be useful to read the DVD-writing HOWTO at http://fy.chalmers.se/~appro/linux/DVD+RW before you use these command-line tools. You can skip over the part in the HOWTO with a detailed explanation of how things are done in the kernel to record DVDs. Read the stuff on the tools, though.

You need to have two packages installed to make DVD recording possible: dvd+rw tools and cdrtools. The dvd+rw tools package includes the growisofs application, which acts as a front end to mkisofs as well as the DVD-formatting utility.

You can use DVD media to record data in two ways. The first is much the same as that used to record a CD in a "session," whereas the second way is to record the data as a true file system using packet writing.

### Session Writing

To record data in a session, you use a two-phase process:

- Format the disc with `dvd+rw-format /dev/scd0` (necessary only the first time you use a disk).

- Write your data to the disc with `growisofs -Z /dev/scd0 -R -J /your_files`.

The `growisofs` command simply streams the data to the disc. For subsequent sessions, use the -M argument instead of -Z. The -Z argument is used only for the initial session recording. If you use -Z on an already used disk, it will erase the existing data.

> **CAUTION**
>
> Some DVDs come preformatted. If this is the case and you format them again, the disc may become useless. Always be sure to read the fine print on the packaging on the DVD+RW before formatting.

> **TIP**
>
> When you write your first session on the DVD, cover at least one gigabyte (1GB). This helps ensure compatibility with other optical drives. DVD players calibrate themselves by attempting to read from specific locations on the disc. Data has to be present for the drive to read it and calibrate itself.
>
> Also, because of limitations in the standard ISO9660 file system in Linux, do not start new sessions of a multisession DVD that would create a new directory past the 4GB boundary. If you do, it will cause the offsets used to point to the files to "wrap around" and point to the wrong files.

### Packet Writing

Packet writing treats the DVD like a hard drive, where you create a file system (like ReiserFS) and "format" the disk. You can then write to it randomly as you would a hard drive. This method, although common on Windows computers, is still experimental for Linux and so is not covered in detail here.

It is possible to pipe data to the `growisofs` command:

```
your_application | growisofs -Z /dev/scd0=/dev/fd/0
```

It's also possible to burn from an existing image (or file, named pipe, or device):

```
growisofs -Z /dev/scd0=image
```

The DVD+RW Tools documentation, found in `/usr/share/doc/dvd+rw-tools`, is required reading before your first use of the program. Try experimenting with DVD-RW media first; DVD-R discs are not quite as cheap as CD-R disks, thus making the penalty for making mistakes somewhat higher.

# TV and Video: Xine and Mplayer

Standard video cards let you see most video resources, as you would expect. What you may not know is that you can turn your monitor into a television screen to receive TV signals with a TV or TV/video combo card. This section describes a sampling of Linux software that works with these content types.

Make sure your cards are properly configured. (See Chapter 4 to configure your hardware cards with YaST and SaX. See Chapter 6, "Launching Your Desktop," for configuring X.)

## TV and Video Hardware

Video support in Linux comes through the V4L (Video for Linux) API, or directly through the X Window System. Support for TV display from video cards with a TV-out jack is poor at this time. TV-only cards are well supported, but you must know the chipset name of your card, not the manufacturer's brand name. The most common chipset is the Brooktree Bt series; the Linux driver is called bttv.

YaST should recognize your card, if it is supported, and load drivers, whether the card is present at your initial SUSE Linux install or is added later. If this doesn't happen, you can always configure the card manually.

To configure the card, you need to identify the chipset. Check YaST. Go to Hardware, then Graphics Card and Monitor, or TV Card.

### Building Your Own Personal Video Recorder

Personal video recorders like TiVo and ReplayTV have changed the way people use television. The VCR introduced the idea of time-shifting broadcast television, but developed the reputation of being so complicated to program that nontechnical folks threw up their hands and gave up. Technical advances have made this easier, but the image of the "guy who can't program his VCR" persists. PVRs automate the hardest part of this task and make it a virtual no-brainer to record both analog and digital TV signals to a hard drive for later viewing.

TiVo itself runs Linux on a PowerPC processor to record shows on its hard drive.

Several open-source projects have been launched to create PVRs on Linux. The most successful of these is the MythTV project. The goal of MythTV is to bring the "mythical digital convergence box" to life, so it has the TiVo features, a web browser, an email client, games, and a music player.

Installing MythTV under SUSE Linux is not for the faint of heart, but it can be done. YaST will help along the way, dealing with various software dependency issues that might not be solved through compiling packages one by one.

> **NOTE**
>
> Another PVR package, Freevo, also runs under SUSE Linux.

**Hardware Requirements**   This is not a project to give your old Pentium II machine a new life. Processing TV signals requires a big and fast microprocessor chip and a good monitor. To make this work, you need modern equipment. Check the PVR Hardware Database at http://pvrhw.goldfish.org/tiki-pvrhwdb.php and compare these systems to the SUSE Hardware Database to pick the best PVR system for you. Hauppage, the maker of several popular TV cards, recommends a Pentium III processor at 733MHz (or 1.8GHz to make DivX video) for its PVR cards. You should also have a high-speed (DSL or cable modem) connection to the Internet to access TV schedule information. In addition, MythTV sets these guidelines:

- 256MB memory

- 40GB (or larger) hard drive

- XFS or JFS file system (which handles large files better than other file systems)

- A video card with a TV-out port

- A video capture card

You have two basic options for video capture: a "frame grabber" that is software driven or a more expensive MPEG encoder. The frame grabber does its encoding using the PC's resources, whereas the onboard encoder does it itself. The trade-off is that the IvyTV drivers needed for the encoder are somewhat troublesome to install.

If you have the right machine, let's start setting it up.

**Setting Up Your PVR**   Follow these steps to build your personal video recorder. Read the online MythTV installation guide before or during your setup. It will be very helpful. Find it at http://www.mythtv.org/docs/mythtv-HOWTO.html.

> **TIP**
>
> These instructions make use of two online tools to update and install software on your SUSE Linux system: YaST Online Update and Apt. Find out more about these in Chapter 21, "Keeping Your System Current: Package Management."

1. If you haven't already, install SUSE Linux. Make sure you have the `qt3`, `qt3-devel`, `qt3-mysql`, `gcc`, `freetype2-devel`, and `mysql` packages installed.

2. Run YaST Online Update to confirm that everything's current.

3. If apt is not yet installed, install it. See Chapter 20 for instructions.

4. Open a shell or console and log in as SuperUser.

**10**

5. Open /etc/apt/sources.list in a text editor and add this line: **rpm http://folk.uio.no/oeysteio/apt suse/9.2-mythtv MythTV**. This site contains MythTV RPMs for SUSE Linux v9.0, 9.1, and 9.2 (change the version number as necessary). If you have an MPEG encoder card, add this line as well: **rpm http://folk.uio.no/oeysteio/apt suse/9.2-ivtv IvyTV** for the IvyTV packages.

6. Type **apt install xmltv zap2it lame mythtv**. This will install MythTV and any other necessary package. This will likely take some time.

7. Setup the Myth MySQL database. Type **mysql -u root < mc.sql** at the shell.

8. Go to http://www.mythtv.org/docs/mythtv-HOWTO.html#toc5.4 and follow the instructions on setting up Zap2It DataDirect to handle your scheduling needs.

9. Decide where in the file system you want to store your recorded video. By default, MythTV stores files in /mnt/store. You may have to create this directory; make sure that at least one user can write to that directory. You may also want to create a user mythtv to be that user. If you prefer to store the files elsewhere, you'll need to edit the MythTV configuration file later.

10. Go to the MythTV setup directory and type **./setup**. Follow the prompts to go through the initial configuration. Accepting the default settings should get you in no trouble.

11. After you have completed the setup, it's time to go back to being an ordinary user. If you have created a separate user, mythtv, log out and log back in as mythtv (otherwise, just exit the SuperUser shell).

12. Running MythTV is a two-step process. First, run mythbackend to open the database, and then run mythfrontend to view your content.

And so you have your own PVR, with no service to buy. There are lots of other options in setting up MythTV; read more about them in the MythTV manual.

# Linux and Your Digital Camera

A digital camera combined with your personal computer is a powerful tool to create, store, edit, print, and share images. You can take your pictures, store them initially on the camera's disk or memory card, and then transfer them to your PC with the camera's USB cable. View or edit the file with your favorite image editor, then email photos to friends and family, post them on your photo blog, or preserve the images on a recordable CD. No fuss, no muss, no film.

Unfortunately, some of the pleasure and convenience associated with digital cameras are lost when running Linux. Most, if not all, of the software bundled with your camera runs only on Windows.

Do not despair, however. SUSE Linux offers many tools to organize and share your photos, and because the digital imaging industry is organized around very common standards, Linux can handle most any task involving your camera.

To begin with, you should have no trouble connecting your camera to your Linux system. Just connect the camera with its Universal Serial Bus (USB) cable to your PC. SUSE Linux should recognize the camera instantly and install the proper drivers. If you have any doubt that your camera is connected, run the following shell command:

```
cat /proc/bus/usb/devices
```

After you have the camera connected, use any file manager to see the image files on your camera. They should be located in /dev/sda1, the first SCSI data device, unless you have a SCSI hard drive installed, in which case the images will be on /dev/sda2.

GNOME has a camera-support tool called gtkam. This is a GTK+ front end to the command-line gphoto software. To run it, go to the Graphics menu and click Digital Camera Tool. The first time, it will ask you to identify your camera model from the list of 500+ cameras it supports. After you have your camera configured, gtkam will help you download your images from the camera to your PC. Just click the thumbnail to select.

KDE fans can use the digiKam tool to handle similar tasks. It also is a KDE-based front end to gphoto, but includes an image editor as well. DigiKam will attempt to autodetect your camera, or you can add it manually. You can create photo albums for specific events.

When your images are on your computer, feel free to run them through The GIMP to enhance them. The GIMP can reduce red-eye problems, crop your photos, change colors, brightness, and contrast, and otherwise doctor up your pictures. See the next section for more fun with The GIMP.

## Webcams

Webcams are typically small low-resolution cameras connected to your computer via a parallel or USB port. The camera can act in two modes: streaming (for a series of images or a moving object) and grabbing (for a single still image). The most common use for webcams includes videoconferencing and the widespread phenomenon of looking in on what's happening on a street corner where a local news organization has set up a camera. Webcams can be used to send almost-live images of assorted people, places, and things to an online correspondent. Perhaps even you've sent off a quick image of yourself—because you can!

You can use any of the video applications that can access a video4linux device to view webcam or still-camera images in SUSE Linux. You can also use GnomeMeeting (discussed in Chapter 16, "Collaborating with Others") as a webcam viewer.

Not all webcams are supported in Linux, and the drivers are based on the chipset used, rather than on the model or manufacturer. Some of the kernel source documentation files in /usr/src/linux-2.6/Documentation/usb contain information about USB webcams and drivers supported in SUSE Linux, including

- ibmcam.txt

- ov511.txt

- `phillips.txt`

- `se401.txt`

- `stv0608.txt`

A good place to start with your webcam is, as always, the Linux Documentation Project. The Webcam HOWTO is located at http://www.tldp.org/HOWTO/Webcam-HOWTO.

## Editing Images with The GIMP

Time was when the GNU Image Manipulation Program (GIMP) was touted as the "killer app" that would drive ordinary desktop users to Linux. A professional image editor whose features rivaled the fabled Adobe Photoshop on Windows that didn't cost several hundred dollars (well, one that didn't cost anything) is just what people need, some analysts thought. It didn't happen exactly that way, but it remains reasonable to say that Linux for the masses wouldn't be here if not for The GIMP.

> **TIP**
>
> To learn more about the role of The GIMP and the toolkit that spawned dozens of GUI products, see the section on GNOME in Chapter 6.

Photographers, animators, web designers, and other artists use The GIMP in all sorts of ways. The nonhuman characters in the *Scooby Doo* movies were created with the help of a GIMP spinoff now called CinePaint.

So what can you do with The GIMP? Just about any photo or other graphic-editing task. The GIMP can import and export more than 30 image formats, including Photoshop's native format. It supports layers (letting you easily add and remove text or other effects from an image) and has all the tools people expect from a modern image editor.

Version 2.2 of The GIMP, released in December 2004, features a more usable interface, better drag-and-drop support, and a shortcut editor.

To run The GIMP from the shell, type `gimp &`. The ampersand (&) launches The GIMP in the background and returns you to the shell prompt.

Otherwise, The GIMP can be found in the Graphics menu in the KDE or GNOME start menus. The first time you run The GIMP, you'll be asked a few startup configuration questions, but then you're on your way.

When you open The GIMP without an image, you'll see the toolbox first; these icons offer the basic utensils for editing an image. Depending on the version installed on your system, more than 30 tool icons could be available to you in the toolbox.

To create a new image, press Ctrl+N (or go to File, New). To open an existing image for editing, press Ctrl+O and an image window appears. Both the toolbox and the image window have their own menus. Open the File menu in either window to open and save graphics and perform other file-management tasks. The Toolbox Extensions menu (Xtns) contains the plug-ins and other enhanced functionality that make The GIMP special.

Right-clicking anywhere in an image window also gives you access to a context menu with a wealth of choices to work with your image (see Figure 10.4).

**FIGURE 10.4**   Just a hint of the choices you have available when right-clicking in a GIMP image.

In the right edge of the menu are two important options, Python-fu and Script-fu. Both offer ways to automate tasks and do all sorts of cool things. Script-fu is the original GIMP scripting language, but because it's based on a relatively obscure programming language, Scheme, it's hard to learn. GIMP 2.0 introduced Python-fu, based on the famous (and famously easy to use and learn) Python scripting language.

The GIMP's Help files are quite good. It doesn't hurt for newbies (either to The GIMP or to image editing in general) to read the manual.

**PHOTOSHOP VERSUS THE GIMP**

Two large obstacles prevent The GIMP from becoming a standard prepress format for dead-tree printers.

The first is Photoshop's licensing for Pantone colors to ensure accurate color matching. Adobe can pay to license Pantone's patented color specification; the all-volunteer GIMP Project cannot. There are GIMP palettes that approximate Pantone colors, but no one can say with certainty if these educated guesses are 100% right.

10

The second problem relates to the differences between how colors look on a computer screen and how they look in a magazine. The GIMP separates colors based on a combination of red, green, and blue (RGB) values. Print publishers use a scheme called CMYK (cyan, magenta, yellow, and "key," or black). In the short term, there is a GIMP plug-in called Separate that provides "minimal support for CMYK." For the long term, developers are working on a new technology, the Generic Graphical Library (GEGL), that will fully support CMYK color separation and other "deep color" issues.

If you produce images for print, these two issues may be critical, and you may need to keep a copy of Photoshop around. Be aware that you can run Photoshop under Crossover Office, the Codeweavers cross-platform tool.

## Graphics Formats

When you work with digital images, there seems to be a million different formats. Despite what you may believe, each format exists for a specific reason, either technical, aesthetic, or legal/financial. Some formats are patented or have patented technology included.

When you're working with editors such as The GIMP, choose the right format for the task at hand. Following is a list of some of the more popular formats, followed by an explanation of why you might want to use (or not use) them.

- BMP—Bitmapped graphics, which are commonly used in Windows. They are large and uncompressed files, good for icons and wallpaper.

- GIF—Graphics Interchange Format. Most graphics on the web once used this format, developed by CompuServe, one of the original online services. GIF uses a patented lossless compression algorithm (LZW) that requires a license to use.

- JPEG—The Joint Photographic Experts Group developed this format for electronic photographs. All digital cameras produce this format by default. The compression scheme loses some data, but provides a sharp image nonetheless.

- PNG—Portable Network Graphics. The open source replacement for GIFs.

- SVG—Scalable Vector Graphics. The Next Big Thing, this web graphics standard is being developed by the World Wide Web Consortium (W3C).

- TIF—Tagged Image File. Often used for printing and publishing.

Sometimes you may not be able to work with a file in its current format. Coming to your rescue are a host of separate image-converter applications that can change an image's format almost instantly. The best known of these, ImageMagick, even does its thing from the command line!

# Gaming on Linux

As the original "hobby" operating system, some Linux users have all their fun just tweaking the OS and their applications. Others need more traditional entertainments. SUSE Linux is fully equipped with assorted options for the gamer in you.

Very few shrink-wrapped commercial PC games are produced for Linux. For the most part, games are developed these days for Windows PCs using the Direct3D graphics engine. The cross-platform OpenGL engine is used for many popular games (like Doom III), but there's a perception that OpenGL is not as muscular.

---

**TIP**

TransGaming Technologies has an engine, Cedega, that converts Direct3D games to OpenGL. This enables Linux users to play as many as 300 Windows and online games, including multi-player role-playing games such as Everquest and Star Wars Galaxies. View the supported games database, with some player ratings, at http://transgaming.org/gamesdb/.

You must subscribe to TransGaming's service, at $5 per month, to get Cedega. Depending on what you play and how often you play it, this might be worth it. See http://www.transgaming.com/ for more information.

---

Many dedicated fans have worked on open-source clones of some classic games, like PacMan, Tetris, and SimCity (called LinCity). And it wouldn't really be a computer without a solitaire game, would it (see Figure 10.5)?

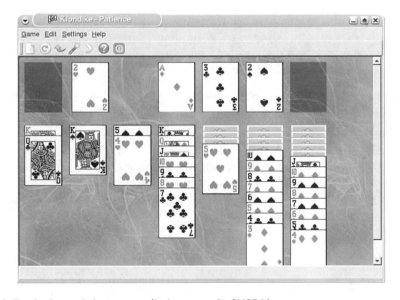

**FIGURE 10.5**    Patience is just one solitaire game in SUSE Linux.

SUSE Linux gives you two solitaire games, KPatience for KDE and PySol—the latter is written in Python. KPatience is installed by default with the KDE-Games package. It has 14 standard games for your amusement. One nice feature is that it will automatically play aces and other scoring cards.

PySol is much flashier, with musical accompaniment (yes, you can turn that off), dozens of games and card sets (sorted by type), and gobs of statistics. It is endlessly configurable to stave off boredom.

10

## KDE Games

KDE comes with 27 games in five categories: Arcade (with 8 games, including adapted classics such as Asteroids and Tron), Board (another 8 choices including chess and backgammon), Card (just three: Poker, Patience, and Skat), Strategy and Tactics (seven games that make you think), and Kids (only one not called "Edutainment": Ktuberling, a Mr. Potato Head editor).

Use the KDE Kicker menu to start any game. Sometimes there will be a configuration screen on first-time use, but most times you can play these right away.

## GNOME Games

The package of games that comes with GNOME is smaller than the KDE collection (just 17), but equally challenging. There's also some overlap, with the usual Tetris clones, disk-flipping, and solitaire games.

One standout is the Yahtzee clone, Tali. This game has great graphics, and you play against five computer opponents by default. This is, of course, configurable. The five dice roll automatically. You click the dice you want to roll (which turn into pumpkins) and click Roll to try to improve your score. After your third roll, you click the category you want to count your score.

GNOME also has a blackjack table for your gambling pleasure. Learn to double-down, split your hand, and other tricks of the trade without risking any real cash. The dealer plays under any of four sets of rules, called Vegas Strip, Vegas Downtown, Atlantic City, or Ameristar. This is set in the game's Preferences.

To play games, go to the GNOME menu, and click Games. All your choices will come up; they are not organized by type.

## Freeciv: A Free Strategy Game

Sid Meier's Civilization is one of the most popular games ever. The chance to build a society from scratch, fight wars, and get to space is irresistible for some. Naturally, some game players run Linux for more serious pursuits. What is interesting is that for some of those players, one of their serious pursuits became creating the game.

The Freeciv project was born in November 1995, about a year after the release of Civilization 1. Freeciv 1.0 came out six weeks later, though a flurry of updates produced v1.0f three weeks later. By the time Civilization III came out in October 2001, Freeciv was up to v1.12, and v2.0 was released in May 2005. SUSE Linux 10 includes v2.04.

You can play by yourself with the computer as your opponent(s), play with friends across a local area network, or use the Freeciv metaserver to play with other folks across the Internet. If you have played the commercial version, you'll be impressed with the similarities, although the quality of the graphics may vary depending on your video card. New players should not be intimidated, because there is a fair amount of help available, both in the game itself and at the Freeciv website (http://www.freeciv.org).

In Freeciv, you are the absolute ruler of your race. You marshal and manage resources to build cities. As in other city-simulation games, you must keep your citizens happy while getting them to produce more wealth, which you then can tax. Meanwhile, you try to increase your scientific and military capacity as you aim to either achieve world domination or build the first rocket to Alpha Centauri.

Most games have just one executable to run; Freeciv has two. To play on your own machine, you first need to run the server application, which contains the maps and most game details. You create AI opponents on the server as well to give you some competition if you're playing alone or with just one or two friends.

New players (especially those who haven't played Civilization) should read the online manuals at the Freeciv website to get a feel for how things work. There are three manuals: more technical, command-oriented manuals for the client and server and a game-playing manual that describes the forces and conditions of the game. The manuals are not complete (especially the client manual), but give you enough of a start to keep going.

## References

- http://www.alsa-project.org/alsa-doc—The Advanced Linux Sound Architecture sound card matrix. Check here for more information on support for your card.

- http://cdb.suse.de—The SUSE Hardware Database. Search here first for your sound and video cards before installing SUSE Linux.

- http://www.linux-sound.org—From music made with Linux to musician mailing lists to player and production software, the jumping-off point for sound and music under Linux.

- http://www.djcj.org/LAU/guide/index.php— The Linux Audio Users Guide.

- http://www.xmms.org/—Home of the X Multimedia System (XMMS). News, downloads, plug-ins, skins, and support for this multifaceted media player.

- http://helixcommunity.org—Many projects related to the open source Helix player, server, and producer for RealPlayer content.

- http://www.vorbis.com—Hows and whys for the Ogg Vorbis audio format.

- http://www.exploits.org/v4l/—Video for Linux information page. Technical information on the V4L APIs, drivers for supported cards, and personal video recorders. Links to software for making video of all types. When typing this URL, note that the last character is an L (as in Video4Linux), not a numeral 1. Should you type the numeral, you get a rather snarky error message.

- http://pvrguides.no-ip.com—Guides to setting up PC-based personal video recorders with MythTV and the VDR system.

- http://www.mythtv.org—The MythTV personal video recorder software. Contains installation instructions and examples of MythTV in action.

- http://anandtech.com/linux/showdoc.aspx?i=2190&p=1—A detailed and honest explanation of a successful MythTV installation on SUSE Linux.

10

- http://www.mplayerhq.hu—The MPlayer headquarters for that varied and full-featured video player.

- http://xinehq.de—The Xine headquarters. News and downloads for this video player.

- http://www.gphoto.org/—Linux Management software for digital camera images.

- http://www.gphoto.org/proj/libgphoto2/support.php—The gphoto list of supported cameras.

- http://www.teaser.fr/~hfiguiere/linux/digicam.html—Digital Camera Support for UNIX, Linux, and BSD. If your camera is not on the gphoto list, this site may help you find out why and offer suggestions.

- http://digikam.sourceforge.net—The KDE digiKam front end for gphoto. Look here for plugins and new versions, which seem to come out every two months.

- http://www.gimp.org—The very well-organized home of the GNU Image Manipulation Program (GIMP). Check out the Tutorials section, with walk-throughs for all skill levels, beginner to expert.

- http://gug.sunsite.dk—The global GIMP User Group. Mailing lists, a large gallery of images and textures, tutorials, and articles to help make you a better GIMPer.

- http://icculus.org/lgfaq—The Linux Gamers' FAQ. Get your questions answered.

- http://www.happypenguin.org—The Linux Game Tome, a catalog of Linux games of all sorts. Player ratings, news, forums, and links.

- http://linuxgames.com—LinuxGames, with all sorts of news related to the topic.

- http://www.kde.org/kdegames—The KDE Gaming area, with descriptions of all the games included with KDE.

- http://www.ggzgamingzone.org—Play Linux games online for free.

- http://www.freeciv.org—The Freeciv wiki site. All things Freeciv, with translations in seven European languages.

CHAPTER **11**

# Going Cross-Platform

Truly one of the great things about Linux is its flexibility. You are not always forced to abandon your old platform or your favorite applications when you make the move to Linux. With enough hard drive space, you can dual boot Windows on a separate partition and share files across file systems. Tools exist that allow you to run many Windows applications directly in Linux. You can even emulate MacOS Classic without a PowerPC.

This chapter is all about using these tools. Some are built in to your SUSE Linux installation, others are freely available for download, and some commercial products are available to purchase as well.

You will learn about the Wine Windows emulation project and its Crossover Office commercial spinoff. Win4Lin is another commercial product that allows you to run Windows 98 or Windows 2000/XP applications directly in Linux. VMware uses a virtual machine approach to installing and running other operating systems and applications. Basilisk II is the MacOS emulator, and DOSBox recaptures some of the earlier days of personal computing. Finally, you'll take a peek at a new project that's been gaining a lot of attention recently, the Xen Virtualization Project.

## Viewing Files from the Windows Side of Your Computer

When you install SUSE Linux on a computer that already has some form of Windows running on it, YaST will offer to run the two operating systems side by side. Linux will then repartition the computer, and the GRUB bootloader adds Windows to its list of boot options.

In this instance, SUSE Linux also creates a /windows directory to make all Windows files accessible to you directly in Linux. Depending on the file systems you are using on either side of your computer, you may not even notice a difference in how a file behaves.

MS-DOS and all versions of Windows up to the introduction of Windows NT ran on the File Allocation Table (FAT) file system. All Linux file systems (ext2, ext3, ReiserFS, XFS, JFS) fully support FAT. That is, you can open files from a FAT formatted volume, edit them, and save them either on the Linux volume or back to the FAT formatted volume. If you edit a Windows file in Linux and save it back to the same directory, you can open that file again in Windows.

The main reason this works so well is that FAT is not a permission-based file system. If you copy a Linux file to a FAT partition, the copy won't have permissions attached to it, but it will be completely readable in the other OS.

Starting with Windows NT, Microsoft created a proprietary permissions-based file system called NTFS, which is the default file system in Windows 2000, 2003, and XP. The transition to this file system has been good for Windows users because NTFS uses disk space more efficiently than FAT, and having permissions on files and directories is more secure. Because Microsoft has not shared many of the details of the file system, Linux support is somewhat less transparent.

Thus, most files on an NTFS volume are read-only on Linux. You can still open and edit these files in a Linux application, but you cannot save the changes back to the NTFS volume. You can, however, save or copy a Linux file to a FAT-formatted floppy or Zip disk, and then open and save to an NTFS volume.

> **NOTE**
>
> You can play most multimedia (music and video) files stored on an NTFS partition in Linux. Because there's no editing/saving going on, the only potential problem lies in support for the format. Linux multimedia player applications such as MPlayer and Helix support some Windows Media features. See Chapter 10, "Sights, Sounds, and Other Fun Things," for more information.

If you edit a lot of files in both operating systems, you should strongly consider creating a small FAT partition to store your data files.

On the other side of the computer, Windows has no native support for reading any Linux file system. Some shareware applications enable you to view files on the Linux Extended File System (ext2 and ext3), but none of these currently support the SUSE Linux default file system: ReiserFS.

▶ Learn more about Linux file systems in Chapter 18, "Managing Files, Volumes, and Drives."

# Emulating Other Operating Systems in Linux: An Overview

Essentially, there are two methods to accomplish the task of running applications across platforms. In the first method, an emulator "translates" an application's calls to one operating system (such as Windows) to another (Linux). In the second method, an application builds a "virtual machine" that creates a second computer inside your computer. The virtual machine then hosts a file system and operating system just as any physical computer does.

In this section, you will learn about three emulators (Wine, DOSBox, and Basilisk II) and two virtual machines (VMware and Win4Lin).

## A Few Misconceptions About Cross-Platform Tools

Nothing's perfect, and it's very hard to reach seamless cross-platform computing nirvana. Before looking closely at each of these tools, you should know a few things that may diminish your excitement at this newfound capability.

- Whatever tool you run from Linux, you won't run your existing Windows applications from the Windows side of your computer. You will install a new instance of the application and will probably have to re-create your settings from scratch.

- You cannot automatically use the same data (such as your Eudora mail queue) for both the Windows side and the Linux side. In many applications, you can import data from one side to the other, but changes made in one copy will not be reflected in the other copy.

- Don't install an emulator or virtual machine to run an application you don't have. All these products will let you "run Word on Linux," but you will need your own copy of Word to install and run. If all you need is a Linux application that will let you open and edit Word documents, use OpenOffice or another of the Linux office suites.

# Using Wine to Run Windows Applications

Choosing a name in the fine GNU recursive-acronym tradition, *Wine Is Not (an) Emulator*, or so it says. Nonetheless, this open source project has been helping Linux users run Windows applications for a long time.

As mentioned in the overview, Wine works by attempting to turn Windows system calls into Linux kernel calls, in part by making the Windows application think it is resting comfortably in a Windows directory.

The Wine environment is targeted for Windows 98, and so applications behave as though they were running under Windows 98.

So far, this is not a problem, but when Microsoft drops support for this operating system, other companies are likely to follow suit. Nonetheless, be careful when buying new applications that you want to run under Wine. Confirm that they will run under Windows 98, and then check the Wine applications database.

## Installing and Configuring Wine

Getting Wine going is a two-step process. First, you must install the Wine package from YaST. This makes the Wine commands available, but does not create the environment or install any software.

An easy way to get things underway is to install the WineTools package from http://www.von-thadden.de/Joachim/WineTools. This gives you a simple GUI tool to configure Wine and install a few essential applications. Install this package via YaST or command line.

---

**NOTE**

Depending on your system and version of Wine, you may get a dependency error for xdialog. You can safely ignore this and install anyway.

---

When you have WineTools installed, go to a shell prompt (as user) and type **wt2**. The WineTools menu (see Figure 11.1) appears.

**FIGURE 11.1**   Wine Tools simplifies your Wine installation.

The WineTools menu is organized so that you run each tool in order and have a fully capable basic installation at the end. Begin with the Base Setup, which will create your fake_windows directories and handle the basic Wine configuration (see Figure 11.2).

**FIGURE 11.2**    Create your base Wine configuration with this menu.

In addition to creating your Wine drive, use this menu to install DCOM98, an essential component for Microsoft Component Object Model (COM) applications, and Internet Explorer. When you've worked your way through this menu, click Main Menu to return.

Continue working through the WineTools menus to install Windows system tools and fonts. Then explore the list of tested software for common, downloadable applications. Although broken down into categories, the list is not comprehensive, but it will give you a good start.

## Installing Windows Applications Under Wine

When you have Wine up and running, installing new applications is no different from installing any others, as long as you remember to keep it within the Wine framework.

Before installing any new Windows application, consult the Wine Applications database at http://appdb.winehq.org. Search for the application you want to install, or browse through the categories. You'll learn here what applications have worked for those who have tried; often included are helpful comments on imperfections, problems installing, and the like. Most, if not all, entries include links to the product website. This is especially helpful for downloadable applications.

Armed with information from the database, you can then install your favorite application. To do so, insert your installation CD-ROM. Open a shell and locate the install program with ls.

```
ls /media/cdrom
```

If the install program is setup.exe, type the following to launch it in Wine:

```
wine D:\setup.exe &
```

The installation program should run the same as it would in Windows. It's probably best to accept the program's default settings during the installation. You can always experiment later.

Downloading applications in Internet Explorer and installing them is identical to the way you would do this in Windows.

## Running Wine

Starting Wine applications can be tricky. Some applications conveniently store an icon in your desktop environment's Wine menu. Others (QuickTime and Opera, for example) even place an icon on your desktop. More often, however, you are going to be working from the shell.

As indicated in the previous section, you then enter something of a land betwixt and between, including drive-letter references. To run Internet Explorer, for example, you need to type the following:

```
wine "C:\Program Files\Internet Explorer\IEXPLORE.EXE " &
```

Make sure the quotation marks, the Windows-style backslashes, the spaces, and the capitalization are all exactly as you see it here.

Two other GUI alternatives exist: The Wine package comes with a very rudimentary file manager called Winefile, and locating and launching files is all it's really good at. Unfortunately, you can't even change the display so that it shows only executables. However, the free and powerful Windows file manager, PowerDesk 5, works nicely (although somewhat imperfectly) in Wine, as you can see in Figure 11.3.

The third option for the GUI inclined is to go to your desktop environment's Control Panel and associate files with the EXE extension with Wine. You can then use Konqueror or Nautilus to locate and run your Wine applications.

## Crossover Office

Crossover Office is a commercial spinoff of the Wine Project. Codeweavers is a company founded by several Wine developers that first created the Crossover Plugin, allowing Internet Explorer plug-ins to run in all the major Linux browsers. This project was followed up with the Crossover Office suite.

Crossover Office allows its users to run Microsoft's flagship products—Office, Internet Explorer, and Visio—along with several other high-profile Windows applications. Early versions of what is now the Novell Linux Desktop (see Appendix A, "Versions of Novell's SUSE Linux," for more information about this product) included Crossover Office, although it was dropped from the current version 9.

**FIGURE 11.3**    You can manage your Wine files easily with this third-party Windows file manager, VCOM PowerDesk 5.

# Running Windows Applications with Win4Lin

Win4Lin, formerly Netraverse, is a company that delivers Windows-on-Linux products for three different audiences:

- Win4Lin 9x allows you to install and run a Windows 98 or Me virtual machine, along with any application.

- Win4Lin Home is a low-cost ($29.95) emulator that uses 64MB of RAM to run its applications.

- Win4Lin Pro is a virtual machine for Windows 2000 and XP that pledges to do for these permission-based operating systems what its sister products do for the consumer line of Windows.

You can order and download all three products directly from Win4Lin. All offer a GUI installation program.

## Installing Win4Lin

After registering and downloading the RPM package from http://www.win4lin.com, open a shell and log in as the SuperUser. Go to the directory you downloaded the package to. Type `rpm -ivh Win4LinPro-<version>.i386.rpm`. This is one of those times when the shell's file completion feature comes in handy, so entering the first few letters of the filename and then tabbing should work.

Next, you must confirm that you have a licensed copy of the target operating system (that is, Windows 95, 98, or Me for Win4Lin 9x/Home; Windows 2000 or XP for Win4Lin Pro). Insert your Windows CD into the drive. While still logged in as the SuperUser, type **loadwinproCD** (for Win4Lin Pro) or **loadwin9xCD** (for Win4Lin 9x/Home). This program will confirm your license and install the necessary components of the OS to your Linux system. You can load more than one OS using this command, provided you have the right CDs.

The third step in the installation is setting up the client environment. Log off as SuperUser and get back to a user account. Now type **installwinpro**. Win4Lin will find the version of Windows you installed and throw its configuration files in your Home directory, under /winpro/configuration (you can specify a different directory using the **-d** switch with this command). It also creates a Windows image file that is the basis for your virtual machine.

After completing the installation, you should back up the image file. Go to the /winpro directory, and type **cp GUEST.IMG GUEST.IMG.backup**. Do this periodically as well, before installing new software or updating Windows.

## Running Win4Lin

Launching Win4Lin is simple enough. From the shell, type **win** (for 9x) or **winpro** (for Pro). This will bring up the virtual machine (see Figure 11.4).

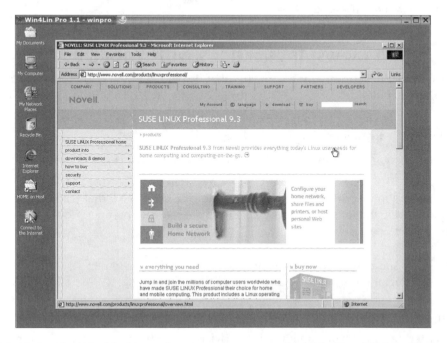

**FIGURE 11.4**    The Win4Lin Pro environment puts a complete Windows 2000 or XP virtual machine at your disposal.

Use the Winsetup tool to install new software and manage Win4Lin settings.

# Running Windows Applications with VMware

VMware Workstation 5.0 is another virtual machine (hence the VM) creator that enables you to run a variety of operating systems at the same time. VMware has separate host packages for Linux and Windows and supports clients for all varieties of Windows and several other Linux distributions. The virtual machine is complete, down to its own BIOS.

The chief problem with VMware is its resource hogginess. Even with a powerful machine with a fast processor and lots of memory, it is difficult to multitask with VMware running. The target audience for VMware primarily consists of cross-platform software developers and testers, along with system administrators. Developers can test their products on a single machine running Red Hat, Fedora Core, SUSE Linux, Novell NetWare, or any and all varieties of Windows. The system administrator can run tests to see what effect the latest Windows Service Pack or antivirus upgrade would have on their system.

This section will focus on running a Windows virtual machine on SUSE Linux.

> **TIP**
>
> Download a free 30-day trial of VMware Workstation at http://www.vmware.com/vmwarestore/newstore/wkst_eval_login.jsp.

## Installing VMware

You have a choice of installation packages for VMware Workstation, either RPM or standard tarball. You can use YaST to install the RPM or extract the tarball as the SuperUser from the shell. Consult the VMware User's Guide (available from the Documentation section of the VMware website) for instructions.

Regardless of how you do the initial package installation, you then run `vmware-config.pl`, the Perl script that will help you configure VMware's host program.

Read the configuration options carefully, but accepting the defaults is okay, too. To ensure that your virtual machines use the same network and Internet access you have with SUSE Linux, use the default Bridged Networking. `Vmware-config.pl` tells you when it has completed its task and returns the prompt to you. When it's finished, exit out of your SuperUser shell and return to the plain user prompt.

## Running VMware

The next step is running VMware and installing a guest OS. From the shell, type **vmware &** (or press Alt+F2 in your desktop environment and type **vmware**) to launch the application. You will be asked for a serial number included in your VMware box or the confirmation email for the downloaded product, and the home screen (see Figure 11.5) will appear.

> **TIP**
>
> You can also launch VMware Workstation from the KDE System menu. Look under Other Programs.

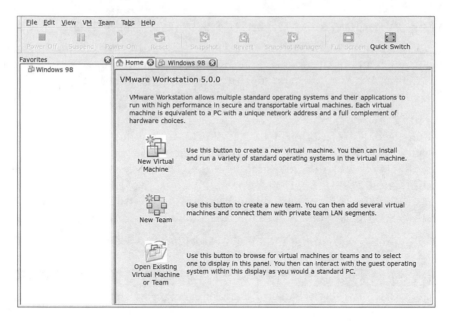

**FIGURE 11.5** Set up a new virtual machine with the VMware home screen.

Click the New Virtual Machine button to begin the process of installing the client OS. Identify the OS you want to install, set up your basic configuration, and you're set.

VMware will add a tab for this virtual machine to the main screen, looking much like Figure 11.6.

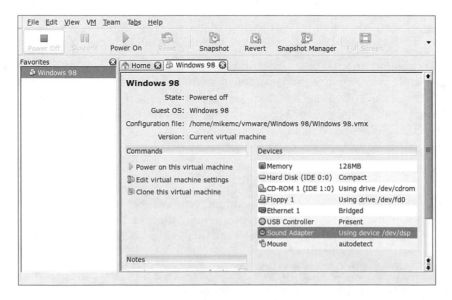

**FIGURE 11.6** When you have configured a virtual machine, use this screen to load it.

Insert the Windows CD into the drive and click Power Up. A window will open as if you have booted, and Windows will install. The virtual machine will take control of your mouse. When the installation is complete, run Windows Update so you can see what updates are required for your computer's operating system, software, and hardware.

Then press Ctrl+Alt to release your mouse back to VMware and your Linux system. Finally, click the Snapshot button to back up the new system. Do this periodically; you can use the Revert button to go back to the last Snapshot if something bad happens along the way.

To install a new application in your virtual machine, power up the VM and then insert your CD. In Windows, the CD should autorun and install as per usual. If it doesn't, run Windows Explorer and locate the installer on the CD.

Running applications may not be 100% as responsive in the VM as in a more normal environment, but it's pretty good. You will be able to discover the same errors in an application that would appear in the standard environment, which makes it good for testing. But games play well, too. See Figure 11.7.

**FIGURE 11.7**  Graphics in a VMware window are as good as anywhere.

Always remember to shut down your client operating system before exiting VMware.

## Emulating a Mac with Basilisk II

The Apple Macintosh operating system, and the computers it powers, generates intense loyalty from its many users.

Many applications programmed for the Mac are indeed great. But because the MacOS was never designed to run on Intel PC chips, building an emulator, or even a virtual machine, is a difficult task. Credit Christian Bauer, the creator of Basilisk II, a free GPLed and stable MacOS Classic emulator, with rising to the challenge.

Basilisk II works on Linux, Solaris, FreeBSD, Windows, Amiga, and BeOS and will emulate any 68K version of MacOS up to 8.1 (although a port has been written for OS X). You need a valid ROM image from your Mac to make this work. This ROM image contains several applications, including the Mac Toolbox and QuickDraw, and is otherwise indispensable.

Basilisk II supports various Mac color displays and peripheral drivers. It will also connect to the Internet and your LAN.

But the task is not for the faint of heart. You will need to create Linux-readable Mac floppies to copy the ROM image. You will need to compile Basilisk II from source. You may have to download and install a new copy of the MacOS. Fortunately, you will find an excellent companion for this journey in "Basilisk II for Linux—Getting It Going from Start to Finish," a tutorial from Marc Hoffman at http://os-emulation.net/basiliskII/ system753_tutorial/linux. An active support forum also exists at http://sourceforge.net/ forum/forum.php?forum_id=6132.

## Using dosemu and DOSBox

DOSBox and the venerable dosemu are DOS emulators you can install with YaST. dosemu can run all sorts of DOS programs, and it comes with a GPL version of DOS, called FreeDOS. DOSBox comes with a graphics package, making it particularly suitable for running games. If you are lucky enough to have a spare copy of Windows 3.x, you can install it under dosemu as well. Both applications can be installed by YaST, and DOSBox inserts itself into the KDE System menu.

dosemu is a little harder to run because it must run outside of X Window System the first time. This is done somewhat easily by launching a virtual console by pressing Ctrl+Alt+F1 (or any of the F keys except 7, which belongs to X).

You'll be asked to log in with your password as User. To launch dosemu, enter the program name **dosemu** at this shell prompt.

You'll be asked for a copy of DOS; pressing Enter will install FreeDOS. By default, your Home directory will be your C drive. You'll then be presented with your C:\ prompt and can run any default program or install your copy of WordPerfect 5.1.

When you're done with the Virtual Console, type **exit** and then press **Ctrl+Alt+F7** to return to your X desktop.

## Xen: The Future of Virtualization?

Since 2003, researchers at Cambridge University in Britain have been working on a new method of virtualizing operating systems. Their project, called Xen, reached a critical mass of support in early 2005.

Unlike VMware, which builds a complete virtual machine, Xen is a *hypervisor*, a layer that doesn't quite go that far. This technology vastly improves the performance of guest operating systems in tests to nearly native performance. This requires each OS kernel to be modified slightly to run on Xen. How SUSE Linux implements this is by using the standard kernel for a standard installation, and putting the Xen virtual machine into /var/tmp/dirinstall, and then using the bootloader application to boot to either the Xen kernel or the standard kernel.

Xen developers have ported several open source kernels, including the 2.4 and 2.6 Linux kernels, NetBSD Unix, FreeBSD Unix, and the Plan9 OS. So you can use Xen today to run several Linux distributions side by side with a copy of FreeBSD to spare. This might be entertaining for some users, but is especially useful to programmers hoping to solve distribution-related problems.

The key question for many users is whether Windows will join the list of supported OSs at some point. License restrictions prevented an early Windows XP port from being released. Intel is expected to release new processors in 2005 that will include a virtualization technology that will help Xen support Windows to some extent. You should not see all the performance you get with directly ported kernels, but the application support on these processors may well exceed Wine's.

SUSE Linux 9.3 was the first Linux distribution to include a copy of Xen, even integrating it into YaST. Open the YaST Software page and you will see the option for Installation to Directory for Xen. When you select this module, a screen very much like the initial YaST install screen (Figure 11.8) will appear.

---

**CAUTION**

Because Xen is relatively new technology, using it is not entirely for the faint of heart. You need to edit your bootloader files manually, and initialize a Xen-specific kernel. Though the risk of losing data is small, it is highly prudent to back up your data before going on this adventure.

---

Notice that the Target Directory where the Xen installation will go is var/tmp/dirinstall. This directory will host the Xen kernel and the associated virtual machine.

YaST will then check its installation source module for the location of its packages. If you have multiple sources (such as a Downloads directory for new RPMs) listed here, you may choose to disable everything but the standard install location, usually meaning your SUSE Linux CD. By default, YaST installs the Standard System with KDE, but you can install any variation of this by clicking the Change button at the bottom of this screen. When you have made your selections, click Next to begin installing the packages into the target directory.

Before trying to access this installation, however, you must edit (as the SuperUser) your /boot/grub/menu.lst file (after first backing it up). Add this entry at the bottom of the file:

```
###Add Xen to the bootlist###
title Xen 2.0
```

```
kernel (hd1,1)/xen.gz dom0_mem=393216
module (hd1,1)/vmlinuz-2.6.11.4-20a-xen root=/dev/hdb3 ro console=tty0
module (hd1,1)/initrd-2.6.11.4-20a-xen
```

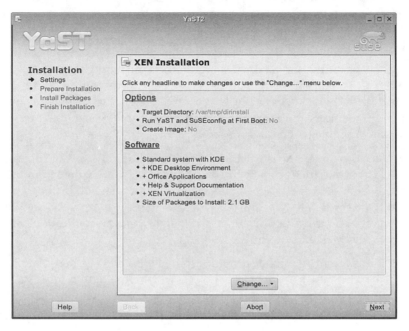

**FIGURE 11.8**    Installing SUSE Linux into a Xen directory via YaST is nearly identical to the standard installation. Use this screen to select the software to install, and to configure Xen-specific options.

Make sure that the numbers inside the (hd) parentheses are identical (1,1) to the first Linux entry, as the directory is located on the same physical hard drive. Save and exit from the editor.

SUSE Linux engineers recommend running these commands as the SuperUser in the shell:

To disable TLS support:

```
mv /lib/tls /lib/tls.disabled
```

To enable xend service:

```
chkconfig xend on
```

To enable xendomains service:

```
chkconfig xendomains on
```

Now create `/var/tmp/dirinstall/etc/fstab` with these values:

```
/dev/sda1                  /                      reiserfs    defaults 1 1
none                    /dev/pts                  devpts   gid=5,mode=620 0 0
none                    /dev/shm                  tmpfs    defaults 0 0
none                    /proc                     proc     defaults 0 0
none                    /sys                      sysfs    defaults 0 0
```

Next, initialize the Xen kernel with these commands (this will likely take some time):

```
chroot /var/tmp/dirinstall/
mkinitrd -s off
```

The `chroot` command moves you into the target directory, so your commands from that point on will apply to the Xen installation, not your running system.

When `mkinitrd` is finished, type `passwd` to assign a Root password for the Xen installation. Lastly, enter these commands to link `/proc/mounts` to `/etc/mtab`:

```
ln -s /proc/mounts /etc/mtab
echo "mount -t proc proc /proc" >> /etc/rc.d/boot.local
echo "ln -s /proc/mounts /etc/mtab" >>/etc/init.d/boot.local
```

You should now be ready to reboot your system. When grub loads the bootloader menu, select Xen 2.0 from the list. Log in as Root with your password, and you should be able to add users (including yourself), and otherwise configure your "new" system.

Xen 3.0, expected late in 2005, will add direct support for 64-bit architectures, though the current 32-bit version 2.0.5 appears to work well enough in 64-bit machines.

## References

- http://www.winehq.org—The Wine Project headquarters. Be sure to vote for your favorite Windows application to be ported using Wine in the Applications Database section.

- http://www.von-thadden.de/Joachim/WineTools—WineTools offers a relatively painless installation of Wine and a number of well-known free applications, including Internet Explorer.

- http://www.codeweavers.com—Codeweavers, Inc., the makers of Crossover Office.

- http://frankscorner.org—This site helps you get the most out of Wine. It includes FAQs and HOWTOs to get you through most problems.

- http://www.vmware.com—VMware Inc., where you can get information and a free 30-day evaluation copy of this virtual machine.

- http://www.win4lin.com—Win4Lin, helping people run Windows 98 applications and now Windows 2000/XP applications.

- http://dosbox.sourceforge.net—The DOSBox site. Check on support for your DOS game and even find downloadable copies of some ancient games.

- http://dosemu.org—The home of dosemu, the DOS emulator.

- http://freedos.org—The FreeDOS project. Assorted applications to use in DOSBox or dosemu.

- http://www.students.uni-mainz.de/bauec002/B2Main.html—Home of the Basilisk II MacOS emulator.

- http://os-emulation.net/basiliskII/system753_tutorial/linux—A tutorial on installing and running Basilisk II on Linux.

- http://www.cl.cam.ac.uk/Research/SRG/netos/xen—The Xen virtual machine monitor project home.

# PART III

## Using the Internet

## IN THIS PART

CHAPTER **12**

# Connecting to the Internet

$A$s it has over the last decade, the Internet is a prime driver of computer sales all over the world. People want to get access to the treasures of the World Wide Web, send email and instant messages to friends and family, learn more about this spam thing they keep hearing about—well, maybe not that.

With all due respect to the SUSE employees in Germany, it is difficult to imagine Linux existing without the Internet bringing together programmers from around the world to work on the kernel and all the other packages that make Linux what it is today. For that reason alone, it makes sense that making a connection to the Internet is a priority and a relatively simple proposition in SUSE Linux.

SUSE Linux provides many tools to access and manage your Internet experience. In the next few chapters, we'll go over the ways to create websites, manage email, upload and download files, and collaborate with others using Instant Messaging, mailing lists, Usenet news, Wikis, and video conferencing.

In this chapter, we will focus on the basics of getting connected, be it through an ordinary dial-up modem or a high-speed Digital Subscriber Line (DSL).

## Basic Connectivity Information

If you already have an Internet connection running under Windows, it is best to gather some information beforehand to make your Linux Internet setup go a little easier. There are still not enough Linux users for many ISPs to pay attention to. Some ISPs remain ignorant of or hostile to the

Linux users they already have. This leads to a general lack of Linux support, especially from the main players.

This means you are not likely to get a shiny CD from your ISP with everything to get you started, but YaST will be there as always to handle that function. The things you need to know most are the following:

- How your IP address is determined—Static or Dynamic (DHCP).

- The IP address(es) for your Domain Name System (DNS) server, especially for dynamic connections.

- The DNS names and IP addresses for your mail and news servers.

- The dial-up phone number for your ISP if you're using a dial-up connection.

- Your credentials, such as your username and password.

Every computer connected to the Internet must have a unique Internet Protocol (IP) address. If everyone who wanted to connect to the Internet required a unique machine to provide that IP address, an ISP would have to buy a separate machine with a separate IP address for every subscriber. Because that is not feasible, and because most people use a dial-up connection that is not always on, a solution was worked out. The vast majority of standard ISP connections use the Dynamic Host Configuration Protocol (DHCP) to assign each logged-in user with an unoccupied server.

> **NOTE**
>
> You'll learn more about TCP/IP and DHCP networking in Chapter 25, "Setting Up Networks and Samba."

An ISP will then get a range of IP addresses that allow it to connect to the Internet. As a user about to configure your system, you may need to find out what that range is. Often this will be in your ISP's documentation booklet. If it's not there and you have a Windows XP box already connected, check the Network Connections in your Control Panel. You should see your connection listed. Double-click to open it, and then click the Support tab. This will tell you whether you are using DHCP for access or DNS service and should tell you all the necessary IP address(es).

You can also get to this information from a Windows command prompt. Go to Programs, Accessories, and then Command Prompt. Type **ipconfig** and you will get the IP Address, Subnet Mask, and Default Gateway addresses. This command is the Windows analog to the Linux `ifconfig` utility, which you will learn more about in the next section and in Chapter 25.

> **NOTE**
>
> Depending on your ISP, the range may not be required to make your connection.

If you have a high-speed connection, you may receive a static IP, but even these are often handled by DHCP. Regardless of your connection type, many ISPs will offer you a static IP address, for a price. Unless you want to directly host a server (mail, FTP, DNS), this is not required.

# Starting with a `localhost` Interface

Before setting up any kind of Internet connection, you'll need to create a dummy interface that the TCP/IP protocol uses to determine the network capability of your machine. This is called the *loopback (lo) interface*, or `localhost`. Many network-aware applications reference this interface as well, so it is important.

What is a loopback interface? To a Linux networking driver, this is a network composed of exactly one computer. The kernel loops back network traffic to and from itself using the 127.0.0.1 IP address.

SUSE Linux should create the `localhost` interface during the initial installation. To confirm this, open a root console and run the `ifconfig` utility to identify your setup. Running this command should generate a response similar to this:

```
lo        Link encap:Local Loopback
          inet addr:127.0.0.1  Mask:255.0.0.0
          inet6 addr: ::1/128 Scope:Host
          UP LOOPBACK RUNNING  MTU:16436  Metric:1
          RX packets:2187 errors:0 dropped:0 overruns:0 frame:0
          TX packets:2187 errors:0 dropped:0 overruns:0 carrier:0
          collisions:0 txqueuelen:0
          RX bytes:114362 (111.6 Kb)  TX bytes:114362 (111.6 Kb)
```

This output tells you that the local loopback interface is active and is assigned the standard IP address for local connections, 127.0.0.1, and a broadcast mask of 255.0.0.0 is used. You even take a small peek into the future, as this version of ifconfig lists an Ipv6 address of `::1/128`. This next version of the Internet Protocol (IP version 6) offers exponentially more IP address space than the existing IP version 4.

## Configuring `localhost` Manually

In the off chance `localhost` was not created during your SUSE Linux installation, it is easy to do yourself.

The `localhost` interface address is stored in a text file called `/etc/hosts`. This file stores all network IP address and hostname information. The kernel and other network utilities reads this to understand how this computer is connected to others.

> **TIP**
>
> You can also access and edit the Hosts file in YaST. Go to `Network Services`, then `Hosts`. Add, edit, or delete hosts here.

When you open this file, you will see a comment that describes the file and the syntax you should follow: IP-Address [tab] Full-Qualified-Hostname [tab] Short-Hostname.

If localhost is not already there, you may add this line:

**127.0.0.1        localhost**

You can leave the Short-Hostname blank. Save and exit. Reopen your root console and use ifconfig and route to create the interface:

**ifconfig lo 127.0.0.1**

This puts the localhost interface in memory, as with all other Linux network interfaces, like an Ethernet (eth0) or dial-up (ppp0) interface.

**route add 127.0.0.1 lo**

This adds the IP address to a routing table the kernel's networking code uses to track routes to different addresses.

Test the new connection by running **ifconfig** again.

You should now be able to run your own loopback test by trying to ping localhost. You should see something like this (we'll use the -c option to count out 3 packets to send):

```
 # ping -c 3 localhost
PING localhost (127.0.0.1) 56(84) bytes of data.
64 bytes from localhost (127.0.0.1): icmp_seq=1 ttl=64 time=0.087 ms
64 bytes from localhost (127.0.0.1): icmp_seq=2 ttl=64 time=0.087 ms
64 bytes from localhost (127.0.0.1): icmp_seq=3 ttl=64 time=0.081 ms

--- localhost ping statistics ---
3 packets transmitted, 3 received, 0% packet loss, time 2000ms
rtt min/avg/max/mdev = 0.081/0.085/0.087/0.003 ms
```

We have completed our prerequisites; now it's time to take on the main course.

# Configuring Your Dial-up Internet Connection

Setting up a dial-up Internet connection under Linux used to be somewhat difficult without a deep knowledge of computer hardware, but YaST has greatly simplified this for the SUSE Linux user.

When you set up a dial-up connection, you're really just using several Internet standard protocols to enable your modem to connect to the ISP through an ordinary phone line. Most dial-up Internet connections use the Point-to-Point Protocol (PPP) because ISPs have found it a fast, efficient way to use TCP/IP over serial (that is, modem) lines. PPP is designed for two-way networking. The TCP/IP protocol suite moves the data.

If you couldn't really conceive of Linux as a successful operating system without the Internet, why was it so hard to set up a dial-up connection in Linux? It's true that Unix (and its Linux cousin) was network-aware from the very beginning, but these were assumed to be machines networked with wires and cards that could have static IP addresses. These workstations were located at research universities, corporate offices, and science labs, where users might log off the network, but the computer would always be there. Unix (and Linux) wasn't ready for computers that had intermittent connections. The protocols for personal computers to connect were kludged together and eventually made to work.

You may not need to entirely understand PPP anymore to dial up to the Internet, but following is a quick primer.

Setting up a dial-up connection is really installing the pppd daemon on your system. This daemon controls the use of PPP. Launching your connection runs two other processes.

The high-level data link control (HDLC) protocol controls the flow of information between your computer and your ISP's server, and the chat routine communicates with the modem, dials the number, and reports on the status of your connection (or occasional lack thereof).

If you want to confirm that pppd is installed, log in as SuperUser (**su**) and run **pppd** with the **--help** argument. You'll see the many parameters you can use to tune your connection, but veering from the defaults can be risky.

> **CAUTION**
>
> Some modems still have a software interface that will not work under Linux. See Chapter 2, "Preparing to Install SUSE Linux," for more information on Winmodems.

## Using YaST to Set Up Your Dial-up Connection

YaST's Network Devices section manages setup wizards for several types of network connections:

- Modem
- Network card
- ISDN
- Fax
- Phone answering machine
- DSL

Although very similar, there are some distinctions. In this section, we'll cover the modem connection. The DSL connection will be in the next section, and the other networking protocols will be covered in Chapter 25.

Begin by opening YaST. In KDE, go to the Kicker menu and choose System, then YaST. You'll be asked for the Root password and YaST will load. Click Network Devices. You'll see the six items previously listed. Click Modem to set up your connection.

YaST should have detected your modem, but you can easily do this if it hasn't. Click Configure under the top screen to launch the Modem Wizard. The first screen should look like Figure 12.1.

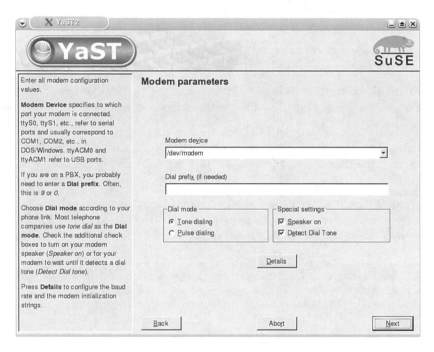

**FIGURE 12.1**    The first modem configuration screen sets the mount point and dial mode.

This screen sets the mount point for the modem and a few initial settings. Using the default /dev/modem mount point is the easiest and should always work, but you can choose a different point from the drop-down menu. If you are in an office where you need to dial 9 to make an outside call, set the Dial Prefix. Modern phone systems nearly always use Tone dialing, so don't change this setting unless you are certain. If you don't like to hear the white noise that accompanies a connecting modem, turn the speaker off (although while you're doing the initial setup, it's a good idea to leave it on until you have confirmed that everything is working properly). If you have call waiting or some other service that changes your dial tone, you may want to uncheck the Detect Dial Tone box so the modem always dials. Only check the Details button if you need to change the default initialization string. When you're finished, click Next to set up your ISP. YaST pulls up a list of Providers in several countries that you can select from. In Figure 12.2, we've selected Earthlink as our provider. Notice that the screen displays the provider's website and support line. If your provider is not listed, click New to add it. Click Next to identify the phone number and other access settings.

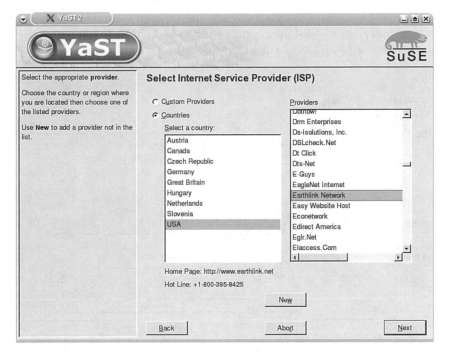

**FIGURE 12.2**    Select your ISP from the list of providers or click New to add yours.

Figure 12.3 shows the ISP configuration screen. You should know at least one local access number for your ISP. Enter it here, along with your username and password. If you want to enter your ISP password each time you dial up, check the Always Ask for Password box. Click Next to configure your connection.

The final configuration screen (see Figure 12.4) defines how you want to manage your connection. The key question to answer here is whether you want applications to be able to start a dial-up connection. This can be a nice thing when you ask your mail client to check mail and it dials up, but can be annoying if, for example, SUSEWatcher wants to check for system updates at 2 a.m. daily and the modem speaker wakes you up. It is also not good if your ISP charges by the minute and an automatic connection does not hang up after completing its task.

By default, Dial on Demand is turned off. Check the box to activate this feature. You need to identify at least one name server (which you should have from your ISP).

Check the Activate Firewall box to prevent all incoming connections from attacking your computer. The Idle Timeout tells how long to wait for a dead connection to revive. By default, if the modem receives no data from the server for five minutes (300 seconds), it will hang up. You can adjust this time to be longer or shorter using the drop-down menu. Setting the Timeout at 0 means the modem will never hang up unless you tell it to.

If you have a static IP address, click the IP Details button to configure it. Uncheck the Dynamic IP box, and enter the static IP address in the Local IP Address box. Click OK to return to the previous screen. Click Next to complete the setup. You should now see your modem and provider listed in the appropriate windows. Should you have multiple ISPs, you must configure each separately. Click Add to start the wizard again.

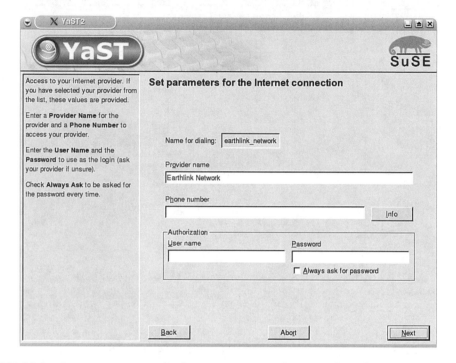

**FIGURE 12.3**    Enter your access number, username, and password on this screen.

When you click Finish, your new settings will be saved and you'll be asked to set up your mail account. See Chapter 15, "Managing Email Servers," for the details of this setup.

Test your new connection in KDE by running KInternet, or in GNOME by running GNOME PPP. It should use the new settings to dial up your ISP and get you going.

---

**TIP**

Another way to test your modem is through a terminal program such as `minicom`. This program is not installed by default, but if you are having problems connecting with your ISP, running `minicom` can help you troubleshoot problems with your modem.

Install `minicom` through YaST, and then run `minicom` from the shell with the `-s` argument to set your modem's serial port:

```
minicom -s
```

Tell `minicom` which serial port your modem is using, and then return to the main screen. Now you can send AT commands (check your modem documentation for examples) and see how the modem responds.

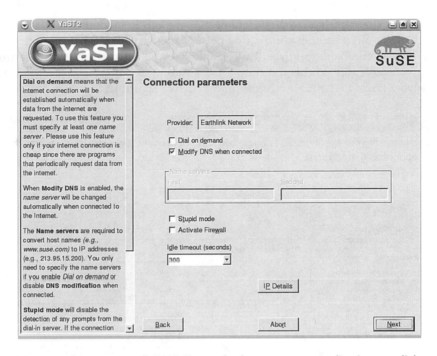

**FIGURE 12.4**  In this screen, tell SUSE Linux whether you want applications to dial-up automatically or only when you ask.

# Configuring a Digital Subscriber Line (DSL) Connection

SUSE Linux supports all flavors of DSL connections, and they can all be set up in the YaST DSL configuration dialog boxes. DSL service generally provides 128KBps to 1.0MBps transfer speeds, transmitting over copper phone lines from a Central Office (CO) to individual subscribers, like you. Many DSL services offer asymmetric speeds, usually offering higher download speeds than upload.

DSL connections require you to have an Ethernet network interface card (NIC) in your computer. If you have multiple computers on a LAN that want to share the connection, you'll need to have at least one other NIC on the machine managing the connection.

Depending on your ISP, you may have a static IP address or use DHCP to assign a new IP address; it also uses a slightly different protocol called PPP Over Ethernet (PPPoE). This is difficult to configure manually through the shell, but YaST greatly simplifies this task.

## Using YaST to Set Up Your DSL Connection

Setting up a DSL connection in YaST is very similar to setting up a modem connection. Begin by opening YaST. In KDE, go to the Kicker menu and choose System, then YaST. You'll be asked for the Root password and YaST will load. Click Network Devices. Click DSL to set up your connection.

The hardware devices involved in a DSL connection are a DSL modem and a network card (usually Ethernet). YaST handles configuring both of these in a DSL Devices page. When you open the DSL configuration page, YaST should have detected your devices during the install, but you can easily do this if it hasn't. Click Add under the top screen to launch the DSL Device Wizard. The first screen should look like Figure 12.5.

> **NOTE**
>
> To check or edit your existing DSL settings, select the device and click Edit. It will display the same options as the Add screen.

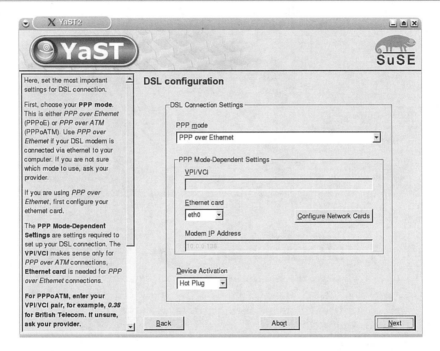

**FIGURE 12.5**    The first DSL configuration screen lets you identify the type of connection and the Ethernet card.

By default, YaST selects PPP Over Ethernet as the default PPP Mode. If your Ethernet card is not listed, you will need to set it up. Click Configure Network Cards to do so.

At first, you will see the overview screen. Figure 12.6 shows you this dialog box. If your card is not listed, click Add to open the configuration dialog box.

The configuration dialog box (see Figure 12.7) sets up your DSL card. It should be labeled as either `eth0` or `eth1`, depending on whether you have an Ethernet LAN card installed in addition to the DSL card.

Setting up for a static IP address is easy. Click the appropriate option button and enter your primary address and subnet mask. If your ISP uses DHCP to set addresses on bootup, you will need to configure other items on this screen.

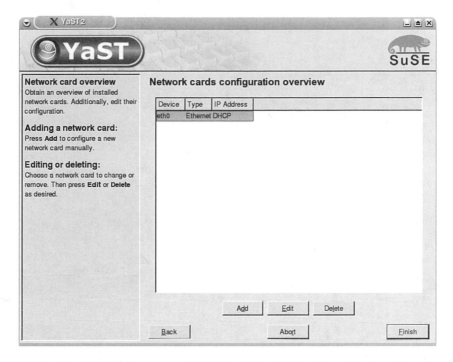

**FIGURE 12.6** Use the Edit button on the Network Cards Configuration Overview page to change the existing settings for your DSL card, or use Add to define a new or undetected card.

Click DHCP Client Options and confirm that Host Name to Send is set to AUTO unless your ISP has specified a hostname. If your card is acting as a router, you may also want to look at the Routing page. You want to enable IP forwarding in this case.

Click Next to save your settings and return to the Network Card overview page, and click Finish to return to the DSL Setup page. When you're finished setting up your hardware, click Next to set up your ISP.

YaST pulls up a much smaller list of DSL Providers in several countries that you may select from in a screen like the one shown in Figure 12.2. If your provider is not listed, click New to add it. Click Next to set your username and password.

Figure 12.8 shows the ISP configuration screen. Enter your username and password. A DSL connection is always on, but when you reboot, the connection is dropped. If you want to enter your ISP password each time you connect, check the Always Ask for Password box. Click Next to configure your connection.

The final DSL provider configuration screen, which is identical to Figure 12.4, defines how you want to manage your connection. There is no real need to set up Dial on Demand, as you are always on. Similarly, you need not worry about the Idle Timeout setting. Do check the Activate Firewall box to prevent all incoming connections from attacking your computer.

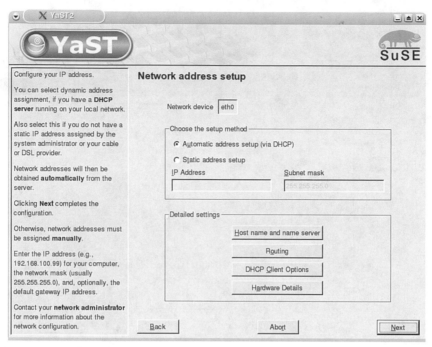

**FIGURE 12.7**    Configure your DSL Ethernet Card with this dialog box.

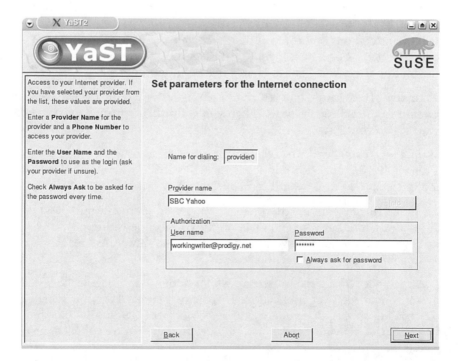

**FIGURE 12.8**    Enter your username and password on this screen.

If you have a static IP address, click the IP Details button to configure this. Uncheck the Dynamic IP box and enter the static IP address in the Local IP Address box. Click OK to return to the previous screen. Click Next to complete the setup.

> **NOTE**
>
> For static addresses, make sure the PPP Mode is set for standard PPP, not PPPoE.

When you click Finish, your new settings will be saved and you'll be asked to set up your mail account. See Chapter 15 for the details of this setup.

## Connecting Your Computer to a Wireless Network

So you're traveling with your SUSE Linux laptop and want to connect to your hotel's wireless network. This can be a problem, but the hurdles can be overcome.

You have basically three problems to deal with when trying to connect to a wireless network:

- Making sure your card is supported, and the proper drivers and firmware are in place.

- Locating the access point.

- Configuring a profile.

This section will cover each of these issues.

### Getting Firmware and Drivers in Place

The first issue can be the easiest to solve. Linux supports many different wireless cards, although not always with every feature that the card supports. Firmware (system code that communicates directly with the card) often must be downloaded separately from a Linux distribution. You can download firmware for ACX100, ACX111, and PrismQT cards directly through YaST Online Update, but these packages do not come with the distribution.

Most wireless card manufacturers still produce only Windows drivers, which can present a major headache for non-Windows users. Too often this requires manual setup and configuration of your network configuration file, `ifcfg-eth2`. This task, however, has been simplified. A second package, `ndiswrapper`, installable through YaST lets you use the Windows drivers directly in Linux.

To make this work, you need the *.inf driver file. If your laptop dual-boots, this file is likely in the \Windows\System folder. It may also have come on a CD with the card, and is otherwise downloadable from the manufacturer's website.

Once you have the INF file, open a shell as the SuperUser, and navigate to the directory where the INF file is. Run this command to confirm that `ndiswrapper` can identify the driver:

```
ndiswrapper -l <driverfilename>.inf
```

You should see a message confirming that `ndis` installed, and the driver is present.

Now you need to make the kernel recognize the driver. This is done through `modprobe`.

```
modprobe ndiswrapper
```

The final step is to add these two commands to your `rc.local` configuration file. The kernel will now load the driver each time at boot.

## Finding an Access Point

Ideally with your drivers in place, you should now be able to scan the area for a nearby access point. If your wireless interface point is `eth2`, you can just type `iwlist eth2 scan` from the shell. You would then need to use `iwconfig` to configure your connection.

There is a KDE tool that can simplify this process, however. The Wireless Assistant will perform the scan and connect you. Download the Wireless Assistant SUSE Linux package from http://linux01.gwdg.de/~pbleser/rpm-navigation.php?cat=/Network/wlassistant and install it through YaST. You can also use apt if you have the suser-guru repository in your `sources.list`.

Launch Wireless Assistant from the KDE Kicker menu, or run it from the shell with **wlassistant**. The first time, it checks for your active network card. The card name should appear in the Device line at the top of the Wireless Assistant screen. It will then scan the area for access points, and display the results of the scan in the main window. Look carefully, as you will also learn the quality of the wireless signal with a star ranking. The WEP column indicates whether a connection supports the relatively secure Wireless Encryption Protocol. This requires a password, but is still a big improvement over allowing open access to whatever comes across the network transom (including any passwords you may send out while you're surfing the Web).

Click the access point you want, and you will be prompted for the Root password on your system. Enter it, click OK, and you're connected.

## Configuring Your Wireless Card

YaST can help you connect to your wireless network as well. If you know the network you want to connect to, using YaST will set things up for you. In YaST, go to Network Devices, then Wireless Network Card. Figure 12.9 will appear.

**FIGURE 12.9**    Configure your wireless card to connect to a stable network here.

At the top of the screen is the network Operating Mode. Nearly all the time, you want to choose Managed mode, as this is a connection with a wireless access point. An ad-hoc network is a peer-to-peer setup with no access point, and Master mode sets up your machine as an access point.

The next line indicates the name of the network you want to connect to. In wireless networking, access points are identified with an Extended Service Set Identifier (ESSID). You should enter the name of your network here, otherwise the card will select the first access point it finds.

The last section deals with authenticating yourself to the network. There are three types of wireless networks, "open" networks that are open to anyone (and that means anyone) without authentication. Generally speaking, you want to leave these networks to the bad guys who will invariably find them. WEP, or "shared key" authentication, is the prevalent, if not superior, option with many wireless networks. When severe holes were found in WEP, a new secure protocol was developed for wireless networks, WiFI Protected Access (WPA). This protocol is still not widely used, but is supported by the Linux kernel and SUSE Linux.

Select the appropriate protocol from the Authentication Mode drop-down menu, then define your pass-key using the mode buttons and the Encryption Key edit box. Selecting a passphrase is the best way to proceed, if you want to have more control over your security. If you select Passphrase, enter a word or a character string from which a key is generated according to the length previously specified. ASCII requests an input of 5 characters for a 64-bit key and 13 characters for a 128-bit key. For Hexadecimal, enter 10 characters for a 64-bit key or 26 characters for a 128-bit key in hexadecimal notation.

---

**TIP***

Tips on creating passwords and passphrases are located in Chapter 19, "Managing Users, Managing Security."

---

You may keep up to four different keys to encrypt the transmitted data. Click Multiple Keys to enter the key configuration dialog. By default, this is set for 128-bit security, but you can lower the level to 64 bit here (not that you should).

In the list area at the bottom of the dialog, up to four different keys can be specified for your computer to use for the encryption. Press Set as Default to define one of them as the default key. Unless you change this, YaST uses the first entered key as the default key. If the standard key is deleted, one of the other keys must be marked manually as the default key.

You should now be successfully connected to your wireless network.

## When to Call Your Internet Service Provider

The lack of official Linux support by the big players in the Internet access business can be a problem, but it can be sidestepped. Many connection problems can be solved by carefully reviewing the documentation in the YaST windows. Others can be solved by the many HOWTO documents at the Linux Documentation Project site, including the ones listed in the Reference section that follows. As always, consult with your Linux User Group (see the "Getting Help: Documentation and Other Sources," section in Chapter 1: "Welcome to SUSE Linux,") to identify Linux-friendly ISPs in your neighborhood.

Dial-up connection problems are usually temporary or involve user error. So before you harass the tech support folks, make sure you haven't fallen into one of these traps.

- If you connect but can't log in successfully, your password could be mistyped. Remember that passwords are case sensitive.

- If the phone number and password are both right, but you still can't log in, check the authentication protocol.

- If nothing works, check the power cords. Is the modem plugged in and connected to the PC with the right jack in the right hole? Things do come loose.

- If everything works properly under Windows on your dual-boot system, but nothing works in Linux, you probably have a Winmodem. Try the Linmodem drivers, or go out and buy a hardware modem.

- This one's good for both dial-up and DSL: If nothing works, and it worked a few minutes/hours ago, and there's no smoke coming out of your machine, it could be a problem at the ISP. If it's a big ISP, they'll know about a glitch quickly. If they're a mom-and-pop local operation, call to report if it just happened; otherwise, give them some time to fix it. Call if the problem persists for hours.

- If you log in okay, but can't browse the Web, it could be a DNS problem. Double-check your DHCP settings and then contact the ISP.

When you contact your ISP, and you know they don't support Linux, try to explain the context of the problem outside of the operating system. It helps to know the Windows counterparts of the Linux (or YaST) dialog boxes you're working with (the Internet Connection Wizard, Network Neighborhood, and the like).

## References

- http://www.tldp.org/HOWTO/HOWTO-INDEX/hardware.html#IIWMODEMS—Linux Documentation Project modems HOWTOs. What you need to know, sometimes in excruciating detail, about ordinary modems, Winmodems, DSL modems, and cable modems. Some of it is outdated, but the revision dates are always posted here.

- http://axion.physics.ubc.ca/ppp-linux.html—Trying to set up PPP manually? This is the place to go, as W. G. Unruh has worked hard to troubleshoot many PPP problems.

- http://cdb.suse.de—The SUSE Hardware database. Check here to see if your modem is officially supported. If your DSL modem is not listed here, don't assume that it won't work. There are not many to choose from.

- http://linmodems.org—A place to learn about software-driven "Winmodems" and attempts to support them in Linux.

- http://start.at/modem— Winmodems Are Not Modems. A large list of modem models to check for Linux compatibility.

- http://www.swcp.com/~jgentry/pers.html—The Linux Dialin Server Setup Guide. A step-by-step approach to setting up your dial-in server.

# Using the Internet: Browsing the Web and Writing Email

When most of us talk about using the Internet, we're usually talking about one of two things: browsing the World Wide Web or reading and sending electronic mail. For some people, these two things are the reason to have a computer in their home. As an operating system that largely owes its success to the existence of the Internet, email and the Web are things Linux does very well.

This and the next few chapters cover SUSE Linux and the Internet. Here you will learn about your many choices in browsing the Web and managing email in SUSE Linux. After that, you'll learn about helping to create the World Wide Web by making a basic website. In later chapters, we'll cover email in depth, show you how to use the net to collaborate with others, transfer files, and administer a web server.

There is a lot of things to do on the Internet, and SUSE Linux is here to help you make the most of it.

## Choosing a Web Browser

Chances are pretty good that you have some experience with browsing the web and don't need anyone to tell you how to do that.

You should know, however, that several browsers are available to you in SUSE Linux. All are under active development and are more secure than Microsoft Internet Explorer (IE). Many folks involved in computer security have urged users to switch from IE, but here's the kicker. In June 2004, the U.S. Computer Emergency Response Team (CERT) issued this recommendation (which is still active at press time): "There are a number of significant vulnerabilities in technologies relating to the IE domain/zone security model, local file system (Local Machine Zone) trust, the Dynamic HTML (DHTML) document object model (in particular, proprietary DHTML features), the HTML Help system, MIME type determination, the graphical user interface (GUI), and ActiveX. It is possible to reduce exposure to these vulnerabilities by using a different web browser, especially when viewing untrusted HTML documents (e.g., web sites, HTML email messages)." (http://www.kb.cert.org/vuls/id/713878)

Here's a quick rundown of names and features.

## Mozilla and Mozilla Firefox

The best known and most popular Linux browsers. As Netscape Communicator, the Mozilla suite was the first dominant commercial browser. Its developers eventually got the open source religion and the suite became the first prominent commercial application to be open-sourced in 1998. While it took over four years to get to the Mozilla 1.0 release, it quickly became the default Linux browser. The v1.7 suite (incidentally the last to bear the Mozilla name) includes an email client, an address book, chat client, and an HTML editor. You can access the other parts of the suite by clicking the appropriate icon in the lower left corner of the browser window.

Some Mozilla developers began to believe that the suite was overkill, and that more people wanted a simple browser that would load quickly and not take up so much memory. The first test version of this browser, then called Phoenix, was released in September 2002. After going through a few name changes and several beta versions, Mozilla Firefox 1.0 came out on November 9, 2004. In its first 99 days, more than 25 million copies of Firefox (for all operating systems) were downloaded.

Both current versions of Mozilla and Firefox offer tabbed browsing (no more separate browser windows unless you want them), effective (and selective) popup ad blockers, and support for RSS and Atom "webfeeds." The latter lets you create "Live Bookmarks" for blogs and other sites that deliver continuing updates. Look for the square orange icon in the lower right corner of Figure 13.1.

Firefox is now installed by default in SUSE Linux, as the Mozilla suite used to be (it's still available via YaST). It remains a quick loading application, but its modular design lets you make it more powerful through the use of extensions. You can get a sense for the variety of these extensions by looking at the Popular Extensions page at Mozilla.org (https://addons.mozilla.org/extensions/showlist.php?application=firefox&category=Popular). These include toolbars for Google and Yahoo searches, the ForecastFox local weather report, the FlashGot download utility, and the StumbleUpon web-surfing utility.

The Mozilla Suite (Figure 13.2) also supports extensions, but its developer community is not as active. In March 2005, the Mozilla Foundation announced that formal development of the suite would end with the 1.7.8 version, but that a new community would continue development of the suite, now called SeaMonkey.

**FIGURE 13.1**    Mozilla Firefox reignited the browser wars in 2004, and is the favorite of many Linux users.

**FIGURE 13.2**    Hail Mighty Mozilla! This browser suite brought forth Firefox, and a host of other Linux browsers.

The open-sourcing of the Netscape/Mozilla browser allowed other developers to create their own visions of a Linux browser. So in many ways, we can thank that team for so much.

## Konqueror

Your KDE file manager is also a fully functional web browser. Click the globe-ish looking icon in the KDE taskbar and Konqueror will open in Web Browsing mode (Figure 13.3). It is also the default KDE browser (though you can change that in the KDE Control Center), so clicking links in most other programs in KDE will open Konqueror. Based on the speedy Mozilla Gecko rendering engine, it also offers excellent cookie management to protect your privacy on the Web.

**FIGURE 13.3**    Konqueror, the KDE web browsing and file management king.

Konqueror is not a perfect browser. It does not import Mozilla or Firefox extensions, though it imports bookmarks and multimedia plug-ins quite well. Text files found on the Web can appear in an editor window, which can make navigation troublesome. If you happen to have a file-manager window open and then open a URL, chances are the browser will open in a new tab in the file-manager window. You then have to detach the tab through the context menu. Some sites, including Novell's, display somewhat strangely. Yet overall, it provides an excellent experience.

---

**TIP**

Maybe the best thing about Konqueror is its bookmark management tool. It is simple to catego-rize your bookmarks as you create them. Konqueror also imports bookmarks from IE, Mozilla, and Opera, making it easy to integrate all your bookmarks in one place, even if you aren't consistently loyal to one browser.

But if you've ever tried to prune your extensive bookmarks list, wishing to remove sites that may not have survived the dot-com era, Konqueror could just be a godsend. In the Bookmark manager, there's a tool that will visit all your bookmarks and let you know if they are still active. This can take some time, but it's well-spent if you have a lot of dead links.

## Epiphany

The default GNOME browser (Figure 13.4) also runs on the Mozilla Gecko engine and has many of the same great features, and a few of its own. It comes with a package of optional extensions and will also run Mozilla extensions.

**FIGURE 13.4**    Epiphany, the GNOME default browser.

Epiphany's developers are keen on building a simple, usable browser. To that end, bookmarks in Epiphany can be placed in multiple categories, and the interface is as clean and customizable as GNOME's.

## Galeon

Galeon begat Epiphany, and the two remain similar, but it has its own nuances. Galeon (Figure 13.5) seeks to be a power user's browser. Google Groups and Image search can be found in the toolbar. Galeon also has excellent cookie and pop-up management for added security. You can go to a website and use the Galeon web menu to approve cookies or pop-ups at that site.

**FIGURE 13.5**    Galeon on the surface looks a lot like Epiphany, but is designed for the power user.

Development on Galeon has suffered somewhat since Galeon's founder, Marco Gritti, left to build Epiphany, but 21 minor versions of Galeon 1.3 have been released in recent years. You can tweak Galeon's preferences extensively, but you'll need a text editor to make most of your changes.

## Opera

This commercial browser (see Figure 13.6), which includes a small advertising window, is responsible for many of the innovations the browsing public now takes for granted. Opera first employed the idea of tabbed browsing, with multiple sites displayed within a single browser window, pop-up ad blocking, strict adherence to standards, and (to somewhat lesser acclaim) advertising-supported software. Though Opera has long sought to support most operating systems, its Linux browser was not released until 2003.

The current version 8.0 includes an email client that also displays RSS feeds (see the weblogging section of Chapter 14, "Creating Basic Websites," for more on RSS) and an Internet Relay Chat (IRC) client. Unfortunately, many sites still don't render properly (and sometimes not at all) in Opera. This has always been a barrier to its adoption.

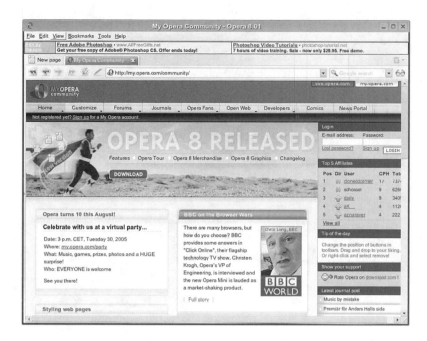

**FIGURE 13.6**    Opera brings its clean look and standards-based engine to Linux.

## Setting Up Your SUSE Linux Email Account

In Chapter 12, "Connecting to the Internet," we covered your modem setup in YaST. After your modem is configured, YaST asks to configure your mail account. This wizard configures your MTA.

If you say Yes to configuring the account, YaST opens the MTA configuration window with something like Figure 13.7.

> **NOTE**
>
> You can also open this wizard from the YaST Network Services page.

By default, YaST enables the default antivirus program, AMaViS. It also lets you set the connection type, based on your earlier setup. If you have an always-on broadband (DSL, cable modem) connection, this should be set as Permanent. Otherwise, select Dial-Up. Click Next to continue.

The Outgoing Mail screen (Figure 13.8) configures Postfix. Start by identifying your SMTP server, which your ISP should provide. You should not need to use the Masquerading features, which allow you to modify the server name in your From line. The Authentication screen lets you identify your ISP Login information if that is required to send mail. Click Next to continue.

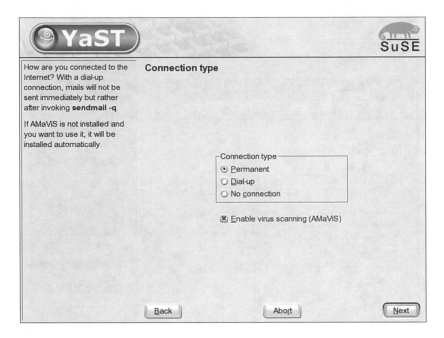

**FIGURE 13.7**    The first YaST mail configuration screen lets you enable the default antivirus program, AMaViS.

> **TIP**
>
> For more information on Masquerading and Authentication, see "MTA Configuration" in Chapter 15, "Managing Email Servers."

The Incoming Mail screen configures Fetchmail. At the top, name your incoming mail (POP3 or IMAP4) server, which you should get from your ISP. Include your login information to simplify getting your mail. Use this screen to identify what local user has access to this account. If you want to tweak your account information to assist Fetchmail, click Details. Point the root mail account to the SuperUser here as well, so that messages coming to root@localhost get seen in your mailbox. Then, set the delivery mode to Procmail if you want to take advantage of this Mail Delivery Agent (MDA) that will aid in the battle against spam (more on this later). Click Finish to save your settings.

> **NOTE**
>
> You can set up your mail account(s) in your mail client if you prefer. YaST will configure only one mail account on a single machine. You will need to configure accounts in the client if you have multiple users or multiple mail accounts.
>
> Configuration screens will differ somewhat in each mail client. But you will always need the same information from your ISP listed here.

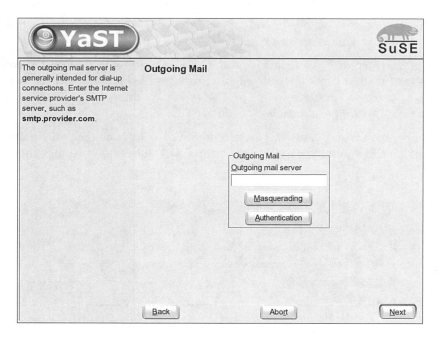

**FIGURE 13.8**    Name your SMTP server on the Outgoing Mail screen.

## Choosing a Mail Client (Mail User Agent)

People spend a lot of time with their email programs. Many get to know their quirks and foibles as well as those of any human being around them. Attachments develop, as do love/hate relationships. Take Microsoft Outlook, for example. Nearly everyone has used it at one time or another.

Maybe you've never used anything but Outlook, but you're now thrown into the Linux world, either by choice or by corporate fiat. Maybe you're a little nervous about the change. Don't be. If you like the way Outlook does things, you can get something that mimics the same Outlook experience that you are accustomed to.

If you've left the Microsoft reservation and want something different, how about a text-based mail client like mutt or pine, or Emacs mail? Want a calendar/to-do list function in your mail client? Sure. Want a Usenet (or RSS) newsreader? You can do that, too. As always, you have choices.

In this section, you will become familiar with the leading Linux email programs: Evolution, Kmail/KOrganizer/Kontact, Mozilla Mail/Thunderbird, Sylpheed, and mutt. Choose one that fits your style and your needs.

### Evolution

Evolution was written by Nat Friedman and the Ximian team to be the Linux alternative to Outlook. Although it is not a reverse-engineering effort, Evolution looks and behaves as much like Outlook as possible. In one package, you have an integrated mail client, a calendar, a to-do list, and an address book.

Evolution was written by Nat Friedman and the Ximian team to be the Linux alternative to Outlook. Although it is not a reverse-engineering effort, Evolution looks and behaves as much like Outlook as possible. In one package, you have an integrated mail client, a calendar, a task list, and an address book (Contacts).

Setting up Evolution is very easy, with a wizard to walk you through the entire process. To set up an email account, type in your name and email address to get things going (Figure 13.9).

**FIGURE 13.9** Setting up basic email information.

Click Forward and select your server type from the drop-down menu. As you can see in Figure 13.10, Evolution supports a variety of mail servers: POP, IMAP, and GroupWise, along with Usenet News.

Click Forward to fill in the third wizard screen (Figure 13.11). Enter the name of your email server in the Host box, and your email account's username. If you want Evolution to remember your ISP password (at the risk of unauthorized people reading and writing email under your name), check the Remember Password box.

Click Forward again. The last Receive Mail setup screen (Figure 13.12) gives you some options: whether Evolution should check mail automatically, and how often; whether to leave retrieved mail on the server (good if your ISP offers a lot of space on the server and web access to your mail); and whether to disable extensions to the POP3 standard. These extensions are rarely needed.

FIGURE 13.10    Select the type of mail server you are connecting to.

FIGURE 13.11    Set up your incoming mail server information.

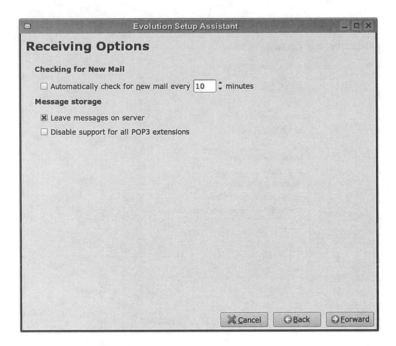

**FIGURE 13.12**    Select receiving mail options.

In the next screen (Figure 13.13), you configure your outgoing (Simple Mail Transport Protocol, SMTP) mail server. Name the server in the Host line. Again choose whether to have Evolution, and remember your password, this time when sending mail.

In the last two screens, you name your account and select your time zone (from a beautifully rendered world map). When you've completed all the setup tasks, click Apply to open Evolution, and then click Send / Receive on the toolbar to get your mail.

Evolution supports creating the standard folders that can help you organize your mail, especially mailing list traffic. You can create filters that send list messages into a folder for reading and storing later. This isn't the interesting thing, because nearly all mail clients do this. Evolution also supports Virtual Folders (vFolders), which allow for unique combinations of relevant data. Say you want to track discussions over several lists on email clients. You can search your existing mail for several keywords, and then make a rule to funnel copies of these discussions into a virtual folder. Go to the Search menu and click Create vFolder from Search. A dialog box appears (Figure 13.14).

In this example, we've selected five possible subjects that should catch a good chunk of the relevant traffic in the lists and newsgroups. We've listed three leading email clients and two variant spellings of "email client." Choosing With All Local Folders in the vFolder Sources at the bottom should pick up Usenet messages, too. Click OK to create the vFolder. Evolution will search the existing messages, and will filter mail and Usenet postings with the matching subjects.

**FIGURE 13.13**     Configure outgoing mail server information.

**FIGURE 13.14**     Configure vFolders in evolution.

Evolution also handles Usenet News in the same environment as mail. Setting up a Usenet feed uses the same wizard as mail, with slightly different requirements. To access newsgroups once you've set up your account, go to Tools, Subscribe to Folders to connect to your news server and select groups to subscribe to. The problem with this method is that you cannot search for groups, but must go through a threaded list of all the groups on the server. Once you make your selections, though, the display is just like your mail client. See Chapter 16, "Collaborating with Others," for more information on Usenet News.

Based on GTK+, Evolution works best under GNOME, but works just fine in KDE. It is the default mail client in the Novell Linux Desktop product designed for the corporate market, in part because of the Ximian Exchange Connector that allows Evolution to get messages from Microsoft Exchange Servers. You'll also notice that Mozilla Firefox launches Evolution when you click an email address on the web, regardless of your default mail setup. Evolution returns the favor when you click a web address as well.

### Organizing Your Life with Evolution Calendar

Evolution is a complete personal information manager, with calendar and task (to-do) list. You can convert email messages to either events or tasks, if you need to.

You can import calendars, from other individuals and from the Web, into Evolution. The calendar supports the iCal standard developed by Apple. Visit http://icalshare.com to see user-contributed calendars on assorted topics, from holidays and history, to local Linux User Group calendars. To import a calendar from iCalShare into Evolution, right-click on the Subscribe link on the website and copy the link to the clipboard. In Evolution, open the calendar and select New Calendar from the toolbar or File menu.

Choose On the Web from the Type drop-down menu, and then paste your copied address in the URL box (delete the default text in this box first). Name the Calendar, and decide how often you want to update it (every 30 minutes is the default, but this is probably overkill for the US Holidays calendar, among others). If you have a dial-up connection, you can also download a calendar file that doesn't constantly ping the web for updates. Click Download Calendar on the website, and save it to a Calendars directory somewhere on your Home directory. When opening the New Calendar dialog box, select On This Computer from the Type drop-down menu (this should be the default). Point to the directory where you saved the calendar, and make it the default folder.

## KDE Personal Information Manager: Kmail/KOrganizer and Kontact

KDE now offers two ways to get your email and personal information managed. If you like Outlook's way of keeping all these functions together in one package, try Kontact. If you prefer that all these things remain independent, and you want separate windows for your calendar and email, each component of the KDE-PIM package will still run separately.

Kontact has six basic components:

- KMail—A full-featured email client with some built-in spam and virus protection, configurable filters to help you organize your mail, and the usual customization features.

- KOrganizer—Calendar and to-do list for the busy person.

- KAddressBook—Holds your Kontacts and integrates with your calendar and mail clients.

- KNotes—A quick-opening, lightweight text editor for reminders and other bits of information.

- KNode—A Usenet newsreader that can access multiple news servers and filter out spam and other worthless material.

- aKregator—A new RSS/Atom feedreader that downloads information from weblogs and news sites for easy reading.

**13**

Besides the main information tools, there are some handy accessories in the KDE-PIM lineup. KPilot (see Chapter 9, "Being Productive: Office Suites and Other Tools") and Kandy are tools to sync your information with your Palm device or mobile phone, respectively. KAlarm notifies you when something important is coming up (or you just have new mail), and KArm is your personal time clock, available to help you figure out where all the time goes (especially if you have billable hours).

Kontact has the Outlook-Today-like Summary page, with calendar and to-do list highlighted, along with a weather report and news feeds. You can choose the components that appear in the Kontact window (so if you don't read Usenet, you don't have to load KNode every time you want to read mail).

> **TIP**
>
> Want to have a Kontact-like experience in Windows? Try Aethera, a Windows PIM from theKompany.com based on the Kontact code. See http://thekompany.com/projects/aethera for more information and the free download.

KMail can deal with those with evil designs on your computer. The KMail Spam Wizard can integrate useful filters for several antispam tools, and the Virus Wizard can also work with four antivirus products: two included with SUSE Linux (ClamAV and H+Bedv Antivir) and two commercial products (Sophos and F-Prot). In addition, KMail has integrated encryption using the GNU Privacy Guard (GPG) available for those messages that need to be secure.

> **TIP**
>
> It's a good idea to keep traffic from each list you're subscribed to in a separate folder. It's much easier to follow threads of a discussion when they aren't interrupted by other messages.

If you use electronic mailing lists, you'll find KMail will help you immensely. KMail is very list-aware. That list-awareness is expressed in many ways:

- Right-click a list message and you can create a filter for that list from the context menu (Create Filter, On Mailing List, <name>).

- KMail will display messages in threads if you like. You can also perform some actions on whole threads: Delete Thread, Ignore Thread (which automatically marks messages in the ignored thread as Read, so you can see them later if you want), and Watch Thread (which marks each new message in the thread with a Watch icon so you don't miss them). You can set this globally in the KMail configure screen or folder by folder.

- Some lists are configured so when you reply to a list message, it goes to the list; others send replies to the message author. In KMail, regardless of how things are set at the list, you can choose where it goes. Press L to reply to the list, press Shift+A to Reply to Author, and plain A replies to All.

- In Folder Properties, KMail (v3.3 and up) will automatically detect the posting address for a list. You can also copy/paste this manually if you prefer.

Do you get buried in mailing list email to the point where you can't read it all, but don't have time to prune the inbox either? KMail's Folder Properties tools can help. Besides the threading and posting functions, Another Folder Property will delete (Expire) old worn-out messages. Right-click a folder and select Properties (or go to the Folder, Properties menu). Click the Old Message Expiry tab to see Figure 13.15.

**FIGURE 13.15**    Prune your Inbox and other folders with the KMail Old Message Expiry property screen.

When you check the Expire Old Messages in This Folder box, you'll see the default settings. They are easily adjusted for your message-reading style. Suppose you're inclined to keep a good tip that you got from a list; you might want to change the Read Mail setting to Never and dump Unread after a proper period (use the drop-down menu to specify whether you want KMail to mark time in Days, Weeks, or Months).

In older versions of KMail, you had to tell the application to expire a single folder or all folders at once. With KMail 3.3, the Expire function works constantly in the background, occasionally delivering a message in the lower-left corner: `Expired x messages in Folder Y`.

### KOrganizer

Kontact also helps you manage your schedule with KOrganizer. Set up events, work on your to-do list, invite people to meetings, and all the other things you expect to do in this type of application.

You can easily turn a to-do item into an event by adding start and end times for the to-do. Drag an email message to an event to attach it.

As with the Evolution calendar, KOrganizer supports the iCal standard, and you can subscribe to or download user-created calendars at iCalShare.com. You can also create your own and share them.

## Mozilla Mail and Thunderbird

The Mozilla Suite that installs by default on your SUSE Linux desktop is more than a browser. A mail and news client, Internet Relay Chat (IRC) program, and HTML editor are all included in the package.

Mozilla project developers are heading in a new direction, separating each of these functions into faster-loading applications with new names. The mail and news client is called Thunderbird, and it is a thing of beauty. Designed to make Outlook Express users comfortable, the interface is very familiar. Setting up mail accounts is simple; creating folders and filters is even more so.

Thunderbird is very security conscious as well. To protect your privacy, the application will not load remote images in HTML-based messages unless you tell it to. Remote images often contain "web bugs" that tell the sender you've opened their message, confirming your email address. The Junk filters are very good.

New features are added first to the standalone products and then are brought into the Mozilla suite. If you prefer to have everything together, Mozilla Mail 1.7 has all the Thunderbird features mentioned previously.

As of this writing, the Mozilla calendar is still in alpha status, but it's on the way.

## Sylpheed

This fast and powerful mail and news client was written by a Japanese programmer, Hiroyuki Yamamoto, with GTK+ for GNOME. Its clean interface is easy to read, although you may want to adjust the spartan default Courier fonts (Figure 13.16).

**FIGURE 13.16**    Sylpheed's clean interface.

Sylpheed has powerful filters, but the dialog boxes to create them are better suited for the technically adept. The same can be said for the other configuration dialog boxes.

Sylpheed will also read Usenet news, but has no calendar function. The address book supports multiple email addresses for one individual and has room for many free-form "user attributes," such as physical addresses, company, title(s), birthdays, and the like.

## mutt

mutt is a text-based mail client that runs directly in the shell.

Originally based on another mail client called elm, mutt has taken on features and ways of doing things from several of its brethren. Hence the name: mutt. The interface is colorful for a text screen and the colors are configurable. You can see it in Figure 13.17.

This client's fans emphasize the power of the client and the ease with which they move through their mail. Like KMail, mutt is highly attuned to mailing-list users, with threading and list-reply options.

SUSE Linux defines a basic systemwide mutt configuration file in /etc/Muttrc. Open it as root to configure mutt for all users on your system, but each user can have his or her own Muttrc in the home directory. It's a relatively big file as configuration files go, so you can see the kind of power you have. It comes well commented, so even newbies can play with some settings. Always make a backup file before you make changes.

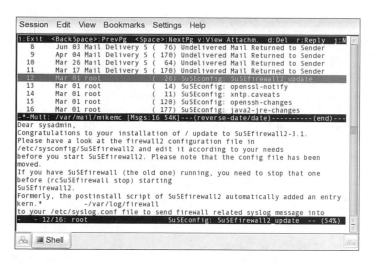

Session   Edit   View   Bookmarks   Settings   Help

```
l:Exit   <BackSpace>:PrevPg   <Space>:NextPg  v:View Attachm.   d:Del   r:Reply   j:N
    8      Jun 03 Mail Delivery S (   76) Undelivered Mail Returned to Sender
    9      Apr 04 Mail Delivery S (  170) Undelivered Mail Returned to Sender
   10      Mar 26 Mail Delivery S (   64) Undelivered Mail Returned to Sender
   11      Mar 17 Mail Delivery S (  170) Undelivered Mail Returned to Sender
   12      Mar 01 root            (   26) SuSEconfig: SuSEfirewall2 update
   13      Mar 01 root            (   14) SuSEconfig: openssl-notify
   14      Mar 01 root            (   11) SuSEconfig: xntp.caveats
   15      Mar 01 root            (  120) SuSEconfig: openssh-changes
   16      Mar 01 root            (  177) SuSEconfig: java2-jre-changes
-*-Mutt: /var/mail/mikemc [Msgs:16 54K]---(reverse-date/date)----------(end)---
Dear sysadmin,
Congratulations to your installation of / update to SuSEfirewall2-3.1.
Please have a look at the firewall2 configuration file in
/etc/sysconfig/SuSEfirewall2 and edit it according to your needs
before you start SuSEfirewall2. Please note that the config file has been
moved.
If you have SuSEfirewall (the old one) running, you need to stop that one
before (rcSuSEfirewall stop) starting
SuSEfirewall2.
Formerly, the postinstall script of SuSEfirewall2 automatically added an entry
kern.*          -/var/log/firewall
to your /etc/syslog.conf file to send firewall related syslog message into
-  - 12/16: root                         SuSEconfig: SuSEfirewall2 update  -- (54%)
```

Shell

**FIGURE 13.17**   The mutt mail client combines features from several of its text-based brethren, such as elm and pine.

At a minimum, you will have to point mutt to your mail server to read mail from your ISP. Use your editor's Find command to locate the POP section of Muttrc; then un-comment and modify the file to your liking.

Navigation between messages in the Index pane and within messages in the Pager is accomplished with arrow keys, the spacebar, and PgUp and PgDown. There are prompts at the top of the pane to remind forgetful users.

Take advantage of the active development team and lively user community, should you get hooked on this client. Start at http://www.mutt.org.

## Sending File Attachments

Some people get confused about email. "If email is just text, and only text, how do people send me fully formatted documents and all those family pictures?" The capability to attach binary files is one of the extensions to SMTP that makes it more useful.

There are several methods for turning a binary file into text for mailing, which are somewhat tied to the operating system you're running. The historic Unix method is called UUEncode/UUDecode (the UU standing for Unix-to-Unix), whereas Macintosh users made BinHex files. Later on, the Multipurpose Internet Mail Extension (MIME) format came in for all operating systems. Nearly every mail client now produced, for whatever OS, can read file attachments that use these formats, and they all can attach files using at least one of these methods without user intervention. That is, you don't have to decide how to encode your attachments.

One deficiency in this encoding and textifying of binary files is that the encoded files are much bigger than the original binary file. Recently, a new format called yEnc has taken the field, claiming to produce smaller, more compressed attachments. Client support for this format is spotty at the time of this writing, but that may change.

13

In the event you find yourself needing to decode one of these files manually, this section will help you with some pertinent details about each format.

When do you need to manually decode an attachment? If you get a message that has a large batch of random digits, characters, and apostrophes in 80-characters-per-line format, that's probably an undecoded attachment. If you see a line at the top of the randomness with a filename, you definitely have an undecoded attachment. See the section "Using UUDeview to Decode a File Attachment" to know what to do with it.

> **NOTE**
>
> Microsoft Exchange Servers use a proprietary format to attach files to Outlook messages. This format, the Transport Neutral Encapsulation Format (TNEF), is read beautifully in Outlook itself, but other clients (regardless of OS) sometimes have a problem, with attachments being labeled with a generic winmail.dat filename.
>
> Progress has been made in viewing these files in Linux mail clients. KDE (and KMail) has a built-in TNEF viewer. Other clients can use the shell utility TNEF to view these files. This utility is available through YaST.

## BinHex

Apple Macintosh users have long used the BinHex format to wrap files. This hasn't changed with the advent of the FreeBSD-based OS X. SUSE Linux users can install UUDeview from YaST to decode these files. This shell utility decodes all manner of attached-file formats, including yEnc and MIME.

## yEnc

This format, with a name derived from smushing together the words "My Encoder," is freely available. Mostly used in the Usenet binaries newsgroups, it can also be used for attaching files to email. The developer, Jürgen Helbring, insists that if you use it in email, you must include the word "yEnc" in the subject heading. This serves both to warn recipients that there is an attachment with this message and to spread the word about the format.

UUDeview will decode these attachments for you. You'll find a list of yEnc-friendly Linux applications at http://www.yenc.org/linux.htm.

## UUEncode/UUDecode

These venerable utilities are included in the sharutils package installed by default in SUSE Linux. If you know you have a UUEncoded file, you can use UUDecode to extract the file. The telltale sign that an attachment has been UUEncoded is that in the top line, along with the filename, is the three-digit permissions indicator.

Suppose the first line in the attachment looks like this:

```
begin 664 vacation027.jpg
```

This tells us that when it's decoded, we'll have a single JPG image, vacation027.jpg, when we're done. You can UUEncode any number of files in a single instance.

When you get an email like this, save it as a file in your home directory. Leave it with no extension (attach1). Then go to your shell and run the UUDecode program:

```
uudecode attach1
```

This will decode the attachment and produce the vacation027.jpg image in your home directory. You should now see this file if you run the ls command, and you should be able to open it. After you've opened the decoded file, delete attach1.

## MIME/Base64

MIME is the general Internet standard for formatting email. It includes the Base64 method for encoding file attachments, as well as messages using non-English characters.

Heinz Tschabitscher at About.com briefly describes what happens when you use Base64: "Base64 encoding takes three bytes, each consisting of eight bits, and represents them as four printable characters in the ASCII standard."

Use UUDeview to decode Base64 attachments.

### Using UUDeview to Decode a File Attachment

What do you do when you find yourself with an undecoded file attachment? Follow these steps.

1. As we did with the preceding UUEncoded message, use the Save As command in your mail client, save this message in your home directory, and call it **attach1** with no extension.

2. Go to a shell or console. Type this command:

```
uudeview -p Documents attach1
```

This will decode the attachment (whatever form was used to encode it) and place the decoded file(s) in your Documents directory. Type **uudeview** (with no switch) to see a list of all the options.

3. Go to the Documents directory (either by cd-ing in the shell or opening a file manager) and open the newly decoded file(s).

After you've opened the decoded file, there is no need to keep the original attachment.

> **NOTE**
>
> When you have decoded a file attachment, you have just turned it back to a binary file. To view or execute it, you still have to open the decoded file(s).

# References

- http://www.mozilla.org—The home port for all things Mozilla, including Firefox, Thunderbird, the Mozilla Suite. Get extensions and themes here.

- http://www.spreadfirefox.com—The community marketing effort for Firefox. Get a link for your own web page, and some ammunition for the war with Internet Explorer.

- http://www.mozilla.org/projects/seamonkey—The next generation of the Mozilla Suite.

- http://konqueror.kde.org—Learn more about both sides of Konqueror.

- http://www.gnome.org/projects/epiphany—Get your Epiphany extensions, and learn more about its features.

- http://galeon.sourceforge.net/Main—The Galeon page.

- http://www.opera.com—Home of the Opera browser. Download the latest version, sign up for OperaMail, and do your own blog, too.

- http://www.gnome.org/projects/evolution—The Evolution home page.

- http://www.mozilla.org/products/thunderbird—The Mozilla Thunderbird page. Links to MozillaZine knowledge base and help forums.

- http://pim.kde.org—Home of the KDE Personal Information Management suite: Kontact, KMail, Korganizer, and the ancillary tools.

- http://sylpheed.good-day.net—Sylpheed, the other GTK-based mail client.

- http://www.mutt.org—The mongrel of text-based email clients.

- http://www.fpx.de/fp/Software/UUDeview—The UUDeview multiformat file attachment decoder. Works with all encoding formats (BinHex, yEnc, MIME, UUEncode). Enjoy the Introduction to Encoding document and get some useful history, too.

- http://www.yenc.org/linux.htm—Linux readers and writers for the yEnc coding format.

- http://email.about.com/cs/standards/a/base64_encoding.htm—An excellent description of Base64 encoding.

CHAPTER **14**

# Creating Basic Websites

The Internet is not just a place to visit. More than ever, it's a place to contribute to.

SUSE Linux can help you build your space on the web. There are tools for everyone to create impressive sites, regardless of your skill level and interest in learning the technology behind it.

The weblog revolution has changed the way many people think about the Internet. The rise of personal weblogs (blogs) has transformed how people communicate with each other, and how they relate to the world—or at least the part of the world that's online.

In this chapter, you will explore the tool choices available to you for producing web pages. Then you'll build a basic informational website with Quanta Plus. We will then explore the various Linux tools for making a personal weblog.

## Choosing a Web Development Tool

The Linux web developer can choose among several good tools. What you choose depends on your skill level and what your comfort level with writing raw HTML is.

### For the Beginner

For the absolute web page beginner, there's nothing better than OpenOffice.org's Writer/Web. OOo offers basic templates (called AutoPilots) for creating several types of pages, including various forms, two-column layouts, and even a photo album style. From the File menu, go to `AutoPilot, Web Page`. Figure 14.1 shows the Web Page AutoPilot dialog box.

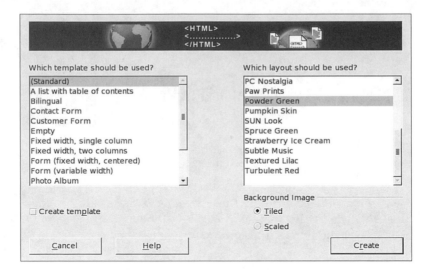

**FIGURE 14.1**    Choose one of many types of page templates with the OpenOffice.org AutoPilot.

> **NOTE**
>
> There are many schools of thought which question whether a beginner is better served by a set of templates or by learning the basic HTML tags. AutoPilot, and similar programs, are useful to a point, but you should still consider studying the basics of HTML if you expect to move beyond the very basics with your web skills.

Many of the background layouts are somewhat garish and difficult to read, but they give you something to start with. Unlike Microsoft Word, Writer/Web delivers very clean and standards-based HTML code.

The standard web page AutoPilot delivers easily editable code for any basic page, with links and navigation graphics, which you can see in Figure 14.2.

A nice touch is the Last Changed note at the bottom of the page. This tells your visitors that the information on your site is current, or perhaps that it is not.

The other office suites included with SUSE Linux all let you write HTML documents, but only OOo helps the novice with something to play with and learn from.

The advantage of using a word processor such as OOo for website creation is that it's a familiar environment. Paragraph styles transfer easily from a standard document to the web, and for the most part it is more WYSIWYG (what you see is what you get) than a specialized editor.

Where the office suites fall short compared to more specialized web-development tools is in creating projects that link pages together in a coherent site. Applications such as Quanta and Bluefish offer advantages that we will explore later.

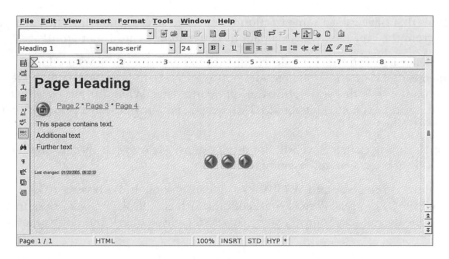

**FIGURE 14.2**  Even a default OpenOffice.org template gives you plenty to work with. Note the navigation graphics, links, and Last Changed notice.

## Browser-Based Page Creators

An alternative to word processors are the browser-based page-creation tools. The genesis for these was Netscape's early decision to include Composer in its suite of Internet tools. This tool is still present in the official Netscape Communicator suite and with its open source Mozilla sibling.

When the Mozilla project decided to break the components of the Netscape suite into sleeker, faster individual applications that still worked well together, some thought Composer might die. Coming to its rescue was Michael Robertson and his team from Linspire (formerly Lindows). They have shepherded the development of a new, simple page-creation tool called nvu (pronounced N-View). It fills the need for a simple tool for new users who don't need to build massive sites with lots of Flash and glitter, but have something to contribute.

## Specialized Web Tools

Next up on the scale are the special tools created for making websites. Like Microsoft FrontPage or Macromedia Dreamweaver, these applications handle all the relevant tasks in building a professional website, with the advantage of being free.

Two of these have become the standard applications for Linux web developers:

- Quanta Plus (now KDE-WebDev) started out as an independent project, but has since become integrated within the KDE desktop.

- Bluefish was created with the Gimp Toolkit (GTK), and is popular with GNOME users. It runs on KDE as well.

Other tools that have gained some traction recently are Screem and Ginf; the latter pulled its name from the ever-reflexive GNU naming convention, "Ginf is not FrontPage."

One difference between the Linux development tools and the Windows products mentioned earlier: These tools are proudly non-WYSIWYG, at least by default, preferring to show you the code first and testing the appearance later. What this means is that you have to know at least a little bit about HTML tagging and how it works before using these tools successfully.

In our forthcoming example, we will not dwell extensively on what specific tags mean, but you will get a sense of how tagging works.

Quanta is not as ruthlessly anti-WYSIWYG as Bluefish, though. With version 3.3, Quanta introduced the VPL (Visual Page Layout) editor, which can display in place of or in a dual view with the default (aka Source) editor. This is still a little buggy, but not bad for a first version.

This is not to say that the only help you get from these tools are some extra toolbars that add a tag when you tell it. Quanta comes with an assortment of templates to handle all the basics of page creation, as you can see in Figure 14.3. No navigation tools are included, though.

**FIGURE 14.3**    Quanta's basic HTML template creates a standard page heading and not much else.

One thing you get with a web tool that you can't get with an ordinary word processor is the support for a variety of web technologies. It is often as easy to create an interactive PHP-based site, or any of several varieties of XML, as it is a static HTML page, if you know what you're doing.

Both tools will also display your pages in most, if not all, prominent Linux web browsers. Bluefish and Quanta each handle this differently, however. Quanta displays pages in its own internal browser and in Konqueror, Mozilla, Netscape, Opera, and Lynx (a text-based browser). Bluefish handles Mozilla, Netscape, Opera, Galeon, and the GNOME default browser. You can add other browsers in the external preferences dialog box. Of course, you must have each browser installed on your system for this feature to work.

---

**TIP**

Do you want to test your pages on Microsoft Internet Explorer without leaving Linux? This is not easy, but it is possible.

Internet Explorer will run under Wine, the Windows emulator, but it takes some work. After installing Wine (via YaST), download Hajime Segawa's script to install Internet Explorer and Windows Media Player from http://sidenet.ddo.jp/winetips/config.html.

Extract the tarball to your home directory, and then read the readme.en file for instructions in how to run the script. When the script is finished, it opens a confirmation page in Internet Explorer, so you know you have a working copy on your system.

Now add Internet Explorer to the browser list in Quanta or Bluefish.

- In Bluefish, go to Edit, Preferences, External Programs. At the top you'll see the browser list. See the line with the Add button? Type **Internet Explorer** there. Under Command, type **wine iexplore %s** (for the current file). Click Add and this will appear in the browser list. Click OK to confirm.

- In Quanta, go to Settings, Configure Actions. Expand the All tree and you will see the View with (browser) settings. This is what you'll base your new action on. Click New Action. Settings are as follows:

  Type: Script

  Text: View with Internet Explorer (You can choose an icon, too.)

  ToolTip (optional): View with Internet Explorer

  Shortcut (Custom): Alt+Shift+F6 (All the others are variations on F6.)

  Detailed Settings:

  sh %scriptdir/externalpreview.sh %pid wine iexplore (To save typing, copy and paste from one of the other Views with choices, and then add **wine iexplore** to the end.)

Leave the other boxes as they are. Click OK to confirm.

---

Both Quanta and Bluefish come with ample documentation for the product and reference manuals for HTML and PHP. Quanta also includes references for JavaScript and cascading style sheets (CSS).

## Übergeek Web Page Tools

You know that a real Linux geek doesn't need a GUI tool to write for the web. It is just markup—hypertext markup at that. Maybe all you need is a text editor and a tag reference guide. Rest assured that every text editor included with SUSE Linux is fully capable of producing perfect HTML code just the way you like it.

Emacs, as per its reputation, not only comes with a web browser, but also has a major mode for Standard Generalized Markup Language (SGML), which means it will help you write to any Document Type Definition (DTD): HTML, XHTML, XML, and so on. Open or create any file with an HTML extension and Emacs will add the relevant menus to your display. All these things work in Xemacs as well.

Vim has a Convert-to-HTML syntax file called 2HTML. Jedit also has a Code2HTML plug-in and plug-ins that will insert tags into your text.

# Practice: Building a Site with Quanta Plus

So you have a lot of knowledge about something and you think other people might be interested. There's no reason not to put up a website with all the stuff you know.

In this section, we will work with Quanta to draw up a site with a few basic pages of information about baseball in Wisconsin.

### Planning Your Site

Ideally, before you build your site, you should do some planning. Most importantly, you have to think about where to store your site; that is, you have to select a web host to keep your pages up. Chances are your ISP offers you some free space, and there are always the free web hosts such as GeoCities, Angelfire, and the like. If you're serious about building a web resource site, you will want to register your domain name and should consider paying for a host. A good web-hosting company will work hard to keep those servers running and your site available to web surfers around the globe.

Another option, particularly if you have a high-speed, always-on connection, would be to host your own site. SUSE Linux includes the Apache web server, so updating your site is a trifling matter. This would be a reason to get a static IP address from your ISP, because your site's availability would be hit-and-miss if the world's DNS servers had to re-locate your site every time you rebooted and got a new DHCP address. For our example, we will self-host the site. See Chapters 26, "Managing Your Apache Web Server," and 27, "Managing Domain Names," for more information on Apache and domain names.

The next thing to consider is what type of information you want to have on your site and how the pages will be organized. A mind-mapping tool like View Your Mind or a flow-charting tool like Dia or Kivio may help you think this out, but quite often, it's time for the old pencil and paper to work its magic.

Our site will have a home page that mostly links to subpages for NCAA Division 1 college baseball, minor league teams in the state, and the state's only Major League franchise, the Milwaukee Brewers. We'll have a history page, for information related to the Milwaukee Braves, the defunct minor league franchises, and the Milwaukee Bears of the Negro National League. Finally, we'll have a listing of folks with Wisconsin ties in the Baseball Hall of Fame in Cooperstown, NY. Figure 14.4 shows a very rough Kivio site plan diagram.

Now it's time to build the site.

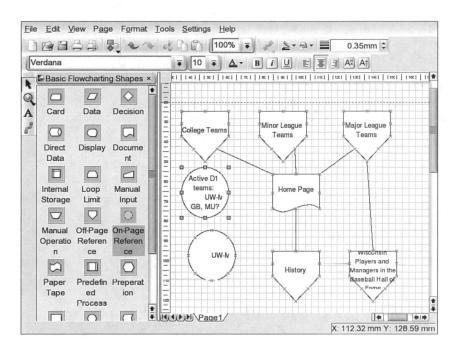

**FIGURE 14.4**   A site plan for the Wisconsin Baseball site.

### Building the Site
The first task in creating our site in Quanta is to create a new project. Go to Project, New Project, and the wizard dialog box shown in Figure 14.5 appears.

Name the project and Quanta fills in the filename. If you already know who your web host is, adjust the Server Settings so Quanta can immediately upload updated files when you ask it. Set the Main Directory; you can store your working files anywhere, but the Documents folder is a fine place. The Templates and Toolbars directories will be placed underneath the Main Directory, although if you have multiple projects going, you may want to have only one of each of these. Finally, if you have an existing site that you want to pull into Quanta, choose Use wget to Download Files from a Site in the Project Sources area. Click Next to locate existing source pages.

What's on the second page (see Figure 14.6) is determined by how you answered the Project Sources question on the first page. Because we have no existing files to bring into the project, there's nothing to do.

Check the Insert Files box at the top, and then add selected files or the entire folder with the appropriate buttons at the bottom.

If you select the option to pull existing files online in the first screen, the New Project Wizard will ask where to look in the Site Source line (unless you've already identified the server in the first screen) and generate a wget command. You can edit the options if you want (run **wget -h** from a shell to see all the options for this program), but clicking Start will retrieve all the files in your site.

14

**FIGURE 14.5**    Creating a new project in Quanta is a three-step process.

**FIGURE 14.6**    Pull existing local files into your new project with this dialog box.

When you've pulled all the existing files into the project, click Next. Your last task is to tell Quanta what type of site you're building. You may also identify yourself (or anyone else) as the site author.

In Figure 14.7, you can see the varieties of DTDs you can use for any given site. For our example, we will use the default HTML 4.0 (Transitional), but you can always select something different from the drop-down menu. We will also stick with the default encoding; you'll rarely have to change that. Also check the Insert global templates box; this will give you quick access to different options for your site. Click Finish to complete your new project.

**FIGURE 14.7**   Quanta lets you select from different DTDs to describe the type of site you're putting up.

The first page in any website is the Index page, where people wind up if they access your domain name. Creating a new project does not automatically open a new page in Quanta, so we need to do that. There are three ways to do this:

- To open a blank page with no header information, click the New Page toolbar icon (or go to File, New).

- Click the Templates icon from the vertical toolbar located to the left of the editor. Go to Pages, HTML_4.01, Basic. Double-click to create the page. You can then fill in the page title yourself.

- Use the Quick Start dialog box. Click the first icon in the Standard toolbar above the editor space. This dialog box (see Figure 14.8) lets you define nearly everything about your page layout.

**FIGURE 14.8**    Create a new page with the Quick Start dialog box.

Enter the title of this page—that is, the title people will see at the top of the browser window when they visit (and also what comes up when they search for your page). Beside the default options, we have also entered keywords, which will help search engines identify the topics the site is about. Separate words and phrases here with commas. Don't overload this tag; if you have more than a few items here, a search engine's spider may decide you're trying to skew the results too heavily, and it may ignore you entirely.

Quanta makes it pretty easy for multiple authors to work on a site. As you can see, you can change several project defaults for each page from this dialog box, including the DTD, the base directory, and the author. If you don't check the boxes, Quanta will create the page using the Project defaults.

When you've finished with the page settings, click OK to confirm. Quanta may ask you if you want the new page to be part of the current project. You should see the editor page looking a lot like Figure 14.9.

> **CAUTION**
>
> The project must be open before you run the Quick Start dialog box, otherwise you won't get the page created properly unless you identify the base directory where the templates are stored.

Adding content is simple. Use the existing toolbars to tag paragraphs either before or after writing your text. Use the Visual Page Layout WYSIWYG editor to see how it looks while you're still working. You can edit from either the Source or the VPL editor. Figure 14.9 shows the start of our page in the VPL editor.

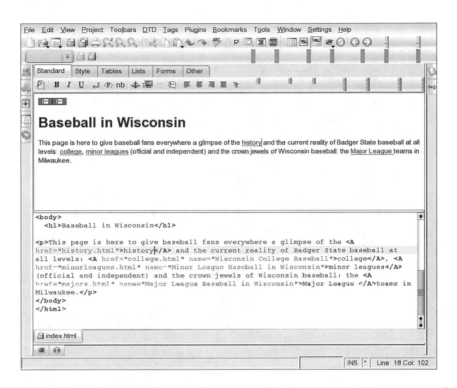

**FIGURE 14.9**    Insert images to liven up the page and include links to other pages on the site.

When you've got a page ready, test it in several browsers to make sure it looks good for everyone. Using the Lynx browser will also indirectly tell you how usable your site is for a blind person using a page reader.

When your site is ready, press F8 (or go to `Project, Upload Project`) to put your handiwork where people can see it. This dialog box shown in Figure 14.10 comes up.

Select (or define) a host server in the Profile Name box. Select the files to upload from the main window (all are selected by default) and click `Proceed`. Quanta will connect with and upload your files and give you a progress report at the bottom of the screen.

# Weblogging with SUSE Linux

Weblogging, or just plain *blogging*, has been around for a relatively long time. The practice managed to claw its way into broad public consciousness in 2004, to the point of being a candidate for *TIME Magazine's* Person of the Year.

Some observers believe that weblogs represent a new form of journalism, as ordinary folks bring their life experiences and perspectives to bear on events large and small and have a potentially global audience to read what they say.

**FIGURE 14.10**    Upload your finished website to your host's servers automatically with Quanta.

Bloggers use their sites in all sorts of ways, serious and trivial:

- Online personal journals, to keep friends and family posted on the latest news.

- A place to share new information (often gleaned from the web itself) about a shared passion.

- Businesspeople are increasingly using blogs to communicate with employees and customers.

- People on the scene at business or technology conferences and similar events report, often in real time, on what's happening to inform those who couldn't be there.

- Political commentators of nearly every persuasion imaginable share news, gossip, and commentary on current events.

- Journalists—professional, amateur, and in between—share information about stories they cover that may not make it into the paper or on the air.

Blogs can be one person's project or have multiple authors. They can be on one topic, broad or narrowly defined, or they can be on whatever pops into an author's head. There are great blogs and poor blogs in all categories. Some are read by thousands every day, but most are read by only a few.

Whatever you want to do with your blog, about the only rule that matters is that a blog home page features posts in reverse chronological order, with the most recent posts at the top of the page. Other characteristics that help differentiate blogs from ordinary websites include the following:

- Blog posts are usually archived and have a link to the URL where the post will be archived when it floats off the home page. This URL, called a *permalink*, is done because bloggers often link to other blog posts to comment on them. With permalinks, and a similar process called TrackBacks, readers can then follow the "conversation" between two or more blogs on the same topic.

- Blogs often have sidebars, called blogrolls, with listings of the bloggers' favorite blogs and other websites.

- Bloggers were among the first to use an XML technology called Really Simple Syndication (RSS) or a competing technology, Atom, to make postings easily accessible. More traditional news outlets are now adding these XML feeds to their sites, and browsers (Firefox, Opera) and portal sites (Yahoo!) are including RSS and Atom readers in their products. See the next section for more on syndication.

- Most blogs encourage interaction between reader and writer. Some blogs permit readers to comment on posts directly on the page. This practice has decreased as spammers began inundating popular bloggers' pages with their wares, but has not disappeared completely.

Not every blog has all these features, and some sites that have these features are not blogs.

Blogging, because it's on the web, is an activity that isn't terribly concerned with operating systems. Many blogs are written directly in a blogger's browser and hosted on the same site. Many bloggers, though, want to separate the writing from the posting, and so use editing tools that run locally on a desktop or laptop and then upload pages to a remote site, just like regular websites.

In this section, we'll review some of the more popular tools that Linux users blog with along with a quick review of some of the popular blog hosts (like Blogger, Typepad, and LiveJournal) that welcome bloggers with all operating systems to participate.

SUSE Linux does not include specific blogging tools in the distribution, although the Quanta team wants you to know that one of the biggest "A-list" blogs, WilWheaton.net, is produced with its tool. Some tools are easy to install; others require a little bit of database or Apache savvy.

## Blogging with Blosxom

Blosxom is an incredibly easy blog-creation tool written by Rael Dornfest, one of the blog founding fathers. Blosxom (pronounced "blossom") is a simple CGI script that sits on your web server and turns ordinary text files into blog posts.

For those with simple blogging needs (mostly plain text, with the occasional hand-created link and styled text), Blosxom is perfect. But don't think that it's just for basic users. With Blosxom's plug-in architecture and easily modified configuration dialog box, you can accomplish many things with your blog.

Blosxom runs as a Common Gateway Interface (CGI) script on your web server, so if you want your blog live on the web at all times, you need to have a host that permits running CGI scripts (most do). You may want to experiment with several tools before settling on one, though. For this, you have the capability to run Apache on your own SUSE Linux Professional system. See Chapter 26 for a more detailed explanation of Apache.

To try Blosxom on your own Apache server, follow these steps to install:

1. Go to http://www.blosxom.com/downloads/blosxom.zip to download Blosxom.

2. Extract blosxom.cgi into the `~/public_html/cgi` directory and make it executable (**chmod 755**).

3. Create a local directory to store your Blosxom posts; Blosxom recommends `~/blosxom`, but you can choose anything you like.

> **CAUTION**
>
> Don't choose a common directory to store your posts in. Blosxom will post to your blog any file in the directory with the appropriate extension (*.txt by default).

4. Open `blosxom.cgi` in a text editor to configure your blog. The first 10 entries in the script describe what Blosxom should do. Name your blog. Give it a description, which can be prosaic (this blog is about growing marigolds) or creative (ruminations on canine lycanthropy and other wizardly things). Set the language. Tell the script where to look for posts (the directory you selected in step 3). You can probably leave the remainder of the entries with their default settings, but consult the manual if you want to know more.

5. Write a test post. Open your text editor and write something. Save it with a .txt extension into the posting directory.

6. Open your favorite web browser and go to the directory where `blosxom.cgi` lives, such as

   `http://home/<username>/public_html/cgi/blosxom.cgi`

7. Your test post should appear, with your blog's title and description, along with the date and time of your post.

For more information on working with your blog, visit the http://www.blosxom.com site.

## Movable Type and Typepad

Movable Type (MT) is considered by many to be the gold-standard weblog application. It has a reputation of being somewhat difficult to install, but it has so many features, it's worth the moderate pain. Many of the more technical-oriented blogs run MT, as do quite a few businesses and news organizations.

Typepad is the Blogger-type hosting service set up by Movable Type's developers. Typepad makes it easy to produce a high-quality MT-type blog without having to manage the installation. They've even made it a going concern by charging a minimal monthly fee ($4.95 as this is written) for basic users.

MT runs on just about every platform and can use any web server or database application you prefer. There is a free version for personal use, but if you want to have multiple authors for your blog, you'll need a paid version (less than $100).

## Blogging with WordPress

WordPress is a very popular system, but a little complex to run. It is driven by a MySQL database, which must be running before you get started. Chances are your web host will support database-driven sites, but you should check in advance.

Similarly, if you want to try out WordPress on your local system first, you will have to get MySQL and PHP set up and running. Use YaST to install the PHP and MySQL packages. See Chapter 29, "Managing Databases," for more information on setting up MySQL.

To set up WordPress

1. Go to http://wordpress.org/latest.tar.gz to download the current version.

2. Extract the tarball to any directory (your home directory will do nicely, as it will create a WordPress directory).

3. Create a WordPress user in YaST. Call it **wpress**.

4. Create a new MySQL database. From a root shell, type **/usr/bin/mysqladmin -p create wordpress**.

5. Log in to the WordPress database: **/usr/local/mysql/bin/mysql -p -u root**

6. Give the WordPress user access to the WordPress database: **GRANT ALL PRIVILEGES ON wordpress TO wpress@localhost IDENTIFIED BY wppass;GRANT ALL PRIVILEGES ON wordpress TO wpress IDENTIFIED BY wppass;**. When this is completed, type **exit** to return to the shell.

7. Either from the shell or your favorite file manager, copy the contents of the WordPress directory that you created in step 2 to the ~/public_html home directory. If you already have content there (or want your blog to be part of your larger site), copy the whole directory over.

8. Open your favorite browser and go to the directory where you extracted WordPress to: http://localhost/wp-admin/install.php. The install screens check that everything is in order and will occasionally ask you a question.

9. WordPress generates a password for the administrator in the install process. Log in to post. You'll see a very nice interface that's pretty straightforward. Fire away!

The WordPress website offers, among other things, plug-ins and templates to further customize your experience.

## Popular Blog Services

The biggest and best-known blogging services generally offer both live-in-your-browser posting and free storage space on their servers for your blog. Some offer the option to email posts, which can be a handy device. Here's a quick overview of what you can do with these services.

### Blogger (www.blogger.com)

The best known, and still the easiest way to get started in the blogosphere. Basic accounts are free, and there are lots of templates to choose from.

In many ways, Blogger is the America Online of the weblog industry; it's where people get started. Blogger blogs run the gamut of styles, but lean toward the personal-journal end of the spectrum.

There are three ways to post. The web-based interface, and using email are the standard ways; you can also create an audio-post via telephone.

### LiveJournal (www.livejournal.com)

LiveJournal started as a way for a group of friends to keep each other posted on their lives. It grew into a large, but still by-invitation-only, community of all kinds of journal-keepers. Today, anyone can get a LiveJournal account and start blogging.

LiveJournals are best known for their mood-indicator and other colorful graphics and lists of connections between users. The LiveJournal code is open source software (visit www.livejournal.org to contact the development team or download the source).

You can post via the web interface or use one of several Linux clients (Kluje for KDE, Logjam and Drivel for GNOME). They also have clients for personal digital assistants (Palm and PocketPC) and cell phones.

### Typepad

As mentioned earlier, Typepad is the hosting service from Movable Type's developers. It is currently available for $4.95 a month for basic users.

## Syndicating Your Blog

As you travel around the Web, you may have seen the little orange rectangles marked XML on certain pages. This is especially true for weblog sites, but increasingly true on regular news sites (CNET News.com, BBC News, Christian Science Monitor, CNN, and Alternet, among others) as well. Perhaps you've clicked the button and saw the equivalent of an HTML source page and wondered what that was for. What you're really seeing is a new way of delivering news and information to you: headline (or full text) syndication of website content.

Publishing a syndicated version of your blog is a great way to gain readers. Most blogging software does this by default, and it is otherwise easy to set up. With syndication, readers can find your blog through blog-search sites like Weblogs.com, Daypop, Feedster, Bloglines, and Syndic8. As a blog reader, syndication also simplifies building collections of blogs to read.

Syndication is about delivering information (also called *newsfeeds*, or just plain *feeds*) from your site to other sites or applications. When you syndicate your site, you can deliver just headlines, full-text rendering of your postings, or some portion of them. Applications called *aggregators*, or feedreaders, ping the server periodically (typically hourly) to see what's new and deliver new content to readers who have subscribed to your feed.

There are two popular formats to syndicate with: RSS and Atom. This is another religious war you can choose to participate in, or not. RSS (also known as Rich Site Summary) is the older format. Development of this format is run by Dave Winer of Userland Software. A group of developers/bloggers decided that RSS wasn't providing the features they wanted and developed the Atom standard. Some blog software supports one standard or the other, some support both. All the aggregators support both standards.

### Reading News and Blogs with Aggregators

Only recently have dedicated newsfeed aggregators begun appearing in Linux. The latest versions of the Firefox and Opera browsers both have aggregators built in. Akregator for KDE is gaining converts, and there are also several excellent online aggregators.

When Firefox arrives at a site with a syndicated feed, an orange button lights up in the lower-right corner of the browser. Click it to create what they call a "Live Bookmark." This is stored with the rest of your bookmarks. When you go to a Live Bookmark, it looks like a folder with the orange icon, with headlines inside the folder. Click a link to go to the permalinked page for that headline.

Opera reads RSS feeds through its built-in mail reader. Subscribing to a feed is as easy as clicking the XML button on a site. Opera will ask you if you want to subscribe; click Yes, and the current headlines will appear. Opera will check for new headlines when it opens.

Akregator is joining the Kontact personal information management suite with KDE 3.4 and is already in pretty good shape. It integrates with Konqueror, but opens articles in its own browser window, rather than having to open Konqueror separately.

If you switch between computers and operating systems frequently, you might like an online aggregator. The best of these is at http://www.bloglines.com. Bloglines works with most browsers (with the exception of Konqueror, which doesn't like the script Bloglines uses to display your feeds). You can organize your feeds into subject folders and add and remove feeds with ease. Bloglines will even look at your current feed lineup and offer recommendations for new blogs that might interest you.

## References

- http://www.openoffice.org—Participate in and get help from the OpenOffice.org project.

- http://www.nvu.com/—The nvu (N-View) project for a Mozilla-based web-authoring tool.

- http://quanta.sourceforge.net—Quanta Plus project page for the KDE web-authoring tool.

- http://kdewebdev.org—The KDE WebDev suite site, for Quanta and its subsidiary tools.

- http://bluefish.openoffice.nl—Bluefish, the GTK-based web-authoring tool.

- http://bfwiki.tellefsen.net—The Bluefish Wiki, where the development team keeps the rest of us posted on what's happening.

- http://www.screem.org—A GNOME/GTK editor for HTML and XML files.

- http://www.ndeepak.info/stuff/vtu/ginf—"Ginf is not FrontPage," another effort to simplify web authoring.

- http://webmonkey.wired.com/webmonkey—The all-purpose online web-design school. Tutorials on various web technologies for all skill levels, from basic HTML to Apache to ColdFusion. Like Wired magazine, occasionally the pages lean to the illegible.

- http://webdesign.about.com—Down-to-earth advice about website design. Free online classes in HTML and cascading style sheets, too.

- http://radio.weblogs.com/0124049—Notes from the Metaverse, the author's technology weblog. Lots of links and news related to open source software and SUSE Linux.

- http://www.planetsuse.org—Planet SUSE, a group blog of SUSE Linux developers.

- http://directory.google.com/Top/Computers/Internet/On_the_Web/Weblogs/Tools—The current directory of blogging tools and services. You'll find something useful here.

- http://www.blosxom.com—Download and learn about Blosxom, the CGI-based blogging tool.

- http://www.billstclair.com/blogmax—The Blogmax extension for Emacs.

- http://wordpress.org—WordPress blog and content-management tool. Very busy and helpful support forums.

- http://www.blogger.com—Still the easiest and cheapest way to start blogging. Now managed by Google.

- http://www.sixapart.com—The company behind Movable Type and Typepad. Access either product from the company blog page.

- http://www.livejournal.com—LiveJournal is a place for more personal blogs and building communities of kindred bloggers.

- http://radio.weblogs.com/0102385/2003/04/24.html#a329—A description of how to run the Windows blog program Radio Userland under Wine.

- http://akregator.sourceforge.net/index.php—The Akregator feedreader for KDE.

# CHAPTER 15

# Managing Email Servers

Is there a single application more essential in making people want to be on the Internet than electronic mail? The idea of dashing off quick notes to colleagues, friends, and family without having to buy envelopes, find stamps, and locate a mailbox—and have the note in the recipient's hands in seconds, not days—it's almost magical, isn't it?

For many of us, that magic has worn off a little. We have to wade through piles of spam, forwarded jokes, and semi-pointless mailing-list postings to get to the really important stuff. And don't get us started on the weekly battle against the latest virus to hit the wild. Email is a blessing, with its share of accompanying curses.

The magic of email happens thanks to a bunch of standards and protocols helped along by a network-aware operating system. In this chapter, you will learn a bit about the mechanics of how email gets from your mailbox to your recipient's mailbox.

You will also learn to set up your email account(s) in YaST and about the different programs you can use to read and send email and handle other information-related tasks. If you're using SUSE Linux email in a multiplatform business environment, you will find the section on connecting with Microsoft Exchange (and finding its alternatives) useful as well.

## How Email Works

When you strip away all the postal metaphors, electronic mail (email) is just plain text sent around a network or between networks. That text is sent from server to server using Simple Mail Transport Protocol (SMTP).

Extensions to this protocol allow for authentication and posting error messages. Mail Transport (or Transfer) Agents (MTAs) work unseen by the user to manage sending and receiving.

There are two sets of rules for receiving mail. If you're getting mail from your Internet Service Provider (ISP), chances are you're using the Post Office Protocol, version 3 (POP3). This protocol sets up rules for downloading mail from a central server (your ISP) to a local client (your hard drive). The POP3 server then deletes the downloaded mail.

The other method for receiving mail is the Internet Mail Access Protocol (IMAP), version 4 generally seen in a corporate environment with users who need email access on the road or via multiple machines. With IMAP, mail is permanently stored on the central server, and users view their mail when they log in to the network.

Somewhat simplified, the following is what happens when you write an email message to occupant@email.net. In the few seconds after you press the Send button in your email client

1. The client sends your text message up to the SMTP server.

2. The server's MTA queries a DNS server to locate the IP address for email.net and queues it for delivery with any other messages that may have come in at the same time.

3. Your SMTP server contacts the MTA at email.net on port 25. When the email.net server acknowledges the contact, your SMTP server sends your message, along with any others directed at email.net. The MTA for the (POP3 or IMAP4) server at email.net checks its list of users to make sure the occupant is there, acknowledges receipt of your message, and closes the connection.

4. The email.net MTA places your message in Occupant's Inbox. If configured that way, Occupant will be notified she has new mail when she logs in.

One of the best things about SMTP is that safeguards are in place so that few messages get lost in the ether. Should you accidentally send your message to ocupant@email.net, the receiving server will send back a No such user error message, and maybe you'll notice your typo before resending. The same thing will happen if the SMTP server does not get an IP address for email.net from the DNS server in step 2. Also, it should be noted that email traffic is *asynchronous,* which means that if some link in the chain of computers is down and not functional, the email will queue up in the server and wait for the connection to be reestablished, only then sending it out to the intended recipients.

Similarly, if the receiving server never acknowledges your SMTP server's contact in step 3, the MTA will notify you that the receiving server is not responding. Depending on the MTA, it may tell you it will try again at another time. If the receiving server still doesn't respond, your MTA will notify you when it has given up; the message is undeliverable.

---

**CAUTION**

Although you can set your mail client to instruct the recipient to confirm receipt of every message you send, don't do this. It's annoying to the recipient. Use this tool sparingly—for your most important messages.

---

# MTA Configuration

When you run the Mail Transfer Agent component in YaST, you are configuring Postfix and Fetchmail. Postfix has been the standard MTA in SUSE Linux since version 8.1. Earlier SUSE Linux versions used the still more widely used Sendmail MTA. Sendmail is notoriously difficult to configure, and Postfix is not. Postfix also handles more traffic faster than Sendmail. Thus, it is not hard to see why the SUSE developers made the switch.

For users, however, there is little difference, because YaST controls the configuration. Creating your own configuration file manually is possible, but can be overwritten with every update because YaST always runs Suseconfig after installing new packages.

In this section, we will deal with the extra screens available in the YaST MTA Wizard. Basic users should stick to the defaults for these settings, but if you want to fine-tune your mail operations, read on.

## Masquerading

Suppose you have a user with a different mail account, and all his mail should come from that account. Use the Local User dialog box to specify the user and the address that should appear in the From line in his email messages.

## Authentication

Some ISPs require a password to send mail using its SMTP servers. If yours is one of them, use this dialog box to identify the server, your username, and your password. If you do not have this information, you may need to require it from your ISP's technical support channels.

## Remote SMTP Connections

Check the Accept Remote SMTP Connections box if this system is a mail server. This will allow your users to send mail through this system.

## Incoming Mail Protocols

As noted earlier, there are two primary ways of receiving mail: POP3 and IMAP. Other protocols can be used to receive/download mail, and they are listed in the drop-down menu. By default, Postfix contacts the server and determines what protocol it uses automatically. The other protocols are the following:

- POP2—Possibly still present on some mail servers, this version of the Post Office Protocol is really old.

- APOP, KPOP—More secure authentication than ordinary POP.

> **NOTE**
>
> Though it is one of the most used services on the network, and has been for quite some time, email remains one of the most insecure services as well. Any security features you can add to the service—including more secure clients—help head off problems before they occur.

- SDPS—The special POP3-compliant protocol used by Demon Internet, an ISP in the United Kingdom.

- ETRN—Short for Extended Turn, an extension to the SMTP mail delivery protocol that allows an SMTP server to request from another SMTP server any email messages it has for a specific domain. ETRN typically is used to retrieve email messages from a mail server that does not have a dedicated connection to the Internet (from webopedia.com).

- ODMR—On Demand Mail Relay.

If your ISP uses one of these different protocols, they should tell you about it. Otherwise, Fetchmail's automatic detection should work fine.

## Delivery Mode

The default here is Directly. To use the Cyrus IMAP server included with SUSE Linux, choose this option from the drop-down menu. To use Procmail to have more control over your mail delivery, choose this option. See the section "Fighting Spam and Viruses" in this chapter for more information.

## Aliases

Aliases enable you to specify unlimited valid email addresses for your local account (but not mail received through your ISP) without having to create a real user with a login. Mail addressed to <alias>@<yourdomainname> (or IP address) is forwarded to one real user account.

Opening the Aliases dialog box displays dozens of default aliases along with the real accounts that the mail to those aliases forwards to. Add to the list and edit or remove existing aliases by selecting the alias you want to work with, and click the appropriate button.

## Virtual Domains

Aliases let you change the username part of an email address. Virtual domains (also called virtual hosting) allow you to change the domain part of the address as well.

Read more about this in Chapter 26, "Managing Your Apache Web Server."

# Fighting Spam and Viruses

Email is incredibly easy to use, and practically cost-free. That's why it's so popular with people. Unfortunately, those same factors are the reasons our mailboxes are inundated every day with dozens, or hundreds, of anonymous messages begging us to refinance our homes, buy various drugs, and enhance the body parts of our choice.

Email is also the favorite mechanism of spreading assorted attacks on our computers and networks through worms, Trojan horses, viruses, and other malware.

Technology columnists, politicians, and ordinary users declare the death of email in the face of this attack. What can we do? Keep trying to fight the battle.

SUSE Linux 9.2 introduced a new antispam wizard that works with your email client to remove unwanted email before it even sullies your mailbox.

Several open source projects aiming to battle spam have sprouted up, and each has its fans: SpamAssassin, Bogofilter, SpamBayes, Assistance-Filter, and GMX are the best known.

KMail and Mozilla Thunderbird both include antispam tools. Thunderbird's is built in, and KMail creates filters to work with the previously mentioned antispam tools.

Finally, there are the old-school methods, using Procmail.

## Antispam Tools

Modern antispam tools use Bayesian filtering to identify words and patterns that are typical in spam messages. They work with MTAs to scan incoming mail and filter it according to its rules.

The biggest problem with these filters is when they pick up *false positives*, good mail (also called Ham) tossed as spam. Some will also still miss a good deal of spam in the bargain. They are trainable, in different ways, so that they improve their detection capabilities as you correct their mistakes.

While you are training your filter, make sure that detected spam gets sent to its own folder and is not deleted immediately. There's no telling how many false positives might be lost otherwise.

To train your filter, create two new folders in your mail client: Not Spam for your false positives and Missed Spam for your false negatives. As new spam comes in, move it manually into your Missed Spam folder. As often as possible (preferably weekly), go through the Spam folder and move Ham into the Not Spam folder. Then run the training tool, which will vary depending on what you're using.

One visit you will want to make is to the Apache SpamAssassin Project at http://spamassassin.apahce.org. This is an open-source software solution (a set of Perl scripts) that runs on the server and stops spam before it ever enters your network. It accomplishes this daunting task using a number of different techniques, including utilizing DNS block-lists, analyzing the header and text, and some statistical methodology.

Using more than one technique to identify spam, this tool has the ability to weed out a vast majority of the spam currently floating about. It is highly recommended that you download the latest build and install it on your servers.

> **NOTE**
>
> One of the worst nightmares that can happen to an administrator is to find that his or her servers have been turned into spam gateways—literally passing spam along at breakneck speed. Many companies are currently offering software products that act as Anti-Spam Gateways, which eliminate spam, phishing attempts, and many viruses before they move beyond the server.

15

The primary benefit that most of these products offer is that they come preconfigured with very little for the administrator to do other than tweak a few settings during installation. Aside from this simplification, they offer little that is not available in SpamAssassin, and it is highly recommended that you investigate this open-source solution and its possibilities before purchasing a similar product.

## Client-Side Spam Filters

The Mozilla Thunderbird team is rightly proud of the Junk filters it has produced. It is easily trained and almost never creates a false positive. Possibly as a result of that mindset, it leaves a lot of false negatives in your box. Fortunately, selecting a message and pressing the J key promptly marks a message as Junk.

The Junk filtering function is not turned on by default. Go to Tools, Junk Mail Controls to turn them on and configure them. You'll see Figure 15.1.

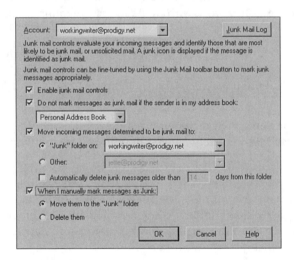

**FIGURE 15.1**    Set up spam (junk) filtering in Thunderbird or Mozilla Mail with this dialog box.

Use this dialog box to automatically whitelist everyone in your address book and tell Thunderbird where to put messages identified as junk. At first, send messages to the Junk folder. When you become confident that there are no false positives (which should not take long), you can change the setting.

## Procmail

Procmail filters (processes) each user's mail as it comes from the server. You can configure it yourself or help one of the other antispam tools work with it. See the README and example files in `/usr/share/doc/packages/procmail` for more details.

## Antivirus Tools

Conventional wisdom is that Linux is virtually virus-proof. This is true, for the most part, but perhaps not forever. Virus writers, from the script kiddies to the more professional criminal types, like to use Outlook as a transmission vector for their tools. Some have even called Outlook a virus-spreading mechanism that also delivers email.

As more people use Linux to get their everyday work done, the evil ones will try to rise to the challenge. How well they succeed depends on how ready for them Linux users (and developers) are when they arrive.

No antivirus tools are installed by default with SUSE Linux. You can configure fetchmail to work with the Mail Delivery Agent called AmaViSd, which will, in turn, work with most antivirus tools.

The most prominent open source antivirus is ClamAV, and several commercial tools are also available for Linux, including F-Prot and Sophos.

# Alternatives to Postfix

One of the last areas where Microsoft has yet to be surpassed by an open-source product is in the area of corporate groupware and messaging. Many businesses use Microsoft Outlook and/or Microsoft Exchange Server to get email, provide calendaring, notes, file sharing, and other collaborative functions. General industry complaints about Exchange Server abound, and they center on issues of scalability, administration (especially backup and restore, where there is a thriving third-party market), and licensing fees.

A "drop-in" alternative needs to have compatibility with Outlook because it's intended to replace Exchange Server in an environment where there are Microsoft desktops in existence using Outlook. A "work-alike" alternative provides similar features to Exchange Server, but does not offer compatibility with the Outlook client itself; the latter is typical of many of the open-source alternatives.

There are several drop-in alternatives, none of which are fully open source because some type of proprietary connector is needed to provide the services to Outlook clients (or provide Exchange services to the Linux Evolution client). For Outlook compatibility, the key seems to be the realization of a full, open implementation of MAPI, Microsoft's Messaging Application Program Interface. That goal is going to be difficult to achieve because MAPI is a poorly documented Microsoft protocol. For Linux-only solutions, the missing ingredient for many alternatives is a usable group calendaring/scheduling system similar in function to that provided by Exchange Server/Outlook.

Of course, independent applications for these functions abound in the open-source world, but one characteristic of groupware is its central administration; another is that all components can share information.

Central to the open-source challenge to Microsoft's dominance in this area is the move toward open standards for messaging, calendaring, and scheduling. The Calendaring Distributed Authoring and Versioning (CalDAV) standard is based on earlier work on

15

distributed authoring and versioning on the Web (WebDAV). With a more orderly, standards-based approach, Exchange's days of dominance may be numbered.

The following sections examine several of the available servers, beginning with Exchange Server itself and moving toward those applications that have increasing incompatibility with it.

## Microsoft Exchange Server

Exchange Server and Outlook seem to be the industry benchmark because of their widespread deployment. They offer a proprietary server providing email, contacts, scheduling, public folders, task lists, journaling, and notes using Outlook as the client and MAPI as the API. If you consider what Exchange offers is the "full" set of features, no other replacement offers 100% of what Exchange does.

## CommuniGate Pro

CommuniGate Pro is a proprietary, drop-in Exchange alternative, providing email, webmail, LDAP directories, a web server, a file server, contacts, and a list server. The CommuniGate Pro MAPI Connector provides access to the server from Outlook and other MAPI-enabled clients.

## Novell GroupWise

GroupWise is Novell's proprietary messaging and calendaring solution. Besides email, it handles instant messaging and task and document management. For the first time, a GroupWise client is being included in SUSE Linux 10.

## Samsung Connect

This is a proprietary, drop-in Exchange alternative. The Samsung Connect server provides what is almost a full replacement for Exchange and will support whatever calendaring standards finally emerge to support Linux.

## OPEN-XCHANGE

OPEN-XCHANGE was SUSE's attempt to enter the groupware market prior to being acquired by Novell. Built mainly around Java-oriented components, OPEN-XCHANGE offers a web-based interface that handles contacts, calendaring, email, and task management. It is based on Cyrus IMAP and Postfix. Working with SUSE Linux Enterprise Server (SLES), OPEN-XCHANGE can also do project management, forums, and bookmarks.

## Kolab/Kroupware

The Kolab initiative began when a German state government approached the KDE developers' group with some funding for a groupware solution. Kolab2 uses Postfix, Cyrus-imap, OpenLDAP, and ProFTPd as its open-source core, and it works best with the Kontact client.

## OpenGroupware (Ogo)

Formerly SKYRiX, OpenGroupware provides groupware and collaboration pieces to any existing email configuration. It provides calendaring, contacts, webmail, task management, resources, and projects and document management. It runs on the SOPE application server.

## phpGroupWare

This may be the best known of several projects based on PHP, which you will learn more about in Chapter 31, "Creating Dynamic Websites." Others include PHProjekt, eGroupware, and more.groupware. It is used with a database management system such as MySQL or PostgreSQL, plus a web server and an IMAP mail server. It provides a web-based calendar, a task list, an address book, email, and it throws in news headlines and a file manager for grins. The problem is that phpGroupWare doesn't really function outside of a browser, leaving the field to more robust clients.

## Hula

Yet another Novell open source initiative, Hula began its life as a proprietary NetMail server. NetMail was open-sourced in spring 2005, and its initial development team spoke openly of rethinking the way people collaborate and making Hula the application to support the ways that people really work. Its stated goal is "to be fun and easy to use, while scaling effortlessly from small groups to large organizations with thousands of members." At the time of this writing, however, version 1.0 was still a ways off.

## Conclusion

As stated earlier, corporate email will not likely change dramatically until an alternative standard is developed. That will likely come out of the discussions at the Internet Engineering Task Force in the coming years. Until then, businesses can and should try some of the existing open-source products, knowing that when the standards arrive, their business will be ready.

# References

- http://www.gnome.org/projects/evolution—The Evolution home page.

- http://www.mozilla.org/products/thunderbird—The Mozilla Thunderbird page. Links to MozillaZine knowledge base and help forums.

- http://pim.kde.org—Home of the KDE Personal Information Management suite: Kontact, KMail, Korganizer, and the ancillary tools.

- http://sylpheed.good-day.net—Sylpheed, the other GTK-based mail client.

- http://www.mutt.org—The mongrel of text-based email clients.

- http://www.fpx.de/fp/Software/UUDeview—The UUDeview multiformat file attachment decoder. Works with all encoding formats (BinHex, yEnc, MIME, UUEncode). Enjoy the Introduction to Encoding document and get some useful history, too.

- http://www.yenc.org/linux.htm—Linux readers and writers for the yEnc coding format.

- http://email.about.com/cs/standards/a/base64_encoding.htm—An excellent description of Base64 encoding.

- http://www.postfix.org/start.html—The Postfix home page. Be sure to click the Web Sites link on the menu to find a mirror site close to you.

- http://www.seaglass.com/postfix/faq.html—The Postfix mailing list FAQ, maintained by Kyle Dent, author of *Postfix: The Definitive Guide*.

- http://www.sendmail.org—The Sendmail home page.

- http://catb.org/~esr/fetchmail—The Fetchmail home page.

- http://www.paulgraham.com/spam.html—Paul Graham's original essay, "A Plan for Spam," outlines the theory of Bayesian filtering.

- http://spamassassin.apache.org—SpamAssassin home page. Check out the wiki pages for downloadable custom rulesets.

- http://bogofilter.org—Eric Raymond's Bogofilter project.

- http://www.nidelven-it.no/articles/introduction_to_thunderbird_5—A good introduction to spam filtering with Mozilla Thunderbird.

- http://www.iki.fi/era/procmail/mini-faq.html—The Procmail FAQ. In his own words, "The author wanted to call this a 'Mini-FAQ' but it keeps getting bigger. There are plans to rename it the 'Bronto-FAQ.'"

- http://pm-doc.sourceforge.net—The Procmail Documentation Project. See the PM-Tips page for sample rulesets/recipes and many other good ideas.

- http://www.clamav.net—Home of the open source Clam antivirus program.

# CHAPTER 16

# Collaborating with Others

So far we have talked a lot about Linux being network-aware. Perhaps the main benefit of computer networking is to advance the ability of humans to network. When humans work together, amazing things get done. SUSE Linux includes a multitude of tools to help you work with other people, whether your collaborators are on the other side of your office or on the other side of the planet.

Several types of collaboration tools are included in SUSE Linux, but you can break them down into two groups:

- Asynchronous communication—Mailing lists, Wikis, and Usenet news

- Real-time communication—Internet Relay Chat, instant messaging, and video conferencing

The advantage of asynchronous (that is, the people involved appear at different times to participate) communication is that it shrinks the physical distance between participants. People do not have to be in the same room at the same time to get things done. Someone in New York can post a message on a global mailing list or newsgroup, and some hours later someone in Bangladesh, who was sleeping when the New Yorker posted, can respond.

The advantage of real-time communication is that it shrinks the response time. With everyone (virtually, at least) in the same room at the same time, questions can get answered instantaneously.

In this chapter, you will learn about all these methods. We covered the basics of email in the previous chapter, so you know how electronic mailing lists work from the user's end, but that's not all there is to know. SUSE Linux has two packages that will manage your own mailing lists: Majordomo and Mailman.

Usenet newsgroups have been part of the fabric of the Internet nearly as long as email and took hold well before the World Wide Web was invented. Although Usenet now has an even bigger problem with spam and malware than email, there remain thriving and helpful communities of Usenet readers and writers that can help you get answers to a multitude of questions for the price of a well-crafted question. Tap into Usenet with one of the news-reading tools discussed here, and then consider hosting your own NNTP server.

More recently, a new collaborative information tool has arisen on the Web. Wikis, short for WikiWiki Web, are web pages that any registered user can edit. Wikis can be places for sharing knowledge and brainstorming ideas, within your team or with your audience. You'll learn more about creating your own wiki pages in this chapter, too.

Real-time communication tools have moved from the realm of teenage time wasters into serious collaboration tools for business. Chat and instant messaging technologies are now used to provide technical support for computer problems, confirm whether marketing and development are in agreement about a product, and even engage in complex business conversations and planning. In this chapter, you'll learn about the variety of Linux tools you can use to engage in this activity.

Do you need to discuss some issues face-to-face with an important out-of-town client? It is no longer necessary to hop on an airplane with an expensive last-minute reservation. Arrange a videoconference instead. Both GNOME and KDE have tools to bridge the gap.

## Usenet News Today

When Usenet began, it was a genuinely new way for Internet pioneers to collaborate with each other. Instead of having to use hit-and-miss methods of finding electronic mailing lists of interest and import to your work, you could set up a server for public bulletin boards where everyone interested in some topic could drop in, find out the latest infor-mation (or "news") about that topic, and drop out again. Anyone who had news could post it there for everyone else's use. People could ask questions and get expert answers, from real people. No one was obligated to read every message, nor would irrelevant post-ings begin to clutter one's mailbox (at a time when disk space was at a premium). What could be better?

For a long time, nothing could. Newsgroups were created on most topics imaginable, organized hierarchically under a few basic categories: Computers (comp), Recreation (rec), Natural Science (sci), Society and Culture (soc), Debate and Controversy (talk), Miscellaneous (misc), and Usenet itself (news).

Anyone could propose to create a new group in these hierarchies, and there are democra-tic procedures in which users vote to approve new groups. This procedure grew oppressive for some people, leading to the rise of the Alternative (alt) hierarchy, where anyone could start a group, and many did (witness the existence of the alt.swedishchef.bork.bork.bork group).

Other hierarchies developed as hardware and software companies delivered Usenet support channels; colleges and universities set up internal newsgroups for students and faculty; and enterprising community-oriented geeks set up newsgroups for their local communities. Some are still functioning today.

Spam first raised its ugly head on Usenet when a pair of immigration attorneys posted an ad for their services in every newsgroup then active. Before the millennium arrived, spam had almost completely obliterated real postings on many groups. But many others are still quite useful.

Chances are good that your ISP offers at least some form of Usenet access. Contact them to find out the address of their Usenet server and the newsgroups they offer (also called their *newsfeed*). Many ISPs are selective in the content of their feed, especially when it comes to the alt groups. These are often seen as the seedier virtual neighborhoods, with pirated software, malware, and less-than-family-friendly text and images abounding. If there is a particular group you're looking for, and it's not included, it can often be added on request.

There are a few public news servers available, and you can find a list of them at http://freenews.maxbaud.net. Unfortunately, spammers often take advantage of this opportunity to peddle their wares, so be careful when using this.

16

### USING GOOGLE GROUPS

Once upon a time, there was DejaNews, the Usenet archive, and it was good. Virtually every Usenet posting going back to the 1980s was included in this free web resource. Then the dot-com era collapsed and DejaNews was endangered. But who should come to the rescue, but the company working so hard to make the Web more useful to humans: Google.

Still technically in beta at this writing, Google Groups is both a way to search through the Usenet archives with all the standard Google search tools and get spam-free web access to all of today's Usenet as well. Google does, of course, place ads on the pages.

Just go to Google Groups (http://groups-beta.google.com) and do a keyword search, or browse groups through the links. With free registration, you can subscribe to favorite groups and create your own public or private Google groups. Figure 16.1 shows the alt.os.linux.suse group in Konqueror.

When reading Usenet postings, your client makes it easy to respond, either by email or as a public follow-up posting. Some clients support multiple "identities" for posting and emailing, so you can choose a different signature or return address.

### CAUTION

Spammers use software "bots" to collect every email address they find on Usenet, so never post a real email address. Use something that a human can read, but a bot would have trouble with, like mynameNO@SPAMmyISP.com.

**FIGURE 16.1**    Google Groups gives you a searchable and browsable Usenet newsfeed on the Web. This is the alt.os.linux.suse group. The standard Google ads appear at the bottom of the page.

# Choosing a Usenet Newsreader

Choices abound in reading Usenet in SUSE Linux. Many email clients can also deliver news. Several standalone clients are also around (Knode/Kontact, Pan, and several text-based choices). Some require you to be online when accessing news, others permit offline reading. Of course, there's also gnus for Emacs.

## Mail/News Clients

Reading email and reading news are very similar tasks: Read and respond, perhaps save for later use. For this reason, the easiest way to keep up may be to use a mail client that supports reading Usenet.

Many email clients do this, including some of the best known: Mozilla Mail/Thunderbird, Evolution, Sylpheed, mutt, and pine. Setting them up to read Usenet is usually just a matter of identifying the Usenet server (often news.<ISPname>.com) and including login information, if authentication is required.

Reading news in a mail client is usually a plain-vanilla experience, without some of the fancier filters used by a standalone news client, but threads are usually supported (if they are supported in mail) and responding to a post operates the same way as email.

Support for binary transfers via Usenet, including images, multimedia files, and programs, tends to be a mixed bag. The yEnc encoding format is much more widespread in Usenet (see Chapter 15, "Managing Email Servers," for more on yEnc), and if your email client doesn't support it, you'll miss out. As many viruses spread via Usenet binaries, this can be a good thing.

## Standalone GUI Newsreaders

Maybe your email client doesn't do news (for example, KMail), or you want something better adapted to the Usenet atmosphere (good binary transfer, bozo filters, and better ways to clear spam). Standalone newsreaders can be a good choice.

As with so many other GUI packages, there are standalone newsreaders for both KDE (KNode) and GNOME (Pan). You can include KNode inside Kontact if you want.

### Pan

Pan runs much like the Windows newsreader Forté Free Agent, but is more advanced. You can read feeds from multiple servers, including the Novell Linux support groups (see Figure 16.2).

**FIGURE 16.2**    Pan is an easy-to-use graphical newsreader that was designed for GNOME but runs everywhere. You can choose to display groups, headers, and messages in a tri-pane format, as shown in this figure, or in tabs, with one pane showing and the others in the background.

Pan supports offline reading, so you don't have to tie up your phone line to read news. This is a multistep process, but one that is easy to get used to.

1. Download headers for the group(s) you're interested in. The headers include (among other things) the subject lines for the postings, who posted, and how long a message is.

2. Select the thread(s) in the group that you want to read.

3. Download the message bodies and go offline (press L or go to File, Work Offline).

When you want to post a message, either by email or to the group, Pan gives you the choice to Send Now (if you're online) or Send Later (for offline use). The Send Later option is also good if you've just composed a really nasty flame and want time to reconsider. When you go back online, go to Post, Send Queued Messages to finish.

> **TIP**
>
> Pan messages marked Send Later are queued in the pan.sendlater folder. To edit or delete a message, choose Folders from the Show Groups pane. Select pan.sendlater and you should see your message in the Headers pane.

Pan has excellent support for Usenet binaries and plays nicely with yEnc. The filters are a little difficult for an ordinary person to decipher, and there is no manual or online help. A team was working on a manual as of this writing.

### KNode

KNode, although not identical to KMail, functions very much like it. As the only part of the Kontact suite not turned on by default, it might be considered something of a weakling; instead it is a fairly muscular client.

Figure 16.3 shows how to configure KNode to receive the official Novell support newsgroups, including the SUSE Linux and Ximian application groups.

> **TIP**
>
> There's an even easier way to subscribe to the Novell support groups: Open http://support.novell.com/forums/2su.html in Konqueror. Click any of the NNTP links on this page, and you'll be asked if you want to follow this link. Click Follow. KDE will open KNode automatically and download the current articles in the selected newsgroup.
>
> Now click the up arrow in Konqueror, and you'll be taken to the main newsgroup page to subscribe to more groups!

Setting up a client to read a particular news server is not hard. Generally all you need is the server name and know whether you need to supply a password (that is, be authenticated) before using it. Some news servers are public, allowing anyone to connect, but most require some identification. By default, news servers use Port 119 to communicate with clients. Like your mail client, if you expect to keep KNode open for awhile and want to check for new articles/postings periodically, you can set the interval here. If you mostly want to read news offline, you should not turn on the interval check.

**FIGURE 16.3**    Configuring KNode for the Novell Support forums. News client server configuration screens are very similar to each other.

KNode also lets you specify an identity to respond to newsgroup articles on a per-account basis. Click the Identity tab to enter in a name, an email address for the From line, and (if you want) a different address in the Reply To field. KNode will use the default settings if you don't say otherwise.

Although not hopeless, KNode works better with text files than with binaries. KNode displays images and supports yEnc. Filters are easier to create than in Pan, especially if you have created filters in KMail.

Go to Settings, Configure KNode, Reading News. Click the Filters tab and you'll see the default filters. Suppose you post questions to Usenet, and you just want to see the follow-up articles to your question. To do this, click New and follow these steps:

1. Name the filter **Follow ups to my questions**. Make sure the Show in Menu box is checked so you can apply the filter easily.

2. Click the drop-down menu to change the Apply On setting to Whole Threads. Leave the Subject area as is.

3. Go down to the From area and type the placeholder variable **%MYNAME** into the box. The filter will then look for articles with your name, as defined in the Identities settings.

4. Click the Status tab and check the Has New Followups box, and then change the setting to True using the drop-down menu. Click OK to create the filter.

16

5. Now go to View, Filter (or click the Filter toolbar icon, which looks like a funnel), and select Has New_Followups to activate your filter on the current group.

## Text-Based Newsreaders

Because there was Usenet almost before there were GUIs, many text-based newsreaders are still in use. Some are even under active development. Included with SUSE Linux are NetNews (nn), InterNetNews (inn), tin, slrn, and suck.

Before starting any of these, you need to set your news server as an environment variable. Do this as user, not as root. From the shell, type the following:

```
export NNTPSERVER=<YourNewsServerDomainName>
```

The next step is to view the groups on your server and subscribe to one or more. This is done by creating a .newsrc file. As an example, let's use slrn. Type the following:

```
slrn -f .jnewsrc - create
```

This configuration file, located at /etc/slrn.rc, is well commented and easy to customize.

When you create the .newsrc file, and, if necessary, log in, slrn will get all the groups available on the server. To subscribe to an interesting group, select it from the list and type a capital **S**. To just see your subscribed groups, type a capital **L**, followed by the Esc key, and then the number **1**.

Figure 16.4 shows slrn in action.

**FIGURE 16.4**    The text-based slrn newsreader displays a set of subscribed groups. Select a group and press Enter to read the messages.

# Collaborating with Wikis

The WikiWikiWeb, taken from the Hawaiian expression for fast, quick, or speedy, was created by Ward Christopher as a way of tapping into the collective knowledge of his circle of friends and co-workers. It combines features of email lists, software documentation tools, and the simple structure of the Web to generate useful, accessible, and frequently updated and reviewed information.

The idea caught on, and people are collaborating with Wikis in all sorts of ways. The best known example of a successful and popular Wiki is Wikipedia.org. Its goal is to produce a basic compendium of human knowledge about most anything. As of February 2005, the English version of Wikipedia was approaching 500,000 articles produced, with at least some articles in some 20 other languages. It has spawned other projects, including WikiQuotes, the Wiktionary, and the Wikinews citizen journalism project.

Dozens of packages have been written to create Wikis with. These packages, called WikiEngines, have varying features. Like blog software, one WikiEngine should meet your needs and idiosyncrasies. Wikipedia uses the MediaWiki engine. SUSE Linux comes with one engine, the Zope-based ZWiki engine. Other engines are easy to get, with varying degrees of installation difficulty. See http://c2.com/cgi/wiki?ChoosingaWiki for help in selecting a package.

## ZWiki

This package builds Wiki functioning on the Zope web application server package. Zope (the Z Object Publishing Environment) was built as an object-oriented tool for creating dynamic websites. It includes a content management framework, its own relational database (and works with other database management systems) and other publishing tools. It is written mostly in the Python scripting language.

Getting ZWiki up and running is a two-step process because you need Zope first. Get Zope installed via YaST, and then go to the Runlevel Editor in YaST (see Chapter 22, "Managing the Boot Process and Other Services," for more information on the Runlevel Editor) to turn on Zope.

Download the latest ZWiki version from http://zwiki.org. New versions are generally released once a month. Extract the tarball to `/var/opt/zope/default/Products` and then reboot the system to launch Zope.

Open a web browser to `http://localhost:8080`, and you should see the Zope welcome message. Click the link for the Zope Management Interface. You'll be asked for a username and password. The SUSE Engineers have created a default user, which is the information you should use the first time. Username: **superuser**, Password: **123**.

From the main screen, use the Select Type to Add drop-down menu to Add ZWiki. Click Add. Figure 16.5 appears.

Give an ID name for the ZMI and a title for your Wiki. Click Create Wiki (and Enter). You'll see the default page in the default skin (see Figure 16.6).

**FIGURE 16.5**   Use the Zope Management Interface to add a ZWiki Web.

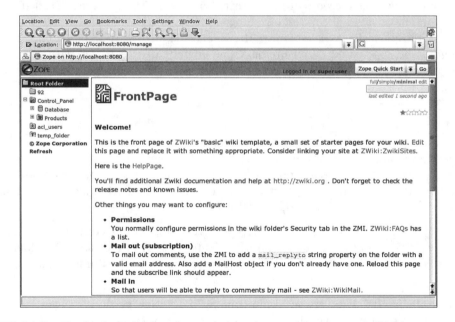

**FIGURE 16.6**   The basic ZWiki template appears when you create a new ZWiki.

Click the Edit link to replace the default text with your own (see Figure 16.7).

> **NOTE**
>
> Learn more about Zope in Chapter 26, "Managing Your Apache Web Server."

ZWiki is flexible in the types of text you can input. It can read and interpret standard HTML, Zope's Document Template Markup Language (DTML), StructuredText (Zope's attempt to simplify the XML documentation standard DocBook for engineers), and standard WikiWikiWeb markup. The latter, which creates a page link for all words with capitals placed inside the word (like WikiWikiWeb or WhyWikiWorks), can be simultaneously very cool and very frustrating.

> **NOTE**
>
> As was mentioned earlier, ZWiki was discussed only because it ships with SUSE Linux. Many other packages/WikiEngines are available and you will want to use the one that best meets your needs. Visit http://c2.com/cgi/wiki?ChoosingaWiki to select a package for your implementation if you want to use something other than ZWiki.

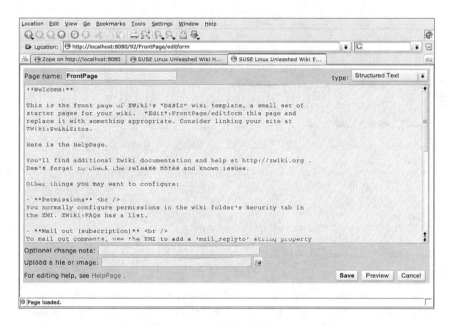

**FIGURE 16.7**   Start typing new material in your WikiEdit page.

# Hosting Electronic Mailing Lists

Mailing lists are a traditional method of asynchronous electronic collaboration. They require no special skills or text formatting abilities from the user, and can serve loads ranging from a small workgroup on a specific project to a global membership of thousands, even millions, of people interested in discussing the World Cup every four years. They are easy to administer, especially if the membership does not change much over time, and can help a website owner draw traffic with a touch of community.

The concept of an automated list is pretty simple: a list is an organized discussion among a group of people. To initiate a discussion (or thread), you can send a single message to the list management software, which then reflects the message to all list subscribers; that is, the people interested in the discussion.

Over the years, there have been several list management tools in use: L-Soft's Listserv, majordomo, and Lyris, to name some of the best known. Recently, an open source package called Mailman has pulled an increasing share of the traffic.

For users, Mailman provides a consistent, web-based interface for managing their own participation, including subscribing/unsubscribing, getting a daily digest of postings, accessing the list archives, turning off the list for vacations, and so on. List administrators get many automated tools that make their jobs easier and less time consuming. Mailman is one of two list-management tools included in SUSE Linux (the other is majordomo).

Mailman keeps track of all subscribers and watches for (and deals with) bouncing messages to some subscribers. It also generates the list archives, if the administrator asks it to.

There is always at least one administrator or moderator for any list—perhaps that is you. That person has access to a special, password-protected administrative web page; there, you can perform your list-god duties, such as

- Manually adding or deleting members, either because you're a nice person or your hand has been forced.

- Writing a Welcome message for new list members with the list ground rules.

- Setting the level of moderation for the list: Do you want to inspect every incoming message, or maybe just a new person's first few postings to certify they're not a spammer in disguise.

- Removing offensive messages from the archives.

## Installing Mailman

YaST does most of the installation tasks, but there are a few configuration steps you must take before you can create a new list on your own system. These steps are explained in the /usr/share/doc/packages/mailman/README.SuSE file. The SUSE team assumes you are using Postfix as your MTA (see Chapter 15) and Apache as your web server (see Chapter 26).

1. In YaST's sysconfig editor (under System), go to Network, Mail, Mailman. (You can also edit /etc/sysconfig/mailman directly.) Identify the following items:

   - MAILMAN_SMTPHOST

   - MAILMAN_DEFAULT_NNTP_HOST

   - MAILMAN_DEFAULT_EMAIL_HOST

   - MAILMAN_DEFAULT_URL_HOST

   - MAILMAN_VIRTUAL_HOSTS

   and run SuSEconfig -module mailman.

2. Call `/usr/lib/mailman/bin/mmsitepass` as user root to set your site master password.

3. As root, edit `/etc/postfix/main.cf`. At the bottom of the file, you will see that YaST has already configured a default alias map: `alias_maps = hash:/etc/aliases, ...,`

4. Add this statement to the line: `hash:/var/lib/mailman/data/aliases`.

5. Return to the root shell and reload postfix with this command: `postfix reload`.

6. Finally, call `/usr/lib/mailman/bin/newlist mailman` as user root to create the master mailing list. This list is needed for the inner workings of Mailman. You will be asked to set up a password as the site administrator; make it easy to remember, but relatively hard to guess.

Now you can use the web interface to set up your list.

> **TIP**
>
> Need a host for your Mailman list? You can find a directory of free and commercial hosts at the Python-friendly Web Hosting page: http://www.python.org/moin/PythonHosting. Look for Mailman in the Services Offered column.

## Running a Mailman List

Mailman files are stored in `/usr/lib/mailman/bin`. They are owned by root, but all members of the Mailman group have execute rights and can run Mailman commands, using either the web interface or from the shell.

Open your browser to http://localhost/admin to see the Mailman web interface. Now you can create and administer lists.

To run Mailman shell commands, change directories to `/usr/lib/mailman/bin` and then run your command. For example, to create a new list, type the following:

```
./newlist
```

The dot-slash is there because the commands are purposely left out of your path for security reasons.

When you create a new list, you'll be prompted to name the list (use all lowercase letters) and give the email address of the list owner. Mailman will send a confirming email to the owner you name. You establish the initial list password in this sequence as well.

You can find the documentation for Mailman in `/usr/share/doc/packages/mailman`. You'll find README files that cover potential problems with various mail transfer agents and operating systems and the current Frequently Asked Questions list. More formal documentation, tailored to different types of users, is at http://www.gnu.org/software/mailman/docs.html. You can read this online or download the PDF or plain-text versions.

# Working with Instant Messengers and Internet Relay Chat

Real-time electronic communication takes two basic forms: Internet Relay Chat (IRC) is like live Usenet, where you go to a group (called a channel) and discuss a topic identified by that channel. Anyone can establish a channel, invite users to participate, set ground rules, and kick users out if they break the rules. Everyone on IRC has a "handle" used to identify them in the chat. Things are relatively anonymous.

Instant Messaging (IM) is a one-on-one process where users can chat with each other without having to visit an IRC channel. Popularized by America Online's Instant Messenger, several networks have since risen to facilitate instant messaging across the Net.

SUSE Linux users can choose from several clients to handle their real-time communication needs, both IRC and IM.

## Internet Relay Chat (IRC)

Like email, the IRC protocol is fundamentally about text. The first IRC clients were based on the command line, and many of these are still in use. But just as plain-text email morphed into HTML-based mail with file attachments and GUI clients, so has IRC.

SUSE Linux includes these IRC clients: Ksirc is the default KDE client (although Kopete works with both IM and IRC networks). Xchat is the X Windows standard IRC client. Kvirc is another KDE-based client, and tkirc is a command-line client based on the tcl-tk language. If you don't already have a favorite, try them all.

> **CAUTION**
>
> For security reasons, never run an IRC client as Root. For the most secure IRC experience, create a special IRC user and always launch your client as that user.

When encountering IRC for the first time, it can be a little intimidating. Unless you know exactly where you're going (as when someone invites you to a specific channel on a particular network), you have a multitude of choices.

Your first choice is the network server. Each client offers a wealth of public IRC servers to connect to (Kopete lists 49 in its wizard; Xchat lists 73). The default lists included with your client can be edited. EFNet is the oldest IRC network, but there are many popular IRC networks, including DALNet and Undernet. Depending on the client, you can connect to multiple servers simultaneously to participate in different channels. If you are looking for Linux support, check out ChatJunkiesNet.

Each server hosts multiple channels/rooms. These are topic areas and can vary constantly. Some channels are always present on a network; others are there only when something is scheduled. You can search the channel list for a topic (especially useful in one of the popular networks, because tens of thousands of channels may be open at any given moment). The list will tell you how many people are logged in on that channel at that moment and give you a description of what the channel is about. You can get a sense of the channel's conversational tone by the description. New users should probably stay away from channels that announce that "Lamers will be SHOT." Most channels are public, but you can set up private channels that require a password. This is configurable in your client.

After you have selected a channel, you can jump right in to the conversation. As you can see in Figure 16.8, the client should display a list of the participants' nicknames in one window, and postings will appear as scrolling text. Introduce yourself, ask a question, or just say "Hi!"

**FIGURE 16.8** An IRC channel window. Postings scroll down in the upper-left pane, and participants are listed in the upper right. Post your message in the bottom editor.

> **NOTE**
>
> IRC can be a pretty nasty environment. Given the relative anonymity of its participants, things can happen here that are not rated PG. Language can be crude and folks can be in chat rooms for every reason imaginable. You may want to watch out if someone starts a conversation asking for your "a/s/l" (age, sex, location). Visit http://www.irc.org/fun_docs/nocuss.html for a humorous take on the language issue, with a few tips on IRC netiquette.
>
> When in IRC, the Golden Rule applies very well. Be respectful to other chatters, don't write in flashing ALL CAPS (even if you want to show off all the things your client can do), and ignore the idiots who act inappropriately.

## Linux Instant Messaging

Instant messaging should be much simpler than IRC, and it can be. The central problem is the multitude of proprietary IM protocols. The three dominant players—AOL Instant

Messenger/ICQ, MSN Messenger, and Yahoo Messenger—all use different methods to connect users of each of their clients.

As long as you and everyone else you want to IM are on the same network, all you need is one account. If you have one friend on a different network, you have to get another account, possibly with another username or password to configure.

You have two ways to solve this dilemma: get a single IM client that supports all the protocols or have all your friends adopt the open-source Jabber protocol and use a Jabber client.

Kopete and GAIM (for KDE and GNOME, respectively) are multiprotocol instant messengers that can run all the previously mentioned systems and leave you active for hours on end. SIM (the simple instant messenger) is an ICQ-only client (as is the command-line licq).

The GAIM configuration window in Figure 16.9 shows the protocol choices you have.

**FIGURE 16.9**    GAIM supports several instant messaging protocols. Choose from the configuration menu.

Jabber is designed to be a universal web-standard IM protocol. Someday the others should all adopt it, but that won't happen soon. If more people used Jabber clients, the day might be hastened. In addition to Kopete and GAIM, KDE has the PSI Jabber client, and GNOME has Gabber.

# Linux Videoconferencing

GnomeMeeting allows Linux users to participate in phone conversations and video conferences from any sufficiently equipped PC with an Internet connection. It uses the H.323 voice-over-IP (VoIP) protocol to transmit voice and (if available) webcam video to and from your location. GnomeMeeting will run on dial-up and broadband connections, although the video will be more troublesome on a slow connection.

You need a working full-duplex-capable sound card, a microphone, a webcam, and a video device to take advantage of all GnomeMeeting's capabilities. If you just want to listen in, the sound card is all you need.

The first time you run GnomeMeeting, a wizard appears that will configure your system. Enter your name, email address, and location, and select your connection type. GnomeMeeting should detect your audio and video devices, and away you go.

When you run GnomeMeeting, you must register with an ILS Directory server to make and receive calls. By default, GnomeMeeting uses the server at http://ils.seconix.com; you can configure a different server if you want. This will put you in the user directory and make you accessible to the world. Tell the people you want to connect with using GnomeMeeting to register with the server as well so you can call them.

> **TIP**
>
> The Skype Voice-over-IP (VoIP) service also works with SUSE Linux. Download the SUSE RPM from http://www.skype.com/go/getskype-linux-qt32.

# References

- http://groups.google.com—Google Groups. Read Usenet on the Web and create groups of your own.

- http://www.isc.org/index.pl?/products/inn—The InterNetNews Usenet server and reader.

- http://slrn.sourceforge.net—"s-lang read news"; the slrn newsreader.

- http://knode.sourceforge.net—KNode newsreader in Kontact and KDE.

- http://pan.rebelbase.com—The Pan newsreader for GNOME.

- http://c2.com/cgi/wiki?WikiWikiWeb—WikiWikiWeb, Ward Cunningham's original collaborative site.

- http://c2.com/cgi/wiki?ChoosingaWiki—Choosing a WikiEngine, with help from Ward Cunningham's assembled masses.

- http://zwiki.org—ZWiki, the Zope-based wiki engine included in SUSE Linux. Docs still in progress.

- http://zopewiki.org/ZopeAndApache—Getting Zope and Apache working together. Helpful when hosting ZWiki on Apache.

- http://twiki.org—Another popular Wiki engine.

- http://en.wikipedia.org—The Wikipedia home page, perhaps the best example of how wikis work.

- http://www.list.org—Home of the Mailman list manager.

16

- http://www.greatcircle.com/majordomo—The Majordomo list manager.

- http://www.siliconexus.com/MajorCool—The web interface for Majordomo.

- http://www.irchelp.org—The place to get help with Internet Relay Chat.

- http://www.irc.org/links.html—IRC clients, channels, networks, and bots. Find them here.

- http://tldp.org/HOWTO/IRC—The Linux IRC mini-HOWTO.

- http://kopete.kde.org—Kopete, the KDE instant messenger and IRC client.

- http://www.jabber.org/user/userguide—The Jabber user guide, for learning about this open-source IM protocol. Jabber.org also hosts a public IM server for you to connect with.

- http://gabber.sourceforge.net—The GNOME Jabber client.

- http://xchat.org—The Xchat home page.

- http://www.licq.org—LICQ, the mother of all Linux instant messengers.

- http://gaim.sourceforge.net—This IM client started as an AOL Instant Messenger (AIM) clone, but now supports most other IM networks as well.

- http://www.gnomemeeting.org—GnomeMeeting videoconferencing home page.

# CHAPTER 17

# Secure File Transfer

In the early days of the Internet, one of the really cool things about it was the capability to transfer files and programs from one computer to another. Using the File Transfer Protocol (FTP), anyone with a modem could connect with and download massive repositories of text files, shareware and freeware applications. People still use FTP all the time, although it is often obscured through the many graphical FTP clients. As you learned in Chapter 3, "Installing SUSE Linux," you can even install SUSE Linux with the help of FTP.

FTP's ease of use comes with a hidden price, however. FTP is not a secure protocol. Virus-laden files and other malware can be easily uploaded to FTP servers and spread across the Net. Unencrypted passwords and email addresses can pass through the network to be harvested by spammers and others with bad intent.

Fortunately, you can use new, more secure applications to get the benefits of FTP in a more secure environment. The Secure Shell (SSH) includes sftp, a more secure FTP client, and scp, the Secure Copy client. Both programs make file transfer safer and are still easy to use.

Another way of moving files around the Internet is by means of peer-to-peer technologies such as BitTorrent and Gnutella. These technologies are apparently as controversial as they are popular, but they use very simple methods of moving data across the network.

This chapter will look closely at file transfer software available in SUSE Linux, using FTP and peer-to-peer technologies. You'll also learn about creating a secure FTP server with SUSE Linux.

The next section discusses FTP clients, and the server information is discussed later.

# Choosing a File Transfer Protocol (FTP) Client

FTP uses a client/server model to move files across a network or across the Internet. It allows for the display of remote file directories. With the right permissions, users can open and edit files on remote directories with FTP as well.

By itself, FTP poses a security risk for both client and server, in part because it allows for login information, including usernames and passwords, to be entered (as well as sent across the network) via clear text. So "anonymous" FTP became a standard practice on the Internet. If clients are not given credentials to use to attach to and manipulate stored data on the FTP server, clients can connect to an FTP site with a generic account by using "anonymous" as the username. A custom developed in which the user's email address was used as a password. This would allow you to log on, but with general rights given to that of an anonymous user. Today, in addition to anonymous FTP, SUSE Linux users can be more secure in their file transfers by using the Secure FTP client that comes with OpenSSH, the free version of the Secure Shell. This section will help you use sftp and other FTP clients.

## Text-Based FTP Clients

It's good to use a text-based FTP client to learn what is actually going on in a file transfer. Dragging and dropping a file from one place to another is a fine way to simplify what is going on, but to understand the half-dozen commands that are being executed when you drag that file over can help you troubleshoot problems.

YaST installs LukemFTP as the default file transfer client for SUSE Linux. This client was written for the NetBSD version of UNIX, and it works quite well. It replaces the standard FTP client, so you can use all the standard FTP commands.

### Common FTP Commands

Following are the most common commands used in a typical FTP session. Be aware that after you have connected with a remote server, most shell navigation commands (cd, ls, and pwd, especially) work nicely.

### Starting and Stopping

- ftp—This command starts the FTP client. You cannot connect without typing this first.

- open—This command connects with the remote FTP site, using either the IP address or the domain name. Type **ftp** at the prompt before using this command.

- close—This closes your connection, but stays in FTP so you can log in to another server.

- bye—This command closes your connection, exits FTP, and returns you to your shell prompt.

- quit—Same as bye. This command closes the connection, exits FTP, and returns you to the shell prompt.

**File Types**

- ascii—Sets a transfer as ASCII text. Use this when sending or receiving text files only.

- bin—Sets a transfer as binary. Use this when uploading programs, images, or compressed archives. Also make sure that any program, image, or archive you download is marked with this tag. Some Windows clients upload files as ASCII by default; these are useless when downloaded later.

**Actions**

- get—Initiates a download of a single file from the remote server to your machine. Syntax: get <filename>.

- put—Initiates an upload of a single file from you to the remote machine. Syntax: put <path/filename>.

- send—Same as put.

- mget—Initiates a download of multiple files from the remote machine to your machine. Accepts wildcards as an argument. See also prompt. Example: mget *.png.

- mput—Initiates an upload of multiple files from you to the remote machine. Like mget, it takes wildcards as an argument. See also prompt. Example: mput *.png.

- prompt—This is an interactive command that gives you some control over mgets and mputs with wildcards. Prompt will ask you before you transfer if you want each matching file. This is especially good if you have a slow connection and find yourself downloading a duplicate, or otherwise unwanted, large file. This option is turned on by default.

- hash—Tells FTP to give you a progress bar of hash marks (#) to indicate how the transfer is going.

FTP includes many other useful commands, which can vary from server to server. If you want to check whether a server supports a particular command, run help after you have connected to your site. You'll get a list (but not a description) of available commands.

> **TIP**
>
> For full descriptions of FTP commands, consult the info page for FTP: **info ftp**. To really dig deep, read the comments in the source code, available on the SUSE Linux DVD.

**Using** lftp **Instead of Plain** ftp

The lftp command is not included with a default SUSE Linux installation, but can be installed by YaST. This can be useful if you have a dial-up connection and a transfer stalls or your connection dies in midtransfer. This package supports restarted downloads (as long as the server does, too) and can also support multiple downloads in a single session with job control.

17

wget

wget is a useful tool for managing noninteractive transfers, such as mirroring remote directories. It works using standard protocols such as FTP and HTTP, and also secure protocols such as HTTPS. Its noninteractivity might not appear to be a blessing, but this feature enables you to download files in the background or write scripts using wget to back up a directory to a remote location. This utility also supports restarted downloads.

Check out the online documentation at http://www.gnu.org/software/wget/manual.

## Using sftp for Secure File Transfers

The Secure FTP client, sftp, was developed as part of the OpenSSH secure shell project to tighten up security problems in some of the fundamental Internet programs. SSH replaced telnet as the remote-connection tool of choice for many users, and sftp does the same for file transfers.

The goal of sftp is not so much to manage the file transfer itself, but to securely transmit login information. This way, files that don't belong in an anonymous FTP directory can still be accessed by those who need them. Instead of connecting with a standard FTP server, sftp connects to the sftp-server component of OpenSSH, allowing for username and password encryption when you log in. sftp does not include all the built-in commands that standard FTP does (you can't use wildcards, for example), but the subset is still quite useful.

If you are concerned that the transfer itself should be secure, you can use the scp (secure copy) command instead of sftp. For this, you'll need to have explicit access to the remote host and also need to know the structure of the file system (that is, where the directory you want to transfer to is located). Secure file transfers are slow because the bits are encrypted, but the lack of speed is well compensated by the peace of mind accompanying the security of the transfer.

Returning to sftp, you can use this only if the remote server has OpenSSH installed. See more on OpenSSH in Chapter 25, "Setting Up Networks and Samba," in the section "Securing Network Services." Secure FTP access is turned on by default in OpenSSH.

Chances are you'll want to use sftp in interactive mode. Enter the IP address or remote hostname with the command to access the remote machine:

```
sftp <IP address>
sftp docs.protek.edu
```

By default, the remote machine will recognize you as the current user on your machine. If you have a different username on the remote machine, use the command a little differently:

```
sftp mmccall@docs.protek.edu
```

It will now connect to docs.protek.edu and identify you with the new username.

sshd is usually configured to run on port 22, and this is where `sftp` tries to connect by default. Some servers can be configured to listen on a different port number, and you can specify that port using the `-o` switch:

```
sftp -oPort2221 mmccall@docs.protek.edu
```

Now you are connected and see a command prompt on the remote machine. To see exactly what commands are available, type **help** or a question mark (**?**) at the prompt. Proceed with your session and `quit` at the end.

## GUI FTP Clients

SUSE Linux includes three standalone graphical FTP clients. Of course, all the web browsers (Konqueror, Epiphany, Mozilla, Galeon, Opera) have FTP clients built in as well. Konqueror in file-management mode (and the Nautilus file manager for GNOME) also has no problem connecting to a remote server and transferring files. Just type the URL for the remote machine into the Location box. In this section, you will learn about gFTP and KBear.

### Using gFTP

The gFTP client for GNOME makes it easy to transfer files from any remote host. When you open it up, you'll see your home directory in the left panel (as you can see in Figure 17.1). When you connect to a remote site, its home directory will appear in the right panel.

**FIGURE 17.1**    gFTP simplifies file transfer with side-by-side directories and drag-and-drop ease.

The program comes with bookmarks for some of the largest FTP file repositories, including the SUSE FTP servers, so you can browse around for interesting files if you're so inclined. If you already know the site you want to connect to, make the connection by typing the address and the additional information into the Host field. After you have connected, you can go to the Bookmarks menu to add this server to your bookmarks for easy access later.

By default, gFTP is set up for anonymous access and delivers your local email address (<username>@linux.local) as the password. You can change the default address in the Options menu, located under FTP. The program also supports sftp and other SSH protocols. To check the settings for secure transfers, go to the FTP menu, and then select Options, SSH.

Figure 17.1 shows the Emacs directory on the GNU project server at the Massachusetts Institute of Technology. At the bottom of the screen, you can see the text stream noting the commands that have been entered. You cannot directly type commands into this window, but all the standard commands are available from the menus. The right-click context menus work well, too.

As always with Linux systems, the default transfer type is Binary, so if you are uploading or downloading a text file, go to the FTP menu and select Ascii.

> **NOTE**
>
> Use the ASCII transfer option only if you are moving plain-text files readable with a text editor. Word processing and spreadsheet files are binaries.

To start a transfer, select a file or group of files and drag them from one directory window to the other. You can also use the arrow buttons in the middle of the screen if the download directory is displayed. You must use the **cd** command to display subdirectories in either window. Select the directory you want to display and use the context menu or the Local or Remote menus (depending on what you're changing) to run the command.

The directory listings are sortable by any of the columns included, so if you want to see the latest additions at the top, click the Date column heading. The columns are also resizable if you can't see everything you want.

When a file is being transferred, it is listed in the transfer window under the directory listings. It will have progress information listed as well. When you have completed your transfers, press Ctrl+Q to issue the bye command and close gFTP.

### Using KBear

Many KDE users prefer using Konqueror to manage remote file transfers and local file-management tasks. If you are more comfortable with a traditional FTP two-panel interface or simply have trouble wrapping your mind around the idea that remote files are just another directory structure, KBear can help. Essentially it opens a series of Konqueror windows that appear side-by-side, with a set of FTP-specific menus to help you along.

The first time you run KBear, you are asked to walk through several screens of a configuration wizard. Newbies may be intimidated, but accepting the default settings should work fine. You can always revisit the settings later from the Configure KBear menu under Settings. (The settings menu can also run the wizard for you again.)

KBear's bookmarks feature is called the Sitemanager, and it includes many of the same sites gFTP does, with some additional KDE-specific locations (KDE.org, Qt). The Sitemanager edit screen will import gFTP and other bookmarks (including WS-FTP for Windows) with just a couple of clicks. Figure 17.2 shows this dialog box.

**FIGURE 17.2**   Import favorite FTP sites to KBear from another FTP client with this dialog box.

KBear supports multiple connections and transactions, although the interface can get cluttered with the Konqueror toolbar at the top of each window. It also supports `sftp` and the other SSH protocols. One helpful tool is the two-click Synchronize Current Directories operation. This is good both for remote backup operations and website updates.

# Peer-to-Peer File Transfer

As controversial as it is popular, peer-to-peer (P2P) file sharing is unlikely to go away anytime soon. As long as Linux serves the "Information wants to be free" crowd (which will be forever), there will be Linux P2P tools.

Two general types of file-sharing protocols exist:

- The traditional, Napster-style model, where files are uploaded and downloaded from one computer to another.

- The BitTorrent model, where large files or packages are downloaded faster by allowing bits to come from several sources and combining them at the end.

Note that all types of files can and do circulate on file-sharing networks, including perfectly legal open-source software. At the same time, be aware that any file can be easily renamed and shared, so that the innocent-looking wav sound effect you pick up may be replaced by an active virus.

In this book, we're not going to examine the legal and moral questions of P2P file sharing. We note that, as of this writing, 6 of the top 10 downloads at the Sourceforge open-source development center (http://sourceforge.net) are file-sharing clients. Whether (and how) you choose to use these tools (as with all the other tools mentioned in this book) is entirely up to you.

SUSE Linux includes several clients that support each of these styles, which you will learn about in the following section.

> **NOTE**
>
> Some of these clients are not in the 64-bit SUSE Linux distribution.

## Napster-Style File Sharing

While recording industry legal attacks against the original Napster application and network have transformed the original concept, there are still many applications and file-sharing networks that have sprung up to meet consumer demands, especially for electronic music files.

Gnutella, eDonkey/Overnet, and FastTrack (aka KaZaa) are perhaps the best known of the file-sharing networks to rise since Napster's fall. What makes them similar to Napster is the user's side of the process.

1.  A user goes online to locate and download a copy of a file (for example, an MP3 music file).

2.  The client connects to the P2P network and searches for the requested file among the shared directories of computers online at that moment.

3.  The client then displays a list of matching files and a little bit of information about the computer the file is on (mainly download speed).

4.  The user selects one copy from the list, and the client downloads the file from the selected computer.

The good thing about the system is that no matter what you're looking for, chances are someone on your network has it. The downside of this model relative to BitTorrent is that you're a prisoner of your partner's connection: No matter how fast your broadband or LAN is, if the person you're sharing with has a flaky dial-up that is only online an hour a day, that's the connection you get. If your client finds another copy of the file on another, faster computer, it will start a new download, but this can mean your hard drive begins to fill up with a bunch of partial downloads of the same file.

KMLDonkey is the KDE-based GUI for MLDonkey, a traditional P2P client that is looking for interoperability with several of these networks. GTK-Gnutella is its GNOME counterpart. They are both a little troublesome to work, but you should be able to avoid some of the pitfalls with this guide.

### KMLDonkey

MLDonkey is a multi-network P2P client, which wants to work with all file sharers the world over. It began as a client for the eDonkey2000 network, now known as the Overnet, but now supports (to varying degrees) the Gnutella and FastTrack networks.

KMLDonkey is the GUI front for this client. Curiously enough, SUSE Linux includes this package, but not the core MLDonkey program—without which KMLDonkey cannot function.

As a would-be KMLDonkey user, you must first go to the MLDonkey website (http://www.mldonkey.org) to download the "core" package and the server lists. Several stable versions of the core MLDonkey package are stored here as tarballs. Download the latest and install it into your home directory. Those who want to ride the bleeding edge can download and compile from CVS here, too. The server lists are included in the mlnet package (in some places also defined as the "core").

When both files have been downloaded, extract the MLDonkey tarball into your home directory. Then extract MLNet into the MLDonkey directory. Now run KMLDonkey, either from the Internet, Peer to Peer menu, or from the shell. If your servers don't appear (or you get a Failed to Connect message), run the MLNet file manually. The servers should now appear in the KMLDonkey window and you should be on your way.

When you connect to the Donkey network servers (the default setting), the main KMLDonkey screen should look like Figure 17.3.

**FIGURE 17.3**    KMLDonkey displays the servers you are currently connected to.

By default, the Servers tab displays all the servers you can connect to. This is useful on a first run when you're trying to make sure something's connecting, but may be tiresome after that. Go to Settings, Configure KMLDonkey to uncheck the Show All Servers box.

Click the Search tab to look for a file. Enter your search keyword(s) at the top and any modifiers further down. The categories are mostly self-explanatory, but if you are looking for an MP3 file, you may want to set a minimum bitrate. This indicates the relative sound quality of a music file. A bitrate of 128 is equivalent to a standard CD recording. The higher the bitrate, the bigger the file, so if you set your "max size" at 500KB and a bitrate of 128KB, you may see files that last only a few seconds.

These are file *sharing* networks, so do your part by designating at least one directory on your system for access to others (and probably not more than that). By default, KMLDonkey shares the Incoming directory where it places its own completed downloads. You can add more by going to the Uploads tab and right-clicking anywhere. Choose Share Directory from the context menu and type the path into the dialog box. Unfortunately, there is no Browse button in this dialog box, so you must type the full path.

### GTK-Gnutella

Gnutella was one of the first decentralized networks to be created. Written by a developer at Nullsoft, the creators of the Winamp MP3 player for Windows, Gnutella was released under the GPL, and only officially available for one day. Nullsoft's owners, then called AOL/TimeWarner, were not pleased by this offering. A community of developers quickly formed to work on the code, and many clients have since been developed to support the Gnutella network.

The Gnutella2 network was created in 2003 and is designed to be a faster and a more efficient protocol than the original Gnutella protocol. Both networks still function.

GTK-Gnutella is a GUI client based on the Gimp Toolkit. It functions much like MLDonkey, but accesses only the two Gnutella networks.

The GTK-Gnutella interface is not exactly a thing of beauty, but it runs nicely. Like KMLDonkey, it first displays the servers you're connected to. To search for something, click in the New Search box and type your keyword(s). You'll be taken immediately to the Search Results window, which you can see in Figure 17.4.

You can modify your search in this window. Click Edit  Filters. Not especially user-friendly, these filter dialog boxes are nonetheless pretty easy to understand. You can set filters for size and name, along with several other parameters.

Select the file(s) you want to download from the search list and click the Download Selected button at the bottom to begin downloading. Searches remain active as long as GTK-Gnutella is running, and whatever main window you're in, you can always see the current results of your search in the Search window below the New Search box.

Settings are also fairly technical in the way they are presented, but if you are not sure what a setting will do, try mousing over the setting; often you'll see a ToolTip with an explanation or hint.

**FIGURE 17.4** The GTK-Gnutella Search Results window. Select your file(s) to download from this list. Note that the Search box on the left displays all your active searches and the number of hits it has generated.

## Wrangling the BitTorrent

Whatis.com describes the most important advantage of BitTorrent as follows: "Rather than having to send a download to each customer requesting it, the distributor or holder of content sends it to one customer who in turn sends it to other customers who together share the pieces of the download back and forth until everyone has the complete download. This makes it possible for the original server to serve many requests for large files without requiring immense amounts of bandwidth."

For the most part, BitTorrent is the sharing format of choice for big collections of archived text, books, and audio and video clips, including entire taped concerts and movies. With SUSE Linux 10, Novell joined the ranks of Linux distributors offering BitTorrent downloads of its ISO images, making it just a little easier to pull down that 3.1GB package.

BitTorrent works a little differently from the traditional file-sharing arrangement discussed in the preceding section. It goes something like this:

1. Someone with content to share creates a .torrent file to wrap the content in. This is done in the BitTorrent client. This person is referred to as the Seed.

2. An announcement is made on a website or mailing list that this torrent (or set of torrents) is available, with instructions given on finding its location.

3. People who want this file point their BitTorrent clients toward the seeded file.

4. Any other clients that have the file (or some pieces of it, depending on the client) and are online contribute bits to every other client that is downloading the same file. This eases the load on the Seed and speeds the download for each client because more bits are coming down at the same time.

17

5.  When a download is complete, it's proper form to remain online and keep your client open for awhile so others can benefit. The client monitors the upload/download ratio and often can turn itself off when you have uploaded as many bits as you've downloaded (that is, a ratio of 1.0:1.0).

Finding torrents is not always an easy task. One site that attempted to be a BitTorrent content clearinghouse shut down after the Motion Picture Association of America threatened a lawsuit. The safe choices are downloading from official sources and getting music from "trade-friendly" artists (think jam bands: Phish, Grateful Dead, Leftover Salmon, String Cheese Incident). An excellent site for the latter is http://bt.etree.org (this is the BitTorrent part of this large music-trading community).

### Azureus, the Java BitTorrent Client

The most manageable BitTorrent client for Linux is a bit of open source Java code called Azureus. Named for a species of frog notable for its blue coloring, Azureus is easy to install and easy to work with.

To install Azureus, head to the download page at http://azureus.sourceforge.net/download.php. Download the appropriate client for your system (choose between the GTK and Motif versions for Intel x86 processors, or the AMD64 or PowerPC versions for those processors). You will get a tarball that you can open with your favorite archiver.

Extract the tarball into your home directory, where it will create an `/Azureus` subdirectory. That's all you need to install the program. To set up Azureus the first time, you need to run the program from the shell. From the home directory, type `./azureus/azureus` to start the Configuration Wizard. The wizard will identify your connection speed and adjust if necessary. Click Next to continue.

The next wizard screen tests the BitTorrent listen port to see if it is available. Click Test to run the test. If it fails, you need to reconfigure the Firewall in YaST or your hardware router to permit regular BitTorrent operations. See the next Tip for more detailed information.

---

**TIP**

BitTorrent works best when other clients have direct access to your bits. BitTorrent clients communicate through port 6881. If you're using the SUSE Firewall, you have to configure it to open the port. Go to the YaST Security and Users module and click Firewall. Click Next twice to get to the Firewall Configuration: Services page. Click the Expert button to add services. In the Additional TCP Services box, type **6881**. Click OK, and port 6881 should be listed under Additional Services at the bottom. Click Next twice more, and then click Finish to confirm your changes.

If you have a hardware router that is your Internet gateway (as is often the case with broadband connections), you may have to configure that to permit BitTorrent communications as well. Visit http://www.portforward.com/routers.htm for helpful information on configuring several popular routers for BitTorrent.

BitTorrent clients will work even if you can't get the listen port open, but your upload/download speeds will suffer.

---

The last screen in the Configuration Wizard asks where to store your .torrent files. Accepting the defaults is perfectly OK. Click Finish to open Azureus.

When you have completed the installation, go back to the Azureus download site to get (via BitTorrent) the latest Java Runtime Environment (JRE). As with the Azureus client, click the appropriate client for your system. The difference is that Azureus will now open up to manage the download instead of your browser. You may even see the Upload Speed column activate as someone else uses some of the bits you've already downloaded.

> **TIP**
>
> When installing any new Java product, it's a good idea to check for a new JRE. Not everyone will have a convenient link like Azureus does. Go to http://www.java.com/en/download to get the latest and greatest. After the new JRE is installed, go to YaST and remove the earlier version.

Azureus has several plug-in enhancements for your BitTorrent experience, and a simple Installation Wizard to obtain and maintain them. Go to the Plugins menu and select Installation Wizard. Select By List from Sourceforge.net to see all the plug-ins download-able from the Azureus site. Click the plug-in name for a description of the tool, and check the box to install it. Click Next, then Finish to begin the download. After it's installed, the Azureus Update Manager will automatically keep both the main program and any installed plug-in current. You'll also notice that plug-ins download into your torrent directory, and you become a seed for the next plug-in download.

## Building an FTP Server

FTP is a client/server process. Most of this chapter has been about the client side because it is most likely that you will be trying to find files for download. In this section, you will learn about SUSE Linux's file-serving capabilities.

As alluded to before, two types of FTP servers exist: Authenticated (or *standard*) servers and Anonymous servers. A standard FTP server requires a valid username and password to give access. Anonymous FTP allows anyone access.

Anonymous servers are convenient for users, but can pose a security threat if not cared for. Fortunately, SUSE Linux uses logical permission schemes and a default configuration that makes it difficult for you to make mistakes.

SUSE Linux users can build both types of FTP servers, but this section will focus on secur-ing an anonymous server with the Very Secure FTP server package, vsftpd.

## Configuring xinetd for Secure File Transfer

Starting an FTP service in SUSE Linux is relatively simple, thanks to YaST. Go to the Network Services section and click Network Services (inetd). Inetd was the original Internet services daemon, but has largely been replaced by xinetd, which allows you to apply individual access policies for different network connection requests, such as FTP.

17

You can choose either package when you install SUSE Linux, but it is much better to select xinetd.

To turn VSFTP on xinetd, first click the Enable button at the top of the Network Services Configuration screen. The various services that can be controlled by xinetd become active and are no longer grayed out. Check the Status column—you can start or configure any of the services marked with three dashes (---). The dashes indicate that a service is inactive; any services that are running now are labeled ON and are also configurable.

Depending on what you have installed, you should see two Services labeled `ftp`, and both should be inactive. Click `vsftpd`, and then click Toggle Status (On or Off) at the bottom. Figure 17.5 displays the screen.

An X should appear in the Change column on the left. Click Finish to start the Server.

**FIGURE 17.5**    Start the Very Secure FTP server in YaST Network Services.

# Configuring Secure File Transfer Servers

The Very Secure FTP main configuration file, `vsftpd.conf`, is located in the `/etc` directory with the rest of the configuration files. You can edit it as Root. The default settings are designed for minimum setup of an Anonymous server. The Anonymous FTP User Settings section of this file sets up the rules for these users. Following are some suggestions:

- If you want to remove Anonymous access and make it an authenticated server, set anonymous_enable to NO.

- To allow Anonymous download of only files that the World (Others) have Read access to, set anon_world_readable_only to YES.

- To allow Anonymous users to upload files to your server, set anon_upload_enable to YES. This line is commented out by default.

- To allow them to create directories, set anon_mkdir_write_enable to YES. Otherwise, set to NO. This line is commented out by default.

- To allow Anonymous users to write (edit and delete) files in the public directories, set anon_other_write_enable to YES. Otherwise, set to NO.

You can make many adjustments while reading this file. Read the man page for vsftpd.conf (or visit http://www.vsftpd.beasts.org/vsftpd_conf.html for the HTML version).

# References

- http://www.vsftpd.beasts.org    The Very Secure FTP.

- http://www.cert.org—The Computer Emergency Response Team. The place to go to learn about current security holes, and the latest "virus alert" email.

- http://www.openssh.org—The open-source Secure Shell home. OpenSSH includes the Secure FTP client.

- http://www.cert.org/tech_tips/anonymous_ftp_config.html—Excellent guidelines for safely setting up an anonymous FTP server.

- http://www.gftp.org—The GNOME FTP client.

- http://kbear.sourceforge.net—A KDE-based FTP client.

- http://www.ncftp.com/ncftp/doc—Documentation for the NcFTP client and server.

- http://wget.sunsite.dk—Wget, the GNU tool for non-interactive (scripted) file transfer.

- http://enterprise.linux.com/article.pl?sid=04/12/20/1910209—A pithy description of what you can do with wget.

- http://www.gnutelliums.com/linux_unix—A list of Unix/Linux Gnutella clients.

- http://gtk-gnutella.sourceforge.net—GTK-Gnutella.

- http://bittorrent.com—Bram Cohen's BitTorrent home page.

- http://azureus.sourceforge.net—Azureus, the Java BitTorrent client.

- http://www.java.com/en/download—Download the latest Java Runtime Environment here.

- http://www.portforward.com/routers.htm—Get help opening your hardware router for BitTorrent.

17

- http://gift.sourceforge.net—The GiFT open-source FastTrack peer-to-peer project.

- http://apollon.sourceforge.net—A GUI for GiFT.

- http://kmldonkey.org—KMLDonkey GUI client.

- http://www.nongnu.org/mldonkey—The home of MLDonkey, where you can download the core program. Front page links to all the file-sharing networks the client supports.

- http://www.mldonkeyworld.com—News, downloads, and support forums for all MLDonkey users.

- http://wiki.etree.org/index.php?page=BitTorrent—The eTree BitTorrent FAQ page, with much good information on BitTorrent clients, how BitTorrent works, and where to find content.

# PART IV

# Basic System Administration

## IN THIS PART

# Managing Files, Volumes, and Drives

In the next four chapters, we will go over the system administration tasks you will have to know, whether you are managing a 1,000 seat network or a single system—your own.

Nearly everything you do in this chapter will be as Root/SuperUser. This is because you're dealing with important system-related issues. As noted previously, when you are working with Root powers, you can do wonderful things quite easily. It is also just as easy to blow your system away. Take care.

Here you will learn about the different file systems SUSE Linux can use to format your drives and other storage devices.

You'll learn about Logical Volume Management (LVM) and how to mount drives and add peripheral storage devices to your system, such as a USB key chain storage device.

Sometimes it's hard to find a file or directory on a big system. Do you wonder if an application you heard about at the Linux User Group meeting is installed on your system? From the standard shell file-finders to the brand new Beagle graphical desktop search tool, you can find things relatively easily with the Linux tools you'll learn about in this chapter.

We'll also tell you about GNU Parted, the partitioning tool included with SUSE Linux.

This information is essential for Linux newbies, and old hands might pick up something new, too.

# Choosing a File System

It's always good to remember that in Unix/Linux, a file system is not just the hierarchy of files and directories accessible through the shell or a GUI file manager.

File systems include the disk format type and the metadata surrounding files and directories. Because everything in Linux is a file with properties, permissions, and other attributes, everything attached to the system (printers, mice, keyboards, files on network servers, remote machines, FTP servers, and so on) is part of the file system.

When we talk of choosing a file system, though, we're talking about disk formats. The Linux kernel and SUSE Linux can work with many file systems. Table 18.1 shows the variety.

**TABLE 18.1**   Linux Compatibility with Various File Systems

| Name | Description | Run Linux Natively | Read from Linux | Copy/Move Files |
| --- | --- | --- | --- | --- |
| ReiserFS | Default SUSE Linux file system. Journaled. | Y | Y | Y |
| ext2 | Extended file system. Default for many older Linux systems. | Y | Y | Y |
| ext3 | ext2 with journal. | Y | Y | Y |
| JFS | IBM Journaled file system. | Y | Y | Y |
| XFS | Journaled file system originally for SGI IRIX, ported to Linux. | Y | Y | Y |
| Minix | The file system Linus Torvalds ported to the x86 platform. | N | Y | Y |
| NFS | Network file system. | N | Y | Y |
| FAT12 | DOS floppy disk format. | N | Y | Y |
| FAT16 | MS-DOS File Allocation Table. | N | Y | Y |
| FAT32/vfat | Windows 9x file system. | N | Y | Y |
| NTFS | Windows NT/2000/XP. | N | Y | NTFS > Linux only. |
| HFS | Macintosh Hierarchical file system. | N | Y | Y |
| ISO9660 | CD-ROM file system. | N | Y | Y |
| UDF | Universal Disk Format for DVD-ROM | N | Y | Y |

## Understanding the Physical Structure of a Disk

All these file systems organize data on a disk in largely the same manner.

The differences between them, especially among the Unix/Linux file systems, are usually related to the speed of retrieval. Disks are organized (or formatted) in blocks. The first block of any disk is the boot sector, which contains a very short program (a few hundred bytes), which will load and start running the operating system.

In the case of a dual-boot system, a bootloading program, such as lilo or grub, will be stored there. All other blocks (sometimes called clusters or sectors) contain the operating system, all your application files, and all your data files that constitute your life.

In Unix and Linux, each block is 1024 bytes by default. A block contains several smaller bits of data:

- A superblock, with redundant information about the complete file system.

- More redundant file system descriptors, useful for reliability and disaster recovery. Also explains why it's really hard to recover when you remove/delete a file in Unix/Linux. All the redundancy disappears, too.

- A bitmap of the block.

- A bitmap of the inode table (see the paragraph following this list for more on inodes).

- Information from the inode table.

- The data itself.

An inode contains all the information needed to identify a file—its attributes and permissions, its location(s) on the disk, its owner, timestamps—except the filename itself (which belongs to the directory).

There is one inode for every file. The inode table performs the same function as the DOS File Allocation Table (FAT). It keeps track of where files are located on the disk for easy retrieval.

## Working with ReiserFS

ReiserFS version 3 is the default file system for SUSE Linux. Created from the ground up by Hans Reiser, it is safer and faster than the old default ext2 file system.

It is a *journaling file system*, meaning it has a file (a journal) that records changes to the file system. Should you have a system crash, a power surge, or some other mishap leading to an unexpected (that is, involuntary) shutdown, recovery will be less traumatic. ReiserFS was the first journaling file system included into the Linux kernel, and it has been supported since kernel version 2.4.1 in January 2001.

If you've ever had Microsoft Windows crash or freeze up, you'll know the pain and agony associated with a nonjournaling file system.

Following the unexpected shutdown, Windows runs its ScanDisk program over your entire hard drive, checking for both bad disk sectors and reestablishing where every file snippet is physically located on the disk. Because broken links might occur, you may have orphaned clusters, a common problem that will result in a loss of data.

Although Linux is a much safer OS with far fewer software-related crashes, Linux users have not been entirely exempt from the involuntary shutdown. When this happens under the ext2 file system, the fsck program also scans the entire file system to make sure no data is lost in the crash. It could also take its time in processing the drive before you can log in.

The journal file makes it tremendously faster and easier to confirm that the disk is not damaged and that data is not lost. The journal knows what changes (saving new data, creating new files, deleting files, updating, and so on) were made to the disk since the last normal shutdown and tells the disk scanner where they are physically located on the disk. The scanner confirms that the location is not damaged and proceeds. This process does not guarantee that no data will be lost in this situation (the journal does not know what you typed since the last save before the crash), but it is in much better shape.

ReiserFS also manages blocks much differently than the Extended Filesystem (ext2, ext3), allowing many small files to share a block. This speeds retrieval and should display small files faster.

Its chief weakness is a problem only for people converting an existing ext2 or ext3 file system to ReiserFS. You must back up all your data and reformat the drive before installing ReiserFS. If you are installing SUSE Linux for the first time on your computer, this is nothing to worry about.

> **NOTE**
>
> The next generation of the ReiserFS, Reiser4, was released in early 2005. The file system, with financial help from the Defense Advanced Research Projects Agency (DARPA), has some advanced security features. These are outlined on the Namesys website: http://www.namesys.com/v4/v4.html#enh_security.
>
> You can expect SUSE Linux to integrate Reiser4 in an upcoming release.

## The Extended File System (ext2, ext3)

The ext2 file system was the standard and default throughout the early years of Linux kernel development. Hardly anyone used anything else until very recently. When ReiserFS first produced a journaling file system, Red Hat and others worked to bring journaling to this file system and ext3 was added to the kernel as of v2.4.16 in November 2001.

Ext3 and ext2 are nearly identical except for the journal file. If you are installing SUSE Linux over an existing ext2 file system, you might want to use ext3 instead of ReiserFS. The chief advantage of the ext3 file system is that it will automatically recognize files on ext2, and reformatting is not required.

## JFS and XFS

IBM's original Journaling File System (JFS) and the XFS file system from SGI (formerly Silicon Graphics, Inc.) are file systems that were designed for other Unix versions now ported to Linux. JFS was the file system of choice for AIX users. SGI created XFS to be the basis for its IRIX systems.

JFS introduced journaling to Linux, and has its own version of `fsck` to handle problem boots. XFS claims superior performance than either JFS or ReiserFS. Perhaps one of these will work for you.

## Choosing a File System

Don't fret endlessly over what file system to choose. All the file systems discussed here are excellent. It is a one-time decision, though. There is some pain involved with changing file systems after installation, especially when moving from ext2 or ext3 to ReiserFS. If you are connected to an existing AIX or IRIX network or you are transitioning from one of these enterprise Unixes, stick with the file system you have.

Otherwise, selecting the default ReiserFS is probably your best choice.

# Creating and Managing File Systems with Expert Partitioner

The first, and perhaps only, time you have to create a new file system on your Linux computer is when you first install the operating system. You learned the basics of how to do this in Chapter 3, "Installing SUSE Linux."

If you add a second hard drive, or have set up a series of mount points that you decide to adjust in one way or another, you can go to the YaST Expert Partitioner tool to handle this task for you.

> **NOTE**
>
> Until GNU Parted came along, partitioning in Unix and Linux was handled by the standard fdisk shell utility. It works a little differently from its DOS namesake, but performs the same essential tasks: creating and modifying the partition table.
>
> The main difference between fdisk and Parted/Expert Partitioner, aside from the GUI, is that fdisk does not preserve existing data. If you tell fdisk to make the root partition 10GB smaller and create a new partition where the old one was, fdisk will do exactly that. If there was data sitting on a block in the last 10GB, it will be overwritten.
>
> Feel free to use fdisk from the shell if you prefer, knowing its limitations.

Expert Partitioner (EP) is a GUI version of GNU Parted integrated into YaST. If you have used either of the Windows third-party partitioning products—PartitionMagic or Partition Commander—you will find EP familiar.

It simplifies the partitioning process and can adjust the partition table without harming existing data. You should know what you're doing before you begin, however. There is a reason it's called *Expert* Partitioner.

> **CAUTION**
>
> Unless you are working with new or otherwise empty drives, Expert Partitioner can ruin some data or even your entire hard drive. This is a very rare occurrence, but if you're making changes to your partition table in the middle of a thunderstorm, power surges can mess things up badly.
>
> Always back up at least your most important files before using EP, even if you are not planning to touch that mount point! And use an Uninterruptible Power Supply (UPS) whenever you have important data of any kind on your computer. This is the minimum protection you need.

18

## Using Expert Partitioner

Now that all the warnings are out of the way, we can begin to work with EP. It is actually a very simple tool. To open it, go to YaST, System, Partitioner. YaST will repeat the warnings you've seen in this section and make you click Yes before opening the tool.

There you will see your current partition table laid out, as shown in Figure 18.1.

**FIGURE 18.1**    Expert Partitioner lets you resize existing partitions and create new ones. The initial screen displays your current partition table.

It's a good idea to have a hard copy of all this information, so write it down in your notebook before making any changes.

In Figure 18.1, you can see that two physical hard drives are on this system: /dev/hda and /dev/sda. Each drive is 74.5GB after formatting. /dev/hda has two Linux partitions, Root (/) and Swap; /dev/sda has one Windows (NTFS) partition, seen here as /windows/C. The Start and End numbers are the block numbers, showing where on the disk each partition/mount point begins and ends.

> **NOTE**
>
> DOS/Windows (and practically all BIOS programs) supports only four primary partitions on a drive. Dual-boot systems have a particular problem with this setup. To get around this limitation, use the idea of turning one primary partition into an "extended partition" that allows you to create multiple "logical partitions," making more efficient drives by making smaller

sectors/blocks. There are few limitations on the number of logical partitions inside an extended partition.

You can install SUSE Linux into an extended partition; this is what YaST does by default. Linux file systems support up to 15 partitions/mount points.

Writing this information down is yet another safety valve in case of emergency, because you can reconstruct the table with the accurate start and end blocks if necessary.

At the bottom of the screen are eight action buttons that correspond to the task at hand. With EP, you can do the following:

- Create a new partition from empty space on the disk.

- Edit an existing drive or partition.

- Delete an existing partition or drive (and all the data on it).

- Resize a partition to make it larger or smaller.

- Manage a logical volume (this is covered later in this chapter).

- Create or manage a RAID volume structure (this is covered in Chapter 20, "Managing Data: Backup, Restoring, and Recovery").

- Encrypt a partition.

- Reread or delete a partition table (under the Expert button).

The following sections walk you through these tasks.

> **NOTE**
>
> When you're working with Expert Partitioner, you can do some experimentation without making changes to your system. Nothing you set up in the EP interface becomes final until you click Apply from the main window (refer to Figure 18.1).

**18**

### Creating a New Partition

Click Create to set up a new partition. Depending on your setup, you will be asked what disk to create the partition on and whether it is a primary or extended partition (see the preceding Note). EP then displays the Create Partition dialog box, shown in Figure 18.2.

Figure 18.2 shows the default settings for this dialog box. In addition to the ReiserFS, you can format the new partition as ext2, ext3, JFS, XFS, or as increased Swap. You can also create a FAT partition readable by Windows. The contents of the Options dialog box changes depending on the file system you choose.

A new partition can use only unformatted space on the physical drive. By default, EP will have this partition fill up the remaining free space, but you can choose to leave some space unformatted (and perhaps ready for another partition) by entering either a specific end cylinder or (as indicated) the size of the partition in megabytes (MB) or gigabytes (GB).

**FIGURE 18.2**    The Create Partition dialog box lets you set all the necessary options for a new Linux partition.

> **TIP**
>
> Check the Encrypt File System box to encrypt all new files created or moved into your new partition. See "Encrypting a Partition or Files" later in this chapter.

The Fstab Options button lets you set up Journaling mode (Ordered is the default), whether a user can mount this partition (No is the default), and whether to mount the partition automatically at startup (Yes is the default). You'll learn more about the fstab file in the "Mounting a File System" section.

The last section is the mount point definition. The default here is /usr, but you can use the drop-down menu or type in a mount point as well.

> **TIP**
>
> If you're adding a FAT partition, make /windows/D (or another drive letter) the mount point.

Click OK to confirm your choices.

### Editing a Partition

When you select an existing partition and click Edit, the dialog box is nearly identical to Figure 18.2. All the options are editable except for the size parameters. You must use the Resize tool to change that.

Why would you edit a partition? If you want to use the Logical Volume Manager (LVM), at least one partition must have the type Ox8e or Ox83. You can set that in this dialog box. You may also want to change the fstab settings for a partition without editing the file by hand. Or you may want to change the mount point for one reason or another, especially with a nonroot partition.

### Deleting a Partition

There are only two reasons to delete a partition with EP: You've copied off all the data and want to recover the space for something else entirely, or you have a nonroot mount point that you don't want to treat as a separate partition anymore.

The latter situation can occur when you define a mount point for /usr or /home to get a faster response from the disk, and the results are disappointing. In that case, move all the files back to the / partition before deleting the mount point.

To use EP to delete a partition, first unmount it with the umount command at the shell prompt. Open EP. Select the partition. Click Delete. You may get a warning, especially if you haven't unmounted or if you accidentally selected the / partition. EP will then mark the partition for deletion. The delete action will not be final until you click Apply. After you do that, the partition will be gone, and the space will be available. See the section on umount later in this chapter.

### Resizing a Partition

This is the trickiest part of the EP process and is the special trick of GNU Parted. The standard Linux fdisk program creates, edits, and deletes partitions. But fdisk, like its DOS/Windows counterpart, is destructive when it performs its functions. fdisk will cheerfully create a new partition where some old data is lying around, but that data will be no more when it's done.

Parted and EP will shrink an existing partition, taking care to preserve existing data and not overwrite it. You can then create new partitions on the empty space remaining.

To resize a partition, select the partition in EP and click Resize. The Resize dialog box (see Figure 18.3) appears.

Use the slider, the spin box, or type in the size (in gigabytes) you want your new partition to be in the Unused Disk box. The second, bottom graphic will show what the disk will look like after the resizing takes place.

If you change your mind, click Do Not Resize to return the settings to where they were. If you are ready to proceed, click OK. The partition will be marked for resizing.

When you have confirmed your intention to resize the large partition, use Create as previously described to create the new partition(s) to fill the newly created space. After you've done that, click Apply to implement the new changes. You can turn back at any time before you click Apply.

### Encrypting a Partition or Files

If you run a business with your computer, you probably have some files that are more sensitive and valuable than others. You want to protect this information from prying eyes. Setting permissions and other access control tools is an important method of securing these files, but some things need even more security. This is especially true with data on laptops and removable hard drives.

**FIGURE 18.3**    Expert Partitioner shows you the amount of space being used by your partition. Use the slider or type in the size you want your new partition to be.

SUSE Linux makes it possible, and relatively easy, to set up an area where files are encrypted within that space. You can set off an entire partition or create an encrypted file system within single files.

You have the option of creating encrypted partitions during the installation process, but you can also do this within EP.

> **CAUTION**
>
> Don't use EP to encrypt a running file system! Adding encryption will destroy any data on a running partition. Always resize another partition and then create a new, encrypted partition using the preceding steps.

To create a single encrypted file to hold secure data, click Crypt File, Create Crypt File in the EP dialog box. Another dialog box (see Figure 18.4) appears.

Enter the path to the file to create along with its intended size. This is set to 50MB by default. Remember that this will be just one file, holding a spreadsheet with your balance sheets, for example. You want this file to be big enough to hold a growing file, but not so big that it encroaches on your capability to store other files. A good rule is to estimate how big that spreadsheet could get over the lifetime of your computer, and then double it.

SUSE recommends accepting the proposed settings for formatting and the file system type (that is, formatting for ext3). Specify the mount point. Decide whether the crypto file system should be mounted during boot in the fstab options. Click OK to mark this file for creation. EP will put this file at the end of the current partition. Your encrypted file will not be created until you click Apply at the end of the process.

**FIGURE 18.4** Use this dialog box to create a single file to hold secure data. When entering the pathname, do not point to an existing file unless you have it backed up.

To access an encrypted partition, you must use the mount command to make the partition visible. You will be asked to supply the password. See the section on the mount command later in the chapter.

### Expert Functions

Two Expert functions round out the EP tasks. If you suspect that the partition table is not showing up correctly in the EP window, click Reread Partition Table.

It's not even close to being a common occurrence, but a bad label can get attached to a disk. If you're having otherwise weird problems on your system, disposing of the label can be a last gasp. Delete Partition Table and Disk Label is the equivalent of waving the white flag and saying goodbye. Along with the bad label, everything else on that partition will disappear as well. Always back up before running this one.

## Mounting a File System

A Linux system doesn't really care what is attached to it at any given moment. Do you want to connect to a printer down the hall, a co-worker's laptop in Australia, a backup mirror on the corporate server in Shanghai, or a floppy disk in your own machine? No problem—with the mount command and the right permissions, all these devices and file systems will appear on your system as if they were all just another part of your computer.

18

If you are the system administrator, you have near-absolute power over what file systems appear on your system, to whom, and when. In practice, this power is exercised through the use of the mount and umount commands, and through the /etc/fstab file governing file systems. In this section, you will learn about each of these tools.

## The mount Command

The mount command loads a file system onto your computer and makes it visible. To mount a floppy disk, for example, insert the disk and then type the following (as SuperUser) at the shell prompt:

```
mount -t vfat /dev/fd0 /media/floppy
```

This is how the syntax breaks down (and you need all this to make it work):

- Type (-t)—This flag and the next item identify the file system type for the platform to be mounted (in this case, the floppy is formatted for FAT32).

- File system—Point to the device partition you are mounting. Floppy disks are, by default, /dev/fd0. This information is set by and retrievable from /etc/fstab (see the section on /fstab later in the chapter).

- Mount Point—Where fstab actually looks for the files. In this case, /media/floppy.

It is a good idea to have all your peripheral file systems (floppy drives, hard drives, USB and serial-port file storage devices, CD-ROM, DVD, and CD-RW drives) connected when you install SUSE Linux. Why? YaST can then identify all these devices and build your /etc/fstab file automatically.

## The umount Command

Most of the time after you have mounted a hard drive or partition, you'll keep it mounted. You're always accessing it. Removable storage media are different; you'll often pop one in, work on files (or copy/move them to your hard drive) and pop it out again. In Linux this is a little more complicated process.

After you have mounted a floppy as described in the last section, before you can put another floppy in the drive, you must unmount the drive. To do this, you must use the umount command (without an N):

```
umount /media/floppy
```

or

```
umount /dev/fd0
```

Before unmounting any file system, make sure that no processes are using files on that file system. You will get an error message if that's the case.

## Using `/etc/fstab` to Automatically Mount File Systems

The default file system mount behavior is set by the FileSystem TABle, or `fstab`. YaST sets this up during the initial installation. You can modify it directly in a text editor (as Root) or use Expert Partitioner's partition editing tool. After you understand the structure of the file, it will be much easier to hand-edit `etc/fstab`, but EP's fstab options page offers a friendlier interface if you are reluctant to hand-edit critical files.

> **TIP**
>
> You can view, but not edit, your fstab file in KdiskFree. This tool lets you see your current disk usage, device type, and mount point. You can mount unmounted file systems as well.

Here is a busy `etc/fstab` file, containing several drives and partitions, along with a CD-RW.

```
/dev/hda2   /               reiserfs  acl,user_xattr     1 1
/dev/sda1  /windows/C       ntfs      ro,users,gid=users,umask=0002,nls=utf8 0 0
/dev/hda1  swap             swap      pri=42             0 0
devpts     /dev/pts         devpts    mode=0620,gid=5    0 0
proc       /proc            proc      defaults           0 0
usbfs      /proc/bus/usb    usbfs     noauto             0 0
sysfs      /sys             sysfs     noauto             0 0
/dev/cdrecorder        /media/cdrecorder      subfs
fs=cdfss,ro,procuid,nosuid,nodev,exec,iocharset=utf8 0 0
/dev/fd0               /media/floppy          subfs
fs=floppyfss,procuid,nodev,nosuid,sync 0 0
```

Each line in the `fstab` file represents another device, file system, or hard drive. The order of items in each line are identical, with six fields altogether. You would guess (correctly) that all the items included in the `mount` syntax discussed earlier appear here. In order, they would be File system, Mount Point, and Type. The other items are various options that you did not set in the earlier simple example of the `mount` command.

The fourth field indicates the mount options for that file system, separated by commas. For example, the Windows drive, `/dev/sda1`, mounts as read-only (`ro`) and all users can mount the drive. If the `user` flag is not set, only Root can mount the file system. `/dev/cdrecorder` includes the `exec` option, which allows you to run binaries from the CD drive. The / (Root) partition uses an Access Control List (ACL) to determine whether binaries can be executed. This means permissions are set at a lower, more fine-grained level than just allowing anyone with access to the partition to execute programs.

The other options listed here are generally specific to that file system. To see all the options that can be used here, see the `mount` and `fstab` man pages.

The last two fields (in the example, all are marked 0 0 except for /, which is 1 1) are digits that other programs use. The fifth field tells `dump`, a venerable Unix backup program, whether to back up the file system when it is run: 1=Yes, 0=No.

18

The last field tells the file system repair tool `fsck` how to interact with each file system: 0=Never, 1=Run at a designated time, 2=Run periodically, but less often than the 1s.

You should not have to edit `/etc/fstab` more than once, but if you have problems with the OS not seeing a file system (CD won't run, can't copy files from a floppy or Zip disk, for example), this is usually the place to start troubleshooting.

# Logical Volume Management (LVM)

The dilemma in partitioning has always been how large to make each partition (also known as a volume). Too often, you just accept a default, or make a wild guess about how much space you'll need for the data you plan to put on your partition. One day, you'll find yourself painfully short of space on one volume, while having a ton of room on another. Wouldn't it be great to have some space that you could allocate on-the-fly, even while a partition was already mounted? Logical Volume Management is a relatively new technology that allows you to use disk space from multiple drives in a single logical volume.

The LVM module in YaST is located under the System page. When you open it the first time, it asks you to create a Volume group. It's best to accept the default and create a System group, but allocate as much space as you want for your Volume group.

A Volume group identifies the Physical Volumes (PVs) on your system. These are the building blocks for your Logical Volumes (LVs). To create a new LV, click Add under the logical volume pane. You will need to specify a size and a file system (like ReiserFS). Click Finish to mount the new volumes.

When it's time to resize your LVs, return to this module. Select the volume you want to shrink and click Edit. Make this volume smaller, and then select the volume you want to expand. Edit it.

LVM works on any Linux file system and can also be used to create more swap space.

With this in mind, let's discuss how you find files within your file system.

# Finding Files

From time to time, you will need to locate a particular file in your file system. With SUSE Linux, you have a variety of tools available to do this. We'll discuss how to use the find, locate, which, and whereis commands, as well as several graphical utilities to track down files.

## Using `find`

The `find` utility does just what its name implies. It's used to find files in your computer's file system. The syntax for using `find` is as follows:

```
find path search_pattern
```

One of the advantages of find is that you can use a variety of search patterns. You can search for a filename, for a specific file type, for files of a particular size, for files that were modified at a certain time, and for files owned by a particular user or group.

These search patterns are created using the following command-line options:

- -name "*file_name*"—This option allows you to search for a filename. You can use a specific filename or you can use a wildcard pattern.

- -size + or - *size*—This option allows you to search for files that are smaller than or larger than the specified size.

- -type *type*—This option allows you to specify whether you are looking for directories (d), files (f), or symbolic links (l).

- -ctime + or - *days*—This option allows you to search for files that were modified more or less than a specified number of days ago.

- -group *group_name*—This option allows you to search for files that are owned by a specific group.

- -user *user_name*—This option allows you to search for files that are owned by a specific user.

For example, suppose you wanted to find a file named myfiles that you think resides in the /home/tux directory on your system. You could enter **find /home/tux -name "myfiles"** at the shell prompt. The find utility will then search the /home/tux path for any file named myfiles, as shown in Figure 18.5.

```
linux:/home/tux # find /home/tux -name "myfile"
/home/tux/myfile
linux:/home/tux # █
```

**FIGURE 18.5**   Using find to search for files.

The find utility, by default, searches all subdirectories beneath the path specified. In the preceding example, you could also enter **find / -name "myfiles"** at the shell prompt and it would find the /home/tux/myfiles file (although it will take much longer). For more information about how to use find, enter **man find** at the shell prompt.

In addition to find, you can also use the locate utility to search for files. Let's look at this utility next.

## Using locate

The find utility works great for locating files in the file system. However, it has one drawback. It finds files by searching through each and every directory beneath the path specified in the command line. This process can be quite slow. For example, if you were to use find to create a search that searched for a specific file from the top of the file system, it may take 10 to 15 minutes (possibly longer) to complete.

As an alternative, you can use the locate utility to search for files. The locate utility operates using an entirely different search mechanism. Instead of searching through directories, it looks for the specified file within its own database of files that are stored in the system.

The locate utility is part of the findutils-locate package. Before you can use locate, you must use YaST to install this package on your system, as shown in Figure 18.6.

**FIGURE 18.6**    Installing locate packages.

After these packages are installed, a database is created in /var/lib called locatedb. A listing of files in your file system is stored in this database. This database is automatically updated every day. If necessary, you can also manually update it by running the updatedb utility from the shell prompt.

With the database updated, you can use the locate utility to search for files within it. The syntax for using locate is relatively simple. You simply run locate and specify the name of the file you want to search for, as shown next:

```
locate file_name
```

For example, if you wanted to search for the myfiles file, you would enter **locate myfiles**, as shown in Figure 18.7.

```
linux:/home/tux # locate myfile
/home/tux/myfile
linux:/home/tux #
```

**FIGURE 18.7**   Using `locate` to find files.

As with `find`, you can view the man page for the `locate` utility to learn more.

In addition to `find` and `locate`, you can also use the `which` command to search for files. Let's review this command next.

## Using `which`

The `which` utility is a handy command for finding the executable files used by system commands. The `which` utility searches for files in a manner similar to the `find` utility. However, `which` searches for files only in the directories contained in the `PATH` variable.

At this point, you've probably noticed that you can run system commands, such as `which`, `locate`, `find`, `cp`, `rm`, and `cd`, regardless of what your current directory in the file system is. That's because the executable files for these commands reside in directories that are included in the `PATH` variable. You can see a listing of these directories by entering **echo $PATH** at the shell prompt, as shown in Figure 18.8.

```
linux:/home/tux # echo $PATH
/usr/sbin:/bin:/usr/bin:/sbin:/usr/X11R6/bin
linux:/home/tux #
```

**FIGURE 18.8**   Viewing directories in the PATH variable.

The `which` utility is used to generate a search that is limited to the directories in the `PATH` variable. For example, if you wanted to find out where the `cp` executable resides, you would enter the following:

**which cp**

The `which` utility then returns the path where `cp` is located, as shown in Figure 18.9.

```
linux:/home/tux # echo $PATH
/usr/sbin:/bin:/usr/bin:/sbin:/usr/X11R6/bin
linux:/home/tux # which cp
/bin/cp
linux:/home/tux #
```

**FIGURE 18.9**   Using **which**.

When working with system commands, you can also use the **whereis** utility. Let's explore this command next.

18

## Using whereis

Like which, the whereis utility is used to find the location in the file system where system commands reside. However, it can return much more information about the file than which can. It not only returns the location of the file, it also returns the location of the man page file and of the source code file (if it exists).

The syntax for using whereis is relatively straightforward. Enter

**whereis *command***

For example, if you wanted to get information about the rm command, you would enter the following:

**whereis rm**

The whereis utility then returns the relevant data, as shown in Figure 18.10.

```
linux:/home/tux # whereis rm
rm: /bin/rm /usr/share/man/man1/rm.1.gz /usr/share/man/man1p/rm.1p.gz
linux:/home/tux # █
```

**FIGURE 18.10**   Using whereis.

If you want to limit the output provided by whereis, you can use the following syntax:

**whereis *option command***

The options you can use include the following:

- **-b**: Returns only the location of the command in the file system.
- **-m**: Returns only the name and location of the command's associated man page files.
- **-s**: Returns only the name and location of the command's associated source code file.

In addition to these command-line utilities, SUSE Linux also includes graphical utilities that can be used to search for files. Let's look at these next.

## Using kfind

The first utility we will explore is **kfind**, which is a graphical version of find that runs within the KDE shell. To use KFind, select K Menu, Find Files/Folders. The screen in Figure 18.11 is displayed.

**FIGURE 18.11**  The kfind interface.

Within this interface, you can configure and execute complex search operations. To do this, complete the following:

1. In the Named field, enter the *name* of the file you want to search for. You can use wildcard characters such as * and ? to expand your search results.

2. In the Look In field, enter the *path* in which kfind should begin its search.

3. If you want kfind to search for the specified file in subdirectories within the specified path, mark Include Subfolders.

4. Select Find. The results of your search are displayed in the field below the search criteria, as shown in Figure 18.12.

**FIGURE 18.12**    **kfind** search results.

In addition to kfind, you can also use a new, more advanced graphical search tool on SUSE Linux: Beagle.

## Using Beagle

Beagle is a search tool that can be used to find different types of information from a variety of data sources associated with your user account. Beagle can search your personal documents, text files (including source code), email, browser history, instant messages, web pages on the Internet, man pages, help files, and media files.

To use Beagle, you must first install the beagle package on your system using YaST, as shown in Figure 18.13.

**FIGURE 18.13**    Installing Beagle.

Be warned; the Beagle package has a number of dependencies that will need to be installed along with it. When you select Accept in YaST, a screen will be displayed listing the additional packages that must be modified or installed to support Beagle, as shown in Figure 18.14.

After you have Beagle installed, the next thing you need to do is start the daemon. It's important that you understand that the Beagle daemon operates in a different manner from other system daemons you may be familiar with. Most other daemons run as either your root user or another specialized user account.

The Beagle daemon, on the other hand, is run from within your individual user account. This is because Beagle searches for data that exists within your own user "space." To start the Beagle daemon, open a terminal session and enter **beagled** at the shell prompt. The daemon will run in the background and begin automatically indexing content available to your user account.

**FIGURE 18.14**    Installing Beagle dependencies.

If you want to customize how the daemon behaves, you can run the Beagle configuration utility by entering **beagle-settings** from the shell prompt. When you do, the screen shown in Figure 18.15 is displayed.

**FIGURE 18.15**    Configuring Beagle indexing and search behavior.

Under the Search tab, you can configure whether `beagled` automatically starts searches and indexing as well as the hotkey sequence required to open the search window. You can configure what `beagled` will index by selecting the Indexing tab, shown in Figure 18.16.

**FIGURE 18.16**    Configuring content to be indexed.

Under this tab, you can configure specific directories that should be indexed and other directories that should not be indexed. By default, all subdirectories of the directories specified are included. As the daemon is running, you can see the content it has indexed by entering **beagle-index-info** at the shell prompt.

Beagle will conduct its searching and indexing operations in the background and run with a low priority so that it doesn't take up excessive amounts of CPU time or hard disk bandwidth. In this mode, the indexing operation could take many hours to complete. However, you can force `beagled` to run at a higher priority and complete the index process much faster. This is done by stopping the daemon, entering **export BEAGLE_EXERCISE_THE_DOG=1** at the shell prompt, and then restarting the daemon.

After your indexing is complete, you can use the Bleeding Edge Search Tool (BEST) to search for data. At the shell prompt, enter `best –show-window`. The screen in Figure 18.17 is displayed.

In the Search Terms field, you can enter the text you want to search for. In the drop-down list, select the data source you want to search, and then select Find.

You can also use a web browser to compose and execute searches. The Beagle daemon includes a small web server application that is enabled by default on port 8888. To access the `beagled` daemon through a browser window, navigate to http://localhost:8888/beagle/search.aspx.

**FIGURE 18.17**    Using BEST to search with Beagle.

With this in mind, let's now discuss some more advanced tasks you can perform with your Linux file system.

# File System Manipulation

For some people, reading books and going to lectures or discussions are the best way to learn new things. For others, playing around on a system is the way to go. If you want to see for yourself how things work in different file systems, try creating a file system using the loopback file system—a special file system that lets you accomplish this interesting and useful feat. You can use the file system you create to experiment with and practice almost all the shell commands found in this chapter with no fear of damaging your system.

> **TIP**
>
> To do this on a larger scale, you can install a basic SUSE Linux system into the Xen virtual machine. Pick a file system, don't install the graphical end, and you have another playground apart from your working system. See the Xen section of Chapter 11, "Going Cross-Platform," for details.

## Creating a File System for Testing

People who run Linux tend to be a tinkerer's lot. They like to try new things and are not afraid of getting under the hood and plumbing the depths of their computers to see what exactly is going on. Although many Linux users have multiple machines (and parts of machines) cluttering up the house, most people have just one computer with a single hard drive to play with. If you then have data on that computer that is really important, you don't want to blow away your operating system on a regular basis after an experiment goes awry. This is perhaps the reason the loopback file system was born. With this handy tool, you can create an image file containing the file system of your choice, and mount it—leaving your "real" file system alone and safe.

You could do this exercise on a floppy or other removable drive, but if you want ample room to play in, working off a hard drive is a better way.

### Step 1—Make a Blank Image File

Use the dd command to create a file with a block size of 1,024 bytes (a megabyte) and create a file that is 10MB in size. You should have enough free space on your drive to accommodate a file that size, of course. You need 10,000 blocks of 1KB (1,024 bits) in this 10MB file, so here's what you type:

```
Dd if=/dev/zero of=/tmp/test-img bs=1024 count=10000
```

The shell responds with

```
10000+0 records in
10000+0 records out
```

### Step 2—Make a File System

Now we need to make the system think the file is a block device instead of an ASCII file, so we use losetup, a utility that associates loop devices with regular files or block devices. You will use the loopback device /dev/loop0. losetup /dev/loop0 /tmp/test-img.

Then format the file with an ext3 file system:

```
mkfs -t ext3 -q /tmp/test-img
```

If prompted that test.img is not a block device, enter **y** to proceed anyway.

### Step 3—Mount the Test File System

Your test file system is ready to go, except that you can't do much with it until it is mounted on your system. Let's start with a mount point, then.

```
mkdir /mnt/image
```

Now we can mount it:

```
mount -o loop /tmp/test.img /mnt/image
```

After mounting the file system, look at it with the df command:

```
df -h /mnt/image
```

And get this response:

```
Filesystem        Size    Used    Avail    Use%    Mounted on
/tmp/test-img     10M     1.1M    9M       2%      /mnt/image
```

To unmount the image:

```
umount /mnt/image
```

You can even back up the image, in case something happens while you're playing:

```
cp /tmp/test-img test-img.bak
```

When you've confirmed that you have a mounted image file, you can create directories, copy files to it, delete files, attempt to recover them, and, generally speaking, do anything you want with this file system. It's a playpen where you can learn valuable lessons with no risk. If you somehow irreparably damage the file system on the image, unmount it, delete it, and start over, perhaps with that backup you just made. So have fun!

Let's now discuss how to mount a read-only partition on a running system.

## Mounting a Read-Only Partition on a Running System

From time to time, you may need to mount a partition in your file system in such a manner that you can view the data that it contains but not be able to make changes to it. This can be accomplished by mounting the partition in *read-only* mode. You can do this in two ways. The first is with the mount command. At the shell prompt, enter

**mount -r device mount_point**

For example, if you had a partition at /dev/sda3 and you wanted to mount it at the /extra directory, you would enter the following:

**mount -r /dev/sda3 /extra**

This is shown in Figure 18.18.

```
linux:/ # mount -r /dev/sda3 /extra
linux:/ # mount
/dev/sda2 on / type reiserfs (rw,acl,user_xattr)
proc on /proc type proc (rw)
sysfs on /sys type sysfs (rw)
tmpfs on /dev/shm type tmpfs (rw)
devpts on /dev/pts type devpts (rw,mode=0620,gid=5)
usbfs on /proc/bus/usb type usbfs (rw)
/dev/fd0 on /media/floppy type subfs (rw,nosuid,nodev,sync,fs=floppyfss,procuid)
/dev/sda3 on /extra type reiserfs (ro)
linux:/ # ▮
```

**FIGURE 18.18**    Mounting a partition in read-only mode.

In Figure 18.18, you can see that the /dev/sda3 partition is mounted in the /extra directory. Notice that when the mount command is subsequently issued without arguments, the mounting for /dev/sda3 is shown with a (ro) designation, indicating that the partition is mounted read-only.

In addition to using mount, you can automatically mount the partition read-only using your fstab file. Simply add ro to the mount options field, as shown in Figure 18.19.

With this in mind, let's now look at mounting an image file as a floppy disk device.

18

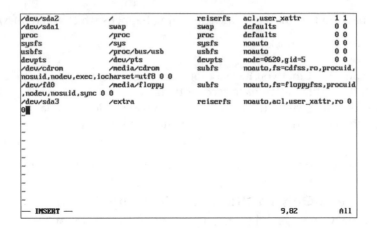

```
/dev/sda2              /                 reiserfs   acl,user_xattr          1 1
/dev/sda1       swap                     swap       defaults                0 0
proc            /proc                    proc       defaults                0 0
sysfs           /sys                     sysfs      noauto                  0 0
usbfs           /proc/bus/usb            usbfs      noauto                  0 0
devpts          /dev/pts                 devpts     mode=0620,gid=5         0 0
/dev/cdrom      /media/cdrom             subfs      noauto,fs=cdfss,ro,procuid,
nosuid,nodev,exec,iocharset=utf8 0 0
/dev/fd0        /media/floppy            subfs      noauto,fs=floppyfss,procuid
,nodev,nosuid,sync 0 0
/dev/sda3       /extra                   reiserfs   noauto,acl,user_xattr,ro 0
0

-
-
-
-
-
-
-
-
— INSERT —                                              9,82        All
```

**FIGURE 18.19**    Mounting a partition in read-only mode using fstab.

## Examining a Floppy Image File

Earlier in this chapter, you learned how to mount floppy disks on your SUSE Linux
system. Using the loopback filesystem, you can also mount an image file as a floppy disk.
This is done by completing the following:

1. Open a terminal session.

2. Switch to your root user.

3. Create the image file by entering **dd if=/dev/zero of=floppy.img bs=512
   count=2880** at the shell prompt.

4. At the shell prompt, enter **losetup /dev/loop0 floppy.img**.

5. Format the file using the MSDOS file system by entering **mkdosfs /dev/loop0** at the
   shell prompt.

6. Mount the image file as a floppy by entering **mount -t msdos /dev/loop0 /media/
   floppy**.

This process is shown in Figure 18.20.

```
linux:~ # dd if=/dev/zero of=floppy.img bs=512 count=2880
2880+0 records in
2880+0 records out
1474560 bytes (1.5 MB) copied, 0.051337 seconds, 28.7 MB/s
linux:~ # losetup /dev/loop0 floppy.img
linux:~ # mkdosfs /dev/loop0
mkdosfs 2.11 (12 Mar 2005)
linux:~ # mount -t msdos /dev/loop0 /media/floppy
linux:~ #
```

**FIGURE 18.20**    Mounting an image file as a floppy.

Before ending this chapter, we need to discuss one more topic: working with character
and block devices. Let's look at this next.

# Managing Files for Character Devices, Block Devices, and Special Devices

As you've probably noticed as we've gone through this chapter, every device in your SUSE Linux system is represented as a file in the /dev directory. Your hard disk drive is represented as a file, such as hda (IDE) or sda (SCSI). Your floppy disk drive is represented as a file, such as fd0. Even your CD-ROM drive is represented by the cdrom file, which is actually a symbolic link to another file, such as hdb or hdc. These files allow your hardware devices to function as one of the following device types:

- **Character devices**—Character devices transfer data in a serial fashion, one piece of information at a time. Modems, keyboards, mice, and terminals are examples of character devices.

- **Block devices**—Block devices are those that, unlike a character device, provide a degree of random access to the data they contain. Hard disk drives, floppy disk drives, and CD/DVD drives are examples of block devices.

Every device in your system needs a driver for the Linux kernel to be able to interface with it. For example, your IDE hard disk drive needs a driver; all SCSI devices in your system need a device driver as well. An important point to remember is that multiple devices of the same type can be serviced by the same kernel driver. For example, if you had three SCSI hard drives in your system, a single instance of the SCSI kernel driver can manage the three physically separate devices.

The Linux kernel keeps track of these different devices using *major* and *minor* device numbers. These numbers are assigned to each device's associated file in /dev. The major number indicates the type of device associated with the file. For example, consider the files displayed in Figure 18.21.

```
brw-rw----  1 root disk 3,   0 Aug 28 14:37 /dev/hda
brw-rw----  1 root disk 3,   1 Aug 28 14:37 /dev/hda1
brw-rw----  1 root disk 3,  10 Aug 28 14:37 /dev/hda10
brw-rw----  1 root disk 3,  11 Aug 28 14:37 /dev/hda11
brw-rw----  1 root disk 3,  12 Aug 28 14:37 /dev/hda12
brw-rw----  1 root disk 3,  13 Aug 28 14:37 /dev/hda13
brw-rw----  1 root disk 3,  14 Aug 28 14:37 /dev/hda14
brw-rw----  1 root disk 3,  15 Aug 28 14:37 /dev/hda15
brw-rw----  1 root disk 3,  16 Aug 28 14:37 /dev/hda16
brw-rw----  1 root disk 3,  17 Aug 28 14:37 /dev/hda17
brw-rw----  1 root disk 3,  18 Aug 28 14:37 /dev/hda18
brw-rw----  1 root disk 3,  19 Aug 28 14:37 /dev/hda19
brw-rw----  1 root disk 3,   2 Aug 28 14:37 /dev/hda2
brw-rw----  1 root disk 3,  20 Aug 28 14:37 /dev/hda20
brw-rw----  1 root disk 3,  21 Aug 28 14:37 /dev/hda21
brw-rw----  1 root disk 3,  22 Aug 28 14:37 /dev/hda22
brw-rw----  1 root disk 3,  23 Aug 28 14:37 /dev/hda23
brw-rw----  1 root disk 3,  24 Aug 28 14:37 /dev/hda24
brw-rw----  1 root disk 3,  25 Aug 28 14:37 /dev/hda25
brw-rw----  1 root disk 3,  26 Aug 28 14:37 /dev/hda26
brw-rw----  1 root disk 3,  27 Aug 28 14:37 /dev/hda27
brw-rw----  1 root disk 3,  28 Aug 28 14:37 /dev/hda28
brw-rw----  1 root disk 3,  29 Aug 28 14:37 /dev/hda29
--More--
```

**FIGURE 18.21**    Major and minor numbers.

18

In Figure 18.21, the `ls  -l` command has been used to display the various IDE device files in /dev, denoted as hda. Notice in the middle of each line in the output of ls that two numbers are displayed. The first number is the major number. All IDE devices have a major number of 3. (SCSI devices have a major number of 8.) The major number identifies which device driver the kernel should use to interface with the particular device.

In Figure 18.21, you will also see a second number listed in the middle of each line of the output of ls. This is the minor number. For example, device file hda has a major number of 3 and a minor number of 0. The minor number identifies the specific node of the device. In Figure 18.21, you can see that device hda1 (the first partition on the master IDE hard drive on the primary IDE channel) has a major number of 3 and a minor number of 1.

In addition, the output of ls, shown in Figure 18.21, indicates the type of device represented by each file. This is indicated by the first character of each line. Notice that each hda line in Figure 18.21 begins with a b. This indicates that the IDE hard disk drives are block devices. By way of comparison, refer to Figure 18.22.

```
linux:/ # ls -l /dev/tty1*
crw-rw----  1 root tty 4,  1 Sep  5 17:36 /dev/tty1
crw--w----  1 root tty 4, 10 Sep  6 09:47 /dev/tty10
crw--w----  1 root tty 4, 11 Aug 28 14:37 /dev/tty11
crw--w----  1 root tty 4, 12 Aug 28 14:37 /dev/tty12
crw--w----  1 root tty 4, 13 Aug 28 14:37 /dev/tty13
crw--w----  1 root tty 4, 14 Aug 28 14:37 /dev/tty14
crw--w----  1 root tty 4, 15 Aug 28 14:37 /dev/tty15
crw--w----  1 root tty 4, 16 Aug 28 14:37 /dev/tty16
crw--w----  1 root tty 4, 17 Aug 28 14:37 /dev/tty17
crw--w----  1 root tty 4, 18 Aug 28 14:37 /dev/tty18
crw--w----  1 root tty 4, 19 Aug 28 14:37 /dev/tty19
linux:/ #
```

**FIGURE 18.22**    Viewing character devices.

The tty devices shown in 18.22 are serial devices. Accordingly, they have a c as the first character in each line of the output of ls, indicating that these files represent character devices.

You can create your own character or block device files. This is done with the mknod utility. The syntax of mknod is as follows:

```
mknod file_name device_type major_number minor_number
```

For example, you could create a new character device named echo with a major number of 33 and a minor number of 0 by entering the following at the shell prompt:

```
mknod /dev/echo c 33 0
```

Major number 33 (character) is reserved for serial cards. You can view a complete list of major numbers and the type of devices they are associated with by viewing the /usr/src/linux-*kernel_version*/Documentation/devices.txt file on your SUSE Linux system.

# References

- http://www.tldp.org/HOWTO/Filesystems-HOWTO.html—Always the place to begin. The file systems HOWTO.

- http://en.wikipedia.org/wiki/Filesystem—Wikipedia on how file systems work in various operating systems.

- http://en.wikipedia.org/wiki/Comparison_of_file_systems—Helpful chart on differences between file systems, with links to the Wikipedia articles on each file system.

- http://www.namesys.com—The group in charge of ReiserFS.

- http://batleth.sapienti-sat.org/projects/FAQs/ext3-faq.html—The Linux ext3 FAQ list. Differences between ext2 and ext3, as well as troubleshooting problems.

- http://oss.sgi.com/projects/xfs—The XFS for Linux site.

- http://www-106.ibm.com/developerworks/linux/library/l-fs9.html—An IBM DeveloperWorks article on XFS.

- http://www-106.ibm.com/developerworks/edu/os-dw-linuxjfs-i.html—A JFS tutorial; free registration with DeveloperWorks required.

- http://sources.redhat.com/lvm2—The Logical Volume Manager home page.

- http://www.tldp.org/HOWTO/LVM-HOWTO—The LVM HOWTO page. Should have information on LVM2 by now.

- http://usalug.org/phpBB2/viewtopic.php?p=33142—Tuning up IDE hard drives with hdparm. A useful tutorial.

- http://www.gnu.org/software/parted—The GNU Parted home page.

- http://www.frccos.com/articlcs/3921—A basic introduction to thc Logical Volume Manager. Includes command-line instructions for building logical volumes.

18

# Managing Users, Managing Security

The heart of Linux security is determining who can use what file and what kind of use is permitted. This is not all there is to making Linux a more secure system, but ultimately what is the purpose of computer security? Keeping the bad guys out of your files.

In this chapter, you will learn about setting up user accounts and creating and managing groups that work together. There are decisions to make about user passwords: Does the user select them, or does the administrator? How strong must passwords be? How often to change them? In this chapter, you'll get advice about security. In short, you'll learn about the human side of system administration.

This stuff is particularly important for system administrators in a multiuser office setting, but even if you are working by yourself, you will need to become familiar with permissions and passwords. This is the area where trouble often starts, and it's the first thing to check when you can't run something.

## User Accounts and Permissions

All Linux systems require one administrator, the Root, and at least one generic user, who can be the same person. The Root is, as noted often here, all powerful. Generic users can be restricted to the point of being able to read only a single file, or have full run of the system as the SuperUser (su). This section will help you better understand how the permissions system works, beyond what you learned in Chapter 5, "Getting Started with SUSE Linux."

## Setting Up User Accounts in YaST

The first user account is set up during the SUSE Linux installation. Adding users is a simple task in YaST.

In YaST, go to Security and Users. Click Edit, Create Users. YaST will review the current user accounts and display them in the first screen (see Figure 19.1).

Besides the standard operations of Adding and Deleting users, you can perform several user-related tasks from this screen:

- Change passwords and access rights for existing users.

- Allow some users to log in without a password.

- View and edit system users (more about this in the next section).

- Set default permissions and groups for new users.

- Set password encryption standards.

- Configure user-related information for Lightweight Directory Access Protocol (LDAP), Samba, Network Information Service (NIS), and Kerberos services.

**FIGURE 19.1**   The YaST User and Group Administration tool.

You will explore some of these options later, but for now you'll create a new user. In this example, you're going to create a user called drone77. Click Add. Figure 19.2 will appear.

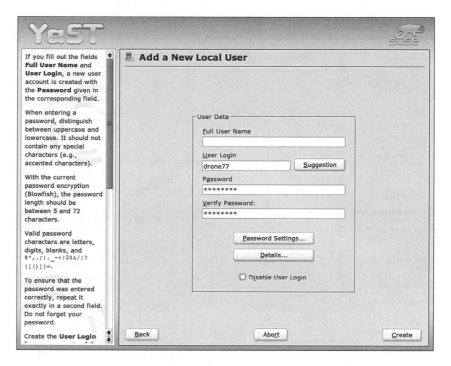

**FIGURE 19.2** Set username and password in the first Add a New Local User screen.

YaST asks for the user's full name. This is not required, but YaST will use this information to provide a suggestion for the system username. Because we already have a username picked out, enter **drone77** on the User Login line. Type an initial password for this user. The Help pane on the left offers some pointers. The password must be between 5 and 72 characters; it is case sensitive (so mix in some capital letters) and can include spaces and just about any character on the keyboard.

To give drone77 a chance to select his own password, you need to set the expiration date. Click Password Settings and Figure 19.3 opens.

The default settings are for a system in which passwords are set once and never changed. This is OK for a single-user system with a modem connection to the Internet, but it's a bad idea if you have an "always on" connection, such as a DSL or cable-modem connection.

Frequent changes of your users' passwords is another way of staying one step ahead of the attackers. A good rule is to reset passwords every 3–6 months. drone77 is set to change passwords every 90 days.

---

**TIP**

Setting the Minimum Number of Days for the Same Password item for greater than 0 prevents users from changing passwords when forced and then immediately changing them back.

---

19

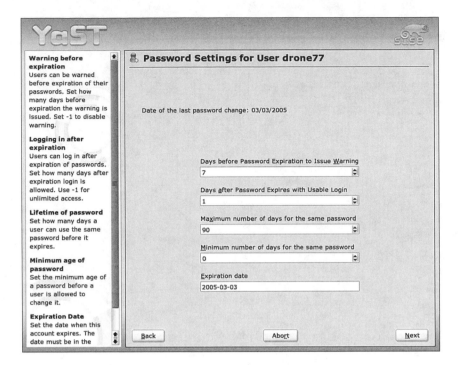

**FIGURE 19.3**    Let the user set a password on first login with these settings.

To let drone77 choose a password on login, you must set the Expiration Date for today, and set the Days After Password Expires with Usable Login to 1 or 0. The Days Before Password Expiration to Issue Warning can stay at the default, but can be adjusted to your preference. The system will then prompt drone77 to change passwords. When that happens, you should return here to delete the Expiration Date.

Click Next when you complete this dialog box to return to the main Add User screen. Click Details to review the other defaults associated with this user. These default settings are generally OK, but there may be items to adjust. In this dialog box, you can set the following:

- User ID (UID)—Every user must have an ID number. Generic users must have UIDs greater than 499; YaST starts at UID 1000 to be safe. You can change this if you want, but do this only when you create the account. Ownership rights are associated with UID numbers, so changing the number will orphan any files outside of the user's home directory.

- Home Directory—By default, this is /home/<username>, but you can change this here. The best reason to change the home directory is if this user is really just a "persona" of another user (like you, for example), who wants to have a single /home directory to store data in.

- Additional User Information—This line is for finger information. For privacy's sake, leave this blank. (see "Changing User Information" in Chapter 5).

- Login Shell—This is the default shell for this user. By default, it's bash. Use the drop-down menu, which has the path to every installed shell on the system, to change shells.

- Default Group and Additional Group Membership—By default, YaST assigns users to the Users group and also to the Dialout and Video groups. You'll learn more about assigning groups in the next section.

When you're through adjusting these settings, click Next to return to the main Add User screen. You can now click Create to add this user to your system. drone77 should now appear on the list of Local Users. Click Finish to return to YaST.

## System Users

Some applications need to own their files and processes to function securely. This is accomplished by creating *system users*. These are usually the daemons that always run in the background (man, lp/print, mail, news, and bin), but also include a few other applications, such as MySQL and the Games user. System users do not log in or have home directories, but they have passwords. They also have control over files that other generic users do not have. System users belong to their own group; that is, bin belongs to the Bin group.

View the list of system users in the User Administration screen by clicking Set Filter and selecting System Users. You should never have to configure these yourself, even as Root.

## RWX: Understanding Permissions

Most of the practicalities of setting permissions were covered in Chapter 5. The focus there is on the *hows* of permissions. It's just a question of assigning Read, Write, and eXecute permissions to the Owner, Group, and World groups. You can do this either from the shell, using the chmod command, or in a GUI file manager. From the shell you can use octals or letter switches.

In this section, the focus is on *why* you want to set permissions in a particular way. Consider that permissions are the heart of security, as previously mentioned, and start with trying to think like a black hat—a would-be attacker. How can you use these three switches—RWX—to your advantage?

- Read—The safest permission to grant is Read. Giving Read access to a file allows viewing the contents of a file. Read access to a directory allows access to the list of files in that directory. In most cases, someone viewing a file (with bad intent or not) is harmless. But what if it's a critical document that needs to be kept from prying eyes? You probably want to encrypt the file as well, but removing the Read option is another step. What if an attacker wants to see if a file known to have a security hole is on your system? An attacker (or a software bot) can do that with World Read access to that directory.

- Write—Giving Write access to a file allows someone to change the content of a file. Write access to a directory means permitting renaming or deletion of existing files and creation of new files in that directory. It's a little easier to see the danger. Give

World Write access to your web-server directory, and your site is a prime candidate for defacement. Give an attacker Write access to your .login file (even without Read access), and someday you won't be able to login because that filename will have been changed. These types of things probably don't happen often, but they are the kinds of mistakes that happen frequently enough to be troublesome.

- Execute—Theoretically, any file in Linux can be made executable by setting this permission. In practice, executable files are standard programs or files that can be used as scripts. In a directory, execute rights are also called *search permission*. It means you can use the directory's name when accessing its files.

# Who Needs What? Managing Groups

Groups are the easy way to handle the "need-to-know" issues that always crop up when dealing with users on a network. Create a group when there is a set of people who need to have similar permission to work on particular files or directories.

As with users, there are two types of groups in SUSE Linux: Local and System. Generally speaking, Local groups are composed of real-life users, and System groups are for managing applications and their files.

Every user on a SUSE Linux system is assigned to the Users group, so common permissions can be set up for everyone. By default, all users are also assigned to the Dialout and Video groups, although this can be changed in YaST.

## Adding Groups

Adding a new Local group to your system is very much like adding a user. From the YaST Security and Users section, choose Edit and Create Groups. You can also come to this page directly from the Edit and Create Users page by clicking the option button. On this page, you will see the existing Local groups (by default, just the Users group). Click Set Filter and then click System Groups to look at those groups instead.

To define a group of writers on this system, click Add to display the screen shown in Figure 19.4.

> **NOTE**
>
> When you are working with Group Administration in YaST, you are actually editing the /etc/group file that stores information about groups on the system. YaST also backs up the old file (as /etc/group.YaST2save) when it makes changes, so you can revert to the old file if you need to.
>
> In addition to YaST, the SuperUser can use several commands to manage groups: groupadd (to add a group), groupdel (to delete a group), gpasswd (to set a group password), and grpck (to check /etc/group for typos) are among the most commonly used.
>
> You can also edit this file directly (as the SuperUser). Back up the file first, as YaST does, and run grpck afterward.

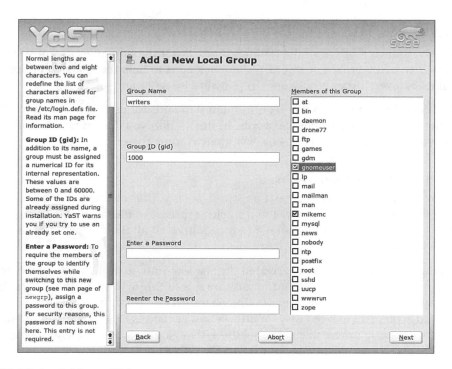

**FIGURE 19.4**    Adding a Writers group.

This process is straightforward. The only thing you have to do is to name the group and identify its members from the list of local and system users on the right. If you want to set a group password for extra security, define that here as well. YaST sets the default Group ID (GID) number starting at 1000. You can change this, but there's no real need to.

When you have checked the box of the members of the group, click Next to create the group and return to the main page. You should see the Writers group on the list of Local Groups, along with its membership. You can add and remove members through this screen, and also through the User screen.

> **NOTE**
>
> Because the User and Group Administration tools share the same page, the Expert Options button appears in both. Except for the Write Changes Now option, nothing here really applies to groups. Use Write Changes Now if you are switching to the User Administration page before leaving YaST.

Click Finish to confirm your changes and close this window. Now you can choose to restrict some files and directories to the Writers group by assigning those files and directories to the Writers group and setting appropriate permissions.

# Passwords: The First Line of Security

Studies have shown that one of the leading causes, if not the primary cause, of system break-ins is an easily broken password. SUSE Linux aims to help the system administrator train all users (even if there's only one) in password integrity and safety.

The YaST Security Settings lets you set minimum standards for user passwords and offer additional ways of securing your passwords. In this section you'll learn how to configure these to your best advantage. First, however, there is some theory to cover.

## The `passwd` and `shadow` Files

A user isn't a user until he or she has a password. Back in the "old days," all user passwords in Unix and Linux were stored in a single `/etc/passwd` file, accessible to anyone with Read access. That's still true, after a fashion, although all the "passwords" are now marked with an X.

In the mid-1990s, John F. Haugh II created the Shadow Suite to deal with the problem of readable passwords, and support for the software spread through the various Linux distributions by 1998. The idea is simple: Keeping plain-text passwords in a single file with World Read access makes it too easy for attackers to get access to passwords. Although making `/etc/passwd` unreadable is one solution, that would cause too many problems. The solution is to put real user passwords in a file only Root can read.

Both `passwd` and `shadow` are database files. `passwd` has seven fields that store the following for each record or user:

- Username
- Password (or holding place)
- UID
- GID
- Finger information
- Path to the home directory
- Default shell

That is, every field included in the YaST User Add screen.

`shadow` has nine fields for each record/user and shares just one with `passwd`: the username. The other fields are

- Encrypted password
- When the password was last changed, expressed as the number of days after January 1, 1970; also known as the *epoch*.
- The number of days before the password can be changed.

- The number of days before the password must be changed.

- The number of days the user gets before being warned the password is about to expire.

- The number of days after a password expires that the account is disabled.

- The number of days (if any) since the epoch that the account has been disabled.

- The last field is reserved for future use; that use has yet to be determined.

These fields are set in the Password Settings dialog box for each user.

## Selecting Passwords

Passwords have become a way of life with just about every computer user. There are system login passwords, web portal passwords, online banking passwords, ATM passwords—the list goes on, possibly forever. Yet it is undeniable that you need all these passwords to protect yourself, your money, your files, and all the other things that we password-protect.

Your Linux files are only as secure as your password, so it's important to select passwords carefully. Following are some very basic tips on making your passwords secure:

- Choose something easy for you to remember, but hard to guess.

- Don't use your name, address, birthday, or other well-known fact about you as a password. The story goes that heiress Paris Hilton had her cell phone's address book hacked when she used her "favorite pet's name" as a password hint. System administrators have been known to check user passwords with a personnel file in their hands, using birth dates, spouse's names, and the like. An unusual combination of some of these characters can be successful, though.

- The longer the password, the better. By default, your system password must be at least five characters. Using the Blowfish password-encryption standard (see the next section for more information on this), your password can be up to 72 characters. It's hard to remember that many, however.

- Always remember: Passwords are case sensitive. Use a combination of upper- and lowercase letters in nontypical locations. It's OK to start your password with a capital letter, but throw some in the miDdLe too.

- Always use a combination of letters, numbers, and special characters. `T3st1n@` is much better than `te$ting`.

The trick is not getting too comfortable with one password, or endless variations on a single theme. Even if you've got what you think is a bulletproof password, come up with a couple more. You just never know when a password-cracking script will get lucky.

## User Authentication Settings with Pluggable Authentication Modules (PAM)

To quote the Linux-PAM System Administrator's Guide:

> It is the purpose of the Linux-PAM project to separate the development of privilege granting software from the development of secure and appropriate authentication schemes. This is accomplished by providing a library of functions that an application may use to request that a user be authenticated.

In short, Pluggable Authentication Modules (PAM) extend the traditional Unix/Linux principle of doing one thing well. If an application needs to confirm (authenticate) a user, they can access the PAM libraries, instead of creating their own mechanism to do so.

> **NOTE**
>
> The Linux-PAM documentation is included in the SUSE Linux Help Center.

The YaST Security Settings serve as the GUI front end for PAM. Go to Security and Users in YaST and then to Security Settings. On the first page, you can choose from three default configurations: Home Workstation (a standalone personal or family computer not connected to the Internet), Networked Workstation (for networked computers, either with other machines on a local area network or with an Internet connection), or Network Server (the highest level of security).

Chances are you will want the Networked Workstation option as a base. You can certainly leave things at that, but perhaps you want to tweak the settings.

Table 19.1 shows the differences in settings between the three default configurations.

**TABLE 19.1**   YaST Default Security Settings

| Setting | Level 1 Home Workstation | Level 2 Networked Workstation | Level 3 Network Server |
|---|---|---|---|
| Checking New Passwords | N | Y | Y |
| Plausibility Test for Password | N | N | N |
| Password Encryption Method | Blowfish | Blowfish | Blowfish |
| Number of Significant Characters in the Password | N/A (applicable only to DES Encryption) | N/A (applicable only to DES Encryption) | N/A (applicable only to DES Encryption) |
| Minimum Acceptable Password Length | 5 | 5 | 6 |
| Minimum Days to Password Change Warning | 0 | 1 | 1 |
| Maximum Days to Password Change Warning | 99999 | 99999 | 99999 |
| Days Before Password Expires Warning | 7 | 14 | 14 |

| Setting | Level 1 Home Workstation | Level 2 Networked Workstation | Level 3 Network Server |
| --- | --- | --- | --- |
| Ctrl+Alt+Del | Reboot | Ignore | Ignore |
| Shutdown Behavior | All Users | Only Root | Only Root |
| Delay After Incorrect Login Attempt | 1 | 6 | 3 |
| Record Failed Logins | Y | Y | Y |
| Record Successful Logins | Y | Y | Y |
| Allow Remote Graphical Login | N | N | N |
| User ID Limitations | 1000–60000 | 1000–60000 | 1000–60000 |
| Group ID Limitations | 1000–60000 | 1000–60000 | 1000–60000 |
| Setting of File Permissions | Easy | Easy | Secure |
| User Launching UpdateDB | Root | Nobody | Nobody |
| Current Dir in Root's Path | Y | N | N |
| Current Dir in Path of Regular Users | Y | N | N |
| Enable Magic SysRq Keys | N | N | N |

To change any of these defaults, you must click Details. YaST will walk you through the four pages of settings.

Some of these items may be perplexing. Read the helpful descriptions for each setting in the left pane of the screen when deciding how to handle each setting. The following list looks at a few:

- Password Plausibility Test—Enforces some of the rules for passwords suggested in the previous section.

- Password Encryption Method—There are three. By default, YaST chooses the Blowfish method at all three levels. This open-source algorithm was developed by security expert Bruce Schneier in 1993 and is faster and safer than the other two choices. Data Encryption Standard (DES) encryption was developed by the U.S. government in the mid-1970s and was the original free encryption algorithm. Passwords using this method are limited to eight characters. MD5 transforms a data string of any length into a shorter, fixed-length value. No two strings of data will produce the same hash value.

- UpdateDB—This program runs daily and works with the `locate` program to quickly find files. If Root runs `UpdateDB`, all files are updated. If the system user Nobody runs `UpdateDB`, only files that Nobody has access to are updated.

- Magic SysRq—The SysRq key is usually located next to the Scroll Lock key on your keyboard. When used with the Alt key, it can permit an orderly shutdown of a crashed system. The bad news is that someone with remote access to your healthy system can bring it down instantly. Given the rarity of system crashes, it is better to leave this disabled.

19

# Monitoring User Activity

Monitoring user activity is part of the sysadmin's duties, and an essential part of tracking how system resources are being used. If you have multiple users on your SUSE Linux system, and especially if you don't, you should become familiar with some of these monitoring tools.

As the all-powerful sysadmin, you can monitor nearly everything your users do on the computer, held back only by the hours in the day. Fortunately for all concerned, even the Bastard Operator From Hell doesn't have time to do this. Any good sysadmin will check in periodically, just to keep the invaders at bay.

## Shell Tools for Watching Users

The acct system accounting package is essential to pull together all the commands you'll need to keep tabs on your system. There are a bunch of handy tools there including sa, accton, and lastcomm.

You may need to start the acct service at startup. To do this, log in as SuperUser and type

```
/etc/init.d/acct start
```

SUSE Linux will now track resource usage in the /var/run/utmp and /var/log/wtmp files. You can access these files with the following commands.

The w command will tell the sysadmin who is logged in, where he or she is logged in at, and what they are up to. No one is able to hide from the SuperUser. The w command can be followed by a specific user's name to show only that user—by default, it will show all current users.

The ac command provides information about the total connect time of a user measured in hours. It accesses the /var/log/wtmp file for the source of its information. To generate a list of users with their login hours, type

```
ac -p
```

Even if you're a sole user, if you log in and out religiously, you might find this command useful. To get a list of total hours logged in on the system for a calendar day, type

```
ac -d
```

> **TIP**
>
> Interestingly, a phenomenon known as "timewarp" can occur, where an entry in the wtmp files jumps back into the past, and ac will show unusual amounts of time accounted for users. Although this can be attributed to some innocuous factors having to do with the system clock, it is worthy of investigation by the sysadmin. It can also be the result of a security breach.

The ac command can prove itself most useful in shell scripts when you want to generate reports on operating system usage to show management what OSes your users run.

The `last` command searches through the `/var/log/wtmp` file and will list all the users logged in and out since that file was first created. The system user `reboot` exists so that you might know who has logged in since the last reboot. A companion to `last` is the `lastb` command, which shows all failed, or bad, logins. It's useful to determine if a legitimate user is having trouble, or if someone is trying to break into your system. The hoped for result of `lastb` is always a message telling you that the btmp log does not exist—meaning there have been not bad/attempted logins.

# Letting Mortals Play at Wizardry: SuperUsers

It has been said here frequently: it is generally a bad idea to log in as Root and do work. Too much damage can be done, and if you're connected to the Internet, you can actually lose control of your system to an attacker. Nonetheless, there are tasks and operations that can be done only by Root, and you may find yourself needing to be Root on a daily basis. Fortunately, there is a built-in solution to this problem: becoming the SuperUser.

There are two ways to perform Root tasks while being logged in as a generic user. The `su` command allows anyone with the Root password to become Root. In a larger system, Root can also assign specific tasks to users without handing out the Root password by implementing the `sudo` command.

### Changing User Identity with `su`

When you run YaST to make changes in your configuration, you are first asked for the Root password. You have just used `su` to become Root.

Whether the task is installing software, troubleshooting problems, or some other system-related issue, you will need this command sooner or later.

> **NOTE**
>
> Although most often run on a system to gain SuperUser access, su is not the "SuperUser" command. It stands for "Substitute User," and you can log in as any other system user with the correct password.

To run `su` from the shell prompt, use this syntax:

```
su <option> <username> <arguments>
```

Typing **su** by itself means you want to log in as Root, and you'll be prompted for the Root password. You'll also retain your own environment settings. To gain Root's environment, type **su -**.

To run a single Root command from the shell and return to your user prompt, use the `-c` switch. Try something like this:

```
su root -c chmod 600 /etc/shadow
```

When you have completed your Root tasks, type **exit** to return to your user prompt.

19

## Using sudo to Grant Root Privileges

When you're the system administrator of a large system with lots of users, you don't want to give out the Root password to everyone who wants to install software on his or her computer. You can solve this problem with SuperUser Do, or sudo.

You configure sudo by editing /etc/sudoers with the special visudo editor. As you might guess, visudo is a version of vi made for use with this file. It checks for parsing errors in your edits, so you should definitely use this, rather than your regular editor (even if you normally work with vi). You may want to return to the vi section of Chapter 5 to review some of the commands if you are not familiar with this editor.

Run su to log in as Root before running visudo. To begin, run visudo with no arguments; that is:

visudo

The default /etc/sudoers file appears in the shell, looking something like this:

```
# sudoers file.
#
# This file MUST be edited with the 'visudo' command as root.
#
# See the sudoers man page for the details on how to write a sudoers file.
#

# Host alias specification

# User alias specification

# Cmnd alias specification

# Defaults specification
Defaults targetpw    # ask for the password of the target user i.e. root
%users ALL=(ALL) ALL # WARNING! Only use this together with 'Defaults targetpw'!

# User privilege specification
# You should not use sudo as root in an SELinux environment
# If you use SELinux, remove the following line
root    ALL=(ALL) ALL

# Uncomment to allow people in group wheel to run all commands
# %wheel    ALL=(ALL)    ALL

# Same thing without a password
# %wheel    ALL=(ALL)    NOPASSWD: ALL
```

```
# Samples
# %users  ALL=/sbin/mount /cdrom,/sbin/umount /cdrom
# %users  localhost=/sbin/shutdown -h now
```

Before editing sudoers, you may want to review the man pages for both sudoers and visudo (sudo itself has a man page as well) for instructions on how to use these files.

Feel free to uncomment any of the default lines to activate them. Instead of editing the default lines, you should add new lines (with a comment to document what you want to do). The basic format of a sudoers line is

```
user host_computer=command
```

The user can also be a group; so, for example, to grant permission to the Writers group to run YaST Online Update, add this line:

```
writers ALL=/sbin/yast2
```

To grant the Writers group this same permission without having to enter a password, add this line:

```
writers ALL=/sbin/yast2 NOPASSWD: ALL
```

When you're finished editing, press **:q** to save changes and return to the shell prompt. Type **exit** to return to your user prompt.

Once configured, sudo is very easy to use. Anyone in the Writers group should now be able to type this command to run YaST:

```
sudo /sbin/yast2
```

Depending on how you set it, writers may be prompted for their own user password to confirm that they are the person that is logged in.

# References

- http://tldp.org/LDP/sag/html—The Linux System Administrator's Guide.

- http://tldp.org/HOWTO/User-Authentication-HOWTO—Setting up passwords.

- http://tldp.org/HOWTO/HOWTO-INDEX/admin.html#ADMSECURITY—The Linux security HOWTOs all in one place. Be sure to read over the Security-HOWTO for an overview.

- http://www.tldp.org/HOWTO/Shadow-Password-HOWTO.html—Explains the shadow password system.

- http://www.novell.com/coolsolutions/feature/11685.html—A brief, but nice, overview of permissions and how to set them in Nautilus/GNOME.

- http://www.gratisoft.us/sudo—The sudo program lets you delegate specific administrative tasks to particular users without turning over the Root password.

- http://www.kernel.org/pub/linux/libs/pam—Pluggable Authentication Modules in Linux.

- http://publib.boulder.ibm.com/infocenter/pseries/index.jsp?topic=/ com.ibm.aix.doc/aixbman/security/pam_overview.htm—This guide to PAM under IBM's flavor of Unix is helpful to Linux users, too.

- http://www-106.ibm.com/developerworks/linux/library/l-sc7.html—This article on "Practical Linux Security" offers an interesting take on handling users.

- http://searchenterpriselinux.techtarget.com/originalContent/0,289142, sid39_gci928466,00.html—This Linux Security Learning Guide is a handy set of articles and links on the range of security topics.

- http://www.schneier.com/blowfish.html—The Blowfish encryption algorithm home page.

- http://linuxgazette.net/issue81/vikas.html—A summary of the Magic SysRq process.

# CHAPTER 20

# Managing Data: Backup, Restoring, and Recovery

Maybe you've heard it a hundred times, perhaps not at all, but it's true: You will lose data one time or another. It's a question of *when*, not *if*.

Bad things happen to good data. A group of computer users in an office working on a Linux file server share data in a folder named SHARE. One of the users accidentally deletes a very important file in that folder that all other users use. No fear—because you backed up the system, a quick restore will be able to get that file back in place, as long as the backup was originally successful. This chapter is about preparing for that eventuality.

## Preparing for Preventing Data Loss

Backing up data is not fun. It takes time and resources, and 99.999 percent of the time it's not productive. For one person, it can be hard to justify taking the time to back up data, buy new storage media, and make sure your existing backups still work. But the day your hard drive decides to join the scrap heap is the day that all that time pays off. That's when you're reminded that backups are like insurance; you hope you never need it, but when you need it, you're really happy it's there.

The trick is knowing how much to back up, what to back up, and how often to back up. This section will help you sort out these issues before you start.

### How to Lose Data

When you think about it, data stored on a computer is a fragile thing. Nothing but ones and zeros stored electromagnetically on a cheap metal platter. The storage industry does a fine job of protecting those digits, but it's almost a wonder that users don't lose more data than they do.

Aside from the times when you consciously press the Delete key or type `rm <filename>` at a shell prompt, when you talk about data loss, this is usually an unintended consequence stemming from various causes. Mother Nature is often at the root of the problem: thunderstorms leading to electrical power surges, tornadoes, floods, hurricanes, and fire can all make data disappear or become useless in an instant.

Floppy disks are fragile things. They can get bounced around enough to damage the disk and corrupt files.

Consider the unstable, buggy program you're using to create new data. When it hangs or crashes, you get a message warning you that `All unsaved data will be lost`.

Hard drives do die, no longer capable of storing your ones and zeros on their platters. Manufacturers even use a rating system of Mean Time Between Failures (MTBF) to quantify the number of hours a hard drive should function. And using wildcards to remove batches of unwanted files can result in wanted files disappearing, too.

Too often, however, data loss results from what technical support people call (privately) "keyboard-to-chair problems"—good old human error. As long as there are humans, no matter how intelligent they happen to be, they will do not-so-intelligent things that can result in some level of data loss. Backups minimize the risk from all these causes of data loss.

## Assessing Your Needs and Resources

In many ways, deciding on a backup strategy is predicated on the answers to two simple questions: What files do I need to back up, and how often do those files change?

The answers get down to a more critical question that lies beneath: What data is important to me?

When you have those issues settled, the question then becomes: What can I afford, in both time and money, to protect that important data? The answers to these questions diminish in importance if you have access to massive amounts of bandwidth or empty warehouses that can store terabytes of data in every square foot of the property. That probably does not describe you, however.

Some backup methods take longer than others, and the same is true for restore methods.

Consider the situation where you have to restore everything. Can you afford to be down as long as it takes to restore using your method? If it's just your machine, will you have to sit there swapping disks in and out every few minutes, or can you automate the process?

These are the questions that will help you formulate your backup strategy. After you have that strategy, it's important to practice it religiously and test it periodically.

Whatever strategy you select, make sure to carry out these practices with similar fervor:

- Have more than one copy of critical data at all times.
- Label the backups using some consistent method (by date, by type of file).

- Store backups in a secure area with consistent temperatures.

- Store critical data somewhere offsite. If all your backups are in your house, and the house catches fire, you're in trouble.

- Try restoring from a backup regularly to make yourself comfortable with the process, and test the medium you're using.

- Test your media. Problems with the CD or defects with the tape can mess things up.

## Choosing a Backup Strategy

Everyone's situation is different, but we can make some generalizations about different types of users and their backup strategies.

- Home users—The critical issue for home users is not rebuilding the operating system and applications. With the SUSE Linux installation CDs, reinstalling the base packages for your system should take about an hour. What is critical is preserving your home directory and your configuration files. Backing up email is optional, depending on the volume and how important you think it is. Configuration files are generally stored in the /etc directory, so backing up /home and /etc is your primary task. If you have applications installed outside of YaST, you should back these up as well. Unless you have critical projects in the works, a weekly backup to a CD-RW or some other external storage drive is all that's required.

- Small Office/Home Office (SOHO)—Like home users, SOHO users can focus on keeping the data in the home directory secure, along with configuration files, business-related mail, and applications installed outside of YaST. SOHO users need to be more rigorous about backups than ordinary home users, because the consequences are greater. Daily backups of important files are a good idea. Because files stored on tape drives are faster to restore than other media, you may want to consider investing in a tape drive, although CDs may be just as good. Redundant drives may also be possible for you.

Many backup strategies are used today, but in this section we'll review some of the more popular ones. Tweak any one of them for your own purposes.

> **CAUTION**
>
> If you are running Windows and Linux on the same computer, don't back up both file systems in one fell swoop. Back up your Linux files with a Linux tool and Windows files in Windows.
>
> YaST System Backup will also back up your partition table. See "Using YaST System Backup," later in this chapter.

**20**

### Simple Strategy

If all you need is to back up a few small documents and some configuration files, you only need a floppy disk or two. Copy the files directly.

If you have a Zip drive or other high-capacity floppy, you can choose to back up the entire Documents directory for each user, plus the /etc directory for all your configuration files. Zip disks come in 100, 250, and 750MB varieties.

With a CD-RW or DVD-RW on hand, you should be able to use K3b to burn the entire home directory for all your users to a single 700MB CD.

The beauty of this strategy is that you can back up files on the spot, simply by copying every changed or new file to your chosen medium, although this is harder to do with a CD. It becomes problematic when your backups grow beyond a single disk. At that point, you'll want to adopt a more formal strategy, as in one of the following.

### Full Backup Periodically

This is the standard backup process where you archive everything to your chosen medium on a weekly, biweekly, or monthly basis. The frequency depends on the importance of the data and how often it changes. Ideally, you can perform this backup to a designated network server, but depending on how much room your files take up, multiple CDs or DVDs may work.

The best way to do this is with archiving software, which is discussed later in the chapter.

### Full Backups with Increments

This is the standard corporate backup routine used in medium-to-large networks. There's no technical reason smaller businesses can't do this, but it may be less necessary. With this strategy, you make a full backup to a tape weekly and back up new and changed files every day.

There are two ways of defining what is "new and changed"—that is, what to include in an incremental backup. The easiest way to do this is to have a single tape (Level 1) reference the last full backup (Level 0) each day. This way, you have to keep track of only two tapes. The danger is that if a lot of things change during a given week, you may run out of tape.

The alternative is to have separate incremental tapes for each day. If you perform your full backup on Friday night, your first increment is Saturday, and it references the full backup. You then remove Friday's tape and insert Sunday's tape, which will include changes since Saturday, and onward to Thursday. So if someone comes to you and asks for the file they accidentally deleted on Wednesday, you can easily find Tuesday's backup tape and restore from there.

It's best to use a professional backup solution, such as Amanda or BRU, for these complicated backups. As a system administrator, then, all you have to worry about is changing tapes. The software handles the actual backup.

## Choosing Your Backup Medium

Leaving aside the warehouse full of terabytes, you need to decide how to store your backed up files. Making a copy of all the files on your hard drive and storing it on another partition on the same drive may be useful in some situations, but not when the drive goes bad.

Given this reality, you must choose another medium to back up your files to. This section gives you a brief overview of your choices and includes some suggestions to help you find the right one for you.

## Mirrors and RAID Arrays

A redundant array of inexpensive disks (RAID) setup offers a system administrator a great opportunity to have a real-time permanent copy of everything on a particular hard drive. Mirrors are additional volumes that contain an exact copy of whatever data is stored on the "parent" volume. Whenever an operation writes data to the parent volume, it is immediately written to the mirror volume as well. If the parent disk were to fail, the mirror disk can immediately take over, ensuring that data isn't lost. With relatively inexpensive hard drives available, this can be a great solution because, as we learned earlier, drives will always eventually fail.

Be aware, though, that mirrors don't check for corrupt files on the parent. They will write corrupt files to their disks as easily as they write good files.

For more information on setting up RAID arrays, see "Setting Up Mirror Disks and RAID Arrays" later in this chapter.

## Removable Storage Media

Using some type of removable media is the standard backup solution for home and SOHO users. Although the 1.4MB floppy disk is slowly disappearing from the computing landscape, other, more robust, choices can make backups less of a painful experience. Anything that helps users get into the backup habit is a good thing.

Besides ordinary floppies, these choices exist for removable storage.

### Zip Drives

SUSE Linux has excellent support for the large capacity floppy drives from Iomega. Coming in 100, 250, and 750MB sizes, these drives can play a role in your backup strategy. These drives also have a choice of connections, serial and USB, which make the drives quite portable. The drive-and-disk combination can be more expensive than comparable CD-R/RW combinations. Zip disks also have a history of experiencing the "click of death," with sudden wiping of the disk. This is not so much of a problem with newer drives, but it still happens.

### USB "Keychain" Drives and Solid-State Portable Drives

Keychain drives (called that because they are so small you can attach them to a keychain) are so cool you might have trouble thinking of them as part of a serious backup program. With these gadgets, you can buy 128MB of storage for around $25 and 1.5GB for around $150. Plug them into a USB port and copy any files you want. Keychain drives use flash memory to store data. USB-based portable hard drives are also coming down in price, with 80GB of storage for about $100, and 400GB for less than $500. SUSE Linux will identify these drives as SCSI storage and mount them like any other volume on your system.

The key thing to remember about both types of drives is that you really need USB v2.0 to make the transfer time worthwhile. Older computers with USB 1.0 ports cannot take advantage of the tremendously higher speeds of the new ports. If you have room for another PCI card in your machine, you can add USB 2.0 ports to your system.

### FireWire Drives

These portable drives use a different interface (IEEE 1394) than the USB drives do, but are otherwise similar. The interface is popular with portable music players and digital cameras. Most of these drives were created for the Macintosh platform, but the Linux kernel supports them.

### CD-RW and Recordable DVD

For newer computers that have some kind of built-in recordable CD or DVD drive, it's hard to debate other choices for your backup. CD-R disks hold 700MB of data and cost less than a dollar; CD-RW (Read-Write) disks are only a little more for the same amount of space.

CDs are durable, compact, and provide a mountable file system. This makes them more versatile than tape for restoring files. They are less fragile than Zip drives and use a more mature technology than the keychain drives. Transfer speeds vary depending on the drive, but all are acceptable. You still have to be careful not to scratch the disk, but they can be protected by jewel cases.

Recordable DVD drives are also now becoming part of new PC installations. DVDs can hold up to 4.4GB of data, and cost around $2. The only issue is that there are two incompatible formats for recordable DVDs: DVD-RW and DVD+RW. You need to know what format your drive supports and buy the appropriate disks. Lately, DVD±RW drives have become available that allow you to use either format.

SUSE Linux provides several command-line tools to burn CDs and DVDs. The k3b utility gives you an excellent GUI interface for these applications, whether you run KDE or GNOME, and supports both DVD formats. To run k3b, simply open a terminal session and enter **kb3** at the shell prompt.

## Network Storage

Although enterprise-level systems can take advantage of Network Attached Storage (NAS) setups, where the backup storage volumes are on the network directly, rather than needing to be restored to a server, there are other options for the rest of us.

- Your Internet Service Provider (ISP) may offer some file storage, either as part of a website package, or straight out.

- Some commercial storage space companies (such as www.xdrive.com) offer space for a monthly fee.

- Google's Gmail service offers a gigabyte of mail storage for free. Richard Jones has written a program that converts some or all of that space into a working Linux file system. Find it at http://richard.jones.name/google-hacks/gmail-filesystem/gmail-filesystem.html.

## Tape Drive Backup

Tape drives have been the standard corporate backup medium for a long time. The TAR archive format for Unix, which groups individual files into a single "tarball" for easy retrieval, stands for *Tape ARchive*. Tape cartridges can hold up to 70GB of data (more if the data is compressed), although capacities can vary.

Tapes are very reliable when maintained, but they do degrade over time. Tape drives can and do fail as well.

> **CAUTION**
>
> Tape drives can be fragile and must be cleaned, aligned, and maintained regularly. Do not risk your data by neglecting these tasks.

# Using YaST System Backup

As always, YaST is here to help simplify the backup task. It will not back up your entire drive, but it can get all the critical files you need to boot your system if your system fails. You can use this tool to create several backup profiles, depending on your strategy.

The System Backup and Restore System tools are both located in the YaST System page. You'll learn more about the Restore tool later in the chapter.

The first time you start System Backup, you will get a blank page. You must first create a backup profile. Go to Profile Management and click Add to create a new profile, as shown in Figure 20.1.

In this section, you learn how to make an initial backup to the home directory for later burning to CD. The first Add Profile screen, Archive Settings, explains a little about the process and asks you where you want to store your backup. Type the full path and name the file in the File Name line, as shown in Figure 20.2.

If you have the Network File System (NFS) running and can back up to a remote volume, click the Network button and select the NFS Server name and your directory in the appropriate boxes.

By default, YaST compresses your system files with the GNUZip (gz) tool and places all the compressed files into a Tape ARchive (TAR). You can also choose to compress with the newer bzip (bz2) archive format, or leave the files uncompressed in another TAR wrapper. If you are using Access Control Lists (ACL), YaST advises using the star format for the subarchives. There's no harm in selecting the defaults, but bzip gets slightly better compression rates than GNUZip.

Click Next to continue.

In the File Selection screen (see Figure 20.3), you are defining files that won't be backed up. By default (and there isn't really any way to change this), YaST backs up every file from packages that have changed since installation. Checking the Backup Files Not Belonging to Any Package box backs up everything, including data files. The Check MD5

**20**

Sum Instead of Time or Size option uses the MD5 hash algorithm to determine whether a file has changed. MD5 transforms a data string of any length into a shorter, fixed-length value. No two strings of data will produce the same hash value. If you don't check this box, YaST will use the last modified date or a changed size to determine whether a file has changed. The latter backup will be faster, but perhaps not as accurate.

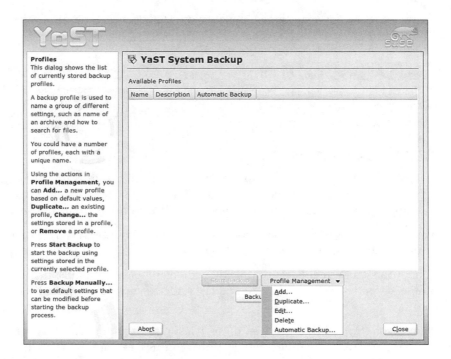

**FIGURE 20.1**    Click Add from the Profile Management menu to create a new profile.

---

**TIP**

You can (and perhaps should) have separate backup profiles for packages, data (files not belonging to any package, with your ~/Mail directory excluded), and mail (with ~/Mail included). See the Search Constraints screen to learn how to take directories out of the backup.

---

If you want to see a list of the files to be backed up before YaST completes the backup, check the Display List of Files Before Creating Archive box. To add a description of this particular backup profile, type in the appropriate box.

If you have a dual-boot system, and the boot manager sits on your hard drive, it is a good idea to back up your partition table. This is not done by default. Click Expert at the bottom of this screen, and then check Back Up Hard Disk System Areas. Clicking Options shows that Back Up Partition Tables is checked automatically when you choose to back up the system areas. If you have an ext2 file system (instead of the default ReiserFS), you can use the Options to back up critical areas of the file system as well.

**FIGURE 20.2**    Define the location for your backup file and choose the type of archive you want to use in this screen.

**FIGURE 20.3**    The File Selection screen defines files that will not be backed up, rather than files that are backed up.

By default, YaST stores the backup archive while it's being built in the /tmp directory. You can change this in the Expert options, but you should need to do this only if that directory is exceedingly low on space.

When you've finished setting the Expert options, click OK to return to the File Selection screen. When you've made all your selections, click Next to continue. The Search Constraints screen (see Figure 20.4) appears.

**FIGURE 20.4**   By default, YaST excludes any Windows volumes, remote directories, the /var directories that store transient information, and other mount points that should not be backed up. You can edit this list and add files matching regular expressions.

The final screen in the Backup Wizard lists directories and file systems to be ignored in the backup process. By default, directories that store transient system information and "alien" file systems such as CDs and floppies that happen to be sitting in their respective drives, Windows volumes, and remote directories are not backed up by default. You can add or delete any directory or file system to or from this exclusion list. You can also exclude files matching a defined regular expression.

Click OK to complete the backup profile. You will return to the main System Backup screen. Click Start Backup to begin the process.

## Backup Software

YaST System Backup covers only vital system files. Many other tools exist to help you back up your more ordinary Linux files. They range from the simple command-line archiver TAR to commercial industrial-strength products like Arkeia and BRU. In this section, you'll learn more about archiving with `tar` and two GUI applications, File Roller and Ark, that will help create archives for backup purposes.

---

**ARCHIVES AND COMPRESSION FORMATS**

Perhaps you've heard of the National Archives, the building in Washington, D.C., where the original Declaration of Independence and millions of other documents are stored. And perhaps you're wondering what that has to do with backup files.

Like the National Archives, the TAR format keeps important files safe and together. It puts a wrapper around a group of files that you designate. Their relationship can be as tight as a group of files that form an executable program or as loose as "the files I want to back up."

If your backup medium is limited in space, you can use a compression program to squeeze out redundant information to shrink a file to take up less space. Programs such as GNUZip and bzip use an algorithm to take text like the word *redundant* to note that it has a pair of Ds and Ns and reduces the size of that word by 11 percent. Taken over an entire document file, these algorithms can save a lot of space counting instances of letters, spaces, and other characters.

You can use TAR and the other compression programs with the shell or use a GUI client. By default, SUSE Linux uses the GNOME Archive Manager to work with archives, but the KDE Ark program works at least as well.

---

## Backups with `tar`

The Tape Archive utility, `tar`, is one of the oldest in the Unix toolkit. It masterfully follows the Unix philosophy of "do one thing well." That thing is grouping files together in one easy-to-transport package. For doing backups, `tar` offers a simple command-line solution. This command archives the whole /etc directory and places the archive in the current directory:

```
tar cvf etc.tar /etc
```

These options create a new archive with the filename `etc.tar` that copies all files in the /etc directory to the archive. As it does this, `tar` is verbose in telling you what it's doing; that is, you'll see a stream of filenames rolling down the shell as each is added to the archive.

If you add the z switch to this command—that is

```
tar cvfz etc.tar /etc
```

You will also compress the files with `Gzip`. Similarly, adding the j switch would use the `bzip` formula.

The `tar` utility can also be used to back up data directly to a tape drive. Most tape drives use a SCSI interface and are accessed through /dev/st*x*; where *x* refers to the number of the tape drive in the system (st0, st1, st2, and so on). For example, if you have a single SCSI tape drive in your system, you would access it through /dev/st0.

To create a backup job and send it to the tape drive, complete the following:

1. Using YaST, make sure your tape drive was detected during boot and that the correct driver was loaded. Usually this isn't a problem, especially if you use a widely recognized SCSI board in your computer (such as those from Adaptec).

2. Insert a tape in your tape drive and wait for it to load and queue up.

3. Open a terminal session.

4. At the shell prompt, enter **tar** *options* **/dev/stx** *path_to_be_backed_up*. For example, to create an archive of the /home directory (and all its subdirectories) on the first SCSI tape drive in the system, you would enter **tar -cvfz /dev/st0 /home**. If the size of the archive exceeds the capacity of your tape, you will need to remove the **-z** option and add the **-M** option. This will allow the tar archive to span across multiple tapes.

5. When the job is complete, you can rewind the tape and eject it at the command prompt using the mt utility. This is done by entering **mt -f /dev/st0 rewoffl**. The mt utility can also be used to perform a number of other tasks with magnetic tapes, such as erasing, rewinding, and fast forwarding. Check out the man page for mt for more information.

A key component of an effective backup strategy is to make sure backups occur regularly. Using the crond daemon, you can configure tar to automatically back up your system at a set time each day (usually later at night when you aren't using the system). This relieves you of the responsibility of remembering to manually start the process. Invariably, the day you forget to run a backup is the day you will end up needing it. Review the tar man page to discover the power and flexibility of this utility, and then put it to work in your backup scheme.

## Using Ark

Ark is a very easy-to-use application that can create or open plain and compressed archives in several formats: tar, gzip, bzip, zip, rar, jar, to name a few. It's the default archive tool if you're using your SUSE Linux system with a KDE shell. As with many applications designed for KDE, it will work under GNOME as well. To create a new archive using Ark, complete the following:

1. Select Kmenu, Utilities, Archiving (assuming you're using KDE).

2. Select File, New.

3. In the Create New Archive screen, enter a *name* for the archive in the Location field.

4. In the Filter field, select the type of archive you want to create. Most of the time, you will probably want to create a gzipped tar archive.

5. Select Save.

6. To add data to the archive, select either Action, Add File or Action, Add Folder.

7. Wait while the files are added to the archive.

Alternatively, you can also create an Ark archive by right-clicking files from within Konqueror and selecting Compress, Compress as *archive_name*.tar.gz from the menu. The new archive will be created and saved in the location you specify.

After it is saved, you can open any existing archive and add files to it. This is helpful if you have some files in other directories. Figure 20.5 shows you how an existing archive appears in the Ark window.

**FIGURE 20.5**    The Gzipped archive for the Azureus BitTorrent client in an Ark window. Notice the directory at the top, with the path included in the filename listing.

## Using GNOME File Roller

File Roller is the default archive tool for SUSE Linux even if you're using the GNOME shell. It integrates well with Nautilus, the GNOME file manager, allowing for drag-and-drop adding of files to new archives.

If you open Nautilus and then File Roller in the same desktop, you can drag files from Nautilus to File Roller. The archiver then asks if you want to create a new archive with the selected files. Click Yes to open the dialog box you see in Figure 20.6.

20

**FIGURE 20.6**    Save a new archive in File Roller.

# Setting Up Mirror Disks and RAID Arrays

If you have two or more hard drives in your computer, one way to preserve files is to have one drive act as a mirror for another. This is the principle behind the RAID concept.

There are several levels of RAID arrays implemented in Linux.

- RAID-0 (Stripe Mode)—Multiple disks combined to appear as a single device. Data is saved in small "stripes" on each disk. This can dramatically increase your system performance because large chunks of data are split up between the drives and read or written concurrently. Unfortunately, RAID-0 doesn't offer any form of data protection. If problems arise on one disk in the array, files on both drives can become corrupted.

- RAID-1 (Mirror)—Data is saved redundantly to all disks in a mirrored array. Instead of splitting data between disks, an exact copy of data being written is saved on multiple drives in the array. Each drive contains a "mirror" of every other drive. Mirroring doesn't improve system performance. However, your chances of retrieving a file stored in a mirrored array are excellent. With most RAID-1 controllers, a mirrored drive can be configured to instantly "take over" in the event that the main drive in the system fails, providing a high degree of data protection.

- RAID-4—Has three or more striped disks included in the array, with one of them storing "parity information." The parity information makes it easier to reconstruct data if one disk in the array fails. In essence, it creates an array that provides the speed of a striped array along with the protection of a mirrored array.

- RAID-5—Same as RAID-4, but parity information is distributed evenly among the disks. As with RAID-4, RAID-5 provides the benefits of both RAID-0 and RAID-1. RAID-5 is more commonly implemented than RAID-4. RAID-5 boards are usually much more expensive than RAID-0 or RAID-1 boards.

- RAID-0+1—Although this is not an official RAID level, many newer RAID controllers provide you with the option of creating a mirrored striped array using four hard disk drives. This provides the speed and redundancy benefits associated with RAID-5 at a much lower cost.

It's important to note here that RAID can be implemented in two ways:

- Hardware—With hardware RAID, you install a special disk interface into an expansion slot in your system to which your hard drives are attached. All RAID configuration tasks are completed using the BIOS of the RAID board. The RAID board itself, then, represents the entire array to the operating system as a single hard disk drive. Using a RAID board is generally considered to provide faster performance than a software RAID solution (although at a higher cost).

- Software—With software RAID, your system's hard disk drives are connected using the standard, non-RAID interface in your system. The operating system, then, is used to create a RAID array using these disks. Software RAID is usually much less expensive than hardware RAID, but is also considered to provide slightly slower performance.

SUSE Linux will support either type of RAID implementation. In fact, setting up a software RAID array on SUSE Linux is quite simple with the YaST Expert Partitioner.

> **CAUTION**
>
> It is always best to set up a RAID array when first installing SUSE Linux so that nothing can happen to your existing data when you're working with the Expert Partitioner.
>
> The steps outlined here apply when you have purchased a drive to serve as your mirror drive after your initial installation. Be sure to back up critical files before starting this process. You will be changing the partition table for your system as part of the setup.

Before installing the new drive, you should convert your Root partition to change the SystemID. Start Expert Partitioner by going to YaST, System, Partitioner. Select your Root partition (marked Linux Native /) and click Edit. In the resulting dialog box, click Do Not Format. Use the drop-down menu to change the File System ID to 0xFD Linux RAID. Click OK to confirm. Click Apply to convert the File System ID.

When the conversion is complete, shut down the system and install the new drive. SUSE Linux should recognize the new hardware and ask how to format it. At this point, you want to create your RAID array (see Figure 20.7).

20

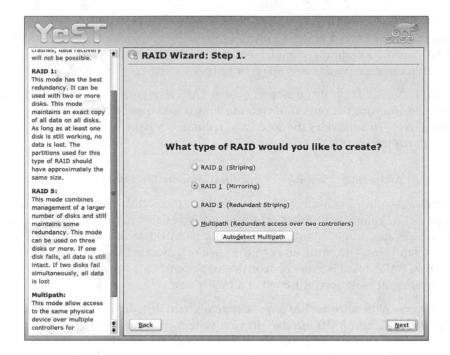

**FIGURE 20.7**    Define the RAID type in the first screen.

---

**CAUTION**

Although it's technically possible to create a software RAID array using two partitions on the same hard disk drive, you should *never* do this. The mirrored or striped partitions should always be located on different disks.

---

You will create a mirror. Click Next to continue.

The second screen (see Figure 20.8) allows you to define the drives you want to mirror. For this example, we created a dummy drive. In a real scenario, the mirror should be at least as large as the active drive. Select both partitions and click Add to create the mirror. Click Next to continue.

The final screen in the RAID Wizard sets options for the mirror (see Figure 20.9). For a mirroring (RAID 1) operation, there's no reason to shift from the defaults. To confirm the settings and return to the main Expert Partitioner screen, click Finish.

When you have finished with the RAID Wizard, click Apply to create the RAID array.

If you chose to use a hardware-based RAID array, you won't have to complete any of these steps. The RAID board will present the array to SUSE Linux as a single hard disk drive. Simply partition and format the logical drive just as you would a physical hard disk drive.

**FIGURE 20.8**    Add partitions to mirror each other in this screen.

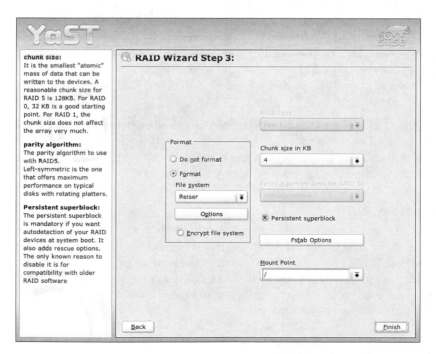

**FIGURE 20.9**    Set options for the mirror drive in the final RAID screen.

# Rescuing a Broken System

When your system is broken and you can't boot, it's a nightmare you don't want to confront. But here you are. Fortunately, you have been backing up regularly and have an archive to restore from. In this section, you'll learn how to get your system back in shape.

## Booting from the SUSE Linux CD

The SUSE Linux installation disk included with this book is bootable and can get you into Rescue mode. First, make sure your BIOS is set to boot from your system's CD/DVD drive before the hard drive. Insert the first SUSE Linux CD into the drive, and boot. You may select Manual Installation to enter special boot parameters under Boot Options, but do this only if you know what you're doing. As you boot from the CD, you will be asked to select the correct language and keyboard layout.

Select Start Installation or System in the main menu.

Select Start Rescue System and identify where the rescue system is located. By default, this is the CD. If you have access to an NFS volume with a Rescue System on it, choose this option. If you have a set of Rescue floppies, see the next section to learn that process.

The Rescue System starts. You can log in as Root with no password. Skip to the "Using System Restore" section to see what to do next.

## Booting from a Rescue Disk Set

YaST will let you make a series of boot disks on floppies that will allow you to boot the rescue system when your CD-ROM drive is down. Go to the System page in YaST to locate the Boot Disk module. The number of floppy disks you will need to complete this operation depends on your system, but usually falls in the range of four to six disks. When you finish making the boot disks, you should return to YaST to make a separate disk containing the Rescue system.

When you need to recover, insert the first boot disk in the drive and then start your computer. You will be asked to insert the Rescue system disk after you boot. As with the CD boot, the Rescue System starts, and you may log in as Root without a password. Proceed to the next section to restore your system.

## Using System Restore

Regardless of how you started the system, after you've gotten into the Rescue system, there is work to be done. To mount your hard drive from the Rescue system, you need to know the device names for your mount points. This is where it comes in handy to have an accessible copy of your /etc/fstab file. By default, your Root mount point is /dev/hda1. You need to carefully mount the system step by step, using the following method. Type the following command:

```
mount /dev/hda1 /mnt
```

This gives you access to the full Root partition. If you have set any other mount points (except for Swap, which is not important here), mount them under the /mnt point as well, as in this command to mount the /usr partition:

```
mount /dev/hda2 /mnt/usr
```

If you have simply misconfigured a configuration file to cause the boot problem, you should now be able to go to /etc and locate the file to reedit back to health. You also have the option to use YaST System Restore to retrieve a backed up file. Follow these steps to use System Restore.

> **NOTE**
>
> Depending on the state of your system, you may get the graphical YaST, where the images in the upcoming figures come from, or the shell version. The menus are identical.

If you prefer to work in a graphical environment (and you can run X), type **startx** to run the X Window System and your preferred environment. Otherwise, just type **yast**.

Use the down arrow to go to the System module, then tab to the components side, and arrow down to Restore System. Press Enter to start the module. Figure 20.10 shows the first Restore screen.

**FIGURE 20.10**   Locate your System Backup file in this screen.

Use this screen to locate your Backup file. In this instance, it's a local file. If you have burned the backup to CD, use the Removable Device option to show that (make sure the disk is in the drive first). Click Next to continue. YaST will read the contents of the backup archive file.

The second screen gives you some basic information on the archive: when it was created, where it is located, and any comments you made about the archive when you created it. To see a list of the packages and files you backed up, click Archive Contents. This is just a list; selecting files and packages to restore happens in the next screen.

By default, YaST restores packages to the / directory (that is, its original location), runs SUSEConfig to make sure everything's in order after the restoration, and reloads your bootloader (if you have one). If you have a good reason to change any of these options, click Expert Options to make those changes. Click Next.

In the final screen, you can select the package(s) and files to restore. By default, YaST restores everything (see Figure 20.11). Choose Deselect All, Select Files to choose your package(s) yourself.

**FIGURE 20.11**    Choose package(s) and files to restore in the final screen.

When you're finished selecting files, click Accept to restore your files. When the process is complete, you return to the shell prompt. Remove the CD from the drive, and type **reboot** to reboot the system normally.

# References

- http://www.tldp.org/HOWTO/Linux-Complete-Backup-and-Recovery-HOWTO—How to back up your system to support a bare-metal recovery.

- http://www.tldp.org/LDP/sag/html—The Linux System Administration Guide. See Chapter 12 on backups.

- http://www.tldp.org/HOWTO/Ext2fs-Undeletion.html—Undeleting files from an Ext2/3 file system.

- http://tldp.org/HOWTO/Software-RAID-HOWTO.html—Learn about software-based RAID arrays in Linux.

- http://amanda.sourceforge.net—The Amanda home page.

- http://www.backupcentral.com—Storage Mountain. Much information and links on backups and other storage-related issues.

- http://linuxgazette.net/104/odonovan.html—An excellent and easy-to-understand article on using rsync and cron for automated backups.

- http://www.k3b.org—The home of K3b, the KDE CD/DVD burning tool.

- http://richard.jones.name/google-hacks/gmail-filesystem/gmail-filesystem.html—The GMailFS program, which allows you to convert your gigabyte of Gmail storage into a working Linux file system.

- http://www.bluehaze.com.au/unix/cdbkup.html—Using a shell script to back up to CD.

- http://www.mondorescue.org—A rescue tool that can produce bootable CDs to restore a broken system.

20

# Keeping Your System Current: Package Management

SUSE Linux makes hundreds of Linux applications available to you with just a few clicks of your mouse. Many of these are installed along with your system, but you can install many more at any time.

New and updated applications are released constantly. Most applications developed for Linux are not produced by a single company needing to get out a new version on a given date to make this quarter's sales projections. They are released when they are ready.

When security issues are discovered in an application, patches can appear within hours. Keeping up with all these changes could be an administrative nightmare, but SUSE Linux makes it easy for you. YaST is, after all, Yet another Setup Tool. The Install/Remove Software and YaST Online Update (YOU) modules are designed exactly to make it easy to install the tools you need and keep them as up-to-date as possible.

In this chapter, you'll learn everything you need to know about installing, removing, and updating your system and its applications. In addition to the YaST software tools, you'll learn how to update your system with the Advanced Package Tool (apt), originally created for the Debian distribution and adapted for use with SUSE Linux.

## Installing Software with YaST

You got a taste of how YaST installs software during the initial system installation. You chose from among four standard installation types: Minimum (command-line only, no X), Minimum Graphical (with X, but no desktop environment), Standard with GNOME, or Standard with KDE. YaST then assembled the packages included in your selection and installed them.

Sooner or later, you will need an application not included in that standard system installation. Unless that application is brand new, chances are you'll find it on the SUSE Linux CDs. This means you're just a few minutes away from having it installed on your system.

Follow these steps to install any new software package(s) from the SUSE Linux installation disks.

After inserting the first SUSE Linux installation CD, start YaST. Enter your SuperUser password and YaST will open to the Software page. Click Software Management. After reading the current package setup, YaST displays the Search page (see Figure 21.1).

**FIGURE 21.1**     Search for a specific package or type of package in this YaST screen.

This is a standard search page, and it is excellent for finding specific applications, either by name or function. You can use Search if, for example, you want to see what Perl modules you have installed and what others are included in the distribution. Enter `perl-` into the Search box (the hyphen is there because all Perl module packages use the syntax `perl-<module name>`).

Sometimes you might want to explore the CDs for interesting applications or to look for a particular type of program. The Package Groups filter lets you do that. Use the drop-down Filter menu to display the Package Groups (see Figure 21.2).

**FIGURE 21.2**   Use the Package Groups filter to browse through a list of similar or complementary applications.

With Package Groups, everything is organized in a tree by type of application. Click a branch to see all the relevant packages. Some branches are further subdivided for a narrower selection, but the Multimedia branch displays everything in CD, Sound, Video, and Other.

Whatever filter you choose, YaST will show all the matching packages in the upper-right pane, with pertinent details. Click any individual package for a more detailed description of that package in the lower-right pane. Installed packages will be checked. To install any others, check the box. You can also right-click any package and choose from the following menu options:

- Install—Selecting this option will install the package.

- Do Not Install—Selecting this option specifies that the package should not be installed.

- Keep—Selecting this option specifies that a previously installed package should remain installed and not be modified.

- Delete—Selecting this option uninstalls the package.

- Update if Newer Version Available—Selecting this option specifies that an already installed package be updated only if a newer version exists in the installation source.

- Update Unconditionally—Selecting this option specifies that the already installed package be updated with the version residing in the installation source, regardless of its version.

- Taboo—Never Install—Selecting this option specifies that the  package is to never be installed.

- Protected—Do Not Modify—Selecting this option specifies that the package is already installed and should not be modified.

You can also configure special installation options without right-clicking the package using the check box.  Clicking the check box next to an installed package once displays the Update icon, which is really a reinstall. Double-clicking the check box marks the package for removal. Some installed packages appear in red type; this means that the version you have installed now is newer than the package on the CD. Choosing Update on these packages will revert the current version to the version on the CD.

When you have finished choosing packages, click Accept to complete the installation. Occasionally, you'll see one of two additional screens. One screen tells you that some other packages will be installed in addition to your selected packages to satisfy some dependencies (see more about dependencies in the next section "The Basics of the Red Hat Package Management System [RPM]"). The other screen indicates that one or more of your selections will conflict with an existing package and offers suggestions about how to deal with the conflict.

YaST then installs the selected packages (see Figure 21.3), processes any other requests made in this session, and runs SUSEConfig to make sure everything's in order. When completed, YaST asks whether you want to install any other packages. Click Install More to do so or click Finish to close the Install module.

You can also use YaST to install a package from the command line. To do this, you must first know the name of the package you want to install. When you do, enter the following:

`yast -i package_name`

For example, if you wanted to install the dosbox package, you would enter the following:

`yast -i dosbox`

Just as when using the Software Management module, installing a package from the command line performs a dependency check and automatically installs any dependent packages required.

After installing any new package, you should always run YOU to check for updated versions of the software. This protects your system against any bug or security problem that may have been discovered and fixed since the last SUSE Linux release; it often gives you new features, as well.

You'll learn more about YOU later in this chapter.

**FIGURE 21.3** YaST Installs the selected packages.

In the preceding example, you used YaST to install additional packages from the SUSE installation CDs. However, you can use YaST to specify other locations from which packages should be installed. You can select an FTP or HTTP server on the Internet, a server on your local network, or a directory on your local hard drive (assuming the packages have been copied there).

Having an alternative installation source can be a lifesaver when you need to install a new package, but have misplaced or damaged your SUSE Linux CDs. Installing from the Internet also ensures that the packages you are installing are the most current available.

Let's take a look at how to add a SUSE mirror site on the Internet as an additional installation source. Complete the following:

1. Open a web browser and navigate to http://www.novell.com/products/ linuxprofessional/downloads/ftp/int_mirrors.html. This website provides a listing of mirror sites you can use as installation sources.

2. Note the URL of the mirror sites closest to you.

3. Start YaST and provide your root password.

4. In YaST, select Software. You will see a module in the right pane called Installation Source, as shown in Figure 21.4.

**FIGURE 21.4**    The YaST Installation Source module.

5. Select Installation Source. The screen in Figure 21.5 is displayed.

**FIGURE 21.5**    Setting the installation source.

Notice in Figure 21.5 that your CD or DVD drive is already configured as your installation source by default.

6. Select Add, FTP or HTTP, depending on the protocol used by the mirror site you've selected. The screen in Figure 21.6 is displayed.

**FIGURE 21.6**   Configuring an FTP mirror as an installation source.

7. Under Protocol, mark the correct protocol for the mirror site you are going to use.

8. In the Server Name field, enter the DNS name or IP address of the mirror server you've selected. For example, if you were going to use the mirror at Oregon State University, you would enter **ftp.oregonstate.edu** in this field. Be sure you don't enter ftp:// or http://.

9. In the Directory on Server field, enter the path to the root of the distribution you want to use, without leading or trailing forward slashes.

10. This part is a little tricky. The issue here is that every mirror site uses a slightly different directory structure. You will need to open a browser window, navigate to the mirror site, and then burrow down through the links until you arrive at the root. For example, on the Oregon State mirror, you would need to delve through to /pub/suse/suse/i386/10.0/ to arrive at the root of the SUSE Linux 10.0 distribution on the site. Then, in the Directory on Server field, you would enter **pub/suse/suse/i386/10.0**.

11. Select OK. You should see the mirror site added as an additional installation source.

12. Ensure the Status of the mirror site is set to On.

13. YaST checks installation sources in the order they appear in this screen. If you want YaST to use the mirror site before your local CD or DVD drive, select your *mirror site* and select Up until it appears first in the list.

14. Select Finish.

---

**NOTE**

If you enter the wrong path, you'll see an error message that states something to the effect of `ERROR(InstSrc:E_no_instsrc_on_media)`. if you see this message, one of two things has happened. Usually, this error occurs when you use a leading or a training forward slash in the directory path. It can also occur if you use the wrong path. Remember that the path must point to the root of the distribution on the mirror site, *not* to the directory where the package files reside.

---

At this point, you can test your new installation source by opening the Software Management module in YaST. When you do, you'll see that the module retrieves its package information from the remote mirror site instead of from your local CD or DVD drive.

With this in mind, we need to relate a little background about applications and packages.

# The Basics of the Red Hat Package Management System (RPM)

The RPM system was inaugurated in 1995 to manage applications in Red Hat Linux 2.0. It was the successor to a collection of Perl scripts that functioned as the earliest Linux packaging tools. Rewritten in the C language in 1996, it quickly became the de facto standard for managing application installations for several distributions, including SUSE Linux.

The basic idea behind RPM is to have a single "pristine" archive of an application's source code that can build packages for different systems and that can track new versions. An RPM database of all available applications is installed on your computer (in `/var/lib/rpm`) and is accessed by YaST and other configuration tools to determine exactly what is on your system, what might be new and updated, and what files each package provides that another package might need to run properly.

This last part, the dependency resolver, is one of the features that made RPM so successful among Linux developers and distributors. When you look at a package in YaST, click the Dependencies tab in the lower-right corner. Here, under Provides, is a list of every file included in the package. After the Provides list, the Requires list tells you every file that this package needs to run, and the Prerequisites list tells you what needs to be installed before you install this package (down to the minimum version number, if necessary). Next up is the list of packages that this package will replace or make obsolete. You have to hope that some other package doesn't require one of these; if it does, you'll get a warning. Finally is a list of conflicts; installing this package will create problems for applications on this list.

RPM packages are now more secure, as packagers can include digital signatures encrypted with GNU Privacy Guard (GnuPG). All packages produced by SUSE Linux are signed, so you know they are genuine.

Interested in packaging your own software with RPM? See Chapter 28, "Using the GNU Compiler Collection and Other Programming Tools."

## Downloading RPM Packages Outside of YaST

SUSE Linux is known for including the largest number of application packages of the major Linux distributions, but it doesn't include every application ever created. Because Linux developers come up with new ideas all the time, there's always something new to try as well.

You can download and install just about any RPM package from any source and run it on your SUSE Linux system.

It's possible that new packages may have some ill effect on your system's stability, but that's rare, especially with RPMs.

When you visit a software repository like `freshmeat.net`, you can see dozens of new and updated applications posted daily. Many developers build RPMs for their applications to make things relatively easy for users to install. Some even build separate RPMs for Red Hat and SUSE users.

You should create a single directory for your downloaded files. It should be in your home directory. Set up your browser(s) to download all files to that directory. The reason to do this is because you can then add that directory to YaST's installation sources and directly install new RPMs in YaST.

To add your `~/download` directory to YaST's installation sources, follow these steps.

1. Open YaST. Select Software, Installation Source.

2. Click Add and select Local Directory from the drop-down menu.

3. Type in, or browse to, the `~/download` directory. Click OK to confirm.

4. YaST will check for a "product," and then give you a message asking you to click Continue to make RPM packages available in the packages section. Do that. The directory should appear in the main window with status On.

Now when you download an RPM package to that directory, you can open YaST's Software Management module and install that package.

KDE/Konqueror users get a bonus convenience when downloading RPMs with the Konqueror web browser. After it is downloaded, Konqueror displays an Install with YaST button. Click it to run YaST's Install module.

# Updating Your System with YaST Online Update (YOU)

An Internet connection is all you need to keep your SUSE Linux system current. This section tells you about using YOU and its companion application, SUSEwatcher, to maintain your system in tip-top shape. Every package posted to a YOU server has been tested by SUSE staff to ensure that it works correctly with your system.

## Running YOU

For the most control over the update process, run YOU manually. You can choose which server to access, which applications to update (or not), and get more information on the patch applied to the application. It takes a little time, but it is not especially complex.

Open YaST and click Online Update. Figure 21.7 will appear.

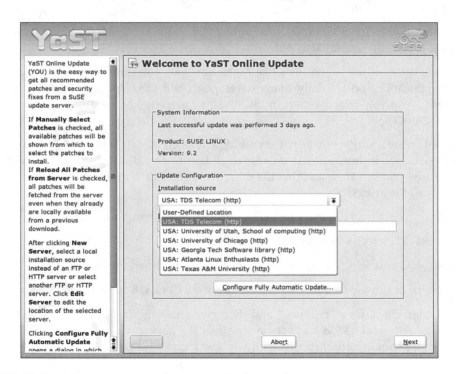

**FIGURE 21.7**   Select a nearby update server for fast service.

For a long time, SUSE maintained just a few online update servers, in Germany and in a few other European locations. YOU always checked for a new list of servers whenever it opened, but the list changed rarely. In early 2004, many more update servers came online, and YOU delivered a geographic list to users.

Select one of the choices from the drop-down menu. You have the option to define a location from the menu, add a new server, or edit the current server address from buttons on this screen. You should rarely, if ever, have to do that.

Click Next to check for updates. YaST will compare its list of currently installed packages to the packages in the Update directory. If there are updates available, you'll see a screen similar to Figure 21.8. At the top of the screen is the list of available updates. Security updates are marked in red. If you had the Select Packages Manually box checked on the Server page, you may see some packages that aren't relevant to your system, but you can install them nonetheless by checking the appropriate box.

**FIGURE 21.8**   The YOU Update screen lists security updates (marked in red) with detailed descriptions of the problem the fix solves.

You can see a detailed description of each patch in the left middle pane. In the case of security patches, this describes the problem solved by the patch. For more mundane updates (bug fixes, new releases, and other patches unrelated to system security), the level of detail in the descriptions runs the gamut. Click Accept to download and install the updated packages.

YOU will download and install the selected packages, giving you an onscreen progress report (see Figure 21.9). When the download is complete, check the Remove Source Packages After Update box to conserve space on your hard drive, and then click Finish to run SUSEConfig and return to the YaST Control Center.

As with installing packages, you can also update your SUSE Linux system from the command line. This is done using the `online_update` command. This utility utilizes the following options:

- -u—Specifies the URL where updates should be downloaded from.

- -g—Download the updates, but don't install them.

- -i—Install downloaded updates.

- -k—Check for new updates.

- -p—Product for which updates should be downloaded.

- -v—Product version for which updates should be downloaded.

- -a—CPU architecture for updates.

- -d—Download updates and simulate installation (for testing).

- -s—Display a list of available updates.

That's all there is to it. With the exception of kernel updates, you should never have to reboot the system to complete an update.

**FIGURE 21.9**    The progress bar keeps you informed on the download and installation process.

## Using SUSEwatcher to Monitor YOU Servers

Since version 8.2, the SUSEwatcher utility monitors your designated YOU server for updates and notifies you when there's something new.

Included in the KDE-SUSE package, SUSEwatcher (and its companion, the Plugger hardware detection utility) sits in the KDE and GNOME panels. Most of the time, you'll just see the green smiling face of the SUSE Linux mascot, Geeko, indicating you are current. But occasionally, the icon will turn an eye-catching red with an exclamation point. This tells you that new security updates are available. More rarely, the icon will turn yellow, indicating that a nonsecurity update has been posted.

Click the SUSEwatcher icon to display the dialog box shown in Figure 21.10. This dialog box is the only settings interface for SUSEwatcher.

**FIGURE 21.10**   SUSEwatcher checks the YOU server for updated software. Click Start Online Update to run YOU.

To run YOU, click Start Online Update. YOU will ask for the SuperUser password and then run normally.

Unless you have a real aversion to taskbar icons, you should have SUSEwatcher set to start automatically. If you have a broadband or LAN connection to the Internet, you should have SUSEwatcher automatically check for updates. It will then check the server once every 24 hours. If you have a modem connection, you have two options: If you want to have the servers checked automatically, you need to have your modem set in YaST to Dial on Demand. See "Configuring Your Dial-Up Internet Connection" in Chapter 12, "Connecting to the Internet," to learn how. If you want to run SUSEwatcher yourself, click the icon regularly and choose Check for Updates from the dialog box.

> **TIP**
>
> Can't find the SUSEwatcher icon? From the KDE menu (or the main menu in GNOME), go to System, Desktop Applet to start SUSEwatcher.

### Automating YOU Updates

Maybe you don't want to know exactly what package is getting updated at any given time. Maybe you don't want to take a few minutes every so often to keep your system secure and updated. You don't have to sacrifice security for a little laziness. YaST can do this for you.

When you open YOU, click Configure Fully Automatic Update. Figure 21.11 appears.

**FIGURE 21.11**    Configure YOU to run daily or weekly and you never have to worry about keeping your system current and secure.

Check the Enable Automatic Update box and the default times appear. If you are more concerned with pulling down security updates, choose to update daily. If you connect to the Internet with a modem, be sure to select a time when you are always online, or configure your modem to Dial on Demand. Click OK to confirm. You can still run YOU manually if, for example, SUSEwatcher identifies a new update.

## Updating Your System with apt

In addition to the RPM system, the APT packaging system developed for the Debian Linux distribution is the other most popular Linux install and update tool. APT's ease of use rates highly. Using APT to install most packages from the command line involves typing `apt-get install <package>` and APT does the rest.

Developers for the Brazilian Linux distribution Conectiva first created `apt4rpm` to bring the benefits of APT to RPM-based distributions. Richard Bos further adapted the program to SUSE's eccentricities. APT is not yet included in the official SUSE distribution, but is readily available from the APT for SUSE website, http://linux01.gwdg.de/apt4rpm. Many APT repositories have also been created to make using APT to download and install new software that much easier.

APT works a lot like YOU. Both applications require the SuperUser to run them; each application accesses the same RPM database when they start up to determine what application packages are installed on your system. To find new versions of current applications, and completely new packages, YaST and APT seek out designated remote servers, but YaST has a list of Novell/SUSE-owned servers that are known to mirror the existing SUSE Linux distribution. APT uses a special server-list file, /etc/apt/sources.list, to access file repositories. APT repositories include mirrors of the SUSE Linux distribution and other sites hosting SUSE-compatible RPMs. With the separate apt4rpm utility, you can even host your own APT repository.

A broader range of packages appear in APT repositories than on the official SUSE servers, and updated versions of many popular applications (web browsers, desktop environments, The GIMP, and the like) appear much faster on the APT repositories than on the SUSE servers. The downside of this speed is that SUSE doesn't put an updated package on the YOU server until it has been tested and functions well under SUSE Linux. It doesn't happen often, but you can run into trouble using new applications installed with APT, although no more trouble than you would experience downloading an RPM from another website yourself and installing it.

To download and install APT, go to the APT for SUSE site and scroll to the Software Installation section. Click the link for your SUSE version and architecture (9.2 for x86 PCs, 9.2-x86_64 for 64-bit processors). Download both the apt and apt-libs packages; then run the YaST Software Management module to install the two packages.

Before you can use APT, you need a sources.list text file to point to SUSE APT repositories. You can find a good default file at the APT for SUSE site in the Advanced Package Tool Configuration section. As before, choose the link for your version and architecture.

**CAUTION**

If you have a 64-bit processor, resist the temptation to add 32-bit apt repositories to your sources.list file. You may discover that there's a "new" 32-bit update for one of your 64-bit packages, and apt will cheerfully download the package and then announce it can't install the new package because the filenames are different.

Save the text file to your home directory, edit the file to your liking, and then copy it as the SuperUser to /etc/apt/sources.list.

**CAUTION**

Many of the repositories included in the sample sources.list file link to experimental packages that may make your system relatively unstable. If you just want to use apt to install stable packages, comment out these sections: kernal-of-the-day kraxel suse-people suse-projects. You may also want to comment out the suser-<name> sections, as well. If you want to keep up with apt upgrades, however, include suser-rbos.

When you have your sources.list file installed, you can run APT. Connect to the Internet and open a shell as the SuperUser. From the shell, gather the list of current files at the repositories by typing the following:

```
apt-get update
```

The first time you run this, it may take a little while, especially if you have a modem connection.

> **NOTE**
>
> Always run update before performing any other operations in apt. New and updated packages can appear in a repository at any time, and any given package may supply a dependency for the package you're using apt to get. Synaptic will do this automatically when you open it (if you haven't updated in the previous 48 hours).

When the repository update is completed, you can install (or update) any package in the repository. One package you might like to start with is the fine GUI front-end for APT, called Synaptic. Type the following:

```
apt-get install synaptic
```

After it is installed, Synaptic adds itself to both the KDE and GNOME System Configuration menus, so you can launch it from there. After prompting you for the SuperUser password, Synaptic will display a YaST-like Search screen, but you might prefer to browse through the list of available updates. In the lower-left corner are four package views, including the Search view you're seeing now. The Sections view corresponds to YaST's sections, and you can see both installed and available packages here. The Status view groups packages by whether they are installed, upgradable, or not installed. Click Status to display this view (see Figure 21.12).

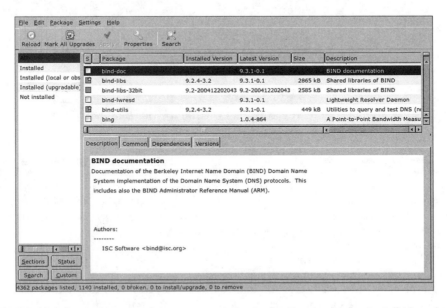

**FIGURE 21.12**    Synaptic makes it easy to manage application packages. Installed packages with available updates have the fill-in check box with a star in the corner.

In the smaller left pane, you'll see five or six status categories. To see all packages with available updates, click Installed (upgradable). Notice that the check box to the left of each package is filled in with a yellow star in the upper-right corner. Click any package to see a description in the right bottom pane. Right-click and choose Mark for Upgrade from the context menu. If you want to upgrade everything on this list, click Mark All Upgrades from the toolbar. As with RPM, Synaptic (and APT as well) may add and remove packages to resolve dependency issues and will tell you before you commit to the changes.

> **CAUTION**
>
> Always check to see that APT is not removing critical packages without replacing them, lest you find yourself unable to boot later. And always back up your system and other critical files like the kernel, the bootloader, your desktop environment, databases, and the like before upgrading major packages.

Before committing to any new update, click the Custom view button, and then click Marked Changes to see the list of packages you are updating, installing, or removing. When you're ready to run APT, click Apply from the toolbar. APT will download all the marked packages and then install them one by one. You will see a progress bar and be notified of any problems. To get more information about the installation process while it is happening, go to Settings, Preferences, and check the Apply Changes in a Terminal Window box.

## Updating Your System with Red Carpet

Ximian started out as a company that built applications for the GNOME desktop, and it did some terrific stuff, especially the Evolution personal information manager. Ximian started branching out from the GNOME focus with an updating product it called Red Carpet. Because Ximian was acquired by Novell a few months before SUSE, Novell has been integrating Ximian products into its own product line. Red Carpet now is the main updating tool for the Novell Linux Desktop. In the guise of Novell ZENWorks Linux Management, Red Carpet also updates the Novell Open Enterprise Server.

Like the other tools covered in this chapter, Red Carpet simplifies the task of updating and installing software for your distribution. Some terminology is different, however. For example, a Red Carpet download site is called a *channel*, to which you *subscribe* to see what's new. You should, nonetheless, find Red Carpet easy to understand and learn.

### Installing Red Carpet

As with APT, Red Carpet is not available through YaST. To get the latest version, visit ftp://ftp.ximian.com/pub/redcarpet2/ with a web browser or FTP client. Choose your SUSE version and architecture (32-bit Intel x86 or 64-bit x86_64).

You will see several RPM packages in this directory. Download these three: `rcd-<version><architecture>.rpm` (this is the daemon that runs in the background), `rug-<version><architecture>.rpm`, and `red-carpet<version><architecture>.rpm`. The combined file size of these three files is about 3MB, so it won't take long to download.

You can use YaST to install these packages, but it may work better to run this from the command line. Log in as SuperUser, change to your download directory, and install the Red Carpet daemon first with this command:

```
rpm rcd-<version><architecture>.rpm
```

You'll see some brief activity, and if successful, the rpm program will return you to the prompt. Repeat the process with the command line and GUI packages.

```
rpm rug-<version><architecture>.rpm
```

```
rpm red-carpet-<version><architecture>.rpm
```

Each should now install and run on your system. The Red Carpet daemon must be running for either of the other programs to work, so there's one last step in your installation. Type **rcd** to complete the installation. The Red Carpet daemon will now run in the background.

## Running Red Carpet from the Command Line (rug)

The fastest way to use Red Carpet to update your system is through the rug command-line utility. As always when installing new software, you should be logged in as the SuperUser when using rug.

Just typing **rug** at the shell prompt will give you a list of rug commands. The first time you run rug, it will locate your existing RPM database, so it knows what is on your system now. To see what channels Red Carpet is using to update your system, type **rug ch**. You should see something like this:

```
subd? | Alias | Name
------+--------------------+---------------------
| redcarpet2 | Red Carpet 2
| rcd-snaps | rcd snapshots
| suse-92-x86_64 | suse-92-x86_64
| suse-92-x86_64-kernel | suse-92-x86_64-kernel
```

The first column, subd?, tells you if you are subscribed to a channel—that is, whether you can access and download from the listed site. In this instance, no channels are subscribed to. Let's sign up for the Red Carpet updates and the SUSE server as well. Type the following:

```
rug sub redcarpet2 suse-92-x86_64
```

Now if you get the channel list again with **rug ch,** you should see this:

```
subd? | Alias | Name
------+--------------------+---------------------
Yes | redcarpet2 | Red Carpet 2
```

```
| rcd-snaps | rcd snapshots
Yes | suse-92-x86_64 | suse-92-x86_64
| suse-92-x86_64-kernel | suse-92-x86_64-kernel
```

> **TIP**
>
> The German server that delivers SUSE packages to APT users also is configured as a Red Carpet service. You can add it as a channel with this command:
>
> rug service-add http://open-carpet.org/services/gwdg/

Now let's look at the GUI client and update the system.

## Updating with the Red Carpet GUI

The Red Carpet graphical application operates very much like Synaptic for APT, rather than the way YaST goes about updating. It uses a tabbed interface to keep you in the know without overwhelming you with lots of material on a page. To begin in KDE, go to System, Configuration, Red Carpet. Red Carpet checks your channels for new stuff and tells you if there are updates for your installed applications (or tells you if you are current).

Click Available Software to see what applications are available in your channels that you have not installed. Use the Section menu to break all the packages down by function, if you are looking for something specific, or just browse through the alphabetical list.

If you find something on this tab that you want, select it and click Mark for Installation. An icon appears and your choice is added to the Pending Actions list on the left (see Figure 21.13).

When you've identified the applications you want to install or update, click Run Now to begin. Red Carpet checks dependencies and lists all tasks to be carried out. Click Continue.

Red Carpet downloads and installs your selection(s). Click OK when it is finished. You will return to the main screen, where you can choose more applications to install, or exit.

> **TIP**
>
> There are so many applications included in the SUSE Linux distribution, sometimes you may not know everything you've installed. Even if you're not the SuperUser, Red Carpet can help you if you just want to see if you have installed that application you just read about in a magazine. Open the Red Carpet graphical application and click Installed Applications.

**FIGURE 21.13**    In Red Carpet, you can see the choices you make in the Pending Actions list on the left.

## Compiling Software from Source

Some programs are too complex or too specialized for the programmer to go to the trouble of creating RPMs for them. So the programmer archives the source code in a tarball and sends it out. Often, simply extracting the code into an appropriate directory is all that's needed to make the application work, as you've seen with several of the blogging tools in Chapter 14, "Creating Basic Websites," and the Azureus BitTorrent client in Chapter 17, "Secure File Transfer."

Other programs must be compiled before they can work. This section will help you do this. Before beginning, you will need to have the GNU Compiler Collection (gcc) installed to handle this task.

First, when compiling new source code, create a new subdirectory in your home directory called source. This will let you compile your code as a user and help prevent any bad (or even malicious) code from harming your system.

Now the task is to extract the archive into the new ~/source directory. You can do this in GNOME File Roller or Ark for KDE, but it will be faster from the shell. Change directory to the ~/download folder (or wherever your source archive is sitting). Depending on the archive format of the original file, type one of the following commands:

```
tar xzvf <package>.tgz -C ~/source
```

```
tar xzvf <package>.tar.gz -C ~/source
```

```
tar xjvf <package>.bz -C ~/source
```

```
tar xjvf <package>.tar.bz2 -C ~/source
```

The first two are different extensions for a `tar`/`gnuzip` archive, whereas the last two were archived using BZip. The `-C` switch extracted the archived files to the `~/source` directory. If you are not sure what archiving method was used, use the `file` command to help you determine the format. Type **`file <package>`**.

Now change to the extracted program directory under the `~/source` directory. Look for a file (usually named in ALL CAPS so you can find it better) called something like README or INSTALL. This file will have detailed instructions on how to compile and make the program work. Chances are these instructions will be some variation on the Configure/Make/Make Install process. This means you will first run a script called `configure`, as follows:

```
./configure
```

This script confirms that all dependencies are met and the build environment is solid. When this script runs successfully, compile the program with the `make` utility included in `gcc`:

```
make
```

Finally, log in as the SuperUser and install the program with the same `make` utility:

```
make install
```

This should safely install your new source program.

## References

- http://www.novell.com/coolsolutions/feature/11504.html—A screenshot-filled YaST tutorial from Novell's Cool Solutions site.

- http://www.suse.de/~sh/YaST2-Package-Manager—Written to explain the big changes in YaST with v8.1, there's a lot of good information here on how YaST works.

- http://portal.suse.com/sdb/en/2003/04/82_susewatcher.html—Documentation for SUSEwatcher, including descriptions for the icons.

- http://www.rpm.org—Home for information on the Red Hat Package Management system. The site includes an online version of Ed Bailey's 2000 book, Maximum RPM.

- http://linux01.gwdg.de/apt4rpm—Everything you need to know to use apt for SUSE Linux.

- http://www.nongnu.org/synaptic—The Synaptic GUI for apt. Download the current source from here, if you can't wait for a new package via apt.

- http://packman.links2linux.org—Excellent repository for packages not yet included in the official distribution. Download directly or use APT.

- http://speakeasy.rpmfind.net—The U.S. mirror for the RPMFind search engine.

- http://rpmseek.com—Find more RPM packages here.

- http://freshmeat.net—A giant repository of Linux and other open source software, organized by date received. Thus, the "freshest meat" is at the top.

# PART V

# Advanced System Administration

## IN THIS PART

CHAPTER **22**

# Managing the Boot Process and Other Services

To begin understanding how your Linux computer works, you need to know how it starts. Booting in Linux is a three-step process, as the computer's basic input/output system (BIOS) starts the machine's hardware without a care as to what operating system its owner (you) wants to run.

It hands control over the machine to a boot manager (such as LILO or GRUB), which does care about finding at least one operating system on the machine.

Finally, you tell the boot manager what file system to run, and it does. The Linux kernel then manages the rest of the session.

In this chapter, you learn exactly what you need to know about the Linux boot process. Some of this information applies to other operating systems, but in this chapter, we focus on starting up and booting SUSE Linux.

Determining which services run in a Linux box partly depends on what kind of Linux box it is. Its system state, or *runlevel*, controls what starts and what doesn't. Ultimately, you have the power, as SuperUser, to define which services run when.

You'll walk through a boot process to see exactly what happens when your computer starts up. You will use the YaST Runlevel Editor to manage services. You'll also look at some of the tools you can use to monitor your system and keep it in tip-top shape.

# Understanding the Boot Process

All x86-type computers, whether running processors from Intel or AMD—no matter what operating system they have—start up the same way. BIOS software that sits on a specialized chip activates all the circuitry on the motherboard, and occasionally other hardware connected to the motherboard, and then goes looking for a boot manager—a piece of software code that starts an operating system. This boot manager code can sit on a hard drive (where it's called the Master Boot Record, or MBR), a floppy disk, a CD-ROM, or even on another computer if the system is using the network file system (NFS). This boot-loader software tells the BIOS where the Linux kernel is located, how to load it into memory, and how to start it.

## Starting to Boot: BIOS to Boot Manager

If all goes well in the hardware initialization, the BIOS locates a special hexadecimal value written to the volume, which makes the volume bootable.

The order in which it looks for this is in the BIOS settings, which you can access by pressing a certain key or key combination while the BIOS is still in command. The traditional order was floppy disk, hard drive, some other place. In recent years, bootable CD-ROMs joined the BIOS options and now should be first on the list.

Any modern BIOS should have considerable flexibility in the devices it searches for a bootable volume, but it always stops looking when it finds the first bootable volume. This is why it's a good idea to remove your SUSE Linux installation CD after adding new software to your system. If you don't, the next time you boot will be to the CD. This is presumably why the CD now has Boot from Hard Drive as the default option on its opening menu.

> **NOTE**
>
> Your BIOS will alert you with a series of beeps if it finds a hardware problem that makes your system unbootable. Each motherboard manufacturer has a different system of generating those beeps, so consult your motherboard manual to learn the code, or contact your PC vendor or manufacturer to try to fix the problem.

When the BIOS finds the bootloader code, it then looks for the MBR, the first sector on the hard drive. This is the most important sector on the disk because the bootloader code (just 446 bytes) and the partition table (64 bytes) reside there. Having properly initialized the hardware, the BIOS can now place the bootloader code into memory and hand over the boot process to the bootloader. The bootloader code that sits in the MBR has one job—to start the full bootloader program, GRUB by default, and load it into memory.

## Choosing a Boot Manager: GRUB Versus LILO

You may not realize it unless you are dual booting multiple operating systems, but after your BIOS starts firing up the fan, the microprocessor chip, and the power supply, a boot manager, or *bootloader*, takes over the process until the kernel starts up.

Linux supports a variety of open-source and proprietary boot managers, but you can install only two with YaST: the Grand Unified Bootloader (GRUB) and the Linux Loader (LILO). GRUB has been the default bootloader for SUSE Linux since v8.2, but LILO still runs quite a few systems, and you may want to use it instead.

LILO succeeded `loadlin` as the primary Linux bootloader and seems to be in the long process of being superseded by GRUB. LILO carries out its single task, booting to a file system, well. It is not quite as flexible nor as configurable as GRUB. Nonetheless, it is still the default bootloader for systems in which the Root partition is installed on CPU-dependent RAID controllers (such as many Promise or Highpoint controllers), Software RAID, or Logical Volume (LVM) managed disk.

The chief difference between the two bootloaders is in how they find and load file systems. LILO looks for a file system based on where the partition table says it is. GRUB can read and identify several file systems (ext2, ext3, ReiserFS, JFS, XFS, Minix, and DOS).

In YaST, the Boot Loader Configuration module is on the System page. You can set LILO as the default if you want and set many other options in this screen (see Figure 22.1). If you prefer, you can edit the file directly by clicking Edit Configuration Files.

**FIGURE 22.1**    Select and configure your bootloader.

By default, GRUB displays a menu, allowing you to boot SUSE Linux from the hard drive, from a floppy drive, or into *fail-safe* mode. Fail-safe mode loads a kernel version with a set of parameters that makes it possible to boot with some hardware problems. If there's another operating system on your computer, GRUB will list this on your boot menu as well. After 8 seconds, GRUB will boot the first item on the menu; that is, SUSE Linux.

> **NOTE**
>
> At the bottom of the GRUB menu, you can specify options for the kernel, if you are so inclined.

You can see how each process builds on the previous one, allowing different operating systems to work on the same hardware.

The GRUB menu you see is controlled by the GRUB configuration file, which is located at /boot/grub/menu.1st. A sample menu.1st file is shown in Figure 22.2.

```
linux:~ # cat /boot/grub/menu.lst
# Modified by YaST2. Last modification on Sun Sep  4 17:52:53 UTC 2005

color white/blue black/light-gray
default 0
timeout 8
gfxmenu (hd0,1)/boot/message

###Don't change this comment - YaST2 identifier: Original name: linux###
title SUSE LINUX 10.0
    root (hd0,1)
    kernel /boot/vmlinuz root=/dev/sda2 vga=0x332 selinux=0    resume=/dev/sda1
 splash=silent showopts
    initrd /boot/initrd

###Don't change this comment - YaST2 identifier: Original name: floppy###
title Floppy
    chainloader (fd0)+1

###Don't change this comment - YaST2 identifier: Original name: failsafe###
title Failsafe -- SUSE LINUX 10.0
    root (hd0,1)
    kernel /boot/vmlinuz root=/dev/sda2 vga=normal showopts ide=nodma apm=off ac
pi=off noresume selinux=0 nosmp noapic maxcpus=0 edd=off 3
    initrd /boot/initrd
linux:~ # 
```

**FIGURE 22.2**   Working with menu.1st.

The first portion of menu.1st defines options for the display of the GRUB menu, such as the color scheme of the menu, the default menu option, and the number of seconds (timeout) before GRUB runs the default menu option.

Following the display options are a list of items that will be displayed in the GRUB menu. Each menu item begins with "title." Notice in Figure 22.2 that this particular GRUB menu will display three items:

- SUSE LINUX 10.0
- Floppy
- Failsafe—SUSE LINUX 10.0

The remaining lines tell GRUB where to find the operating system files needed to run Linux. These include the following:

- root: This command sets the current root device to the specified device.

- kernel: This command loads the primary boot image from the boot image file.

- initrd: This command loads an initial ramdisk for the boot image.

To configure how GRUB boots your system, you can either manually edit menu.1st with a text editor, or you can use the YaST System, Boot Loader module, shown in Figure 22.3.

**FIGURE 22.3**   Configuring GRUB in YaST.

As you can see in Figure 22.3, each of your menu items is displayed in the Section Management screen. Here you can add, delete, or modify your GRUB menu items, as shown in Figure 22.4.

In this screen, you can edit your menu item name, the kernel file, initial ramdisk file, root device, and VGA mode, as well as optional kernel parameters.

> **NOTE**
>
> In addition to manually editing the menu.1st file and using YaST, you can also use the GRUB shell to configure how your system boots. Simply enter **grub** at the shell prompt. To learn how to manipulate GRUB from the shell, see the grub man page.

## Loading the Kernel

When GRUB hands over the process to the SUSE Linux kernel, it leaves the scene. The kernel now takes charge, putting up the message Uncompressing Linux…; it is present and available to you until you shut down the system. While the kernel boots, SUSE Linux puts up a nice blue wallpaper to hide all the boring text that scrolls by as the kernel initializes first your peripheral hardware, then the hard drive and attending file systems, followed by the serial ports. Press the Esc key to watch the boot process unfold.

**FIGURE 22.4**    Modifying a GRUB menu item in YaST.

As a user, or even as an administrator, you don't have much direct interaction with the Linux kernel. You run applications, which occasionally interact with the kernel to get things done. In the kernel's view of things, an application is simply a process, one of many it deals with. The father of all processes, which the kernel loads soon after the kernel itself loads, is called init, located in the /sbin directory. The rest of the boot process (and later, the shutdown process) is really handled by init, not the kernel. All other processes are started by init or one of its child processes. Init is centrally configured by the /etc/inittab file.

After activating the serial ports, the kernel runs a series of boot scripts, located at /etc/rc.d/boot.d, which activates (and, if required, mounts) still more devices and local file systems.

Then boot.clock sets up the system clock, ldconfig identifies the current time zone, and local networking interfaces are turned on via boot.sysctrl, boot.localnet (for the loopback interface), and boot.isapnp.

Finally, the kernel's System Boot Control declares

```
The system has been set up
```

and runs /etc/init.d/boot.local. This program invokes the appropriate runlevel for the system. There is much more on runlevels in the next section, but a standard networked desktop will launch Runlevel 5 as it hits the home stretch of the boot process.

At Runlevel 5, networking services are started and various other services and the system logs come online. The sound driver, keyboard maps, CUPS printer interfaces, mail transfer agent, and xinetd Internet services come next.

Finally, the kernel starts the X Window System and the display manager (KDM by default) that allows the user to log in. Logging in loads the desired desktop, and you're done.

> **NOTE**
>
> To closely examine your most recent boot process, open /var/log/boot.msg in a text editor, or open the YaST View Startup Log module from the Misc page.

## System Services and Runlevels

There are several ways to start and stop services. SUSE Linux uses the *runlevel* method that originated with Unix System V. Runlevels determine when, or if, a service runs. They also determine the order in which services are started.

Runlevels, generally speaking, identify the type of use for the computer. Table 22.1 explains the different runlevels in SUSE Linux; notice that they correspond somewhat directly to the basic choices of software installations presented to you during the initial installation of SUSE Linux.

The minimum installation is roughly equivalent to Single User Mode, Runlevel 1, whereas the minimum graphical install corresponds to Runlevel 3. The gluttons who want a graphical desktop use Runlevel 5, the whole enchilada.

**TABLE 22.1**    Runlevels

| Runlevel | Description |
| --- | --- |
| 0 | System Halt, system shutdown. |
| 1 | Single User, or rescue, mode. Only root can log in. |
| 2 | Local Multiuser mode without remote networking. |
| 3 | Full Multiuser mode with network. |
| 4 | Not used. |
| 5 | Full Multiuser mode with network and X display manager (also fail-safe mode when booted directly from the boot prompt). |
| 6 | Reboot. |

While the system is running, you can actually change your current runlevel. When you change runlevels, all services essential to your current runlevel are stopped and the services essential to the new runlevel are started.

To do this, enter the init command at a shell prompt, followed by the runlevel number you want to switch to. For example, if you want to switch from runlevel 5 (complete with

X and a desktop environment) to runlevel 3 (the minimal graphical environment), you would complete the following:

- Open a terminal session and switch to your root user account.

- At the shell prompt, run the init script for runlevel 3 by entering **init 3**.

When you do this, init consults the /etc/inittab configuration file and runs /etc/ init.d/rc with 3 (the new runlevel) as a parameter. The rc utility runs stop scripts for every service missing a start script in /etc/init.d/rc3.d, but having a stop script in /etc/init.d/rc5.d.

Stop scripts have filenames that begin with K (for "kill"), and start scripts begin with S (for "start"). The numbers following the letter indicate an order for each script to be executed. This prevents files with some dependencies from crashing before they stop.

After all the unnecessary runlevel 5 scripts have been stopped, the start scripts run for services needed in runlevel 3 but not in runlevel 5.

When you installed SUSE Linux, you were given the option to set your system's default run level. By default, this is runlevel 5. This is usually the best option for most users. However, suppose it isn't the right choice for you. Suppose you want to use your SUSE Linux system as a server (which it can do very well) and you don't want the CPU spending unneeded cycles redrawing your graphical screens. You would prefer it to boot, by default, to a text-based prompt while retaining the capability to run your graphical desktop when needed. In this situation, runlevel 3 would be a better choice.

You can set your default runlevel in two ways. First, you can edit your /etc/inittab configuration file with a text editor, as shown in Figure 22.5.

```
#
# /etc/inittab
#
# Copyright (c) 1996-2002 SuSE Linux AG, Nuernberg, Germany.  All rights reserve
d.
#
# Author: Florian La Roche, 1996
# Please send feedback to http://www.suse.de/feedback
#
# This is the main configuration file of /sbin/init, which
# is executed by the kernel on startup. It describes what
# scripts are used for the different run-levels.
#
# All scripts for runlevel changes are in /etc/init.d/.
#
# This file may be modified by SuSEconfig unless CHECK_INITTAB
# in /etc/sysconfig/suseconfig is set to "no"
#

# The default runlevel is defined here
id:5:initdefault:

# First script to be executed, if not booting in emergency (-b) mode
si::bootwait:/etc/init.d/boot

"/etc/inittab" 97L, 2926C                              1,1          Top
```

**FIGURE 22.5**    Editing the /etc/inittab file.

Notice that about three-fourths of the way down the screen, a line reads as follows:

`id:5:initdefault:`

This line specifies which runlevel your system should boot to by default. If you want to change this to runlevel 3, you should complete the following:

1. Open a terminal session and switch to your root user account.

2. At the shell prompt, enter **vi /etc/inittab**.

3. Arrow down to the `id:5:initdefault:` line in the file.

4. Press Ins.

5. Change the 5 to a **3**.

6. Press Esc.

7. Enter **:exit**.

8. Reboot your system.

When the system boots, it will enter runlevel 3, as shown in Figure 22.6.

**FIGURE 22.6**    Booting into runlevel 3.

When it's finished booting, your system will display a simple, text-based screen asking you to authenticate. After logging in, you can optionally start your graphical environment by entering **startx** from the shell prompt.

The second way you can change your default run level is with YaST. If you're not comfortable using Linux text editing tools, you can let YaST do the work for you. To change your default runlevel using YaST, complete the following:

1. Start YaST and navigate to the System, System Services (Runlevel) module.

2. Select Expert Mode. The screen in Figure 22.7 is displayed.

**FIGURE 22.7** Changing the default runlevel in YaST.

3. In the Set Default Runlevel After Booting drop-down list, select the default *runlevel* for your system.

4. Select Finish.

The next time you restart your system, it will boot to the default runlevel you configured.

# Controlling Services at Boot with the YaST Runlevel Editor

YaST provides a startlingly easy way for system administrators to manage which services run at boot. The YaST Runlevel Editor module is easy to understand and gives you important information about each service. The start/stop process is nothing more than a mouse click.

How wonderful, you're thinking. A nice change. Experienced system administrators may cringe a little, though. It is so easy to destroy your system. The help text to the left of the Runlevel Editor, shown in Figure 22.8, offers a relatively calm warning: The runlevel editor is an expert tool. Only change settings if you know what you are doing, otherwise your system might not function properly afterwards.

That's fine as far as it goes. The Caution box coming up next may be closer to the point.

> **CAUTION**
>
> You can render your system unbootable if you do not take particular care when starting new services, and especially when stopping existing services.
>
> Using the Runlevel Editor in Expert Mode is potentially more dangerous. Don't change the runlevel for a service without very good reason.
>
> Always review the changes you made before closing the Runlevel Editor. They will not take effect until you reboot your computer, so you can prevent catastrophic errors if necessary.

**FIGURE 22.8**    The YaST Runlevel Editor makes it incredibly easy to turn services on and off. Great care must be taken so that you do not disrupt your system's functioning.

## Using the Runlevel Editor

When you open the Runlevel Editor module from the YaST System page, a list of all available services appears. The second column tells you whether this service currently is loaded at boot, and the third column offers a brief description of each service. Click a service, such as `freshclam` in Figure 22.9, and see a more detailed description in the bottom pane.

To start a service when you next boot your system, select it from the list and click Enable. To turn a service off, select it and click Disable. Review your changes and click Finish to confirm them. Reboot your computer to force the changes.

## Expert Mode

Click the Expert Mode button to display the additional options (see Figure 22.9). The first thing you may notice are the boot scripts and other services listed here. When in Expert Mode, you really need to know what you're doing, and you get much less hand holding as far as descriptions of each service.

**FIGURE 22.9**   The Runlevel Editor Expert Mode lets you start and stop services, set different runlevels for individual services, and set the default runlevel on boot.

In Expert Mode, you can do the following:

- Change the default runlevel on boot.
- Identify which service can run on each runlevel, from boot to shutdown and everything in between.
- Start, Stop, or Restart any service without rebooting.
- Enable all services on boot.

As in Simple Mode, the editing process is straightforward. Use the drop-down menu to select the default runlevel. Select a service to make changes. Click the Start/Stop/Refresh menu to act on a service now: Start a service not currently running, Stop a running service, or Refresh (stop, if necessary, then start) a service.

Use the check boxes near the bottom of the screen to change the runlevel of a selected service. B runs a service at boot. S runs a service at shutdown.

Notice that when you change from Simple Mode to Expert Mode, the second column changes from Enabled to Running. This lets you use the Start/Stop/Refresh menu. The Set/Reset menu lets you Enable or Disable individual services and adds a third option: Enable All Services.

Make your changes, review them carefully, and then click Finish to confirm your changes.

## Manually Starting and Stopping Services

If you change the configuration file for a particular service, you usually have to stop and restart the service to use the new configuration. When making changes to the X server, it is often worthwhile to change from Runlevel 5 to Runlevel 3 to test the changes, then switch back to reenable the display manager. This way, if you make a mistake, you can fix it and get it right without having to reboot every time.

To stop, start, or restart any service, open a shell as the SuperUser. To see if your ALSA sound server is running, type the following:

```
/etc/init.d/alsasound status
```

The script will report its status. It should report

```
ALSA sound driver loaded.              running
```

To stop and restart the service, type

```
/etc/init.d/alsasound restart
```

and the following should appear:

```
Shutting down sound driver              done
Starting sound driver:  via82xx         done
Restoring the previous sound setting    done
```

As noted in the previous section, you can also use the YaST Runlevel Editor in Expert Mode to start, stop, or restart any service.

## System Monitoring Tools

SUSE Linux and the two desktop environments offer several tools, both graphical and shell based, to help you manage and monitor your system.

## KSysGuard

Windows users sooner or later become familiar with the Task Manager tool, if for no other reason than to close out some application that is "not responding" to the user or the operating system. Those who make the switch to SUSE Linux will feel comfortable the first time they open the KDE equivalent: KSysGuard. The good news is you rarely, if ever, have to run this program to make a program behave (or, failing that, go away).

Although KSysGuard looks like and behaves much like Task Manager, *do not* press Ctrl+Alt+Delete to bring it up. The famous Three Finger Salute just brings up a shutdown dialog box. You can launch this application from the shell by typing **ksysguard** or going to System, Monitors in the KDE menu.

KSysGuard offers two types of information by default in its tabbed window. The System Load tab (see Figure 22.10) gives you a graphical view of several system processes. You can adjust the information this tab displays using the menus on the left side. The Process Table (see Figure 22.11) has a list of every process currently running on your system, with many details on its status. If you find an application hung up, you can locate its process(es) here and (with the right permissions) kill it.

> **NOTE**
>
> If a problem application is owned by Root, you can write down the Process ID (PID) number, log in as SuperUser in a shell, and type **kill <PID>** to end that process.

**FIGURE 22.10**    See what's happening on your system with the System Load monitors in KSysGuard.

To add a new set of monitors to KSysGuard, go to the File, New menu (or press Ctrl+N) and select a set of monitors from the menu on the left.

**FIGURE 22.11** Kill problem applications in the Process Table.

## KDiskFree and KwikDisk

Short on disk space? Need to know when to modify your partitions or logical volumes? KwikDisk can sit in your KDE system tray and tell you what disks are currently mounted and how much space each has remaining. By default, it will also pop up a warning box when a disk is getting full.

To put KwikDisk in your tray, right-click in an empty spot on the tray. Choose Add to Panel, Application, System, Desktop Applet to find KwikDisk.

KwikDisk is the watchdog for a larger program, KDiskFree, which gives you similar information from your /etc/fstab file and lets you mount and unmount drives with a right-click.

## GKrellM

This is an oddly wonderful little program that can be just geek eye candy, but also can be a very powerful and informative tool at your disposal.

GKrellM (see Figure 22.12) is a GTK-based monitor that uses krells to display its information. Krells? Joe Barr at NewsForge.com tracked down this definition: "A krell is a unit of measurement used in the horizontal display of various measurements. If you were monitoring the amplifier in the movie Spinal Tap, for example, while it was running wide open, krells would be seen along the entire length of the meter."

By default, the program will pull information from the /proc directory and tell you several important things about your computer, including

- What sort of use your CPU is getting.

- The number of users (both "live" and system) logged in and the processes running.

- When the hard drive is being accessed, and for how much data at a time.

- Your network connection speed.

- A graph of your Random Access Memory usage, both hardware RAM and your Swap partition.

- The very top of the display gives you your machine name and the date and time. On the bottom is a running total of how long you have been logged in (the uptime total).

**FIGURE 22.12**    GKrellM helps you visualize what is happening on your computer.

Right-click any monitor to configure that monitor. Right-click on an edge to bring up the GKrellM Configuration screens. Insert any monitor you'd like from the lengthy list of choices.

GKrellM has been blessed with devoted users who have written plug-ins for nearly everything you might like to do with the application. And in its eye-candy role, there are themes you can download to change colors and some behaviors. Access all these at the application website, http://www.gkrellm.net.

## References

- http://www.linuxgazette.com/issue70/ghosh.html—This Linux Gazette article, "Bootstrapping Linux," offers much detail on the BIOS and MBR.

- http://www.lostcircuits.com/advice/bios2/1.shtml—The LostCircuits BIOS Guide. The site itself is a bit ad heavy, but there is excellent information on various BIOS settings.

- http://www.rojakpot.com/freebog.aspx—"The Definitive BIOS Optimization Guide," another excellent site with plain-language explanations of many BIOS settings. Useful no matter what OS you use.

- http://www-106.ibm.com/developerworks/linux/library/l-slack.html—Joe Brockmeier explains the Slackware Linux boot process, which is not so different from SUSE Linux.

- http://linux-newbie.sunsite.dk—The Linux Newbie Administrator Guide. Very helpful.

- http://www.troubleshooters.com/linux/grub/grub.htm—"GRUB from the Ground Up," a fine explanation of how to create a GRUB boot floppy and boot it on a disabled machine.

- http://www.gnu.org/software/grub/manual—The GRUB manual in various formats.

- http://tldp.org/HOWTO/LILO.html—The LILO Mini HOWTO.

- http://tldp.org/LDP/lame/LAME/linux-admin-made-easy—Linux Administration Made Easy. See Section 4.8 on booting with LILO.

- http://www.linux.com/article.pl?sid=04/05/17/1832239—A brief review of KSysGuard.

- http://docs.kde.org/en/3.3/kdebase/ksysguard—The KSysGuard Handbook.

- http://www.gkrellm.net—The home of GKrellM.

22

CHAPTER **23**

# Securing Your Machines

It's an old story, but will remain true for the foreseeable future: The only method of keeping a computer 100% secure is to lock it in a room and never turn it on. The one thing computers do best is also the most dangerous thing about them—they collect, store, and display information. Your job as system administrator is to ensure to the best of your ability that particular bits of information are displayed only to people and machines you want those bits displayed to.

With its permission-based file system, Unix and Linux make a good start on protecting your data from the bad guys. But the more connections your computer makes to other computers, first to a local area network, then to a wide area network, and finally to the Internet, the more chances your data have to be compromised.

In today's world of interconnected computers and "always-on" access to the Internet, the importance of maintaining a secure computer has never been greater. There may be some truly dangerous "cyber-terrorists" out there working at bringing down society as we know it, but these are not the people you have to protect your machine from. The ordinary computer user has to put up with the script kiddies (young folks who want to prove their alleged computer prowess by running prewritten programs that break into other people's systems), disgruntled employees, and fast-spreading viruses and worms. Unfortunately, that's more than enough to keep you busy for quite some time.

In earlier chapters, you've learned some basic skills for protecting your computer with permissions (Chapter 19, "Managing Users, Managing Security"), fighting viruses (Chapter 15, "Managing Email Servers"), and transferring files securely (Chapter 17, "Secure File Transfer"). In this chapter, the focus is on other tools to protect yourself and your information. You will also become prepared for the worst, having some idea of what to do when your carefully laid security strategy is somehow penetrated.

# Understanding Computer Attacks

There are many ways to divide up the types of computer attacks, but perhaps the easiest to understand is the internal attack, where someone has access to a computer on the local area network, versus the external attack, which occurs over the Internet. The distinction is important because it clarifies the relative danger your system is in. Chances are excellent that your local network is protected quite well by the system of permissions, along with the trust you place in your users to not damage the system. Unless you are in the habit of hanging around with the bad guys and giving them access to your system, you shouldn't have to spend a great deal of time protecting your system against your users.

It's that outside world that you must worry about most. In a world—and Internet—filled with millions upon millions of people, some percentage (usually small) will be evil. The Internet makes it possible for machines to connect on a vast scale, and any single machine can be attacked by people located anywhere on the planet. Within minutes of making first contact with the Internet, some machines can be attacked, although usually not successfully. Don't let your machines be counted among the victims.

This situation is not a result of malicious users lying in wait for your IP address to do something interesting. Instead, canny virus writers have created worms that exploit a vulnerability, take control of a machine, and then spread it to other machines around them. As a result, more attacks today are the result of these autohacking tools. There are really only a handful of the truly evil out there; however, as with most human endeavors, if you're really the target of someone's attack, you probably cannot prevent it without a massive effort.

Scripts come in another flavor as well: prewritten code that exploits a vulnerability and gives its users special privileges on the compromised machine. These scripts are rarely used by their creators. They get posted online for the aforementioned script kiddies, who use them to invade vulnerable systems and brag about it to their friends.

Your job as a system administrator is to keep your computers and local networks from being compromised by worms, script kiddies, and the more serious attacks conducted by more experienced criminals. Your users (even if it's just you) want to use the computer to accomplish great things and not worry about the firefights outside. Wearing your sysadmin hat, you can accomplish this task.

Regardless of the source of the attack, you can follow a five-step checklist to secure your SUSE Linux box:

1. Assess your vulnerability. Decide what machines can be attacked, what services they are running, and who has access to them.

2. Configure the server for maximum security. Install only what you need, run only what you must, and configure a local firewall.

3. Secure physical access to the server.

4. Create worst-case–scenario policies.

5. Keep up to date with security issues.

You'll learn more about each step in the following sections. You must implement all the steps.

## Assessing Your Vulnerability

It is a common mistake for people to assume that switching on a firewall makes them safe. Although there's no question that switching on a firewall is an important step to take, it is not a solution and never has been. Each system has distinct security needs, and taking the time to customize its security layout will give you maximum protection and best performance.

Following are the most common security mistakes people make:

- Installing every package—SUSE Linux 10 has 3 gigabytes of software included in the distribution. If a machine is not going to be an FTP server, you probably don't need to have the server installed on it. YaST makes it easy to configure your installation so that you can remove unnecessary packages and get the ones you will use.

- Enabling unused services—Do you really require the capability to access your system remotely? Do you want people to upload files to your machine? If not, don't run SSH or FTP. Always think about what you use, whether that service is open to the Internet, and whether you need it.

- Disabling the local firewall on the grounds that your server already has a firewall installed—When it comes to firewalls, more is better. Your computer is your castle. Put up a wide moat with a long drawbridge, followed by a thick wall, followed by another thick wall 10 feet away from the first one. Make it hard to access, and it won't be worth the time it takes for your attacker to continue.

- Letting your machine give out more information than it needs to—Earlier we talked about the unfortunate, if inevitable, demise of `finger` as a useful tool to find out about other users on the network. Now it's just another way to hack into someone's system.

- Keeping the door to the server room unlocked—Less common in IT shops these days, but still a bad idea. Even if your sysadmins live in the server room (and with Linux servers, that really shouldn't be—they work best unattended), the room should be locked whenever no one is inside.

- Being careless with your wireless network—Wireless networking is convenient and helpful, but the standards were not developed with security in mind. Someday, this is likely to improve. We're not there yet.

After you have ruled out these common problems, you're on to the real problem. How can the bad guys attack your machine? What can people access from the outside? This comes down to the question of what applications and services face the Internet, and what ports do they run on?

The best way to find answers to these questions is through the Nmap networking utility. This little tool will scan the ports of any machine on your network, or all of them, and tell you which ones are open at that moment. Any service you have installed that responds to Nmap's query is pointed out, and you may, in turn, choose to lock down ports that should not be open.

SUSE Linux does not install Nmap by default, but you can install the command-line version and a GUI front-end called Nmap-gtk through YaST. Other GUIs are available at the Nmap website, http://www.insecure.org/nmap.

Although you can use the shell version, it is much easier to configure and see the results of Nmap's work in the GUI (Figure 23.1). It is also better to run Nmap as the SuperUser, because you will get more information that way. To launch Nmap-gtk, log in as the SuperUser and type **xnmap &**.

**FIGURE 23.1**    Nmap scans ports to see what is open and vulnerable.

The best way to run Nmap, especially the first time, is to use the SYN Stealth scan (on by default when you launch it as SuperUser) with OS Detection and Version Probe on. By default, Nmap scans the localhost (127.0.0.1), but you can add or change targets by typing the IP address(es) into the Target(s) edit box. The first time you run Nmap, you should click the Scanned Ports box to change the scan range from a few default ports; select All from the drop-down menu. This scan takes a little longer, but gives you a more complete picture of your status. As you adjust your options in the GUI, you'll see the actual shell command being built at the bottom of the window. You could, if so inclined, copy this command to a text file and run it as a shell script later on.

When you have made your selections, click Scan. Nmap tests each port to determine whether it responds. If it does, Nmap asks the application at that port for version information and displays that to the Nmap screen. You then get results like those displayed in Figure 23.1. Ideally, there will be no surprises on the list. If there are surprises, or you decide that there are some unnecessary services on the list, you can take action.

You can log your Nmap scan by going to Save Log in the File menu and choosing a location from the menu. To view the log file later, go to Open Log from the File menu.

If you just have one or a few machines on the network, you probably need to run Nmap only once a year, or if you suspect your system is compromised. Sysadmins of larger networks should run Nmap regularly as part of their general maintenance regimen.

> **CAUTION**
>
> Peer-to-peer file sharing networks such as Gnutella and BitTorrent usually require you to open ports on your firewall to speed up, or even access, the network. Recognize that you may be compromising your security when you participate in these networks. Be wary when downloading files from these sources. although as of this writing, no significant worm has propagated itself through peer-to-peer networks, it could easily happen. Not every file with a certain name contains the content you may be expecting after you get it downloaded.

# Protecting Your Machine

After you have disabled all the unnecessary services on your system, what remains is a core set of connections and programs that you want to keep. Don't think you're done, though. It's time to consider what to do about your wireless network and the physical security of your servers.

## Securing a Wireless Network

Wireless networking under the 802.11 standards is not built with security in mind. The practice of *wardriving*, where folks drive around with wireless-equipped laptops looking for a hotspot, tells you most of what you need to know about the security of the average wireless network. It's one thing to use random wireless hotspots to surf the web on the road, it's quite another to intercept packets of data transferring across someone's wireless network. This is potentially a serious problem that you need to be concerned about. Great progress has been made in the last few years, but this problem has not been solved yet. If an attacker is in your neighborhood and knows the frequency that your network uses, you have a nightmare on your hands. It should also be noted that the encryption standard of most wireless NICs is weaker than you need and should not be considered part of your security plan.

---

**TIP**

Whenever you are running on a wireless LAN, always run Open-SSH tools to protect yourself and your data. SSH passwords are not transmitted as plain text, and your sessions are encrypted.

This is especially true if you are accessing public WiFi access points. Many hosting providers don't (or haven't until recently) provided secure email, and your username/password combination is sent in plain text across the network every time you check your mail.

If you have your own network, it should be secured with the Wired Equivalent Privacy (WEP) algorithm. You not only want to protect your personal workstation/desktop/whatever information, but you also want to protect your credentials on any servers you connect to.

---

Whether or not your network is wired, the better the physical security of your computers, the more secure your network will be. Keep wireless transmitters (routers, switches, and the like) as close to the center of your building as possible. Do your own wardriving around the building to see if anyone just walking around can access your network, and shut things down tighter if you can.

It does not take much to hook up a wireless access point to a legitimate network hub, and then whoever sets up that point can compromise your entire network. Be wary and scan for them regularly.

### Another Word on Passwords and Physical Security

This is one of those messages that it's difficult to emphasize too much: Secure passwords and secure machines are the first line of defense against electronic break-ins. Follow the password rules outlined in Chapter 19, especially if you're the Root user. Having access to the Root account is the holy grail for an attacker. Protect that account and that password with everything you have. Enforce the password standards mercilessly on your users as well.

If you are the sysadmin on a company SUSE Linux server, be aware that changes in people's employment status can create problems for you. Former employees are often the source of attacks on servers. Have a policy in place for what happens to user accounts when someone leaves your company. That policy need not be draconian, but it should be fair to all concerned. Make sure everyone knows what it is, and enforce it consistently.

## Configuring the SUSE Firewall

If you connect to the Internet, even with a modem and dial-up connection, you need a firewall to protect you from attack. Fortunately, SUSE Linux includes an excellent firewall to help you. Go to YaST Security and Users and click the Firewall module to start the process.

The first screen in this wizard (see Figure 23.2) asks for the interfaces you want to protect.

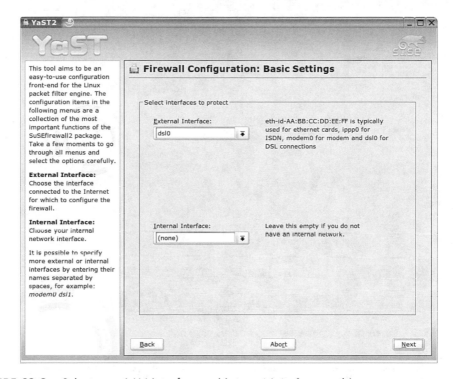

**FIGURE 23.2**    Select your LAN interface and Internet interface on this screen.

The External Interface is your Internet connection. The Internal Interface is your LAN card. Use the drop-down menu to select or change an interface from the default. Click Next to continue.

The second wizard page (see Figure 23.3) is used mainly for systems with active server components that need ports open to communicate with their clients. If you are using a web server (Apache or similar), a mail server, or any other server on the list, check the appropriate box.

> **NOTE**
>
> If you install a server package through YaST Network Services, the install wizard will always ask you to open the firewall so it can function properly.

If an Internet application needs a specific port opened, you can click the Expert button to open that port.

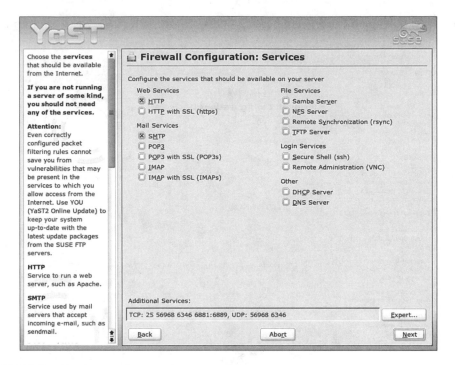

**FIGURE 23.3**    Open ports for any servers on this screen.

---

**CAUTION**

Anytime you open a port in your firewall, remember that every open port is a "hole" you are drilling that an attacker can breach. There are always good reasons for opening a port. Make sure you have a good reason before you drill the hole.

---

Click Next to continue.

The Features page comes up next. Going with the defaults here is usually best. If this machine is only going to be a router, check the Forward Traffic and Do Masquerading box. If you want other computers on your LAN to have only the same access to services on your computer that the rest of the Internet has, check Protect from Internal Network.

The last screen sets up what information the firewall logs contain. Unless you are trying to troubleshoot a specific problem, it's a bad idea to log every packet, or even every dropped packet. Stick to the defaults here. Click Finish to activate the firewall.

The configuration file adds a script to the boot process so the firewall loads each time you boot. To turn off the firewall, reopen the module and select Stop Firewall and Remove from Boot Process.

## Other Security Utilities to Consider

In addition to the tools mentioned thus far, you should also consider adding some basic Linux security tools to your toolbox. These include the following:

- Tripwire—This is one of the best file system monitoring tools around. It records information about important files (such as checksums) in a database. If anything changes in those files, Tripwire will catch the change when it runs (configure it as often as you like with cron) and will alert you. More information on Tripwire can be found at http://www.tripwire.org.

- Snort—This is a sniffer that monitors network packets and can be used to alert you to suspicious activity. Acting as an intrusion detection system, it can offer you the first warning that a possible attack is underway. More information on Snort can be found at http://www.snort.org.

- PortSentry—Like Snort, PortSentry acts as an intrusion-detection system by looking for suspicious activity. It differs from Snort in that it tries to find this activity by focusing on attempts aimed at the local computer and not on the network as a whole. It also offers the capability to block ports, and thus functions as a firewall as well. More information on PortSentry can be found at http://sourceforge.net/projects/sentrytools.

> **NOTE**
>
> Although it has been implied, it is important to note that any network is only as strong as the weakest element on it. To have a secure network, it is important to keep all workstations secure.

## What to Do if You've Been Hacked

Humor books aside, it is never fun trying to come up with worst-case scenarios, and it's even less fun trying to figure out how to survive them. Thinking about the day someone breaks into your carefully protected, what-seemed-secure network and compromises your system is harder still. Yet thinking about it ahead of time can ease the stress of that day and can also put that day further into the future.

You can take courses and even get certified in disaster recovery management, also called business continuity. So the suggestions offered here just scrape the surface, but following are some ideas to help you think out and plan for the day that no one wants to come—and how to survive and recover from it. The job you save may be your own.

- Don't just shut the network down. If the attack has ended, you let the attacker know you're on to him by yanking the cord. Give the security team a chance to catch the perpetrator if he returns.

- Not everyone needs to know you've been attacked. If the attack came from inside, it wouldn't be a good idea to tell all the employees.

- Head over to http://www.rootkit.nl/projects/rootkit_hunter.html and pick up a copy of the Rootkit Hunter. Rootkits are programs attackers leave behind so they can mess you up again. They are designed to hide themselves, but this application can help you find them. The bad news is that if a rootkit is found, you have to wipe the machine and start over.

- After you've thought about it and decided the compromised machine is not really required on the network, take the machine offline. You may decide that the chances of your attacker coming back are slim, and so you don't want to try luring him back.

- Start reviewing your log files, and store them somewhere else. Because log files can be edited—they are just text files, after all—there may still be useful information in them that can help you track down the attacker.

- Check /etc/passwd for unauthorized users. Although you should be using shadow to store your genuine user passwords, invaders often create new users in /etc/passwd in hopes that some applications just check that file to confirm permissions. If you see a user you don't recognize or can't verify, remove it immediately.

- Run lsof to obtain a list of open files. The -p option can be used to specify a process ID number (such as a suspected user's shell) to limit the display to only those open files associated with them.

- Run ps aux to check for unusual programs running on the system, and watch your cron job listing, too.

- Check on /srv/www and make sure all your web pages are present, accounted for, and unchanged.

- Check the contents of .bash_history in each of your user's home directories. Look for attempts to log in as the SuperUser or Root. If you find them, don't put that user under suspicion automatically; that user may have just been the unlucky account the attacker reached.

- If you have a prior relationship with a security company, call them in right away. They can find things in the log files that an untrained observer won't.

- Bring those backup tapes back and start checking them. Just because you noticed this attack doesn't necessarily mean it was the first time.

- If you haven't done so already, develop a more formal disaster recovery plan!

## Keeping Up to Date on Linux Security Issues

It's no surprise that computer security is a hot topic on the Web. You can find a lot about it in the technology news sites and most Linux-oriented news sites as well. Two sites you should be familiar with are

- LinuxSecurity.com—This is primarily a news service that scours the web for security-related information and commissions articles for its site as well. Every Monday morning, you can get the Linux Security Week newsletter in your inbox, with all the security warnings issued in the previous week so you can keep your system safe. The site also hosts Security HOWTOs, a glossary of security terms, and the comments and forums you expect on a PHP-driven website.

- SecurityFocus.com—Possibly the best general site on computer security and the host of the famous BugTraq mailing list. This extremely high-traffic list is often the first place the public learns of newly exposed application vulnerabilities. They also host a Focus on Linux list and offer an RSS feed for its news content and vulnerability announcements.

To keep up with the latest security updates for SUSE Linux, keep your SUSEwatcher application in your desktop taskbar, too. This will help you keep your system as secure as the SUSE/Novell engineers can make it.

## References

- http://www.insecure.org/nmap—The Nmap home page. There is a lot of general information about network security here, as well as official and user-generated documentation.

- http://www.rootkit.nl/projects/rootkit_hunter.html—Analyze whether an attacker left behind tools to wreak more havoc on your system.

- http://www.securityfocus.com—Keep up with security issues on all platforms.

- http://www.linuxsecurity.com—Focus on Linux security problems and solutions.

# Kernel and Module Management

Previously you learned what happens when you start your Linux computer: The BIOS wakes up all the electronics on the motherboard and finds a bootloader. The bootloader checks the hard drive to find a kernel. The kernel does everything else. But what is a kernel?

Stripped to its essentials, the kernel really *is* the operating system. It is the piece of software that allows humans to interact with otherwise inanimate pieces of plastic, silicon, and other precious metals. The Linux kernel is Linux. Distributions such as SUSE Linux, Debian, Fedora Core, and Ubuntu package different sets of applications, update mechanisms, and configurations. The reason they are all Linux is because they distribute the Linux kernel released by Linus Torvalds and developed by an amazing crew of kernel hackers.

In this chapter, you will learn how to get your hands on the kernel source, how to manage kernel modules, how and when to patch the kernel, and how to troubleshoot problems with the kernel.

The vast majority of SUSE Linux users will find that the precompiled kernels the SUSE engineers provide more than satisfies their needs. These kernels are available through YaST (as is the kernel source code). SUSE Linux is designed for the tinkerer, though. If you think you can be a kernel hacker, SUSE Linux can help you find out.

Even if you're a little fearful at the idea of messing with the kernel, you should read the first two sections of the chapter to know a little bit about the history of the kernel and how it works. Someday you just might pick up a brand-new piece of hardware for which a Linux driver was added to the kernel snapshot last week. Go all the way through this chapter, and you'll know exactly what to do to get it working.

# Linus's Baby: The Linux Kernel

At the bottom of most Linux-related web pages and at the front of this (and just about every other) Linux book, there is a notice: Linux is a registered trademark by Linus Torvalds. In most cases in the larger world, posting such a notice is just another silly requirement imposed by lawyers on publishers and web designers. For this book, at least, it is but one way to acknowledge the debt we all owe to the Finnish programmer who started it all.

While the GNU Project to develop a free Unix-based operating system had been working on a functioning kernel for years, Torvalds wanted to do his computer science homework at home. So in August 1991, he ported the teaching operating system called Minix to the Intel 80386 platform and offered the code to readers of the Usenet newsgroup, comp.os.minix.

## The Linux Source Tree

The kernel source code lives in a group of directories called the kernel source tree. This tree's structure is important because the process of compiling the kernel is automated.

When you compile a kernel, `make` is actually running a series of scripts. The scripts, *makefiles*, expect to find pieces of the kernel code in specific places. If they are not there, the makefile breaks, and the kernel is incomplete. You will learn how to compile a kernel with `make` later in the chapter.

You don't need the kernel source code on your system for Linux to run—you just need the compiled kernel binaries for that. If you ever want to compile a kernel, you need to install the `kernel-sources` package from YaST.

The sources are stored in `/usr/src/linux`, which contains several directories; the most important for you is the Documentation directory. In these files, you should find just about everything you need to know about the kernel and its various modules. In the subdirectories, you'll find text files with detailed information about all the various drivers for peripherals, file systems, and networking tasks patched into the kernel. These documents are written for programmers, but the advanced user can often glean much useful information as well.

## Types of Kernels

There was a time when Linux kernels were monolithic—a single block of code with all the instructions for the processor, motherboard, and other hardware specified within.

When changing hardware, you had to recompile the kernel to include the drivers for the new piece and remove the old drivers. This was important because unnecessary kernel modules took up memory, which was at a premium.

As the kernel code grew larger and the number of devices that you could add to a computer increased, recompiling became a nearly unbearable chore. So kernel hackers developed a new building method to solve the problem. Device drivers became modules that could be loaded and unloaded into the kernel when you needed them. With this modular approach, all the kernel code could be compiled at once, with most of the code compiled into modules. Adding new hardware involved loading a module in place of rebuilding the whole kernel.

The standard SUSE Linux kernel has some drivers compiled inline, as part of the kernel itself. These are the drivers required during the boot process. Kernel modules are loaded after login.

> **NOTE**
>
> Commonly, drivers for SCSI disk drives that you intend to boot are inline. If they aren't, you couldn't access the drive.
>
> Ingenuity has gotten around this problem of needing inline drivers, however. You can use `initrd` to start a RAM disk. This creates a small kernel and the appropriate device driver, which accesses the device and loads the actual kernel. More about this later in the chapter.

Some code can be only inline or in a module (for technical reasons), but most code can be compiled either way. With fast modern processors and cheap memory, the performance differences are negligible, but they are of concern when installing Linux on an older, slower machine.

When compiling a kernel, you select inline or modular loading during the `make config` step that you'll learn more about later. Unless you have a specific reason to do otherwise, you should always choose modular loading when asked.

## Managing Modules

When you are using a modular kernel, you need to load and unload the modules, automatically whenever possible. You may need to pass parameters on to modules when you load them, such as memory addresses or interrupt codes. In this section, you'll learn about the tools Linux offers to manage your kernel modules.

Use any of these module management tools to get your kernel to bend to your will. All of them have man pages to help out, if necessary.

- `lsmod`—As `ls` provides a list of files and directories, so `lsmod` gives you a list of loaded kernel modules. This is usually a long list, so you should develop the habit of piping the command through `less`, the GNU pager.

- `insmod`—Load (insert) a specified module into the kernel. If the module you want to load is installed in a directory other than under `/lib/modules`, be sure to specify the full path when running this command. Several options are offered for this command; the most useful is `-f`, which forces the module to be loaded.

- `rmmod`—Unload (remove) a specified module (or more than one) from the running kernel.

- depmod—Creates a dependency file (`/lib/modules/<kernelversion>/modules.dep`) for individual modules. Many kernel modules need other modules to load first; that is, they are dependent on another module to work. During the system boot, `depmod` `-A` is run very soon after the kernel starts up to sort out the order in which modules load. The `-A` switch is there so a new dependency file is created only when there is a change in modules.

- modprobe—Perhaps the most used module tool, `modprobe` combines `insmod` and `rmmod`. `modprobe` uses the dependency file created by another tool, `depmod`, to automatically load or unload (with the `-f` switch) a module.

- modinfo—Get a module's name, author, license type, and perhaps other information from a module's object file—that is, if the author included any information in the object file. Modules contributed by SUSE engineers include information on whether the module is officially supported.

- /etc/modprobe.conf—Not a command, but a file that contains module variables. These variables control how `modprobe` and `depmod` behave.

## When to Recompile

There was a time when all SUSE Linux users were warned to take a blood oath never to recompile a SUSE kernel. The SUSE engineers had worked endlessly to make sure everything worked just so and had the best device drivers you could get. Compiling new modules into this carefully balanced and functional kernel could lead to disaster.

Today, SUSE Linux is designed to be an "enthusiast's" (read "tinkerer's") version of the operating system. So as a user, you are almost expected to want to tweak every setting to squeeze the most amount of performance and individuality you can get out of your computer. There's even a kernel-of-the-day directory on the SUSE server that is accessible for any user via YOU and APT. Don't ever use this on a production system, but if you *really* like the bleeding edge of development, you can be there every day.

Nonetheless, the vast majority of SUSE Linux users can (and should) rely on the kernel shipped (and occasionally updated) by SUSE. Those engineers have not been slacking on the job; they still work endlessly to make sure your system is as stable and as high performing as it could possibly be. When security holes are discovered in the kernel, a patched kernel will be in the YOU servers almost instantly.

> **TIP**
>
> To learn more about SUSE's process in building kernels, check out `/usr/src/linux/`
> `README.SUSE`. This file is included in the `kernelsources` package.

When should you violate the Don't Recompile a SUSE Kernel rule? You are permitted to come up with your own exceptions, but these three are probably the best reasons:

- To accommodate a really new, or obscure, piece of hardware.

- To update your entire system before a precompiled kernel is available. That is, you need a newly released kernel with a device driver that will finally solve a longstanding printer problem.

- If you are running SUSE on an older computer and you need to optimize the kernel to run on the older hardware.

As noted earlier, you can pick up RPM packages for new kernels by way of the SUSE kernel-of-the-day repositories. Include this repository in your apt sources.list file or use YaST to get it. This will simplify the installation process.

> **CAUTION**
>
> Always back up data before manually compiling a new kernel. You never know what can happen when you are essentially upgrading your OS.

After your new kernel is installed, reboot your system to load the new kernel.

> **NOTE**
>
> When you use YaST to install a new kernel (whether you're doing it yourself or YOU is getting a security patch), YaST will warn you about running the lilo bootloader before rebooting. It is safe to ignore this warning. Remember the default SUSE Linux bootloader is grub.

# Kernel Versions

In the preceding section, I mentioned the kernel-of-the-day repository. The very existence of this place gives you a sense of the pace of development of the kernel. As new features are added, bugs are fixed, and new technology is incorporated into the code base; new iterations of the kernel are coming out all the time.

This is the reason why kernel version numbers are so complicated. With most applications, versioning is a relatively simple operation, with a major version number indicating lots of new features (or, in the case of commercial applications, at least enough to justify paying for an upgrade), and one or two digits after the dot indicating bug fix updates.

For example, SUSE Linux Professional 9.2 shipped with kernel version 2.6.8-24.10. You can break this down into these sections:

- Major version—Currently at 2.

- Minor version—Currently at 6. Even-numbered minor versions are stable kernels; development releases are odd numbered.

- Sublevel number—This is the current iteration of the kernel. If you visit www.kernel.org, you'll see it listed as the stable version. This number changes much more often than the first two. In this case, it's 8.

- Patch level—When there is a dash after the sublevel, the next number represents the number of times small patches have been added by members of the kernel team. Here, it's 24.

- Extraversion level—This number represents the work the SUSE engineers have done with the latest patch. Here, it's 10. Generally, this work addresses code issues in the "stock" kernel and additional hardware support.

To see what kernel version you're running, type **uname  -r** at the shell prompt.

> **NOTE**
>
> Alan Cox has taken on many responsibilities within the kernel hacking team. One of those tasks (though considerably less official) is releasing periodic "ac" patches distinguished by the -ac marker at the end of the kernel version. Stored and downloadable at http://www.kernel.org/ pub/linux/kernel/people/alan/, these patches include hints at what's being cooked up by the team working on the test kernel. Experimenters can join in the testing.

## Getting New Kernel Sources

The Linux kernel has always been available free for the download. You can obtain kernel tarballs with your favorite FTP client or web browser from ftp.kernel.org or (preferably) one of the 116 (and counting) mirrors listed at http://www.kernel.org/mirrors. A kernel compressed by `bzip2` is around 35MB, while the same tarball compressed with `gzip` is around 42MB.

In the v2.6 download directory, you will find a plethora of download choices (see Figure 24.1 for a browser-eye view).

These include all the sublevel versions of the 2.6 kernel, compressed with different tools, along with digital signature files (with the `.sign` extension) to validate the kernel as official. "Patch" versions, with just the patches from that iteration, are also stored here (you'll learn about these in the next section). The directory also has changelog files for each iteration, indicating the changes from the previous release.

To download a full kernel, select the version you want, with the compression format you're most comfortable with. The SUSE Linux GUI archive programs can handle both `gzip` and `bzip2` formats, so you can get the smaller `bzip2` file.

After it is downloaded, move the package to a directory other than `/usr/src` (keeping it in your download directory is perfectly fine) and extract it to your home directory. From the shell, the command for a `bzip2` file is **tar -xjvf    linux-2.6.10.tar.bz2,** and for a gzip archive, type **tar -xzvf Linux-2.6.10.tar.gz**.

> **TIP**
>
> Use your Tab key to take advantage of your shell's file-completion feature when extracting a downloaded kernel. In the preceding example, type **tar -xjvf linux** and then press Tab to complete the filename.

```
linux-2.6.8.1.tar.sign      14-Aug-2004 06:13  248   tar archive
linux-2.6.8.tar.bz2         14-Aug-2004 01:09  34M   tar archive
linux-2.6.8.tar.bz2.sign    14-Aug-2004 01:09  248   tar archive
linux-2.6.8.tar.gz          14-Aug-2004 01:09  43M   GZIP compressed docume>
linux-2.6.8.tar.gz.sign     14-Aug-2004 01:09  248   GZIP compressed docume>
linux-2.6.8.tar.sign        14-Aug-2004 01:09  248   tar archive
linux-2.6.9.tar.bz2         18-Oct-2004 17:09  35M   tar archive
linux-2.6.9.tar.bz2.sign    18-Oct-2004 17:09  248   tar archive
linux-2.6.9.tar.gz          18-Oct-2004 17:09  43M   GZIP compressed docume>
linux-2.6.9.tar.gz.sign     18-Oct-2004 17:09  248   GZIP compressed docume>
linux-2.6.9.tar.sign        18-Oct-2004 17:09  248   tar archive
linux-2.6.10.tar.bz2        24-Dec-2004 16:38  35M   tar archive
linux-2.6.10.tar.bz2.sign   24-Dec-2004 16:38  248   tar archive
linux-2.6.10.tar.gz         24-Dec-2004 16:38  44M   GZIP compressed docume>
linux-2.6.10.tar.gz.sign    24-Dec-2004 16:38  248   GZIP compressed docume>
linux-2.6.10.tar.sign       24-Dec-2004 16:38  248   tar archive
linux-2.6.11.1.tar.bz2      08-Mar-2005 18:59  35M   tar archive
linux-2.6.11.1.tar.bz2.sign 08-Mar-2005 18:59  248   tar archive
linux-2.6.11.1.tar.gz       08-Mar-2005 18:59  44M   GZIP compressed docume>
linux-2.6.11.1.tar.gz.sign  08-Mar-2005 18:59  248   GZIP compressed docume>
```

**FIGURE 24.1**    This selection of a kernel mirror FTP directory shows the variety of download options.

Once the source tarball is unpacked, you will see a new directory with the correct kernel version number. Copy or move this directory (as the SuperUser) to /usr/src. Create a symbolic link (also known as a *symlink*) of linux-2.6 to the new kernel. From the shell, type the following:

```
rm /usr/src/linux-2.6
ln -s /usr/src/linux-2.6.10 /usr/src/linux-2.6
```

When you create this symlink, you can get creative, allowing multiple kernel versions to be compiled and tailored for different functions. Change the symlink to the kernel directory you want to work on.

> **CAUTION**
>
> The correct symlink is critical to have make work properly. Always have the symlink point to the version of the kernel sources you're working with.

## Patching the Kernel

If you have a slow modem connection to the Internet, downloading a whole 35MB kernel may be quite a chore. As previously mentioned, the kernel mirror download directory will also have smaller patch files with only the changes since the last iteration.

> **NOTE**
>
> You need to have an installed kernel-sources package from the SUSE Linux disk (or another full version of the kernel source in /usr/src/linux) to use patch files.

In doing this, you may be trading one chore for another, however. If you are using version 2.6.1, for example, and the patch containing the module you need is version 2.6.11, you can't just apply the 2.6.11 patch file and go on your merry way. You must apply all the intermediate patch files, in the order they were released (first 2.6.2, then 2.6.3, on up to 2.6.11).

For simplicity's sake, download your patches to a /patch directory in the source tree. You will need Write privileges on the directory to do this.

If you need to patch several versions at once, as in the previous example, there is help. The patch-kernel script is located in the /usr/src/linux/scripts folder. This script applies all the necessary patches to bring your kernel up to the latest version.

> **TIP**
>
> Before running the patch-kernel script, back up your existing kernel source files, just in case something goes wrong.

The syntax for the patch-kernel script is

```
patch-kernel <source-dir> <patch-dir> stopversion
```

The source directory defaults to /usr/source/linux if you don't specify it here, and the patch directory defaults to the current working directory. So if you are patching version 2.6.1 to version 2.6.10, and the patches are all in /usr/src/linux-2.6.1/patch, type this:

```
scripts/patch-kernel /usr/src/linux-2.6.1 /usr/src/linux-2.6.1/patch
```

The script applies all the patches in the /patch directory and then creates a 2.6.10 code tree. If you're working from a clean stock kernel, you should have an error-free process. If something goes wrong, the script will create files with the patch number with a .rej extension (or just a # sign), indicating which patch failed. If this happens, you need to troubleshoot it yourself, a task for the experienced C programmer familiar with the kernel source.

Whether you have assembled the kernel from the SUSE Linux disk by downloading a full version or a patch, you are now ready to compile this new code tree.

# Compiling the Kernel

When you've downloaded a fresh kernel, or patched your existing sources, you need to compile the new kernel to use the new functionality. *Compiling* from source means transforming human-readable text/code into binary, machine-readable form. Compiling a kernel also means taking those binary files and putting them where they belong in /boot and /lib and then notifying GRUB (or LILO) of the changes.

The good news is that you have your old buddy make to automate nearly the whole compile process for you. By following these steps, you can compile and install a custom kernel just for you.

1. Back up your data, just in case.

2. Make sure you have a working boot disk with the old kernel on it, just in case something goes wrong. See the following note to learn how to create one.

> **NOTE**
>
> Before making any changes to your current, running kernel, make sure you have a backup copy. SUSE recommends using the installation CD to boot in an emergency, but what if the CD drive is inaccessible? It's good to have a floppy backup as well.
>
> YaST once allowed you to make a boot disk directly, but the kernel has grown too large to fit on a single floppy, complicating the task. It is still possible to create a bootable kernel with five floppies, using this process:
>
> If you need to format the disks first, use
>
> ```
> fdformat /dev/fd0u1440
> ```
>
> Mount the SUSE Linux CD1 (for example, to /media/cdrom):
>
> ```
> mount -tiso9660 /dev/cdrom /media/cdrom
> ```
>
> Change to the boot directory on the CD:
>
> ```
> cd /media/cdrom/boot
> ```
>
> Create the boot disk with the following command:
>
> ```
> dd if=/media/cdrom/boot/bootdisk of=/dev/fd0 bs=8k
> ```
>
> The README file in the CD's /boot directory will give you more information on including kernel modules on additional floppies.

3. Backup the .config file, if it exists, just in case. Type (as SuperUser) `cp .config .config.bak`.

4. Run `make mrproper` to prepare the kernel source tree, cleaning out any old files or binaries. `make mrproper` will delete the .config file. Restore it.

5. Edit the makefile to change the EXTRAVERSION number.

6. Modify the kernel configuration file with `make xconfig` (or the interface of your choice).

7. Run `make dep` to create code dependencies used later in the process.

8. Run `make clean` to prepare the sources for actual compilation.

9. Run `make bzImage` to create a binary image of the kernel.

**24**

> **NOTE**
>
> Several make directive choices exist to create this image, but the most common are the following:
>
> - zImage makes an uncompressed kernel image.
> - bzImage creates a compressed image. Some BIOS's cannot parse large images, and this image accommodates that requirement.
> - bzDisk creates a compressed image and places it on a floppy disk for testing purposes. Make sure you have a floppy in your drive before running this directive. You won't be prompted.

10. Run make modules to compile any modules your new kernel needs.

11. Run make modules_install to install the modules in /lib/modules and create dependency files.

12. Run make install to automatically copy the kernel to /boot, create any other files it needs, and modify the bootloader to boot the new kernel by default.

13. Open a text editor and verify the changes made to /boot/grub/grub.conf; fix if necessary. If you happen to be running LILO as your bootloader, check /etc/lilo.conf and rerun /sbin/lilo if you make any changes.

14. Reboot and test the new kernel.

# Troubleshooting Problems

Compiling a kernel is a complex operation, and things can go wrong. Chances are, you will see error messages printed on the screen when something does go wrong. Some of these messages will show up in the /var/log/messages file, which you can look at in any text editor. Other messages may appear in other error logs as well. First thing: Don't panic! Many (if not quite all) problems can be solved with proper research.

## Errors During Compile

It's rare that a kernel doesn't compile, but there's always a chance that something slips through the testing process.

A more likely scenario is that the compile crashes before completion when you attempt to experiment with new and untested code. Trying to add support for a newer device to an older kernel can also sometimes result in a compile crash.

It's also possible for you to end up with a *tainted kernel*. A tainted kernel is one where you have introduced a module that isn't covered by the GPL or similar license. This can happen when you're using hardware that requires a proprietary module (such as Nvidia display adapters). If you compile the kernel with one of these proprietary modules, you will see taint warnings.

Should you run into this situation, you're down to two options: Remove the offending module and wait for a solution from the kernel hackers, or try fixing the error yourself.

Most folks might want to take the safer course and wait for a fix, but if you think you might like to help hack the kernel, this is your opportunity. Finding a solution not only solves your problem, it might help millions of users down the road.

If you run into this problem and want to explore it, your first step is to contact the maintainer of the kernel section that did not compile. Go to `/usr/src/linux/MAINTAINERS` to find the person in charge. Ask if the team is aware of your problem. If necessary, you could post a problem to the appropriate mailing list, but before doing this, look at the If Something Goes Wrong section of the `/usr/src/linux/README` file.

### Runtime Errors, Bootloader Problems, and Kernel Oops

If the kernel compiles, but crashes after you restart your computer, you have runtime errors. Error messages will appear on the screen (you can see them after you've turned off the SUSE boot screen by pressing Esc) or in the `/var/log/messages` file. Bootloader problems will be displayed on the screen, without a log file. *Kernel oops* are errors in a running kernel, with the errors written to `/var/log/messages`.

In these situations, Google is your friend. Chances are quite good that someone else has seen the error message(s) you have, and there are likely documented solutions out there. Head to your favorite search engine and type in the error message with quotes around it. Be aware that Google has a 10-word limit on search terms, so you may need to focus on the keywords in the error message.

Most problems that surface after compiling a new kernel are bootloader-related. If you are running the LILO bootloader and forget to run `/sbin/lilo` after configuring the new kernel, it will have problems. See the LILO mini-HOWTO at the Linux Documentation Project (http://www.tldp.org/HOWTO/LILO.html) for diagnostic aids and solutions to most LILO problems. The GRUB manual is also online, at http://www.gnu.org/software/grub/manual.

## Kernel Tuning with `sysctl`

As the kernel developed over time, developers sought a way to fine-tune some of the kernel parameters. Before `sysctl`, those parameters had to be changed in the kernel configuration and then you had to recompile the kernel.

The `sysctl` utility can change some parameters of a running kernel. It does this through the `/proc` file system, a "virtual window" into the running kernel. Although it might appear that a group of directories and files exist under `/proc`, that's only a representation of parts of the kernel, referred to as variables. We can display a list of the variables as shown in the following:

```
 sysctl -A
```

```
kernel.HZ = 1000
kernel.min-timeslice = 1000
kernel.def-timeslice = 21000
kernel.ngroups_max = 65536
kernel.printk_ratelimit_burst = 10
```

```
kernel.printk_ratelimit = 5
kernel.panic_on_oops = 0
kernel.pid_max = 32768
kernel.overflowgid = 65534
kernel.overflowuid = 65534
kernel.pty.nr = 5
kernel.pty.max = 4096
kernel.random.uuid = 7e576126-6356-4159-afd3-4de6a0227736
kernel.random.boot_id = 152ee742-ef9d-49c5-a271-cb98662ddc7e
kernel.random.write_wakeup_threshold = 128
kernel.random.read_wakeup_threshold = 64
```

This is just a partial listing of some kernel settings—the whole list runs about 20 pages.

> **NOTE**
>
> To see the full list of variables, enter **sysctl -A** at the shell prompt. You can learn more about working with the kernel by reviewing the kernel API documentation at http://kernelnewbies.org/documents/kdoc/kernel-api/linuxkernelapi.html.

If you want to change a value, use the -w (write) switch:

```
sysctl -w kernel.pid_max=35000
```

We've increased the maximum PID (process ID) number with this command.

This change is good only for the current session. If you find a setting is useful, save it to the /etc/sysctl.conf file. The syntax is identical to the shell command:

```
kernel.pid_max=35000
```

This tool is more interesting to kernel hackers than to most users, but it is a potentially powerful tool.

# References

- http://www.kernel.org—The Linux Kernel Archives. Where to find the latest kernel and more information.

- http://www.kernel.org/mirrors—Download the kernel from a server near you.

- http://www.kernel-traffic.org—The Kernel Traffic newsletter, a weekly summary of what's happening on the Kernel mailing list.

- http://www.gnu.org—GNU's not Unix. The home of many kernel-related projects. Get software and documentation here, and a healthy dose of free-software philosophy.

- http://www.gnu.org/software/make/manual/make.html—The make manual. This utility is much more than a source-code build environment.

- http://kniggit.net/wwol26.html—The Wonderful World of Linux 2.6, a guide to the latest version of the kernel by Joseph Pranevich.

- http://www.kernelnewbies.org—For people who want to try their hand at kernel hacking. The Kernel Newbies host an IRC chat channel, #kernelnewbies, and a wiki from this site.

- http://tldp.org/LDP/lki—Linux Kernel 2.4 Internals Guide. Get into more depth about how the kernel works.

- http://tldp.org/HOWTO/HOWTO-INDEX/os.html#OSKERNEL—These HOWTOs explore the kernel in several ways.

- http://minix1.hampshire.edu—Al Woodhull's Minix site. Learn more about Linux's "parent" OS.

- http://www.cs.vu.nl/~ast/minix.html—The official Minix site.

- http://jungla.dit.upm.es/~jmseyas/linux/kernel/hackers-docs.html—Its origins are similar to those of a FAQ document, but this annotated "Index of Documentation for People Interested in Writing and/or Understanding the Linux Kernel" is more of a reference guide, with pointers to an abundance of useful kernel information.

- http://kerneltrap.org—"Your Ultimate Source for Kernel News."

- http://www.gnu.org/software/grub/manual—The GRUB manual.

- http://www.tldp.org/HOWTO/LILO.html—The LILO mini-HOWTO.

24

# Setting Up Networks and Samba

Before it was known for almost anything else, Linux made its name in networking. Your Linux computer can connect with almost any operating system under the sun—MacOS (both flavors), all Unix flavors, and even Windows (with Samba's help). Linux servers can be easily and quickly deployed in heterogeneous networks and will run pretty much forever without a crash or reboot.

SUSE Linux differs from SUSE Linux Enterprise Server (SLES) mostly in that SLES tends to offer a more server-friendly implementation—often with older but more stable packages. SUSE Linux has more than enough power and flexibility to manage your home or small-to-medium business servers. This chapter will help you get going.

You will learn some basic Linux networking concepts and how to configure your network interface cards (NICs) and other network devices with YaST.

## Networking with TCP/IP

Unix networking is based on the same stack of protocols that powers the Internet (well, perhaps it's the other way around): the Transmission Control Protocol/Internet Protocol (TCP/IP) suite. In addition to the two namesake protocols, the TCP/IP suite includes the User Datagram Protocol (UDP).

The purpose of these protocols is to move data around in *packets*. These are tiny little chunks of data created at the transmitting end and moving at the speed of light toward the receiving machine. Packets move faster and more accurately to their destination than one hunk of data would. Under TCP/IP, all data travels via IP packets from one IP address to another IP address.

IP packets wouldn't be able to travel very far if there was no way for two machines to connect with each other. TCP provides that connection-based protocol. When a TCP connection is made, the data stream is broken up by IP into packets, and it travels to the second machine. TCP then reassembles the packets back into a whole stream, figures out what type of data it is, and approaches the appropriate port for that data type (port 110 for POP email servers, as an example).

Where does UDP fit in the scheme of things here? It is a connectionless protocol. Applications that use UDP just choose a destination and start sending. UDP is usually used for small amounts of data or on fast and reliable networks. Some peer-to-peer networks also use UDP.

## TCP/IP Addressing

One thing to get straight at the beginning: local area network (LAN) addressing is distinct from Internet addressing, even if they are based on the same protocol stack. This can lead to some level of confusion, in part because in Unix, even a standalone computer that never interacts with another machine still has a loopback IP address.

Internet IP addresses (also known as "public" IP addresses) are assigned by an addressing body like the American Registry for Internet Numbers (ARIN), which is the body for the United States. Internet Service Providers (ISPs) and other entities requiring blocks of IP addresses apply to ARIN and similar institutions. The addressing body then assigns the requested blocks, which are, in turn, assigned to the ISP's subscribers. These addressing bodies are needed because every machine on the Internet at a given moment requires a distinct IP address. You'll see later, when you learn about DHCP, that one IP address can be any number of physical machines.

LAN IP addresses are assigned by the system administrator so that each physical machine attached to the network has a distinct address. As a result, your computer can have three identities or addresses at once: its loopback address (the one-computer network), its LAN address (and if a computer can connect to several networks, it can have several LAN addresses), and its public Internet address.

▶ Learn more about setting up loopback connections in Chapter 12, "Connecting to the Internet."

Standard TCP/IP addressing under version 4 of the protocol is expressed as a series of 4 decimal numbers separated by dots, as in 187.0.15.255. These represent a 32-bit binary value, and each of the four sets of numbers are called an *octet*. Each octet includes a number range from 0 to 255. The first octet usually signifies what *class* the network belongs to. There are three classes of networks:

- Class A networks have a first octet in the range of 1–126, and the last three octets define the host. Each Class A network has up to 16,777,214 hosts. Of these, the 10 octet is reserved for local networks (127.0.0.0 is reserved for the loopback range).

- Class B networks have a first octet in the range of 128–191. In this range, the 128 octet is also reserved for local networks. The first two octets belong to the network, the last two to the host. There are 16,382 Class B networks, with 65,534 possible hosts.

- Class C networks have a first octet in the range of 192–223. In this range, the 192 octet is also reserved for local networks. The first three octets belong to the network, with only the last octet belonging to the host. Thus, there are 2,097,150 possible Class C networks, but each network can have only 254 hosts.

Two other network classes are irrelevant to this discussion. Class D network addresses are reserved for multicast addresses, and Class E addresses are experimental.

These classes are standard, but a *netmask* also defines your network class. The netmask shows what part of an IP address represents the network and which represents the host. Common netmasks for the different classes are the following:

- Class A      255.0.0.0

- Class B      255.255.0.0

- Class C      255.255.255.0

There's more information on netmasks in the "Network Organization" section later in the chapter.

The allocation of IPv4 addresses is reaching the breaking point. Class A networks are full. Class B is nearly there, and you can guess where Class C is, too. Something needed to be done, and it was. Welcome Internet Protocol, version 6.

> **NOTE**
>
> Many years ago, it was thought that we would run out of IP addresses in a very short time. This led to the need and demand for IPv6. What was not anticipated or foreseen, though, was the creation and widespread adoption of technologies such as Network Address Translation, which enable multiple clients to share the same IP address. Because of their extensive use, the transition to IPv6 has moved much slower than it otherwise would have.

## The Next Step: Internet Protocol, Version 6 (IPv6) Addressing

It's easy to see the need for IPv6. Just think of how many different machines you use to access the Internet today: desktop PC, laptop, personal digital assistant, or cell phone with email and Web access. Thinking about getting a Voice over IP (VoIP) phone? Now consider the prospect of widespread Internet use in the global South: Brazil, China, India, South Africa. All these devices need addresses, not to mention the "smart houses" and web-enabled refrigerators the dreamers have speculated about.

IPv6 fixes this problem by using 128-bit addresses using hexadecimal numbers, producing a truly mammoth number, equaling $3.4 \times 10^{38}$ potential addresses. Instead of four octets, IPv6 addresses has eight hexadecimal groups. Four groups belong to the network and four groups to the host.

Like the global transition to the metric system, moving to IPv6 has been a long process. The initial standard was adopted in 1994, but the vast majority of Internet connections still use the old standard. Many networking utilities, firmware, and parts of some (non-Linux) operating systems will need rewriting to fully support IPv6.

You can use IPv6 to set up your internal network. SUSE Linux supports IPv6 and includes many utilities to use the new network. Consult the Linux+IPv6 HOWTO at http://www.tldp.org/HOWTO/Linux+IPv6-HOWTO for more information.

## Ports

Network servers rarely have just one dedicated task. For example, web servers handle standard pages and secure pages, and perhaps an FTP volume as well. For this reason, applications are assigned *ports* by the Internet Assigned Numbers Authority (IANA) to make "direct" connections for specific services. These ports help TCP/IP distinguish services so data gets to the right application. You've seen references to these ports elsewhere in this book: Web browsers access port 80, POP email clients look for port 110 to get mail, FTP servers use port 21, and BitTorrent uses port 6881. You can see these common ports in the /etc/services file and online at http://www.iana.org/assignments/port-numbers.

As a system administrator, you can assign ports on your server to different applications by editing its configuration file. This can occasionally thwart remote attacks on a common port, but it requires you to notify your legitimate remote users to connect to the new port instead of the common port.

# Network Organization

Organizing your addressing becomes more problematic the bigger your network gets. If you have fewer than 254 devices needing an IP address, you're pretty much home free with a Class C network. But after that it can get interesting. There are some workarounds, though, which is what this section is about.

## Subnetting

Class A and B networks can include separate networks called *subnets*. These subnets are specified in the second (in Class A networks) or third (Class B) octets. One computer with an address of 172.19.25.0 and another of 172.19.120.5 would be on the same Class B network (172.19), but on different subnets. These two computers would need a router or switch to communicate. Subnets can be useful to separate workgroups.

## Netmasks

Subnet masks, or just plain netmasks, are used by TCP/IP to show which octets are owned by the network and which are owned by the host. You saw the standard netmasks earlier in the chapter. You can use customized netmasks to organize subnets to fit your needs. Even if you have a single Class C address, you can use netmasks to create subnets: Make that last octet a number greater than zero.

## Network Address Translation (NAT)

NAT is a service that makes it possible for a server to translate between hosts on a network using private addresses and one or more public addresses. Usually, the router running NAT services all the clients on a network segment and shares a single registered IP address among all of them. This allows the hosts to essentially hide behind the router and a firewall is created at the network layer.

# Hardware Devices in Networking

Standalone PCs require several hardware devices to network with other PCs, servers, peripherals, and the outside world. This section reviews the most essential and explains how to get it going on your system.

## Network Interface Cards (NICs)

Unless a computer can interface with a network, there is no network. That's what NICs are for. Each NIC has a unique address known as the Media Access Control (MAC) address that identifies the NIC. This hardware address is used by DHCP and several other protocols to identify a machine. NICs come in several flavors, depending on the method (or *topology*) they use to connect with other NICs. With the exception of some wireless NICs, SUSE Linux supports nearly every card on the market, regardless of topology. These topologies are discussed in the sections that follow.

### Token Ring

One of the older networking technologies, developed by IBM. As you would think, the network is set up in a ring, with each host passing around a single token. When a host receives the token, it can transmit data. The maximum transfer speed of a token ring NIC is 16Mbps (16 million bits per second). It uses an *unshielded twisted pair* (UTP) cable.

### 10BaseT Ethernet

There are other forms of Ethernet NICs, but this was the standard for a long time. Ethernet hosts link in a star pattern to a hub at the center. The hub must be within 100 meters of any host. Data goes through the hub to all the hosts, but packets are processed only by the appropriate host. Transfer speed is 10Mbps. 10BaseT also uses UTP cable.

### 100BaseT Ethernet

This simple upgrade to the 10BaseT standard is easy for administrators to handle, offering much faster transfer rates than 10BaseT with little more exertion than replacing NICs and hubs. As you might guess, 100BaseT NICs have a transfer speed of 100Mbps. It requires Category 5 UTP cable.

### Fiber Optic and Gigabit Ethernet

If you are building a network for the first time or have a big budget, you should consider these cards. Fiber optic cable is relatively expensive, but it delivers data much faster. This is due, in part, to fiber's capability to transmit digital data directly, without needing to convert to analog for transmission across metal wires. Gigabit Ethernet delivered over fiber optic cable transfers data at 1000Mbps.

### Wireless NICs

With all the hype and discussion of wireless networking, it's easy to forget that wired networks are still faster. Nonetheless, the convenience and cost can make wireless very attractive even for networking desktop PCs. This is especially true for new networks where the wiring is not already in place.

As with any new technology, Linux support is not 100% there yet, but it is catching up quite nicely. There's more on wireless networking later in this chapter.

## Network Cable

In practical terms, there are two general types of network cables in use today: UTP and fiber optic. Six categories of UTP cable are available, and each has a different purpose:

- Category 1—Your telephone wire, used for voice transmission.

- Category 2—A token ring cable, with transfer speed of 4Mbps.

- Category 3—A 10BaseT cable, with transfer speed of 10Mbps.

- Category 4—For modern token ring networks, transfer speed is 16Mbps.

- Category 5—The most widely used UTP cable today. Transfer speed is up to 100Mbps.

- Category 6—This cable also has a transfer speed of 100Mbps and comes in two forms: stranded, for runs up to 25 meters, and solid, for up to 100 meters.

Fiber optic cable is used frequently in wide area networks (WANs) because it will transmit data up to 62 miles at 100Mbps. It is free of electromagnetic interference, and it is more secure.

## Hubs

Hubs connect several hosts in a star network topology. They can have any number of connection ports, but typically they come in 4-, 8-, 16-, 24- and 48-port configurations. Hubs allow you to easily expand a network. Need more connections? Just buy another hub. Hubs can even connect with other hubs through an *uplink* port; the connected hubs then act as a single hub. Troubleshooting problems is also a little easier because if one host goes down, it doesn't take the whole network with it.

## Routers and Bridges

Routers and bridges connect your network to its subnets and to other networks. They do this using different methods.

Bridges, or *dumb gateways*, connect subnets, relaying information without any filtering. This lack of filtering makes it a bad way to connect to the Internet. All the data traveling through those pipes at any given moment don't really belong on your network. Bridges are useful if one subnet is getting overburdened with traffic, though. Another subnet can lighten the load.

Routers are designed to connect networks to other networks and the Internet. They filter data so you can block certain ports that you don't need. Routers tend to be more expensive than bridges, but for home and small business use, DSL packages often come with routers for around $100.

## Initializing New Network Hardware

In SUSE Linux, hardware detection is largely automated. During the initial installation, YaST recognizes your NIC and other hardware and initializes it.

If YaST does not automatically identify your card, you can set this up manually in the Network Cards module. Open YaST, go to Network Devices, Network Cards. The Configuration screen pops up, with any detected cards in the bottom half. Click Configure to set up the new card. Figure 25.1 appears.

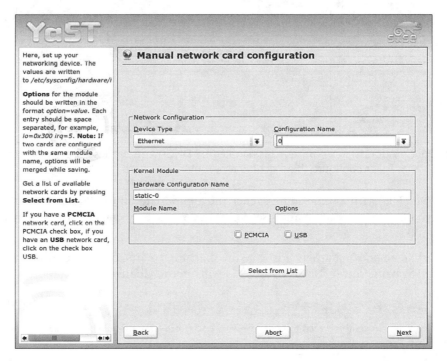

**FIGURE 25.1**   Choose Select from List to find your network card, or enter NIC information yourself.

Click Select from List to locate your card from a list. Doing this identifies the kernel Module Name to load. If your card is not on the list, consult your NIC's manual for configuration information. If your NIC is connected either by PCMCIA (typical for laptops) or USB, click the appropriate box. Click Next to continue.

In this screen, you'll set up your addressing. Figure 25.2 shows a NIC configured for DHCP.

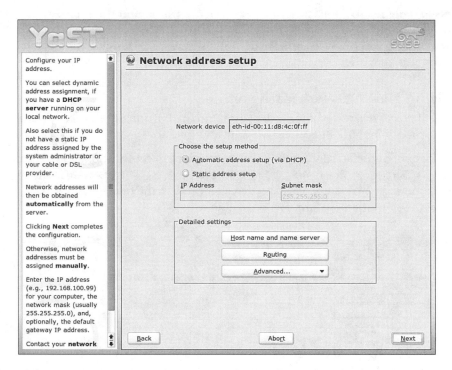

**FIGURE 25.2**    Addressing for this card is handled by DHCP. You can also use this screen to set up a static address or configure this machine as a router.

To set up the NIC with a static address, click the appropriate button. Enter the static address; you'll see the subnet mask is set for 255.255.255.0 by default. You can change this if you like.

Click Host Name and Name Server to give the machine a name on the network and, identify a domain name server (DNS). Figure 25.3 will appear. Change settings and click OK.

> **NOTE**
>
> You can also access this screen through the DNS and Host Name module under YaST Network Services.

In the Advanced Settings, you can set a Maximum Transfer Unit (MTU) for this card, choose when to load the NIC if you don't want to start at boot, and allow users to adjust NIC settings in the Detailed Settings menu. You can also add multiple addresses through aliases. Unless you have specific reasons for doing any of the above, you shouldn't, because the defaults will work well.

Click Next to return to the main screen and click Finish to confirm your settings. You will need to reboot to activate your card.

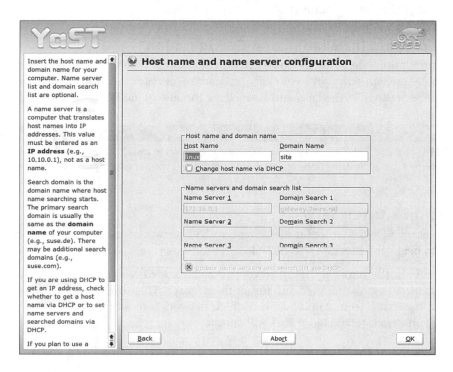

**FIGURE 25.3**    Give this machine a name and identify a domain name server for its Internet connection.

# Dynamic Host Configuration Protocol (DHCP)

As you might guess, DHCP allows a network administrator to configure TCP/IP parameters for each host on the network when the host connects to the network. The network administrator can assign an IP address to a NIC, set DNS entries, and configure default routing and gateway information for each host. In this section, you'll learn how to use DHCP to assign an IP address, and how to set up a DHCP server with YaST.

## How DHCP Works

DHCP basically holds identifying information for each client that might connect to the network, and so offers persistent storage of network parameters. This information typically includes Subnet, hostnames and addresses, and specific hardware addresses.

DHCP also allocates temporary and permanent IP addresses to clients and hosts. A temporary assignment is called a *lease*. When a lease elapses, a client can ask for an extension or return it to the server. DHCP can also allocate infinite leases for permanent connections, assuming it has enough addresses to spare.

For the network administrator, DHCP simplifies life immensely because it automates the allocation of IP addresses. No more accidentally assigning duplicate addresses or worrying about managing a limited number of available addresses.

## DHCP Software Installation and Configuration

During installation, YaST will set up DHCP for your system when it configures the NIC. This actually puts an entry into your /etc/sysconfig/network file. You can access and change some settings in the DNS and Host Name module in YaST Network Services.

> **NOTE**
>
> YaST uses a DHCP client called dhcpcd. You have the option to install the DHCP-client package from the Internet Systems Consortium as well, which gives you some command-line options.

## Setting Up a DHCP Server

You can set up a DHCP server on the system in YaST Network Services as well. Click the module to begin the process. This module sets up the /etc/dhcpd.conf file.

If you don't already have the DHCP Server package installed, you'll be prompted to insert the SUSE Linux installation media to install the package. Then the Configuration Wizard begins. In the first screen, you'll be asked which network interface to use for your server. Select one and click Next. Figure 25.4 will appear.

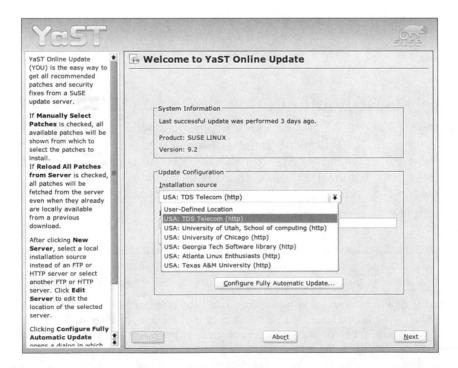

**FIGURE 25.4**   Enter your addressing information here.

The essential information to be entered here is the domain name this server will administer, the IP addresses for the DNS server(s) you're using, and the default gateway. As you see here, the default lease time for each host is 4 hours. This is adjustable here. If you want DHCP to handle addressing for your print server, enter its information here, too. Click Next to continue.

This screen (Figure 25.5) gives the server the address block it has to work with. Enter the first and last addresses it can assign. You can also adjust the default lease time and set a maximum time beyond which extensions cannot be granted. Click Next to continue.

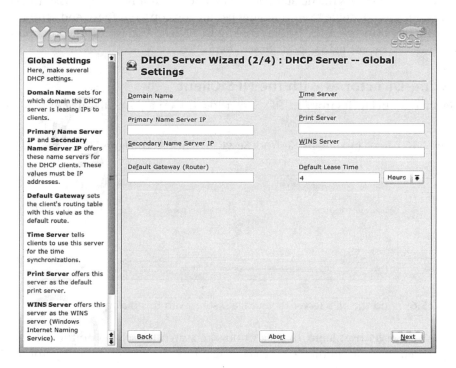

**FIGURE 25.5**    Enter the range of IP addresses the DHCP server can assign here.

In the last wizard screen, you'll be asked whether to start the server on boot or only when you ask it to start. To start the server, click Detailed Settings and then click Start DHCP Server Now. Click Finish to exit the wizard.

## Using the Network File System

The Network File System (NFS) is a way for different computers on the same network to share files transparently, as if volumes and directories were all on the same computer. If a user happens to work on multiple machines, NFS allows that user to log in and access the home directory using any computer on the network.

Any computer on the network can have an NFS server, an NFS client, or both. The necessary packages are installed by default with SUSE Linux.

## Starting and Configuring the NFS Server

To start the NFS Server on any network computer, run the NFS Server module in YaST Network Services. On the first screen, click Start NFS Server and check the Open Port in Firewall box, if necessary. Click Next to identify (export) directories to other machines.

To include a directory on the server, click Add Directory in the middle of the screen. Enter the full path of the directory or browse to it. Click OK and you will see some options. By default, all hosts on the network can see this directory, but you may limit that.

The options box includes the default permissions: ro (read-only), root_squash (prevents Root from another machine from changing permissions on your files), and sync (which requires the server to save a file before replying to a client request for it). Other options can be set here; consult man exports to see them.

## Importing Directories with the NFS Client

Adding shared directories from an NFS Server to work on a particular machine is a snap in YaST.

Open the NFS Client module in Network Services. Click Add. Figure 25.6 appears.

**FIGURE 25.6**    Add the NFS server to your file system with this dialog box.

Enter the NFS server hostname (or click Choose to search for servers on the network). Select a shared directory in the Remote Filesystem box and name a mount point (perhaps /nfs) on your local system. Click OK to confirm your choices, and click Finish to edit your /etc/fstab file to include the remote directory among the mount options for this machine.

# Playing Nice with Microsoft Windows with Samba

It may not be inevitable anymore, but there just might be one computer, or 100, running Microsoft Windows on your network. Despite vastly different file systems, it is possible, even easy, to enable those Windows machines to access files on the Linux machines. Samba uses the Server Message Block (SMB) protocol to perform this miracle. As far as the Windows PCs are concerned, you even have a C drive.

Samba is a very complex application with excellent documentation. The Samba HOWTO Collection and Reference Guide runs nearly 600 pages. *Samba Unleashed* is more than double that. The complexity comes from having an impressive amount of options.

Running a default Samba installation is pretty simple, however. It's like a lot of Linux applications. You can tweak Samba endlessly to make it work exactly the way you want, or you can just let it do its thing.

On the positive side, Samba functionality is installed and enable by default with SUSE Linux. In Konqueror, you can change the location to smb://*windowshost* and see the shared resources available to you there without further intervention necessary. You can easily manage Samba settings through YaST beneath Network Services.

If a bare minimum installation of the operating system was done, and not all of the necessary Samba components were installed on your workstation, you can always start YaST, choose Software, Install and Remove Software, and search for the Samba packages.

## Securing Network Services

SUSE Linux uses xinetd, the eXtended Internet Services Daemon, to secure network services and keep the bad guys out.

xinetd is a more secure version of the original Internet Services Daemon, inetd. It is designed in particular to protect your network from denial of service (DoS) attacks. A DoS attack occurs when someone tries to saturate a server's resources with repeated requests for services. You can limit the number of incoming connections with xinetd to something manageable.

To configure xinetd, go to the YaST Network Services page and select the xinetd module. YaST is actually reading from and writing to the /etc/xinetd.conf configuration file. Here you can set up your access control lists to allow (or deny) particular IP addresses and domain names from making requests on your network.

You can also restrict access to only some services with xinetd.

As an administrator, you should always know the services that you are offering the reason for such. Security on a server and security on a workstation are often approached from two different angles—this need not be the case, but it does provide two opposing views of how to approach the issue.

On a server, often all services are turned off and then only the ones that are needed are turned on. For example, as the server needs to host a web, appropriate services for that are turned on. If someone balks that they cannot access something they have a legitimate need to, and it is ascertained that they should be able to do so, then the appropriate services for that are turned on as well. Services are enabled one at a time as needed until it is known exactly what the server needs and this becomes the set of offerings.

With a workstation, often you start with a host of services enabled. You then start turning them off one a time until you get to the point where you are unable to do a task and enable the one in question once more.

Both approaches work and are useful in different scenarios. The key to both is careful research and good documentation.

25

# References

- http://arin.net—The American Registry for Internet Numbers, the body that assigns public IP addresses for the United States.

- http://www.ietf.org/rfc.html—Search for, or get a list of, Internet Engineering Task Force Requests for Comment.

- http://www.deepspace6.net—A resource clearinghouse for information on Linux and the new Internet Protocol. Good links and documentation pages.

- http://www.tldp.org/HOWTO/Linux+IPv6-HOWTO—The Linux IPv6 HOWTO.

- http://www.ietf.org/rfc/rfc2460.txt—The IPv6 Standard document.

- http://linuxreviews.org/features/ipv6—Interesting article on "Why You Want IPv6."

- http://www.iana.org/assignments/port-numbers—Learn what ports are assigned to what applications at the Internet Assigned Numbers Authority site.

- http://directory.google.com/Top/Computers/Software/Internet/Servers/ Address_Management/Dynamic_DNS_Services/—The place to find Dynamic DNS service providers.

- http://www.isc.org/sw/dhcp—The keepers of the SUSE Linux default DHCP server package and the optional client. You can view the current DHCP README file online at the ISC site.

- http://dhcp-monger.est-unique.net/wakka.php?wiki=Welcome—The DHCP-Mongers Wiki. Read man pages, search the mailing lists, submit new information.

- http://nfs.sourceforge.net—The Network File System project page, including FAQ list.

- http://www.samba.org—The Samba home page. See the HOWTO collection and Samba-By-Example Guide in the Documentation section.

- http://www.wi-fizone.org—Find a wireless hotspot wherever you may be at this site, sponsored by the WiFi Alliance trade group.

- http://standards.ieee.org/getieee802—Get the official IEEE standard document for any 802.xx networking specification here. This runs the gamut from Ethernet (802.3) to WiFi (802.11) and beyond.

- http://portal.suse.com/sdb/en/2002/11/wavelan.html—Wireless network setup from the SUSE Support Database.

- http://www.hpl.hp.com/personal/Jean_Tourrilhes/Linux/Wireless.html—Much good material on Linux Wireless Networking.

- http://www.securityfocus.com/unix—This comprehensive security site offers security news, mailing lists, and even some firewall rule sets.

- http://www.linuxsecurity.com—Get the weekly Linux Advisory Watch and Linux Security Week newsletters to keep up with the latest information and patches. Tutorials for beginners and articles for security professionals.

- http://www.insecure.org—The home of the nmap security scanner.

- http://www.ethereal.com—The freeware Ethereal network protocol analyzer and packet sniffer.

# CHAPTER 26

# Managing Your Apache Web Server

There is no World Wide Web without web servers, more accurately called *httpd* servers. And there is no more popular web server than the open-source Apache server.

In Chapter 14, "Creating Basic Websites," you played a little bit with Apache in setting up a test system for your website and blog. Here we will go into more detail on the topics of setting up and administering your web server.

## What Is Apache?

In the beginning there was the National Center for Supercomputing Applications (NCSA). Although the World Wide Web was first invented by Sir Tim Berners-Lee while he was at the then Conseil Européen pour la Recherche Nucléaire (CERN) in Switzerland, the Web could not become what it has without two practical additions: a server and a browser. The pioneers for both these applications were at NCSA at the University of Illinois.

A web server is nothing more than an application that runs silently in the background, listening for incoming requests from another computer for a particular document. After it receives a request, the server responds with the document, using the Hypertext Transfer Protocol (HTTP). The NCSA developed the first popular server application, HTTPd, but eventually lost interest in the project. Development on HTTPd formally ended in 1998.

A group of users and developers continued to work on the open-source code for HTTPd, fixing bugs and adding features in a haphazard way. Things were formalized when Bob Behlendorf and Cliff Skolnick set up a site where these

HTTPd patches could all go. Before long (or so the legend goes), "a patchy server" got a formal name, Apache.

Marc Andreessen and others on the HTTPd team also worked on NCSA Mosaic, the first successful browser application. Andreessen went on to produce a commercial application that built on the Mosaic code, Netscape Navigator.

Over the years, Apache has become by far the most popular web server application. Netcraft has been monitoring server usage since October 1995, when HTTPd was still number 1. Apache has been the most popular server since October 1996 and has steadily increased its market share.

The Apache Software Foundation (ASF) was incorporated in 1999 as the official guardians of the project. Today it has a board of directors elected annually by ASF members. It hosts two dozen web-related software projects that share the open-source Apache License.

The Apache 2.0 web server was released in 2002 and is included in your SUSE Linux disk. You can also download source code directly from the project website, http://httpd.apache.org/download.cgi, and build it yourself.

# Installing Apache

You can install Apache through YaST like any other package. This is by far the easiest way. When you search for Apache in YaST, you'll see a couple dozen packages, including several modules and Perl scripts that are optional but that may be useful to you.

When you install Apache 2.x, you will need one of the multiprocessing module (MPM) packages to run the server. The MPM is the component responsible for listening for network connections, accepting the request, and passing it to children processes for handling. There are two module packages available, apache2_prefork and apache2_worker, but only one can be loaded into the server at a given time.

The apache2_worker MPM handles requests using threads and is more geared toward use on a multiprocessor system. It is more advanced than the apache_prefork MPM, which instead handles requests using forked processes. The worker MPM has also been known to wreak havoc with some older modules. It's important to select the correct MPM based on your needs and hardware.

Be sure to install the `apache2-example-pages` as well. This will let you test whether Apache is working immediately after installation.

If you prefer to get under the hood and see exactly what is going on, however, you can still compile your web server from source code.

## Building Apache from the Source Code

You can get the latest stable source code from the Apache download site at http://httpd.apache.org/download.cgi. This page will point you to a mirror site that changes constantly. You can choose from a tarball, called `httpd-<version-number>.tar`, compressed with either gzip or bzip2. These archives are a few megabytes each and should not take too long to download, even with a dial-up connection.

> **CAUTION**
>
> Installing Apache from source can be a difficult task. Before attempting to do this, you should be very comfortable with your knowledge of your system and how all the various parts work together. You should know what to do in case of a problem. Much less can go wrong when you install via YaST, or even by using the standard Red Hat Package Managers (RPMs), and you can always uninstall an errant RPM package. That is not the case with source code.

After the download is complete, you should extract the archive into a safe temporary directory, such as /tmp. The archive creates a new httpd_<version-number> directory to store its files. This directory will contain a README, a LICENSE, and an INSTALL file.

The README file lists introductory information about the httpd server itself, where to find the latest version and documentation, acknowledgements, and whom to contact if you want to become involved or report a bug. The LICENSE file enumerates the terms and conditions for use and redistribution of the server software. The INSTALL file gives a quick overview at the installation process. Be sure to check out these files before attempting to build Apache.

Apache relies heavily on the use of autoconf and libtool, and although you could compile Apache the old-fashioned way by editing Makefile templates, you'll find it easier to use the configure script that comes in the tarball. To do this, open a shell (as a regular user), change directories to the location of the extracted tarball (that is, /tmp/httpd_<version-number> if you're following along), and then type the following command:

```
./configure --help
```

The script will output a list of configuration options you can use to fine-tune the compile process and Apache's setup. After you've read through the list and determined which options best suit you, run the configure script again:

```
./configure --prefix=/usr/local/httpd2 --with-mpm=prefork --enable-so //
    --enable-rewrite
```

The files will be placed in /usr/include/apache2 by default when the compiled httpd is installed, so you may want to specify a different directory using the prefix option as I did earlier. Keeping Apache's binary, scripts, configuration files, and modules all together is a good idea and makes things easier if you later need to upgrade or remove the server.

The configure script generates the necessary Makefile to compile the server. Type **make** to begin compiling the source code. After the code has been compiled, log in as the SuperUser and type **make install** to complete the installation and install the files under the directory you specified with configure's prefix option.

You can now configure your server. See the "Runtime Server Configuration Settings" section later in this chapter for ways to do that.

26

> **TIP**
>
> If you have already installed Apache and want to upgrade to a newer source version, try creating symlinks from the old installation to the new extracted directory.

# Starting and Stopping Apache

Now you've installed Apache with its default configuration. SUSE Linux provides a default home page, /srv/www/htdocs/index.html, in English and several other languages to test whether Apache is working properly. The proper way to run Apache is to have the web server run after booting, network configuration, and any firewall loading. The YaST Runlevel Editor takes care of this for you. This module is located on the YaST System page. See "Using the Runlevel Editor" in Chapter 22, "Managing the Boot Process and Other Services."

> **TIP**
>
> In the Advanced mode of the Runlevel Editor, make sure Apache is set to load at Runlevels 3 and 5.

After that is done, open any browser to http://localhost. If you have installed the sample pages package, you should see Figure 26.1.

**FIGURE 26.1**    If Apache is installed correctly, you'll get this test page when pointing a browser to http://localhost.

You can also use a wrapper script, apachectl, to start and stop the Apache server without having to reboot the entire machine. This comes in handy when you tweak httpd's configuration and need to restart the service for the changes to take effect. The script is found in the same directory as the httpd binary and in its simplest incantation, followed by start, restart, graceful, or stop:

```
./apachectl start
```

Intuitively, start and stop will start and stop the server, respectively. You can use restart to stop and immediately start the server again, or use graceful to give Apache a chance to finish any tasks it's performing before stopping (a graceful stop).

## Runtime Server Configuration Settings

Running Apache with its default settings should suit most uses. There are some tweaks you can make to customize Apache to your own liking or needs. If you installed Apache using YaST, Apache's standard configuration file is stored in /etc/Apache2/httpd.conf. If you installed Apache manually, the httpd.conf file will reside in the etc subdirectory of whatever you specified as Apache's base directory using configure's prefix option. You can either use SUSEConfig or edit this file directly to customize your server.

The SUSEConfig editor is located on the YaST System page. To configure Apache, go to Network, WWW, Apache2. Open the tree (click the + sign) to view the settings. These include the following:

- **APACHE_HTTPD_CONF**—Use this setting to specify a different configuration file than the default httpd.conf.

- **APACHE_MPM**—Multiprocessing modules are compiled into Apache and handle tasks such as network and process management. Remember, Apache can use only one MPM at a time. You can have both MPMs installed, but this setting determines which MPM is used. By default, SUSE Linux installs the prefork MPM.

- **APACHE_SERVERADMIN**—Useful only if APACHE_SERVERSIGNATURE is set to email. This setting lists the administrator's email address. The default is webmaster@<hostname>, where <hostname> is taken from the HOSTS file.

- **APACHE_SERVERNAME**—This is an important setting, especially if the server is open to the Internet and not just your LAN. Use this to define your fully qualified domain name, such as www.susefan.com, because this is the name your server will return when pinged. You don't need to set this if the machine's canonical name (that is, what SUSE calls your machine) is fine with you; Apache will use this by default. If you administer your own DNS (see the next chapter for information on how to do that), be sure to add an alias for your host. Otherwise, ask the manager of your DNS (your ISP, for example) to set this name.

- **APACHE_CONF_INCLUDE_FILES**—Create a custom configuration file and name it httpd.conf.local. Use this setting to have Apache use the custom configuration file in addition to the default. You can add multiple files separated by spaces.

26

- `APACHE_CONF_INCLUDE_DIRS`—Suppose you have a server application and its configuration file installs to a directory other than /etc/Apache2. Use this setting to allow Apache to read this configuration file. You can add multiple directories separated by spaces.

- `APACHE_MODULES`—This is where modules installed by YaST are activated. Look over the Description text for hints on various modules.

- `APACHE_SERVER_FLAGS`—This is the equivalent of starting Apache from the command line with various switches to turn features on and off. Review the Apache man page to see a list of switches/flags you can enter here.

- `APACHE_START_TIMEOUT`—By default, if the kernel tries to start Apache during boot, and Apache does not start in 2 seconds, it will report a timeout. You can extend this time (if, for example, you have some security features added that will slow response time) here.

- `APACHE_SERVERSIGNATURE`—This starts a footer at the bottom of any server-generated error page. By default, this includes the server name and Apache version number. If you want to include a contact point for the user to find you, set this to email and enter an email address at `APACHE_SERVERADMIN`. If you prefer that nothing appear, set this to no.

- `APACHE_LOGLEVEL`—This defines what gets entered into the server logs by setting the minimum level. By default, this is set at warn, so only problems that generate warnings (or worse) are entered. Informational messages are screened out. You should change this only if you are trying to troubleshoot a problem that might generate a lower-level message.

- `APACHE_ACCESS_LOG`—The location of your access log. Who is visiting?

- `APACHE_USE_CANONICAL_NAME`—This is turned off by default; turn it on so Apache delivers the ServerName listed earlier. Use the DNS setting to let the domain name server handle requests for the server name.

- `APACHE_SERVERTOKENS`—This tells Apache how much information it delivers about itself when asked. The default is the OS it is running on. You can set this higher or lower.

- `APACHE_EXTENDED_STATUS`—You can get additional information in your server status reports with this option turned on, but recording it will slow the server down some.

- `APACHE_BUFFERED_LOGS`—Use this to get Apache to store several log entries in memory and write them together to disk, rather than writing them after each request. On some systems, this may result in more efficient disk access and hence higher performance. It may be set only once for the entire server; it cannot be configured per virtual host.

- `APACHE_TIMEOUT`—How long, in seconds, Apache attempts to process a request before giving up. By default, this is set at 300 seconds (5 minutes).

### Additional Settings in `httpd.conf`

Most important Apache settings can be configured in `/etc/sysconfig`, but some must be edited in Apache's own configuration file, `/etc/Apache2/httpd.conf`. Consult the Apache documentation for a listing of all the settings, also called directives, but you should consider changing the following defaults:

- `DocumentRoot`—This should be set to the top directory that you want to serve files from. The default is `/srv/www/htdocs`.

- `MaxClients`—The maximum number of concurrent clients (that is, visiting browsers). The default is 150, but it probably should be set with consideration to the amount of traffic you expect.

- `Port`—Where Apache listens for traffic. This is set by default at port 80, the assigned port for HTTP traffic. This may also be set to port 8080 depending on your intended setup.

- `Directory`—Set directory permissions with this directive.

- `DirectoryIndex`—The file(s) Apache looks for when a request is made for the index or listing of a directory. Several documents can be listed (so you can list such files as `index.php`, `index.shtml`, `index.htm`, `index.txt`, and so on) and the server will return the first one in the list that it finds. If none of the documents exist, then, depending on how you've configured things, Apache may try to generate its own directory listing.

- `UserDir`—In every user's home directory, there is a subdirectory called `public_html`. To have Apache recognize files in this directory, set it here. The address for these pages would be http://<servername>/~<username>.

## File System Authentication and Access Control

You may have some documents in your web directory that you don't want the whole world to have access to. From a user's standpoint, you've often come across pages that require a password or that simply tell you that you aren't authorized to use this page. In this section, you'll learn how to protect parts of your site from prying eyes through user authentication and authorization.

### Restricting Access with `allow` and `deny`

Apache lets you restrict access to your site based on IP addresses or hostnames. This is done through directives in `httpd.conf` called `allow` and `deny`.

Suppose you plan to host an `apt` package repository at `susefan.com/pub/`, but you don't want anyone outside of `susefan.com` downloading its files with a browser. You would add these lines to `httpd.conf`:

```
<Location /pub>
    SetHandler pub
```

```
      Order deny, allow
      Deny from all
      Allow from susefan.com
</Location>
```

Note the four statements. First, we told Apache that when someone tries to access the /pub directory, it needs to check whether the person is allowed. Then we set the order for Apache to check—first process the deny statements and then the allow statements. In this case, the statements are easy to follow: Deny everyone, unless the request originates from a host within the susefan.com domain.

You can describe your limits for either deny or allow in six ways:

- all affects everyone.

- A full or partial IP address, such as 192.168.1.101 or 192.168.1. This is preferred over a domain name because it's faster to process.

- A full or partial host or domain name, such as susefan.com. This is a little slower than an IP address because Apache must do a DNS lookup to confirm the host.

- A network/netmask pair such as 192.168.1.0/255.255.1.0.

- A network address in the classless interdomain routing (CIDR) form, such as 192.168.1.0/24.

- An environment variable, such as env=allowed_hosts.

## Authentication

Many organizations have a members-only section of their website where information is stored that the rest of the world can't access. To see the information in such a restricted area, users must prove they are authorized to do so, usually by providing a username and password.

Apache Basic Authentication is the most common authentication method used, probably because it is quite straightforward in its approach. When someone attempts to access a protected page, Apache asks for a username and a password. It then verifies the username and password and if successful, Apache serves the request.

> **CAUTION**
>
> Basic Authentication does not encrypt the password when you type it in, so don't use valuable passwords (such as your login password) for your protected page.
>
> Similarly, webmasters should not use Basic Authentication for highly sensitive data. You have the option of using Apache Digest Authentication (which is more secure, but not always supported by browsers), using SSL/TSL or finding some more secure means of making the data available to a selected group. Consult the Apache documentation for information on Digest Authentication.

The first step in implementing Basic Authentication is to create a plain-text list of user-names and passwords. This is done using htpasswd2, a script included with the Apache2 package and installed to the same directory as httpd and apachectl. You should store these passwords away from your main Apache installation directory, making it harder for rogue applications to find them, so make a new directory (as the SuperUser) to hold this file, such as /usr/local/httpd2/passwd first.

> **NOTE**
>
> Basic Authentication is implemented with the mod_auth module. In the unlikely event that you get a command not found error message when running htpasswd2, make sure this module is installed.

When you have created this directory, type this command to create a new hidden password file, with the first user included:

```
./htpasswd -c  /usr/local/httpd2/passwd/.htpasswd mikemc
```

You'll be prompted twice for this user's password:

```
New password:
Re-type new password:
Adding password for user mikemc
```

To add new users to this file, use the same command without the -c switch (that creates a new file):

```
./htpasswd /usr/local/httpd2/passwd/.htpasswd newuser
```

Next, you need to tell Apache to refer to .htpasswd when serving a protected page. You do this in one of two ways: directly through httpd.conf or by creating a new .htaccess file. The .htaccess file should be located in the directory you want to protect; in the example used in the allow/deny section, this would be /pub/.htaccess. In httpd.conf, you would create a new section labeled <Directory /pub>. Either way, the syntax is the same. Use these four directives:

```
AuthType Basic
AuthName "Members Only"
AuthUserFile /usr/local/httpd2/passwd/.htpasswd
Require user mikemc
```

Here the AuthType is Basic because we're using Basic Authentication (the option would be set to Digest if mod_auth-digest was used). The AuthName can be anything and identifies the "realm" or category of that page. In this case, all pages with the AuthName Members Only would have the same password. Thus, when the browser went to another page marked Members Only, it could deliver the same password without forcing the user to retype it in an endless series of pop-up dialog boxes. The AuthUserFile points to

26

the .htpasswd file containing the usernames and passwords. The Require directive specifies the user(s) allowed to access the page.

If, instead of one person having access to a resource, you want to create a group of users with the same level of access, create a group file named .htgroup in any text editor with the Group Name and a list of users. Save it in the same directory as .htpasswd. The entry in .htgroup file should look like this:

```
Members: mikemc robsh ltorvalds svillinski
```

The concept of the two files are similar to Linux's /etc/passwd and /etc/group files; .htpasswd stores each username and password hash, and .htgroup aggregates usernames into logical groups. Each group member needs to have a password listed in .htpasswd before access is allowed.

Now edit your .htaccess file so that your group has access.

```
AuthType Basic
AuthName "Members Only"
AuthUserFile /usr/local/httpd2/passwd/.htpasswd
AuthGroupFile /usr/local/httpd2/passwd/.htgroups
Require group Members
```

Everyone in the Members group would now have access to all pages with the "Members Only" realm.

> **NOTE**
>
> You can create as many groups as you want in your .htgroups file. Each entry is a single line listing all its members together, separated only by a space.

## Apache Modules

It should not surprise you that the "patchy" server does most of its work through modules. After all, it's this very modular design that has enabled it to become a powerful, flexible web server. Some 50 core modules are included in the Apache2 package, and a couple dozen more are included in the SUSE Linux distribution. All are installable with YaST. In addition, nearly 400 modules are stored in the Apache Module Registry, http://modules.apache.org. The following is but a brief sampling of modules available for Apache:

- bw_mod—Limits the number of simultaneous connections and bandwidth usage for virtual hosts and directories.

- mod_auth_mysql—Adds MySQL database-based authentication.

- mod_bt—Extends Apache to handle the BitTorrent protocol and act as a tracker.

- mod_clamav—Scans files for viruses with ClamAV before serving them to the client.

- `mod_ftpd`—Extends Apache to handle FTP transactions.

- `mod_gnutls`—An alternative to mod_ssl that provides the capability to use SSL/TLS.

- `mod_mono`—Serves ASP.NET client applications in a non-Windows environment with Mono.

- `mod_perl`—Processes embedded Perl code before serving a document.

- `mod_php4`—Processes embedded PHP code before serving a document.

- `mod_python`—Processes embedded Python code before serving a document.

- `mod_rewrite`—Manipulates URL addresses according to rules written using regular expressions.

- `mod_ruby`—Processes embedded Ruby code before serving a document.

- `mod_so`—Enables usage of modules linked at runtime in contrast to only those statically compiled.

- `mod_ssl`—Adds the capability to establish and communicate across SSL/TSL connections.

- `mod_websh`—Processes embedded Tcl code before serving a document.

- `mod_xslt`—A filter that transforms XML files into other formats on-the-fly by applying XSLT stylesheets.

Each module adds new directives that can be added to your configuration files. Make sure the module is compatible with your Apache installation, though. Changes made to Apache between versions 1.3.x and 2.x break some modules. All that information, including the module's installation procedures and the new configuration directives they make available, can be found either in the module's or Apache's documentation.

## Virtual Hosting

Apache lets you host several domains with a single instance of the server, a process referred to as *virtual hosting*. This service can be a godsend for the system administrator overseeing an installation with limited resources, such as hardware, static IP addresses, or even time to monitor several server setups. Virtual hosting is implemented through several directives included in `httpd.conf`.

> **NOTE**
>
> The `mod_vhost_alias` module is another virtual hosting tool included with the core Apache package. It is designed for use by ISPs and other large sites.

There are two ways to implement virtual hosts in Apache: name-based and IP-address–based hosting. This section covers both options.

In either case, you must first tell Apache the IP addresses that have multiple domains associated with them. You can either use a specific IP address or the * variable to indicate that Apache should consider any request it receives as a candidate for virtual hosting. Open `httpd.conf` and type

```
NameVirtualHost *
```

## Name-Based Virtual Hosting

According to the HTTP/1.1 specification, when a client seeks out a document from a server, it includes the expected domain in its request. Although various domains may resolve to the same IP address with a DNS query, the domain names in the HTTP requests will still be different. This is the basic principle of name-based virtual hosting.

This type of virtual hosting (also known as *vhosting*) is the easiest and most popular way to handle hosting multiple domains. With this method, you need only one IP address to host several domain names. Apache receives a request, examines it to identify the desired domain, and obliges with the proper page.

You'll need to add `VirtualHost` sections in the configuration file for each domain name after the NameVirtualHost directive. For example, if you want to host a personal site at www.YourName.com and a second site, www.susefan.com, this is how you would enter them in `httpd.conf`:

```
<VirtualHost *>
    ServerName www.YourName.com
    DocumentRoot /srv/www/htdocs/YourName.com
    ServerAdmin webmaster@YourName.com
    ErrorLog /var/log/apache2/www.YourName.com-error_log
    CustomLog /var/log/apache2/www.YourName.com-access_log common
</VirtualHost>

<VirtualHost *>
    ServerName www.susefan.com
    DocumentRoot /srv/www/htdocs/susefan.com
    ServerAdmin webmaster@susefan.com
    ScriptAlias /srv/www/htdocs/susefan.com/cgi-bin
    ErrorLog /var/log/apache2/www.susefan.com-error_log
    CustomLog /var/log/apache2/www.susefan.com-access_log common
</VirtualHost>
```

> **CAUTION**
>
> Although SSL/TSL have not been discussed, it is still worth mentioning that Apache cannot distinguish different security certificates for name-based virtual hosts. This is because SSL/TSL operates at a socket level, and the request has already been encrypted by the time Apache receives it. This may cause warnings to be triggered by the client's browser, depending on the common name listed by the certificate. In these cases, IP-Address–Based virtual hosting is recommended.

As the server receives the request, it will scan through the configuration file seeking a virtual host entry's ServerName or ServerAlias directive that matches the expected domain. If no matching entry can be found, the first virtual host is used. The virtual host first inherits the directives set earlier in the `httpd.conf` file and then overrides those explicitly set for the host.

In the preceding example, www.YourName.com will use whatever ScriptAlias value is defined in the base configuration, whereas www.susefan.com will use `/srv/www/htdocs/susefan.com/cgi-bin`.

## IP-Address–Based Virtual Hosting

Hosting multiple IP addresses is a little more complex than hosting multiple names, but it is more widely supported. All but a very few ancient browsers (that is, those browsers that support only HTTP/1.0) support name-based vhosts, but if you want to be universal, this is the way to go.

> **NOTE**
>
> Kernel support for multi-IP-hosting, called IP aliasing, must be enabled for these commands to work. This is the default setting for SUSE Linux.

Setting up IP-based vhosting is a two-step process. First, you must identify the addresses to use. As the SuperUser, run `ifconfig` to find the Internet address (listed here as `inet addr`) attached to `eth0`, your Ethernet connection. It should show up similar to the following:

```
inet addr:172.26.1.33
```

Then use `ifconfig` to bind more addresses to the network interface:

```
/sbin/ifconfig eth0:0 172.26.1.40
/sbin/ifconfig eth0:1 172.16.1.41
```

Now you can enter the same VirtualHost statements in `httpd.conf` as you did when using names, with only the VirtualHost statement changed:

```
<VirtualHost 172.26.1.40>
    ServerName www.YourName.com
    DocumentRoot /srv/www/htdocs/YourName.com
    ServerAdmin webmaster@YourName.com
    ErrorLog /var/log/apache2/www.YourName.com-error_log
    CustomLog /var/log/apache2/www.YourName.com-access_log common
</VirtualHost>

<VirtualHost 172.26.1.41>
    ServerName www.susefan.com
    DocumentRoot /srv/www/htdocs/susefan.com
```

```
    ServerAdmin webmaster@susefan.com
    ScriptAlias /srv/www.htdocs/susefan.com/cgi-bin
    ErrorLog /var/log/apache2/www.susefan.com-error_log
    CustomLog /var/log/apache2/www.susefan.com-access_log common
</VirtualHost>
```

# Dynamic Content

Active content on a web page can range from a simple form or opinion poll, to a search-engine results page, to a portal with personalized news content.

Apache offers three methods of generating active content: common gateway interface (CGI) scripts, server-side includes (SSI), and active content modules such as mod_perl.

Chapter 31, "Programming Dynamic Websites," covers the creative end of making active content. This section is a brief introduction into the nuts and bolts of delivering this content to users.

## CGI Programs

CGI is a specification that allows a web server to execute programs and scripts that reside on the web server and return their output back to the client. CGI programming is the most common method of generating dynamic content for the web. Almost any language can be used, although Perl, Python, and C tend to be the most popular.

The easiest (and most secure) way to activate the CGI capabilities of Apache is to create a special directory that will contain all the scripts, and specify it using the ScriptAlias directive. Traditionally, the name of the directory is cgi-bin. Apache will try to run any file that resides in that directory ll file residing in the directory set with ScriptAlias.

Remember, these programs must be executable by the system Apache user. When you place your programs there, the permissions must be set to permit this:

```
chmod 755 program.cgi
```

Another way to enable CGI is to add +ExecCGI to the directory's Options directive and then set a handler for files with certain extensions. These changes can be made either in the http.conf or .htaccess file:

```
Options +ExecCGI
AddHandler cgi-script .cgi .pl
```

In the preceding code, files in the directory with a .cgi or .pl extension will be handled as CGI scripts. Apache will execute the scripts and return the results to the requesting client.

## Server-Side Includes

SSI are specially crafted comments called *elements*, which are embedded in a web page and interpreted by Apache. They can be used to include the contents of other files, display environment variables (such as the current date and time) or a file's timestamp, and produce program outputs.

To enable SSI, mod_include must be available to Apache, and you must add +Includes to the directory's Options directive either in http.conf or in .htaccess:

```
Options +Includes
```

There are then two methods for identifying a file for processing as an SSI document. The first is to specify a file extension, traditionally .shtml, and associate a handler to process files that end with that extension:

```
AddType text/html   .shtml
AddHandler server-parsed   .shtml
```

The directives may be placed in either the http.conf or a .htaccess file. When set, Apache will process all files with the .shtml extension for SSI elements before returning the results to the requesting client.

The second method for identifying a file is by turning on the XBitHack directive and setting the execute permission bit on any SSI file. Again, they may be set either in .htaccess or httpd.conf.

```
XBitHack on
```

With XBitHack turned on, Apache will parse all files that the user has permission to execute, regardless of the file's extension.

## Active Content Modules

If you find yourself writing a lot of CGI scripts in a particular interpreted language, it might be beneficial to see if a module exists that integrates the language's interpreter with Apache. For example, you would probably do better in the long run using the mod_perl Apache module instead of processing your Perl-powered pages through CGI. When you call a script from Apache, the Perl interpreter process starts, does its work, and then eventually stops. You can just imagine what that does to your system's resources if you have 20 scripts running simultaneously, even if just for a few seconds. When you channel those scripts through a module, everything is handled by one native interpreter. This makes everything go faster—and safer.

The downside is that mod_perl is much fussier about errors. Apache doesn't really mind if you don't release a resource programmatically, because it shuts down the script before that becomes a problem. In a module, errors accumulate and become real problems. The upside is that you will become a better programmer as a result of fixing all these problems.

26

Some languages are specifically designed to be run through an Apache module, such as PHP. PHP can be used to process scripts through CGI; the language's documentation encourages the use of an Apache module over the CGI implementation.

SUSE Linux provides Apache modules for four scripting languages: mod_perl, mod_python, mod_php4, and mod_ruby.

▶ **SEE** Chapter 30, "Using Perl and Python," and Chapter 31, "Programming Dynamic Websites," for more information about using these languages.

# Other Web Servers

Apache may be number one in the web server business, but it is not the only one. Aside from IIS (a commercial web server product from Microsoft), several general-purpose web servers can run on Linux. Specialized web servers, such as the various Wiki engines, the Zope application server, and J2EE application servers, also run on Linux.

This section covers some of the server products that will run on SUSE Linux.

### thttpd

This tiny server (only 129KB), included in SUSE Linux and installable via YaST, aims to be a simple, small, fast, and secure web server. It's not as feature rich as Apache or other server applications, but it does support CGI, Basic Authentication, virtual hosting, and bandwidth throttling.

### Caudium WebServer

The Caudium WebServer is on par with Apache but again with different strengths and weaknesses. It is a nonforking, threaded web server. It offers a web-based configuration interface, templating with the RoXen Macro Language (RXML), Pike code embedding, and the Supports Database, a method through which the requesting browser's capabilities can be identified without using JavaScript in the web document. Caudium is not distributed with SUSE, but its source code can be downloaded from the project's home page.

### Xitami

Xitami is a small, multithreaded and modular web server application that can also handle FTP requests. It supports direct support for CGI scripts written in Perl, Awk and Python, Basic Authentication, virtual hosting, on-the-fly server configuration, and server-side XML processing. Xitami is not distributed with SUSE, but the project's source code can be downloaded from its website.

### Zope

Zope is an open-source web-application server written mostly in Python. It is included in SUSE Linux and is installable via YaST. (You learned a little about Zope, including how to install it, when you installed ZWiki in Chapter 16, "Collaborating with Others.")

Zope is an excellent content management framework and is geared toward serving dynamic pages. Zope can do its own web serving and has many of the same modules to do its work that Apache does, but it is often used together with Apache.

The best thing about Zope as a web server is that the simple web-based interface makes configuration much easier than with Apache.

## ColdFusion

Macromedia's ColdFusion server bills itself as a fast way to create powerful web-based applications. It can run as a standalone application server, integrate with Apache, or work in conjunction with other J2EE solutions to serve CFML documents. The main benefits of the ColdFusion server is its Java underpinnings, which allow developers to use third-party Java code in their Internet applications, and tight integration with Macromedia's other technologies. Free trial and developer versions are available from the company's website.

## TomCat

The TomCat servlet container is part of the Apache Foundation's open-source Jakarta project and embodies the industry's standard implementation for the servlets and JSP interfaces. It can be configured as a standalone application server or integrated with Apache to serve JSP pages. TomCat can handle CGI and SSL requests when acting as a standalone server. Other benefits are its Single Sign On feature and web-based configuration interface. TomCat can be downloaded from the project's website.

# References

- http://www.apache.org—The Apache Software Foundation umbrella site. Access all Apache projects from here.
- http://httpd.apache.org—The place to start for information on the Apache Web Server. News, downloads, FAQs. Check the Docs subproject for a PDF user's guide.
- http://modules.apache.org—The Apache Module Registry. Locate modules to install, and contribute modules you've created.
- http://www.apachetoday.com—A little cluttered and ad ridden, but ServerWatch's Apache Today site is still an excellent source of Apache news and tutorials.
- http://tldp.org/HOWTO/HOWTO-INDEX/apps.html#SERVERHTTP—An index of web server-related HOWTOs, mostly dealing with Apache, but a few others, too.
- http://susefaq.sourceforge.net/faq/apache.html—The Unofficial SUSE FAQ list includes useful SUSE-specific Apache information.
- http://news.netcraft.com/archives/web_server_survey.html—The monthly Netcraft survey of popular web servers. As this is being written, nearly 70 percent of the Web runs on Apache.
- http://modpython.org—Home of the mod_python Apache module.

- http://hoohoo.ncsa.uiuc.edu/cgi/—Information on the common gateway interface.

- http://modruby.net—The `mod_ruby` page.

- http://www.acme.com/software/thttpd—Home of `thttpd`.

- http://caudium.net/—The Caudium WebServer home page.

- http://www.xitami.com/—The Xitami website.

- http://www.zope.org—All the latest and greatest from the Zope community.

- http://www.macromedia.com/software/coldfusion/—Web page at Macromedia promoting the ColdFusion MX server.

- http://jakarta.apache.org/tomcat/—The Java Servlet and JSP server released through the Apache Free Software Foundation.

# CHAPTER 27

# Managing Domain Names

The domain name system (DNS) is the lifeblood of the Internet. Without DNS, we would all be forced to remember TCP/IP addresses to get to websites, get to our email, buy merchandise, or look up information in a search engine. To go to www.novell.com to learn more about SUSE, for example, you would have to remember 130.57.4.27. Why attempt to remember a set of numbers such as this when you can remember www.novell.com/ linux? The DNS brings a level of simplicity into surfing the Web and doing work with SUSE Linux. In this chapter we will learn how DNS is used with SUSE Linux. Of course, there are ways around this—by editing your HOSTS file, for example, to make the lack of DNS bearable by adding a local DNS database to your personal system—but for the most part, if you don't want to update this file each time you want to use DNS, make certain you implement a DNS server in your enterprise so that you can remember www.novell.com, instead of 130.57.4.27.

In Chapter 12, "Connecting to the Internet," you learned how to connect to the Internet. In Chapter 25, "Setting Up Networks and Samba," you learned about TCP/IP fundamentals. In this chapter, you will build on the concepts of the Internet and TCP/IP and learn about the DNS, how it is configured on your SUSE Linux system, and how to modify it if needed. In this chapter, you will also learn how to set up SUSE Linux as a DNS client in YaST, edit DNS configuration files, use tools such as nslookup to gather information, and finally, learn the fundamentals of using Linux as a DNS server.

# Essential DNS Concepts

The DNS is a distributed and hierarchical database whose function is to resolve hostnames to IP addresses. As mentioned earlier, this is really the only reason DNS is used. As a matter of fact, using DNS adds latency and complexity to any configuration management you need to do, such as changing the DNS information itself. Because the DNS database is "distributed," those changes need to replicate through the DNS system, whether it is hosted locally within your network privately, whether it is a public DNS server communication with other public DNS servers to replicate changes, or a hybrid of both. DNS is worth every ounce of issue you may derive from it, so let's start by taking a look at how to configure it locally on your SUSE Linux system so that you can use and test it.

In the following example and illustration, DNS will be shown step by step and simplified as much as possible, although entire books are dedicated to the subject because of its depth and complexity.

In this example, your hostname is the website www.novell.com. Suppose that you would like to visit the Linux section of the website to find out more about SUSE Linux. The website's IP address is 130.57.4.27. You are currently on a home laptop running SUSE Linux. You open a web browser (Konqueror, for example) and attempt to visit the www.novell.com site by entering the easy-to-remember Uniform Resource Locator (URL) of www.novell.com. Consider the following steps, shown in Figure 27.1, that are taken when you enter a domain name into your web browser:

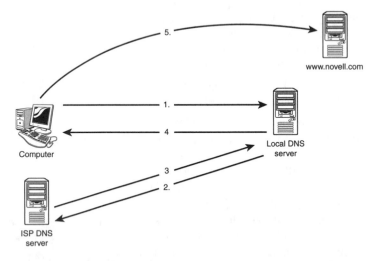

**FIGURE 27.1**    Viewing a simple DNS design.

1. Your local system (with help from you, of course) wants to get to www.novell.com. To do this, it needs to know what Novell's website IP address is and because it does not, it asks its locally configured hosts file to resolve the DNS name—novell.com. This local system currently does not have any entries in the hosts file; therefore, the manually configured DNS server (the local DNS server) will attempt to resolve it.

2. This is the first time this site has been requested; therefore, the domain is unknown by the local DNS server and the request needs to be "forwarded" from the local DNS server to the ISP's DNS server, which does know that www.novell.com resolves to 130.57.4.27. The ISP's DNS servers are public servers.

3. After the full URL of http://www.novell.com is placed in the Location field, requested by Konqueror, and resolved to an IP address of 130.57.4.27, that information is then cached in the local DNS server so that if this request is again brought up, it will be quicker to resolve.

4. Now that www.novell.com has been resolved to the local DNS server, the answer of 130.57.4.27 is given to the client.

5. The client now can connect via the Internet to the www.novell.com website and browse it for SUSE Linux help or other information.

In this scenario, you had a DNS server and a DNS client. In this chapter you will learn about both—how to set up and install SUSE Linux to handle both tasks. The DNS client is the host that is requesting DNS information that is provided by a DNS database, either local to the system itself (hosts), as shown in Figure 27.2, or on a server configured to provide such information. First, let's view the local database on the SUSE Linux system. You can find the hosts file off of the root of the operating system, in the etc directory. (Later in this chapter, you will learn how to configure this with YaST.)

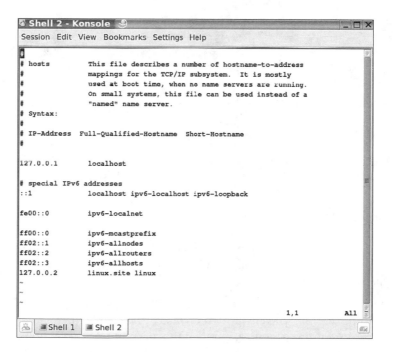

**FIGURE 27.2** Viewing a Linux HOSTS file.

The server with BIND installed is called a DNS server. Let's continue discussing what DNS is, its inner workings, and how it works with Linux.

## DNS Hierarchy

After you understand how the DNS is used for communication, you should also understand how it's entered as a URL into a computer web browser such as Konqueror. Figure 27.3 shows a standard web browser with a URL inserted.

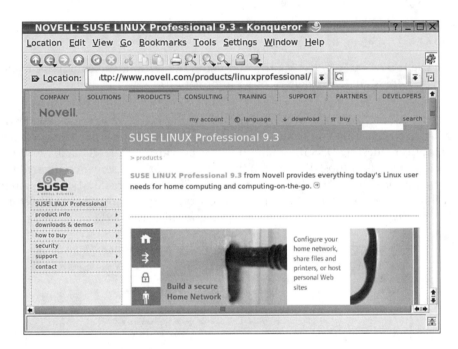

**FIGURE 27.3**   Finding help online.

To understand the DNS, you have to understand what it is you are looking for when you enter a URL such as the one shown here. For instance, the URL for Novell's home page for SUSE Linux is found in the location field as the following:

```
http://www.novell.com/products/linuxprofessional/
```

Because URLs and web browsing are not this chapter's focus, let's just quickly review them so we can get into DNS in more detail. First is the protocol that you will be using, which is HTTP (Hypertext Transfer Protocol).

HTTP is nothing more than a protocol that is used to transmit files over the World Wide Web (WWW) using port 80. The entry www.novell.com is a fully qualified domain name, or FQDN. An FQDN consists of a host, a domain name, and a top-level domain (TLD). These are all shown in the URL www.novell.com. In this example, www is the host (this entry is not always required), novell is the second-level domain, and the .com is the TLD. Although it's not seen, a period also follows .com, which would make the FQDN appear as www.novell.com. The trailing period shows the root. You do not have to add this period, but it's okay if you do. Most people don't even know that it exists. Some browsers append the entry, some ignore it; either way, it works.

TLDs are explained as follows. In Figure 27.4, you can see a few TLDs with second-level domains following.

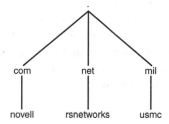

**FIGURE 27.4**    Viewing a sample DNS hierarchy.

For this example, take a look at the following three URLS:

- http://www.novell.com
- http://www.rsnetworks.net
- http://www.usmc.mil

You may see after you enter some of the URLs (www.usmc.mil, for example) that although it works, it is replaced by a different URL in the Location field of your web browser. In this example, www.usmc.mil has been redirected to a new, longer URL. Both URLs lead to the home page, or index page, of the website; the URL is being redirected by the web server's internal configuration.

In these examples, the highest level of the DNS hierarchy is Root. A single period (.) represents the Root domain, as shown in the illustration.

You can also see that the TLD is .com, .net, and .mil. In the early 1980s, about a half-dozen main TLDs were designated for use. Domain names may be registered in three of the most commonly used TLDs, which are .com, .net, and .org. There are many others, but most serve limited purposes. Table 27.1 lists some of the most common TLDs.

**TABLE 27.1**    Common Top-Level Domains

| | |
|---|---|
| .com | The TLD of .com represents the word "commercial." It is the most widely used and accepted domain name in use today—worldwide. |
| .net | The TLD of .net represents the word "network." It is most commonly used by Internet Service Providers (ISPs), hosting companies, or other businesses that are directly involved in the infrastructure of the Internet. |
| .org | The TLD of .org represents the word "organization." It is used mostly by not-for-profit groups. |

27

**TABLE 27.1**   Continued

| | |
|---|---|
| .edu | The TLD of .edu represents the word "education." It is used mostly for colleges, schools, and educational facilities worldwide. |
| .mil | The TLD of .mil represents the word "military." It is mostly used to denote military branches, such as the Navy and the Marine Corps. |
| .biz | The TLD of .biz represents the word "business." It is used mostly to show a small-business website, although most times, .com is preferred only because it's more commonly known to the general public. |
| .info | The TLD of .info represents the word "information." It is used mostly to show informational-based websites such as directories, phone books, or any other form of service that provides information to the general public or private groups. |
| .gov | The TLD of .gov represents the word "government." It is used mostly to show government agencies and departments. |

> **NOTE**
>
> The original seven TLD were .com, .edu, .gov, .int, .mil, .net, and .org. In 2001 and 2002, the other entries were introduced. In addition to these, countries have always had TLDs available for their use as well—.au for Australia, and so on. In recent years, a few countries have opted to make their domains available for use by anyone—these include .tv for Tuvalu, .ws for Western Samoa, and .cc for the Cocos Islands.

Note that these are just guidelines; you can purchase and use just about any URL as long as it is available. You may find, just by the fact that the domain name is not available for sale, that many of your good ideas for names are already taken.

> **NOTE**
>
> You can find more information on TLDs at the following URL: http://www.icann.org/tlds/.

Now you should feel very comfortable with the DNS hierarchy when you see a URL such as www.novell.com.

DNS maps friendly names to IP addresses. It is similar to a phone book, pairing hostnames and IP addresses much in the same way as people's names are paired with their telephone numbers. The internal structure of that phone book is the DNS hierarchy. Now that you understand how DNS is structured, let's dive into the internals of it.

## Zones

The DNS database contains zones. These are called *zone files,* which contain resource records (explained in the next section). A DNS zone file is also a database. There are two standard zone types: forward lookup zones and reverse lookup zones. A forward lookup zone allows for a resource name to IP address resolution—for example, looking up the IP address of www.novell.com.

A reverse lookup zone, if you haven't already guessed, does the opposite, which is allowing for IP address to resource name resolution—for example, determining a hostname from only the IP address. Both zones need to be built, created, and managed by a system administrator. The reverse lookup zone is contained in a domain known as in-addr.arpa.

## Records

When you're building a DNS infrastructure, after you have the TLD, the second-level domain, and a zone database created on the DNS server, it's important to then add records to it. Records are nothing more than files that hold data that the DNS server queries. Each domain that is created always contains resource records containing information about the DNS infrastructure you are managing, especially by default. Some records are made by default when you install DNS for the first time. There are many types of DNS database records. The most common database record is the A (Address) record, which maps a hostname and an IP address. This is the primary method of DNS resolution. A records are responsible for most of the DNS communication and resolution in use with DNS. The DNS forward lookup zones are populated with a variety of resource records. The most common resource records are listed in Table 27.2.

**TABLE 27.2**   Commonly Used DNS Records

| | |
|---|---|
| A (Address) record | The Address record contains the hostname to IP address mapping for the particular host. The majority of the records in the zone will be host A Address records. |
| PTR (Pointer) record | The Pointer record is used for reverse lookups. This file is merely a pointer to another location. |
| MX (Mail Exchanger) record | The Mail Exchanger record identifies the domain's preferred mail servers. |
| CNAME (Canonical Name) record | Also known as an *alias*. Canonical Name must be used with an existing A record; it provides an alias type name to map to the original A records IP address. |

Now that you understand the fundamentals of DNS and how it works for you as a client, let's look at how to configure it on SUSE Linux.

# Configuring DNS with YaST2

Configuring DNS with YaST is an easy process when you configure the client. Remember from our earlier discussion that the DNS resolution process is used for simplicity, allowing a client to use an easy-to-remember name instead of what it really needs to use, which is the IP address. You use the domain name; the client (when configured properly) gets that information from its local database (hosts) or from an external distributed one, such as DNS. To configure your client with DNS, you will need to know the following from your ISP or your local systems administrator:

- The IP address of the DNS server(s)

- The correct domain name(s)

That's it! It's that simple to set up DNS on your local client. It's even easier if you have Dynamic Host Configuration Protocol (DHCP) in use. DHCP can be used to automatically update the DNS information on your client if you have a DHCP server installed on your network, or if your ISP (most likely the case) provides you with the DNS information you need through the DHCP server you get your initial IP address from when you connect to a network. To configure DNS manually, use the following steps. To get to the DNS configuration pages, simply open YaST and navigate to the Network Services menu in the YaST Control Center, as shown in Figure 27.5.

**FIGURE 27.5**    Configuring DNS with YaST.

Make sure you are logged in as Root or are able to use the root account to make your changes. When you open YaST, YaST will take a moment to initialize its network configuration. After it is completed, if this is the first time you are entering this section of YaST, you may be prompted to edit DNS information manually. A warning will pop up to let you know that although you may be getting ready to make a manual entry, the DNS information was already configured by DHCP, as shown in Figure 27.6.

You can choose to either Accept or Modify the contents. Accepting will gray out all configurable sections except for the host and domain name sections at the top of the DNS configuration window. If you click Modify, you will be given a chance to edit the settings manually. If you are unsure of what you are doing, you may want to write down the settings you are changing so that you have a way to get back to the original configuration. If you change your DNS settings, it's likely you will no longer be able to access the Internet anymore from your SUSE Linux system. To manually change the settings, select Modify and insert the information you desire, such as a new hostname and domain name for your computer, or the Name Server list and domain search listing you have laid out in Figure 27.7.

The resolver configuration file (/etc/resolv.conf) has been temporarily modified by dhcpcd. You have two options:

1. Modify the current (changed!) version of the file
2. Press 'Accept' now and continue editing other (non-resolver) data. You could return to this dialog later when the above service has terminated.

Accept    Modify

**FIGURE 27.6**    Viewing a DNS resolver warning.

**FIGURE 27.7**    Host Name and Name Server Configuration page.

27

A name server is a computer that translates hostnames into IP addresses, and that is what the three name servers seen here are doing. If you remember the example in the beginning of this chapter, this section should make more sense—you are configuring the client to get its information from one of the three servers listed here. Why three? Usually you would have a primary, a secondary, and a tertiary name server to get information from. For disaster recovery purposes it's common to have more than one single DNS server to rely on. Relying on a single DNS server means all your eggs are in one basket, and if an egg cracks, you are out of name resolution! As you can see from this simple example, it's common to have multiple DNS server settings to rely on.

> **NOTE**
>
> Although I have manually changed these settings, I have also left the check box checked to Update Name Servers and Search List via DHCP solely because that's how it's configured currently in a SOHO. You would want to remove this setting if you were manually adding your servers and did not want it overwritten by a DHCP server configuration.

The domain search list is the list of domain names where hostname searching begins— and hopefully ends with the proper name resolution applied to the client. You can add multiple names in the search list, although it's commonly seen, and used, with only one domain name. That's it! Make sure that you click the Finish button at the bottom of the Host Name and Name Server Configuration window. When you finish, you will be able to use those settings when attempting to resolve names on the Internet, such as www.novell.com.

## Hosts File

Multiple files on your SUSE Linux system will allow you to modify DNS information. To work with the hosts file, which we have already discussed and worked with in the /etc directory, we will look at how to use YaST to make those same changes. As you saw earlier, open YaST and navigate to the Network Services menu in the YaST Control Center. Then select Host Names. A dialog box opens as shown in Figure 27.8.

In this section you can change the hosts file from YaST, whereas we saw it edited in the vi editor before. You can do either, whichever is easier for you, depending on which tool you feel the most comfortable using to make your edits. If you are new to Linux, you should attempt to learn both, although the YaST way is easier than the vi editor at the shell prompt.

**FIGURE 27.8**   Viewing the Host Configuration.

# Basic DNS Tools

To test your new DNS configuration, you can either attempt to access the Internet, or if you want to be a little more technical, you can use tools such as nslookup or dig. In this section of the chapter, you'll take a look at both tools.

The dig tool has been around for a long time on Unix systems and serves a very important function. The dig tool stands for Domain Internet Groper. dig is a Unix-based program that allows users to learn information from a DNS site by querying it. You can see from Figure 27.9 that dig has, in fact, found quite a bit of information on www.novell.com.

> **NOTE**
>
> In Figure 27.9, the default gateway address has been blackened out to protect the identity of the system. You will not see a black bar on your screen as you do here.

You can also use nslookup, a tool that you may be familiar with when using Microsoft Windows products, such as Windows XP. SUSE Linux also uses the nslookup command as follows:

```
linux:~ # nslookup
> www.novell.com
Server:        167.2.1.1
Address:       167.2.1.1#53
```

27

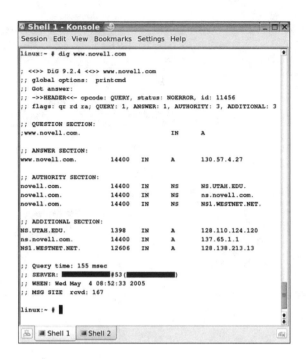

**FIGURE 27.9**    Using dig.

The nonauthoritative answer follows:

```
Name:   www.novell.com
Address: 130.57.4.27
```

The next step is to use the set command, which will show you all of your DNS server assignments. By typing **set all**, you can see your primary, secondary, and other DNS servers, as well as other settings changes you can make with this command:

```
> set all
Default server: 167.2.1.1
Address: 167.2.1.1#53
Default server: 167.2.1.2
Address: 167.2.1.2#53

Set Options
  novc                 nodebug            nod2
  search               recurse
  timeout = 0          retry = 2          port = 53
  querytype = A        class = IN
  srchlist = rsnetworks.net
> exit
```

You can type **exit** and select a carriage return to quit. This will bring you back to the Linux prompt so you can work again at the shell prompt. These tools will help you to verify and test your DNS service, either locally or against a DNS server.

Now that you understand some of the fundamentals of the DNS and have learned how to configure it on a client and test it, it's time to delve into the real power of SUSE Linux and turn it into a DNS server.

## Configuring Name Servers with BIND

Before we dig (pun intended) deeper into how to configure DNS as a server-based service on your SUSE Linux system, a word on the service itself—BIND.

BIND stands for Berkeley Internet Name Domain or Daemon. BIND is software developed by the University of California at Berkeley, as the name implies. BIND is a full service DNS solution that allows clients to get name resolution information as requested. Although an entire book can be dedicated to Unix- and Linux-based DNS, for purposes of this chapter, we will not get too involved with BIND's history and current status. In this section we will cover the basics. If you want more information, the following URLs explain DNS, BIND, and how to configure BIND to the smallest detail:

- http://www.tldp.org/HOWTO/DNS-HOWTO.html#toc1

- http://www.isc.org/index.pl?/sw/bind/

BIND is one of the most used and commonly seen forms of DNS on the Internet today. In fact, most service providers use only BIND because of their lack of trust and the proprietary nature of the Windows-based DNS server products.

Now that you are familiar with BIND, let's look at how to configure your system with it. Up until now you have worked with SUSE Linux as a client of DNS. Next, you will make SUSE Linux function as the server that the clients query to get their DNS resolution information. Let's look at how this is done.

First, you need to verify that DNS is installed on your SUSE Linux system. To verify, open up YaST. On the left pane of the YaST Control Center, select Software. Then select Install and Remove Software. In Figure 27.10, you can see under the Network Services section that BIND is either installed, or it is not. Here, for this example, it has already been installed.

After DNS is installed, open YaST if it is not already opened; select the DNS Server icon that will allow you to configure DNS settings on your SUSE Linux system.

Next, you need to configure DNS. To configure DNS manually you can use YaST to install the base system and then configure it as well. To get to the DNS configuration pages, open YaST and navigate to the Network Services menu in the YaST Control Center.

You can use the DNS Server section of YaST to configure a DNS server for your local network. When you start the module for the first time, a wizard will prompt you about making changes on your forwarder. A forwarder is used to send your request to the next server that will be able to answer the request and then cache it on the forwarding server, which will most likely be "Internet facing" and have a publicly assigned IP address.

**FIGURE 27.10**    Using YaST to install DNS.

Next, consider the following. Because you've set up the client, you are now setting up the server. If you remember from previous examples, the DNS server, if not a root server, will still need to get its information from a public Internet-based DNS server. The server you are creating now with your SUSE Linux system is a local DNS server that will be used in your local environment (or network), and it will have to query another DNS server for its name resolution information because it is not a public Internet-based DNS server. You can, in fact, set it up as an Internet-based DNS server, but because doing so is outside the scope of this book, this chapter will not be able to cover all those details in depth. There are many more steps to configuring a DNS solution, and there are many ways you can set it up, allowing you to meet just about any name resolution scenario placed before you.

To set your SUSE Linux system as a Local DNS server, you can bypass the forwarder configuration by clicking Next. You do not have to set a forwarder. Remember, a forwarder is nothing more than setting your local DNS server as a nonroot DNS server that will query a root server if it does not know the answer to a query. When you starting the module for the first time, see the dialog box shown in Figure 27.11, DNS Server Installation—Forwarder Settings.

Click Next to enter the other DNS server configuration settings areas, such as where you will build new A records.

**FIGURE 27.11**     Changing the forwarder setting.

After you have clicked Next, you will be shown the DNS Zone section where you can add a new zone. A default of example.com is shown in Figure 27.12.

**FIGURE 27.12**     Viewing DNS Zone information.

This particular dialog box consists of several parts and is responsible for managing of zone files, adding new zones, or removing a zone. To add a zone, add or change the current zone name of example.com. The type of zone will be the master because it's the first zone you are making. After you make more zones, you will be given an option to make a slave domain. A slave is a DNS server that will get its main information from the master server. Read and writes can be done on the master; the slave is read-only and gets its configuration information from the master.

To add a reverse zone you have to know to add the extension to your zone, such as 10.1.1.in-addr.arpa. The name must end in .in-addr.arpa and you will need to add this manually. Select Edit Zone to configure other settings of an existing zone. To remove a zone, you can select Delete Zone. If you decide to edit a zone, you can select Edit Zone.

Inside the zone, you can change many settings, such as adding records. To add a simple A record so you can have basic name resolution, click the Records tab and add a new resource record. (Resource records were covered earlier in the chapter; now you can add one manually.) To add a record, add the hostname (without the domain name) to the Record Key. The Type is an A record (the Domain Name Translation). The Value is the IP address you want to use. By clicking Add, you will have successfully added your first resource record beyond what may have been made during the installation, such as the SOA record, or Start of Authority, which is a record that will indicate the start point or point of originating authority for information stored in the zone just created. The SOA resource record is the first record created when adding a new zone. This is a great example of a record that is made for you (see Figure 27.13).

**FIGURE 27.13**   Using the Zone Editor.

Now that you understand how to add records and adjust the zone file database, click Back to go back to the original DNS Zones configuration page. You can also click OK to finish, but you are not quite finished with your configurations.

Clicking Next from the DNS Zones dialog box will bring you to the Finish Wizard. The reason why you didn't want to bypass this screen by clicking OK is that you want to modify the DNS server startup options and behavior. For instance, do you want the server started now, or when you boot up? Or do you want to set it for manual start? Either way, you can adjust these settings in the DNS Server Installation Finish Wizard. When you're done, click Finish to run your new DNS server. You can also click Expert Options to get more options to choose from, including a section where you can adjust your logging settings, which is covered next.

# Logging

Now that you have your DNS Server installed, you will want to set up logging so you can help find problems and aid your troubleshooting process if needed. It's recommended to turn on logging only as needed, but as long as you are checking often and saving old log files, checking them and analyzing them for issues or problems, you can leave it on.

There are many things you can log, as shown in Figure 27.14, and there are multiple options you can choose from.

**FIGURE 27.14**   Viewing SUSE log settings.

To specify the location where the logging data is stored, look under Log Type in the DNS Server Logging dialog box. By clicking the Browse button, you can select a new location to store the file. It's recommended that you click Browse anyway and make a new directory called DNSLOG, for example, so that you can save all your files in one location. As a handy side note, from the example shown here, I have named the file in a way that dates it, because if you save files, you will need a way to recall what files have what information in them. You'll also need to know when they were created so that you have a way to track back to a specific time or date. Either way, make sure you have a system in place that allows you to organize your data so that it's easy to retrieve.

If you choose Log to a System Log, you can now log to the system log, which is stored in /var/log/messages. Also, make sure you set the log correctly, including its size, which should be set to about 5–10MBs, depending on how much information you want to store based on your logging selections. Zone transfers are the only entries to be logged, and they are being logged to an independent file named DNS052005, which stands for DNS log, 05 (month of May), and the year 2005. You can use any example that comes to mind, or use this one if it works for you and your business or personal needs.

## Summary

Remember that DNS is nothing more than a naming system and protocol used not only by companies worldwide in their internal networks, but also for the publicly accessible Internet. DNS is used to add a human quality to finding data on the network—www.novell.com or 130.57.4.27—as mentioned earlier. However, www.novell.com is much easier to remember than a set of numbers. You can move Domain Names around easily, but IP addresses are not so portable.

There is much to know about DNS; like SUSE Linux, you can set up the system as a DNS client or a DNS server. YaST will help you configure both.

## References

- http://www.tldp.org/HOWTO/DNS-HOWTO.html#toc1—The Linux Documentation Project. This is an in-depth DNS HOWTO with DNS general information as well.

- http://www.isc.org/index.pl?/sw/bind/—Internet Systems Consortium, Inc. (ISC) is a nonprofit public benefit corporation dedicated to supporting the infrastructure of the universal connected self-organizing Internet. This is an in-depth DNS/BIND HOWTO with DNS/BIND general information as well.

- http://www.arin.net—American Registry for Internet Numbers. A nonprofit registry responsible for the administration and registration of Internet Protocol (IP) numbers in North and South America, South Africa, the Caribbean, and all other regions administered currently managed by Network Solutions, Inc.

- http://www.isc.org/bind.html—Berkeley Internet Name Domain information direct. BIND software, developed by the University of California at Berkeley, implements a DNS server and a resolver library that enables clients to store and retrieve resources or objects and share this information with other resources on the network. This link covers BIND in detail.

- http://www.iana.org/—Internet Assigned Numbers Authority. IANA is a government-funded authority that assigns and distributes international domain names and IP numbers or Internet addresses and oversees the Internet software protocols of the officially sanctioned root servers.

- http://www.internic.net/—A registry responsible for name assignment within the following TLDs: COM, EDU, NET, GOV, and ORG.

# PART VI

# Programming

## IN THIS PART

# Using the GNU Compiler Collection and Other Programming Tools

Although GNU/Linux is many things, it has been and always will be a programmer's plaything. The GNU Project began with a C compiler and a text editor. Linux began as a porting project. Although the intertwined projects have grown considerably beyond their hobbyist roots, they will never completely outgrow them.

In this and the next few chapters, you'll learn about the tools SUSE Linux provides both the beginning programmer and the most seasoned software engineer. From simple compilers to full-blown integrated development environments (IDEs), Linux can help you program in dozens of languages and in an environment best suited to your style.

Open-source development isn't always a solitary task, however. Concurrent Versions System (CVS) and Subversion each make it easier to collaborate with others. And after you've created a quality program, you may want to make it readily available and easy to install for the public at large. For that, there are several solutions, most notably the Red Hat Package Manager (RPM).

This chapter focuses on some of the tools available for programming in C, C++, and Java. You'll also learn about a trio of Linux IDEs: Eclipse, KDevelop, and Anjuta. You'll see how CVS and Subversion can be used to manage your source code and collaborate with other programmers. Finally, you'll learn how you can use RPM to disseminate your final product.

This is not a book on how to program complex software programs, and novices should not expect to learn more than the barest rudiments here. Learning programming is a worthwhile, if challenging, pursuit. It is also one of the best ways to "give back" to the Linux community for all the wonderful applications you're using with your copy of SUSE Linux. If you are intrigued by what you read in this and in the coming chapters, there are more than a few good books on the subject, some of which will be highlighted here.

# Basic Programming in C Under Linux

Unix and the C programming language have been partners from the very beginning. The vast majority of Unix and Linux code (including the Linux kernel) is written in C, and that tradition continues. C is a platform-neutral language; the code is not dependent on any particular system architecture.

C is a compiled language, so you won't need any other special programs to run your applications aside from the editor and compiler you use to write it. Interpreted languages, such as Perl and Python, need a separate program known as an *interpreter* to run.

You first enter your C program's statements (called *source code*) into a text file. This code is then fed to a *compiler* that translates the source code you've written into a binary file—the ones and zeros that the machine can read. Often, a *linker* is used to connect the program with other system libraries or with other programs.

As you saw in Chapter 5, "Getting Started with SUSE Linux," SUSE Linux offers a variety of text editors. Most contain special features for programming in assorted languages, such as highlighting commands in different colors and checking for mismatched parentheses and brackets. Programmers will also find the following essential tools in SUSE Linux:

- The GNU Compiler Collection, which will compile and link programs written in seven programming languages.

- The GNU Debugger (gdb), which identifies and helps you troubleshoot problematic code.

- The Make utility, which pulls multiple source-code files into a single working package.

- Autoconf, which allows a programmer to create customized compiling and installation configurations for a program's source code.

> **NOTE**
>
> These programming tools are not installed by default when you install SUSE Linux. You can easily get them using YaST, and they must be installed before any of the programs mentioned in this chapter will work on your system.

## A Simple C Program

C program source code files come in two types: *header*, or *include*, files and programs or procedural files. Standard C program files have a *.c extension and contain at least one *function*. Functions are a set of commands a program carries out to accomplish its tasks. Header files have an *.h extension and carry variable descriptions, declarations, and other data common to all source files in the project.

Writing simple programs in C is a six-step process:

1. Open your favorite text editor.

2. Type the source code.

3. Save the file with the appropriate extension (.c for a program or .h for a header file).

4. Repeat steps 2 and 3 as necessary if your application's source code will be broken down into multiple files.

5. Compile the program with GCC.

6. Run the program and then debug any problems.

Since time immemorial, the first program taught to students of a new language is called "Hello World" and consists of printing those two words on your screen. It's a short program, but its aim is to demonstrate the basic syntax of the language. We will follow the steps listed previously to write a "Hello World" program in C.

Open your favorite text editor and write the following source code text, exactly as you see it. Press Enter to insert a new line after the final brace.

```
#include <stdio.h>
int main(int argc, char* argv[]){
    printf("Hello, World.\n");
    return 0;
}
```

Details vary from editor to editor, but chances are good that your braces are highlighted in color, as is the quoted phrase. Now save this file as a plain text document named hello.c to a source directory, either in Home (/~/source) or in Documents (/~/Documents/source).

## Using the GNU Compiler Collection

The GNU C Compiler (GCC), first written by Richard Stallman in 1987, has grown over time to support six other languages: Ada, C++, Fortran, Java, Objective-C, and Objective-C++. This is why the official name changed to the GNU Compiler Collection. Version 4.0 came out in April 2005.

Open a shell, change to the directory you saved your program to, and compile your program:

```
gcc -o hello hello.c
```

28

> **TIP**
>
> Your editor may have a direct link or command to run the compiler, so you can test your program without leaving the editor. Consult the editor's documentation.

> **TIP**
>
> The GCC determines which compiler to use based on the file extension of your source code. Table 28.1 shows common extensions for the supported languages. You can override this behavior by using the -x option (see man 1 gcc for more information).

**TABLE 28.1**    GCC Expected File Extensions for Source Codes

| Language | Extension |
| --- | --- |
| Ada | Source: .ads, .adb |
| C | Source: .c |
| | Header: .h |
| C++ | Source: .C, .cc, .cp, .CPP, .cpp, .c++, .cxx |
| | Header: .H, .hh |
| Fortran | Source: .F, .FPP, .fpp, .r |
| Objective-C | Source: .m |
| | Header: .h |
| Objective-C++ | Source: .M |
| | Header: .h |

The compiler creates an executable program called `hello` from the source file, `hello.c`. Heed any warnings you may get from the compiler. If you get any, you've mistyped something or forgot to press Enter (new line) at the end of the code. If necessary, compile again until you get a fresh prompt with no feedback. GCC delivers only bad news; if things work, it just does its thing.

If you look in the directory you will see a new file called `hello` with no extension. Now you can run the program:

```
./hello
Hello, World.
```

What did you do? You saved the source code with a .c extension to note what language this code is written in. The compiler created the executable `hello` (the name specified by the –o option), and then you executed the program. Because the program is not located in one of the standard executable directories, `usr/bin` or `/usr/local/bin`, you must use the dot-slash "execute" command in the directory where the program is located.

Additional GCC language front ends exist for Pascal, Modula-2, Modula-3, Mercury, VHDL, and PL/I; these are developed by teams separate from the GCC team and are not available via YaST. The Objective-C++ component is also missing from SUSE. You can access these languages at http://gcc.gnu.org/frontends.html.

# Building Java Applications with Eclipse

IBM has been a big backer of the Java language since its birth in the mid-1990s, and possibly even a bigger backer of Linux and open-source software since the turn of the twenty-first century. It isn't a big surprise that as a result, the IBM-sponsored Eclipse Java development platform is open source and works well in Linux.

Eclipse began as, and basically still is, an environment for building applications in the Java language. Because it is endlessly extensible with plug-ins, much more can be done with it. Developers regularly use it to program in Python, PHP, and other languages.

The Eclipse package that you install with SUSE Linux contains these core features: the Eclipse Java Development Tool (JDT), the Plug-In Development Environment (PDE), and the Eclipse Software Development Kit (SDK). SUSE Linux also includes the Ant build application, the JDI debugger, the JUnit testing framework, and a refactoring tool. Other plug-ins are installable through the Eclipse Update Manager, a YaST-like tool that checks for new software versions and installs them.

> **TIP**
>
> Using the Eclipse Update Manager with SUSE Linux can be troublesome at first, but it is not exceptionally difficult to fix.
>
> When YaST installs Eclipse, all the files and directories are owned by Root and the group Root. The average user has access only by default, but the Eclipse Update Manager needs write access to create and update files in the /usr/share/eclipse directory.
>
> You solve this problem by logging in as the SuperUser and creating a new system user called **eclipse**, and a group of the same name, with the new user as its only member.
>
> Finally, because Root owns this directory and its branches, you need to adjust the permissions for /usr/share/eclipse. Go to this directory and type: **chgrp -R eclipse \***. This makes the eclipse group responsible for the directory and all its subdirectories. Now you can use chmod to allow this group to read and write files in the same directories: chmod -R 661 \*. You should now be able to run Update Manager without any trouble.

**28**

## Using the Eclipse Workbench

The first time you run Eclipse, you'll get a Welcome screen. Feel free to walk through the tutorials and examples offered there, and when you're done, click Workbench to get started.

> **TIP**
>
> Eclipse uses the Mozilla browser to deliver its online help, including the Welcome to Eclipse tutorials. If you don't have Mozilla installed, or if you prefer a different browser, go to Preferences in the Window menu in the Eclipse Workbench. Under Help, choose Custom Browser and identify your preferred application.

In Figure 28.1, you can see a sample "Hello World" program written in Java in the Eclipse Workbench. We'll go into the program in more detail later, but the Workbench gives you quite a lot at your fingertips.

In the upper-left corner is the Package Explorer, which lets you move around and open files in your project editor. The editor is in the center. You can have any number of files open in the editor at any given moment, but only one active at a time. You'll see any others in a tab in this area. In the upper-right corner is the Outliner, which shows each element in the active program. Clicking any item in the Outliner highlights that element in the editor.

Across the bottom, Eclipse watches for problems in your code and flags them for you. If your program displays some text on your shell (also known as the console), it will display a Console tab as well.

**FIGURE 28.1**    The Eclipse Workbench puts many tools at your fingertips.

## Creating a Small Java Application in Eclipse

Perspectives are a set of related views and windows that help complete the task at hand. Each Perspective is tailored to a specific task. By default, Eclipse displays the Resource Perspective, with which you can start creating any sort of project. The Java Perspective was shown earlier in Figure 28.1.

You can change Perspectives by going to the Window menu and selecting Open Perspective. The default list of choices changes depending on the Perspective you're starting from, but you can always display the entire list of Perspectives with the Other option.

For our "Hello World" example, begin by selecting the Java Perspective. Eclipse will respond by moving the default windows around a little bit to set up the Java Perspective layout. You can further customize this view by maximizing windows, adding others, and closing some (if you find a particular setup useful, you can save a custom Perspective as well from Window, Save Perspective As).

You will need a new project to store your code in. Go to File, New, Project (or use the New Project toolbar button), and a wizard appears. Create a new Java Project, and name it **Hello World** (spaces are permitted in project names). You can further specify build settings, but that's for projects more complex than this one and the defaults will suit us fine.

Now your program (actually a Java class) can be created. Go to File, New, Class to launch the Class Wizard. Name it **HelloWorld**, this time with no space. You should also define a package, because the use of the default package is discouraged (a package puts the class in a folder with related classes). The convention for the Eclipse Platform is to use **org.eclipse** as the default; for this one, use **org.eclipse.hello**. Check the box to create a void main method stub, and then click Finish. You'll see the result, HelloWorld.java, in the Java editor window.

The Main() function needs something to do. In the Outliner, click main(string[]). You'll see main highlighted in the editor. Go to the end of the line (with the left brace) and press Enter. Type **System.out.println("Hello World!");**. Your code should resemble the following:

```
package org.eclipse.hello;

public class HelloWorld {
    public static void main(String[] args) {
        System.out.println("Hello World!");
    }
}
```

When you've finished entering your code, go ahead and save your work either with File, Save or the Ctrl+S key combination.

Now it's time to run the program. Make sure HelloWorld.java is selected in the Package Explorer window on the left. Go to Run, Run As, Java Application. If all has gone well, you should see the Console window open on the bottom, as shown in Figure 28.1, displaying Hello World. If you have any problems, you can use the Debug view to help you sort it out.

Eclipse offers you an easy way to export your project when it's time to finally release it. To export our new Hello World application as a JAR file, make sure the Hello World project's root is selected in the Package Explorer pane and select File, Export. The Export Wizard will appear.

The first step of the wizard will prompt your for the type of export; select JAR file and click Next. Continue through the steps, ensuring that you set the export destination for your archive, and specify the main entry class. Eclipse will package your application and you can share it now with whomever you please.

## Using the KDevelop Integrated Development Environment

KDevelop began as an IDE to rapidly produce C++ code for use in KDE projects. Since its inception it has grown to support 13 compiled and scripting languages. It is not part of the standard SUSE Linux installation, but you can install the necessary packages in YaST.

KDevelop automates many of the tasks needed to create new programs. In fact, you won't even need to write anything yourself to produce a "Hello World" program in several languages! You will, however, get a sense of how such a program is built in the real-world KDE environment. Let's walk through the process of creating quality, free GUI software for KDE.

Begin by opening KDevelop; it's located in the KDE menu under Development, Integrated Environment. A clean screen appears. Go to the Project menu and select New Project. A wizard appears. You'll see the array of available languages and default projects. Open the C++ tree and then the KDE branch. Scroll down to Simple KDE Application. When you select this option, a screenshot and description will display in the right panel, as shown in Figure 28.2.

**FIGURE 28.2**    Select a project and name it in the first KDevelop New Project Wizard screen.

Name the project **KHello**. Note that the Final Location line will revise itself. If you don't already have a source directory in your home directory, use the Browse button to create one. Click Next to continue.

The second screen sets general information about you, the developer, and defines the license this program will carry. By default, KDevelop selects the GPL, but you can use the drop-down menu (as shown in Figure 28.3) to choose another license if you like.

**FIGURE 28.3** Choose from a variety of open-source licenses.

KDevelop pulls your name and email address from your KDE settings, but these fields are completely editable. It is a very good idea to include a valid email address, if not necessarily your primary one, with your free software, so users can contact you with bug reports and the like. Click Next to continue.

The third and fourth screens set up your header file and your program template. Both include the standard GPL announcement, regardless of what license you selected in the previous screen. You may want to edit or delete this if you are using a different license (you may also add other text to your header file or CPP file in these templates). When you are finished editing the templates, click Finish to create HelloWorld.cpp.

KDevelop displays its code in what it calls the IDEAl user interface (see Figure 28.4). You can adjust this in the Settings if it's not to your liking.

If you use Execute Program from the Build menu, KDevelop will ask to run Automake and Configure first. This is good practice. KDevelop will do that and then run the application.

28

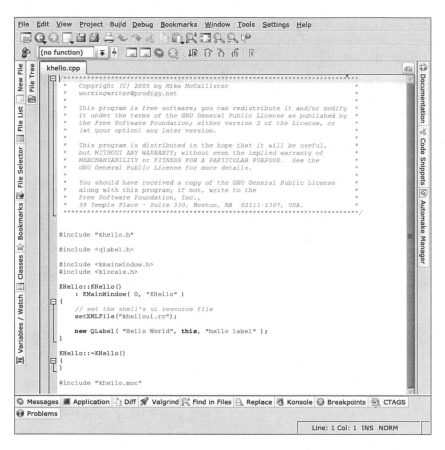

**FIGURE 28.4**    KDevelop generates a complete "Hello World" KDE program in C++ and displays it in this window.

After the program runs, click the File Selector tab on the left side of the KDevelop window. These files were all created by the wizard and are standard pieces of Linux applications. Click any file and it will open in the editor. In your real programs, be nice to your users. Modify the INSTALL file if users need to do something unusual to get your program working. Include README information and NEWS on this version's progress. If you have specific plans for the program, by all means share those plans in the TODO file.

## Using Anjuta to Create GNOME Applications

Anjuta is a relatively new tool to help create GTK+ and GNOME applications with C and C++. It works with the Glade-2 GUI generator for GTK/GNOME and other packages to create nice-looking GNOME applications. As we saw with KDevelop, writing a Hello World application here won't require us to write any code. We'll get a sense though of how an application can be written in Anjuta.

You can install Anjuta with YaST, but the package dependency information is incomplete, so it does not install all the packages it needs. To be safe, try installing the `-devel` packages in the YaST Development libraries. Under Install and Remove Software, click the Package Groups display from the drop-down menu at the top. Go to Development, Libraries, GNOME. Many packages there will be called `<PackageName>-devel`. These packages contain all the necessary files to create (that is, develop) new programs.

When you open Anjuta, you have the choice of creating a new project, importing an existing project, or opening an existing Anjuta project or file. Click the Application Wizard button to begin a new project, and the screen shown in Figure 28.5 appears.

**FIGURE 28.5**    Select a new project type in the first screen.

In the second screen (see Figure 28.6), you select the name of the project and the language to be used. Project names are one word and are duplicated in the Project Target box.

The third screen asks you to describe your project. You can be pretty long-winded if you choose. In the final settings screen (see Figure 28.7), you set up where to put your program in the GNOME menu, as well as several other items. Enabling `gettext` support allows you to internationalize your application with other human languages. You may also specify an icon for your application if you want it to appear in the GNOME Application menu.

Confirm the settings you want the project to have and apply them to generate Yet Another Hello World program. Anjuta now runs its own Autogen program, which generates a `configure` file based on the wizard settings (see Figure 28.8).

28

**FIGURE 28.6**    In Anjuta, project names are one word, and you can code in both C and C++.

**FIGURE 28.7**    Make final adjustments and choose an icon in the project settings here.

After Anjuta has generated the source code and a configure script, you must compile and build the application before you can run it. Go to the Build menu and select Compile. You should not get any errors. Then go back to the Build menu and select Build All. After the application has been compiled and built, from the same menu, select Execute. You should see a terminal pop open with "Hello World!" and instructions on how to close the window.

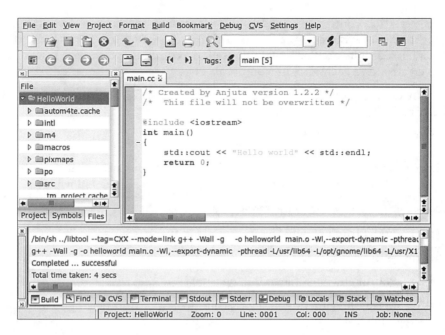

**FIGURE 28.8**   When Anjuta generates source code, you still must compile, build, and execute the code.

## Managing Collective Software Development with CVS and Subversion

The original revision control system (rcs) utility has features to manage small application projects, but when an application grows larger or is maintained by several developers, a better tool is needed. The Concurrent Versions System (CVS) arose to manage a corps of far-flung open-source developers and files that can potentially change on a minute-by-minute basis.

CVS controls the source code by storing it exclusively in one place, called a *repository*, and setting rules for access to the files. A CVS repository from the client perspective is like an FTP site or other remote access directory. It contains all the files in a particular development project. The difference between CVS and FTP is that a CVS repository is like a library, and FTP is like a bookstore. To work on a file or set of files, you must check them out of the repository and check your changes back in (or *commit* your changes, in the CVS vernacular). The administrators of the repository can decide whether more than one person can check out a file at a time, how to process multiple changes, when to build the new version of the application, and what files will be included.

With CVS, you can get a complete record of changes in files without having multiple copies taking up space on your hard drive or server volume. Source files can be compared against the list of changes between versions, and any version can be reconstructed for review. Because any version can be reconstructed at any time, bugs can be tracked more easily and better test cases can be developed.

28

Incidentally, version control isn't good only for software projects. Any electronic file that undergoes frequent revisions or that is grouped with other files in a larger entity (for example, a book and its chapters) might do well to exist in a repository. It is reasonably simple to create a CVS repository on your local drive.

Create a base directory for all your CVS projects, such as ~/**cvsroot**. Then point CVS to that directory:

```
cvs -d ~/cvsroot
```

You can now add files and directories (projects) to cvsroot, which can, in turn, be versioned over time using CVS. The six key CVS commands are the following:

- add—Commit a new file to the repository.
- import—Add a batch of new files or projects to the repository.
- checkout—Get a file to edit.
- commit—Return an edited file to the repository.
- remove—Make files currently in the repository disappear (other copies may exist elsewhere, however).
- update—In a local repository, confirm that everything is current. In a remote repository, get the latest changes in your working directory.

CVS isn't perfect, however, and in 2001 some CVS developers moved to another project, Subversion, which they hoped would solve some of CVS's nagging problems. This project, designed to eventually replace CVS as the open-source project management tool of choice, released version 1.0 in 2004 and has won many converts.

Both CVS and Subversion work in substantially the same way. Subversion adds several new features, including the capability to track versions of directories, a binary differencing algorithm, and more efficient branching and tagging of new versions of files.

Both CVS and Subversion are command-line applications, but Cervisia provides a GUI front-end to CVS and Subversion for KDE users. It can be used either as a standalone application or integrated into a Konqueror window. Cervisia allows you to connect to your repository and update and work directly with it. Eclipse also has a CVS plug-in that works the same way.

## Creating RPM Packages

You have created this wonderful piece of software that you want to share with the rest of the Linux world. Because you are a kind and considerate programmer, you want to make it easy for nonprogrammers to install and run it on their systems. The best way to do this, especially on a SUSE Linux system, is to build an installation package with RPM.

You learned the basics of the RPM system in Chapter 21, "Keeping Your System Current: Package Management." That section looked at RPM from the user's standpoint: the standard way of installing software on SUSE Linux. In this section, you'll get a brief introduction to how to create RPM packages from your source code. You'll find a more detailed approach, with everything you need to know, by reading Ed Bailey's *Maximum RPM* at http://www.rpm.org/max-rpm.

You can make an RPM package out of any program for which you have working source code. This means you can use programs you have created, but also any other open source program you think needs an RPM. Helping to package new RPMs for a project is an easy, excellent way to contribute to the open-source community. The process is quite simple:

1. Obtain the source code for the application.

2. Build the program source.

3. If necessary, make a patch including any changes required to build the code successfully if the original would not build on your system.

4. Ensure that the necessary RPM-specific directories exist somewhere on your system: BUILD, SOURCES, SPECS, RPMS, and SRPMS.

5. Create a spec file for your package.

6. Build the RPM package.

7. Test the package.

As a sample project, let's make an RPM for the "Hello World" application you wrote using KDevelop.

## Making a Spec File

Because you already have a working KHello program compiled from source, the first three steps in the process are complete. The key step is creating the spec file that tells the rpm application how to install KHello on someone's system. The spec file can be created using any text editor.

There are eight sections in an RPM spec file: a header, a prep section, a build instruction section, an installation section, file cleanup, pre- and post-installation and optional uninstallation scripts, a list of files in the package, and a changelog.

The header section gives a basic description of the package and has a number of elements. Following is our header section for KHello:

```
Summary: "Hello World" for KDE
Name: khello
Version: 0.1
Release: 1
Copyright: GPL
Group: Applications/Games
```

```
Source: /home/mikemc/source/KHello/KHello.tgz
Distribution: SuSE Linux

%description
KHello prints the words "Hello World" in a KDE window.
```

The summary element is a one-line description of our RPM package. The application's name and version are identified using name and version, respectively. A release number is used to identify sequential bug fixes if the extent of the recoding doesn't warrant a version increase. The program's licensing can be specified with copyright. The group element is used to identify which section under the K menu a shortcut icon will be placed.

The source element should point to a pristine copy of our source code (without any patches applied). More than one file can be specified by using source0, source1, source2, and so on. If you did need to apply a patch, those should be listed in the same manner as the source code using the Patch element.

The %description allows us to insert a complete description of what our application does; it can take up more than one line if necessary.

With our header section complete, we can now turn our attention to the prep session. The prep session consists of an sh script to prepare the working directory and source code. We can also use predefined RPM macros to perform common tasks. All we'll need to have in our prep section is a reference to RPM's %setup macro:

```
%prep
%setup
```

If you had a patch file, you would also want to reference the %patch macro on a separate line after %setup.

The Build section is relatively straightforward. You should put any commands here that you would need to use to build the software after you had untarred the source, patched it, and cd'ed into the directory. This is just another set of commands passed to sh, so any legal sh commands can go here (including comments).

Your current working directory is reset in each of these sections to the top level of the source directory, so keep that in mind. You can cd into subdirectories if necessary.

```
%build
make
```

The Install section works much the same way as Build. Ideally, you can run make install, but if the Makefile doesn't provide the capability to automatically install an application, it will be necessary to write the sh script to accomplish this here.

```
%install
Make install
```

The Cleanup section is used mostly for testing purposes. Use the `%clean` macro to remove any leftover files from the `BuildRoot` directory before running a second time.

You can run pre- or post-installation scripts by using the `%pre` or `%post` macros in this section. Similarly, you can run scripts before or after an uninstallation using `%preun` or `%postun`.

All the files included in your package must be listed in the Files section. You will generate a file list in your first test build, which you can then copy to this section. There are also some macros to help with this listing, which you can find at http://www.rpm.org/ RPM-HOWTO/build.html.

The last section of the spec file is a changelog, listing new features and fixes in this version. Each entry begins with a standard string:

```
*date +"%a %b %d %Y" <YourName> <YourEmailAddress>
```

A subsequent line begins with a – and lists the changes. For our example, because you're just at the first version, type something like **First version**. You can enter anything, but the changelog should be as informative as possible.

```
%changelog
*Fri Sep 30 2005 mikemc mikemc@susefan.com
- Created first version.
```

Save this file in the KHello directory, and you're just about ready to go.

## Listing Files and Generating Patches

The contents of `%files` are critical because if a file is not listed, it will not be included in the final RPM package. One way to generate a good file list for your spec file is to get the source to build cleanly without using RPM. To do this, unpack the sources and preserve the directory by changing its name to `KHello.orig`. Then unpack the source again so you have two directories. Go into the KHello source directory and build it.

If you had to edit any code, you'll need a patch. After you get things to build, clean out the source directory from any files that were made from the `configure` script. Then `cd` back out of the source directory to its parent. Use the diff utility to create a patch file:

```
diff -uNr KHello.orig KHello > KHello-bugfix.patch
```

This will create a patch for you that you can use in your spec file. Note that the `buxfix` that you see in the patch name is just an identifier. You might want to use something more descriptive as to *why* you had to make a patch. It's also a good idea to look at the patch file you are creating before using it to make sure no binaries were included by accident. Afterward, copy the file list generated by the build into your spec file.

## Building and Testing Your RPM Package

Now that you have a useful spec file, it's time to copy your files to their proper place in the RPM directories created earlier and build your RPM. The original sources and patches should be copied to the SOURCES directory and the spec file is copied to the SPEC directory.

Build the RPM by entering into the SPEC directory and issuing this command:

```
rpm -ba khello.spec
```

The command will build both a binary RPM and a source RPM. If you want only a binary package built, use the `-bb` argument instead, or use `-bs` if you want only a source package.

RPM will use the BUILD directory to compile the application from the source code and patches and then place the finished binary package file in RPMS. The finished source package file will be placed in SRPMS. With some good fortune, you should now be able to change into the RPMS directory and run `rpm -ivh khello.rpm` to install your new package.

If possible, try installing the package on at least one other computer. After you have successfully built your RPM, register at freshmeat.net and announce your new application!

## Other Linux Programming Resources

This very brief introduction to the tools of programming cannot possibly scratch the surface of what you need to know to get started in the field. If you have further interest in programming, here are a few of the better books on bookstore shelves:

- *Sams Teach Yourself C++ in 21 Days*, by Bradley Jones and Jesse Liberty
- *The C++ Programming Language*, by Bjarne Stroustrup
- *Sams Teach Yourself C in 21 Days*, by Bradley Jones and Peter Aitken
- *The C Programming Language*, by Brian W. Kernighan and Dennis M. Ritchie
- *Sams Teach Yourself Java 2 in 21 Days*, by Rogers Cadenhead and Laura Lemay
- *Eclipse Kick Start*, by Carlos Valcarcel
- *Eclipse in Action*, by David Gallardo, Ed Burnette, and Robert McGovern

## References

- http://gcc.gnu.org—Home of the GNU Compiler Collection.
- http://gcc.gnu.org/frontends.html—Front ends for other languages available for GCC.
- http://www.gnu.org/software/autoconf—The Autoconf configuration utility.
- http://gcc.gnu.org/java—GCC's Java compiler, GCJ.
- http://subversion.tigris.org—The very well-designed Subversion site.

- http://svnbook.red-bean.com/en/1.0—The online book, *Version Control with Subversion.*

- https://www.cvshome.org—The CVS site, secure and also well organized.

- http://www.linux.ie/articles/tutorials/cvs.php—A somewhat cheeky CVS tutorial.

- http://eclipse.org—The hub of the Eclipse community. Everything you need to get going and keep going.

- http://www.eclipseplugincentral.com—The place to find your needed Eclipse plug-ins, with news, too.

- http://www-128.ibm.com/developerworks/java/jdk/eclipse/—The IBM Development Package for Eclipse. Includes the IBM Java Development Kit optimized for Eclipse.

- http://www.kdevelop.org—News, forums, documentation, and a real-time chart indicating the number of downloads per hour of this IDE.

- http://anjuta.sourceforge.net—The GNOME/GTK+ IDE.

- http://www.digitalfanatics.org/projects/qt_tutorial—Tutorial for C++ developers to learn Qt.

- http://doc.trolltech.com/3.3—The official reference documentation for the current version of Qt.

- http://www.rpm.org—Home for information on the Red Hat Package Management system. The site includes an online version of Ed Bailey's 2000 book, *Maximum RPM.*

- http://www.rpm.org/RPM-HOWTO—An excellent guide to creating an RPM.

28

# Managing Databases

In this chapter, we look at database creation and client access with SUSE Linux. Databases can be considered digital phonebooks—when there is a need for highly organized storage of a massive amount of information, a database is called for. There are very special requirements associated with databases; therefore, it shouldn't seem strange that it takes special software to create a storage system that is highly organized by items such as fields, records, and tables. Databases (if optimized and running properly) can store massive amounts of data, such as logging information for a web server. The blending of Apache web server software, the PHP scripting language, and the MySQL database engine is basically what fuels most of today's website development. PHP will be covered in Chapter 31, "Creating Dynamic Websites."

This chapter is only an introduction to these two technologies. Entire publications have been dedicated to the topic of building databases, especially with MySQL, one of today's hottest web-based database technologies in use.

Your operating system comes with an open-source database that is very popular with today's web development teams—MySQL. This chapter covers the installation and configuration of MySQL as well as how to access a MySQL database with a client.

## What Is a Relational Database?

A database is a collection of information organized in such a way that a computer program can quickly select desired pieces of data based on a query that you provide. As previously mentioned, databases are the storage sites for the world's data.

Database services are based on a client/server model. In SUSE Linux, you can install components based on that model for both the client and the server portions of the database. You can install a database server by installing MySQL. You can also use various database clients to access the database service running on your system.

By installing the service, you install the software needed to run, operate, and manage database protocols such as SQL. SQL stands for Structured (or Standard) Query Language; it is a standard language for accessing and manipulating databases. SQL defines statements that can be used to retrieve and update data in a database, such as SELECT, UPDATE, DELETE, INSERT, and WHERE.

You can access a MySQL database in various ways—via the command prompt using the mysql command, using specialized client software such as Knoda, or through a web browser.

Before getting too far into this chapter, we need to discuss how databases work. There are two general types of databases: flat-file databases, which are much like your /etc/passwd file, and relational databases, which are much more complex and require much more "structure" to organize them. Flat-file databases are poor performers and are not truly scalable. A flat-file database is the opposite of a relational database, which is hierarchical. Relational databases, on the other hand, are specialized to handle large amounts of data. They are scalable, which means that they grow well, unlike their flat-file counterparts.

Relational databases are organized by fields, records, and tables. In a relational database, a field is a single piece of information. A record is one complete set of fields, and a table is a collection of records. This is essentially what makes up the logical structure of databases.

In a database, each table is identified by a name, such as *Contacts*. Each table contains records, also called rows, that contain the actual database data. For example, suppose we were to define a table called Contacts and create the following three records:

```
Last          First       Address         City          State
Coughanour    David       578 E. 200 N.   Santaquin     Utah
Johnson       Brian       113 N. 1111 E.  Rigby         Idaho
Corry         Jason       57 E. Wrangler  San Antonio   Texas
```

Using the SQL language, you can create queries that return specific data from the database. For example, suppose you were to compose the following query:

```
SELECT Last FROM Contacts
```

The database would return the following data:

```
Last
Coughanour
Johnson
Corry
```

In addition to creating queries, the SQL language also allows you to update, insert, and delete records. This is done using the following commands:

- SELECT—Retrieves information from a table

- UPDATE— Modifies information in a table

- DELETE—Removes information from a table

- INSERT INTO—Adds new data to a table

In addition to manipulating data within a table, SQL commands can also be used to manage the table itself. This is done using the following commands:

- CREATE TABLE—Creates a new table

- ALTER TABLE—Modifies an existing table

- DROP TABLE—Deletes an existing table

A key feature of a relational database is that you can create "relations" between tables, which enables you to create powerful interrelated data sets. A relational database is also known as a relational database management system (or RDBMS). RDBMS is a type of database management system (DBMS), but this one focuses on the relational model just discussed.

When you install the database service with YaST, you can create the system of fields and such where the data will be stored and organized in a way that information can be managed efficiently. If data is managed this way, it is quick to retrieve and easier to manage, mine, and control.

# Implementing MySQL

MySQL is a freely downloadable open-source RDBMS that uses SQL. Before continuing, you need to understand that there are two versions of MySQL:

- MySQL—This is the "standard" version of MySQL that is included with your SUSE Linux distribution.

- MySQL-Max DB—This is the "heavy duty" version of MySQL that is designed for use by large enterprises.

In this section, we're going to focus on MySQL. You'll learn how to install and configure MySQL on your SUSE Linux system.

## Installing MySQL

Most likely (especially if you installed SUSE Linux with a minimal amount of services), you will not have MySQL installed because it's not installed by default. As long as you have the installation CD-ROMs, you can install it quickly and easily using the YaST Software Management module, as shown in Figure 29.1.

29

**FIGURE 29.1**    Using YaST to install MySQL.

To install MySQL on your system, complete the following:

1. Run YaST and navigate to Software, Software Management.

2. In the Search field, enter **mysql**; then select Search.

3. In the Package column, select the following packages, as shown in Figure 29.1:

    - mysql

    - mysql-administrator

    - mysql-client

    - mysql-shared

There are many other MySQL-related packages that you could install. Most of these packages, such as apache2-mod_auth_mysql, are used to enhance the functionality of the MySQL service. You can, optionally, install these packages as well:

1. In the Search field, enter **knoda**; then select Search. The knoda package provides a database client that can be used to access your MySQL server.

2. Mark the knoda package in the right frame.

3. Select Accept.

4. When prompted that the packages are installed, select Finish.

When you are done with your installation, you are highly encouraged to run the YaST online update so that you can patch up your databases with any new tools, security fixes, or patches that may be available. You may also be interested in viewing the www.MySQL.com website for the latest version of the product. You can download the source files in an RPM package and install the latest version if your needs require it.

After installing MySQL, a number of initial configuration tasks must be completed before you begin working with your first database table. We'll look at these tasks next.

## Completing MySQL Initial Configuration Tasks

After installing your MySQL packages, you need to do the following:

- Initialize the grant tables.

- Start the MySQL server.

- Secure the MySQL user accounts.

Let's discuss how to do each of these.

### Initializing the Grant Tables

One of the first tasks you need to complete is to set up your MySQL server's grant tables. To understand the grant tables, you must first understand that MySQL access controls, including user accounts and permissions, are managed from within the MySQL service itself. This is done using five tables within the MySQL database:

- user—This table is used to specify whether a specific user is allowed to connect to the MySQL server.

- db—This table is used to define which databases a user is allowed to access.

- host—This table is used to define which hosts are allowed to access a given database.

- tables_priv—This table is used to define access privileges for a given table.

- columns_priv—This table is used to define access privileges for specified columns of data for a given table.

These tables must be initialized before you can use MySQL. This is done by running the mysql_install_db script from a shell prompt. To do this, complete the following:

1. Open a terminal session and switch to your Root user account.

2. At the shell prompt, enter **cd /usr/bin**.

3. At the shell prompt enter **./mysql_install_db**.

Grant tables are then installed and initialized, as shown in Figure 29.2.

29

**FIGURE 29.2**    Initializing the grant tables.

You need to run mysql_install_db only once after initially installing the MySQL packages. The script creates the database's data directory, the grant tables, and a test database that can be used to test your implementation. The utility also creates entries in the grant tables for two MySQL user accounts:

- root

- anonymous-user

---

**NOTE**

It's important that you understand that MySQL has its own user accounts that are separate from your SUSE Linux system's user accounts. Even though MySQL uses an account named root, it's not the same as the root account on your Linux system. The MySQL database runs on your system as a Linux system user account named mysql, which is created when the MySQL packages are installed.

---

With the grant tables initialized, you now need to start the MySQL service. Let's review how to do this next.

### Starting the MySQL Server

You can start the MySQL service on your server by entering the following command from the shell prompt:

```
mysqld_safe --user=mysql &
```

The --user option specifies which Linux system account the MySQL server should run as. The ampersand at the end of the command indicates that the process should run in the background. You may have to wait for a few minutes for the server to finish loading.

---

**NOTE**

You can also start the server by entering **rcmysql start** at the shell prompt.

---

To verify that the server is running, enter the following command at the shell prompt:

`mysqladmin version`

You should see output similar to that shown in Figure 29.3.

```
linux:~ # mysqladmin version

mysqladmin  Ver 8.41 Distrib 4.1.13, for suse-linux on i686
Copyright (C) 2000 MySQL AB & MySQL Finland AB & TCX DataKonsult AB
This software comes with ABSOLUTELY NO WARRANTY. This is free software,
and you are welcome to modify and redistribute it under the GPL license

Server version          4.1.13
Protocol version        10
Connection              Localhost via UNIX socket
UNIX socket             /var/lib/mysql/mysql.sock
Uptime:                 5 min 29 sec

Threads: 1  Questions: 3  Slow queries: 0  Opens: 11  Flush tables: 1  Open tabl
es: 0  Queries per second avg: 0.009
linux:~ #
```

**FIGURE 29.3**    Verifying that MySQL is running.

> **NOTE**
>
> The commands presented in this subsection assume that you haven't created a password for your MySQL Root user account yet (we'll talk about how to that later in the chapter). If, by chance, you've already created a Root user account, you'll have to use the following syntax for the commands presented here:
>
> *command* -h localhost -u root -p *option*
>
> For example, to perform the preceding test, you would enter the following:
>
> mysqladmin -h localhost -u root -p version

If you want to make sure your MySQL service automatically starts at boot, open YaST and navigate to the System, System Services (Runlevel) module and configure the mysql daemon to start at the desired runlevels (probably 3 and 5).

At this point, you can execute several tests to verify that the MySQL server is functioning properly. Complete the following:

1. At the shell prompt, view the databases currently on the server by entering **/mysqlshow**. You should see the databases shown in Figure 29.4 displayed.

```
linux:~ # mysqlshow

+-----------+
| Databases |
+-----------+
| mysql     |
| test      |
+-----------+
linux:~ #
```

**FIGURE 29.4**    Viewing MySQL databases.

> **NOTE**
>
> The MySQL database contains the grant tables discussed earlier. The test database is an empty database that you can experiment with as you learn how to use MySQL.

2. View the tables contained within the MySQL database by entering **mysqlshow mysql**. You should see the tables shown in Figure 29.5.

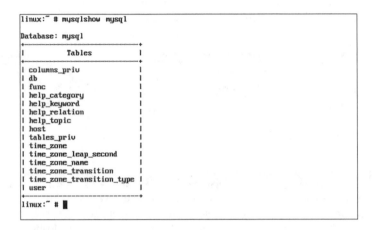

```
linux:~ # mysqlshow mysql

Database: mysql
+------------------------------+
|           Tables             |
+------------------------------+
| columns_priv                 |
| db                           |
| func                         |
| help_category                |
| help_keyword                 |
| help_relation                |
| help_topic                   |
| host                         |
| tables_priv                  |
| time_zone                    |
| time_zone_leap_second        |
| time_zone_name               |
| time_zone_transition         |
| time_zone_transition_type    |
| user                         |
+------------------------------+
linux:~ #
```

**FIGURE 29.5**   Viewing tables within a MySQL database.

Now that you're sure the MySQL server is running properly, you need to work with your MySQL user accounts. Notice in Figure 29.2 that you are prompted, after initializing the grant tables, to secure your MySQL Root user account. We'll talk about how to do this next.

### Securing the MySQL User Accounts

After running msql_install_db, your root MySQL user account is created but has no password, allowing anyone access to your MySQL server. This is something you should change as soon as possible. To do this, complete the following:

1. Open a terminal session and switch to your Root user account.

2. Verify that your MySQL server is currently running.

3. Create a password for your MySQL Root user by completing the following:

   - At the shell prompt, enter **mysqladmin -u root password '*your_new_password*'**.

   - At the shell prompt, enter **mysqladmin -u root -h *your_system_hostname* password *your_mysql_root_password***.

Now that your MySQL server has been installed and initialized, you can learn how to use the MySQL Control Center.

## Using the MySQL Control Center

Because the services are installed on your Linux system, let's look at how to manage them. First, you will have to open the MySQL Control Center. This can be found by launching your KDE Menu to the Office, Database section. You will see that you now have access to both the console and Knoda. Select the mysqlcc shortcut to open the Control Center, as shown in Figure 29.6.

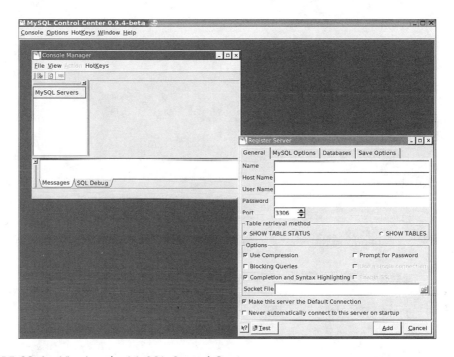

**FIGURE 29.6**    Viewing the MySQL Control Center.

After you open the Control Center, which includes the Console Manager, you will immediately need to add your own server (or a remote one) as a manageable server in the console in the Register Server dialog box shown in Figure 29.6. To do this, add your server by entering the required information, as shown in Figure 29.7.

The Name field is the name of the manageable entity in the MySQL Console Manager. The Host Name is very important. If you don't know what your host's name is, you can use YaST again in the Network Services section under the DNS and Host Name section. When you are done adding your client server (which, by the way, can be either MySQL or PostgreSQL if you change the driver), click Add to add your server to the console, as shown in Figure 29.8.

If your server is up and operational, all you need to do is connect a client to it to test it.

29

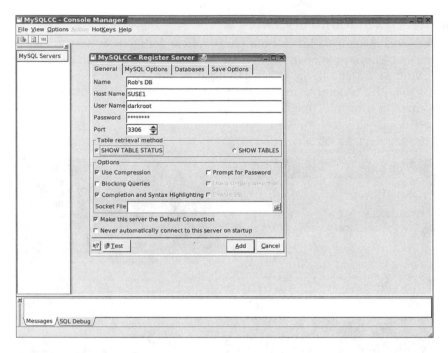

**FIGURE 29.7**    Configuring the MySQL server.

**FIGURE 29.8**    Viewing the configured MySQL server.

# Connecting to a MySQL Database with a Database Client

Now that you have installed and configured your database, you will need to connect to it and access data. This can be done in many ways. For instance, you can use the plethora of tools from the command line—some tools are proprietary, some open source. You can also use most standard web browsers. You can also use tools such as the MySQL Control Center, as seen in the previous section, or another client, called Knoda, that comes with your SUSE Linux CD-ROMs.

Let's begin by learning how to use a simple command-line database client called MySQL Monitor.

## Using the MySQL Monitor Database Client

The MySQL Monitor client allows you to connect to a MySQL server and manipulate its databases. To establish a connection, complete the following:

1. Open a terminal session and switch to your Root user account.

2. At the shell prompt, enter **mysql -h localhost -u root -p**.

> **NOTE**
>
> This command assumes you are connecting to a database running on the same system. You can use the -h option to specify a different hostname if the MySQL database you want to connect to is running on a different system.

3. When prompted, enter the password you created previously for your MySQL Root user account. The screen shown in Figure 29.9 is displayed.

```
linux:~ # mysql -h localhost -u root -p
Enter password:
Welcome to the MySQL monitor.  Commands end with ; or \g.
Your MySQL connection id is 13 to server version: 4.1.13

Type 'help;' or '\h' for help. Type '\c' to clear the buffer.

mysql> █
```

**FIGURE 29.9**   Using mysql.

Notice that the shell prompt has been replaced with a mysql prompt, indicating that mysql is running. From this prompt, you can enter commands to manage and manipulate your databases.

For example, suppose you want to create a new database named *contacts*, create a table within it, and insert data into the table. You can do this by completing the following:

1. At the mysql prompt, enter **CREATE DATABASE contacts;**. You should be prompted that the database has been created.

2. To tell the mysql client to use the database you just created, enter **USE contacts** at the mysql prompt. The utility should respond with Database changed.

3. To see the tables that have been defined by default within the contacts database, enter **SHOW TABLES;** at the mysql prompt. It should report Empty set, indicating that no tables have been defined.

   At this point, things get a little more complex. You will need to use the CREATE TABLE command to create the table. That's easy enough; however, you will also need to define your table's columns in the command as well. To do this, you first need to define the columns that you want to include in the table. Then you need to decide what kind of data will be stored in each column as well as how long the data in the table will be.

4. In the table we're building here, let's suppose we want four columns:

   • first

   • last

   • phone

   • lastcontact

   We know that the first and last columns will contain alphabetical characters of an undetermined length. We know that phone will contain 10 numbers with two hyphens (*area_code-prefix-number*). The lastcontact column will contain the date of last contact. In the next step, you will enter the CREATE TABLE command that will create a table named *vendors* and format these columns.

5. At the mysql prompt, enter **CREATE TABLE vendors (first VARCHAR(15), last VARCHAR(15), phone CHAR(12), lastcontact DATE);**.

6. Verify that the table and columns were created correctly by entering **DESCRIBE vendors;** at the mysql prompt. You should see that the vendors table and its associated columns were created, as shown in Figure 29.10.

```
mysql> DESCRIBE vendors;
+-------------+-------------+------+-----+---------+-------+
| Field       | Type        | Null | Key | Default | Extra |
+-------------+-------------+------+-----+---------+-------+
| first       | varchar(15) | YES  |     | NULL    |       |
| last        | varchar(15) | YES  |     | NULL    |       |
| phone       | varchar(12) | YES  |     | NULL    |       |
| lastcontact | date        | YES  |     | NULL    |       |
+-------------+-------------+------+-----+---------+-------+
4 rows in set (0.04 sec)

mysql>
```

**FIGURE 29.10**   Creating the vendors table.

Notice in Figure 29.9 that each column is null, indicating that no data has been added to the table. In the next step, you will use mysql to add a vendor named Diana Nelson, whose phone number is 801-555-1234 and was last contacted on July 24, 2005.

7. To insert the preceding data into the table, enter **INSERT INTO vendors VALUES ('Diana','Nelson','801-555-1234','2005-07-24');** at the mysql prompt. The utility should prompt you that the query was OK and that one row was affected.

8. To view the data in your table, enter **SELECT * FROM vendors;** at the mysql prompt. Your MySQL server should respond with all the data in the table, as shown in Figure 29.11.

```
mysql> SELECT * FROM vendors;
+-------+--------+--------------+-------------+
| first | last   | phone        | lastcontact |
+-------+--------+--------------+-------------+
| Diana | Nelson | 801-555-1234 | 2005-07-24  |
+-------+--------+--------------+-------------+
1 row in set (0.00 sec)

mysql> █
```

**FIGURE 29.11**    Displaying the contents of the vendors table.

You've just built a very basic MySQL database and table. This is only a small taste of what you can do with MySQL. If you want to learn more advanced MySQL skills, visit http://www.mysql.com.

Let's now take a look at the Knoda database client.

Knoda is a database front end for MySQL and PostgreSQL and contains a generic ODBC driver. You can use it for creating tables and databases, forms, reports, and queries. Knoda has also an export/import filter for CSV files. The package contains a general library with dialog boxes for the handling of databases, which can be used in other applications. It can be accessed by going to the KDE menu and selecting Office, Database, Knoda. You can see the Knoda client version 0.7 in Figure 29.12.

To configure the client, you can select mysql from the drop-down box so that the MySQL database can be accessed and managed with the Knoda client. To adjust the client, click the Options button on the Knoda client. The Preferences dialog box opens, as shown in Figure 29.13.

To attach to the database, click the Connect button on the Knoda client. This will either connect you to or stop you from connecting to the MySQL database. Most times, problems will be miniscule. Other times, the issues (and what you need to do to resolve them) could take weeks. Working in the world of programming and development will take some time, practice, and patience. If you have problems connecting to your database, try rebooting your system and checking inetd for the running service or the local firewall to make sure that MySQL ports are able to be used by the system.

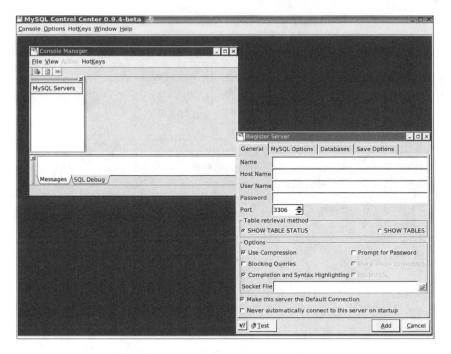

**FIGURE 29.12**    Using the Knoda client.

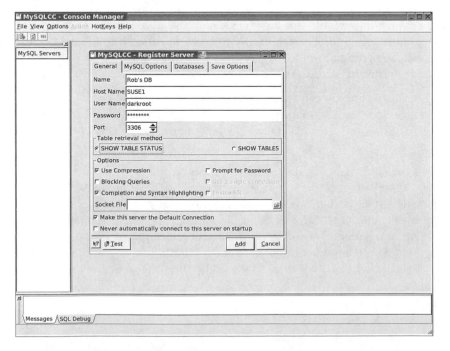

**FIGURE 29.13**    Setting the Knoda client preferences.

# Optimizing MySQL

Tuning your MySQL server for increased performance is exceptionally easy to do, simply because you can see huge speed increases by getting your queries right. But this chapter isn't about traveling up the learning curve, it's about quick tips that will make things work better now. MySQL can do that, too, as long as your system has enough RAM.

The key is understanding how MySQL's buffers work—there are buffers and caches for all sorts of things, and finding out how full they are is crucial to maximizing performance. MySQL performs best when it is making full use of its buffers, which in turn places a heavy demand on system RAM. Unless you have 4GB of RAM or more, you don't have enough capacity to set very high values for all your buffers. Picking and choosing is required.

## Measuring Key Buffer Usage

When you add indexes to your data, it enables MySQL to find data faster. However, ideally you want to have these indexes stored in RAM for maximum speed, and the key_buffer_size variables define how much RAM MySQL can allocate for index key caching. If MySQL cannot store its indexes in RAM, you will experience serious performance problems. Fortunately, most databases have relatively small key buffer requirements, but you should measure your usage to see what work needs to be done.

To do this, log in to MySQL and type **SHOW STATUS LINE '\key_read' ;**. That returns all the status fields that describe the hit rate of your key buffer. You should get two rows back: Key_reads and Key_read_requests, which are the number of keys being read from disk and the number of keys being read from the key buffer. From these two numbers you can calculate the percentage of requests being filled from RAM and from disk, using this simple equation:

```
100 - (Key_reads / Key_read_requests) x 100)
```

That is, you divide Key_reads by Key_read_requests, multiply the result by 100, and then subtract the result from 100. Plug in some numbers and you can get a result. Suppose Key_reads is 1,000 and Key_read_requests is 100,000. Divide 1,000 by 100,000 to get 0.01. Move the decimal point two spaces to the right to multiply by 100 and get 1.0. 100 – 1 = 99; this is the percentage of requests being filled from RAM. Be happy.

Most people should be looking to get more than 95% of their requests served from RAM. The primary exception to this rule is if you update or delete rows often. It's hard to cache something that's always changing, and MySQL won't do it. If your database is largely read-only, the ratio should be closer to 98%. Lower figures mean you might need to bump up the size of your key buffer.

If you are seeing problems, the next step is to check how much of your current key buffer is being used. Use the SHOW VARIABLES command and look up the value of the key_buffer_size variable. It is probably something like 8388600, which is eight million bytes, or 8MB. Use the SHOW STATUS command to look up the value of Key_blocks_used.

You can now determine how much of your key buffer is being used by multiplying Key_blocks_used by 1,024, dividing by key_buffer_size, and multiplying by 100. So if Key_blocks_used is 8,000, you multiply that by 1,024 to get 8,192,000; dividing that by key_buffer_size (8388600) gets us to 0.97656. Multiplying that by 100 gives us a key buffer ratio of 97.656, or nearly 98% of your key buffer is being used.

Now to the important part. You have figured out that you are reading lots of keys from disk, and you also now know that the reason for reading from disk is almost certainly because you do not have enough RAM allocated to the key buffer. The general rule: Allocate whatever RAM you can spare to the key buffer, up to 25% of everything you have. This translates to about 128MB on a 512MB system. Beyond that, you will go the opposite way, slowing things down immeasurably if you have to access Swap for the key buffer.

Open /etc/my.cnf in your text editor and look for the line that contains key_buffer_size. If it is not there, create one under the line [mysqld]. When you set the new value, don't be arbitrary about it. Try doubling what you have there now (or 16MB if it's a new line); see how that goes. To set 16MB as the key buffer size, the line should look like this:

```
[mysqld]
set variable = key_buffer_size=16M
datadir=/var/lib/mysql
```

Restart your MySQL server with rcmysql restart, and then go back into MySQL and run SHOW VARIABLES again to see the key_buffer_size. It should be 16773120 if you have it set to 16MB. Because MySQL just got reset, all its values for key hits and the like will also have been reset. You need to let it run for awhile so you can assess how much has changed. If you have a test system you can run, so much the better.

After your database has been accessed with normal usage for a short while (if you get frequent accesses, this might be only a few minutes), recalculate how much of the key buffer is being used. If you get another high score, double the size again, restart, and retest. Keep trying until your key buffer usage is below 50%, or you find out you don't have enough RAM to do this properly. Again, never use more than 25% of your physical RAM for the key buffer.

## Using the Query Cache

Newer versions of MySQL allow you to cache the results of queries so that if new queries come in that use the same SQL, the result can be served from RAM. In some ways, the query cache is quite intelligent. If, for example, part of the result changes because of another query, the cached results are thrown away and recalculated next time. However, in other ways it is very simple. For example, it uses cached results only if the new query is the same as a cached query, even down to the capitalization of the SQL.

The query cache works well in most scenarios. If your site has an equal mix of reading and writing, the query cache will do its best but will not be optimal. If your site is mostly reading with few writes, more queries will be cached (and for longer), thus improving overall performance.

You need to find out whether you have the query cache enabled before we try anything else. To do this, use SHOW VARIABLES and look up the value of have_query_cache. If all is well, you should get YES back, meaning the query cache is enabled. Look for the values of query_cache_size (the amount of RAM allocated to the query cache) and query_cache_limit (the maximum result size that should be cached). These should be set at something like 8388608 (8MB) and 1048576 (1MB).

An 8MB query cache should be enough for most people, but if you are storing an especially large amount of data, consider doubling that. You should never need a query cache of more than 32MB, though.

Next, type **SHOW STATUS LIKE 'Qcache%';** to see all the status information about the query cache. You should see values for eight variables from which we can determine the current use of the query cache.

Add the totals of Qcache_hits, Qcache_inserts, and Qcache_not_cached. This gives you the total number of queries received. Dividing Qcache_hits by the total queries and multiplying the result by 100 gives you the percentage of queries being served from the query cache. The higher the number, the better off you are. If the gods smile upon you, it will be in the mid-to-high 90s.

Using the query cache does not incur much of a performance hit. When MySQL calculates the result of a query normally, it simply throws it away when the connection closes. With the query cache, it hangs on to those queries, so there's no extra work being done.

## Miscellaneous Tweaks

If you have tuned your key buffer and optimized your query cache and still find your site struggling, there are a handful of smaller changes you can make that will add speed to your database.

When reading tables, MySQL has to open the file that stores the table data. How many files it keeps open at a time is defined by the table_cache setting, which is set to 64 by default. You can increase this setting if you have more than 64 tables, but be aware that there are limits on how many files can be open at a time. Think things out before exceeding 64 tables in a database.

The other thing that is tweakable is the size of the read buffer, which is controlled by read_buffer_size and read_buffer_rnd_size. Both of these are allocated per connection, meaning you need to exercise care to have large numbers. Whatever you choose, read_buffer_rnd_size should be three to four times the size of read_buffer_size. If read_buffer_size is 1MB (a good size for a very large database), read_buffer_rnd_size should be 4MB.

## Query Optimization

The biggest speed-ups can be seen by reprogramming your SQL statements so they are more efficient. If you follow these steps, your server will thank you.

- Select as little data as possible—only the fields you need.

- If you only need a few fields, use LIMIT to select the number you need.

29

- Declare fields as NOT NULL when creating tables to save space and increase speed.

- Provide default values for fields, and use them where you can.

- Be very careful with table joins because they are the easiest way to write inefficient queries.

- If you must use joins, be sure you join on fields that are indexed.

- Find and fix slow queries. Add `log-long-format` and `log-slow-queries = /var/loog/slow-queries.log` to your `/etc/my.cnf` file, under [mysqld], and MySQL will tell you about queries that took a long time to complete.

- Use OPTIMIZE TABLE tablename to defragment tables and refresh the indexes.

## Summary

In this chapter we looked at deploying a hierarchical database using SUSE Linux. You can install MySQL and have a fully functional database operating within minutes. After it is installed and configured, you can use the `mysql` or `knoda` clients to access the database.

## References

- http://www.mysql.com/—The MySQL database home page, with news, downloads, and documentation.

- http://dev.mysql.com/doc/—MySQL database home page's documentation repository. If you want to learn more about MySQL, visit the documentation center.

- http://www.postgresql.org/—PostgreSQL database home pages. PostgreSQL is one of the world's most advanced open-source databases supporting almost all SQL constructs, including subselects, transactions, user-defined types, and so on.

- http://www.postgresql.org/docs/—PostgreSQL database home page's documentation repository. You can start here to find a wealth of PostgreSQL information available online. This section of the website contains current and archived manuals for PostgreSQL users and administrators.

- http://www.knoda.org/—The home page to download the newest Knoda client or learn more about it.

# CHAPTER 30

# Using Perl and Python

The primary open-source web-development tools are often lumped together as a makeshift suite called LAMP: Linux, Apache, MySQL, and Perl/Python/PHP. Linux and Apache provide the base to deliver your web-based application; MySQL provides convenient data access; and scripting languages such as Perl, Python, and PHP handle much of the "heavy lifting" involved in working with the data and presenting it to the end uscr.

The massive growth of the Web in the early 1990s fueled an interest in getting interesting things online quickly. The Common Gateway Interface (CGI) offered developers a way to produce dynamic content and add interaction to the Web by allowing a user to remotely execute a remote script or program on the server and returning the results. Many programmers had experience with Larry Wall's Practical Extraction and Report Language (Perl), so it was a natural choice to use in CGI programming. Perl quickly became the language of choice and it continues to play an important role in today's Internet.

Perl can be a difficult language to learn, but it is easy to use after you understand how it works. It is highly flexible, with more than one way to do just about anything. That flexibility is what makes it a little complicated.

Python is younger than Perl, but they have many things in common. They are both interpreted languages, have active cultures that center around the language and the philosophy behind it, and within their respective cultures, fun is a big component. Python is object oriented and has a cleaner syntax than Perl. Python has contributed substantially to the Web, not only as a scripting language, but also serving as the building blocks for applications such as Zope and BitTorrent.

In this chapter, you'll get an overview of both languages and learn how to begin using them in SUSE Linux.

# What Is Perl?

Perl is an interpreted scripting language written in the mid-1980s to help system administrators automate some of their tasks. It has grown from there. It is essentially a procedure-based language, but it does support object orientation.

Because of its power and flexibility, Perl goes by many nicknames: the Swiss Army Chainsaw, bash on steroids, and so on. What is interesting about Perl is that nearly all of its code and syntax is borrowed from other languages. If you're well versed in computer languages, you'll likely see pieces of C, bash, BASIC, awk, and sed reflected in Perl.

You might be surprised at how ubiquitous Perl is on your system. Do a file search for `*.pl` on your entire system and you are likely to find hundreds of Perl scripts with this extension. Look at the directories these files sit in, and you'll see how critical Perl is to this operating system and its application developers.

There are two guiding principles in the Perl movement: Perl "makes easy things easy, and hard things possible," and There Is More Than One Way To Do It (TIMTOWTDI, also known as the "Tim Toady" principle). Remember these ideas and you will go far.

> **NOTE**
>
> A grammar note: Perl is an interpreted language whose syntax is run through the `perl` interpreter. The language is always referred to with a capital P (Perl). The interpreter is always referred to as `perl` (small P). Thus shall it be here.

# Perl Variables and Data Structures

Variables in Perl come in three types: scalar, arrays, and hashes.

- Scalar variables are those that hold a single value. Scalars are preceded by a $ sign in the code. Some assignment statement examples using scalar variables are

  ```
  $x = 5;
  $pi = 3.14159;
  $animal = "dog";
  ```

- Arrays are numerically indexed lists of scalar data. Arrays are identified in Perl by the @ sign. An example of an array is

  ```
  @months = ("January", "February", "March", "April", "May", "June", "July",
      "August", "September", "October", "November", "December");
  ```

- Hashes are collections of scalar values arranged in key/value pairs. Hashes are identified with a % sign. An example of a hash is

  ```
  %birthdays = ("mom" => "SEP 06", "jean" => "JUN 01", "marc" => "JUN 16");
  ```

Scalars can be strings or numbers and can change from one type to the other, depending on the operator. If an operator expects a number, Perl will see the value as a number, and if an operator expects a string, Perl will see a string. This lets you concentrate less on the difference between numbers and strings, as long as you get the operator right (you'll learn about operators in the next section).

Arrays follow the same syntactical conventions as scalars. Each scalar value that makes up an array can be referred to as $<array>[index#], where, in this case, # is a numerical index. The index begins at 0, meaning that the first item in the list is 0, the second is 1, and so on.

Hashes were originally called *associative arrays*. The => identifier is called a *fat comma* because it behaves much like a comma in other contexts. In fact, commas could be used to define the preceding hash, but the fat commas make it more legible. Compare:

```
%birthdays = ("mom", "SEP 06", "jean", "JUN 01", "marc", "JUN 16");
```

## Operators and Other Statements

Programming has always been about manipulating data, so you can't do much with all these variables unless you have some operators to work on them. There are three main types of operators in Perl: comparison, compound, and arithmetic operators.

*Comparison* operators compare the value of one operation or statement with that of another to see if the overall statement resolves to either "true" or "false." A different course of action can be followed within the program, depending on how statements resolve. Table 30.1 lists the comparison operators offered by Perl. You'll notice that the operators are different for numerals and strings.

**TABLE 30.1**   Perl Comparison Operators

| Meaning | Numeric Operator | String Operator |
| --- | --- | --- |
| Equal to | == | eq |
| Less than | < | lt |
| Greater than | > | gt |
| Less than or equal to | <= | le |
| Greater than or equal to | >= | ge |
| Not equal to | != | ne |
| Returns -1 if less than, 0 if equal, and 1 if greater than | <=> | cmp |
| Range between first and second operands | .. | |
| Matched by regular expression | | =~ |
| Not matched by regular expression | | !~ |

*Compound* operators are largely identical to Boolean operators and can be combined with other operator types into more complex forms of results. These are listed in Table 30.2.

**TABLE 30.2** Perl Compound Operators

| Meaning | Operator |
| --- | --- |
| Logical AND | && |
| Logical OR | ;; |
| Logical NOT | ! |
| Group these compound statements | () |

*Arithmetic* operators can be used to perform all sorts of mathematical operations on variables. These are listed in Table 30.3.

**TABLE 30.3** Perl Arithmetic Operators

| Meaning | Operator |
| --- | --- |
| Raises x to the y power | x**y |
| Calculates the remainder of x/y | x%y |
| Adds x to y | x+y |
| Subtracts y from x | x-y |
| Multiplies x times y | x*y |
| Divides x by y | x/y |
| Negates y | -y |
| Increments y by 1 and uses value | ++y |
| Uses value of y and then increments by 1 | y++ |
| Decrements y by 1 and uses value | --y |
| Uses value of y and then decrements by 1 | y++ |
| Assigns value of y to x | x=y |

# Regular Expressions

Many Linux applications use regular expressions to simplify searches. In Perl, regular expressions have been taken to the level of an art form.

Statements with regular expressions use several of the same symbols that wildcards and operators use, but for slightly different reasons. Regular expressions use symbols to match patterns in text.

Some folks suggest that Perl regular expressions even represent a small programming language of its own. When you open the perlrequick man page (a brief introduction to regular expressions in Perl), this idea is reinforced by using a "Hello World!" example. To find the word World in "Hello World", use this line in a Perl script:

```
print "It matches\n" if "Hello World" =~ /World/;
```

This script tells Perl to find (=~) the expression World in the Hello World string and then print the words "It matches" with a newline (\n) if it is found.

Any scalar can be matched against a regular expression in a script. This offers a wealth of possibilities to locate and manipulate data. The trick is learning the shorthand involved in getting it. This shorthand includes the *metacharacters* that represent search terms and operators. It's because regular expression patterns are made up of metacharacters that some people find cryptic and difficult to decipher.

Table 30.4 shows you some of the primary metacharacters and their uses in Perl. If you are familiar with regular expressions and wildcards in the shell or other applications, watch carefully for differences in Perl's metacharacter usage.

**TABLE 30.4**   Some Perl Metacharacters

| Meaning | Metacharacter |
| --- | --- |
| Match any single character (except a newline). | . |
| Match the preceding character(s), any number of times. | * |
| Match the preceding character(s), one or more times. | + |
| The preceding character(s) may not be in the string, but it will still match if the other requirements are present. | ? |
| Boolean OR statement. | \| |
| Text matches if a tab character is present. | \t |
| Pattern matches if it is at the beginning of a line. | ^ |
| Pattern matches if it is at the end of a line. | $ |
| Match a letter, number, or underscore. | \w |
| Match a number. | \d |
| Match any whitespace character such as a space, tab, or newline. | \s |
| Escape any metacharacter into an ordinary character. | \ |

In addition to searching and matching text segments and character patterns, regular expressions can also be used to validate user input. The form of expected input is expressed as a regular expression against which the input is compared.

```
my $email = <STDIN>;
print "Input is in valid format" if
    $email =~ \[A-Za-z0-9._%-]+@[A-Za-z0-9._%-]+\.[A-Za-z]{2,4}\
```

This is just a taste of how to use regular expressions in Perl. Read over the perlrequick and perlretut man pages for a more in-depth look, or check out *Teach Yourself Regular Expressions in 10 Minutes* by Ben Forta and published by Sams Publishing.

# Perl Modules and CPAN

The Unix philosophy of creating and using small programs that do one thing well, often in conjunction with other similar programs, has led to the largely modular design of even the most complicated applications. So it is with Perl. Perl does much of its work through modules that plug in to the Perl environment. Many Perl modules are installed with the basic Perl installation, and dozens more are optionally installable through YaST.

One important component included in the base Perl installation is the marvelous CPAN.pm module. CPAN.pm makes it easy to download and install other modules from

CPAN, the Comprehensive Perl Archive Network. CPAN is a large repository of Perl modules, reusable code, and documentation. There you can find more Perl goodies than you can imagine.

CPAN is always accessible from the Web at http://www.cpan.org, and you can search and download modules directly with your browser. But for ease of installation, the Perl CPAN module can't be beat.

Log in as SuperUser and type

```
perl -MCPAN -e shell
```

The first time you run CPAN, you'll go through a configuration dialog. Accepting the default configuration options is usually the right thing to do, but you'll still want to read through everything carefully. You can always modify the configuration later on if you have to by entering **o conf init** at the cpan> prompt.

After configuring your system, CPAN will ask about your location and find a nearby download mirror. This speeds up your transfer and doesn't use as much bandwidth. After you've selected one or more mirror sites, you will see the cpan> prompt. You can now search CPAN for something useful.

Let's look for an update for SpamAssassin. Type **h** to see a list of available commands. Reading the help screen, we see that regular expressions can be used to search for a specific module. To search for our updated package with the regular expression, spam, type

```
m /spam/
```

> **TIP**
>
> On each visit to the CPAN mirror, run `reload index` to ensure that you can access the latest modules to hit the mirror.

The CPAN module searches the database for modules that fit and then lists the matching modules. Among them is the `Mail::SpamAssassin` module (and several child modules). To download and install this module, type

```
install Mail::SpamAssassin
```

CPAN will download the module, configure it for your system, and run `make` and `make install` all at once. If you prefer to download now and install later, use the `get` command instead of `install`. The `h` or `?` command is always at your side to help you decide what to do next.

> **TIP**
>
> The CPAN module offers a command history if ReadLine support is enabled. If it is, you can use your up and down arrows to repeat or edit a recent command.

When you have found and installed all the modules you want, type **q** at the cpan> prompt to quit the module and return to the SuperUser prompt.

## The Future of Perl

Perl 6 has been under development since the year 2000 and may be near release when you read this. It is a nearly complete rewrite of the interpreter's code, with numerous changes. The biggest change is the new Parrot interpreter, through which all Perl 6 code will pass. This virtual machine is designed to support not just Perl 6, but Perl 5, Python, and several other scripting languages as well.

Following are a few highlights of the effects on the core Perl language itself:

- Perl 6 will be more strongly typed, allowing you to specify both the storage type and implementation type of a variable.

- Sigils will be simplified. In the new version of Perl, sigils will cease to be adjectives and become an indivisible part of the nouns themselves.

- Case statements are simpler, too. How does one single control statement sound? It's called given, and it is used like this:

```
$val = 'G4';
given $val {
 when 'A4' { print "paper" }
 when 'B4' { print "prior" }
 when 'C4' {  die "BOOM!" }
 default { print "huh??" }
}
```

Many Perl 6 features can already be accessed using various Perl 5 modules available from CPAN.

## What Is Python?

It's still a defining image. In May 2000, *Linux Journal* did a special supplement on the Python language, and the editors wanted to do something fun for the cover. There wasn't the budget for the Knights Who Say "Ni," the Minister of Silly Walks was unavailable, and perhaps they couldn't find a cross-dressing lumberjack for a photo shoot. Yet they needed something Pythonesque to get the right mood. Someone remembered a sketch with an organist in the middle of a field near the ocean, and a legend was born. The supplement featured a long side-shot of a man sitting at a (computer) keyboard with his bowtie on— and nothing else. And the letters poured in. Take a look at http://www.linuxjournal.com/article/4106.

There may have been some folks who didn't get it (indeed there will always be some folks who don't get it), but one thing that Python (the language) and the people who use it aim to do is dispel the myth of the humorless geek. The language is named, after all, for the immortal stars of the British sketch show "Monty Python's Flying Circus." Yet for all the silliness inherent in Python culture, the language is responsible for some very hard-working tools.

Quality assurance teams for both computer hardware and software use Python scripts to get their products ready for release. Search engines (including Google) use Python to perform their tasks. Web designers and bloggers use Python-based tools Zope and Plone to generate their content. Top-flight scientists in geophysics, electromagnetics, and fluid dynamics use the SciPy library in their research.

Python programmers are very productive because the language is easy to grasp, and it doesn't take much to get going. It puts an emphasis on creating human-readable code and being explicit about what is going on in the code. The language handles many house-keeping activities, such as I/O, memory management, data typing, and variable binding, with aplomb.

The next section tells you a little bit about programming in Python and the tools available to you in SUSE Linux.

## Python Variables and Data Structures

Python has four variable types: scalars, lists, tuples, and dictionaries.

- Scalar variables are those that hold a single value, much the same as in Perl. Although unlike Perl, numeric and string types are segregated and no extra symbols are prefixed to variables in Python. Examples of numeric and string scalar variable assignments are

```
x = 5
pi = 3.14159
animal = "dog"
```

- Lists are numerically indexed lists of objects. They can be made up of any combination of things you choose, such as scalar data, dictionaries, tuples, and even other lists. An example of a list assignment is

```
months = ["January", "February", "March", "April", "May", "June",
➥ "July", "August", "September", "October", "November", "December"]
```

- Tuples are almost identical to lists, except they are immutable. That means unlike a list, which you can change and modify any way you like, you cannot change a tuple.

- Dictionaries are associatively indexed arrays comparable to Perl's hashes. They are a collection of objects or values arranged in key/value pairs. An example of a dictionary assignment is

```
birthdays = {"mom" : "SEP 06", "jean" : "JUN 01", "marc" : "JUN 16"}
```

# Indentation

Every programming language has a way of organizing the code so it appears in readable chunks—whitespace, braces, explicit line termination (such as the semicolon in C). Python uses indents as a formal part of the language, and lines end with a hard return.

The rules on indentation are simple. Be consistent in how you indent. Use the same number of spaces to indent a block of code. If you need a statement that spans more than one line, use the backslash (\) to continue the line. Here's an example of Python's indentation rule at work:

```
file = open("./data.txt", "r")
while 1:
  line = file.readline()
  if not line:
    break
  print line,
file.close
```

Python's indentation rules may take a little getting used to if you're coming from another programming language such as Perl, but they will make your code more readable and thus easier to maintain. With any project, it's good to keep in mind that you may not always be the person in charge of the code, and memory fades, so make it readable at all times.

# Extreme Object Orientation

In Python, *everything* is an object. They have identities, types, and values, but also inherent properties and methods. For example, you can determine the index of a given substring using a string object's index method:

```
import string
greeting = "Hello World! It's nice to meet you!"
location = greeting.index("nice")
print location
```

You can create your own objects with the `class` statement. User-defined classes can have class variables and class methods, which govern all instances of the class. Each instance of a class can, in turn, have its own instance variables that don't apply to other instances.

# Python IDEs and the Interactive Shell

Several IDEs are available to help developers write their scripts and programs. Although many are cross-language, some are primarily written for working with Python. Two such examples of the latter are IDLE and SPE.

IDLE, short for Integrated DeveLopment Environment, is part of the basic Python distribution. It is coded in Python itself and uses the Tkinter toolkit to create its graphical interface. Don't let its barebones appearance fool you, however—IDLE offers syntax high-lighting, smart indents, a multiple-undo history, a partial debugger, call tips, and an interactive shell.

A very popular Python IDE is SPE, which stands for Stani's Python Editor. It's written in Python and uses wxPython as its interface toolkit. SPE offers more features than IDLE, including sticky notes, a regular expressions assistant, a UML viewer, and a class explorer window.

Other cross-language editors used for Python development include jEdit (a popular IDE written in Java), Eclipse, and Anjuta (both discussed in Chapter 28, "Using the GNU Compiler Collection and Other Programming Tools").

Calling python from a console with no command-line arguments will start Python's inter-active shell, so you don't need to fire up a full-fledged IDE or even a text editor to test out your ideas in Python. You can enter statements at the shell prompt and it will immediately interpret them. Sending an EOF character (usually the Ctrl+D key combination) will exit the interactive shell.

## References

- http://www.perl.com—The source for Perl. News, articles, blogs and the like.

- http://www.perl.org—The Perl Directory. Links to the Perl universe.

- http://www.cpan.org—The Comprehensive Perl Archive Network. CPAN is the place to download modules and other gotta-have Perl stuff. If you write something useful, upload it here.

- http://use.perl.org—The Perl news center. Find out about conferences, user group meetings, and assorted fun facts.

- http://learn.perl.org—Where to begin with Perl online. Tutorials, book recommendations for all levels of expertise, and a beginner's mailing list.

- http://www.tpj.com—The Perl Journal, the monthly magazine.

- http://www.pm.org—PerlMongers user groups.

- http://dev.perl.org/perl6—The Perl 6 hub. Get overall design information here and the latest on development of Perl 6 and the Parrot interpreter.

- http://python.org—The center of the Python universe. Just about everything Python links here.

- http://www.pythonware.com/daily—The Daily Python—Python news and comment from around the Web and the blogosphere.

- http://www.python.org/moin/BeginnersGuide—For new programmers, a Python guide.

- http://docs.python.org/tut/tut.html—This tutorial promises to teach you Python in an afternoon.

- http://www.amk.ca/python/howto—A collection of Python HOWTO documents, including how to use regular expressions in Python.

- http://www.die-offenbachs.de/detlev/eric3.html—Home for the Eric Python IDE.

- http://www.pyzine.com—An online Python technical journal.

- http://en.wikipedia.org/wiki/Python_programming_language—A long and detailed entry, and a worthy introduction to the Python language.

- http://pythonide.stani.be/—Home of Stani's Python Editor.

- http://www.jedit.org/—A programmer's text editor written in Java that offers support for Python development.

30

# Creating Dynamic Websites

Websites that remain stagnant and don't change will most likely suffer and lose traffic. See it once and you never have to go back. Give a user a reason to come back—news, community, downloading, commentary—and not only will one person keep coming back, her friends will visit, too. You'll get links from other places, and then Google finds you faster. It's a simple formula.

You could manually code large chunks of the site every day, but a far easier solution is to use PHP, the PHP Hypertext Preprocessor, to easily create and maintain lively, interactive sites that people will want to visit regularly. Some 20 million domains use PHP to generate their sites, and the number increases nearly every month.

In Chapter 14, "Creating Basic Websites," you created a basic static website with tools included in SUSE Linux. In this chapter, you'll learn how to use PHP to make that site more interactive and appealing. Then you'll let your users talk among themselves with a forum.

## Using PHP

PHP is the result of another lazy programmer's effort to simplify his life. Back in 1994, Rasmus Lerdorf wanted to eliminate some of the drudgery associated with updating his personal web page. Lerdorf wrote some Perl scripts to generate HTML tags based on some C code. In June 1995, he announced the existence of the Personal Home Page (PHP) tools, version 1.0, in a Usenet CGI newsgroup. Those tools have since evolved into a full-fledged scripting language with a powerful engine, Zend, and a large community of developers hacking the code. You can read more about the history of PHP at http://php.net/history.

The PHP Home Page at www.php.net defines PHP as "a widely used general-purpose scripting language that is especially suited for Web development and can be embedded into HTML. Much of its syntax is borrowed from C, Java and Perl with a couple of unique PHP-specific features thrown in." It is open source and works on the server side to generate its content. PHP often works with databases such as MySQL and PostgreSQL to generate content.

PHP boasts a command-line interpreter as well as modules that work with just about any web server out there, but we will focus on PHP's `mod_php4` module for Apache. Similarly, PHP works with just about any database management system, but we will focus on MySQL.

> **NOTE**
>
> PHP 5.0 was released in July 2004, but was not included in the standard SUSE Linux distribution until v9.3 in April 2005. The instructions in this book apply to PHP 4, but nothing should be substantially different in the new version. See the section "The Future with PHP 5" for information on PHP 5's new features.

PHP is extensible through the PHP Extension and Application Repository (PEAR) and the PHP Extension Community Library (PECL), both hosted at php.net.

## Installing PHP

The core PHP package, mod_php, and many PHP extensions are installable through YaST, making it easy to use PHP on a local Apache server setup. The core PHP package installs the basics of the language, which work from a command line. If you plan on using PHP in a CGI capacity, this is fine—but this isn't the recommended (nor most beneficial) way. The apache_mod_php package is an Apache module that will allow you to process and serve HTML pages with embedded PHP code. You'll want to install both the core and mod_php packages.

To confirm that PHP is properly installed on your system, open a text editor and write this line:

```
<?php phpinfo(); ?>
```

Save the file as `/srv/www/htdocs/test.php`. Now open a web browser to http://localhost/test.php. Figure 31.1 should appear.

If you don't get the PHP info page, make sure the script was typed correctly, and then see if Apache is running by going to `http://localhost`. If Apache is not running, check the Runlevel Editor in YaST.

Look carefully at the info page. You will see which PHP extensions are installed, where your `php.ini` configuration file is stored (by default in `/etc`), and a fairly detailed configuration report.

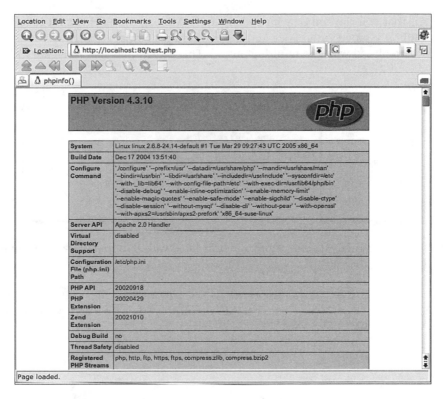

**FIGURE 31.1**    If PHP is properly configured on your system, this page should appear in your web browser after writing the test file.

If you are using a web-hosting vendor, make sure that PHP is supported before uploading PHP pages to your site. Finding a host with PHP support should not be difficult, but many PHP-related websites, like the PHP Resource Index at http://php.resourceindex.com, include pointers to PHP-friendly hosts.

Before writing any PHP code, you should also check that your favorite text editor or IDE supports PHP code highlighting and the like. All the web-authoring tools included in SUSE Linux (Bluefish, Quanta Plus, and Nvu) support PHP (although Nvu has some quirks, see http://www.viapanda.com/nvuphp.html for details). Emacs needs a separate php-mode, downloadable from Sourceforge.net (http://sourceforge.net/projects/php-mode). There are also PHP helper scripts for VIM at vim.org.

## Writing PHP Scripts

You've already written your first PHP script—the one-line `test.php` script you used to test your installation in the earlier section. There's more to learn than that, of course, and this is what you'll do in this section.

The PHP interpreter basically treats any documents fed to it as text and echos back the contents, unless it finds code set between special opening and closing tags. The neat thing about this is that you can embed your code in an HTML page and PHP won't touch your HTML. It will only process your code and the end result is a final HTML document with the PHP code replaced with the resulting output. This is demonstrated in Figure 31.2.

**FIGURE 31.2**    PHP interprets only your code delineated with <?php and ?>. The end result is a complete HTML document.

PHP's include function is used to import the contents of another file. This allows you to include other PHP scripts or even other HTML files into your scripts and use PHP to template your website:

```
<html>
<h1>Welcome!</h1>
<?php include "menu.html"; ?>
<img src="img/me.jpg" alt="picture of me" />
<p>Welcome to my website.  Here you'll learn all sorts of neat stuff about
me.  Here's some of the things that are going on in my life right now:</p>
<?php include "events.html"; ?>
<p>Thanks for stopping by!</p>
<hr />
<?php include "footer.html"; ?>
</html>
```

Variables are used in PHP to store information in memory that the script may need. They are identified by a $ and are not strictly typed like variables in other languages. This means a variable can hold a number, a string, or anything else that you may want to alias.

PHP also offers a variety of mathematical and logical operators to compare variables. By using them with PHP's flow control structures, you can write scripts that follow different paths, depending on the value of the variables. Table 31.1 shows some of the operators available in PHP.

```
<?php
  $forecast = "rain";
  $times = 17;
  if ($weater == "rain") {
      echo "I've already told you ";
```

```
    echo $times;
    echo " times... if it's going to rain you should bring your umbrella!";
}
if ($weather != "rain") {
    echo "Have a nice day!";
}
?>
```

**TABLE 31.1**    Selected PHP Operators

| Meaning | Operator | Example |
|---|---|---|
| Assignment | = | $x = $y |
| Add | + | $x + $y |
| Subtract | - | $x - $y |
| Multiply | * | $x * $y |
| Divide | / | $x / $y |
| Calculates the remainder | % | $x % $y |
| Negation | - | -$x |
| Increment by 1 | ++ | $x++ |
| Decrement by 1 | -- | $x-- |
| Equal to | == | $x == $y |
| Exactly equal to | === | $x === $y |
| Less than | < | $x < $y |
| Greater than | > | $x > $y |
| Less than or equal to | <= | $x <= $y |
| Greater than or equal to | >= | $x >= $y |
| Not equal to | != | $x != $y |
| Logical NOT | ! | !$x |
| Logical AND | && | $x && $y |
| Logical OR | \|\| | $x \|\| $y |
| Group | () | ($x = 5) && ($y = $z) |

PHP also has looping structures that can be used to cycle through a section of code any number of times. This saves you the time of having to explicitly write the same section of code over and over. Here's an example that will zip through and write out all the numbers between 1 and 10,000—each on a separate line:

```
<?php
  $x = 1;
  while (x >= 10000) {
      echo $x;
      echo "<br />";
      $x++;
  }
?>
```

Many predefined functions are available in PHP to help manipulate data, explore strings of text, and even generate graphical images and PDF files. From its simple Perl days, PHP has grown to be a very useful and robust scripting language. I highly recommend exploring the documentation available at http://www.php.net to learn more about the power of PHP.

## Adding More Functions to PHP

PHP can be extended in a similar manner as Apache, where a modular design permits adding new features and functionality by linking in new modules. The PECL library is a set of modules that can link into the language's core. The new functions they provide are then available as any of PHP's built-in functions.

PEAR is a collection of reusable, open-source code for use in your PHP applications. The code is organized as a selection of files that act as wrappers giving convenient access to various PHP functions or extending PHP in some way. The files are collectively known as a *package*.

Both PECL modules and PEAR packages can be installed using the pear utility. Calling pear without any arguments will display a list of commands pear understands. The install argument followed by the package or module name will install it; the uninstall argument similarly will uninstall the component.

```
./pear install Mail
downloading Mail-1.1.8.tgz ...
Starting to download Mail-1.1.8.tgz (16,196 bytes)
......done: 16,196 bytes
install ok: Mail 1.1.8
```

## The Future with PHP 5

PHP version 5.0 was released in June 2004 and was included with SUSE Linux Professional beginning with version 9.3.

PHP 5 features enhanced support for Extensible Markup Language (XML), using the libxml2 toolkit. Strong support exists for all XML-related technologies, but many are especially excited about the potential for ordinary users to create fully rendered PHP objects using the SimpleXML parser. With SimpleXML, you can read, write, or iterate over your XML file with ease in accessing elements and attributes.

If you're interested in building web services applications with PHP, there is new support for Simple Object Access Protocol (SOAP).

For programmers, the chief difference between the two versions is the introduction of object-oriented programming tools in the Zend Engine. PHP has had some object modeling available since version 3, but some experienced object-oriented programmers had problems with unusual syntax. In PHP 5, among the changes welcomed by programmers used to working with objects are the following:

- You can use common access modifiers to limit access to certain classes and properties.

- Constructor and destructor methods of dealing with objects are more consistent and easier to use.

- A new `final` class declaration limits overloading inheritance.

- Objects can be cloned with the `clone` keyword.

- Classes may have constant values.

Other new enhancements include extensions that add support for the SQLite portable database library and HTML Tidy, a marvelous tool that cleans up your HTML and other markup code. You can also download a new Perl extension to support writing Perl in your PHP documents.

Visit http://www.zend.com/php5/whats-new.php for a more complete listing of the new features in PHP 5.

# Setting Up an Interactive Site with WordPress

One way to generate interest in—and traffic to—your website is by publishing a weblog. Although still primarily a weblog-creation tool, WordPress can also be thought of as a way to easily generate discussion on virtually any topic of interest without having to resort to relatively complicated forum or bulletin board systems. In this section we'll see how this free PHP application can be used to set up an interactive website.

## Installing WordPress

> **NOTE**
>
> We'll be able to go through the installation of WordPress in only a cursory fashion. For detailed installation instructions, check out the Installing WordPress page of the WordPress Codex at http://codex.wordpress.org/Installing_WordPress.

The latest version of WordPress can be downloaded from the WordPress website at http://wordpress.org. After you've obtained the archive, go ahead and unzip it.

```
tar zxvf latest.tar.gz
```

A wordpress directory will be created and the archive's contents extracted into it. You can then move this directory to a location that's web accessible, such as /srv/www/htdocs.

```
mv wordpress /srv/www/htdocs
```

WordPress requires a database to store the contents people post. You can configure the database using phpMyAdmin. If necessary, create a new database for WordPress, a new database user named wordpress and a corresponding password, and give all access privileges on the database to the wordpress user.

Next we need to make sure WordPress knows about the database we've set up and how to connect to it. Rename the wp-config-sample.php to **wp-config.php**, and then open it with a text editor. Look for the section of code that looks like the following:

```
// ** MySQL settings ** //
define('DB_NAME', 'wordpress');      // The name of the database
define('DB_USER', 'username');       // Your MySQL username
define('DB_PASSWORD', 'password');   // ...and password
define('DB_HOST', 'localhost');      //99% chance you won't need to change this
```

Replace the values next to DB_NAME, DB_USER, and DB_PASSWORD with the correct data determined by how you set up WordPress's database earlier:

```
// ** MySQL settings ** //
define('DB_NAME', 'wordpress');      // The name of the database
define('DB_USER', 'wordpress');      // Your MySQL username
define('DB_PASSWORD', 's3cr3t');     // ...and password
define('DB_HOST', 'localhost');      //99% chance you won't need to change this
```

Save your changes and then open your web browser to http://localhosthost/wp-admin/install.php. This will launch the installation script that will guide you through the rest of WordPress's setup.

## Overseeing Users' Access to WordPress

WordPress allows an administrator to add users who can post directly to a site and to regulate comments from readers. How much interactivity you want is almost entirely up to you. By default, WordPress permits much dialog and commentary among the poster(s), but this is quite configurable. Log in to your WordPress site and you'll be presented with the site administration tool. Click Options, Discussion to set your ground rules.

If you want to ban comments altogether, uncheck the Allow People to Post Comments on the Article box at the top of this Options page. When you scroll down to the Before a Comment Appears section, you can choose to moderate every comment, require a name and email address for every comment author, or require that everyone's first comment be approved. In the latter case, after any comment is approved, the author can offer comments on any post.

When you have set the default behavior for comments, click Manage at the top of the menu and then click Comments. This page lets you search for and edit particular comments if someone gets out of line or if you want to reply directly. If you have chosen to moderate comments, click Awaiting Moderation to complete that task.

Another great feature of the weblog culture is the cross-discussion among weblog authors. WordPress by default attempts to notify the owners of articles you link to when you post. It also supports "pingbacks and trackbacks," so that other blogs can notify you when they write about your articles.

Now click Links at the top of the screen. A blogroll is another way of allowing your readers to learn more about you and interact with other sites you think are important, interesting, or otherwise worth visiting. By default, WordPress includes a blogroll pointing to many WordPress developers, but it shows you how easy it is to set up a blogroll for your site.

Click Add Link to manually link to a site. Use the edit boxes to specify the Universal Resource Indicator (URI), the "real name" of the site, and a description. Create categories for your links in the Link Categories page and specify them for each link. You can also offer a more detailed description of your relationship with the site you're linking to.

As you can see, you can do a lot with WordPress to promote interactivity with your readers.

## Setting Up a Web-Based Community Forum

One of the best ways to keep users coming back to a site is to make the site more interactive and offer your visitors the opportunity to discuss the topic of your site through a bulletin board or forum system. PHP makes it easy to bring a forum into your site. One of the more popular bulletin board packages, phpBB, is free and available at http://www.phpbb.com.

### Installing phpBB

To install phpBB, go to http://www.phpbb.com/downloads.php to get the latest version. You get a choice of archive formats, so choose any one. Extract the archive to /srv/www/htdocs. It will create a /phpBB2 directory.

Change the permissions on /srv/www/htdocs/phpBB2/config.php to 0666 so everyone can read and write to this file. Then create a new MySQL database for phpBB. Create the user bbuser, set a password, and grant it full access privileges to the new database.

In a browser, type **http://localhost/phpBB2/install/install.php** into the address line. The installation portion of the system will appear, as illustrated in Figure 31.3.

Be sure to fill in all the requested information. Under Basic Configuration, make sure you have the correct database type listed. By default, it selects MySQL 3.x, but you will have MySQL 4.x installed on your system and an option to download 5.x from the MySQL website, www.MySQL.com. In Database Configuration, identify the database and the user you created for phpBB.

In the Admin Configuration section, tell phpBB how to identify you as the administrator of the bulletin board. At the bottom of the screen, click Start Install. The program will connect to your database and create the admin user for phpBB. Click Finish Installation.

For security reasons, you will now want to delete the /contrib and /install subdirectories. If these files are on the public web server, you put your entire bulletin board system at risk. When you've done this, refresh your browser to be taken to a sample forum page.

**FIGURE 31.3**    Start configuring your forum system with the Install page.

## Configuring phpBB and Creating Forums

The initial phpBB setup includes a dummy domain name and description text, along with a Test forum. This is mostly to give you something to look at. At the bottom of the forum page, click Go to Administration Panel to begin configuring your bulletin board for real.

You'll be taken to the Admin Index, which will have very interesting stats about your forums when they go live. But we want to start with the General Configuration settings, located under General Admin on the menu list on the left. In Figure 31.4, you'll see that the Site Name and Site Description have been adjusted. Most of the other defaults here are OK for an initial setup. Review everything else here and click Submit when you're happy.

Now it's time to create some forums. Under Forum Admin, click Management. You can set up categories and topics for your forums here. Type a category name, such as *Wisconsin Baseball Today* into the New Category edit box, and then click Create New Category.

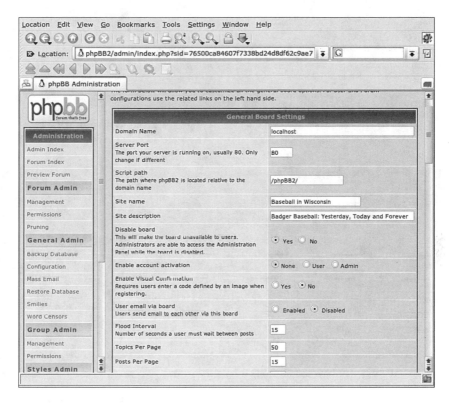

**FIGURE 31.4**  Give your forum a name and description, among other things, in the General Configuration settings.

You'll need to define some more specific forum topics next. Type a forum topic, such as *Milwaukee Brewers*, into the New Forum box (as shown in Figure 31.5) and click Create New Forum.

A dialog box appears (see Figure 31.6), where you can add a description for this topic. You may want to set some limits on the discussion in the Description as well. Review the other settings and click Create New Forum when ready.

After you've set up your real categories and topics, it's safe to delete the Test category. Click Forum Index under Administration, and you'll get a look at what visitors will see when they come by. It should look something like Figure 31.7.

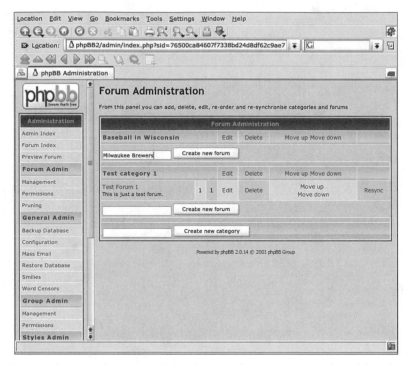

**FIGURE 31.5**    When you have a category for your forums, you need to define forum topics.

**FIGURE 31.6**    Describe your forum topic in this dialog box.

**FIGURE 31.7**    You're ready for visitors.

## References

- http://www.php.net—The PHP home page.

- http://www.zend.com—Zend Technologies, owners of the Zend scripting engines at the heart of PHP 4 and 5.

- http://www.phpbuilder.com—Tutorial and news site.

- http://codewalkers.com—A site offering tutorials, code, reviews, and support forums for programming with PHP and MySQL.

- http://php.resourceindex.com—The PHP Resource Index. The main draw for this site is the thousands of ready-made PHP scripts, functions, and classes. You can also find links to other tutorials and the larger PHP community.

- http://weberdev.com—More code, tutorials, weblogs.

- http://www.hotscripts.com—Scripts for every webmaster's need, mostly in PHP, but also in Perl, Python, JavaScripts, and even some in C and C++. Updated constantly, this is a great place to look for something interesting.

- http://phpdeveloper.org—News and forums for all types of PHP coders.

- http://www.thelinuxconsultancy.co.uk/phpeditors.php—A filterable (by OS and license type) list of editors and IDEs that support PHP coding.

- http://forums.devnetwork.net—The PHP Developers Network web forums.

- http://www.planet-php.net—A collection of PHP-related weblogs.

- http://www.viapanda.com/nvuphp.html—A FAQ outlining problems with using PHP in the Nvu web-authoring application, with some workarounds.

- http://phpnuke.org—One of the original PHP-based content-management systems.

- http://www.wordpress.org—The WordPress personal publishing system.

- http://www.phpbb.com—phpBB, a popular PHP-based community forum system.

# CHAPTER 32

# Performance Tuning

Squeezing extra performance out of your hardware might sound like a pointless task, given how inexpensive hard drives and memory have become over time. To a certain degree this is true, for most folks at least. But as we've said before, Linux users are tinkerers at heart. Many of us will gladly spend hours to make our computers work harder, faster, and smarter. Like the amateur auto mechanics of generations past, a cottage industry of overclockers and performance zealots has risen among the hordes of geekdom. And with the capability that Linux and other open-source software gives you to look under the hood and see for yourself what's going on, you can find the way to squeeze that last bit of juice out of an application.

The amount of benefit you can get by optimizing your system varies, depending on what kinds of tasks you are trying to perform. Even with all the shortcuts built in to any modern word processor, no software tricks will make your fingers type any faster in OpenOffice.org under SUSE Linux than in Microsoft Word in Windows. In the next few pages, we will look at ways to get a little more oomph out of your SUSE Linux system.

You should understand that optimization is not an absolute term. You can do almost anything to improve performance for a computer or specific application, and still have room to get even more out of it. But after a while, the law of diminishing returns starts kicking in, and you start working too hard to get not much back. So use these tips and methods, but remember that the reason you want to improve your performance is not for its own sake. You want to get some work done, too.

Nowhere else is the auto mechanic metaphor more appropriate than among the folks who muck around at the lowest levels of their systems. These are the folks who break down specification lists and performance metrics and consider them all a challenge to get more out of them than they were promised. This section is for these folks.

Before you undertake any of this type of work with Linux, keep a couple things in mind. First, perform a benchmark on your system before you start tweaking it. A good package to use for this task is hdbench, available from http://www.hdbench.net. Another good benchmarking tool is bonnie. The bonnie utility is available on your SUSE Linux CDs.

Many other packages are available as well. If you visit http://www.freshmeat.net, you can search for the term **"benchmark"** and find a variety of packages. If you happen to be a programmer, you can probably develop your own benchmarking tests, and perhaps you want to offer those to the Linux community after they've been tested a few times on your own system.

Second, tweak one thing at a time. If something bad happens (and tweaking is all about finding the limits, after all), make it something that's easy to trace. Log in your book what works, what doesn't work, and what breaks. Then move on to the next thing.

If you're going to find the limits of your system, have two things ready at all times: a good backup of your important data and the batch of six boot floppy disks to rescue your system if you need to. If you haven't yet, go to the YaST System page and launch the Create a Boot, Rescue, or Module Floppy module to perform this absolutely essential task.

Let's begin by discussing how to optimize the services running on your system.

# Optimizing Services

One of the most basic (and most frequently overlooked) tasks in optimizing the performance of a Linux system is to scrutinize the services it's running. Put very simply, the more services you have running, the slower the system will perform.

SUSE Linux is a true multitasking operating system. It's capable of running many process at the same time on a single CPU. However, the process of suspending one running process and running another one places a heavy load on the system CPU. The more times this happens, the slower the system runs. You can monitor how frequently this happens using the vmstat utility from the shell prompt. Sample output from vmstat is shown in Figure 32.1.

Notice under the System heading that there are two columns: in and cs. The in column displays the number of *interrupt requests* (either hardware or software generated) the CPU has processed each second. The cs column displays the number of *context switches* the CPU has had to deal with each second.

> **NOTE**
>
> An interrupt is a signal received by the CPU indicating that something (usually hardware) in the system needs its attention. A context switch occurs when the CPU has to suspend one running process and run another. Both of these events are CPU intensive.

```
linux:~ # vmstat 1
procs -----------memory---------- ---swap-- -----io---- --system-- -----cpu-----
 r  b   swpd   free   buff  cache   si   so    bi    bo   in    cs us sy id wa
 1  0  57328   6836  10772  46488   18   16   461    71  302   262  7 18 55 21
 0  0  57328   6836  10772  46488    0    0     0     0  256   120  0  2 98  0
 0  0  57328   6836  10772  46488    0    0     0     0  251   107  1  2 97  0
 0  0  57328   6836  10772  46488    0    0     0     0  307   165  4  5 91  0
 0  0  57328   6836  10772  46488    0    0     0     0  251   104  0  1 99  0
 0  0  57328   6548  10808  46488    0    0     0    64  261   130  2 13 84  1
 0  0  57328   6548  10808  46488    0    0     0     0  251   103  1  0 99  0
 0  0  57328   6548  10808  46488    0    0     0     0  255   115  2  2 96  0
 0  0  57328   6548  10808  46488    0    0     0     0  251    95  0  2 98  0
 0  0  57328   6548  10808  46488    0    0     0     0  255   107  2  1 97  0
```

**FIGURE 32.1**    Using `vmstat` to view system performance.

A certain number of these events is unavoidable. For example, every time you move the mouse or type a key on the keyboard, you generate an interrupt request. However, the number of these events, especially context switches, can be reduced by running only those services that you actually need.

When your system was installed, the installation program made many assumptions about what services should be automatically run at boot. Most of these services are necessary for your system to run properly. However, some of them aren't. To see what's running on your system, open YaST and navigate to the System, System Service (runlevel) module, as shown in Figure 32.2.

For example, notice in Figure 32.2 that the Postfix MTA (Mail Transfer Agent) is configured to automatically start at runlevels 3 and 5. Postfix is a popular email daemon that is widely implemented by many organizations to provide a powerful mail solution.

However, on your personal SUSE Linux system, there's a pretty good chance that you don't need it, especially if you're using an external ISP for email services. In this case, you can stop the Postfix MTA and configure it to not start at boot, thereby reducing the load on your CPU. In this example, you can stop the service by entering **rcpostfix stop** at the shell prompt. Then you can use the Runlevel Editor in YaST to disable Postfix at boot.

> **CAUTION**
>
> Don't get too carried away shutting down services. You might be tempted to stop services that you don't recognize. Most of these services actually are needed for your system to run properly. Only disable a service after you have thoroughly researched what it does and are confident that it isn't required.

**FIGURE 32.2** Viewing services configuration in YaST.

# Using PowerTweak

We begin this exercise by calling attention to a native SUSE Linux tool called PowerTweak. The Linux version of this application began life when SuSE engineer David Jones began work on a PCI Bridges kernel hack and later heard that the developer of a Windows shareware program called PowerTweak was looking for someone to port the tool to Linux. The deal was made, and PowerTweak was brought to Linux.

The program became a YaST module in SUSE Linux v8.1 and has been there ever since. Like the /etc/sysconfig Editor module (from which it steals its user interface), PowerTweak allows you to change assorted settings in the kernel, file system, network, and swap file to improve performance. The difference between the two modules is that PowerTweak writes its own configuration file, /etc/powertweak/tweaks, and then runs a daemon to implement the changes you make. This makes it a little easier to back out if a change breaks your system.

Figure 32.3 displays the PowerTweak module interface. To open it, go to the YaST System page and click PowerTweak. If you don't have the appropriate packages installed already, YaST asks if you want to install them (there's an extras package, too, with additional goodies).

In the left pane of the PowerTweak window is a tree full of devices and items you can tweak. Select one to display and edit in the right pane. There is guidance on what to do, to a varying degree, for each item in the display window. To make a change, type the value you want into the Edit box. Sometimes a drop-down menu will appear to direct your changes.

**FIGURE 32.3**   The YaST PowerTweak module.

Click Finish to approve the change or Abort to leave without making changes.

For example, suppose your SUSE Linux system gets a lot of heavy use. You start seeing errors indicating that the system is running out of file handles. You do some research and discover that this can be alleviated by increasing the value of the `fs/file-max` parameter. To do this, you would complete the following:

1. Start YaST and select System, PowerTweak.

2. Navigate to VFS Subsystem, Core, fs/file-max. The screen in Figure 32.4 is displayed.

3. In the Setting Of field, enter a new *value* for fs/file-max. In this case, the default value of 4096 will be increased to 12066.

4. Select Finish.

With any parameter displayed in PowerTweak, you can view a description of what the parameter does along with a possible range of values you can use.

With this in mind, let's next look at tuning the performance of the hard disk drives in your system.

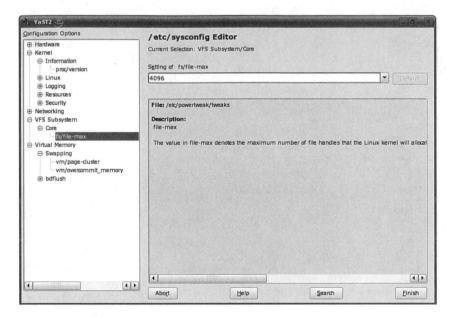

**FIGURE 32.4**    Setting the value of fs/file-max in PowerTweak.

# Tuning Hard Disk Drives

In addition to managing running processes and using PowerTweak, you should also consider tuning the performance of the hard disk drive in your SUSE Linux system. Input/output operations on the hard drive represent some of the most time-intensive operations your Linux kernel will have to complete as it goes about its business. Because of these, hard disk operations can become a significant bottleneck in your system.

The slow speed of hard disk operations are because hard disk drives themselves are inherently slow when compared to other storage devices such as RAM or SRAM cache. A hard disk drive is composed of mechanical devices—motors, platters, and actuator arms—that require a certain amount of time to complete their tasks.

However, there are some things you can do improve the performance of the drives in your system. The first aspect you need to consider is the type of drive you use in your computer. Let's talk about this topic next.

## Choosing the Best Hardware

Not all hard disk drives are the same. The quality of the drive you choose can make a big difference in the overall performance of your system. When selecting a drive, you should keep the following points in mind:

- Drive Interface—Most desktop systems sold today use Integrated Drive Electronics (IDE) hard drives. (The newer generation of IDE drives are called  Advanced Technology Attachment [ATA] drives.) These drives are inexpensive to manufacture and can store a large amount of data, hence their popularity.

Unfortunately, IDE/ATA drives have some serious shortcomings that you should keep in mind. First, the IDE controller on the master drive requires a lot of CPU time to read or write data. Although IDE drives may have a high data-transfer rate, the CPU is going to have to do a lot of work to make it happen.

Second, remember that each IDE channel on your system (the primary and the secondary channels) can each have two IDE devices connected to it, resulting in a total of four drives in a typical system. Keep in mind that many different types of IDE drives have been manufactured over the years. Early IDE drives transmitted data at around only 15MBps. Later-generation IDE drives can transfer data at speeds up to 133MBps. If you connect an older, slower drive to an IDE channel with a newer drive, the newer drive will slow down to the speed of the old drive. The entire channel will operate at the speed of the slowed device connected to it.

Finally, attaching two devices to the same IDE/ATA channel can slow things down because a single drive controller must manage two devices. If you choose to use IDE/ATA, you will get the best performance if you install a single device on each channel.

If you want the best performance possible from your disk subsystem, you should consider using either a Serial ATA (SATA) or Small Computer System Interface (SCSI) disk controller and drive. Both of these systems address many of the shortcomings of IDE and provide better performance.

- Data Transfer Rate—Over the years, many types of hard disk interfaces have been manufactured. Some interfaces are faster than others with respect to the amount of data they can transfer. If you choose to use an IDE/ATA disk interface, be sure to select either an ATA100 or ATA133 system.

  If you choose SCSI, you might find your choices a little more complicated. Over the years, a variety of SCSI standards have been implemented, including SCSI I, SCSI II, and SCSI III. Within the SCSI II and III standards, you can choose from Fast, Wide, and Fast/Wide options. Although the variations can get confusing, you'll get the best performance from a SCSI III Fast/Wide adapter and hard disk combination.

  If you go with SATA, you can choose between SATA150, which transfers data at 150MBps, and SATA300, which transfers data at 300MBps. As with the other disk options, the faster the drive and controller, the faster the performance of your system.

- Disk Rotation Speed—Remember that hard disks are mechanical devices. The speed at which data can be read or written is heavily dependent on how fast the platters inside the disk rotate. The faster the rotation speed, the faster data can be read or written. Low-end, inexpensive drives rotate at around 3500 RPMs. Midrange disks rotate at around 5000 RPMs. Fast disks rotate at 7200 or even 10000 RPMs. The faster the rotation, the better your system performance will be.

After you've selected the best drive for your system, you can then tune your drive for its best performance. Let's talk about how to do this next.

## Tuning Hard Drive Parameters at Boot

One way to tune your hard drive involves adjusting the settings in your BIOS. Every BIOS seems different, and in any case is not Linux, so consult your motherboard manual before proceeding. Take every precaution, and make sure the BIOS sees all your drives. Change one setting at a time.

Linux does offer a limited means to interact with BIOS settings during the boot period (mostly to override them).

Other options include these commands, which can be used to force IDE controllers and drives to be optimally configured. Your mileage may vary, but they have worked for some. You can get more information in the Bootprompt HOWTO at the Linux Documentation Project. Consider the following:

idex=dma   This will force DMA support to be turned on for the primary IDE bus, where x=0, or the secondary bus, where x=1.

idex=autotune   This command will attempt to tune the interface for optimal performance.

idex=ata66   If you have ATA66 drives and controllers, this command will enable support for them.

hdx=ide-scsi   This command will enable SCSI emulation of an IDE drive. This is required for some CD-RW drives to work properly in Write mode, and it might provide some performance improvements for regular CD-R drives as well.

idebus=xx   This can be any number from 20–66; autodetection is attempted, but this can set it manually if dmesg says that it isn't autodetected correctly, or if you have it set in the BIOS to a different value (overclocked). Most PCI controllers will be happy with 33.

pci=biosirq   Some motherboards might cause Linux to generate an error message saying that you should use this. Look in dmesg for it; if you do not see it, you don't need to use it.

These options can be sent to the kernel at startup by pressing F2 at the GRUB menu and entering them in the Boot Options Field. You can also use the YaST Bootloader module to insert these parameters into /boot/grub/menu.lst. To do this, complete the following:

1. Run YaST and navigate to System, bootloader.

2. In the Section Management tab, select the menu item you want to add these options to.

3. Select Edit.

4. In the Other Kernel Parameters field, enter the *option* you want to include.

5. Select OK.

6. Select Finish.

You can also use the hdparm utility to tune your drive. Let's talk about how to do that next.

## The hdparm **Command**

The hdparm utility can be used by the SuperUser to set and tune the settings for IDE hard drives. You would do this to tune the drives for optimal performance.

Once a kernel patch and associated support program, hdparm is now included with SUSE Linux. You should only experiment with the drives mounted read-only because some settings can damage some file systems when used improperly. Evidence of this can be seen when typing the hdparm command without any arguments. This displays the program's help; look at all the options marked DANGEROUS:

```
hdparm - get/set hard disk parameters - version v5.9


Usage:  hdparm  [options] [device] ..


Options:
 -a    get/set fs readahead
 -A    set drive read-lookahead flag (0/1)
 -b    get/set bus state (0 == off, 1 == on, 2 == tristate)
 -B    set Advanced Power Management setting (1-255)
 -c    get/set IDE 32-bit IO setting
 -C    check IDE power mode status
 -d    get/set using_dma flag (0/1)
--direct  use O_DIRECT to bypass page cache for timings
 -D    enable/disable drive defect management
 -E    set cd-rom drive speed
 -f    flush buffer cache for device on exit
 -g    display drive geometry
 -h    display terse usage information
 -i    display drive identification
 -I    detailed/current information directly from drive
--Istdin  reads identify data from stdin as ASCII hex
--Istdout writes identify data to stdout as ASCII hex
 -k    get/set keep_settings_over_reset flag (0/1)
 -K    set drive keep_features_over_reset flag (0/1)
 -L    set drive doorlock (0/1) (removable harddisks only)
 -M    get/set acoustic management (0-254, 128: quiet, 254: fast) (EXPERIMENTAL)
 -m    get/set multiple sector count
 -n    get/set ignore-write-errors flag (0/1)
 -p    set PIO mode on IDE interface chipset (0,1,2,3,4,...)
 -P    set drive prefetch count
 -q    change next setting quietly
 -Q    get/set DMA tagged-queuing depth (if supported)
 -r    get/set device  readonly flag (DANGEROUS to set)
 -R    register an IDE interface (DANGEROUS)
 -S    set standby (spindown) timeout
```

32

```
-t    perform device read timings
-T    perform cache read timings
-u    get/set unmaskinq flag (0/1)
```

> **NOTE**
>
> Setting the -u option to 1 can result in a significant boost in the performance of the system. However, some IDE drives don't support this parameter.

```
-U    un-register an IDE interface (DANGEROUS)
-v    defaults; same as -mcudkrag for IDE drives
-V    display program version and exit immediately
-w    perform device reset (DANGEROUS)
-W    set drive write-caching flag (0/1) (DANGEROUS)
-x    tristate device for hotswap (0/1) (DANGEROUS)
-X    set IDE xfer mode (DANGEROUS)
-y    put IDE drive in standby mode
-Y    put IDE drive to sleep
-Z    disable Seagate auto-powersaving mode
-z    re-read partition table
```

As you can see, the general format of the command is this:

```
hdparm <option> <device>
```

This tests an IDE hard drive:

```
hdparm -tT /dev/hda
```

Be sure to replace /dev/hda with the mount point of your hard drive (usually with a number added, such as dev/hda1). hdparm will then run two tests—cached reads and buffered disk reads. A good IDE hard drive should be getting 400–500MB/sec for the first test and 20–30MB/sec for the second. Note your scores, and then try this command:

```
hdparm -a16 -d1 -u1 -c1 /dev/hda
```

After you've made these changes (take another look at the help to see what you're doing), test the drive again. The numbers should increase. If so, run this command:

```
hdparm -a16 -d1 -u1 -c1 -k1 /dev/hda
```

The -k1 option saves the settings, and uses them on subsequent boots.

Read over the man page for more information about the multitude of options previously listed. Be aware that the SUSE engineers do their best to optimize all the settings before shipping the distribution. Because they cannot anticipate every configuration, however, it's worth a try to see what you can get on your own, if you're so inclined.

You can also increase performance by disabling file access time. Let's look at how to do that next.

### Disabling File Access Time

Whenever Linux reads a file, it changes the last access time—known as the atime. This is also true for your web server. If you are getting hit by 50 requests per second, your hard drive will be updating the atime 50 times a second. If you don't really need to know when a file was last accessed, you can disable atime by modifying /etc/fstab to include the noatime attribute for the file system.

With an ext2/ext3 file system, you can also use the chattr (change attribute) command to turn off atime changes by directory with this command:

```
chattr -R +A <directory_path>
```

The -R switch makes the command operate recursively through the subdirectories of the specified directory.

With this in mind, let's now discuss how to spread out the disk load on your system.

### Spreading Out the Load

With a Linux system, certain directories and partitions are used more heavily than others. These include the swap partition, /var, /tmp, and /home. Placing all these on the same hard disk can slow down performance.

To increase performance, they should be spread across multiple hard disk drives. If possible, the performance can be increased by installing multiple hard drives in your system and creating separate partitions for /var, /tmp, and /home, distributing them (along with the swap partition) across the drives.

> **NOTE**
>
> In an ideal world, you would place each of these partitions on a separate hard drive to achieve the maximum level of performance.

Doing this distributes the read/write load across multiple drives, allowing multiple operations to occur simultaneously.

## References

- http://www.coker.com.au/bonnie++—bonnie, a benchmarking tool for Linux file systems, with links to similar tools for RAID systems and SMTP servers.

- http://powertweak.sourceforge.net—The home of Linux PowerTweak. Some history, and an overview of the project.

# Command-Line Master Class

Throughout this book, we've talked a lot about getting things done in both GUI and command-line environments. It's not difficult to understand that for most users (and that's probably an understatement), the point-and-click interface is the best and easiest way to use a computer. Graphical desktop environments represent the future of Linux as an everyday operating system. Yet, the shell still represents the fastest and most powerful way to use a Linux computer. Once you have mastered the shell and its available tools, there's an amazing amount of stuff you can do with just a few keystrokes.

The Linux shell can be a black box for the average user. Actually, in most cases, it *is* a black box with a white cursor unless you're running the rxvt X terminal, where the colors are reversed. But in the hands of an experienced Linux geek, pipes and redirects and regular expressions and all the things that make the shell special can fulfill the promise of personal computing in ways that just don't compare to the GUI experience.

In the early days of Linux, one of the taglines used to bring people over described that promise: "Put the power of a workstation in your PC." Before Linux matured, you had to spend tens of thousands of dollars to buy a machine that had enough resources to run a commercial Unix variant. Linux brought that power within reach of most users. And the seat of that power is in the command line.

This chapter aims to make you a master of shell arcana, at least on a small scale. There might be some repetition of earlier lessons, but repetition can be a good thing when learning something new. By the end, you'll be able to do a few amazing things, and perhaps acquire the taste to do more. Have fun!

# Some Basic Commands

There are hundreds, maybe even thousands, of commands that the Linux shell can process. But a typical power user is familiar with just a handful. These would include

- cat—Prints the contents of a file. Any text file can be viewed, with the default output being displayed on the monitor.

- cd—Change directories. When this command is used without any options, it changes from the current directory to the home directory of the user.

- chmod—Change modules (file access permissions).

> **TIP**
>
> The chmod utility can work with octal permissions—such as 777—or alpha—such as rwx.

- cp—Copies files and directories.

- du—Displays disk usage.

- emacs—A multi-purpose text editor (with the kitchen sink thrown in).

- find—Searches for files and can be used with many different options. For example, to find all files beginning with the three letters "ins" and list them, the command would be: find . -name ins* -print.

- gcc—The GNU Compiler Collection; makes programs out of source code.

- grep—Searches for a string within input, a file, directory, or anything else specified.

> **TIP**
>
> A newer version of grep that offers a few more pattern-matching options is egrep.

- ln—Creates symbolic link (symlink) between files.

- locate—Finds files from an index.

- ls—Lists files in a directory. Options can be used with it to change the display in a great many ways, including showing hidden files (-a), in reverse order (-r), in long format (-l), and so on.

- make—Compiles and installs programs.

- man—The manual page reader that displays man pages (help files) for utilities, special files, and other entries.

- mkdir—Creates (makes) directories.

- mv—Moves files or directories.

- ps—Lists processes for the current user or all users.

- rm—Removes (deletes) files and directories.

> **NOTE**
>
> Of all the utilities available in Linux—and there are a multitude of them—one of the most dangerous is rm. In Linux, files are not merely flagged as deleted when rm is used, they are truly gone and there is not an undo feature. Be very careful when using this utility.

- ssh—The Secure Shell; connects to other machines.
- tail—Displays the last lines of a file. The opposite of this is head, which displays the first lines of a file.
- top—Shows resource usage in a constantly updated display.
- vim—A text editor.
- which—Displays the location of a command by looking through the PATH statement to find the first executable that you will encounter.
- xargs—Executes commands from its input. This is often used in conjunction with find to run commands on files once they have been found to match a specific pattern. For example, to find all files created by the user named "skipper" and look within them for the word "original", the command would be: find / -user skipper -type f | xargs grep -i original.

Gaining a basic understanding of what these commands do and how they can interact with each other is essential if you want to become a real wizard of the shell. This doesn't mean you have to know every option switch and types of usage, but you need to get to a situation and know what tool or tool chain is most likely to get you out of that situation.

> **NOTE**
>
> Every one of these commands (and practically all the others discussed in this book) will work in SUSE Linux, regardless of what shell you choose. Some shells have more commands built in than others, but you need not worry about dependency issues in choosing a shell.

Some of these commands are really larger applications. You learned about text editors and links in some depth in Chapter 5, "Getting Started with SUSE Linux," and about gcc and make in Chapter 28, "Using the GNU Compiler Collection and Other Programming Tools." The rest are seemingly simple instructions that reveal the shell's power when you look closely at them. That is our task here, with the aim of giving you the confidence needd to be able to mix them together to create your own commands and solve your own problems.

## Displaying the Contents of a File with cat

One of the first shell commands a Unix or Linux user learns is cat, which displays the contents of a file in the shell. This is useful both because you don't have to open a text editor or similar application to see whether a certain file contains a certain string, and because you can display the results of another command as text.

The standard use of cat is to display a file like this:

cat myfile.txt

There are two commonly used options that go with cat. You can include line numbering in cat by adding the -n switch. Adding -s displays one blank line at a time. This means if you have a file with a lot of blank lines interspersed with a few lines of text, cat will "squeeze" out all the extra blank lines, and print a line of text, a blank line (which can represent many more blank lines), more text, another blank line, more text, and so on.

You can combine these two switches as well, as in this command, that displays the output of /proc/cpuinfo, showing you information about your CPU:

cat -sn /proc/cpuinfo

If you run this command yourself, you will see the list of items has each line numbered, and a single numbered blank line at the bottom. The file itself may have as many blank lines at the bottom as it wants; cat will only display (and count) the first one.

Finally, you can use cat to string together multiple files, and then perform operations on all of them without having to cut and paste them all together, like this:

cat -s myfile.txt muotherfile.txt

Incidentally, some users are surprised to learn that cat does not abbreviate "catalog" or some other familiar word beginning with those three letters. cat's job is to concatenate the contents of files, as we've seen in the last example.

## Making and Changing Directories with mkdir and cd

Creating new directories is a pretty simple task with mkdir. Just type the command and the name of the new directory, and if you have write permission to the new directory's parent, it will create it without a word. If you are a lazy typist, be aware that md works just as well as the more formal mkdir.

Just don't get ahead of yourself. If you want to create two directories at once, this is not always possible. While it is quite permissible to create two new directories using mkdir UserDocs Music, mkdir will complain if you try to create Music/CDs, if the Music directory does not exist already.

But wait, there's a solution to this problem. Try this command:

mkdir -p /Music/CDs

With the -p switch, mkdir creates the parent directory, Music, then the child, CDs.

As long as we're speaking of CDs, let's switch gears and talk about changing directories. Now this cd seems like a pretty straightforward, no-frills type of command. But there are ways to maneuver quickly through your file system knowing some of cd's switches.

If you have experience with a DOS command line, you probably already know how to use .. to get to the parent directory. You may even know that cd / will take you to the Root (/) directory. What you may not know is that cd - will take you to the last directory you were in before now. You also may not know that using the tilde like this: cd ~ will always take you to your home directory. Play with these until you get comfortable moving around.

## Changing File Access Permissions with chmod

What you learned earlier about chmod can be greatly extended through one simple parameter: -c. This instructs chmod to display a list of all the changes it made as part of its operation, which means we can capture the output and use it for other purposes.

This switch is not a command history, but that can be a good thing. If you want a file to have certain permissions, but are not sure what the current permissions are, you can run this command. If no results display, nothing changed.

Another interesting switch is the --reference switch. Say you want all files in the current directory to have the same permissions as /home/myfile.txt, you can run this:

```
chmod --reference ~/myfile.txt *
```

The -R switch (note the capitalization) makes your command recursive through all the files and subdirectories of the current directory. If you happen to have trouble writing new files to your /home directory, run chmod -R 000 /home to make all files and subdirectories read/write to their owner.

## Copying, Moving, and Renaming Files with cp and mv

Managing your files and directories from the shell is pretty straightforward, and mastering the basics of cp and mv doesn't take much. But let's look at a couple of switches that will indeed help you.

To copy a file or group of files from one directory to another is simple:

```
cp *.txt ~/Documents
```

This copies all text files from the current directory to the /home/<username>/Documents directory. All well and good, but what if there's one text file already in /Documents with the same name as one of the files you're copying? Perhaps you ought to consider more creative filename conventions, but cp's default behavior in this instance is to overwrite the existing file.

One of two switches will solve this problem for you. The -i switch makes cp an interactive command, and prompts you before overwriting an existing file. Perhaps even better (at least if you know the two files are really different versions of the same file) is the -u switch, which tells cp to only copy the file if it is newer than the file in the destination directory. This is also useful when synchronizing directories, say from your laptop to your desktop. Both of these switches work with mv, making it useful in both contexts.

One other thing about mv: It is the command you use to rename a file in Linux. Where you would normally include a destination path for your move operation, just type the new name. The shell will "move" the file to the new name.

## Displaying Disk Usage with du

The du command displays the size of each file and directory that is inside the current directory. Its most basic usage is as easy as it gets:

```
du
```

With this command, you get a long list of directories and the amount of space their files take up. Add the -a switch, and you get an even longer list, with the size of each individual file. One problem with this is that du outputs its sizes in bytes, which is excellent on the accuracy scale, but can get annoying if you have video files with tens or even hundreds of megabytes on the list. Coming to the rescue is the -h switch, making the results more human-readable, if perhaps not so precise. Big files now read as 27M (for megabyte).

Combining these two switches, along with the -c switch, which gives you a total size, gives you a very nice list of files and their sizes.

```
du -ahc /home/mikemc
```

## Searching for Strings with grep

grep is one of those legendary Linux tools, a tool that genuine wizards employ with regularity. It is unquestionably a powerful tool for finding things. You use it to find text of any sort, whether in files or in standard input. Standard usage is simple:

```
grep -r "some text" *
```

This searches through all the files in the current directory and its subdirectories for a string "some text." (The -r switch makes it recursive. Note that unlike chmod, the r here is lowercase.) When grep is finished, it will display matching lines along with the name of the file the line is contained in. If you don't want to see the matching line, use the -1 switch. This displays all the files with text that matches, but none of the matching text.

You can also use regular expressions for your search terms (see Chapter 29, "Managing Databases," for more on regular expressions).

Here are a few more useful switches:

- -v—Inverts your search, so grep -v "some text" * looks for files that do not contain the search phrase.
- -i—Changes grep's default case-sensitivity.
- -c—Delivers a count of matching lines without naming files or displaying lines. Works with -v as well, to count non-matching lines.
- -n—Displays the line number of the matching line(s) in the file.

You'll see an important use for grep later when we look at piping together commands.

## Finding Files from an Index with `locate`

The `find` command is a good tool, but it can be startlingly slow. That's where `locate` comes in. This is just a wonderful tool, one that speeds the process immensely. This program uses a database that indexes your directory. The key to succeeding with `locate` is to update this database regularly.

> **NOTE**
>
> `locate` is the only command in this listing not installed by default in SUSE Linux. You can install the `findutils-locate` package in YaST, however. When you install it, SUSE Linux will automatically update the index database nightly.

All you have to do then is run this command:

```
locate <filename>
```

You will quickly get a list of every directory that file appears in. The only downside is that you can only search for a filename, not any other property of the file. Once you've found it, of course, you can use other commands to get more information about it if you need it.

## Listing Files in the Current Directory with `ls`

You use `ls` by itself to get a plain list of files in the current (or specified) directory. You can also use all the standard wildcards to find particular files or types of files.

Listing files is a pretty straightforward process, but displaying the results can be problematic. The `ls` command offers many ways to display and use your results. Here are some of the standard switches for `ls`:

- `-a`—Include hidden files
- `-h`—Display file sizes in kilobytes (K) and megabytes (M)
- `-l`—Displays the "long" listing, like the Details view of a GUI file manager
- `-r`—Reverse order
- `-R`—Recursively list directories (again, uppercase like `chmod`, not lowercase like `grep`)
- `-s`—Shows file and directory sizes
- `--sort`—Sorts the listing

## Reading Man Pages with `man`

Reading man pages themselves are a simple task, at least if you can understand the sometimes too-dense geekspeak that contribute to the notion that Linux has a steep learning curve. But leaving the language barrier aside, it can be difficult to move around in a man page, unless you know that you're in the paging program called `less`. This is the enhanced version of the original Unix pager, called `more`.

33

The purpose of a pager is to deal with the pesky problem of display output that takes up more than one screen in a shell. If you run `cat` in a standard command-line window (not an X terminal with a scroll bar), unless the file is awfully short, you will only see the last part of the file. Using `less <filename>` allows you to use your keyboard to scroll through the contents of a file, like a man page.

Navigating in `less` is mostly intuitive. The arrow keys, Page Up and Page Down, work as you would expect them to, and the space bar acts much the same as Page Down (as in a web browser). Pressing Home takes you to the top of the file, and End takes you to the bottom.

There are a few interesting ways to get around in `less`, though. If you want to see Line 27 of this man page, just type `27g`. You can also use percentages; to move to the 87% mark of the page, type `87p`. You can even do a text search by pressing the forward slash (/) and typing your search term(s). To see the next match, type / and Enter. To search backward, use the question mark (?) instead of the slash.

Finally, always remember to press `q` to quit your man page and return to the shell prompt.

## Listing Processes with `ps`

There are few more powerful commands at your disposal than `ps`, which can tell you an extraordinary amount of things about your machine and how it runs. The tricky thing about `ps` is that it doesn't use a hyphen with its command switches, so you have to keep that in mind when you run it.

The purpose of `ps` is to give you a list of all processes attached to the current terminal, which is likely to be your PC, but could be something else if you're logged in remotely. This, in fact, makes `ps` a useful command when you are logged in to a remote machine. You may not know what tools you have access to, and `ps` will tell you. One of the standard uses for `ps` is to see a list of all processes for all users; use the a switch. To see all processes for all users, whether they are attached to the current terminal or not, use `ps ax`.

In Chapter 22, "Managing the Boot Process and Other Services," you saw the KSysGuard system monitor application display processes in a tree pattern, showing the relationships between processes. Think you can't get that in a shell? Wrong! Try `ps u` to get "user-oriented output."

There is a ton of options that you can use with `ps` to get a handle on your machine. Check out the man page for a detailed listing.

## Deleting Files and Directories with `rm`

Way back at the beginning of the book, you were warned about `rm`. If you have forgotten, it bears repeating. If you are logged in as Root, and type `rm -rf /`, you can kiss your system goodbye. While the best way to protect yourself against this eventuality is to only log in as Root (or more precisely the SuperUser) when you absolutely have to, there is a backup plan. You should implement this right away, too.

Sticky fingers at the keyboard are more of a problem than bad intentions when it comes to the problem of over-deleting. Using `rm -rf <directoryname>` is not necessarily evil, either. All you are doing is saying "Yes, I really mean to delete this directory (and everything underneath it with the -r switch), don't warn me." But if you start typing the path `rm -rf /home/<formeruser>` and accidentally put a space after that first slash, you are indeed asking for trouble. You've gone from deleting the home directory of an old user to deleting / …and then the old user.

The way to protect yourself is to include the `--preserve-root` switch every time you use rm. You aren't even required to remember this tip. Right now, just add this line to the `.bashrc` file in your home directory (and the .rc configuration file of any other shell you might use):

```
alias rm='rm --preserve-root'
```

Now you don't have to think about it again. Each time you run rm, it will know not to ever delete the / directory.

### Displaying the Last Lines of a File with `tail`

Are you seeing something funky going on with your machine? Do you want to check a log file to see what might be up? You can do this by reading active log files with `tail`. This command displays the last few lines of a file and updates as new lines are added. To have `tail` monitor your system log's security messages, try this:

```
tail -f /var/log/secure
```

The -f switch has `tail` "follow" the progress of the file, and deliver each new message as it is generated. To keep it running as long as the log generates messages, add the PID number (which you can get from ps) of the log you're following and add it to the command thusly:

```
tail -f ---pid<PID#> /var/log/secure
```

Now see what's going on!

### Displaying Resource Usage with `top`

This is another way to get a handle on what's happening on your system. More precisely, it seeks to identify the biggest resource hogs at a given moment, so if your system has slowed to a crawl, you can determine and terminate whatever process is killing your system.

You are best off running `top` as the SuperUser, because you never know who owns the bad-acting process. You don't actually need any switches to get `top` running properly. After you type `top` at the prompt, it will open and display a list of processes sorted with the most CPU-intensive tasks at the top. Unfortunately, those processes don't have names in the `top` display.

To kill the process at the top of the list, type k and enter the PID. You are prompted for a signal number (the manner in which you want the process killed), with 15 as the default. This signals the process politely, asking it to shut down. Those apps that are not wildly out of control comply with the request. If your unruly process doesn't terminate, repeat the process, only this time send the not-so-polite Signal 9 (terminate and terminate NOW).

### Displaying the Location of a Command with `which`

One last quickie: Do you want to know the physical location of a command or application? Type `which mkdir`, and you'll discover that the `mkdir` command sits in `/bin/mkdir`. How useful.

## Combining Commands Together

So far, we have only been using commands individually, and for the most part that's what you'll be doing in practice. What gives Linux its real power, though, is when users string commands together, to build on the results of one tool to get even more done. There are even commands that serve as glue to hold these more complex tool chains together.

All the commands we have looked at here print their information to the screen, but the target can be flexible. There are two ways to control where output should go: piping and redirection. Pipes connect one program's output and the next program's input. Instead of displaying results on the screen, a command will send results to another program, which manipulates the information it gains to get even better results for the user. Output redirection works in a similar way, but works best when creating new files. We'll look first at pipes, and then at redirection.

There's a Freeciv game going on, and you need to know who's in it. Let's take two of the commands we learned about earlier in this chapter at find out:

```
ps aux | grep freeciv
```

What you did was create a list of processes live on the system right now. That list, including additional information about the processes (including the owner of each process), was sent to grep. It looked at that list and looked for lines containing the word "freeciv." grep then identified the matching lines and told you who owned the active clients, and who owned the server as well.

Earlier, we used du to develop a good list of all the files on the system. Wouldn't it be nice to have that in a file that we could then manipulate further down the road? Simple enough:

```
du -ahc /home/mikemc > du.txt
```

If we wanted a running total of who was playing Freeciv at any given moment, we could start a cron job to run our ps | grep pipe, and then add a third command:

```
ps aux | grep freeciv > players.txt
```

Simple, yet a pretty good illustration of just what we can do.

# References

- http://www.gnu.org—The spiritual home of the free-software OS movement. Learn much about command-line tools here.

- http://www.linuxdevcenter.com/linux/cmd—The alphabetical directory of Linux commands. Information on 515 (and counting) Linux commands.

- http://tuxfiles.org/linuxhelp/cli.html—Newbie-oriented help on assorted command-line topics.

- http://linuxcommand.org—You have Linux installed and running. The GUI is working fine, but you are getting tired of changing your desktop themes. You keep seeing this "terminal" thing. Don't worry, we'll show you what to do.

- http://justlinux.com/nhf/Shells/Basic_Console_Commands.html—More on the commands listed here.

33

# PART VII

# Appendices

## IN THIS PART

# Versions of Novell's SUSE Linux

Congratulations! By reading this book, you have successfully navigated your way through the SUSE Linux operating system and learned quite a bit about it. Perhaps now you are looking for more information about your current version or other versions that may suit your needs better, such as the server version of the SUSE Linux operating system—which is called the SUSE Linux Enterprise Server (or SLES); it is more of a server class system and fits the needs of a server operating system better. The version of SUSE we covered in this book was based on SUSE Linux 10, which is considered a desktop class operating system. In this appendix, we will take a look at the current version of SUSE Linux, version 10, as well as the related family of SUSE and Novell products.

> **NOTE**
>
> To find out about Novell's support and development of Linux in general, visit the following URL. The Novell/Linux website is chock full of documentation and information you can use to help you to make a wise decision on what version of Linux to deploy, based on your personal, and perhaps your business, needs.
>
> ```
> http://www.novell.com/linux/index.html
> ```

## SUSE Linux 10

Currently in version 10.0, SUSE Linux is a state-of-the art desktop operating system that provides you with tools for productivity, a connection to the Internet, and much more. SUSE has always been well known for having the biggest distribution among the "majors." Hundreds of open-source applications are bundled with SUSE Linux—so many that it takes five CD-ROMs (or 2 DVDs) to hold them all. Half of that includes the source code for the applications, but still more applications than you will probably ever use are available. Some of the available tools are meant for hard-core development of the system. If your personal or business needs change and you need some other software tool to get things done (one of the plethora of tools you have learned within this book, for example), odds are you do not have to pull out your checkbook to get the functionality you need. You need only to fire up YaST and search for the appropriate tool, and in minutes you're ready to go.

---

**NOTE**

You can view an online list of SUSE Linux's installed programs. You can also look at each package that comes with SUSE Linux and view the details.

`http://www.novell.com/products/linuxpackages/professional/index.html`

---

The product offerings keep expanding to include more office-based productivity and collaboration tools as well as programming, development, and networking tools; the list goes on.

---

**NOTE**

SUSE Linux also comes with two complete office suites (OpenOffice.org and KOffice), a minisuite (GNOMEOffice, with AbiWord word processor, gnome-db database, and Gnumeric spreadsheet), two industrial-strength open-source relational database management systems (PostgreSQL and MySQL), two financial programs (GnuCash and KMyMoney), two personal information managers (Ximian Evolution and Kontact), and just about everything you need to be productive.

---

You can also call SUSE Linux a very solid development tool for programmers who work with Linux and Unix, C++, LAMP, and so on. Programmers at all skill and experience levels will find practically all the necessary tools for their craft within SUSE Linux. There are text editors galore, starting with the venerable GNU Emacs and vim and including many others of more recent vintage, the GNU C Compiler (gcc), support for Perl, Python, Ruby, PHP, Java, and just about any other language you can think of, and at least two integrated development environments (IDEs) in KDevelop and Eclipse. Manage your large projects with the Concurrent Versioning System (CVS) or Subversion, too.

In addition to all these applications, plus all the routine commands, fonts, and eye candy that you would want in a desktop system, SUSE Linux comes with extensive printed documentation. The Administration Guide covers the installation and other system administration tasks for those with root privileges. The User Guide is a friendlier manual that covers configuring and using a desktop environment, office applications, electronic mail, and other tools. You can read the full contents of both these books through the SUSE Help Center as well.

SUSE Linux is updated with point releases twice a year, but because applications get revised with bug fixes, security fixes, and feature enhancements all the time, you can stay on the cutting edge. Many developers package their applications using the Red Hat Package Management System (RPM). SUSE has always used this method to build its distribution, and many SUSE-specific RPMs have been written. You can use the YaST Online Update (YOU) or the Advanced Package Tool (APT) created for Debian systems and adapted for RPM as well, but RPM is definitely the most commonly used. Whichever you choose, you will be able to package your applications with ease using SUSE Linux.

### Version 10.0

As of the writing of this book, SUSE Linux is at version 10.0. From the authors' experience with it, it's clear that version 10.0 is a solid, reliable, and secure desktop operating system. The current version is easy to install, easy to configure, and very stable.

Because SUSE Linux is primarily a desktop operating system, you can expect to see it function solidly as you browse the Web, send email, chat with friends via an Instant Messaging program, design and post web pages, organize digital photos, play movies, and create documents, web pages, and spreadsheets. You can even use it to host a blog or develop your own applications.

Although it's not intended for business deployments, SUSE Linux 10.0 provides corporate evaluators with an excellent first look at technologies such as XEN (virtualization), OpenOffice 2.0 (productivity suite), Beagle (desktop search), and Mono (open-source development environment). These technologies, when refined and fully supported, may appear in future Novell enterprise Linux offerings.

> **NOTE**
>
> While not yet finalized, as of this writing it is expected that SUSE 10.0 will be available in both a downloadable and a boxed version.

## SUSE Linux Enterprise Server (SLES)

SUSE LINUX Enterprise Server (SLES) 9 is an enterprise class operating system that will allow you to apply a "server" component to your SUSE Linux knowledge. As discussed within the book, SUSE Linux is primarily used for a desktop operating system. If you need more advanced components and services, such as the capability to cluster your systems so that in the event one of them fails, the other takes over, adding a level of reliability to your system. Tools such as this will not be found anywhere but on the "enterprise" version of the OS. SLES allows you to perform application tuning and offers advanced networking features and more.

You can use SLES as a step upgrade to OES. OES is Novell's Open Enterprise Server, or OES. With OES, you would need a base operating system in place first, and that's where SLES comes in. Like most other Novell-based operating systems used in the server-class arena, you will need to install a base OS and then apply the application-based topping, which would be OES.

A

# Novell Linux Desktop (NLD)

Novell Linux Desktop (NLD) is a desktop operating system intended for use in the corporate environment. Built upon SUSE Linux, it includes all the features you find there—including YaST, YOU, OpenOffice, and all others. What truly sets it apart from SUSE Linux—and other Linux desktop operating systems— is that it comes with support from Novell. NLD is not sold through retail channels, but marketed directly to Novell customers through the support/sales channel and along with a service agreement detailing the support you expect and will receive.

As of this writing, NLD 9 is the latest version of the operating system, but 10.0 is in development.

# Open Enterprise Server (OES)

The Novell OES is a secure, highly available suite of services that provides proven networking, communication, collaboration, and application services in an open, easy-to-deploy environment. Some of the common components of OES (that bring it above the base version of SLES) include the Novell NetWare kernel, all services currently in NetWare 6.5, and additional enhancements that are in development. This includes Novell's top-of-the line file, print, and directory services.

> **NOTE**
>
> You can learn more about the Novell Open Enterprise Server by visiting the home page at the following URL.
>
> http://www.novell.com/products/openenterpriseserver/index.html

The Novell OES incorporates the latest NetWare NOS services and functionality, as well as the complete SUSE Linux Enterprise Server 9 operating system (Intel-based x86 platform) all under one roof.

With Novell OES, users receive much of the same as they do with SUSE Linux, except as mentioned earlier; the Novell OES is built specifically for server-based services such as the following:

- Advanced file and storage services
- High-availability services (such as Clustering)
- Advanced management services and tools
- Advanced networking and productivity services
- Advanced identity-management and security services

Those who are familiar with NetWare (especially version 6.x) will notice that many of the tools used for NetWare, such as iFolder, iPrint, and iManager, as well as Novell Storage Services (NSS), can be used on Linux.

To find out more about Novell's OES (or SUSE Linux for the desktop), visit Novell's website for more information.

# APPENDIX B

# SUSE and Linux Internet Resources

Now that you are very familiar with the operation of SUSE Linux, you should learn more about it by visiting and researching many freely available online resources. The Internet is an excellent resource to find information on Unix and Linux, especially if you are new to it and need to find information quickly.

With the purchase of SUSE by Novell, a new world of opportunities has opened to you. As you work to learn your new desktop environment, master the shell prompt, or just learn more about Linux in general, many opportunities have opened up for the Linux desktop movement with the release of SUSE Linux. Not only is SUSE Linux now being developed by a company that has had a long-standing success as a server-based platform, it's being supported by it as well. Novell has spent a lot of time making sure that the online documentation is being developed and the operating system is receiving the support it needs. Beyond the support you may get from Novell, SUSE is also supported well on the public Internet, which is what we will be covering in this appendix.

In Chapter 1, "Welcome to SUSE Linux," the book started by giving you places online to search if you have issues. For instance, Chapter 1 covered Novell SUSE online help and where to find Linux User Groups (LUGs). As we mentioned, *Linux Gazette* magazine hosts the Groups of Linux Users Everywhere (GLUE) site at http://glue.linuxgazette.com. Organized geographically, you can browse through the listings or search from the main page. Every group has an email contact, and many have a URL listed.

This appendix builds on that first chapter, expanding the list of information you can search for online and keeping it all in an easy-to-use reference. The listing of information provided here is merely a gateway into the endless sea of what information is really out there if you search hard enough for it. Do be aware that although these sites can be helpful, it is up to you to verify the legitimacy of each website you visit. Sites such as Novell.com will most likely have more (and probably more accurate) information than a website run by a hobbyist. Make sure you use web references carefully and verify your sources of information if you are unsure.

After you venture out on the Internet to research, make sure you continue your studies with Unix and Linux in general and practice as much as possible while researching. Remember, the more you practice, the easier it gets, and after you know commands cold, how to navigate the system, and where things are kept, your control of Unix strengthens.

Beware of buggy and virus-filled software on the Internet. There is so much to learn about Unix and Linux that you can literally search for months and come up with new sources of information daily. Make sure you do not download software that is a virus, or Trojan, or another form of malware. Make sure you check that you download software from legitimate sources. Keep your antivirus software (and any other form of antispyware software you may be running) updated and patched. You may also want to be aware of (and watch out for) "orphanware." This is software that is created by an entity that basically ends support for the product (for whatever reason) and leaves it, and you, orphaned—without a solution.

In this appendix, you will find a list of Internet resources for learning about the topics covered in this book and expand on where you may be able to find even more information on your version of Linux, or for other general Linux-based information.

## Novell SUSE Linux Reference

In Chapter 1 we covered the basics of where you can find SUSE Linux-specific help. You can get help by using the documentation sources that come with the SUSE Linux operating system, including the Help Center, which is used to find information for you by searching the documentation that comes with the version of Linux you just installed, such as 9.3.

Because documentation and other sources with more than 1,000 programs are included in the distribution, even a book this size cannot cover the basics of everything in your copy of SUSE Linux. There are plenty of places to go to learn more about Linux and help you troubleshoot problems with applications. Printed documentation and, as previously mentioned, the SUSE Help Center will help you find many of the answers to general questions you may have that cannot be answered within this book. You can also try to use SUSE Online Support using the SUSE website at http://www.novell.com/products/linuxprofessional/support/. This support system is a great resource for getting help. The first set of menus is for paid support. The second set is for Do-It-Yourself online support.

When you're trying to find a solution for a problem, click Support Database from the main Support menu, or just go directly to the Support Database at http://portal.suse.com/sdb/en/index.html.

This database is searchable, either via keyword or full text. Besides German and English, the database exists in French, Spanish, Czech, and Hungarian (Magyar). The Online Support menu on the main support page links to some interesting HOWTO documents, showing you step by step how to handle issues great and small, from partitioning your hard drive to comparing HTML editors to encrypting email.

At http://www.opensuse.org you'll find a great deal of information related to SUSE and the Open Source movement. Not only will you find documentation and other links here, but this is also where betas and development releases are usually posted. You can report bugs, participate as a developer, and do much more.

Man pages are also a great way to get help when you need it. If you are running SUSE Linux and find you need help, try the man pages. Man pages are compressed text files, located in /usr/share/doc. They are usually tersely written (usually by their programmers), with information listed under particular categories specified by convention. These include a command reference, a summary of what each option/switch does, and the author of the page or the program. Occasionally, there are known bug statements.

## Mailing Lists

You can use general Linux or SUSE-specific mailing lists to find more help if needed.

```
http://lists.suse.com/
```

```
http://www.suse.com/en/private/support/online_help/mailinglists/
```

## Unix General Reference

The following links are Unix specific or Unix vendors that will help you find general Unix-based information.

```
http://www.ugu.com/
http://www.unix.org/
http://www.sco.com/
http://www.unixreview.com/
http://www.freebsd.org/
```

## General Linux Resources

For a wide array of free Unix and Linux (SUSE and so on) white papers and other help, visit rsnetworks.net.

```
http://www.rsnetworks.net/masterunixquickly/
```

The Linux Documentation Project is a great source for HOWTO guides and other information on a variety of Linux topics.

```
http://www.tldp.org/
```

Linux on Laptops offers information for installing Linux on specific makes and models of laptop computers.

`http://www.linux-laptop.net/`

Find a LUG near you. Linux user groups often sponsor "install fests." You bring your PC and they'll help you install Linux on it. In addition, LUGs have interesting guest speakers at their meetings.

`http://lugww.counter.li.org/`

The GNU Project and the Free Software Foundation contain source code and documentation for many of the utilities used in Linux distributions.

`http://www.gnu.org/`

## Linux News Reference

`http://slashdot.org`
`http://www.linuxgazette.com/`
`http://www.linuxworld.com`
`http://www.linux.com/`
`http://www.linuxjournal.com/`
`http://www.linuxquestions.org/`

## Linux Search Reference

`http://www.novell.com/linux/`
`http://www.google.com/linux`
`http://portal.suse.com/sdb/en/index.html`

Use the preceding online search engines (or your other vendor-specific or non-vendor-specific ones) and search on keywords.

Keywords examples: **suse**, **linux**, **ftp**, **nfs**, **rpm**, **distribution**, **iso images**, **novell**, **unix**.

SUSE Linux package listing can be found online at Novell's website.

`http://www.novell.com/products/linuxpackages/professional/diff_cd_dvd.html`

## General Web Link Reference

In the next section of the appendix, we will take a look at the references listed by category. If you have an issue with editing and want to learn more about the vi editor, search the appendix for the heading on editing, for example.

## SUSE and Linux Internet Resources

Each chapter in this book includes a reference section with links to more or related information to the subject of the chapter. Use it to build a set of bookmarks to help you learn more about Linux in general and SUSE Linux in particular.

In this section, the references have been broken down into three major sections: systems administration, which cover X Window, Office applications, and so on; network and security references, which cover tutorials and information on IP addressing, name services, and so on; and programming and LAMP references, which, if you are getting into development on Linux, will surely help you out in your development efforts.

Following are a few general sites to look at first before you delve too deeply into other online sources. These will prove to be some of your best bets.

- http://www-1.ibm.com/linux/—The Linux portal at IBM. News, reports, and white papers related to this important Linux player. Check the SUSE Linux link under "Linux Distributors" for material related to IBM support for SUSE Linux products.

- http://www.suse.com/—The English-language home of SUSE Linux. News, downloads, support.

- http://www.suse.com/us/private/support—Search the support database, read HOWTOs, subscribe to a mailing list.

- http://portal.suse.com/sdb/en—Direct link to the SUSE support database.

## Installation, Disk Tools, and General Systems Administration

This set of links points to useful resources on installing Linux, booting, partitioning, and other installation and system-management tools.

- http://irc.freenode.net—A great starting place to go for information about SUSE, Linux, or anything related.

- http://linux.dell.com—Home of the Dell Linux Community. Dell is focused on Enterprise Linux and will sell you servers with either SUSE Linux Enterprise Server or Red Hat Enterprise Server, but the community site offers mailing lists to support Linux users on desktops and laptops as well.

- http://linuxshop.ru/linuxbegin/win-lin-soft-en/table.shtml—Look here for Linux equivalents of Windows applications.

- http://cdb.suse.de—The SUSE hardware compatibility database.

- http://www.linuxprinting.org—Want to see if your printer works in Linux? Here's the place.

- http://www.linux-usb.org—The Linux-USB project, with information on supported devices and drivers.

- http://www.qbik.ch/usb/devices—The Linux USB devices database; search here for compatible devices.

B

- `http://www.linmodems.org`—Linux drivers for software-based modems.

- `http://www.linuxcertified.com` and `http://emperorlinux.com`—Two companies that deliver laptops with Linux preinstalled.

- `http://linux-laptop.net`—More information on Linux-friendly laptops.

- `http://www.linux1394.org`—The Linux FireWire project, with information on drivers for these devices.

- `http://elks.sourceforge.net`—The Embeddable Linux Kernel Subset, an attempt to build some Linux functionality that will run on an Intel 286 and earlier processor.

- `http://www.lnx-bbc.org`—Home of the Linux Bootable Business Card project, producing a "live CD" in the shape of standard business card.

- `http://www.gnu.org/software/parted/parted.html`—Home of GNU Parted, the free-software disk partitioning tool.

- `http://tldp.org/HOWTO/Installation-HOWTO/index.html`—From 2000, this Linux Installation HOWTO was written by programming guru Eric S. Raymond.

- `http://www.gnu.org/software/grub`—The GRUB bootloader home page.

- `http://www.pathname.com/fhs`—Probably more than you want to know about the new Linux Filesystem Hierarchy Standard.

- `http://standards.ieee.org/regauth/posix`—The IEEE POSIX information page.

- `http://cnswww.cns.cwru.edu/~chet/bash/bashtop.html`—Chet Ramey's bash page. He is the current maintainer of the bash project.

- `http://www.tldp.org/LDP/Bash-Beginners-Guide/html/`—The Bash Beginners Guide as a web page. If you visit www.tldp.org/Guides you can get this in other formats, along with other excellent Linux resources.

- `http://www.tcsh.org/Welcome`—The tcsh Wiki. Learn more and contribute your own knowledge about this C Shell.

- `http://www.zsh.org/`—Home of the Z Shell. Select a nearby mirror.

- `http://www-106.ibm.com/developerworks/linux/library/l-z.html`—Good introduction to the Z Shell from IBM.

- `http://www.ibiblio.org/mc/`—Home of the Midnight Commander. Screenshots, FAQs, and a to-do list for the developers.

- `http://www.dotfiles.com/`—Explore contributed configuration files for various shells, editors, and other tools.

- `http://www.shelldorado.com/`—Heiner's Shelldorado. Much scripting information for all shells, but a good introduction, too.

- `http://www.gnu.org/software/emacs/emacs.html`—The GNU/Emacs home page.

- `http://www.dotemacs.de/`—The "very unofficial dotemacs home." Explore the many ways to configure your Emacs.

- `http://www.emacswiki.org`—Find new modules and helpful people here.

- `http://www.vim.org/`—The Vim home page.

- `http://vimdoc.sourceforge.net/`—Where to find documentation of all sorts for Vim.

- `http://www.yzis.org/`—The new project from the developers of Kvim for the K Desktop Environment. The yzis editor is a new editor based on vim.

- `http://sourceforge.net/projects/joe-editor/`—The home for Joe's Own Editor.

- `http://jedit.org/`—The Java-based editor.

- `http://linux.about.com/od/embedded/l/blnewbie_toc.htm`—The Linux Newbie Administrator Guide. A basic overview.

- `http://www.gratisoft.us/sudo/`—The sudo main page. Downloads, documentation, and resources for this command.

- `http://www.x.org`—The X.org Foundation, the hub of X Window System development activity.

- `http://freedesktop.org`—The effort to produce minimum standards for free desktop software. Not a formal standards body, but a "collaboration zone" where projects are hosted and KDE and GNOME developers can discuss concerns.

- `http://www.kde.org`—The home of the K Desktop Environment. Well-organized site, with links to nearly everything relevant to KDE.

- `http://dot.kde.org`—The KDE News site, with links to online articles about KDE and its applications, along with press releases and the like.

- `http://www.gnome.org`—The GNOME home.

- `http://www.gnomedesktop.org`—"Footnotes," the GNOME News site.

- `http://www.novell.com/linux/ximian.html`—The Ximian area of Novell.com. Information about Evolution, Mono, and the Ximian Desktop.

- `http://xwinman.org`—An Internet hub for learning about and trying Window Managers for X.

- `http://www.gnomefiles.org/app.php?soft_id=599`—Metacity.

- `http://sawmill.sourceforge.net`—Sawfish is a window manager for the X Window System. It was formerly known as Sawmill.

- `http://www.windowmaker.org`—WindowMaker is a window manager used in Linux.

- `http://icesoundmanager.sourceforge.net/IcePref2`—IceWM is an advanced Linux configuration tool.

- `http://www.cryptonomicon.com/beginning.html`—The Neal Stephenson essay, "In the Beginning Was the Command Line." See also an authorized "update" by Garrett Birkel, "The Command Line in 2004," at `http://home.earthlink.net/~android606/commandline`.

- `http://www.gnu.org/software/bash`—The official bash site at the GNU Project. Download the latest, and read the Introduction to Bash.

- `http://cnswww.cns.cwru.edu/~chet/bash/bashtop.html`—Chet Ramey's bash site. Ramey is the current bash maintainer. Looks very much like the official page, but also has the bash FAQ list.

- `http://www.tldp.org/LDP/Bash-Beginners-Guide/html`—A bash guide for beginners.

- `http://ldp.nllgg.nl/LDP/abs/html`—The Advanced bash scripting guide. "This tutorial assumes no previous knowledge of scripting or programming, but progresses rapidly toward an intermediate/advanced level of instruction." Read online, or download the PDF or the SGML source.

- `http://www.filibeto.org/sun/lib/development/shell/config_the_bash_shell.html`—Configuring the bash shell.

- `http://www.justlinux.com/nhf/Shells/Basic_Console_Commands.html`—Learn these commands and you can be comfortable saying you know bash "well enough."

- `http://www.kornshell.com/doc`—Assorted documentation for the commercial Korn shell, ksh.

- `http://www.tcsh.org`—The tcsh wiki. Although it does not contain a wealth of information, check out the FAQ and TipsNTricks page. You can also subscribe to the two tcsh mailing lists from here.

- `http://www.faqs.org/faqs/unix-faq/shell/csh-whynot`—Perl guru Tom Christiansen's famous 1996 essay, "Csh Programming Considered Harmful." Why it's a bad idea to script in the C Shell.

- `http://www.zsh.org`—Home of the Z Shell. Very useful.

- `http://www.OpenOffice.org`—The home of the open-source productivity suite. Extended documentation, a knowledge base, and links to the various mailing lists that keep this project running.

- `http://wwws.sun.com/software/star/staroffice/`—OpenOffice.org's commercial big brother, produced and marketed by Sun Microsystems. This version includes a database and a few other closed-source widgets and tools.

- `http://www.taming-openoffice-org.com/`—Aimed at the person who wants to get more out of OOo. Many valuable tips, links, and pointers to other books that cover OOo in depth.

- `http://www.KOffice.org`—The KDE Office Suite home. Downloads, news, mailing lists, and archives.

- `http://www.gnome.org/gnome-office`—The umbrella home for the GO Suite.

- `http://www.abisource.com`—The AbiWord page.

- `http://www.gnumeric.org`—The Gnumeric page.

- `http://www.softmaker.de/index_en.htm`—Softmaker Office.

- `http://en.hancom.com/products/hancomoffice20.html`—Hancom Office.

- `http://kmymoney2.sourceforge.net/index.html`—Kmymoney.

- `http://www.gnucash.org`—GnuCash.

- `http://www.scribus.net`—Home of the Scribus desktop publishing tool. Be sure to check out the detailed and very helpful tutorial at docs.scribus.net.

- `http://www.gnome.org/projects/dia/`—The Dia diagramming tool. Useful documentation not included in the package.

- `http://www.insilmaril.de/vym/`—The View Your Mind page. Written in VYM and exported to HTML. Nice way to see how the program works.

- `http://www.alsa-project.org/alsa-doc`—The Advanced Linux Sound Architecture sound card matrix. Check here for more information on support for your card.

- `http://www.linux-sound.org`—From music made with Linux to musician mailing lists to player and production software, the jumping-off point for sound and music under Linux.

- `http://www.xmms.org/`—Home of the X Multimedia System (XMMS). News, downloads, plug-ins, skins, and support for this multifaceted media player.

- `http://www.vorbis.com`—Hows and whys for the Ogg Vorbis audio format.

- `http://www.exploits.org/v4l/`—Video for Linux information page. Technical information on the V4L APIs, drivers for supported cards, and personal video recorders. Links to software for making video of all types. When typing this URL out, know that the last character is an L (as in Video4Linux), not a numeral 1. Should you type the numeral, you get a rather snarky error message.

- `http://www.mythtv.org`—The MythTV personal video recorder software. Installation instructions, examples of MythTV in action.

- `http://anandtech.com/linux/showdoc.aspx?i=2190&p=1`—A detailed and honest explanation of a successful MythTV installation on SUSE Linux.

- `http://www.mplayerhq.hu`—The MPlayer headquarters for that varied and full-featured video player.

- `http://xinehq.de`—The Xine headquarters; news and downloads for this video player.

- `http://www.gphoto.org/`—Linux Management software for digital camera images.

- `http://www.gphoto.org/proj/libgphoto2/support.php`—The gphoto list of supported cameras.

- `http://www.teaser.fr/~hfiguiere/linux/digicam.html`—Digital Camera Support for Unix, Linux, and BSD. If your camera is not on the gphoto list, this site may help you find out why and offer suggestions.

- `http://digikam.sourceforge.net`—The KDE digiKam front end for gphoto. Look here for plug-ins and new versions, which seem to come out every two months.

- `http://www.gimp.org`—The very well organized home of The GNU Image Manipulation Program (GIMP). Check out the Tutorials section, with walk-throughs for all skill levels, beginner to expert.

- `http://gug.sunsite.dk`—The global GIMP User Group. Mailing lists, a large gallery of images and textures, tutorials, and articles to help make you a better GIMPer.

- `http://icculus.org/lgfaq`—The Linux Gamers' FAQ; get your questions answered.

- `http://www.happypenguin.org`—The Linux Game Tome, a catalog of Linux games of all sorts. Player ratings, news, forums, and links.

- `http://linuxgames.com`—LinuxGames, with all sorts of news related to the topic.

- `http://www.kde.org/kdegames`—The KDE Gaming area, with descriptions of all the games included with KDE.

- `http://www.ggzgamingzone.org`—Play Linux games online for free.

- `http://www.freeciv.org`—The Freeciv wiki site. All things Freeciv, with translations in seven languages.

- `http://www.winehq.org`—The Wine Project headquarters. Be sure to vote for your favorite Windows application to be ported using Wine in the Applications Database section.

- `http://www.von-thadden.de/Joachim/WineTools`—WineTools offers a relatively painless installation of Wine and a bunch of well-known free applications, including Internet Explorer.

- `http://www.codeweavers.com`—Codeweavers, Inc., the makers of Crossover Office.

- `http://frankscorner.org`—This site helps you get the most out of Wine. Contains FAQs and HOWTOs to get you through most problems.

- `http://www.vmware.com`—WMWare Inc., where you can get information and a free 30-day evaluation copy of this virtual machine.

- `http://www.win4lin.com`—Win4Lin, helping people run Windows 98 applications, and now Windows 2000/XP applications.

- `http://dosbox.sourceforge.net`—The DOSBox site. Check on support for your DOS game, even find downloadable copies of some ancient games.

- `http://dosemu.org`—The home of DOSEmu, the DOS emulator.

- `http://freedos.org`—The FreeDOS project. Assorted applications to use in DOSBox or dosemu.

- `http://os-emulation.net/basiliskII/system753_tutorial/linux`—A tutorial on installing and running Basilisk II on Linux.

- `http://www.cl.cam.ac.uk/Research/SRG/netos/xen`—The Xen virtual machine monitor project home.

- `http://www.tldp.org/HOWTO/Filesystems-HOWTO.html`—Always the place to begin. The file systems HOWTO.

- `http://en.wikipedia.org/wiki/Filesystem`—Wikipedia on how file systems work in various operating systems.

- `http://en.wikipedia.org/wiki/Comparison_of_file_systems`—Helpful chart on differences between file systems, with links to the Wikipedia articles on each file system.

- `http://www.namesys.com`—The Group in charge of ReiserFS.

- `http://batleth.sapienti-sat.org/projects/FAQs/ext3-faq.html`—The Linux ext3 FAQ list. Differences between ext2 and ext3, and troubleshooting problems.

- `http://oss.sgi.com/projects/xfs`—The XFS for Linux site.

- `http://sources.redhat.com/lvm2`—The Logical Volume Manager home page.

- `http://www.tldp.org/HOWTO/LVM-HOWTO`—The LVM HOWTO page. Should have information on LVM2 by now.

- `http://usalug.org/phpBB2/viewtopic.php?p=33142`—Tuning up IDE hard drives with hdparm. A useful tutorial.

- `http://www.gnu.org/software/parted`—The GNU Parted home page.

- `http://www.nvu.com/`—The nvu (N-View) project for a Mozilla-based web-authoring tool.

- `http://quanta.sourceforge.net`—Quanta Plus project page for the KDE web-authoring tool.

- `http://kdewebdev.org`—The KDE WebDev suite site. For Quanta and its subsidiary tools.

- `http://bluefish.openoffice.nl`—Bluefish, the GTK-based web-authoring tool.

- `http://bfwiki.tellefsen.net`—The Bluefish Wiki, where the development team keeps the rest of us posted on what's happening.

- `http://www.screem.org`—A GNOME/GTK editor for HTML and XML files.

- `http://www.ndeepak.info/stuff/vtu/ginf`—"Ginf is not FrontPage," another effort to simplify web authoring.

B

- `http://webmonkey.wired.com/webmonkey`—The all-purpose online web-design school. Tutorials on various web technologies for all skill levels, from basic HTML to Apache to ColdFusion. Like Wired magazine, occasionally the pages lean to the illegible.

- `http://webdesign.about.com`—Down-to-earth advice about website design. Free online classes in HTML and cascading style sheets, too.

- `http://radio.weblogs.com/0124049`—"Notes from the Metaverse," the author's technology weblog. Lots of links and news related to open-source software and SUSE Linux.

- `http://www.planetsuse.org`—Planet SUSE, a group blog of SUSE Linux developers.

- `http://directory.google.com/Top/Computers/Internet/On_the_Web/Weblogs/Tools`—The current directory of blogging tools and services. You'll find something useful here.

- `http://www.blosxom.com`—Download and learn about Blosxom, the CGI-based blogging tool.

- `http://www.billstclair.com/blogmax`—The Blogmax extension for Emacs.

- `http://wordpress.org`—WordPress blog and content management tool. Very busy and helpful support forums.

- `http://www.blogger.com`—Still the easiest and cheapest way to start blogging. Now managed by Google.

- `http://www.sixapart.com`—The company behind Movable Type and Typepad. Access either product from the company blog page.

- `http://www.livejournal.com`—LiveJournal is a place for more personal blogs and building communities of kindred bloggers.

- `http://radio.weblogs.com/0102385/2003/04/24.html#a329`—A description of how to run the Windows blog program Radio Userland under Wine.

- `http://www.gnome.org/projects/evolution`—The Evolution home page.

- `http://www.mozilla.org/products/thunderbird`—The Mozilla Thunderbird page. Links to MozillaZine knowledge base and help forums.

- `http://pim.kde.org`—Home of the KDE Personal Information Management suite: Kontact, KMail, Korganizer, and the ancillary tools.

- `http://sylpheed.good-day.net`—Sylpheed, the other GTK-based mail client.

- `http://www.mutt.org`—The mongrel of text-based email clients.

- `http://www.fpx.de/fp/Software/UUDeview`—The UUDeview multiformat file attachment decoder. Works with all encoding formats (BinHex, yEnc, MIME, UUEncode). Enjoy the "Introduction to Encoding" document and get some useful history, too.

- `http://www.yenc.org/linux.htm`—Linux readers and writers for the yEnc coding format.

- `http://email.about.com/cs/standards/a/base64_encoding.htm`—An excellent description of base64 encoding.

- `http://www.postfix.org/start.html`—The Postfix home page. Be sure to click the Web Sites link on the menu to find a mirror site close to you.

- `http://www.seaglass.com/postfix/faq.html`—The Postfix mailing list FAQ, maintained by Kyle Dent, author of *Postfix: The Definitive Guide*.

- `http://www.sendmail.org`—The Sendmail home page.

- `http://catb.org/~esr/fetchmail`—The Fetchmail home page.

- `http://www.paulgraham.com/spam.html`—Paul Graham's original essay, "A Plan for Spam," outlines the theory of Bayesian filtering.

- `http://spamassassin.apache.org`—SpamAssassin home page. Check out the wiki pages for downloadable custom rulesets.

- `http://bogofilter.org`—Eric Raymond's Bogofilter project.

- `http://www.nidelven-it.no/articles/introduction_to_thunderbird_5`—A good introduction to spam filtering with Mozilla Thunderbird.

- `http://www.iki.fi/era/procmail/mini-faq.html`—The Procmail FAQ. In his own words, "The author wanted to call this a 'Mini-FAQ' but it keeps getting bigger. There are plans to rename it the 'Bronto-FAQ.'"

- `http://pm-doc.sourceforge.net`—The Procmail Documentation Project. See the PM-Tips page for sample rulesets/recipes and many other good ideas.

- `http://www.clamav.net`—Home of the open source Clam antivirus program.

- `http://groups.google.com`—Google Groups. Read Usenet on the Web and create groups of your own.

- `http://www.isc.org/index.pl?/products/inn`—The InterNetNews Usenet server and reader.

- `http://slrn.sourceforge.net`—"s-lang read news"; the slrn newsreader.

- `http://knode.sourceforge.net`—KNode newsreader in Kontact and KDE.

- `http://pan.rebelbase.com`—The Pan newsreader for GNOME.

- `http://c2.com/cgi/wiki?WikiWikiWeb`—WikiWikiWeb, Ward Cunningham's original collaborative site.

- `http://c2.com/cgi/wiki?ChoosingaWiki`—Choosing a WikiEngine, with help from Ward Cunningham's assembled masses.

- `http://zwiki.org`—ZWiki, the Zope-based wiki engine included in SUSE Linux. Docs still in progress.

- `http://twiki.org`—Another popular Wiki engine.

- `http://en.wikipedia.org`—The Wikipedia home page, perhaps the best example of how wikis work.

- `http://www.list.org`—Home of the Mailman list manager.

- `http://www.greatcircle.com/majordomo`—The Majordomo list manager.

- `http://www.siliconexus.com/MajorCool`—The web interface for Majordomo.

- `http://www.irchelp.org`—The place to get help with Internet Relay Chat.

- `http://www.irc.org/links.html`—IRC clients, channels, networks, and bots. Find them here.

- `http://tldp.org/HOWTO/IRC`—The Linux IRC mini-HOWTO.

- `http://kopete.kde.org`—Kopete, the KDE instant messenger and IRC client.

- `http://www.jabber.org/user/userguide`—The Jabber user guide, for learning about this open source IM protocol. Jabber.org also hosts a public IM server for you to connect with.

- `http://gabber.sourceforge.net`—The GNOME Jabber client.

- `http://xchat.org`—The Xchat home page.

- `http://www.licq.org`—LICQ, the mother of all Linux instant messengers.

- `http://gaim.sourceforge.net`—This IM client started as just an AOL Instant Messenger (AIM) clone, but now supports most other IM networks as well.

- `http://www.gnomemeeting.org`—GnomeMeeting videoconferencing home page.

- `http://www.kernel.org`—The Linux Kernel Archives. Where to find the latest kernel and more information.

- `http://www.kernel.org/mirrors`—Download the kernel from a server near you.

- `http://www.kernel-traffic.org`—The Kernel Traffic newsletter, a weekly summary of what's happening on the Kernel mailing list.

- `http://www.gnu.org`—GNU's not Unix. The home of many kernel-related projects. Get software and documentation here and a healthy dose of free-software philosophy.

- `http://www.gnu.org/software/make/manual/make.html`—The make manual. This utility is much more than a source-code build environment.

- `http://kniggit.net/wwol26.html`—The Wonderful World of Linux 2.6, a guide to the latest version of the kernel by Joseph Pranevich.

- `http://www.kernelnewbies.org`—For people who want to try their hand at kernel hacking. The Kernel Newbies host an IRC chat channel, #kernelnewbies, and a wiki from this site.

- `http://tldp.org/LDP/lki`—Linux Kernel 2.4 Internals Guide. Get into more depth about how the kernel works.

- `http://tldp.org/HOWTO/HOWTO-INDEX/os.html#OSKERNEL`—These HOWTOs explore the kernel in several ways.

- `http://minix1.hampshire.edu`—Al Woodhull's Minix site. Learn more about Linux's "parent" OS.

- `http://www.cs.vu.nl/~ast/minix.html`—The official Minix site.

- `http://jungla.dit.upm.es/~jmseyas/linux/kernel/hackers-docs.html`—Its origins are similar to those of a FAQ document, but this annotated "Index of Documentation for People Interested in Writing and/or Understanding the Linux Kernel" is more of a reference guide, with pointers to an abundance of useful kernel information.

- `http://kerneltrap.org`—"Your Ultimate Source for Kernel News."

- `http://www.gnu.org/software/grub/manual`—The GRUB manual.

- `http://www.tldp.org/HOWTO/LILO.html`—The LILO mini-HOWTO.

- `http://www.tldp.org/HOWTO/Linux-Complete-Backup-and-Recovery-HOWTO`—How to back up your system to support a bare-metal recovery.

- `http://www.tldp.org/LDP/sag/html`—The Linux System Administration Guide. See Chapter 12 on backups.

- `http://www.tldp.org/HOWTO/Ext2fs-Undeletion.html`—Undeleting files from an Ext2/3 file system.

- `http://amanda.sourceforge.net`—The Amanda home page.

- `http://www.backupcentral.com`—Storage Mountain, with much information and links on backups and other storage-related issues.

- `http://linuxgazette.net/104/odonovan.html`—An excellent and easy-to-understand article on using rsync and cron for automated backups.

- `http://www.k3b.org`—The home of K3B, the KDE CD/DVD burning tool.

- `http://richard.jones.name/google-hacks/gmail-filesystem/gmail-filesystem.html`—The GMailFS program, which allows you to convert your gigabyte of Gmail storage into a working Linux file system.

- `http://www.bluehaze.com.au/unix/cdbkup.html`—Using a shell script to back up to CD.

- `http://www.mondorescue.org`—A rescue tool that can produce bootable CDs to restore a broken system.

B

- `http://www.novell.com/coolsolutions/feature/11504.html`—A screenshot-filled YaST tutorial from Novell's Cool Solutions site.

- `http://www.suse.de/~sh/YaST2-Package-Manager`—Written to explain the big changes in YaST with v8.1, there's a lot of good information here on how YaST works.

- `http://portal.suse.com/sdb/en/2003/04/82_susewatcher.html`—Documentation for SUSEwatcher, including descriptions for the icons.

- `http://www.rpm.org`—Home for information on the Red Hat Package Management system. The site includes an online version of Ed Bailey's 2000 book, *Maximum RPM*.

- `http://www.nongnu.org/synaptic`—The Synaptic GUI for apt. Download the current source from here if you can't wait for a new package via apt.

- `http://packman.links2linux.org`—Excellent repository for packages not yet included in the official distribution. Download directly or use APT.

- `http://rpmseek.com`—Find more RPM packages here.

- `http://freshmeat.net`—A giant repository of Linux and other open-source software, organized by date received. Thus, the "freshest meat" is at the top.

- `http://www.lostcircuits.com/advice/bios2/1.shtml`—The LostCircuits BIOS Guide. The site itself is a bit ad heavy, but there is excellent information on various BIOS settings.

- `http://www-106.ibm.com/developerworks/linux/library/l-slack.html`—Joe Brockmeier explains the Slackware Linux boot process, which is not so different from SUSE Linux.

- `http://linux-newbie.sunsite.dk`—The Linux Newbie Administrator Guide. Very helpful.

- `http://www.troubleshooters.com/linux/grub/grub.htm`—"GRUB from the Ground Up," a fine explanation of how to create a GRUB boot floppy and boot it on a disabled machine.

- `http://www.gnu.org/software/grub/manual`—The GRUB manual, in various formats.

- `http://tldp.org/HOWTO/LILO.html`—The LILO Mini-HOWTO.

- `http://tldp.org/LDP/lame/LAME/linux-admin-made-easy`—Linux Administration Made Easy. See Section 4.8 on booting with LILO.

- `http://www.linux.com/article.pl?sid=04/05/17/1832239`—A brief review of KSysGuard.

- `http://docs.kde.org/en/3.3/kdebase/ksysguard`—The KSysGuard Handbook.

- `http://www.gkrellm.net`—The home of GKrellM.

# Linux Networking and Security Reference

This set of links points to useful resources on IP addressing, networking, and securing Linux.

- `http://arin.net`—The American Registry for Internet Numbers, the body that assigns public IP addresses for the United States.

- `http://www.ietf.org/rfc.html`—Search for, or get a list of, Internet Engineering Task Force Requests for Comment.

- `http://www.tldp.org/HOWTO/Linux+IPv6-HOWTO`—The Linux IPv6 HOWTO.

- `http://www.ietf.org/rfc/rfc2460.txt`—The IPv6 Standard document.

- `http://linuxreviews.org/features/ipv6`—Interesting article on "Why You Want IPv6."

- `http://www.iana.org/assignments/port-numbers`—Learn what ports are assigned to what applications at the Internet Assigned Numbers Authority site.

- `http://directory.google.com/Top/Computers/Software/Internet/Servers/Address_Management/Dynamic_DNS_Services/`—The place to find Dynamic DNS service providers.

- `http://www.isc.org/sw/dhcp`—The keepers of the SUSE Linux default DHCP server package and the optional client. You can view the current DHCP README file online at the ISC site.

- `http://dhcp-monger.est-unique.net/wakka.php?wiki=Welcome`—The DHCP-Mongers Wiki. Read man pages, search the mailing lists, submit new information.

- `http://nfs.sourceforge.net`—The Network File System project page, including FAQ list.

- `http://www.samba.org`—The Samba home page. See the HOWTO collection and Samba-By-Example Guide in the Documentation section.

- `http://www.wi-fizone.org`—Find a wireless hotspot wherever you may be at this site, sponsored by the Wi-Fi Alliance trade group.

- `http://standards.ieee.org/getieee802`—Get the official IEEE standard document for any 802.xx networking specification here. This runs the gamut from Ethernet (802.3) to WiFi (802.11) and beyond.

- `http://portal.suse.com/sdb/en/2002/11/wavelan.html`—Wireless network setup from the SUSE Support Database.

- `http://www.hpl.hp.com/personal/Jean_Tourrilhes/Linux/Wireless.html`—Much good material on Linux Wireless Networking.

- `http://www.securityfocus.com/unix`—This comprehensive security site offers security news, mailing lists, and even some firewall rule sets.

B

- `http://www.linuxsecurity.com`—Get the weekly Linux Advisory Watch and Linux Security Week newsletters to keep up with the latest information and patches. Tutorials for beginners and articles for security professionals.

- `http://www.insecure.org`—The home of the `nmap` security scanner.

- `http://www.ethereal.com`—The freeware Ethereal network protocol analyzer and packet sniffer.

- `http://www.tldp.org/HOWTO/DNS-HOWTO.html#toc1`—The Linux Documentation Project. This is an in-depth DNS how to with DNS general information as well.

- `http://www.isc.org/index.pl?/sw/bind/`—Internet Systems Consortium, Inc. (ISC) is a nonprofit public benefit corporation dedicated to supporting the infrastructure of the universal connected self-organizing Internet. This is an in-depth DNS/BIND how to with DNS/BIND general information as well.

- `http://www.arin.net`—American Registry for Internet Numbers. A nonprofit registry responsible for the administration and registration of Internet Protocol (IP) numbers in North and South America, South Africa, the Caribbean, and all other regions administered currently by Network Solutions, Inc.

- `http://www.isc.org/bind.html`—Berkeley Internet Name Domain information direct. BIND software, developed by the University of California at Berkeley, implements a DNS server and a resolver library that enables clients to store and retrieve resources or objects and share this information with other resources on the network. This link covers BIND in detailed information.

- `http://www.iana.org/`—Internet Assigned Numbers Authority. IANA is a government-funded authority that assigns and distributes international domain names and IP numbers or Internet addresses and oversees the Internet software protocols of the officially sanctioned root servers.

- `http://www.internic.net/`—A registry responsible for name assignment within the following top level domains: COM, EDU, NET, GOV, and ORG.

- `http://linuxprinting.org`—A central compendium of information on printing in Linux. Download official and unofficial open-source drivers. Read the recommendations in the Suggested Printer List when you're in the market for a new printer. Ask questions in the forums.

- `http://h10018.www1.hp.com/wwsolutions/linux/products/printing_imaging`—Hewlett Packard's Linux driver efforts.

- `http://www.tldp.org/HOWTO/Printing-HOWTO`—From the page: "A collection of information on how to generate, preview, print and fax anything under GNU/Linux."

- `http://www.cups.org`—The place to keep up with the Common Unix Printing System.

- `http://www.pwg.org/ipp`—The IETF Printer Working Group's page on the Internet Printing Protocol (IPP), used by CUPS. Very technical, but a good FAQ.

- `http://www.ghostscript.com`—The Ghostscript news and community page. New release announcements and a community component based on "diary entries."

- `http://www.cs.wisc.edu/~ghost`—The ghostscript home page.

- `http://www.adobe.com/products/acrobat`—Learn more about Acrobat and PDF from the official site. You can also download the free Reader here.

- `http://solutions.brother.com/linux/en_us`—The Brother Linux support and driver status page.

- `http://www.bluetooth.com`—The Bluetooth website.

- `http://www.holtmann.org/linux/bluetooth`—Marcel Holtmann's Linux and Bluetooth page. Articles in English and German, plus downloads.

- `http://www.cs.ucl.ac.uk/staff/s.zachariadis/btpalmlinux.html`—A guide to connecting your Palm PDA to your PC with Bluetooth.

- `http://tuxmobil.org`—The place to get information on Linux on all sorts of mobile hardware: laptops, PDAs, and cell phones. Monthly newsletter as well.

- `http://tuxmobil.org/Infrared-HOWTO/Infrared-HOWTO.html`—The Linux Infrared HOWTO. Configuring and using IrDA.

- `http://linux-laptop.net`—Another portable Linux site.

- `http://www.sane-project.org`—Home of the Linux scanner driver project "Scanner Access Now Easy." Search to see whether your scanner is supported by Linux.

- `http://www.ntp.org`—Network Time Protocol home.

- `http://ntp.isc.org/bin/view/Servers/WebHome`—The Public NTP Server list. Find a NTP server to connect to. Much more helpful information, too.

- `http://www.cpqlinux.com/acpi-howto.html`—The Linux ACPI HOWTO.

- `http://www.tldp.org/HOWTO/HOWTO-INDEX/hardware.html#HWMODEMS`—Linux Documentation Project modems HOWTOs. What you need to know, sometimes in excruciating detail, about ordinary modems, Winmodems, DSL modems, and cable modems. Some of it is outdated, but the revision dates are always posted here.

- `http://axion.physics.ubc.ca/ppp-linux.html`—Trying to set up PPP manually? This is the place to go, as W.G. Unruh has worked hard to troubleshoot many PPP problems.

- `http://linmodems.org`—A place to learn about software-driven "Winmodems" and attempts to support them in Linux.

- `http://start.at/modem`—"Winmodems are not Modems." A large list of modem models to check for Linux compatibility.

B

- `http://www.swcp.com/~jgentry/pers.html`—The Linux Dial-in Server Setup Guide. A step-by-step approach to setting up your dial-in server.

- `http://www.vsftpd.beasts.org`—The Very Secure FTP.

- `http://www.cert.org`—The Computer Emergency Response Team. The place to go to learn about current security holes and the latest "virus alert" email.

- `http://www.openssh.org`—The open-source Secure Shell home. OpenSSH includes the Secure FTP client.

- `http://www.cert.org/tech_tips/anonymous_ftp_config.html`—Excellent guidelines for safely setting up an anonymous FTP server.

- `http://www.gftp.org`—The GNOME FTP client.

- `http://kbear.sourceforge.net`—A KDE-based FTP client.

- `http://www.ncftp.com/ncftp/doc`—Documentation for the NcFTP client and server.

- `http://wget.sunsite.dk`—Wget, the GNU tool for noninteractive (scripted) file transfer.

- `http://enterprise.linux.com/article.pl?sid=04/12/20/1910209`—A pithy description of what you can do with wget.

- `http://www.gnutelliums.com/linux_unix`—A list of Unix/Linux Gnutella clients.

- `http://gtk-gnutella.sourceforge.net`—GTK-Gnutella.

- `http://bittorrent.com`—Bram Cohen's BitTorrent home page.

- `http://azureus.sourceforge.net`—Azureus, the Java BitTorrent client.

- `http://gift.sourceforge.net`—The GiFT open-source FastTrack peer-to-peer project.

- `http://apollon.sourceforge.net`—A GUI for GiFT.

- `http://kmldonkey.org`—KMLDonkey GUI client.

- `http://www.nongnu.org/mldonkey`—The home of MLDonkey, where you can download the core program. Front page links to all the file-sharing networks the client supports.

- `http://www.mldonkeyworld.com`—News, downloads, and support forums for all MLDonkey users.

- `http://wiki.etree.org/index.php?page=BitTorrent`—The eTree BitTorrent FAQ page, with much good information on BitTorrent clients, how BitTorrent works, and where to find content.

- `http://tldp.org/LDP/sag/html`—The Linux System Administrator's Guide.

- `http://tldp.org/HOWTO/User-Authentication-HOWTO`—Setting up passwords.

- `http://tldp.org/HOWTO/HOWTO-INDEX/admin.html#ADMSECURITY`—The Linux security HOWTOs all in one place. Be sure to read over the Security-HOWTO for an overview.

- `http://www.tldp.org/HOWTO/Shadow-Password-HOWTO.html`—Explains the shadow password system.

- `http://www.novell.com/coolsolutions/feature/11685.html`—A brief, but nice, overview of permissions and how to set them in Nautilus/GNOME.

- `http://www.gratisoft.us/sudo`—SuperUser Do lets you delegate specific administrative tasks to particular users without turning over the Root password.

- `http://www.kernel.org/pub/linux/libs/pam`—Pluggable Authentication Modules in Linux.

- `http://publib.boulder.ibm.com/infocenter/pseries/index.jsp?topic=/com.ibm.aix.doc/aixbman/security/pam_overview.htm`—This guide to PAM under IBM's flavor of Unix is helpful to Linux users, too.

- `http://www-106.ibm.com/developerworks/linux/library/l-sc7.html`—This article on "Practical Linux Security" offers an interesting take on handling users.

- `http://searchenterpriselinux.techtarget.com/originalContent/0,289142,sid39_gci928466,00.html`—This Linux Security Learning Guide is a handy set of articles and links on the range of security topics.

- `http://www.schneier.com/blowfish.html`—The Blowfish encryption algorithm home page.

- `http://linuxgazette.net/issue81/vikas.html`—A summary of the Magic SysRq process.

- `http://www.learntosubnet.com`—A good source on learning how to use IP addresses and subnet them. Good (and free) lessons on how to work with IP addressing and name services.

## LAMP and Other Programming References

The following links and resources are for you if you need to find more information on programming with Linux, web development, LAMP, and so on.

- `http://www.apache.org`—The Apache Software Foundation umbrella site. Access all Apache projects from here.

- `http://httpd.apache.org`—The place to start for information on the Apache Web Server. News, downloads, FAQs. Check the Docs subproject for a PDF user's guide.

- `http://modules.apache.org`—The Apache Module Registry. Locate modules to install, and contribute modules you've created.

- `http://www.apachetoday.com`—A little cluttered and ad ridden, but ServerWatch's Apache Today site is still an excellent source of Apache news and tutorials.

- `http://tldp.org/HOWTO/HOWTO-INDEX/apps.html#SERVERHTTP`—An index of web-server–related HOWTOs. Mostly dealing with Apache, but a few others, too.

- `http://susefaq.sourceforge.net/faq/apache.html`—The Unofficial SUSE FAQ list includes useful SUSE-specific Apache information.

- `http://news.netcraft.com/archives/web_server_survey.html`—The monthly Netcraft survey of popular web servers. As this is being written, nearly 70 percent of the Web runs on Apache.

- `http://modpython.org`—Home of the `mod_python` Apache module.

- `http://modruby.net`—The `mod_ruby` page.

- `http://www.acme.com/software/thttpd`—Home of `thttpd`.

- `https://helix-server.helixcommunity.org`—The open-source streaming media server.

- `http://www.zope.org`—All the latest and greatest from the Zope community.

- `http://gcc.gnu.org`—Home of the GNU Compiler Collection.

- `http://gcc.gnu.org/gcc-4.0/changes.html`—What's new in GCC 4.0.

- `http://www.gnu.org/software/autoconf`—The Autoconf configuration utility.

- `http://gcc.gnu.org/java`—GCC's Java compiler, GCJ.

- `http://subversion.tigris.org`—The very well-designed Subversion site.

- `http://svnbook.red-bean.com/en/1.0`—The online book *Version Control with Subversion*.

- `https://www.cvshome.org`—The CVS site, secure and also well organized.

- `http://www.linux.ie/articles/tutorials/cvs.php`—A somewhat cheeky CVS tutorial.

- `http://eclipse.org`—The hub of the Eclipse community. Everything you need to get going and stay going.

- `http://www.eclipseplugincentral.com`—The place to find your needed Eclipse plug-ins, with news, too.

- `http://www.kdevelop.org`—News, forums, documentation, and a real-time chart indicating the number of downloads per hour of this IDE.

- `http://anjuta.sourceforge.net`—The GNOME/GTK+ IDE.

- `http://www.digitalfanatics.org/projects/qt_tutorial`—Tutorial for C++ developers to learn Qt.

- http://doc.trolltech.com/3.3—The official reference documentation for the current version of Qt.

- http://www.rpm.org—Home for information on the Red Hat Package Management system. The site includes an online version of Ed Bailey's 2000 book, *Maximum RPM*.

- http://www.mysql.com/—MySQL database home page. The World's Most Popular Open Source Database. The software's official home page with news, downloads, and documentation.

- http://dev.mysql.com/doc/—MySQL database home page's documentation repository. If you want to learn more about MySQL, visit the documentation center.

- http://www.postgresql.org/—PostgreSQL database home pages. PostgreSQL is one of the world's most advanced open-source database supporting almost all SQL constructs, including subselects, transactions, user-defined types, and so on.

- http://www.postgresql.org/docs/—PostgreSQL database home pages documentation repository. There is a wealth of PostgreSQL information available online and it can be found here to start with. This section of the website contains current and archived manuals for PostgreSQL users and administrators.

- http://www.knoda.org/—The home page to download the newest Knoda client or learn more about it.

- http://www.perl.com—"The Source for Perl." News, articles, blogs, and the like.

- http://www.perl.org—The Perl Directory. Links to the Perl universe.

- http://www.cpan.org—The Comprehensive Perl Archive Network. CPAN is the place to download modules and other gotta-have Perl stuff. If you write something useful, upload it here.

- http://use.perl.org—The Perl news center. Find out about conferences, user group meetings, and assorted fun facts.

- http://learn.perl.org—Where to begin with Perl online. Tutorials, book recommendations for all levels of expertise, and a beginner's mailing list.

- http://www.tpj.com—*The Perl Journal*, the monthly magazine.

- http://www.pm.org—PerlMongers user groups.

- http://dev.perl.org/perl6—The Perl 6 hub. Get overall design information here and the latest on development of Perl 6 and the Parrot interpreter.

- http://python.org—The center of the Python universe. Just about everything Python links here.

- http://www.pythonware.com/daily—The Daily Python URL, Python news and comment from around the Web and the blogosphere.

- http://www.python.org/moin/BeginnersGuide—For new programmers, a Python guide.

- `http://docs.python.org/tut/tut.html`—This tutorial promises to teach you Python in an afternoon.

- `http://www.die-offenbachs.de/detlev/eric3.html`—Home for the Eric Python IDE.

- `http://www.pyzine.com`—An online Python technical journal.

- `http://en.wikipedia.org/wiki/Python_programming_language`—A long and detailed entry, and a worthy introduction to the Python language.

- `http://www.php.net`—The PHP home page.

- `http://www.phpbuilder.com`—Tutorial and news site.

- `http://codewalkers.com`—Another news site, with the occasional PHP coding contest with interesting challenges and real prizes.

- `http://php.resourceindex.com`—The PHP Resource Index. The main draw for this site is the thousands of ready-made PHP scripts, functions, and classes. You can also find links to other tutorials and the larger PHP community.

- `http://www.zend.com`—Zend Technologies, owners of the Zend scripting engine at the heart of PHP 4 and 5.

- `http://weberdev.com`—More code, tutorials, weblogs.

- `http://www.hotscripts.com`—Scripts for every webmaster's need, mostly in PHP, but also in Perl, Python, JavaScripts, and even some in C and C++. Updated constantly, this is a great place to look for something interesting.

- `http://phpdeveloper.org`—News and forums for all types of PHP coders.

- `http://www.thelinuxconsultancy.co.uk/phpeditors.php`—A filterable (by OS and license type) list of editors and IDEs that support PHP coding.

- `http://forums.devnetwork.net`—The PHP Developers Network web forums.

- `http://www.planet-php.net`—A collection of PHP-related weblogs.

- `http://www.viapanda.com/nvuphp.html`—A FAQ outlining problems with using PHP in the Nvu web-authoring application, with some workarounds.

- `http://phpnuke.org`—One of the original PHP-based content management systems.

- `http://www.phpbb.com`—phpBB, a popular PHP-based community forum system.

# Worldwide Linux Newsgroups

In the last section of this appendix, we will look at the newsgroups you can participate in to find out more about Linux.

| | |
|---|---|
| linux.appletalk | linux.dev.localbus |
| linux.apps.bbsdev | linux.dev.lugnuts |
| linux.apps.flexfax | linux.dev.mca |
| linux.apps.linux.bbs | linux.dev.mgr |
| linux.apps.seyon | linux.dev.msdos |
| linux.apps.seyon.development | linux.dev.net |
| linux.apps.xword | linux.dev.new-lists |
| linux.bbs.rocat | linux.dev.newbies |
| linux.debian.alpha | linux.dev.normal |
| linux.debian.announce | linux.dev.nys |
| linux.debian.bugs | linux.dev.oasg |
| linux.debian.changes | linux.dev.oi |
| linux.debian.devel | linux.dev.opengl |
| linux.debian.policy | linux.dev.pkg |
| linux.debian.user | linux.dev.ppp |
| linux.dev.680x0 | linux.dev.qag |
| linux.dev.admin | linux.dev.raid |
| linux.dev.apps | linux.dev.scsi |
| linux.dev.atm | linux.dev.serial |
| linux.dev.bbs | linux.dev.seyon |
| linux.dev.c-programming | linux.dev.sound |
| linux.dev.config | linux.dev.standards |
| linux.dev.debian | linux.dev.svgalib |
| linux.dev.diald | linux.dev.tape |
| linux.dev.doc | linux.dev.term |
| linux.dev.fido | linux.dev.userfs |
| linux.dev.fsf | linux.dev.uucp |
| linux.dev.fsstnd | linux.dev.wabi |
| linux.dev.ftp | linux.dev.word |
| linux.dev.gcc | linux.dev.x11 |
| linux.dev.hams | linux.fido.ifmail |
| linux.dev.ibcs2 | linux.free-widgets.announce |
| linux.dev.interviews | linux.free-widgets.development |
| linux.dev.ipx | linux.i18n |
| linux.dev.isdn | linux.jobs |
| linux.dev.japanese | linux.largesites |
| linux.dev.kernel | linux.local.chicago |
| linux.dev.laptop | linux.local.nova-scotia |
| linux.dev.linuxbsd | linux.local.silicon-valley |
| linux.dev.linuxnews | linux.motif.clone.lesstif |
| linux.dev.linuxss | linux.net.atm |

B

linux.net.masqarade

linux.new-tty

linux.news.groups

linux.ports.alpha

linux.ports.hp-pa

linux.ports.powerpc

linux.postgres

linux.redhat.applixware

linux.redhat.axp

linux.redhat.devel

linux.redhat.digest

linux.redhat.install

linux.redhat.list

linux.redhat.misc

linux.redhat.pam

linux.redhat.ppp

linux.redhat.rpm

linux.redhat.sparc

linux.samba

linux.samba.announce

linux.scsi.ncr53c8xx

linux.sdk

linux.sources.kernel

linux.test

linux.test.moderated

linux.wine.users

> **NOTE**
>
> Internet Resources change often. If you are unable to find any of the resources listed in this appendix, visit your favorite online search engine and use the search techniques listed in the beginning of this appendix to find the information you are looking for.

# Index

## SYMBOLS

## NUMBERS

## A

# C

*How can we make this index more useful? Email us at indexes@samspublishing.com*

*How can we make this index more useful? Email us at indexes@samspublishing.com*

# H

*How can we make this index more useful? Email us at indexes@samspublishing.com*

# M

*How can we make this index more useful? Email us at indexes@samspublishing.com*

*How can we make this index more useful? Email us at indexes@samspublishing.com*

# Q – R

# T

# X – Y – Z

# What's on the DVD

The book's DVD-ROM contains the complete binary version of SUSE Linux 10.0—the equivalent of five CDs.

## Amusements
- FreeCiv
- KDE Game Collection
- Maelstrom
- SuperTux
- Tux Racer
- Xboard

## Development

### Languages
- Bison
- Flex
- GCC
- Guile
- Java
- Mono
- Perl
- Python
- Ruby
- Tcl
- TK

### Tools
- Ant
- Autoconf
- Automake
- cscope
- CVS
- DDD
- DejaGnu
- ElectricFence
- Expect
- GDB
- Libtool
- Ltrace
- Make
- Strace
- Subversion

### Documentation
- BIND Documentation
- HTML Documentation for the GNU C Library
- GNOME 2.x Desktop Documentation
- Linux and POSIX manual pages
- Linux Documentation Project man pages
- Qt 3 Development Kit and man pages
- Samba documentation
- SuSE Help System

## Documentation
**(continued)**
- Xen Virtualization documentation
- Online manuals for X11

## Hardware
- a2ps
- ALSA
- Bluetooth firmware and libraries
- CUPS
- Printer filters
- GNOME Printing Architecture
- gPhoto
- GTKam
- hdparm
- KDE Digital Camera application
- Kooka
- klipsi
- LIRC
- mgetty
- motv (Video4Linux TV application)
- PCI Utilities
- SCSI Tools
- sendfax
- wireless-tools
- xpp
- XSane

## Productivity

### Archiving
- Bzip
- cpio
- GNU Zip Compression Utilities
- konserve
- Pack Program
- Pax
- Star
- Unzip
- Zip

### Databases
- db-utils
- Knoda
- GNU Data Access (GDA) Library
- C++ Client Library for PostgreSQL

## Databases
**(continued)**
- Mergeant
- MySQL
- PostgreSQL
- Rekall
- SQLite
- UnixODBC
- XBase

## Editors
- ed
- GNU Emacs
- AUC TeX
- flim
- Gedit
- jEdit
- JOE
- Mined
- PicoTeXmacs
- ViM
- XSLIDe

## File Utilities
- GNU Find
- KDE Utility Programs
- Midnight Commander
- Nautilus

## Graphics
- AutoTrace
- Blender
- Dia
- Eye Of GNOME
- FontForge
- F-Spot
- GIMP
- GNUPlot
- Gpdf
- GpsDrive
- ImageMagick
- Base Libraries for KDE Graphics Applications
- KimDaba
- netpbm
- GNU Ocrad
- Skencil

## Multimedia
- ALSA Tools
- amaroK
- arts
- aumix
- banshee

## Multimedia
**(continued)**
- cdparanoia
- CDRDAO
- Cdrecord
- Cecilia
- dvd+rw-tools
- FluidSynth
- K3b
- Kaffeine
- KDE Multimedia Applications
- Kino
- Mkisofs
- RealPlayer
- Rythmbox
- Sound-juicer
- SOX
- Totem
- Xine

## Networking
- Apache 2
- BIND
- BitTorrent
- Bogofilter
- Curl
- Dante
- DHCP client/server
- Dirmngr
- EPIC
- Epiphany
- Ethereal
- Evolution
- Fetchmail
- Finger
- Flash Player
- FreeRADIUS
- Gaim'
- GnomeICU
- GnuPG 2
- Grepmail
- htdig
- imap
- INN
- iproute2
- iptables
- iputils
- krb5
- Lynx
- Mail
- MediaWiki